"We Shall Independent Be"

AFRICAN AMERICAN

PLACE MAKING

AND THE STRUGGLE

TO CLAIM SPACE IN

THE UNITED STATES

edited by
ANGEL DAVID NIEVES
and LESLIE M. ALEXANDER

UNIVERSITY PRESS OF COLORADO

© 2008 by the University Press of Colorado

Published by the University Press of Colorado
5589 Arapahoe Avenue, Suite 206C
Boulder, Colorado 80303

The University Press of Colorado is a proud member of
the Association of American University Presses.

The University Press of Colorado is a cooperative publishing enterprise supported, in part,
by Adams State College, Colorado State University, Fort Lewis College, Mesa State College,
Metropolitan State College of Denver, University of Colorado, University of Northern Colorado,
and Western State College of Colorado.

The paper used in this publication meets the minimum requirements of the American
National Standard for Information Sciences—Permanence of Paper for Printed Library Materials.
ANSI Z39.48-1992

Library of Congress Cataloging-in-Publication Data

"We shall independent be" : African American place making and the struggle to claim space in the
United States / edited by Angel David Nieves and Leslie M. Alexander.
    p. cm.
  Includes bibliographical references and index.
  ISBN 978-0-87081-906-3 (hardcover : alk. paper) 1. African Americans—Social conditions.
2. African Americans—Civil rights—History. 3. Place (Philosophy)—Social aspects—United
States—History. 4. African American neighborhoods—History. 5. Community life—United
States—History. 6. City planning—United States—History. 7. Human geography—United
States—History. 8. Social ecology—United States—History. 9. United States—Race relations. 10.
United States—History, Local. I. Nieves, Angel David. II. Alexander, Leslie M.
  E185.86.W434 2008
  305.896′073—dc22

                                        2008001304

Design by Daniel Pratt

17   16   15   14   13   12   11   10   09   08   10   9   8   7   6   5   4   3   2   1

To all those who have struggled to claim a place for themselves.

CONTENTS

VI. CHURCHES AND SACRED SPACES

I first thank our many talented essayists without whose intellectual gifts, patience, and understanding this book would never have been realized. My co-editor, Leslie M. Alexander, and I are grateful that they remained committed to the project and have seen it through to publication.

I must also thank our former University Press of Colorado acquisitions editor, Kerry Callahan, under whose watch the compiling and editing of the manuscript began more than five years ago. Her insights, coupled with her unwavering support of the project, were invaluable to us as first-time editors. Darrin Pratt, director of the University Press of Colorado, has been most supportive and patient with his two young authors, in spite of delays encountered on the way. We offer our sincerest thanks to him and his amazingly talented staff, including Laura Furney, Daniel Pratt, and Ann Wendland.

The institutional and personal debts we owe are almost too many to list given the size and scope of the project. Staff and faculty colleagues at the University of Colorado at Boulder were generous with their time, support, and friendship. Here I must thank David N. Pellow, Lisa Sun-Hee Park, Elisa Fascio,

Deborah Hollis, Karen Moreira, Christine Yoshinaga-Itano, Lisa Penaloza, Erika Doss, José Martínez, Lane Hirabayashi, and Evelyn Hu-DeHart. My apologies to any librarians and scholars at CU-Boulder, the University of Maryland, and the Ohio State University we have neglected to thank, and our apologies for any omissions.

A core cohort of Ethnic Studies majors at CU-Boulder comprised some of the most dedicated and socially conscious students a new professor could wish for in his first years of teaching: Owen Balint, Alicia Brown, JoAnna Cintron, David Jiménez, Kerry Kite, Mary Lettau, Ginnie Logan, Allison Lott, Jessica Luciano, Leah McFail, Cara McKinley, Tangie Sutton, Brooke Takala, and Jolene Wallace. My first undergraduate advisee, Robb Hernández, a part of that same cohort, deserves special mention because of his commitment to rigorous scholarship and activism on behalf of students of color. He has renewed my faith in student activism.

At the School of Architecture, Planning & Preservation at the University of Maryland, College Park, Ann Petrone deserves special mention for offering me guidance and freely availing me with her unique strength. Steve Boyle and Patti Cossard somehow made life inexplicably easier with their sincere friendship, humor, and hard work on my behalf. The unending support and leadership of Alex Chen, Jim Cohen, Marie Howland, Mary Konsoulis, Guido Francescato, Steve Hurtt, Gary Bowden, Garth Rockcastle, Lee Waldrep, and Brooke Wortham have been particularly notable. Isabelle Gournay has also been a real friend and colleague—in every sense of those words and more. Donald Linebaugh, director of the Program in Historic Preservation there, has never wavered in his support of innovative scholarship and teaching. A great deal is owed to him and the program. Students in Historic Preservation at College Park, including Stephanie Frank, Romola Ghulamali, Laura Mancuso, Cristina Miranda-Cornejo, Darsey Nicklasson, Ben Riniker, Suzanne Stasivlatis, Stephanie Ryberg, Najah Gabriel, Tahani Share, Rei Harada, Joy Tober, Mary Seng, Jennifer Sherrock, Susan Fite, and Casey Gallagher, have also been generous with their encouragement. Robert E. Waters Jr., went out of his way to provide institutional and financial support for my many endeavors and to him I extend a very special thanks.

No one could ask for a better friend and mentor in academe than Mary Corbin Sies. Her generosity, academic leadership, and rigorous attention to scholarship are boundless, and to her I offer my profuse thanks.

From the Consortium on Race, Gender, and Ethnicity (CRGE), Bonnie Thornton Dill, Ruth Zambrana, and Amy McLaughlin have provided generous financial, emotional, and spiritual support over the past several years. They have also provided me an extended academic family outside the school. Without CRGE, I might never have come into close personal and scholarly contact with the most dedicated group of colleagues committed to social justice in the academy a person could ever hope for, including Elsa Barkley Brown, Lynn Bolles, Neil Fraistat, Psyche Williams-Forson, Sharon Harley, Katie King, Matt Kirschenbaum, Marilee Lindemann, Doug Reside, Ana Patricia Rodríguez, Debbie Rosenfelt, Paul Shackel, Martha Nell Smith, Nancy Struna, Laura Nichols, Daryle Williams, and Clyde Woods. Patrick Grzanka, Shana Kent, Tanesha Leathers, Greg P. Lord, Tyrone Stewart, Allison Merritt, Maria Cristina García, Mary N. Woods, James E. Turner, Lynette Boswell, Kirsten Crase, and Yolanda Reyes have all contributed to this book and have enriched my scholarship in ways they may never fully understand. Val Brown, Grace Criscuoli, Dawn Green, Wendy Hall, Monica Herrera, Krista Johnson, Julie Jarvis-Myers, Lil Roberts, and Cindy Woo have provided me with the very best administrative support possible, despite the many challenges of working in the large and impersonal bureaucracy of a university. They are all very special to me.

I'd like to thank my colleague Jefferson Pinder for kindly permitting me the use of his brilliant collage painting "Curb Blues (Katrina landscape)," from 2006, as a cover illustration. I now find myself surrounded by some of the most thoughtful, caring, and courageous women of color humanly possible who are also eminent scholars in their respective fields, including Maria Cristina García, Michelle R. Scott, Gabriela Sandoval, Isabel Martínez, Jennifer Wilks, Jean Kim, and Susie Lee. Leslie Alexander has been consistently generous with her time and friendship while providing her love at critical moments.

I also extend my greatest thanks and eternal love to my life partner, Richard Foote. It is impossible to articulate through prose what his encouragement has meant to me as an academic. I am particularly indebted to Richard for his support during the editing of this book. I also thank my parents and sister for their support and love.

We have other companions we wish to acknowledge. As we wrote this essay, my co-editor Leslie was forced to put her dog, Sasha, to sleep after a diagnosis of inoperable cancer. As dog lovers, we also dedicate this book to Sasha's memory. My own four-legged friend, Mitzy, has helped me to maintain my equilibrium and kept me in good humor with her unique devotion and love.

ADN, COLLEGE PARK, MARYLAND

Professor Alexander also thanks all the family members and friends who have supported her during her academic career. Special gratitude goes to Sandy Alexander, Michelle Alexander, Carter Stewart, Nicole Stewart, Jonathan Stewart, Corinne Stewart, Margaret Washington, Robert L. Harris Jr., James Turner, Mwalimu Abdul Nanji, Jacqueline Melton-Scott, the late Don Ohadike, Hasan Kwame Jeffries, and her co-editor Angel David Nieves. She is also deeply indebted to those who provided intellectual and financial support: the Ford Foundation, the Anonymous Donor Fellowship, the Sage Fellowship, the Cornell Graduate School, the New York Historical Society (especially Cynthia Copeland), the New York Municipal Archives, and the staff of the Cornell Library. She is especially grateful for the Ford Foundation's annual conferences, where she gained strength and encouragement from the multitude of scholars engaged in inspiring research. Last, but definitely not least, Professor Alexander offers love and gratitude to the memories of John Alexander and Sasha Alexander.

LMA, COLUMBUS, OHIO

"We Shall Independent Be"

Angel David Nieves

Cultural Landscapes of Resistance and Self-Definition for the Race

Interdisciplinary Approaches to a Socio-Spatial Race History

> Perhaps if we learn more of what has happened and why it hap-
> pened, we'll learn more of who we really are. And perhaps if we
> learn more about our unwritten history, we won't be so vulnerable
> to the capriciousness of events as we are today. And in the process
> of becoming more aware of ourselves we will recognize that one
> of the functions of our vernacular culture is that of preparing for
> the emergence of the unexpected, whether it takes the form of the
> disastrous or the marvelous.
>
> RALPH ELLISON, *GOING TO THE TERRITORY*[1]

The above quote outlines the very premise of this volume—that from an African
American–centered perspective one can document, record, and interpret the
"unwritten history" of African American "space making" while focusing on the
multiple processes of Black self-determination. The essays in this volume consider African Americans' attempts to claim a "space" for themselves within the
complex social, economic, and political fabric of U.S. dominant culture from the
antebellum era through the present. As such, drawing on the diverse fields of
urban studies, cultural landscape studies, architectural history, women's studies,
planning history, human geography, history, and others provides us with a means
of examining the historical significance of race and place to African Americans
in their struggle for self-definition. Although some of the contributors work outside the discipline of African American studies, their individual essays fall within
the parameters of scholarship emerging in this interdisciplinary and multidisciplinary field.

Despite attempts in the last two decades to focus on a more inclusive American social history through the lens of multiculturalism, institutions of higher learning continue to perpetuate pedagogies of "veiled" white supremacy with regard to African American agency and self-determination. The discourse surrounding multiculturalism (now labeled "cultural diversity") also reflects the holdovers of past educational policy decisions and curricula that fail to come to terms with the troubled American past of human bondage and racialized oppression. Although some might argue that we have made significant strides in academe since the Civil Rights Movement, many others would argue that African American scholarship is still situated in the recovery phase and awaits the documentation of countless undiscovered texts and narratives. However, neglecting the experiences of Blacks in shaping the American cultural landscape can no longer be attributed to their supposed absence from the historical record.

Although this volume challenges our assumptions about African American space making through new and innovative scholarship, so much of it would not have been possible without questioning basic methodological assumptions of what constitutes "legitimate" sources of evidence in each of their respective fields. In addition to emphasizing the usual newspaper, archival, and statistical accounts, it is important that attention is drawn to such rarely used sources as burial grounds, artifacts, and other aspects of material culture. Few anthologies are as suggestive as to how everyday, but less visible, spaces such as cemeteries, courtrooms, dance halls, and public transport provide valid sources for sociohistorical research. Little-understood environments, such as the Black suburb, and so-called natural environments, such as forests and swamps, reflect a change in our notions of space and spatial formations as immutable, static, or neutral.

In uncovering or recovering this history, the essayists in this volume contend that examining the physical, social, and intellectual spaces created by African Americans will offer us new forms of historical evidence, methodologies, and analyses. Clearly, past attempts to enslave and suppress African Americans have been met with collective resistance, spurring African Americans to offer up new strategies for redefining self-identity through their own histories and narratives. The essays in this volume provide insights into the still largely unexamined ways in which African Americans have succeeded in mapping cultural landscapes of resistance and self-definition for the race.[2]

This introductory essay seeks to outline our rationale for the volume as a whole and to suggest means by which we might explore a range of subjects across time-period, discipline, and more traditional thematic boundaries. These chapters, evidence of rich and varied scholarship, appear (at least on the surface) to be centered on very different subjects, and with little or no connection between them, as their subjects range from the draft riots of the antebellum

North to desegregation in the twentieth-century South, and from the racialized space of leisure and street entertainment to indoor musical venues. Examined more closely, however, it becomes clear that the contributors all grapple with some shared fundamental questions: How was it that Black people created community for themselves, and how, despite their indelible imprint on the American landscape, did they seek to set aside a place for themselves in an American society that was often hostile to their presence? Race and racism figure prominently in the collection because they "do not emerge unprompted from individual minds, but are thoroughly embedded in our collective everyday lives [past and present] and in the very structures of our social, political, and economic activities."[3]

Certain spaces have long figured prominently in research on the African American experience. Existing traditions in African American historiography previously emphasized the impact of the rural plantation and later the urban ghetto on the culture and politics of the Black community. Such prior studies emphasized the role of whites as the literal architects of these spatial archetypes, but for their own betterment African Americans sought to play a role in the construction of both environments.[4]

Scholarship examining the impact of Africans Americans on space and place making has emerged as a critical field of inquiry in the humanities and social sciences only within the last thirty years or so, particularly in the study of human geography, material culture, and the landscape. Despite an outcry from politically minded academics inspired by the Civil Rights Movement, it was only in the late 1960s that scholars began to apply methods of spatial analysis to the lived experiences of African Americans and their varying forms of cultural production. For example, geographers in the late 1960s and early 1970s prodded their discipline and related fields to address the pressing needs of African Americans in their research for greater "social ends."[5] By the late 1970s, anthropologists and historians began linking culture and landscape to the explosion of works in the Black Arts movement. By the 1980s and 1990s, the "spatial turn" in social theory began challenging the notion of space as static, dead, or even neutral, influenced as it was by emerging scholarship in culture and social resistance. Initially, theorists like Henri Lefebvre, Edward Soja, Michel Foucault, M. M. Bakhtin, and David Harvey reconceptualized space as socially constructed, often linking it to broader social relations and the inherent structures of the capitalist state. An earlier generation of scholars, some trained in architecture and many of whom were initially labeled "radical geographers" by mainstream scholars—men such as John Brickerhoff Jackson, John Kirkland Wright, and David Lowenthal—had recognized as early as the 1940s that, by examining the widest breadth of American vernacular cultures, an understanding of cultural landscapes could effectively provide a critique of power relations and their resulting social constructions.[6]

Unfortunately, few of these early works in geography or landscape studies considered the particularities of race and social politics outside the rubric of a problem-oriented or "social ills" pathology model. Even today, there is relatively little literature that critically considers African Americans as active agents of their own social change through space making in the face of racial segregation or political disenfranchisement.[7] By the 1980s, historian Armstead Robinson, in his essay "Plans Dat Comed from God," addressed the question of how newly freed slaves managed the problems of self-help and institution building in Memphis, Tennessee, during the period of Reconstruction. His work broke with traditional disciplinary boundaries by articulating the significance of space making among working-class African Americans and women reformers.[8] Robinson's innovative work began to rethink and theorize about the contributions of African Americans to the built environment. Although a subsequent generation of geographers and landscape studies scholars like Pierce Lewis argued that "the human landscape is our unwitting autobiography, reflecting our tastes, our values, our aspirations, and even our fears, in tangible, visible form,"[9] very little work has considered African Americans actively shaping the built environment through an interdisciplinary framework, or as actors with significant spatial agency, until now.[10]

It was only in the early 1990s that a group of publications from African American studies scholars—historians and Black feminists—considered how space and the "efforts of poor and racial-ethnic groups and individuals to deconstruct racism and shape space [broadly defined] in their own interests" changed our theoretical understandings of race and cultural landscapes.[11] Robin D.G. Kelley's essay " 'We Are Not What We Seem': Rethinking Black Working Class Opposition in the Jim Crow South," appearing in the *Journal of American History* (1993), outlined a "research agenda that might allow us to render visible hidden forms of resistance, to examine how class, gender, and race shape working-class consciousness."[12] Both Robinson and Kelley argued that, after decades of oppression, Blacks responded through their own unique form of resistance in shaping everyday spaces and places. Kelley writes: "[P]olitics was not separate from lived experience or the imagined world of what is possible. It was the many battles to roll back constraints, to exercise power over, or to create space within the institutions and social relationships that dominated their lives."[13]

A third important essay by historians Elsa Barkley Brown and Gregg D. Kimball, "Mapping the Terrain of Black Richmond" in the *Journal of Urban History* (1995), closely examined the built environment of Richmond at the nexus between cultural geography and the field of Black studies. As Brown and Kimball have argued, "historians have [now] focused on intracommunity relations, raising new questions about the dynamics of spatial relations among African Americans." They add, "Exploring the cultural meanings of black urban space has opened up new understandings for us and presented us with new problems of interpretation and presentation."[14] These essays by Armstead, Kelley, and Brown and Kimball changed the ways in which we look at Black activism and suggested methods of a cultural mapping of those sites that were all-important to a rising Black working-class consciousness and political activism—not only in the Jim Crow South but across the historical spectrum of the African American experience. How then might we come to consider the buildings, homes, and institution-building efforts as the cultural markers of a new race history and the coded signifiers of resistance to oppression?

When reading the essays in this volume, the editors could not help but reflect upon W.E.B. Du Bois's classic (if admittedly overcited) reference to double-consciousness—a sense that African Americans had of being both Black and American—and their struggle to reconcile these warring identities. However, invoking the idea of Du Bois's double-consciousness somewhat elides the multiple forms of identity and consciousness that this volume underscores. Du Bois's idea of double-consciousness deserves to be explicitly challenged, particularly his emphasis on the dual black-white racial divide. This volume does not treat the various internal conflicts and cleavages that attended Black space making, particularly the very complicated class and gender dimensions of African American space making. It is also impossible to overlook in several of the essays in this book how so much of African American activism involves the creation of multi-class and gender alliances and movements within the Black community. By focusing on the creation of community and the contestation over space, these essays reflect that very double-consciousness and its many variants and reveal that Black people across time and location have sought to create space in American society in a way that both reflected their community ethics and asserted their right to exist in a society that rejected their equality and citizenship. Keeping such themes in mind was important to us as we began the process of sorting through the many essays now included in this collection. Expanding our own understanding of space and place making was critical and, as a result, presented alternative ways of understanding the Black experience.

Since the arrival of the first Africans in the Americas, the United States has been dominated by a racial caste system based largely on issues of landownership and property rights. Citizenship and membership in the new republic required legislation over property and, in turn, over the space of our new nation. American nationalism was uniquely, and almost entirely, tied to racial identity and the material practices that came to define early notions of "whiteness" among the first European Americans. "Blackness" took on very real and spatialized characteristics with the development of chattel slavery in the United States across a forced African diaspora. It was not just documenting physical space—

Africans in the New World were generally not at liberty to own property—but it was, rather, the intellectual and spiritual spaces of resistance and self-definition that became critical to this anthology. For example, if we recall accounts of the brutal voyage of the Middle Passage, we cannot forget those countless Africans who took their own lives by jumping overboard. They believed, through their own unique form of spirituality, that the ocean's waters would return them to their homeland in Africa as they died. The editors have sought to engage in a broader conversation about the ways in which "space" has been appropriated, defined, and redefined by African Americans despite the strictures embedded in racial classification.

Understanding that space was not a static construct, to be marked by simple physical boundaries or even by architecture, has helped us to envision the collection more broadly in terms of the African American search for social justice. Essays are grouped into six broad categories: community building, intellectual and political space, segregated spaces, schools and educational spaces, urban space and leisure, and churches and sacred spaces. Of course, what complicates and enriches these stories is the reality that within the Black community, there were multiple types of space, not just public and private but home and family space, economic space, community space, and political space, to name just a few. The essays in each category often defy our imposed classifications because of the complex inter- and multidisciplinary approaches with which contributors have engaged their subject matter. Some of the section categories overlap, an intended consequence of not following traditional periodization. In these essays, two themes emerge and play out similarly despite temporal or geographical boundaries: the idea of how Black community space was made and the problems of white hostility or social contestation toward these Black spaces. As all of these essays indicate, areas that were dominated by Black people socially, economically, or politically became highly contested—both within the Black community and as the result of white hostility. Essays by Alexander, Bachin, Nieves, Scott, and Wiese have in part appeared in previous publications but depart from their earlier versions to address questions of space more broadly. Each of these works was, and continues to be, among the very best work to date.

I. COMMUNITY BUILDING

The first chapter, "Community and Institution Building in Antebellum New York: The Story of Seneca Village, 1825–1857" by co-editor and historian Leslie M. Alexander, maintains that Seneca Village, a community located on a portion of the site that became New York's most celebrated park—Central Park—was a critical symbol of self-determination to antebellum Blacks. Seneca Village was established around 1825 as an autonomous Black community, eventually comprising numerous homes, gardens, churches, schools, and cemeteries. It was also home to a burgeoning number of free Black activists led by Andrew Williams and Epiphany Davis, active members of the African Society for Mutual Relief. Interestingly, the African Society emphasized the importance of accumulating real estate and hoped it might inspire the creation of a strong Black neighborhood in Upper Manhattan. By the 1850s, Seneca Village had blossomed into a flourishing community that stretched from Eighty-first Street to Eighty-ninth Street and lay between Seventh and Eighth Avenues. Alexander argues that Seneca Village offered its residents the prospect of their own political enfranchisement and a concrete alternative to the ongoing debates over emigration. Denied equal justice and the rights of citizenship in the new republic, Black New Yorkers knew that there was much hostility toward their existence as a freed people. Yet, owning their separate community offered them a sense of racial cohesion and pride in their history as Africans. Unfortunately, a group of white New Yorkers including Mayor Fernando Wood plotted the destruction of Seneca Village, in part because of their inability to accept Black New Yorkers as free and equal citizens. The mayor and his supporters eventually replaced the neighborhood with something more beneficial to their interests—a public park with a booming real estate market at its edges that would benefit New York's white elite. Money was not the only reason for removing a thriving Black community like Seneca Village: rather the link between landownership in Seneca Village and voting rights meant equal suffrage or power for Blacks, which was anathema to Fernando Wood. Mayor Wood also knew that local state senator James Beekman was an ardent supporter of colonization and Black removal from the United States, allowing him to act easily in favor of Central Park's creation.

In antebellum New York, race plays a significant role in demarcating the physical boundaries and early development of most American cities. In Chapter 2, "Contesting Space in Antebellum New York: Black Community, City Neighborhoods, and the Draft Riots of 1863," literary historian and critic Carla L. Peterson illustrates how the Black community in antebellum New York was both a social space and a physical space where Black folk came together as community builders to establish their own institutions such as schools, homes, and churches. Despite the fact that the Black population was dispersed throughout the city, Black New Yorkers created a community with its own social, sacred, and political space. Unfortunately for the Black community, their progress was not lost on their enemies, and these Black institutions, too, became targets of racial enmity. The most obvious form of racial hostility is exemplified in Peterson's description of the 1863 draft riots, when white mob violence focused exclusively on destroying Black institutions and symbols of Black social and economic progress.

Peterson makes clear that the draft riots were far more complicated than Black vs. white, and that some African Americans moved through their different worlds in ways that made them less of a target to whites than others.

By the twentieth century, the power of community-based organizations could not be overlooked, particularly those that emerged primarily as African American organizations, often battling to overcome the redlining of neighborhoods and the many mechanisms of racial segregation that came with the search for housing. In Chapter 3, "Self-Determination: Race, Space, and Chicago's Woodlawn Organization in the 1960s," historian Mark Santow examines the emergence of one of the largest and most powerful African American community groups in the nation, the Temporary Woodlawn Organization (TWO). Through an examination of Woodlawn and TWO in the 1950s and 1960s, this essay explores the politics of racial geography in postwar America. Santow argues that Americans today continue to define place, property, and community largely in racial terms, affecting how racial and political identities and interests are formed, how problems and inequalities are viewed, and what solutions are seen as both possible and desirable. The relationship between place and race—or what he calls "racial geopolitics"—has been at the center of ideologies and strategies surrounding both the protection of racial privilege and the search for racial justice. Santow makes the larger point about the ambivalent victory of segregated self-determination over integrated diffusion of power.

II. INTELLECTUAL AND POLITICAL SPACE

The struggle over space and the ways in which African Americans have attempted to build community in the face of racial discrimination are reserved not only for the tangible or physical elements of the built environment; space becomes just as significant when we consider its relationship to a form of geopolitics and ideology. With any social movement, as can be demonstrated among antislavery or desegregation activists, comes the emergence of a deeply rooted intellectual project that seeks to justify collective action. In Chapter 4, "A Recess from Jim Crow: Luther P. Jackson, the Teachers, and the Movement for Racial Justice," historian Michael Dennis examines the way in which Luther P. Jackson, a professor at Virginia State College in Petersburg, stitched together his voting rights advocacy and his drive for advancing African American political action while serving as secretary of civic education in the Virginia Teachers Association. After launching the Virginia Voters League, one of several southern organizations committed to mobilizing the African American vote in the 1930s, Jackson turned to the schools as the vehicles of political consciousness–raising during the war years. Working alongside cooperative principals, Jackson promoted political awareness among African American teachers and students, using the classroom as the physical and temporal space to achieve his goals. Jackson built spaces where African Americans could imagine and express their notions of political freedom. This process of reclaiming schools and building independent organizations committed to civil rights proved indispensable to the Black Freedom Struggle.

Flying in the face of the legal system's efforts to restrict the rights of citizenship to landowners, free Blacks of both genders used the space of the courtroom to argue for their legal rights. This use of the courtroom in the antebellum North meant that Blacks were not only exercising a sense of their own self-worth but also tentatively defining their access to citizenship. In Chapter 5, "Claiming the Courtroom: Space, Race, and Law, 1808–1856," historian Scott Hancock examines how enslaved and free Black women and men in Massachusetts began participating in the legal arena within a generation of the colony's founding. (Their role in this highly contentious public space changed significantly after general emancipation in the late eighteenth century.) However, with Black litigants claiming the lower courts as public space within which they had a right to operate, African Americans appeared there as both defendants and plaintiffs with increasing frequency well into the nineteenth century. The lower courts thus emerged as a public arena that proved useful for managing conflict both among Blacks and with whites. As Black leaders claimed the space of the courts to wrestle for rights through litigation, they also attempted to use a rhetoric of rights to create a safe public space for Black people in the polity.

A direct result of the Civil Rights Movement was that an African American citizenry was now able to further promote its own intellectual project of self-empowerment and self-reliance through a kind of race consciousness. Antecedents like the African Society for Mutual Relief and the American Negro Academy were not part of a discontinuous legacy of intellectually based institutions fostering radical agendas. In Chapter 6, "'Liberated Grounds': The Institute of the Black World and Black Intellectual Space," Black studies scholar Derrick White looks at the Institute of the Black World (IBW), founded in 1969 in conjunction with the Martin Luther King Center in Atlanta, Georgia. The IBW was founded with the idea that Black intellectuals could use their minds "in service of the Black community." White examines the intellectual space sought and created by the Institute of the Black World for the development of Black consciousness during the Black Power era. The essay also examines the ideological rupture with the Martin Luther King Center and the re-establishment of ties with radical activists across the African diaspora, such as C.L.R. James, Walter Rodney, and Sylvia Wynter. Ultimately, White examines the decline in the late 1970s of IBW as a Black think tank and the impact the loss of this intellectual space has had on the development of future grassroots protest movements among African Americans.

III. SEGREGATED SPACES

In recent years, a proliferation of works on commemoration has often ignored its meaning to the African American community, particularly for those persons living in the rural South. Continuing debates over a proposed memorial to American slavery in the nation's capitol and the building of a national museum in honor of the African American experience highlight our uneasiness over dealing with the legacy of forced enslavement. A 1994 mock slave auction in Colonial Williamsburg, Virginia, was greeted with much hostility and criticism for portraying the harsh realities of the auction block. In Chapter 7, "Subverting Heritage and Memory: Investigating Luray's 'Ol' Slave Auction Block,'" American studies scholar Ann Denkler looks at a counterdedication to a purported slave auction block in Luray, Virginia. Her essay suggests that the current definitions of public history are only relevant and fitting for white mainstream history, and that when studying African American culture, we need to consider new approaches and methodologies that look at African American "public" history in more "private" settings. For Denkler, sites such as the home, the church, the "hidden" sites interpreted as part of white heritage only, or those sites in remote parts of the larger cultural landscape all await reinterpretation. Interestingly, Denkler uncovered information on the history of African American tourism in and to the Luray area, locating an extant structure that housed traveling African Americans and whites in the 1950s and was known as the "Black Holiday Inn." Located in the remote foothills outside of town, "Miss Martha's" (as it is called in the community) offered a safe haven for those who could not stay or eat on the Main Street of Luray. Miss Martha's reveals how racial segregation affected almost every aspect of Black and white lives, even in their travels. Travel became yet another system of control that told African American tourists they could only visit, eat, and stay in certain places. The African American tourism experience was separate but not equal, was experienced in more private settings, and, to this day, remains undocumented in the mainstream tourism scholarship, which is oblivious to racial context.

The struggle over landownership and property rights plagued most major American cities in the interwar period, particularly throughout the urban South. Despite protective covenants and the redlining of most traditionally white neighborhoods, African Americans pushed the boundaries of residential segregation as early as the mid- to late 1940s. In Chapter 8, " 'Going Colored': The Struggle over Race and Residence in the Urban South," historian Kevin M. Kruse details that, throughout the early decades of the twentieth century, Atlanta city leaders did everything in their power to create a strict structure of residential segregation. Although their political and legal maneuverings greatly tended to confine the city's Black community, they failed to contain it completely. By the late 1940s, large numbers of Blacks in Atlanta began to move beyond the neighborhoods reserved for them and, in so doing, threatened to move beyond the "place" designated for them as well. The first steps in this African American search for space began in the neighborhood of Mozley Park. Although the area seemed a small and insignificant part of town, this one neighborhood proved to be, in fact, a crucial battleground in the city's larger struggles over race and residence in the latter part of the twentieth century. Indeed, the "racial transition" of Mozley Park was critically important for African American claims to space in the city. Throughout Mozley Park's "transition troubles" in the late 1940s and early 1950s, Black leaders learned to shape and reshape their approach to residential desegregation, forging cautious compromises with city officials as they went. White residents, meanwhile, staged a strong "defense" of their neighborhood in the streets, in the courts, and at city hall. Ultimately, unable to stem the course of Black expansion, white residents abandoned their neighborhood in a bitter, scorched-earth retreat and became martyrs for other whites across the city. In the end, Blacks and whites alike formed lasting impressions and misinterpretations of what they believed had happened in Mozley Park.

America's obsession with the suburban ideal (or the "suburban nation") in the late twentieth century is something that cannot be denied or overlooked as we begin to address the rapid decline of those first-ring streetcar suburbs closest to our major metropolitan centers. Unfortunately, little is known about African American efforts to also lay claim to the making of early suburbs in the years prior to the mid-nineteenth century. In Chapter 9, "The Other Suburbanites: African American Suburbanization in the North Before 1950," urban planning historian Andrew Wiese argues that working-class African Americans played important roles in shaping the American suburban pattern before 1950. Although Black families had articulated a number of the values long associated with white suburbanization—desires for home ownership and preferences for family-centered communities and semi-rural landscapes among them—they also pursued a distinctive suburban vision rooted in their experiences, aspirations, and incomes as working-class migrants from the rural and small-town South. Through their efforts to build homes, raise institutions, and care for families, they created places that were distinctly African American and participated in the wider social process of metropolitan decentralization known as suburbanization.

African American attempts to shape the patterns of their residential space begin as early as the eighteenth century with the founding of breakaway maroon communities outside the control of European and European American planters. As such, the natural landscape becomes an important part of enslaved African Americans' attempts to craft their own spaces of resistance outside the gaze of white hostility and violence. In Chapter 10, "Hidden Away in the Woods and

Swamps: Slavery, Fugitive Slaves, and Swamplands in the Southeastern Border-lands, 1739–1845," environmental historian Megan Kate Nelson argues that from 1739 to 1845, European and European American communities saw swamplands in the southeastern borderlands of the United States as sites where they could exercise control over nature and power over other people—especially enslaved Africans and African Americans. Forcibly transported to these southeastern bor-derlands to work as slaves on rice plantations, Africans and African Americans saw swamplands quite differently. They were regarded and used as sites of ref-uge and places where the enslaved could lead lives potentially independent of their masters and cruel overseers. Nelson argues convincingly that, although European Americans espoused "ecolocal" theories connecting race, disease, and environment to establish and bolster slavery in the borderlands for their own benefit, slaves developed their own separate ecolocal culture and often subverted European American desires over their bodies. In the swamplands, Africans and African Americans shaped their own lives both within and outside the strictures of the slave system in unique and important ways.

IV. SCHOOLS AND EDUCATIONAL SPACES

Dozens of community-based efforts have begun around the South to find and save the schools built between 1913 and 1932 with Julius Rosenwald's seed money. The National Trust for Historic Preservation has assigned the Rosenwald schools to its list of the eleven most endangered historic places in America—bringing new attention to the importance of establishing model programs for African American education in the early twentieth-century rural South. The various preservation and conservation efforts now under way across states like Alabama, Maryland, and the Carolinas (to name a few) have implemented adaptive reuse methods as a way of reinvigorating these building sites for new community uses. In Chapter 11, "Rosenwald Schools in the Southern Landscape," architectural historian Mary S. Hoffschwelle details the work of the Julius Rosenwald Fund Rural School Building Program that brought together philanthropists, professional educators, archi-tects, and Black and white rural citizens to create new schools for Black children in the South. Rosenwald schools were the products of a collaboration between Julius Rosenwald, the president of Sears, Roebuck, and Company, and Booker T. Washington, principal of the Tuskegee Institute in Alabama. Washington had turned to Rosenwald in 1912 for money to build six one-room schools as a pilot program for improving Black opportunities and race relations in rural Alabama. Within five years this modest request had mushroomed into a regional program that by its conclusion in 1932 had contributed to the construction of 5,357 school buildings in the South. Rosenwald school designs, distributed free of charge and published in national school plan books, set standards for white school buildings as well. These simple modern buildings were among the first public schoolhouses for Black children ever constructed, and African Americans regarded these as true measures of progress for the race. Hoffschwelle traces the process by which rural African Americans used the Rosenwald Fund program to secure a permanent place in the public landscape of the modern South.

Black women reformers used built environments not only as sites of containment and refuge but also as sites to demonstrate their agency over the design of the educational landscape, thus providing evidence as to how architecture communicates both political protest and self-determination. In Chapter 12, "'We Are Too Busy Making History . . . to Write History': African American Women, Constructions of Nation, and the Built Environment in the New South, 1892–1968," co-editor and public historian Angel David Nieves posits that African American women's educational reform efforts of the 1890s were a primary force in creating a Black nationalist forum through the design and construction of normal and industrial schools in the South. He contends that these women reformers were in fact modeling a kind of "political architecture" through the building of these race-based vernacular landscapes. In many ways these physical environments became a spatialized reflection of their own solutions for social justice. Such women insisted on helping to rebuild their race through higher education and used the space of school reform as a vehicle for establishing a social countermovement.

Community organizing has been critical to urban-based protest movements by African Americans against powerful, traditionally white institutions like those college campuses or universities found adjacent to minority communities. Privately run institutions of higher education have long been involved in redeveloping these neighborhoods under the guise of white benevolence, all the while gaining new investment property—and hence fostering even further hostility and mistrust between communities. In Chapter 13, "Gym Crow Must Go: The 1960s Struggle Between Columbia University and Its New York City Neighbors," historian Stefan Bradley focuses on the 1960s conflict over the New York City parkland that played out among Black community residents, city officials, and Columbia University. With parkland precious to all of these actors, the controversy eventually escalated to a point where Columbia, a largely white institution, was forced to submit to the will of the Black community—something rare in U.S. history. Columbia University had acted as many white institutions did during the 1950s and 1960s when it disregarded the needs of the Black residents who surrounded the school and made plans to construct a new gymnasium in Morningside Park, the strip of land separating the university enclave from Harlem. Permission to build the gymnasium was granted by the city contingent upon the university making the facility available for community use. After learning of the university's plans for separate entrances and sections for university affiliates and community members, some community leaders began referring to the structure as "Gym Crow," remarking that the spatial scheme of the structure was reminiscent of those built during the era of legal segregation. With the Black community and Columbia University's own student body joining in protest in spring 1968, Columbia was eventually pressured into abandoning its plans for a gym in Morningside Park. This victory against Columbia allowed community residents to retain ownership and sovereignty over a space that they considered their own and, in a larger sense, showed that Black communities were not necessarily powerless against predominantly white American institutions.

V. URBAN SPACE AND LEISURE

Race uplift efforts for the betterment of African Americans were not always regarded as uniformly benign, particularly regarding efforts to suppress an emerging Black entertainment industry. There it spectacularly failed to recognize the importance of varying forms of cultural production like jazz and the blues to a burgeoning working-class consciousness. Although race uplift is usually depicted as a movement designed to improve conditions for Black people, was there a downside to uplift? Could race uplift even be construed as anti-community? In Chapter 14, "Mapping out Spaces of Race Pride: The Social Geography of Leisure on the South Side of Chicago, 1900–1919," urban historian Robin F. Bachin recounts the story of the 1919 Chicago race riot, a violent and deadly battle that had an enduring legacy in structuring race relations in Chicago for decades. On a steamy July afternoon, two African American boys were enjoying a swim in Lake Michigan at the Black Twenty-fifth Street beach. But when young Eugene Williams's raft drifted past the invisible barrier separating the Black beach from the white one to the south, white youths began stoning Williams, leaving him to drown in the lake and setting off several days of brutality. Bachin maintains that the events of the riot, and the way they unfolded, highlight the central role played by spatial geography in the city as it contributed to long-standing racial animosity. When Williams inadvertently traversed the dividing line on his raft, he brought to light a boundary more elusive but no less well inscribed than the one separating the two beaches. He had challenged the racial boundaries between public spaces in Chicago, those boundaries that echoed the racial separation in the workplace and in residential areas. This essay examines the sites of leisure in the Black Belt where leisure, "vice," and race pride all intersected, revealing the curious physical and cultural proximity of spaces of respectability and vice.

Social equality was deeply connected to notions of citizenship, and the establishment of streetcar lines in most American cities provided access to downtown civic life. Passage on streetcar lines for African Americans helped desegregate spaces across the city, changing the ways in which African Americans interacted in the public realm. In Chapter 15, "Rights of Passage: The Integration of Philadelphia's Streetcars and Contested Definitions of Public Space, 1857–1867," urban historian Michael Kahan's description of Black Philadelphia's antebellum community is strikingly similar to Peterson's depiction of New York City during the same period. Although Philadelphia's Black community was larger, it was similarly dispersed throughout the city, and its members created a sense of community by forming organizations and institutions designed to uplift the race. Yet Kahan reminds us that it was also a community limited by the rules of segregation. Kahan's study also demonstrates the depth of white hostility toward Black racial progress, noting the abundance of race riots in antebellum Philadelphia as well as the virulent opposition to the integration of public spaces. Kahan's essay is not primarily about residential dispersal or community organizations but more about the problematic construction of "public interest" in the United States.

White politicians, the clergy, and social reformers often used the discourse of public morality and disease to contain working-class African Americans' efforts to establish their own entertainment districts. Black ministers and reformers similarly challenged these Black-owned institutions, often failing to recognize the contradiction between promoting Black businesses and controlling what kind of businesses could be created. In Chapter 16, "The 'Sweetest Street in the World': Recreational Life on Chattanooga's Ninth Street," public historian Michelle R. Scott argues that the recreational needs of the Black community were met in the heart of Black Chattanooga in the shops, taverns, and theaters of the East Ninth Street commercial district. In the case of Chattanooga, this district became the site where Black folk relocating from the Deep South re-created a sense of community by convening and socializing in the space of a few square blocks. Scott maintains that entertainment's segregated nature during this period allowed Black residents of Chattanooga to enjoy parades and musical entertainment within their own autonomous environment. Here performers such as Bessie Smith and Roland Hayes managed to transform public city space into theater/performance space. In addition, Scott compellingly describes the ways in which saloons became the sites where Black Chattanoogans were able to organize politically, such as in response to threats of racial violence after the lynching of Ed Johnson. Scott articulates the various ways in which Blacks in Chattanooga benefited socially, economically, and politically from the Ninth Street district. Curiously, Blacks joined whites in criticizing the district's entertainments, citing the immorality of minstrel and variety shows and calling into question the ways in which Black working-class spaces were viewed across racial lines.

VI. CHURCHES AND SACRED SPACES

The effort to commemorate the Civil Rights Movement among memorial activists has been met with some hostility in "New South" cities like Selma, Alabama, and Atlanta, Georgia. Clashes with local leaders of the Ku Klux Klan have brought new attention to the ways in which political actors attach their own agendas to these memorial landscapes—on both sides of the racial divide.[15] In Chapter 17, "Putting the Movement in Its Place: The Politics of Public Spaces Dedicated to the Civil Rights Movement," human geographer Owen J. Dwyer attempts to redress scholarship that either distorted or ignored the contributions of African Americans to American history by examining, in particular, those cities across the South that are presently in the throes of commemorating the Civil Rights Movement of the 1950s and 1960s. Installed in places once dominated by pledges of "massive resistance" to integration, museums, monuments, and street signs dedicated to the movement—understood collectively as the movement's memorial landscape—prompt questions as to how the country's collective memory has changed over the past two decades. Likewise, the absence of civil rights memorials from the traditional locales of public history raises questions as to the contemporary politics of place associated with civil rights commemoration. Dwyer argues that most civil rights memorials are located amidst the decimated remains of segregation-era Black business districts. Surrounded by low-end retail establishments, impacted ghettos, and urban renewal–era vacant lots, these memorials straddle the border between commemoration and confinement insofar as they raise the question, do these public spaces celebrate the history associated with these places or are they confined to them? His essay examines the location and design of civil rights memorials in Atlanta, Georgia; Birmingham, Alabama; and Memphis, Tennessee. Created over the past two decades, these memorials are the largest and most popular of several dozen associated with the Civil Rights Movement. Dwyer concludes that the meaning(s) and authority of the memorial landscape remain a contested terrain, mutually constituted with contemporary politics of race, urban development, and memory.

Cemeteries, burial grounds, and church teachings were all linked to the common space held in highest regard among African Americans as a symbol of their struggle for freedom: the rural church. The rural church provided African Americans emerging from slavery with their very first institutions, laying the foundations for many secular organizations that would work toward race betterment and social welfare. In Chapter 18, "Sacred Spaces of Faith, Community, and Resistance: Rural African American Churches in Jim Crow Tennessee," architectural historian Carroll Van West argues that rural African American churches are historical artifacts of the creation, development, persistence, and continuity of three vital and interrelated components of African American heritage: ethnic identity, religion, and education. After emancipation, the actual places or locations of historic rural African American churches signified the establishment of a sacred place where community institutions would be nurtured, where cemeteries would be established, and where rituals of culture and identity would be perpetuated and protected. As Jim Crow segregation intensified, churches became ever more important rallying centers for African American culture and the centers of the twentieth-century Civil Rights Movement. Van West outlines the significance of rural churches as sites of memory, culture, and identity to Tennessee's African American communities.

Claiming spiritual space was critically important to African Americans as they sought comfort from the shackles of forced enslavement in antebellum America. Emancipation for many Blacks was believed to be a direct result of their status as a "chosen people"—closely following the teachings found in the Christian tradition. Questions as to the image of God and the strong belief of his role in making humankind in his own image led many to believe that He was in fact Black. In Chapter 19, "'In Our Image, After Our Likeness': The Meaning of a Black Deity in the African American Protest Tradition, 1880–1970," religious historian Patrick Q. Mason establishes the correlation between strong beliefs in the racial identity of a Black deity and social protest movements among male reformers. Beginning with Henry McNeal Turner's fearless declaration that "God is a Negro," the idea of a Black God and Jesus emerged as an important strand in African Americans' multi-faceted struggle against the idolatry of whiteness that surrounded them in American society. A racialized deity was employed by Blacks in two separate but related attempts to claim "space," both metaphysical and physical. First, the distinctive African American interpretation of Christianity that culminated in the rise of Black theology in the late 1960s and 1970s was built on the cultural, intellectual, and theological space carved out by the proponents of and believers in a racialized God. Second, the notion of a Black deity helped to reclaim the dignity and sanctity of the Black body that had been brutalized and desecrated by centuries of racist ideology and practice formalized in the institutions of slavery and Jim Crow. For African Americans, argues Mason, denying God's whiteness and asserting his Blackness thus played an important role in the movement to assert the dignity, and even divinity, of the Black body.

Elsewhere, on Saturday morning, October 4, 2003, the remains of 419 colonial-era enslaved and free African Americans were ceremonially lowered into the newly dedicated African Burial Ground in New York's Lower Manhattan. There, Maya Angelou, speaking on behalf of the long-dead African ancestors, intoned: "You may bury me in the bottom of Manhattan. I will rise. My people will get me. I will rise out of the huts of history's shame."[16] Angelou, an African

American woman, recalled how women suffered some of the worst treatment under decades of forced chattel slavery and suggested turning the shame of enslavement into a triumph over the horrors of the past. For New York City–based activists the burial ground represents a spiritual link to Africa—a link that activists and reformers beginning as early as the eighteenth century embraced through the use of the term "African" in the names of religious and secular institutions they helped found. Reclaiming Africa as a spiritual homeland or space continues today as the burial ground takes on symbolic importance to Africans across the diaspora. In Chapter 20, "Reclaiming Space: The African Burial Ground in New York City," African art historian Andrea E. Frohne reconsiders the African Burial Ground located in Lower Manhattan, used by Africans and people of African descent from approximately 1700 until 1790. A portion of the burial ground was unearthed in 1991 when the General Services Administration (GSA) began construction of a thirty-four-story federal office building at 290 Broadway. Containing anywhere from 10,000 to 20,000 bodies, the African Burial Ground covered some five to six acres in an area that today lies in Lower Manhattan's Civic Center. Throughout the 1990s and to the present, African Americans and others expressing concern for the site fought the GSA for the proper treatment of the interment space. The burial ground became contested terrain at many levels—local, national, and even global. Frohne introduces the term "spirituality of space" as a way to explore an African-centered understanding of spirituality and cosmology at the site. For Frohne, the "spirituality of space" can be understood as a personal or collective interaction, recognition, or reference to a spiritual entity in a space or cultural landscape. Instead of letting the notion of spirituality stand alone, it is conjoined with a less static understanding of space as a way to ground the metaphysical qualities alongside the physical and to concentrate here on the specific location of the African Burial Ground. She then considers how the burial ground has been reclaimed in terms of its physical space as a place of memory making, self-definition, and renewed political activism among Black New Yorkers.

The essays in this volume provide important tools in our continued attempts to understand the complex racialized landscapes African Americans were creating in their quest for self-determination. As historical archaeologist David G. Orr suggests, "cultural landscapes are the most complex 'manuscripts' given to us from the past."[17] In order to understand these complex manuscripts, we must begin to fully acknowledge the contributions African Americans have made in shaping the American landscape. We intend these essays to provide new methodological tools toward that end. Ralph Ellison once warned against efforts to bury parts of our unwritten history: "By pushing significant details of our experience into the underground of unwritten history, we not only overlook much which is positive, but we blur our conceptions of where and who we are. . . . It is as though we dread to acknowledge the complex, pluralistic nature of our society, and as a result we find ourselves stumbling upon our true national identity under circumstances in which we least expect to do so."[18] Ultimately, these essays will help us shift our understanding of African American space making to the foreground and promote our appreciation of the broader American cultural landscape.

NOTES

This chapter title was the title of our "Crossroads of Culture" 2004 American Studies Association Conference panel presentation including Drs. Carla Peterson, Michael Kahan, Michelle R. Scott, and Robin Bachin. The editors want to thank Robb Hernandez, Allison Merritt, and Richard Foote for their assistance in helping prepare the manuscript for publication. The impetus for capitalizing "black" and not "white" is intentional. Black with a capital "B" is a purposeful recognition of the struggles African Americans endured during enslavement and their collective sensibilities in the postemancipation period to rebuild a sense of self-identity. African Americans shared a sense of pride and honor for their many accomplishments despite the terror and racial hatred waged against them in the years immediately following Reconstruction. Numerous newspaper accounts, journals, and novels written by African American men and women suggest their aspirations for the future as a "race" during the transition from enslavement to freedom.

1. Ellison, *Going to the Territory* (New York: Random House, 1986). This is Ellison's compilation of sixteen essays written between 1957 and 1985.

2. Two significant works that look at similar issues are Lesley Naa Norle Lokko, ed., *White Papers, Black Marks: Architecture, Race, Culture* (Minneapolis: University of Minnesota Press, 2000); and Craig E. Barton, ed., *Sites of Memory: Perspectives on Architecture and Race* (New York: Princeton Architectural Press, 2001). Both Lokko and Barton consider the role of race and memory in architecture. Also see a special issue forum of the *Journal of Planning History* 1, no. 3 (August 2002), co-edited by Gail Lee Dubrow and Mary Corbin Sies.

3. Richard H. Schein, "Race, Racism, and Geography," *The Professional Geographer* 54, no. 1 (2002): 2.

4. Wendell E. Pritchett, guest editor, "Special Section: On Black Milwaukee," *Journal of Urban History* 33, no. 4 (May 2007): 539–567.

5. Owen J. Dwyer, "Geographical Research About African Americans: A Survey of Journals, 1911–1995," *Professional Geographer* 49, no. 4 (1997): 441, 446.

6. John Kirkland Wright, "Terrae Incognitae: The Place of Imagination in Geography," *Annals of the American Association of Geographers* 37 (1947): 1–15; David Lowenthal, "Geography, Experience, and Imagination: Toward a Geographical Epistemology," *Annals of the American Association of Geographers* 51, no. 3 (1961): 241–260; Janet Conway, *Identity, Place, Knowledge: Social Movements Contesting Globalization* (Halifax, Nova Scotia: Fernwood Publishing, 2004), 35–39. This line of argument departs significantly from previous scholarship suggesting "radical geographers" only emerged in the 1970s.

7. For a more recent discussion that begins to address these issues, see Dianne Harris, "Little White Houses: Critical Race Theory and the Interpretation of Ordinary Dwellings

in the United States, 1945–1960," a paper presented at the conference "Reconceptualizing the History of the Built Environment in North America," Charles Warren Center, Cambridge, MA, April 2005, 1. Most recently, Richard Schein has edited a volume titled *Landscape and Race in the United States* (New York: Routledge, 2006).

8. Armstead L. Robinson, "'Plans Dat Comed from God': Institution Building and the Emergence of Black Leadership in Reconstruction Memphis, 1865–1880," in *The Web of Southern Social Relations: Women, Family, & Education*, ed. John Wakelyn et al. (Athens: University of Georgia Press, 1985), 182–183.

9. Pierce Lewis, "Axioms for Reading the Landscape: Some Guides to the American Scene," in *The Interpretation of Ordinary Landscapes: Geographical Essays*, ed. D. W. Meinig (New York: Oxford University Press, 1979), 12.

10. This is not to suggest that the work of folklorists Henry Glassie, John Michael Vlach, and others has not been influential. The work of scholars Dell Upton, Leland Ferguson, and Richard Westmacott has made a significant contribution to our ways of examining meaning and power on the American landscape as they impact ethnic and racially marginalized subgroups. Several works have emerged from across a variety of fields that have also begun this kind of work. These include works by Gail Lee Dubrow, Grey Gundaker, Dianne Harris, Dolores Hayden, Lynn Horiuchi, Michelle Scott (Chapter 16, in this volume), Andrew Wiese (Chapter 9, in this volume), and Clyde Woods.

11. Mary Corbin Sies, "Regenerating Scholarship on Race and the Built Environment," a paper presented at the conference "Reconceptualizing the History of the Built Environment in North America," Charles Warren Center, Cambridge, MA, April 2005, 4, 6. In particular, also see works by Bonnie T. Dill, bell hooks, and Patricia Hill Collins, particularly on intersectionality. For a recent discussion on intersectionality, see Leslie McCall, "The Complexity of Intersectionality," *Signs: Journal of Women in Culture and Society* 30, no. 3 (2005): 1771–1800. Feminist geographers have also made important theoretical links between place and gender. See the work of Doreen Massey, Linda McDowell, Gillian Rose, and Elizabeth Grosz. Unfortunately much of that work fails to address the significance of race.

12. Robin D.G. Kelley, "'We Are Not What We Seem': Rethinking Black Working Class Opposition in the Jim Crow South," *Journal of American History* 80, no. 1 (1993): 76.

13. Ibid., 78.

14. Elsa Barkley Brown and Gregg D. Kimball, "Mapping the Terrain of Black Richmond," *Journal of Urban History* 21, no. 3 (March 1995): 316. This and other essays appear in Kenneth W. Goings and Raymond A. Mohl, eds., *The New African American Urban History* (Thousand Oaks, CA: Sage, 1996).

15. Steven Hoelscher and Derek H. Alderman, "Memory and Place: Geographies of a Critical Relationship," *Social & Cultural Geography* 5, no. 3 (September 2003): 352.

16. Office of Public Education and Interpretation of the African Burial Ground (OPEI), "The African Burial Ground: Return to the Past to Build the Future," http://www.africanburialground.gov/ABG_AnAfricanAmericanHomecoming.htm (August 3, 2005).

17. David G. Orr, "Preface: Landscapes of Conflict," *Historical Archaeologist* 37, no. 3 (2003): 1.

18. Ellison, *Going to the Territory*, 591, 595.

PART I

Community Building

Leslie M. Alexander

Community and Institution Building in Antebellum New York

The Story of Seneca Village, 1825–1857

On a brisk autumn day in 1871, workers made a shocking discovery while plowing up the ground in New York City's newly established Central Park. As they labored to uproot trees near the Eighty-fifth Street entrance, landscapers uncovered two coffins; one enclosed the body of a Black man. According to an article in the *New York Herald*, the unearthing of this burial ground was a mystery because no one remembered the existence of a cemetery in that area.[1] Apparently, less than fifteen years after the residents of Seneca Village were driven from their land, their story had already been forgotten by most New Yorkers.[2] Indeed, even in light of this burial site, no mention was made of the thriving community whose ruins and cemeteries lay beneath the hallowed land, and most New Yorkers never realized that the creation of Central Park had cost an entire community its homes, churches, and burial grounds. Dismissed as a shantytown or ignored entirely, Seneca Village nearly disappeared from New York City's history.[3]

Although generally forgotten, Seneca Village was a crucial symbol to the Black community during the antebellum era. To this group of newly emancipated New Yorkers, Seneca Village reflected their commitment to building institutions in the United States, the attainment of political power, and all their hopes for the future. For Black New Yorkers, then, Seneca Village was much more than a thriving neighborhood; it was a symbol of the success their people could achieve and their potential destiny in the United States.[4] Beginning in 1825, residents labored for over thirty years to construct homes, gardens, churches, schools, and cemeteries in an effort to create a sense of permanence for free Black people in America. The success of Seneca Village, however, could not remain a secret forever, as at least a few White New Yorkers became disturbed and threatened by the notion of a strong autonomous Black community. Consistent with the white backlash during the 1850s, politicians commenced an attack against Seneca Village that ultimately decimated a community and the dreams of its residents. This chapter tells the story of Seneca Village, the Black people who made it a home, and the movement to destroy it that culminated in the creation of Central Park.

The tale of Seneca Village begins rather modestly, with a few small plots of land and a group of committed Black activists. Prior to the Civil War, most New York City residents lived below Forty-second Street in the expanding, yet overcrowded, urban milieu. The territory stretching north of the city was still mostly rural and unpopulated. Loyalists had owned much of that region prior to the Revolutionary War but abandoned the land following British withdrawal. In the early national era, the few men who owned these large tracts of land used them primarily for agricultural purposes. However, in 1825, landowner John Whitehead made a crucial decision that created a new possibility for Black New Yorkers. Whitehead, who owned property between Eighty-fifth and Eighty-eighth Streets near Seventh Avenue, chose to parcel off his land and sell individual plots to interested buyers. Perhaps to Whitehead's surprise, an unexpected group of people began to purchase his estate. Attracted by inexpensive land and the opportunity to create a community, Black New Yorkers began to invest in Upper Manhattan Island. Andrew Williams and Epiphany Davis purchased the first plots from the Whiteheads in September 1825; on September 27, Williams selected three lots for which he paid $125, and Davis purchased twelve lots for $578. Shortly thereafter, the African Methodist Episcopal (AME) Zion congregation chose six adjoining tracts. From this initial activity, the community of Seneca Village was born.[5]

It was no coincidence that Andrew Williams, Epiphany Davis, and the AME Zion Church purchased their land simultaneously. Since the dawn of emancipation, Black New Yorkers had worked within institutions like AME Zion Church and the African Society for Mutual Relief to accumulate property and build a viable Black community. In 1800, four years after their split from the white-dominated John St. Methodist Church, the African Methodists bought a sizable plot of land on the corner of Church and Leonard Streets, where they erected a new edifice to accommodate their congregation. What is most important about this action is not the simple construction of a church building. On the contrary, the significance of their activities can only be understood by examining the ways in which constructing a church reflected their commitment to African American place making. For the African Methodists, institution building was a vital component of racial advancement, a philosophy that was especially evident in their articles of incorporation. Members of the African Methodist Episcopal Church clearly stated that only "Africans or their descendants" could officially join the membership or be elected as church trustees. Likewise, they decided the church building was forever to be the property of "our African brethren and the descendants of the African race."[6] In their minds, then, the church symbolized the ability of newly emancipated African peoples to create a permanent institution that would serve the race in future generations.

In the years that followed, other Black religious institutions, like St. Philip's Episcopal Church and Abyssinian Baptist Church, emulated the African Methodists by accumulating property and erecting their own buildings. However, in a foreshadowing of the attack on Seneca Village, White New Yorkers mercilessly attacked these Black establishments because they were the physical manifestations of Black autonomy. Deeply resentful of any evidence of Black progress and permanence, they demonstrated their disapproval through routine physical assaults on the congregants and arson attacks. Between 1810 and 1821, "mysterious fires" destroyed the African Methodist Episcopal Church and St. Philip's Episcopal Church, and, along with the Abyssinian Baptist Church, these institutions were targeted during the 1834 anti-abolition riot.[7]

Yet despite the persistent threat of violence, Black New Yorkers remained determined to accumulate land, erect institutions, and create a sense of permanence for their race.[8] The African Society, for example, began to purchase real estate to inspire the creation of a strong Black neighborhood. On August 18, 1820, African Society members purchased a plot of land on which they constructed a meetinghouse. Members were quite pleased with its location for two revealing reasons. First, its position in the heart of the Black community allowed their building to become a community center for the entire Black population. In fact, they erected their lodge with the intention that it would also "accommodate other societies." Perhaps even more importantly, the African Society selected that site in hopes that, as the shipping industry expanded, the Black neighborhood would become "one of the most valuable locations in the city." However, as the organization's historian later reflected, "the change so confidently expected did not transpire, and the hope of our members never realized itself," as commerce expanded in the opposite direction. Regardless, the African Society members' planning and intentions demonstrated their dedication to community solidarity and economic autonomy. For many Blacks, their efforts must have been a symbolic representation of permanence and their hope that Black people could have a prosperous future in the United States.[9]

Thus, by 1825, when Black New Yorkers saw the opportunity to establish a neighborhood in Upper Manhattan Island, it is not surprising that they responded with enthusiasm. In fact, its earliest residents were part of the existing legacy of African American institution building in the city. Andrew Williams and Epiphany Davis were not only AME Zion Church congregants but also charter members of the African Society. Within weeks of their investment in northern Manhattan, other African Society members, like Samuel Hardenburgh, soon joined Williams and Davis. As a result, the African Society's real estate ventures did not end in Lower Manhattan; African Society members, followed by an array of Black New Yorkers, slowly migrated northward to establish the community of Seneca Village.

In less than fifteen years, as residents constructed homes, gardens, and barns, Seneca Village expanded considerably. According to the 1838 map of the community, there was a variety of property ownership, ranging from those who owned several plots with grand homes to those who inhabited a single plot with a small cottage. For example, African Society member Epiphany Davis owned seventeen plots of land and constructed two three-story homes on his property, which must have been the envy of the community. Likewise, George Root controlled nine plots upon which he constructed several buildings; in addition to a barn, stable, and shed, Root built a two-story piazza that stretched the entire length of one tract. Andrew Williams only owned three plots, but he erected two buildings that were over two stories high. Yet despite these impressive displays, there were many properties that stood empty or only contained a small building city officials described as a "shack." William Pease was one such landowner; he purchased a single lot but was unable to afford the construction of an impressive building. Black female property owners Sarah and Cornelia Reed were in similar circumstances; they probably waited impatiently for the day when they would be able to build on their land and permanently inhabit the burgeoning community of Seneca Village. Pease and the Reeds represented a portion of the Black population who longed to be property owners but struggled against poverty. These stories reflected the diversity within New York's Black community and also the burning desire to create a unified Black neighborhood regardless of economic status.[10]

Although Seneca Village's popularity was clearly growing among Black New Yorkers, it is difficult to determine exactly how many people lived in the community. According to the 1855 census, there were 264 people living there; however, it is likely that the number was much higher. Many Seneca Village landowners do not appear in the 1855 census, despite the fact that they had constructed homes and likely lived on their land. In addition, official reports indicated that there were over 300 homes in Seneca Village by 1857, and it seems unlikely that there would be 300 homes and only 264 residents.[11] Further complicating the situation is the possibility that Seneca Village was used as a haven for fugitive slaves during the antebellum era. Many Seneca Village residents were connected to various political movements, including the Underground Railroad and the protection of fugitives. Obviously, fugitives seeking refuge in the community would not appear in the census. This combination of factors probably skewed the report on Seneca Village's population.

Regardless of the actual number of residents, however, Seneca Village blossomed into a flourishing community during the 1850s. The neighborhood stretched from Eighty-first Street to Eighty-ninth Street, between Seventh and Eighth Avenues, and, in the upper region, there was extensive farmland with barns, stables, and several two-story homes. The property owned by longtime residents like Andrew Williams, Epiphany Davis, and George Root continued to prosper, as did the land owned by Henry Garnett, who owned two adjoining plots of land containing a barn, a stable, two sheds, and two houses. One of Garnett's homes was particularly impressive, towering three stories high and including a basement and a porch.[12] Reflecting their desire to establish an independent, self-sustaining community, many residents cultivated gardens to provide food for themselves and fellow community members. According to one newspaper report, Seneca Village contained numerous homes "of various degrees of excellence . . . a number of these have fine kitchen gardens, and some of the side-hill slopes are adorned with cabbage, and melon-patches, with hills of corn and cucumbers, and beds of beets, parsnips, and other garden delicacies."[13] Most striking, however, was the increasing number of affluent Black New Yorkers who invested in Seneca Village. George Webster and Charles Silvan, a Haitian immigrant, each owned property worth over $2,000 whereas O. P. McCollin and William Mathews controlled plots valued at $1,000 each. The fact that property values often exceeded the necessary amount to qualify for voting rights reinforced the image of Seneca Village as a community where Black folks were beginning to thrive despite the legacy of slavery.[14]

Although men like Charles Silvan, George Root, and George Webster reflected the wealth in Seneca Village, there were many regular folks who simply viewed the community as their home and labored to build something permanent.

Many families likely came to Seneca Village hoping to create a positive future for their children. Upon arriving in New York State in 1855, Richard and Mary Thompson, for example, purchased land in the community, and their children, Alfred and Catherine, found respectable work there as a cartman and a school-teacher, respectively. Likewise, Solomon Hutchings, who was unable to afford his own land, rented a house in the neighborhood and brought his family to the community to seek opportunity. Eventually, he was employed as a common laborer and his daughter helped support the family as a domestic. Rare among the community residents were women like Sarah Wilson, a single, fifty-nine-year-old Black woman employed as a washerwoman, who managed to acquire a plot of land and construct a home worth $500. Wilson was even financially secure enough to adopt a young girl, Catherine Treadwell, and provide for her education.[15] The examples of these struggling Seneca Villagers demonstrated that many Black folks were deeply inspired by this community's potential and flocked there in hopes of forging a better life. In many ways, their dreams were initially realized; most Seneca Villagers' property was only worth about $500, but this was still rather impressive for the antebellum era. Compared with the experience of the many Black New Yorkers who were crowded into attics and cellars in the Five Points district, Seneca Village must have seemed a veritable mecca and a symbol of what the Black community could eventually attain.

Seneca Village residents were members of a burgeoning community, a neighborhood that reflected their hopes for a prosperous future as free people. Most notably, Seneca Village contained many institutions like churches and schools, which were symbols of the Black community's longevity and fortitude. Continuing their tradition of independence and activism, the Zion Church estab-lished a branch in Seneca Village in the early years of the community's existence. Known after 1848 as the African Methodist Episcopal Zion Branch Militant, the Seneca Village congregants worked tirelessly to develop a sense of permanence in their new home. By 1838, they had raised enough money to construct a church and, by 1853, there were over 100 regular attendees with 30 permanent mem-bers. They also created a cemetery, where they could properly pay homage to their ancestors. In August 1853, the congregation held a ceremony to honor the placement of the cornerstone of their new church, a symbolic representation of the permanent structure they would eventually erect. Elder Christopher Rush, the superintendent of African churches who had participated in the famous 1796 move toward religious independence, presided over the proceedings. Rush laid the cornerstone of the church; his presence signified the importance of the church not only to Seneca Village but also to New York City's entire Black community.[16]

Although not as large and influential as the AME Zion Branch Militant, other religious institutions soon joined the community. As early as 1840, there were reports of a church called African Union in New York City with a small presence in Seneca Village. African Union was apparently an "independent sect of Methodists" that was affiliated with a main body in Delaware. Its New York City headquarters were located downtown near Fifteenth Street and, according to the *Colored American* newspaper, its 100-member congregation was composed of a "plain and exemplary people." Although its congregations may have been smaller than most Black churches in New York City, African Union managed to establish a branch in Seneca Village with a "small frame building." Under the Rev. James Barney's leadership, African Union Church settled near the AME Zion Church and offered religious salvation to the residents of Seneca Village.[17] They also followed the African Methodists' example of creating a cemetery for the interment of their people. Although the records from AME Zion Branch Militant and African Union Churches did not survive, these institutions were profoundly important to Black Seneca Villagers because they represented the continuation of the movement to build autonomous Black organizations and create a lasting legacy for the Black community.

Adjacent to the Zion and African Union Churches was a third church called All Angels. Unlike Zion and African Union, All Angels was not a typical Black church because it did not have any official affiliation or connection with the Black community. In fact, it was under the leadership of a white minister, Thomas M.C. Peters, and affiliated with St. Michael's Protestant Episcopal Church. Even more, All Angels Church had a biracial and multiethnic congregation that included Black people, like the Stairs and Riddles families, alongside Irish residents, like Margaret McIntay and the Cassidy family. All Angels was certainly unique in its day, for most Black New Yorkers did not worship with whites in the antebellum era. However, the existence of All Angels was a testament to a new social and political reality. By 1855, German and Irish immigrants had moved into New York City, and some found their way to the area surrounding Seneca Village. Three Irish families, the Lanes, the Berrys, and the Foleys, moved near Seneca Villagers Sarah Wilson and William Pease.[18] Although most European immigrants remained in the area just south of Seneca Village, many joined All Angels' congregation, which, by the 1850s, had a sizable wooden building that was two stories high.[19] The arrival of these families in the neighborhood illustrated a different kind of hope. For although All Angels did not reflect the efforts at Black autonomy evident elsewhere in the community, since Black and white New Yorkers worshiped and were apparently buried together, it offered the vision that the races could eventually coexist peacefully, a goal that many Black activists longed for.

Black Seneca Villagers' dreams were also realized in their efforts to improve education among their people; by the 1850s, the community contained two schools. Of course Black activists in New York City gave considerable attention to the education of their youth throughout the early national and antebellum eras, hopeful that knowledge was the key to racial uplift and community progress. This mission continued in Seneca Village partly as the result of the AME Zion Church, which offered space in its basement for one of the schools.[20] In addition, there was a branch of the African Free School, although, by the 1850s, the school was under the control of the public school system and was known as Colored School No. 3. Under the leadership of seventeen-year-old Black Seneca Villager Catherine Thompson, Colored School No. 3 was an impressive institution; despite the fact that it was housed in an "old building," it was extremely "well attended."[21] Although little else is known about these educational endeavors, they were clear evidence of the Black community's continuing commitment to the future of the race.

Seneca Village was much more than a collection of residents, homes, churches, and schools. These individuals and buildings together formed a community: a collective movement that symbolized the hope and possibility of Black New Yorkers, who valued African pride and racial consciousness and aspired to create lasting Black institutions and attain political power. Seneca Village was home to a community of Black New Yorkers who were truly "Africa's Children," those who recognized that they were descendants of Africa and yet were determined to build a future for themselves in the United States. Seneca Village's mere existence gives tremendous insight into the Black experience in New York City, but it is crucial to try to understand the *meaning* of Seneca Village because it may shed light on Black New Yorkers' hopes, dreams, and political perspectives during the antebellum era.

Although most Black activists by the 1850s had ceased their public admiration for Africa, their ideological connection to their homeland never fully disappeared. Admittedly, many Black activists had grown so concerned with public perception that they either avoided the subject of Africa or openly denounced their African identity, hoping to convince white Americans that Black people could be true and loyal Americans.[22] Nevertheless, there is evidence that Seneca Villagers remained attached to their African heritage and espoused a sense of racial consciousness. Indeed, individual residents maintained a connection to Africa and carried the memory of their people's history with them in various ways. In a powerful demonstration of the power of Black history and the community's desire to remember their past, Epiphany Davis's will contained a special stipulation for the future edification of his family.

Written in 1843, the document demanded that, upon his death, Davis's daughter Ann should receive a "picture called a section of a slave ship."[23] The now-famous illustration depicts the Middle Passage's horrors, showing how

Africans were packed into floating torture chambers and reduced to chattel bondage in the Americas. Abolitionists had used this picture for years to raise public consciousness about the need to abolish the ghastly slave trade and the system of slavery. Davis, however, hung this picture in his home as a constant reminder of the Black community's history and struggle. Moreover, he obviously recognized the importance of passing these memories and stories on to future generations so they would always remember that they were children of Africa, men and women who had endured slavery and risen to be free people.

Epiphany Davis was not the only member of the community who honored his African heritage. Samuel Hardenburgh, who was among the earliest Seneca Village residents, rose to fame in Black New York for his regular appearance as the grand marshal in community parades. Black parades were especially significant because, as scholar Sterling Stuckey has indicated, they proudly exhibited African culture and race pride. Eileen Southern and Josephine Wright concurred with Stuckey, arguing that processions incorporated African elements such as marching, drumming, singing in "the various languages of Africa," and displaying colors and banners. Likewise, Mitch Kachun noted that African cultural forms "had a significant impact on the style and content of their celebrations."[24] Indeed, in New York City, ritual celebration, music, and Black pride formed the foundation of Black parades and allowed the community to celebrate their unique cultural legacy.[25]

As a member of the African Society, Hardenburgh routinely reflected his connection to African culture by continuing the tradition of parading; he marched with the African Society on many occasions and also in the Emancipation Day celebration in 1827. For decades, Hardenburgh delighted Black New Yorkers by riding through the streets of New York, dressed in elaborate garb, flanked by various assistants, and carrying a drawn sword in his hand. Even after legal emancipation, when some members of the Black leadership denounced parading and other public displays of African culture, Hardenburgh insisted upon continuing the tradition, a choice that indicated he could not surrender his commitment to African celebrations. Hardenburgh must have carried his boldness and his connection to Africa with him to Seneca Village and, along with Epiphany Davis, influenced community members to remember and celebrate their African heritage.[26]

Even more than their enduring connection to Africa, however, Seneca Villagers demonstrated a distinct racial consciousness that acknowledged their unique identity as Black people in the United States. Their political and racial perspectives were particularly evident during the 1853 ceremony held to lay the cornerstone for the African Methodist Episcopal Zion Church. During the proceedings, the Rev. Christopher Rush and Seneca Village residents buried several items within the cornerstone to preserve some meaningful items for future generations to unearth. Along with a hymnbook and copy of the discipline from the AME Zion faith, they included a text from the Epistle of Peter, chapter one, verse six.[27] Within this passage was a powerful testimony to the Black experience in the United States: "Wherein ye greatly rejoice, though now for a season . . . ye are in heaviness through manifold temptations."[28] This verse spoke of an abiding faith despite adversity; it reminded the Black congregation that although they might be surrounded with the "heaviness" of racial oppression, they always have reason to rejoice and receive salvation. This passage demonstrated the community's passionate belief in God, but it also reflected a racial consciousness, an awareness that they were an oppressed people that would ultimately transcend their experience.

Although the Epistle of Peter suggested a spiritual transcendence that would rescue Black folks from their worldly pain, in a temporal sense the community of Seneca Village provided a tangible escape from racial persecution. Faced with the American Colonization Society's repeated efforts to forcibly remove Black people from the United States, Black New Yorkers viewed Seneca Village as an independent autonomous Black community, a permanent home that would serve as a beacon to the free Black community, symbolizing their right to remain in the United States and obtain the rights and equality they so justly deserved. Certainly, there must have been a level of pride among Seneca Villagers in the late 1840s and early 1850s, as they surveyed their community and saw the potential of their people and the future of the race. Especially within the context of Black activism in antebellum New York, the establishment of Seneca Village was the most powerful example of the Black community's strivings to build a sense of stability for their people in spite of the hostile American environment. Although they were denied equal justice and the rights of citizenship, Black New Yorkers apparently believed that, through this community, they could assert their commitment to remain in the United States and win the battle for justice. Moreover, it reminded other Black people that their diligence would be rewarded and that, despite obstacles, they could rise to be free. In direct opposition to colonization schemes, Seneca Village gave Black New Yorkers hope for their future in the United States.

The existence of Seneca Village also offered protection from racial hostility in an even more concrete sense. Although the anti-abolition riot of 1834 had revealed the vulnerability of the Black community in New York City and reminded them of their tenuous freedom, Seneca Village was removed from the center of activity and contained a group of Black activists committed to protecting their people. In fact it was Seneca Villager Epiphany Davis who wrote to the mayor, prophesying danger and pleading for protection.[29] Obviously, the mayor ignored his warning but, once the 1834 race riot began to rage in Lower Manhattan, the tiny community of Seneca Village remained safely out of harm's way. Perhaps the growth in the region by 1838 reflected an exodus of the riot victims who, bolstered by an increasing consciousness that Black New Yorkers needed to create an independent, safe alternative to city life, sought a refuge from the devastating violence.

Beyond potential race riots, Seneca Village offered safety for Black people fleeing another kind of persecution. Throughout the antebellum era, fugitive slaves flocked to the North, seeking asylum and an end to the horrors of enslavement. Black activists in New York had a tradition of protecting fugitives, and there is evidence that Seneca Village was used as a safe haven for those escaping slavery.

Located a few miles from New York City, Seneca Village was ideally situated away from the constant gaze of its enemies. City officials were unable to regularly patrol the community and, therefore, it offered prime conditions for concealing fugitives. People could blend in easily and hide until it was safe to move them further out of danger. Beyond the practicality of location, we also know that individual residents of Seneca Village were active in efforts to assist fugitives. The African Society, which was influential in establishing Seneca Village, was reputed to be active in the Underground Railroad and apparently had a secret chamber in the basement of their meetinghouse for such purposes.[30] Through the African Society, Seneca Villagers were also connected to men like Charles Ray, James McCune Smith, John J. Zuille, and Albro Lyons, who were known conductors on the Underground Railroad. In 1842, African Society member Albro Lyons moved into Seneca Village. Lyons had been particularly involved in the cause of fugitives; as his daughter later reported, his operation of the Colored Sailors Home was a cover for harboring fugitives, and he was also active in the movement to free alleged fugitive James Hamlet in 1850.[31] Since the nature of assisting fugitives necessitated complete secrecy, we may never know the full role of Seneca Village in the Underground Railroad. It is clear, however, that the community had compelling links to the Underground Railroad and its setting provided the perfect opportunity to harbor fugitives and assist abolitionist efforts.

Seneca Village's role in Black political activism was not limited to its involvement in the abolitionist movement; its very existence bolstered the struggle for Black voting rights. Indeed, perhaps the most obvious benefit of Seneca Village was the potential it offered for political enfranchisement. According to the New York State Legislature's ruling in 1821, Black people had restricted access to the suffrage contingent if they owned property worth at least $250. Thus, landownership was the key to political power and represented the only path to gaining political influence for the Black community. In fact, throughout the antebellum era, a few activists recommended the accumulation of property as a method to advance their cause. As evidenced by one of the resolutions that emerged from the 1840 New York State convention, Black leaders had concluded that since property ownership "secures to us the elective franchise, we do, therefore, strongly recommend to our people throughout the State to become possessors of the soil, inasmuch as that not only elevates them to the rights of freemen, but increases the political power in the State, in favor of our political and social elevation."[32] Black New Yorkers echoed a similar sentiment at an anti-colonization meeting in 1852. In one of the resolutions asserting the rights of Black people to remain in the United States, Black activist George Downing argued that they should "obtain real estate, and thus, if possible, be even more indissolubly linked with the soil." Recognizing the connection between property ownership and political power, Downing linked his real estate recommendation with a resolution declaring that the community should renew their efforts to gain the suffrage.[33] Downing was, in fact, simply articulating a point that Seneca Villagers already knew: property ownership gave Black male New Yorkers access to the vote and, thus, acquiring land in Seneca Village offered the possibility of gaining access to the political rights they so fervently desired.

Unfortunately, Seneca Village's strengths were not lost on the Black community's enemies. A few white New Yorkers, who were concerned about the creation of Black institutions and the potential power of these newly freed people, apparently were determined to destroy this burgeoning community. Prompted by a disturbing combination of racism and greed, a group of white politicians, including Mayor Fernando Wood, plotted the destruction of Seneca Village and eventually succeeded. Unwilling to accept Black New Yorkers as free and equal citizens, Mayor Wood was consumed by a mission to decimate Seneca Village and replace the neighborhood with something more beneficial to his interests. The opportunity to destroy Seneca Village and simultaneously improve his financial holdings presented itself beginning in the late 1840s. In order to justify the destruction of Seneca Village, politicians must have realized they would need public support; but what issue could they find to inspire the residents of New York? The answer to that crucial question appeared thanks to the well-intentioned comments of Andrew Jackson Downing.

Downing, a staunch advocate of city parks, wrote extensively about the benefits of creating public space to improve the urban environment. As early as 1848, he published an article arguing that New York City would be the perfect home for a grand park that would be open to "every man, woman, and child in the city." Further, he maintained that such an establishment would promote "social freedom" by allowing interaction between various classes within the city.[34] Less than a year later Downing advanced his proposition again, stating that New York City could potentially become the home to the "finest park" in the region.[35] As one contemporary observer later reflected, Downing's articles were the "actual beginning of the Central Park, the birth of the idea."[36] Although his motivations appeared to be pure, Downing's words served as the impetus behind a movement that eventually led to the destruction of Seneca Village.

Significantly, the early movements to establish a park in New York City did not immediately threaten Seneca Village's existence. Convinced that a public garden would improve conditions in the city, Mayor Kingsland passed a resolution in July 1851, stating that the area known as Jones Woods near the East River would be transformed into a park for the enjoyment of the entire city.[37] Yet Mayor Kingsland came under instantaneous criticism from Andrew Downing. Although Downing supported the basic concepts of the initiative, he argued that the location was too small and the unfortunate selection was the result of the "narrow sighted frugality of the common council." Downing maintained that Jones Woods was not large enough to be anything other than a "child's playground" and suggested that the Common Council consider the area above Thirty-ninth Street. This region, Downing argued, would have enough space to "have broad reaches of park and pleasure grounds, with a real feeling of the breadth and beauty of green fields, the perfume and freshness of nature."[38] There is no evidence that Downing knew anything of Seneca Village, but if he did, he apparently felt that the creation of a city park took precedence over the homes, churches, schools, and cemeteries in Seneca Village's burgeoning Black community.

Following Downing's article, the Common Council reversed their position on developing Jones Woods into a city park and, on August 5, 1851, they selected "the piece of ground lying between Fifth and Eighth Avenues, Fifty-Ninth and One Hundred Sixth Streets, for the purpose indicated over that known as Jones Woods." Thus, the Common Council slated Seneca Village for destruction to transform the area into a public garden. From the beginning, however, their decision was plagued by difficulty. First, the land in that region was considered undesirable for the creation of a park; one report in particular described the lands south of Seneca Village as "rocky" and "swampy." After further investigation, Central Park's Board of Commissioners determined that the region was "a pestilential spot, where rank vegetation and miasmatic odors taint every breath of air."[39] And the conditions of the land were not the only problem. By 1853, perhaps motivated out of a selfish desire to have the park located in their own neighborhood, many New York City residents opposed the creation of Central Park, arguing that Jones Woods was a more beneficial selection. As a result, thousands of New Yorkers signed a petition asking that the Common

Council reconsider its decision and immediately create the park at Jones Woods. According to the petitioners, "The time to consummate this desirable object should be no longer delayed" and work should begin quickly on the property "so eligibly situated."[40]

The mayor ignored the hostile opposition, and the legislature passed an act to seize the land above Thirty-ninth Street, including Seneca Village. Just three months after the AME Zion congregation laid the cornerstone to their new church, the Common Council appointed five commissioners to take the land and oversee implementing the plan to establish the park. Their plans were delayed, however, when petitions forced an investigation of the movement against Central Park, forcing the Common Council to temporarily suspend activity. Following an extensive review, a subcommittee passed a resolution to "destroy" the plans for Central Park above Thirty-ninth Street and return to the site at Jones Woods. Perhaps this was a time of hope for Seneca Villagers, because it appeared that their community would be spared. But their dreams were quickly shattered with the stroke of a pen. In a remarkable demonstration of mayoral power, the new city leader Fernando Wood vetoed the resolution and continued with the plans for Central Park.[41]

Mayor Wood's decision is crucial, because it suggests a possible conspiracy behind the creation of Central Park. Although the land was undesirable and public opinion favored Jones Woods, the mayor made a unilateral decision to continue with the plans for Central Park. What could have inspired him to reach such a conclusion? Apparently, significant political incentives prompted him to establish Central Park: namely, to raise property values in the surrounding area and to destroy Seneca Village. The first motivation is quite simple to understand; Mayor Wood owned property in a neighborhood adjoining Seneca Village and had a strong financial investment in the creation of Central Park. Cognizant that the value of his property would dramatically increase following the establishment of the park, Wood had an obvious personal stake in Central Park's creation. Indeed, once Seneca Village was eliminated, Mayor Fernando Wood's land value skyrocketed from a few hundred dollars to over $10,000.[42]

Yet, financial gain was not the only motivation in the story of Central Park's creation. Unfortunately, both Mayor Fernando Wood and New York senator James Beekman were committed to eradicating the free Black population from the North. Although Senator Beekman was initially in favor of the Jones Woods location because of his own financial self-interest (he owned land near Jones Woods), he did not oppose the elimination of Seneca Village because he was an ardent supporter of colonization and Black removal from the United States.[43] When Senator Munroe appeared on the congressional floor in 1852, he delivered a powerful address that revealed Beekman's support for the colonization movement: "[T]he honorable Senator from the 5th (Mr. Beekman) has become deeply interested in the Colonization Society. He tells us his whole heart is in it." Senator Munroe concluded that the "direct effect" of the Colonization Society was the degradation of the Black community, the denial of social and political rights, the strengthening of the domestic slave trade, and the perpetuation of the system of slavery. Even more, he was convinced that supporters of colonization believed in the "incapacity, the unfitness of the colored man to our institutions." Thus, despite Senator Beekman's being described as a "friend" to the Black community, it was clear that he harbored dangerous political perspectives regarding the future of the Black race in America.[44] As a result, although Beekman supported the Jones Woods location, he did not actively defend Seneca Village; instead, his colonizationist politics drove him to ignore a productive and successful Black community in the United States at his own financial expense.

If Beekman's colonizationist tendencies were not disturbing enough, Mayor Fernando Wood had an even more troubling record on racial matters. To begin, while a congressman from 1841 to 1843, Wood routinely opposed the removal of property qualifications from Black voting. As a result, he must have found it particularly disconcerting that the vast majority of Seneca Villagers were able to gain voting rights through property ownership. Even more alarming, in 1857 (the same year as Seneca Village's final destruction) Wood strongly supported the *Dred Scott* decision that upheld notions of Black inferiority and stated that Black people could never be full citizens. In addition, Wood called for an end to antislavery agitation in Kansas and supported the extension of slavery into newly acquired U.S. territories. Wood was especially enraged by radicals in the Republican Party who supported Black rights and pushed to censure Republicans for attempting to secure equal suffrage for Black people. Specifically, he denounced radical Republicans for promising "lazy, unfit blacks immediate suffrage, high pay and social superiority."[45]

Many of Wood's most alarming racial views came to light *after* Seneca Village was demolished, but they are important to chronicle because they illuminate deeply held racist beliefs that Wood carried with him as he decided Seneca Village's fate. By 1860, Fernando Wood's attitude toward Black people was fully revealed. Not only did he become a devout apologist for slavery but he also publicly insisted that the abolitionists' commitment to Black freedom and equality was eroding American society. According to Wood, the only way to save the country was to "extinguish the followers of the anti-slavery fiend stalking the country." Further, he fueled fears that Black Republicans were advocating for a violent overthrow of slavery and prophesied that such a conflict would destroy the Black population. During a speech he delivered to Democratic Party members, Wood reinforced notions of Black inferiority, stating that any successful armed rebellion would eventually lead to the "annihilation of the black race, which could not fend for itself."[46] Scholar Ernest McKay has argued that Wood's racial philosophy stemmed from an extended period of time he spent in Virginia, where he became accustomed to southern ways. As McKay explained: "[Wood] saw nothing wrong with slavery. Neither the cruelty nor the immorality of the system troubled him."[47] Ultimately, Wood's racial politics influenced many of his political views and resulted in his extreme opposition to the Civil War.

Known as a "Peace Democrat," Wood was adamantly opposed to the possibility of war and fought to make any and all concessions to the South in order to keep them in the Union. As one scholar wrote, "As mayor he had made it clear his sympathies lay with the seceding cotton states."[48] In fact, Wood publicly argued that most New Yorkers did not hold strong antislavery views because New York City's wealth relied upon "the continuance of slave labor and the prosperity of the slave master."[49] When it became apparent that compromise between the North and South was hopeless, Wood advocated for an extreme measure, suggesting that New York City secede from the Union and become an entirely independent entity. On January 6, 1861, Wood appeared before the city's Common Council and presented his radical plan. His argument was based on the notion that since the city of New York was heavily dependent on the southern economy, New Yorkers must take action to protect their interests: "With our aggrieved brethren of the Slave States, we have friendly relations and a common sympathy. . . . While other portions of our State have unfortunately been imbued with the fanatical spirit which actuates a portion of the people of New England, the city of New York has unfalteringly preserved the integrity of its principles of adherence to the compromises of the Constitution and the equal rights of the people of all the States." What is particularly striking about this quote is the way in which Wood openly sided with the view that the North was wrongly persecuting the South and that the rights of individual states were being violated. He also suggested that New York City residents should continue to resist the "fanatical" abolitionist views of others in the region. As a result, Wood maintained that New York City must embrace a policy of separation in order to defend its financial holdings and political principles: "New York, as a *Free City*, may shed the only light and hope of a future reconstruction of our once blessed Confederacy."[50]

Of course New York City ultimately remained in the Union, yet Wood did not temper his views during the war. He continued to oppose Republican efforts to improve the status of free Blacks or liberate anyone enslaved in the South. In particular, he objected to the 1862 Confiscation Act, widely considered as the predecessor of the Emancipation Proclamation, which provided freedom to all enslaved people who took refuge behind Union lines and stated that

Confederates who did not surrender within sixty days of the act's passage would be punished by having their slaves emancipated. Wood's biographer explained his view on confiscation succinctly when he wrote: "Confiscation had a logical extension, the divisive issue of ending slavery and its relationship to defining the status of freed blacks. . . . Based on racism, constitutional conservatism and his belief that freeing slaves foiled compromise, he fought against any alteration of the prewar South's social order. As a result, Wood did not accept the legitimacy of the 1862 Confiscation Act . . . [or] the Emancipation Proclamation, and vehemently opposed anything that might create black equality." Wood's opposition to Black equality became even more virulent during the war after his brother became the publisher of the *New York Daily News*. The paper soon became the Wood brothers' mouthpiece and, in June and July of 1863, the paper regularly spewed racist propaganda against the war and the draft. In fact, the two brothers were ultimately blamed for instigating the 1863 draft riots that decimated Black institutions and resulted in the killing and torturing of hundreds of Black people.[51]

Late in 1863, Fernando Wood was elected to the House of Representatives, where he unilaterally opposed all legislation designed to advance the cause of Black people. He began by voting against the Thirteenth Amendment, which outlawed slavery because, as he argued on the floor of Congress, "The Almighty has fixed the distinction of the races; the Almighty has made the black man inferior, and, sir, by no legislation, by no partisan success, by no military power, can you wipe out this distinction." He continued on his anti-Black rampage by voting against numerous other bills, including one granting homesteads for emancipated Blacks and another offering equal pay and treatment for Black troops. He even attempted to prevent Montana from becoming a state because it allowed Blacks to vote. His final act of racial injustice was to deliver an "emotional speech" in defense of the Ku Klux Klan, arguing that Klan members should not be prevented from their terror campaigns in the South.[52]

To say that Fernando Wood opposed Black advancement, voting rights, and equality is an understatement; thus, there should be no doubt that his racist views influenced his desire to remove Seneca Village. When Mayor Wood evoked the power of eminent domain and seized the land Seneca Village occupied, he was motivated by financial gain and racism. Initially passed in 1853, the decision became final in July 1855 and Seneca Village officially became the property of the city. According to the rule of eminent domain, the city had the right to deprive citizens of their land if it could be established that "the public good demands taking private property."[53] Yet, the "public good" was not always obvious to the citizens in whose benefit such actions were supposedly taken. Thus, in an effort to gain popular support, Central Park supporters still launched a propaganda campaign against Seneca Village to validate their actions. In their annual reports, the Central Park Board of Commissioners described Seneca Village in highly negative terms, arguing that "a suburb more filthy, squalid, and disgusting can hardly be imagined." They further suggested that most residents were engaged in illegal activities and living in wretched conditions.[54] Historians of Central Park perpetuated the myth that the community was simply a gathering of squatters and thieves.[55] What the Board of Commissioners and future scholars failed to note, however, was that such descriptions were actually in reference to the "southern portion of the site," not the community of Seneca Village.[56] Seneca Village was, contrary to popular belief, a beautiful community composed primarily of families. A newspaper report had to concede that the area occupied by Black people was a "pleasing" and "neat" settlement.[57]

Regardless of the reality of Seneca Village, the propaganda was enough to justify the seizure of the land and the removal of its occupants. By 1855, the Common Council began the process of destroying Seneca Village and ultimately assumed control of over 7,500 plots of land in Upper Manhattan. There were delays along the way, because the law of eminent domain allowed Seneca Villagers to remonstrate against their treatment by contesting the city's assessment of property values. According to the law, the city had to compensate landowners for the value of their land but, unfortunately for Seneca Villagers, the city was allowed to determine that price.[58] In the initial appraisal, the city announced that it would pay just over $1 million for the land it had taken. This figure was clearly unfair, because the *New York Sun* newspaper had reported in 1851 that the land in that ward was valued at nearly $7 million.[59]

As a result, and contrary to the popular notion that Seneca Villagers did not oppose their expulsion, the community organized and bombarded the Common Council with petitions appealing to the city government to reverse its decision.[60] The petitioners fell into two general categories: those who did not want to surrender their property regardless of compensation and those who felt that they deserved more money for their property.[61] Andrew Williams, a founding resident of Seneca Village, was among the petitioners who argued that the city was not paying a reasonable amount for his property because the city offered only $2,335 and he knew that it was valued at over $4,000.[62] It is unknown what individual compromises the city eventually made with Andrew Williams and other Seneca Villagers, but the Common Council ultimately paid over $5 million for the entire ward above Forty-second Street.

Obviously, Seneca Villagers were not sufficiently reimbursed for the loss of their property; even if they had received a cash payment commensurate with the value of their land, how could money replace the community they had labored to build? For its residents, Seneca Village was a symbol of their sustained efforts to create a place for themselves and their people. To Black New Yorkers throughout the city, it was an icon of their creativity and their social, economic, and political progress. Its destruction must have been devastating to both the residents and the entire Black community. Yet, when Seneca Village was slated for destruction, residents were told to vacate the premises in February 1856.[63]

Significantly, despite the Common Council's proclamations, many Seneca Villagers refused to leave. Apparently aware that their removal was the result of a conspiracy, some Black residents remained in their homes. According to the *New York Daily Times*, when the police attempted to remove them, these residents claimed that this decision was motivated by something more than a desire to create a city park: "The policemen find it difficult to persuade them out of the idea which has possessed their simple minds, that the sole object of the authorities in making the Park is to procure their expulsion from the homes which they occupy."[64] Although the city newspaper condescendingly accused the Seneca Villagers of having "simple minds," the residents were clearly far more astute than anyone guessed. Only through hindsight can we now see that the Black community was correct; the decimation of Seneca Village was the result of a plot to undermine the potential of the Black population and satisfy racist men like Fernando Wood.

Despite the political awareness of the Seneca Villagers, they could not save their community. In August 1857, another announcement was released, demanding that they abandon their homes immediately.[65] The police violently removed the remaining resisters the following month. As the *New York Tribune* reported nearly a decade later, the raid on Seneca Village could "not be forgotten. . . . [M]any a brilliant and stirring fight was had during the campaign. But the supremacy of the law was upheld by the policeman's bludgeons."[66]

The final battle to save Seneca Village was long and bloody but ultimately concluded in a devastating loss for the Black community. Despite their determination to remain and continue the project they had commenced, Seneca Villagers were ultimately forced from their community. One can only imagine the scene as these Black pioneers left their homes, schools, churches, and cemeteries, suddenly adrift without a community. For three decades, Seneca Village had served as a beacon of hope to free Blacks throughout the city but, through an act of racism and greed, it was unjustly and violently extinguished.

NOTES

Essay adapted from the publication *African or American? Black Identity and Political Activism in New York City, 1784–1861.* Copyright 2008 by the Board of Trustees of the University of Illinois. Used with permission of the University of Illinois Press.

1. *New York Herald*, August 11, 1871.

2. There is significant confusion surrounding the community's name. The rector of St. Michael's Church maintained that the area was known as Seneca Village; however, there is no other evidence that the community actually used that name. Others refer to the region as "Yorkville" or occasionally mention the derogatory name "Nigger Village." If the community was in fact called Seneca Village, the most common question is why Seneca? We may never know the answer to that query. Various scholars who heard my presentations on this topic at academic conferences initially suggested that the name was a reference to the Native Americans who originally inhabited that land, particularly because an old Native American trail passed nearby. However, we know that the Senecas did not live on Manhattan Island and had no significant connection to that region. Therefore, I have proposed that the name "Seneca" could refer to the Roman philosopher who wrote extensively about the rights of humans to freedom and liberty. Black New Yorkers who had been educated at the African Free Schools were trained in Classical philosophy and would likely have been exposed to Seneca's ideas. Perhaps inspired by the ideal of liberty and equality, Black residents adopted the name "Seneca" to reflect their hope for their community's potential.

3. The truth about Seneca Village began to be revealed following a brief mention of the community in Roy Rosenzweig and Elizabeth Blackmar's study of Central Park, *The Park and the People: A History of Central Park* (Ithaca: Cornell University Press, 1992). Inspired by this citation, Cynthia Copeland at the New-York Historical Society (NYHS) began to investigate the community and constructed an exhibit that became one of the most popular events at the NYHS. Since then, other scholars of Black New York have mentioned Seneca Village briefly; however, there has still not been an extensive historical investigation of this important and influential neighborhood. For other discussions of Seneca Village, see Craig Wilder, *In the Company of Black Men: The African Influence on African American Culture in New York City* (New York: New York University Press, 2001), 101–102; Leslie M. Harris, *In the Shadow of Slavery: African Americans in New York City, 1626–1863* (Chicago: University of Chicago Press, 2003), 266–267.

4. Of course Seneca Village was not the first effort by Black New Yorkers to establish an independent community in the state. In 1846, after white abolitionist Gerrit Smith announced that he would donate 120,000 acres of land in upstate New York to 3,000 Black New Yorkers, there was an aborted attempt to create a community called "Timbucto." For more, see John Stauffer, *The Black Hearts of Men: Radical Abolitionists and the Transformation of Race* (Cambridge, MA: Harvard University Press, 2002), 139–145, 157–158.

5. New York City, Tax Records 1825, New York Municipal Archives.

6. John Jamison Moore, *History of the African Methodist Episcopal Zion Church in America, Founded in 1796, in the City of New York* (York, PA: Teacher's Journal Office, 1884), 15–18, 22–23; William J. Walls, *The African Methodist Episcopal Zion Church: Reality of the Black Church* (Charlotte, NC: AME Zion Publishing House, 1974), 47–50; Jonathan Greenleaf, *A History of the Churches of All Denominations in the City of New York, from the First Settlement to the Year 1846* (New York: E. French, 1846), 321.

7. New York City Common Council, *Minutes of the Common Council of the City of New York, 1784–1831* (New York: City of New York, 1917), 4:389; 5:272, 278; 7:729; 9:40; 6:274; B. F. DeCosta, *Three Score and Ten: The Story of St. Philip's Church of New York City:*

A Discourse Delivered in the New Church West 25th Street at Its Opening Sunday Morning, February 17, 1889 (New York: Printed for the Parish, 1889), 28; *New York Evening Post*, July 12, 1834; *New York American*, July 12, 1834; Tyler Anbinder, *Five Points: The 19th Century New York City Neighborhood That Invented Tap Dance, Stole Elections, and Became the World's Most Notorious Slum* (New York: Plume, Penguin Putnam Books, 2001), 11–12. For more on the 1834 riot, see Paul Gilje, *The Road to Mobocracy: Popular Disorder in New York City, 1763–1834* (Chapel Hill: University of North Carolina Press, 1987); J. T. Headley, *The Great Riots of New York, 1712–1873* (Miami: Mnemosyne, 1969); Linda Kerber, "Abolitionists and Amalgamators: The New York City Riots of 1834," *New York History* 48 (1967): 28–39; Leonard L. Richards, *"Gentlemen of Property and Standing": Anti-Abolition Mobs in Jacksonian America* (New York: Oxford University Press, 1970); Eugene Portlette Southall, "Arthur Tappan and the Anti-Slavery Movement," *Journal of Negro History* 47 (1967): 28–39.

8. Another example of an institution-building effort, and the opposition it inspired, was apparent in the creation of African Grove Theatre, a leisure and entertainment spot that was established in 1821 and destroyed in 1829. For more, see Alexander, *African or American?*; Gilje, *Road to Mobocracy*; George A. Thompson Jr., *A Documentary History of the African Theatre* (Evanston, IL: Northwestern University Press, 1998); Shane White, *Stories of Freedom in Black New York* (Cambridge, MA: Harvard University Press, 2002).

9. John J. Zuille, *Historical Sketch of the New York African Society for Mutual Relief* (New York: n.p., compiled 1892–1893), 16; Alexander, *African or American?*; Wilder, *In the Company of Black Men*, 105–106.

10. Gardner A. Sage, Manhattan Square Benefit Map, 1838. According to this map, there were over 200 plots of land in Seneca Village, but many of them had not yet been developed.

11. Board of Commissioners of Central Park, *Second Annual Report of the Board of Commissioners of the Central Park* (New York: William C. Bryant and Co., 1859), 60.

12. New York Common Council, *Central Park: Memorial of the Common Council of the City of New York to the Legislature Approved June 11th, 1853* (New York: n.p., 1853). After considerable investigation, there does not appear to be any relationship between this Henry Garnett and well-known activist Henry Highland Garnet.

13. *New York Tribune*, August 14, 1857.

14. Information compiled from the 1855 Census, New York County, 22nd Ward, 3rd District.

15. Ibid.

16. *New York Tribune*, August 5, 1853.

17. *Colored American,* March 28, 1840.

18. 1855 Census, New York County, 22nd Ward, 3rd District.

19. All Angels Parish Church Records, 1849–1850.

20. *New York Tribune*, August 5, 1853.

21. *Anglo African Magazine*, July 1859. By 1856, perhaps aware of the impending doom, Black activists recommended that Colored School No. 3 be combined with Colored School No. 4 in Harlem.

22. For more on this shift in identity, see Alexander, *African or American?*, chapters 4–6.

23. For Epiphany Davis's will, see the collection of wills in the City of New York, Liber no. 101, New York Municipal Archives.

24. Sterling Stuckey, *Slave Culture: Nationalist Theory and the Foundations of Black America* (New York: Oxford University Press, 1987), 142–144; Eileen Southern and Josephine Wright, *Images: Iconography of Music in African American Culture (1770s–1920s)* (New York: Garland, 2000), 28; Mitch Kachun, *Festivals of Freedom: Memory and Meaning in African American Emancipation Celebrations, 1808–1915* (Amherst: University of Massachusetts Press, 2003), 22. Stuckey noted that these activities were found among African peoples throughout the West Indies and Canada as late as the 1850s. Shane White and Graham White also conceded that "northern blacks infused these events with their own cultural imperatives, creating something fresh." Shane White and Graham White, *Stylin': African American Expressive Culture from Its Beginnings to the Zoot Suit* (Ithaca, NY: Cornell University Press, 1998), 101.

25. Sterling Stuckey, *Going Through the Storm: The Influence of African American Art in History* (New York: Oxford University Press, 1994), 55, 60–65, 74.

26. For discussions of Samuel Hardenburgh's participation in Black parades, see Alexander, *African or American?*, chapters 2–3; Henry Highland Garnet, *A Memorial Discourse Delivered in the Hall of the House of Representatives, Washington City, D.C., on Sabbath, February 12, 1865, with an introduction by James McCune Smith, M.D.* (Philadelphia: J. M. Wilson, 1865), 24; Sterling Stuckey, *Slave Culture: Nationalist Theory and the Foundations of Black America* (New York: Oxford University Press, 1987), 143–144; Shane White, " 'It Was a Proud Day': African Americans, Festivals and Parades in the North, 1741–1834," *Journal of American History* 81, no. 1 (June 1994): 44.

27. *New York Tribune*, August 5, 1853.

28. *The Holy Bible, Containing the Old and New Testaments in the King James Version*, First Epistle of Peter, I:6 (Nashville: Thomas Nelson Publishers, 1977).

29. Mayor's Papers, 1834, New York Municipal Archives.

30. Walter N. Beekman, *Address by Walter N. Beekman, Vice President, New York African Society for Mutual Relief* (Brooklyn: n.p., 1946), 6.

31. Dorothy Sterling, *We Are Your Sisters: Black Women in the Nineteenth Century* (New York: W. W. Norton & Company, 1984), 220–221; Lewis Tappan, *The Fugitive Slave Bill: Its History and Unconstitutionality with an Account of the Seizure and Enslavement of James Hamlet, and His Subsequent Restoration to Liberty* (New York: n.p., 1850), 36.

32. Philip S. Foner and George Walker, eds., *Proceedings of the Black State Conventions, 1840–1865* (Philadelphia: Temple University Press, 1979), 10.

33. *Frederick Douglass Paper*, February 5, 1852.

34. Andrew Downing, "A Talk About Public Parks and Gardens," *The Horticulturist, and Journal of Rural Art and Rural Taste* 3, no. 4 (October 1848): 155.

35. Andrew Downing, "Public Cemeteries and Public Gardens," *The Horticulturist, and Journal of Rural Art and Rural Taste* 4, no. 1 (July 1849): 12.

36. Charles H. Haswell, *Reminiscences of an Octogenarian of the City of New York, 1816 to 1860* (New York: Harper and Brothers, 1897), 465. Roy Rosenzweig and Elizabeth Blackmar noted that William Cullen Bryant also issued an appeal for a park in 1844 and therefore preceded Downing by five years. Rosenzweig and Blackmar, *Park and the People*, 15–17. However, it seems that Downing's appeal was the immediate impetus for creating a park.

37. Board of Commissioners of Central Park, *First Annual Report on the Improvement of the Central Park, New York* (New York: Charles Baker, Printer, 1857), 6; Rosenzweig and Blackmar, *Park and the People*, 18.

38. Andrew Downing, "The New York Park," *The Horticulturist,* and *Journal of Rural Art and Rural Taste* 8 (August 1, 1851): 346–347.

39. Board of Commissioners of Central Park, *First Annual Report*, 6, 11–12.

40. James W. Beekman Papers, Jones Woods Petitions, New York City, 1853.

41. Board of Commissioners of Central Park, *First Annual Report*, 7–8; Rosenzweig and Blackmar, *Park and the People*, 56.

42. Fernando Wood's Tax Records, 1855–1860, Bureau of Old Records, New York City Municipal Archives. A book published in 1913 also noted the dramatic rise in property values in 1858 and 1859 following the establishment of Central Park. Henry Collins Brown, *Old New York: Yesterday and Today* (New York: Privately Printed for Valentine's Manual, 1922), 140–152.

43. James Beekman was one of the primary supporters of the Jones Woods location because he was a sizable-property owner in that area, and he believed that his real estate value would increase dramatically. Rosenzweig and Blackmar, *Park and the People*, 21, 30–33, 51–53.

44. *Frederick Douglass Paper*, April 22, 1852.

45. Jerome Mushkat, *Fernando Wood: A Political Biography* (Kent, OH: Kent State University Press, 1990), 164, 170, 161.

46. Fernando Wood, *Speech of Fernando Wood Delivered Before the Meeting of the National Democratic Delegation to the Charleston Convention at Syracuse, February 7, 1860* (New York: n.p., 1860); Mushkat, *Fernando Wood*, 100.

47. Ernest A. McKay, *The Civil War and New York City* (Syracuse, NY: Syracuse University Press, 1991), 13.

48. James McCague, *The Second Rebellion: The Story of the New York City Draft Riots of 1863* (New York: Dial Press, 1968), 43.

49. McKay, *The Civil War and New York City*, 14.

50. *New York Times*, January 8, 1861 (emphasis in original).

51. Mushkat, *Fernando Wood*, 143–144, 137–138. Historian Iver Bernstein also noted Wood was hailed as a hero by the mobs during the riot. Iver Bernstein, *The New York City Draft Riots: Their Significance for American Society and Politics in the Age of the Civil War* (New York: Oxford University Press, 1990), 26. It is also important to note that, later in 1863, Wood was honored by the New Jersey Democratic Party and he joined in a toast celebrating the days when "Liberty wore white face, and America was not a negro." *New York Times*, November 25, 1863.

52. Mushkat, *Fernando Wood*, 153, 146, 185.

53. Board of Commissioners of Central Park, *First Annual Report*, 103. The policy of eminent domain was originally passed in 1807 and became the justification behind various "urban renewal" programs, including an attempt to rid New York City of perceived "undesirables" in the notorious Five Points region. For more on this effort, see Elizabeth Blackmar, *Manhattan for Rent, 1785–1850* (Ithaca, NY: Cornell University Press, 1989), 175.

54. Board of Commissioners of Central Park, *Second Annual Report*, 60.

55. In 1967, the curator of Central Park argued that the area was a "discouraging sight" filled mostly with squatters' shacks and hog farms. Henry Hope Reed, *Central Park: A History and a Guide* (New York: Clarkson N. Potter, 1967), 19–20. Even as recently as 1992 another scholar perpetuated this negative image of Seneca Village, writing that the area was occupied by 5,000 or more "scavengers" who huddled in trenches and caves in a barren wasteland. Laurie Watters, *A Year in Central Park* (New York: Rizzoli, 1992), 15.

56. Board of Commissioners of Central Park, *Second Annual Report*, 60.

57. *New York Daily Times*, July 9, 1856.

58. Board of Commissioners of Central Park, *First Annual Report*, 93.

59. *New York Sun*, July 12, 1851.

60. According to Elizabeth Blackmar and Roy Rosenzweig, the residents of Seneca Village accepted their fate and quietly relinquished their land. Rosenzweig and Blackmar, *The Park and Its People*, 53.

61. Board of Commissioners of Central Park, *First Annual Report*, 105.

62. Andrew Williams's Affidavit of Petition, 1856, Bureau of Old Records, New York City Municipal Archives.

63. Board of Commissioners of Central Park, *First Annual Report*, 7.

64. *New York Daily Times*, July 9, 1856.

65. *New York Tribune*, August 27, 1857.

66. *New York Times*, August 17, 1866.

Carla L. Peterson

Contesting Space in Antebellum New York

Black Community, City Neighborhoods, and the Draft Riots of 1863

> In 1849 Mr. Lyons became the proprietor of the Seaman's Home for colored
> sailors. In connection with this he kept a sailor's outfitting store until the time of
> the draft riots in 1863. Being a prominent man and always fighting the oppres-
> sion of his race, the mob threatened to hang him. Three times he alone repulsed
> dastardly attempts to wreck his home, but was compelled to flee to a police sta-
> tion to save his life, being pursued through the streets by a howling mob.
>
> OBITUARY, *NEW YORK AGE,* JANUARY 9, 1896

> Mr. White carried on the business of druggist and chemist at Frankfort and
> Gold Streets for nearly forty-seven years. . . . Scores of poor families were
> befriended and helped by him. . . . Those whom he helped had a chance to show
> their gratitude during the draft riots of 1863. When the riot was at its height a
> crowd of men gathered at White's store to defend it from attack. Mr. White was
> warned by some of the business men that he would be wise if he hid himself.
> He said: "What have I to fear? Even if these men here could not protect me,
> there are as many men among the rioters who would fight for me as there are
> those who would injure me." Not the slightest attempt was made to harm him
> or his property.
>
> OBITUARY, *NEW YORK TIMES,* FEBRUARY 19, 1891

This is a story about antebellum New York and the bitter contestation over
space that defined much of the city's history and culminated in the draft riots
of July 1863. Considered to be one of the most violent civil insurrections in
U.S. history, the draft riots pitted working-class white men—largely Irish and
Catholic—against the city's political leadership, social elite, and most especially
black population. My story centers on two African American men—Albro Lyons

(1814–1896) and Philip Augustus White (1823–1891)—who lived through those tumultuous days and on what happened to them and their homes as well as to their places of work and worship. I did not pick these two men out of the archives at random: Philip Augustus White was my paternal great-grandfather and his wife was a niece of Albro Lyons. They lie at the heart of a larger project I am currently working on: a history of the everyday social, cultural, and work life of nineteenth-century black New Yorkers captured through the lens of family history.

My archival exploration into the lives of ordinary African Americans in nineteenth-century New York has uncovered new and as yet untold stories about the draft riots that are far less familiar than the more conventional narratives of black victimization. In these stories, space plays a critical role. I argue that Albro Lyons's and Philip White's vastly divergent experiences during the draft riots were shaped by each man's relationship to the various city spaces he inhabited. Their experiences provide a blueprint for the varying ways in which black New Yorkers worked to mark out and negotiate spaces for themselves before, during, and after the Civil War. They underscore how the claiming of space is always a process, and the meanings of space unstable, contested, and in constant need of negotiation. Beyond the concerns of the black community, the draft riots also represent a pivotal moment in the history of the entire city. The violence that erupted in July 1863 reshaped the urban landscape, realigning boundaries and reforming spaces increasingly demarcated by race and class.

Born in New York in 1814, Albro Lyons attended the African Free School on Mulberry Street, which had been established in the late eighteenth century by New York's Manumission Society. His schoolmates included many students who would later become prominent African American leaders, such as James McCune Smith, Henry Highland Garnet, Alexander Crummell, Charles and Patrick Reason, and George Downing. By the 1830s, these young men were active participants in community affairs. Lyons was a member of the African Society for Mutual Relief, the Philomathean Literary Society, the New York Society for the Promotion of Education Among Colored Children, and the Hamilton Lodge and had several times been elected delegate to represent New York City at various annual conventions of colored people. He worshiped at St. Philip's Episcopal Church, one of the city's earliest and most prominent black churches. Initially located on Collect (later Centre) Street, it moved in 1857 to Mulberry Street where its close proximity to police headquarters led to its occupation as a barrack during the draft riots. After trying a variety of trades, Lyons opened a Seaman's Home for Colored Sailors on Pearl Street in 1849. As Leslie Alexander notes in Chapter 1, at that time Lyons was among the black New Yorkers who had taken up residence in Seneca Village. In the mid-1850s,

Lyons moved his family to Vandewater Street in Lower Manhattan into a building that also housed his Seaman's Home and was reputed to be a station on the Underground Railroad.[1]

Given the small size of New York's black community, it was inevitable that Lyons and White should become friends. They might have met through their mutual acquaintance James McCune Smith, or perhaps as congregants at St. Philip's, or maybe in their collaborative work for the Society for the Promotion of Education Among Colored Children. Philip White was born in Hoboken, New Jersey, in 1823. According to his marriage certificate, his father came from England and his mother from Jamaica, but thus far I have found no record that explains why or how they came to the United States. An obituary published in the *New York Age* notes that White's father died early, leaving the family impoverished and his son "thrown upon his own resources." Throughout the 1830s, White attended the African Free School No. 2 on Laurens Street. In 1840, he became an apprentice in the drugstore of James McCune Smith, who had recently returned to New York after obtaining a medical degree from the University of Glasgow. Proprietor of a thriving pharmaceutical and medical practice, McCune Smith was also the physician for the Colored Orphan Asylum. White then went on to attend the College of Pharmacy of the City of New York, from which he graduated in 1844, the first African American student to do so. That same year he became a communicant at St. Philip's Episcopal Church and a few years later opened a drugstore on Frankfort Street in the city's Fourth Ward. By 1858, he had moved his store to the corner of Frankfort and Gold Streets and was living on nearby Vandewater Street. White devoted his energy during these years to his business, to his social activist causes such as his secretaryship of the New York Society for the Promotion of Education Among Colored Children, and to St. Philip's. The close proximity of White's and Lyons's homes to one another undoubtedly cemented the friendship between the two men. In 1867, White married Lyons's niece, Elizabeth Guignon, who had lived with the Lyons family as a child.[2]

Despite White's and Lyons's personal achievements, most black New Yorkers suffered from intense racial discrimination that severely constrained their lives. Slavery did not end in the state until 1827, but even after its abolition, "blackbirders" roamed the streets, anxious to capture escaped slaves, or even free or emancipated blacks who could not provide proof of their status, and remand them into slavery. Those blacks who remained in the city felt the sting of racial prejudice in every facet of their lives. Transferred from the Manumission Society to the city's Public School Society in the early 1830s, the African Free Schools offered an increasingly poor education. The Public School Society demoted all but one of the schools to the primary level, discharged black teachers who had been responsible for the more advanced grades, and abandoned the use of spelling books.[3] Even those black New Yorkers who were able to obtain some schooling could find work only as unskilled laborers—women as domestics, laundresses, and charwomen; men as servants, laborers, or more fortunately as coachmen and cooks. Without the possibility of economic advancement, they remained mired in poverty, living in crowded and unhygienic housing that resulted in a high incidence of disease and early mortality rates. Finally, even well-to-do blacks found the few civil rights they had curtailed; in 1821, for example, most black men were disfranchised when the state legislature imposed a $250 bond on New York voters.[4]

By mid-century, black New Yorkers could readily claim that they were being assaulted from below and above. From below, antagonism came from the city's white working class, in particular from the Irish who, like African Americans, faced discrimination in schooling, jobs, and housing and suffered equally from the ravages of poverty and disease. Thrown together at the bottom of the socio-economic ladder, the two groups lived in proximity to one another and were closely associated in the minds of other urban dwellers. Historian Noel Ignatiev has perceptively analyzed how the Irish gradually disassociated themselves from and turned against their black brethren in order to improve their own economic lot and achieve citizenship. They came to regard blackness as a sign of degradation inextricably linked to slavery. Eager to improve their status by distinguishing themselves from blacks so that they could place themselves in a relatively superior position, the Irish fiercely upheld their status as white persons, as free people, and as wage laborers, and sought to purify the spaces they inhabited—both work and social—of all black presence.[5]

Antagonism against blacks also came from above from a significant segment of the city's ruling commercial and political elite. New York Democrats, for example, believed that their economic interests were tied to the South and were thus disinclined to help or protect African Americans. In the late 1850s, they managed to elect Fernando Wood as mayor. Once in office, Wood suggested that were the Union to dissolve, New York should become a free city. In the 1862 election, Wood and fellow Peace Democrat Horatio Seymour campaigned on the slogan that the emancipation of slaves substituted "niggerism for nationality." Wood won a congressional seat and Seymour was elected governor.[6] This hostility against blacks eventually came to a boil and erupted during the draft riots of July 1863.

The impetus for the draft riots was the federal government's decision to draft soldiers into the Union army during the Civil War. In March 1863, Congress passed the National Conscription Act decreeing that all male citizens between the ages of twenty and thirty-five were to be enrolled in the military and a lottery would determine who would actually serve. But the act also allowed exemption from service to those able to provide an acceptable substitute or pay $300, thus ensuring that the poor rather than the rich would go to war. New York's white working-class population—native-born, Irish, and German—initially supported the war, seeing it as a source of employment and also as an act of good citizenship. But a variety of factors gradually led them to withdraw their support. They were disillusioned by the mounting number of war deaths; frustrated by rising prices and falling wages; resentful of the government's power; fearful of economic competition from blacks and especially of the specter of ex-slave labor flooding the North after a Union victory; and, finally, angry that they were being asked to risk their lives in an armed conflict in which neither those whom they held responsible for the war—the political elites—nor those who they believed to be the cause of the war—blacks—were participants. On July 13, they took to the streets and rioted.[7]

Historians have extensively documented the ways in which the draft riots took shape and evolved over a five-day period. From today's perspective, the riots may be seen as a contestation over city spaces as the mob endeavored to seize control of the city's infrastructure, invade and police neighborhoods and workplaces in order to rid them of a black presence, and finally destroy black property. On the first day the rioters were a composite crowd of native-born, Irish, German, Protestant, and Catholic men from different parts of the city. They were mostly journeymen in the older artisan trades and seemed mainly intent on destroying government property—municipal and federal buildings, telegraph lines, railroads and streetcar tracks, ferries, and bridges—in a daring attempt to contest and perhaps even take over the entire space of the city. By the second day, however, the riot took a new turn as the artisans and Germans retreated, and workers in the new industrial occupations and common laborers—mostly Irish Catholic—took over, venting their anger against the wealthy and the ruling elites in a wholesale destruction of private property.[8]

But throughout the conflict, rioters reserved their special animus for New York's black population, particularly targeting black individuals and property, including homes. On Wednesday night, a crowd of about 100 Irishmen destroyed two rows of houses on York Street, leaving the homes without doors or glass in the windows but with heaps of stones piled on the stoops and floors of the rooms.[9] Similar scenes could be found on the East Side. Several seamen's boardinghouses on Roosevelt Street close to Vandewater in the Fourth Ward suffered assaults similar to that on Albro Lyons's home, which will be discussed later in this chapter; not only were the houses looted and burned, but owners and boarders alike were stripped of their clothes and forced to run naked through the streets to safety as the mob directly targeted black men, women, and children.[10]

Part of the animosity was economic. White longshoremen living around the piers began patrolling the dock area as early as Monday. They issued a statement proclaiming that work on the docks was reserved for white laborers alone and attacked black men caught in the vicinity.[11] On Wednesday night, one Charles Jackson was apprehended as he walked along West Street. He was kicked in the face and ribs, cut in the throat, and thrown into the water to drown. Miraculously, he survived and was rescued the next day.[12] Yet, work antagonisms alone cannot explain the assaults against black individuals. As often as not, neighbor turned against neighbor. In one particularly horrifying incident, an Irish laborer living on West Twenty-seventh Street broke into a house on the corner of Twenty-seventh and Seventh Avenue inhabited by Abraham Franklin, a crippled black coachman, and his sister. He and his fellow rioters dragged them from the house, beat and kicked them, and then hanged Franklin from a lamppost. The mob scattered when soldiers appeared, cut Franklin's body down, and rescued his sister. As soon as they left, however, the body was hoisted up again, only to be taken down later and dragged through the streets by its genitals.[13]

READING SPACE

In tracing the fate of the Colored Orphan Asylum, St. Philip's Episcopal Church, and two individuals—Albro Lyons and Philip White—this essay seeks to look beyond the often reiterated anecdotes to construct a more complex picture of the draft riots. Like others, I begin by underscoring the tremendous significance of city space for all New Yorkers, whether white or black, well-to-do or poor. But we need deeper analysis of the complexity of space for black New Yorkers, who were not only members of their local neighborhoods but also part of New York's black community. I argue that Lyons and White inhabited such spaces in dramatically different ways. The choices each man made serve as a metonym for the ways in which African Americans in antebellum New York sought to create spaces of their own and endow them with special meaning, all the while finding their claims repeatedly contested and in constant need of negotiation.

Space in this instance is not merely physical or geographical but is marked by human relationships; it is social and political. Michel de Certeau's concept of "strategy" proves useful here to an understanding of how space is inhabited and worked on. De Certeau defines "strategy" quite simply as the manipulation of power relationships. A strategy necessitates, first of all, "subjects" in possession of what he calls "will and power," which might be a business or an institution of knowledge. Second, it requires a "place" that can be delimited "as its *own.*" From this place, subjects establish relations with what de Certeau terms an "exteriority" composed of collaborative or hostile forces—perhaps customers, or competitors and enemies—that must then be managed. To do so requires distinguishing the delimited place of will and power from its surrounding environment. In other words, a strategy represents "an effort to delimit one's own place in a world bewitched by the invisible [or not so invisible] powers of the Other."[14]

The (utopian) hope is that such manipulation of relations with outside forces will result in "mastery." In its most concrete form, mastery is the ownership of place. But another of its forms might be mastery through sight; through a panoptic practice, the subject transforms foreign forces into objects that he can observe, measure, and ultimately control. Most ambitiously, mastery represents the triumph of place over time, the "ability to transform the uncertainties of history into readable spaces."[15] By seeking to delimit places of will and power of their own within their city environment, black New Yorkers sought to transform the uncertainties of history into readable spaces. My reading of specific incidents that occurred during the draft riots attempts to do the same, although I remain acutely aware that such readability can never fully be achieved. Like the spaces of the city, the spaces of history remain unstable and subject to negotiation.

Albro Lyons and Philip White lived in both the black community and their local city neighborhood. The black community is a strategy in which members carved out delimited spaces from the surrounding hostile environment in order to gain greater control over their lives. From the late eighteenth century on, black New Yorkers came together to establish institutions of their own—churches; mutual aid societies; literary, political, and educational organizations. On a material level, the creation and maintenance of such institutions constituted their will and power. On the level of consciousness, they came to embody what Raymond Williams has called a "knowable community" defined by a "grammar of morality."[16] Here, this grammar is rooted in a group identity born out of a shared racial history, a belief in common interests culminating in collective action, and a desire to preserve common historical memories. Ideally, the black community enables the mastery of place over the vagaries of history.

New York's antebellum black community as strategy had its limitations, however. Threats came from without as white New Yorkers challenged blacks' claims to delimited place, or as some black institutions found themselves still dependent on the patronage of benevolent white religious and abolitionist groups. Fault lines also existed within the black community. For one, its members were not a monolithic group but constituted a heterogeneous population divided by class, color, place of origin, religion, gender, and so forth. For another, New York's black community was not spatially bounded; rather, its inhabitants as well as its institutions were scattered throughout the city's lower wards. Such geographical diversity necessarily resulted in additional interests and affiliations outside of the black community. Thus, the black community was never fully stable and its will and power never fully secure. During the draft riots, the threats to it were even more devastating.

Black New Yorkers also lived in city neighborhoods—specific bounded locales that can be geographically mapped but are also defined by a set of social relations. In the early antebellum period, New York neighborhoods were highly heterogeneous in terms of class, race, and ethnicity. People tended to live in close proximity to their workplace so that neighborhoods brought together employers and employees, the well-to-do and the poor, the native-born, African Americans, Irish, and Germans.[17] Thus, black New Yorkers lived in neighborhoods that were neither identical to the black community nor racialized. These gave rise to a different kind of knowable community, one that was largely based on face-to-face contacts. Such neighborhood relationships can lead to physical and social intimacy. They invite the mastery of place through close observation of neighbors, streets, and buildings just as they encourage the forging of social and emotional bonds. But they can also lead to hostility, as evidenced by the mob attacks on black neighbors during the draft riots. Moreover, the boundaries of neighborhood are never fixed and absolute; they are porous and vulnerable to intrusion by strangers.

As black New Yorkers, Albro Lyons and Philip White sought to delimit places of their own within both the black community *and* their city neighborhood. The historical record indicates that their vastly contrasting experiences during the draft riots were shaped by their differing conduct as both private *and* public figures within these spaces.

THE BLACK COMMUNITY: THE COLORED ORPHAN ASYLUM AND ST. PHILIP'S EPISCOPAL CHURCH

Among black New Yorkers' earliest community institutions were churches like the African Methodist Episcopal Zion Church at Leonard and Duane Streets and St. Philip's Episcopal Church, whose first location was on Collect Street; literary societies like the Philomathean Society on Duane Street and the Phoenix Society on West Broadway; newspaper offices like those of *Freedom's Journal* on Church Street and *The Colored American* on Pearl Street; the African Society for Mutual Relief on Orange Street (later renamed Baxter); many Seaman's Homes for colored sailors, like Albro Lyons's, near the docks on the Lower East Side; and James McCune Smith's pharmacy on West Broadway, which was an important meeting place for black activists.

In fact, the term "black community" bears closer analysis. Some of these institutions, like the African Society for Mutual Relief, were determined to safeguard their autonomy and remained independent from white control. But others, seeking to forge cultural bonds with white society, did accept aid from white patrons. The Phoenixonian Literary Society was funded in part by Arthur Tappan and accepted some white members; as the tenth parish of Trinity Church, St. Philip's received regular stipends from the mother church.[18] Still other organizations were fully dependent on white benevolence; in fact, although caring exclusively for black children, the Colored Orphan Asylum was created and operated by a group of white women. Finally, New York's black community had originally been localized in Lower Manhattan's Sixth Ward, but under urban pressures it gradually became aspatial—or "unbounded," to use a term employed by historian Kenneth Scherzer—and spread out over several wards and neighborhoods.[19]

Through these institutions, black New Yorkers sought to delimit places of their own. But their vulnerability became all too apparent during the draft riots when many were invaded by outside hostile forces that challenged their very existence. The fate of the Colored Orphan Asylum, repeatedly described in historical accounts, offers a conventional narrative of black victimization. One of the most important benevolent institutions for African Americans, the asylum had been established by a group of white women in a building located at Fifth Avenue and Forty-third Street. It took care of some 200 orphans in the black community between the ages of four and twelve. In 1843, its board of managers appointed James McCune Smith as the orphanage's doctor. According to contemporaneous accounts, about 400 rioters entered the house "and immediately proceeded to pitch out beds, chairs, tables, and every species of furniture, which were eagerly seized by the crowd below, and carried off. When all was taken, the house was then set on fire."[20] Black New Yorkers might well have felt a certain ambivalence toward the Colored Orphan Asylum since it both provided relief to the most vulnerable among them *and* reminded them of their necessary dependence on white benevolence. But the rioting mob felt no ambivalence. To them, the asylum symbolized undeserved white largesse toward blacks and intimated undeserved possibilities of black upward mobility.

In contrast, the fate suffered by St. Philip's Episcopal Church, where Albro Lyons, Philip White, James McCune Smith, and many of their friends worshipped, offers a less conventional story and serves to remind us of the strikingly different forms that violence may take. In its minutes of August 4, 1863, the church's vestry poignantly described the desecration of its sanctuary:

> It . . . was our pleasure and duty to be permitted to assemble ourselves in our sanctuary on the Sunday of July 12th for our usual devotions and humble praise and thanksgiving. But on the succeeding day July 13th 1863 anarchy and confusion took the place of law and order and for several days pillage, arson, murder reigned supreme in our midst. Men, women, and children having seemingly, suddenly become transformed into the vilest and savagest of

fiends. During the reign of this state of affairs, at a late hour Tuesday night July 14th 1863 the police authorities took possession of our parish to quarter military who had been summoned hither to bring order over chaos, restore law and maintain the peace of the city. Thus our parish has been in their possession since the above mentioned date until Friday noon July 31st 1863. In consequence of such occupation our church has been greatly defaced and damaged and left in an untenable condition requiring thorough renovation.[21]

St. Philip's origins explain the deep shock that permeates the vestry's account. The church had been born out of the desire of Trinity Church's black parishioners to delimit a space of their own. As early as 1795, they appealed to the church vestry for help "to purchase a piece of ground as a burial place to bury black persons of every denomination and description whatever in this city whether bond or free."[22] In 1807 they requested permission to receive religious instruction geared specifically to their own needs. In 1814, the African Catechetical Institution was formed, followed in 1818 by St. Philip's itself as Trinity's tenth parish. Its first building was erected on a plot of land on Collect Street between Anthony and Lombard Streets in 1819. Destroyed by fire in 1821, it was rebuilt in brick on the same spot in 1823.[23]

The desire of Trinity's black congregants for a place of their own in which to honor the dead and make better Christians of the living was the impetus for the founding of many black churches during this period; such delimited spaces made it possible for African-descended Christians to develop their own culturally specific value system, or "grammar of morality." The creation of St. Philip's as a morally delimited space was even more remarkable given the degradation of its surrounding environment. Its location was on the edge of the Sixth Ward's notorious Five Points district, characterized by Charles Dickens as a place where "poverty, wretchedness, and vice are rife enough . . . debauchery has made the very houses prematurely old . . . all that is loathsome drooping and decayed is here."[24] When Albro Lyons and Philip White joined the church in later years, its parishioners were a socially and economically diverse group. Some were unskilled laborers working as washers, laborers, or porters; others were engaged in skilled trades as barbers, shoemakers, or tailors; and still others—White and Lyons among them—were entrepreneurs. In addition to fulfilling its original purpose as a place of worship, commemoration, and catechism, St. Philip's, like other black churches, was a site of social activism. Beginning in 1848, the New York Society for the Promotion of Education Among Colored Children rented rooms in the church's basement to house a primary school for black children; in addition, collections were taken periodically for the Colored Orphan Asylum.[25]

Several factors converged, however, to undermine St. Philip's as a strategy. First of all, many white New Yorkers strongly contested its self-assertive claims as a delimited place. The most egregious event was the assault on the church during the anti-abolitionist riot of 1834. To racist New Yorkers, abolition evoked basic fears, most especially the specter of economic competition and racial amalgamation; thus, it took little to provoke them. The pretext for this riot was a meeting held in the nearby Chatham Street Chapel, a house of worship initially organized by Arthur and Lewis Tappan, brothers and prominent members of the American Anti-Slavery Society, to extend "benevolent Christianity" to the poverty-stricken inhabitants of Five Points. In July 1834, the Tappans, at the behest of a group of black leaders, agreed to host a service in the chapel commemorating New York State's emancipation law of 1827. The gathering brought together blacks and whites, and Lewis Tappan read the society's Declaration of Sentiments. Angry rioters interrupted the service, and they did so again a few nights later when members of the New York Sacred Music Society objected to the presence of the choirs of St. Philip's and the First Colored Presbyterian Church in their chapel stalls. The rioting expanded to St. Philip's as the mob invaded it, smashing the stained-glass windows, burning the walnut pews, demolishing the organ, pulling down the altar, ripping its table apart, breaking the flower vases, and shredding the chancel carpet, altar hangings, and vestments.[26]

Second, St. Philip's continued dependence on Trinity also undermined the parishioners' ability to master place and environment. The church never owned the land on Collect Street; rather, it was obtained through a sixty-year lease from George Lorillard, one of Trinity's wealthiest members. Moreover, throughout the years, St. Philip's received substantial annual stipends from Trinity. Finally, it occupied a marginal place within the institutions of Episcopalianism. From its inception, St. Philip's was excluded from membership in the New York State diocesan convention, which was supposed to be a reflection of church unity; not to be a part of the convention meant not to be a part of the denomination.[27]

To its parishioners, St. Philip's represented above all sacred space. As such, it endowed the concept of a delimited place with new meaning, offering an experience of place and time dramatically different from that which characterized the secular world. Religious scholars have suggested that within the sacred world the material realities of place function as a means of apprehending the divine, of interpreting the higher order of things. Sacred space thus encompasses a sense of both place and placelessness, of particularity and universality. It opens up onto a transcendent sense of timelessness; it becomes the embodiment of eternal time.[28]

The physical space of the church is thus a manifestation of divinity. This was certainly true for the congregants of St. Philip's. They expressed their reverence of God by insisting on having a building of their own, which they lovingly endeavored to improve. Contemporaries described the Federal-style brick church erected in 1823 as a "neat brick building, 70 × 40, containing 3,000 square feet," with no exterior sign such as a steeple or cross to indicate that it was a place of worship. Its interior was "characterized by simplicity, good taste, and economy."[29] But the reports of the damage done during the 1834 riot suggest that in the intervening years, considerable money and effort had been expended to beautify it. In the mid-1850s, in response to the increasing delocalization of the black community in general and the church's membership in particular, the vestry decided to move uptown. In 1857 the church purchased a Methodist church building on Mulberry Street in the Fourteenth Ward, and once again, parishioners set about improving their church's interior. The vestry, for example, authorized the creation of a subcommittee, which included Albro Lyons, to secure a chandelier for the new building.[30]

For St. Philip's parishioners, the sacred space of their church also embodied specifically Episcopalian traditions. We need, then, to reconsider the church's strategy from yet another perspective, that is, as a bold attempt on the part of a black institution to delimit a place of its own *within* a white institutional space. St. Philip's congregants expressed their denominational belonging most explicitly through their insistence on admission to the diocesan convention. The vestry waged a bitter ten-year battle in order to obtain membership. Year after year, it sent a delegation to the convention only to be denied admission. It was 1853 before St. Philip's three delegates—Philip White among them—would be seated.[31]

More immediately, St Philip's parishioners reaffirmed their identity as Episcopalians through adoption of High Church doctrine and practices that were being promoted by New York's Bishop Hobart. High Church belief asserted that Episcopal bishops could trace their lineage in an unbroken chain of succession back to earlier Christian bishops and hence to the apostles themselves.[32] In thus turning to the past, High Churchmen revived ideas of tradition, order, and ritual that they believed had been lost under liberalizing tendencies within Anglicanism and mandated a return to more formalistic ritual as well as to Gothic architecture. Embracing High Church ideals was thus another way in which St. Philip's lay claim to being an integral part of ancient Anglican tradition. Continuing its efforts to improve their new building, the vestry formed a second subcommittee, of which Lyons was once again a member, to determine how best to alter the church's chancel "to make it conform to the usage of the Protestant Episcopal Church."[33] Finally, parishioners also expressed their sense of Episcopalian belonging in the High Church rituals of their weekly services. A reporter described a service held in 1862 as "reverentially impressive, solemn, and imposing." He first took note of the altar, which was "brilliantly illuminated with tapers in pyramidical candelabra," and then went on to detail the service itself; during the Evening

Prayer, the officiating minister read the First and Second Lessons and the congregation then sang the "Cantate Domino," the "Benedic, anima mea," the "Gloria in Excelsis," and the 105th Psalm.[34] In thus insisting on admission to the diocesan convention and adopting High Church ideals, St. Philip's parishioners defiantly asserted their rightful place within Anglican tradition. In so doing, they sought to transform the uncertainties of history into readable spaces.

History, however, invaded St. Philip's in the form of the draft riots of 1863. The church was not overrun by the Irish mob, although parishioners might well have feared that it would meet the same fate it ultimately did in 1834. Its location on Mulberry Street across from the New York Police Department headquarters protected it from attack. Yet, ironically, it opened the church to another form of violence—occupation by military troops brought in to help restore order. As the vestry minutes of August 4 attest, the congregation's sense of the desecration of their sacred space was no less intense. It immediately set about restoring the sanctuary and appealed to city and federal authorities for aid. But it was only after months of protracted negotiations that St. Philip's was reimbursed approximately $1,500 of the $2,500 that the repairs had cost.[35]

No extant records exist to tell us how city and federal agencies viewed the matter. Perhaps their reaction was similar to the contempt heaped upon members of the African Methodist Episcopal Church, which had also been used as an army barrack. An 1887 account of the riots written by William Stoddard, a former volunteer special (member of a temporary militia) indicates the extent to which the municipal authorities operated according to a grammar of morality dramatically different from that of St. Philip's congregants. They grudgingly agreed to pay the African Methodist Episcopal Church for new carpets as well as new books for the Sunday School library "on the ground that the unrighteous police, soldiery, and 'specials' had read up forever all there was left of the old" but drew the line "with a good deal of quiet fun" at reimbursement for the Sunday collections missed when the church was undergoing repairs. Stoddard cynically concluded, "That church and the Orphan Asylum both made money by the mob, but in somewhat different ways."[36]

For the parishioners of the African Methodist Episcopal Church and St. Philip's, the sense of violation must have been manifold. To them, the damage done was both physical and psychological. They must have been dismayed by the lack of emotional support from those responsible for protecting them and appalled by the defilement of a sacred space that more than any other had conferred stability on the uncertainties of their daily lives. Thus, the St. Philip's vestry ended its August 4 minutes by fervently anticipating the day when "we and our fellow parishioners may once again through God's providence be permitted to draw near and assemble in our old, accustomed, beloved, and familiar spots in united prayer, to mingle our voices in praise and thanksgiving to 'God our refuge.'"[37] The reparations demanded by the church, then, were not only material and financial but spiritual and psychic as well.

THE NEIGHBORHOOD OF THE "SWAMP": ALBRO LYONS AND PHILIP WHITE

Albro Lyons and Philip White were not among those parishioners responsible for St. Philip's move uptown. They both resided on Vandewater Street in the city's Fourth Ward, Lyons at number 20 and White at number 40. This street lay in an area located south of the Five Points district and extending to the East River; once a marshland, it was commonly called the Swamp. At the time of the draft riots, Lyons's Seaman's Home was in his residence and the Seaman's General Outfitting Store he owned was close by on Roosevelt Street, and White's drugstore was a couple of blocks away on the corner of Frankfort and Gold Streets.[38] In addition to Lyons's and White's participation in the affairs of the black community, we need then to consider their place in the neighborhood of the Swamp as well.

As we have seen, by the mid-nineteenth century, New York's black community had become aspatial and delocalized. To a certain extent, it fits Benedict Anderson's concept of an "imagined community" in which members "will never know most of their fellow-members, meet them, or even hear of them, yet in the minds of each lives the image of their communion." In contrast, the city neighborhood is localized, bounded, and defined by particular landmarks and objects. It is simultaneously a delimited geographical space and a social space created by daily interaction among neighbors. In Benedict Anderson's terms, it more closely approximates "the primordial village of face-to-face contact" characterized by the "particularistic ties of kinship and clientship."[39] Neighborhood interactions revolve around family and kin networks but also entail practices of work, trade, and property rental or ownership. These face-to-face interactions readily facilitate the implementation of strategy, the mastery that comes from visual familiarity with one's environment or more ideally from possession of one's own delimited place.

The neighborhood space is also marked, however, by other contacts that have a potentially destabilizing effect. For one, even though the neighborhood is localized, its boundaries are porous and subject to invasion by strangers. For another, if neighborliness connotes intimacy, it can also lead to hostility. In *Civilization and Its Discontents*, Freud noted that in personal relationships the neighbor "has more claim to my hostility and even my hatred"; he is "someone who tempts [me] to satisfy [my] aggressiveness on him." Freud termed such hatred among territorially adjacent communities "the narcissism of minor differences" and defined it as the aggressive feeling of one community toward a related neighboring one in order to solidify group cohesion.[40] We can thus readily see how at moments of historical crisis, forces in the surrounding environment can threaten and destabilize a delimited place.

According to Edwin Burrows and Mike Wallace, in 1861 the Fourth Ward was the most densely populated place on earth, containing 290,000 people per square mile.[41] Although less notorious than Five Points, it was just as much of a slum: in appallingly overcrowded conditions, its inhabitants suffered from poverty, malnutrition, poor sanitation, and disease. They were subjected to the yellow fever epidemic of 1822 and outbreaks of cholera in 1832 and 1849; tuberculosis and venereal disease remained chronic problems. Like other neighborhoods in Lower Manhattan, the Swamp was defined primarily by the kinds of industries that were located there and by the people who worked in them. Shipbuilding industries dominated the waterfront area along with associated trades such as boardinghouses and outfitting stores for sailors like those Lyons owned, as well as grog shops and brothels that catered to sailors' more pleasurable needs.[42] Adjacent to the waterfront was the area of the Swamp proper where Philip White's drugstore was located. This area specialized in leather tanning and other related industries. Many of New York's old merchant class had made their fortune tanning leather and storing hides in warehouses around Frankfort Street until the ill effects of the leather-making process led the city to close down the yards.[43]

In early antebellum New York, workplace and residence were often in close proximity to one another in neighborhoods like the Swamp. Manufacturers and workers alike often lived in the same neighborhood, as did workers of different ethnic and racial backgrounds; class and racial/ethnic differentiation occurred within buildings and blocks rather than from neighborhood to neighborhood. In this sense, the Swamp was no different from other city neighborhoods, bringing together well-to-do manufacturers and merchants, skilled tradesmen and artisans, and unskilled laborers, native-born populations, whites, blacks, and immigrants. By the early 1860s, however, the area had become increasingly working-class and Irish. Blacks were now concentrated in wards to the north and west; and although merchants still maintained their businesses in the Swamp, they had begun to move their households to residential enclaves in a gradual process completed in the 1870s.[44]

Albro Lyons and Philip White lived within the double context of the black community and the local neighborhood of the Swamp. Both men were dedicated to their own personal socioeconomic advancement just as they were both committed to serving their community. It was their different methods of regulating their private and public affairs within their neighborhood that account for their vastly disparate experiences during the draft riots. Lyons's place on

Vandewater Street brought together both private and public functions: it was at once domestic space (family home), economic space (Seaman's Home), and black community space (a station on the Underground Railroad). In an unpublished autobiographical sketch, one of Lyons's daughters, Maritcha, described how the multiple functions of her home made it especially suitable as a stopping point for runaway slaves: "Father's connection with the underground railroad brought many strange faces to our house, for it was semi-public and persons could go in and out without attracting special attention."[45] By the mid-1850s, Lyons had accumulated a sizable estate and was not hesitant about displaying his wealth. Property assessment records indicate that in 1862 the house was valued at $5,500. It was described as a "fine brick building." Located directly next door to the home of the widow of George Gilpin, an "Old Swamper" who had kept a leather store on Frankfort Street, Lyons's home might well have been originally occupied by one of New York's old merchants.[46]

In her autobiographical sketch, Maritcha Lyons gave a vivid account of how the "rabble" launched three attacks on the home before finally gutting it. In the first, windowpanes were broken, shutters smashed, and the front door partially demolished; in the second, her father fired a pistol to disperse the crowd; in the third, the mob successfully penetrated the house.[47] After its destruction, Lyons submitted claims for compensation to the Merchants Relief Committee, a group composed of some of the city's most prominent citizens, seeking to help victims of the riots. They itemize the value of his possessions in exquisite detail—an English rug appraised at $15, a French mechanical column lamp at $23, an oil painting at $40, a looking glass with a gilt frame at $20, and so forth. The fact that Lyons was able to recover from this private association approximately the same amount that the city and federal governments reimbursed St. Philip's ($1,500) confirms his substantial wealth.[48]

A convergence of factors helps to explain the assault on Lyons's house. To Lyons, his home represented a haven for his family and members of the wider black community as well as a well-deserved reward for successful entrepreneurship. To the Irish rioters, however, it was a harsh reminder of their own lack of will and power, of their inability to delimit places of their own. Their attack had multiple meanings. First, it struck at the very heart of the black domestic household. Second, it was directed against black property and wealth, the manifestations of which could only seem ostentatious and illegitimate to the mob. Third, it was designed to destroy a black workplace and threaten black sailors inclined to seek "white" work on the docks. And, finally, it sought to eliminate a black community institution dedicated to antislavery work. Maritcha Lyons does not say whether the mob was composed of neighbors or strangers or both. What is particularly significant, however, is that Lyons's neighbors found no compelling reason to come to his aid. In both his establishment of a colored Seaman's Home and his social activism, Lyons had chosen to cater exclusively to the black community. Thus, he had been unable—or unwilling—to translate his daily face-to-face contacts within his local neighborhood into particularistic ties that might have motivated those around him to come to his defense.

On the day of the final assault on the home, John W. Rode, a sergeant from the fourth precinct, sent Lyons a note in which he wrote: "I cannot say today what will occur tomorrow. I will be at said drugstore at 3 o'clock this day with horse and wagon."[49] I can only surmise that the named drugstore was Philip White's and that Sergeant Rode believed it to be a safe haven from which he could effect the rescue of the Lyons family. White's very different construction of a social space for himself within the neighborhood of the Swamp accounts for both his personal safety and the preservation of his property during the riots. To a lesser degree than Lyons, and perhaps not quite as visibly, White was an active member of the black community. He was several times elected to the St. Philip's vestry and was secretary of the New York Society for the Promotion of Education Among Colored Children from 1851 until at least 1865. But it was his drugstore and his position as local druggist that enabled White to delimit his own place of will and power within the Swamp.

White's trade—and his success at it—may be seen as a form of power. In antebellum America, pharmacy occupied a fluid status as a field midway between a trade and a profession. No special training was required to become a druggist and no restrictive legislation existed to regulate the compounding and selling of drugs. Rather, pharmacy was regarded as an entrepreneurial field in which any ambitious young man, even of the lower classes, could readily make a name for himself. In 1829, however, concern over the lack of regulation of pharmaceutical practices led a group of pharmacists to come together and found the College of Pharmacy of the City of New York.[50] The career of Constantine Adamson, one of the college's founders, provides an excellent example of the possibilities pharmacy offered. An Englishman, he had been a soldier, seaman, and lumber trader before coming to the United States and turning to pharmacy. After the foundation of the college, Adamson served as one of its trustees and presidents.[51]

Philip White undoubtedly turned to pharmacy not only to help the sick and the poor around him but also to advance his own socioeconomic agenda, taking advantage of its entrepreneurial possibilities and its relative lack of racism. The highly international nature of American pharmacy might well account for its relatively relaxed attitudes about race. As the best pharmaceutical training was in Europe, many Americans went there to study, and conversely many European pharmacists immigrated to the United States. Finally, White probably chose to attend the College of Pharmacy of the City of New York both to hone his skills as a druggist and to become part of a professional network of businessmen whose acquaintance might stand him in good stead in later years.

White's drugstore occupied an important space within both the black community and the local neighborhood. For their part, African Americans were highly appreciative of the success of their businessmen. In the February 11, 1848, issue of *The North Star*, William C. Nell noted that he had "visited the Apothecary's Hall of Dr. James McCune Smith in West Broadway, as also the establishment of Mr. Philip White in Frankfort Street, both of whom are practical men and conduct their business, preparing medicines, etc. etc. with as much readiness and skill as any other disciple of Galen and Hippocrates. . . . [They] are proving their capacity, as I believe, to their pecuniary benefit, and at the same time thus elevating the character of those with whom they are identified by complexion."[52] To Nell, these two drugstores were sterling examples of modern black professionalism, entrepreneurship, and adherence to the Protestant ethic of hard work.

But White's drugstore was also a part of the local neighborhood of the Swamp. Both the physical space of the store and his actual practice as druggist enabled White to master his environment. Like other druggists of his time, White would have marked out the interior space of his store with great care. Similar to today's drugstore, the antebellum drugstore sold toilet articles and perfumery as well as hardware items, such as window glass, paints, oils, and mirrors. Many also sold liquor, ostensibly for medicinal purposes although more often for consumption as a beverage.[53] But the drugstore's main business was selling drugs that were compounded right there on the premises. In this work, the druggist and his apprentice carried out multiple tasks since "in many instances the hands that received and opened the case of rhubarb, opium or assafoetida fresh from off the ship, in turn dispensed these remedies in pillbox or vial to the suffering invalid."[54] They prepared the drugs at the prescription counter, which functioned as a kind of laboratory; estimates indicate that forty-eight out of every one hundred drugs were manufactured on the spot.[55] The prescription case held everything that was necessary for filling a prescription: extracts made from plants such as belladonna, digitalis, poppy, and hollyhock, as well as "every preparation of mercury, iodine, potash, quinine, iron, etc. with tinctures, waters, acids, and syrups, scales spatulas, labels and corks, records such as the United States Dispensatory, and reference works of various authorities."[56] It was here that the druggist or his apprentice "assorted, garbled, and powdered" the drugs, in the process "enjoying a wholesome development of muscle through wielding the ponderous pestle, handling the sieves and working the screw press."[57]

In the beginning at least, Philip White would have performed such tasks himself. Thus, to a much greater extent than Lyons, his labor would have been highly visible as his neighbors could see him day after day, working behind his prescription counter, and could appreciate his dedication to his work. As a druggist, moreover, White was a provider in the city's service industry. From his own perspective, he was a small-business owner, self-employed, and independent. He also possessed a certain degree of social prestige and had open before him the possibility of upward mobility, which might eventually culminate in property ownership. From the point of view of his neighbors in the Swamp, he was a healer in a community ravaged by chronic illness and disease. Consequently, White sought, in ways that Lyons either could not or would not, to serve his immediate neighborhood by building up particularistic ties of clientship. His obituary in the *New York Times* gives us a good sense of how he achieved these ends; it reported that White "was never unmindful of the poor, and the services and material of his store were willingly given without pay to any one who needed them. . . . His acts of kindness and charity were numerous, and scores of poor families were befriended and helped by him not only with medicines, but with food and money. Those whom he helped had a chance to show their gratitude during the draft riots of 1863."[58]

The *New York Times* obituary attributed to White the comment that he felt certain of protection not only by those standing guard at his drugstore but also by "many men among the rioters." This statement suggests that the mob was at least in part composed of neighbors prepared to destroy black property— perhaps Albro Lyons's home—but determined to "fight" for his. White's strategy throughout the 1850s consisted then of delimiting a neighborhood place in which he could bring together potentially antagonistic groups of blacks and Irish and provide useful service to each of them. In his drugstore, White successfully forged a relationship of mutual interdependence between himself and his neighbors in which benevolence and self-interest were inextricably intertwined for the benefit of all concerned. If White took care of his customers, giving away medicines for free, he was, through this act of benevolence, maintaining the stability of the neighborhood in which he both lived and worked and protecting his own position with it. In turn, if his poor Irish neighbors accepted his benevolence, they were ultimately able to repay him by protecting him during the riots; in so doing, they also ensured that the drugstore on which they depended so heavily would survive the riots and continue to serve them. Here the particularistic ties of clientship made possible the formation of neighborhood bonds that transcended divisions of race, class, and ethnicity.

Yet White's relationship to his neighborhood community was far more complex than his poor Irish neighbors ever imagined. Unbeknownst to them, he had gained the confidence of the businessmen of the Swamp whose support eventually allowed him to engage in a wholesale drug business. As the *Times* obituary noted:

> His industry and obliging disposition won for him also the favor of business men in the Swamp, many of whom took pains to put trade in his way until he was firmly established. The opportunities thus opened to him included some wholesale orders which led him into that branch of the business. It soon became so profitable that he bought the store property and was rated prosperous. He clung to the retail branch of his business even after he became a wholesale dealer, few in the neighborhood indeed knowing for some years that he had interests beyond the counter.[59]

White's work, then, extended beyond his visible role as a local service pro-vider to the more invisible, aspatial, and impersonal (but far more lucrative) business of wholesale dealer. And yet, as the obituary notes, White's ability to advance in his trade was enabled by the particularistic ties he had forged with businessmen in the Swamp and also, quite possibly, by contacts he had made and nurtured over the years through the College of Pharmacy. We might want to attribute the businessmen's interest in White to a combination of paternalistic attitudes, racial guilt, and self-serving feelings of benevolence, but it is just as likely that they too aspired to community stability at a time of rampant poverty, disease, social unrest, and political uncertainty.

White may be seen, then, as a transitional figure between local shopkeeper and emergent capitalizing manufacturer. In this position he was able to improve his socioeconomic status while allowing it to remain hidden from those who might have resented his rapid upward mobility. White's experiences within the space of the neighborhood were defined then not so much by his race and class as by his neighbors' *perceptions* of them. To his poor Irish customers, he was above all a hardworking shopkeeper whose generosity compelled their loyalty. To the businessmen of the Swamp, he was an entrepreneurial young man whose business prospects they wanted to help improve. To both groups, his drugstore and his practice as druggist contributed to the welfare of their neighborhood, which they did not want to see undermined.

The draft riots and their aftermath underscore the degree to which claims to space by members of a subordinated group are so often subject to contesta-tion and negotiation, and the meanings of these spaces multiple and unstable. To varying degrees, the fate of the Colored Orphan Asylum, St. Philip's, and Albro Lyons's home tells a fairly typical story of black victimization: the success of white mob violence in attacking and destroying black institutions and prop-erty on the one hand, the inability of African Americans to delimit their own places of will and power on the other. In contrast, Philip White's experiences were atypical. The survival of his drugstore points to the extraordinary success of his manipulation of space as strategy in the midst of a hostile environment; so far, the archives have not uncovered similar events that might have happened to other African Americans during the riots. And although White's story is that of one single individual and occurred within the context of personal rather than systemic relationships, it might well provide us with a countermodel of racism that allows us to imagine new cross-racial alliances and interactions within this country's tangled web of race relations.

Lyons's and White's postbellum lives further indicate how black New Yorkers both continued to delimit places of their own and experienced space as unfixed and unstable. Shaken by the harrowing events of the draft riots, Lyons left New York and moved his family to Rhode Island; it would be many years before he would return and settle in Brooklyn. White continued to live in the Swamp until the building of the Brooklyn Bridge destroyed Vandewater Street, forcing him to move to Brooklyn in 1870 but allowing him to maintain his drugstore until his death in 1891. Lyons's and White's move to Brooklyn was in fact part of a broader exodus of black New Yorkers to Brooklyn, resulting in the creation of a black middle-class neighborhood in the Williamsburg area. Although a mark of the residential segregation that has so plagued the nation's race relations, this bounded neighborhood must also be seen as a protective response to the racial violence suffered by black New Yorkers during the draft riots and as a renewed effort to carve out their own spaces of will and power.

One result of this migration to Brooklyn was the further spatial separation of blacks from their community institutions. White continued his work on behalf of St. Philip's Church, focusing in particular on its financial health; he effectively took the business skills he had learned and the money he had earned from his neighborhood drugstore and reinvested them in a black community institution. Neither neighborhood nor church was to remain spatially fixed, however. In yet another new intra-urban migration of black New Yorkers, St. Philip's moved further uptown to West Twenty-fifth Street in 1886 and finally relocated to Harlem in the early decades of the twentieth century. It is Harlem's twentieth-century spatial formation that has come to function for so many as a metonym for the overlapping identity of black neighborhood and black community. But in so doing, we risk forgetting the far richer and more complex history of black New Yorkers' claims to space.

NOTES

1. Obituary, *New York Age*, January 9, 1896.
2. Undated newspaper clipping, Rhoda Golden Freeman Research Collection, Schomburg Center for Research in Black Culture, New York Public Library.

3. Rhoda Golden Freeman, *The Free Negro in Antebellum New York* (New York: Garland, 1994), 245–246.

4. Dixon Ryan Fox, "The Negro Vote in Old New York," *Political Science Quarterly* 30 (June 1917): 258–262.

5. Noel Ignatiev, *How the Irish Became White* (New York: Routledge, 1995), 96–100, 111–112.

6. Edwin G. Burrows and Mike Wallace, *Gotham: A History of New York City to 1898* (New York: Oxford University Press, 1999), 867, 886.

7. Iver Bernstein, *The New York City Draft Riots: Their Significance for American Society and Politics in the Age of the Civil War* (New York: Oxford University Press, 1990), 7–28.

8. Ibid., 5, 20–26.

9. *Report of the Committee of Merchants for the Relief of Colored People Suffering from the Late Riots in the City of New York* (New York: George A. Whitehorne Printer, 1863), 23.

10. Adrian Cook, *The Armies of the Street: The New York City Draft Riots of 1863* (Lexington: University Press of Kentucky, 1974), 78–80.

11. Bernstein, *New York City Draft Riots*, 27.

12. *Report of the Committee of Merchants*, 21.

13. Cook, *Armies of the Street*, 143.

14. Ibid.

15. Michel de Certeau, *The Practice of Everyday Life*, trans. Steven Rendell (Berkeley: University of California Press, 1984), 35–36.

16. Raymond Williams, *The Country and the City* (New York: Oxford University Press, 1973), 166.

17. Kenneth A. Scherzer, *The Unbounded Community: Neighborhood Life and Social Structure in New York City, 1830–1875* (Durham, NC: Duke University Press, 1992), 6–14.

18. Daniel Perlman, "Organizations of the Free Negro in New York City, 1800–1860," *Journal of Negro History* 56 (1971): 191.

19. Scherzer, *Unbounded Community*, 169.

20. *Report of the Committee of Merchants*, 23–25.

21. *St. Philip's Episcopal Church Vestry Minutes,* August 4, 1863, Manuscript Division, Schomburg Center for Research in Black Culture, New York Public Library.

22. *Trinity Church Vestry Minutes*, April 13, 1795, Trinity Church Archives.

23. Benjamin F. De Costa, *Three Score and Ten: The Story of St. Philip's Church* (New York, Printed for the Parish, 1889), 17–29.

24. Quoted in Tyler Anbinder, *Five Points* (New York: Free Press, 2001), 32–33.

25. *St. Philip's Episcopal Church Vestry Minutes*, January 9, 1849; August 12, 1845.

26. John H. Hewitt, Jr., *Protest and Progress: New York's First Black Episcopal Church Fights Racism* (New York: Garland Publishing, 2000), 41–47.

27. Craig Townsend, *An Inexpedient Time: Race and Religion Among New York City Episcopalians* (Ann Arbor, MI: UMI Dissertation Services, 1998), 211.

28. Philip Sheldrake, *Spaces for the Sacred: Place, Memory, and Identity* (Baltimore, MD: Johns Hopkins University Press, 2001), 30, 56, 153.

29. De Costa, *Three Score and Ten*, 29.

30. *St. Philip's Episcopal Church Vestry Minutes*, May 16, 1859.

31. Ibid., October 11, 1853.

32. Townsend, *Inexpedient Time*, 22.

33. *St. Philip's Episcopal Church Vestry Minutes*, June 14, 1859.

34. St. Philip's Episcopal Church Clipping File, St. John the Divine Archives.

35. De Costa, *Three Score and Ten*, 39–40.

36. William Osborn Stoddard, *The Volcano Under the City* (New York: Fords, Howard & Hulbert, 1887), 12–22.

37. *St. Philip's Episcopal Church Vestry Minutes,* August 4, 1863.

38. *Brooklyn Eagle,* June 19, 1951.

39. Benedict Anderson, *Imagined Communities: Reflections on the Origin and Spread of Nationalism* (New York: Verso, 1991), 6.

40. Sigmund Freud, *Civilization and Its Discontents*, trans. James Strachey (New York: W. W. Norton & Company, 1962), 67, 69, 72.

41. Burrows and Wallace, *Gotham*, 883.

42. Scherzer, *Unbounded Community*, 31, 66.

43. Joseph Alfred Scoville, *The Old Merchants of New York City*, 5 vols. (New York: Carlton, 1864), 1:251–258; Ann L. Buttenwieser, "Exalted Spaces: Recapturing the Glorious Underpinnings of the Brooklyn Bridge," *South Street Seaport Museum Magazine* (Fall 1983): 25–26.

44. Scherzer, *Unbounded Community*, 51, 95.

45. Maritcha Lyons, "Memories of Yesterdays, All of Which I Saw and Part of Which I Was—An Autobiography," Harry Albro Williamson Papers, Schomburg Center for Research in Black Culture, New York Public Library, 46.

46. Scoville, *Old Merchants of New York City*, 1:279.

47. Lyons, "Memories of Yesterdays," 8–9.

48. Harry Albro Williamson Papers, Schomburg Center for Research in Black Culture.

49. Ibid.

50. Curt Wimmer, *The College of Pharmacy of the City of New York* (Baltimore: Read-Taylor, 1929), 20–21.

51. "Memoir of Constantine Adamson," *American Journal of Pharmacy* 17 (1846–1847): 248–251.

52. *North Star*, February 11, 1848.

53. Wimmer, *College of Pharmacy*, 121–122.

54. Edward Parish, "On the Relations of the Several Classes of Druggists and Pharmacists to the Colleges of Pharmacy," *American Journal of Pharmacy* (November 1871): 482.

55. Edward Parish, "Pharmacy as a Business," *American Pharmaceutical Association* (1856): 61.

56. Wimmer, *College of Pharmacy*, 122.

57. Parish, "On the Relations of the Several Classes," 481.

58. Obituary, *New York Times*, February 19, 1891.

59. Ibid.

Mark Santow

Self-Determination

Race, Space, and Chicago's Woodlawn Organization in the 1960s

> Before I built a wall I'd ask to know
> What I was walling in or walling out
> And to whom I was like to give offense.
> Something there is that doesn't love a wall,
> That wants it down.
>
> ROBERT FROST, "MENDING WALLS"

> When the president of TWO goes anywhere to bargain, he has a collective leadership beside him and huge numbers of people behind him. He goes into battle with a real weapon, the weapon of the poor—their numbers. What does it mean to have that support? It means that he and those that support him are *free men* in every sense of the word. We have paid heavily over the past five years for our self-determination. We in TWO believe that dignity is more important than money . . . you have made me *proud* to be a part of TWO. . . . You have made me proud—more than I can say—to be a Negro. And finally, you have made me proud to be a man.
>
> PRESIDENT LYNWARD STEVENSON, 1966

In the three decades following the end of World War II, U.S. cities underwent extraordinary demographic transformations that had profound consequences for political alignments, racial identities, and the social geography of metropolitan areas. The Great Migration of African Americans from the South to the urban Northeast and Midwest began during World War I, lapsed during the Depression

decade, and then began again in the 1940s. It continued until the end of the sixties, changing forever both the nature and spatial expression of American race
relations. The process of black "invasion" and white flight—what journalist
M. W. Newman referred to in 1960 as "Chicago's Great Question"—was (and
is) of vital importance for understanding the racial and political dynamics of
metropolitan areas in postwar America. Even a brief perusal of city newspapers
from the late 1950s and early 1960s reveals that the "Great Question" was hardly
specific to Chicago in either its existence or its importance.[1]

Racial transition and flight have been a common multi-generational experience for millions of Americans, white and black. These experiences, and the
structural inequalities to which they are recursively related, serve as both the
foundation of modern American urban and suburban politics and the prism
through which many whites and blacks map metropolitan space, create racial
and territorial identities, and consider the possibilities and probabilities of social
change. Americans today continue to define place, property, and community
largely in racial terms, affecting how racial and political identities and interests
are formed, how problems and inequalities are viewed, and what solutions are
seen as both possible and desirable.[2]

Woodlawn, on the South Side of Chicago, was a community that experienced extraordinarily rapid racial transition in the 1950s and the emergence of
one of the largest and most powerful African American community groups in
the nation, the Temporary Woodlawn Organization (TWO), in the 1960s. This
essay will examine the history of TWO, its relationship to 1960s federal poverty
programs, and the politics of racial geography in the postwar era. TWO, a creation of community organizer Saul Alinsky and his Industrial Areas Foundation
(IAF), was organized in 1960 around the concept of self-determination. The
group articulated and attempted to implement a localized, participatory, and
communitarian attack on the problems of Chicago's growing South Side ghetto
by claiming and utilizing a racialized sense of territorial identity and interest.[3]

TWO attempted to foster an alternative racial geography that lay some-
where between fostering individual social and geographic mobility (the focus
of most 1960s anti-poverty programs) and "gilding the ghetto" (the focus of
Chicago's black political leadership). In the process, it raised a fundamental question with which this nation still struggles: Is integration and racial dispersion
the best way to improve the lives of urban African Americans by fostering individual social (and geographic) mobility? Or are community control and neighborhood self-determination the best method for dealing with the devastating
consequences of America's racial history?[4]

The story of TWO reveals the limits of place-based approaches to the problems of cities in which geography and politics are deeply tied to racial identities

and interests. The spatiality of race has been at the heart of race relations in the twentieth century. The relationship between place and race has been at the center of ideologies and strategies surrounding both the protection of racial privilege and the search for racial justice. This relationship thus has played a critical role in American politics, in the formation of racial identities, and in the way cities and their suburbs look, function, and relate to one another. Because of TWO's emphasis on neighborhood control, local efficacy, and territorially based identity and interests, its successes and failures in dealing with the politics of race and place in the postwar American city not only help explain the social history of urban race relations in recent decades but also speak to the enduring dilemmas embedded in the search for democratic, humane, and realistic solutions to the persistent problems of the American metropolis.

RACE AND PLACE IN URBAN AMERICA

What does it mean to speak of the importance of "place"? Even a brief journey through America's largest cities reveals an unmistakable connection between where (and how) people live and who they are. Most urban residents can quickly identify where various groups live in their home city. The "other side of the tracks," the "inner" city, "white flight," the "Black Belt"—all of these terms are geographic or spatial in nature, at once describing places but also people and social processes. Urban scholars generally refer to this relationship among place, identity, and social structure as "social geography." The conception of space is critically important for understanding urban life in general and race relations in particular. People don't experience racial hierarchy in general; they experience it in particular places and at particular times. One of the ways in which social structures and hierarchies shape people's lives, possibilities, and worldviews is through space. It is a critical part of the concrete lived world and of how people are constituted as social actors. In a certain sense, exploring the politics of social geography allows us to see how social structures affect real lives—and, in turn, how those politics reproduce or challenge those structures. Particularly with regard to race, what power is and how it is experienced and cognitively understood are tied to how it is spatialized—how it finds its way into the built environment, where people live, and how they think of property, community, and social belonging. Race has helped to shape the contours of urban space, whereas the spatial development of metropolitan areas along racial lines has deeply affected patterns of both group and identity formation.

"Whiteness" has also been defined and defended through its spatial expressions and the close connections among race, property, and citizenship. This can be seen through political and legal phenomena, such as exclusionary zoning and racially restrictive covenants, and in more localized actions, such as the organization of "keep-'em-out" homeowner groups, the use of violence to keep neighborhoods white, and white flight. More generally, it can be seen in the widespread association of "responsible" homeownership, citizenship, safety, community, and stable property values with whiteness—an association generally reinforced by federal policy, the courts, and housing market actors and institutions throughout the twentieth century. When people speak of "the old neighborhood" or argue over when or why the neighborhood "went," they are providing evidence of the inseparability of race and place.[5]

Geographies of power are historical creations, the product of past and present political conflicts—geopolitics, as legal scholar David Delaney calls them.[6] Geographical themes like space, place, and mobility have played a pivotal role in the history of race relations in the United States, from slavery to the present. From the Fugitive Slave Law of 1850 to the busing controversies of the 1970s, from the legally enforced racial etiquette of the Jim Crow South in the late nineteenth century to "white flight" in the late twentieth century, race has been tied to place, mobility, and territory. Segregation and integration are spatial processes, and ghettoes and exclusive suburbs are spatial entities.

Interestingly, divisions within black political thought have reflected these processes, often differing over both the possible and desirable connections between space and power and what Delaney calls the "spatial conditions of liberation."[7] This is evident in pre–Civil War debates over colonization (sending American blacks to Africa). It was, later in the century, part of challenging the Jim Crow project, which assigned legal and racial meaning to "determinable segments of the physical world" and consequences to crossing lines.[8] The differences between Booker T. Washington and W.E.B. Du Bois were in part spatial, with Washington focusing on institution building and accommodating himself to the fact of segregation, and Du Bois insisting that separate could never be equal.

By the mid-sixties, prominent participants in the Civil Rights Movement began to disagree profoundly about the best path to racial justice. These divisions appeared to be about whether class or race was the salient social category for formulating both the desired end of the movement and the means by which to achieve it. In fact, however, the differences were as much about the spatial conditions of black liberation as they were about race and class. Did the movement need to focus on local struggles based on racial and geographic consciousness? Or did it need to think more broadly and build alliances with working-class whites outside the ghetto in order to bring about a redistribution of wealth? Was racial integration necessary for the achievement of equal opportunity and social justice? Or were racial solidarity and community power sufficient? TWO, in formulating its philosophy of self-determination, took these views seriously and sought to merge them. In many cases, TWO began to work its way through their practical implications well before they became the focus of national discussion.[9]

While the social history of white resistance to black newcomers in the first two decades after World War II has been well examined, we have few accounts of how urban blacks constructed community and identity in the wake of white flight. The critical importance of the politics of racial geography for the distribution of primary social goods in the United States demands a more complete story. TWO was organized on the South Side of Chicago in the wake of white flight in Woodlawn. Its story weaves through many of the larger events, ideas, and mobilizations of the turbulent 1960s—from the Freedom Rides to the Chicago Freedom Movement, to the War on Poverty, to Black Nationalism and community control. TWO and its members sought to define and institutionalize the organization's philosophy of self-determination. In the process, they struggled to articulate a relationship between race and place that moved beyond both integration and separatism.

WOODLAWN AND THE BIRTH OF TWO

Woodlawn has a varied and interesting geographical history. By World War I, when a small group of blacks began to establish a relatively stable community in the area's western section, Woodlawn had become a "residentially mature" area made up mostly of two-, three-, and four-story brick apartment buildings. The wartime production boom brought with it a vast increase in newcomers, as many single men and women working in the Loop downtown took up residence in the old hotels built for the 1893 Columbian Exposition, as well as in a growing number of boardinghouses and apartment hotels. By 1920, the area off of Sixty-third Street (the main thoroughfare) had become largely populated by transients; building owners began to convert single-family homes into multi-unit kitchenettes. By 1940, Sixty-third was built up with cheap shops, taverns, and transient hotels, and the area between Sixty-third and the Midway had mostly become a "kitchenette" district.[10] Woodlawn had also begun to develop a reputation as the "center of vice" on the South Side, although the commercial district around Sixty-third and Cottage Grove continued to be a profitable (if somewhat seedy) area into the 1950s.[11]

Although popular belief among the South Side's white homeowners blamed the deterioration of the area on the influx of blacks, its decline had in fact started earlier. Indeed, whites fleeing the increasingly rundown eastern section of Woodlawn in the 1940s and 1950s created an opening for house-poor black families seeking to escape the ghetto. Its further decline as the black population increased was largely attributable to its aging housing stock, the dual housing market, and racial discrimination in the credit and labor markets. When it came to the politics of racial geography, however, correlation was frequently confused with causation.

With the Second Great Migration, housing pressures and racial transition in Woodlawn increased with terrific speed, as whites quickly vacated the central district. The first black families, according to local clergy, were "well-to-do stable families seeking relief from the intolerable housing and social conditions of the ghetto further north and west," but scare tactics, panic selling, kitchenette conversions, and "tavern activity" soon followed.[12] As late as 1950, Greater Woodlawn had been only 31.4 percent black; ten years later, blacks made up 89.1 percent of Woodlawn's population.[13] Much of that population turnover occurred after 1957.[14] As of March 1960, 87 percent of Woodlawn residents had moved into their homes in the preceding six years.[15] Housing was both overcrowded and in poor condition: the Welfare Council of Metropolitan Chicago determined that only 51 percent of housing units in Woodlawn were "sound" in 1960, as opposed to 77.3 percent for the city as a whole.[16] The speed of racial turnover left local social organizations—including churches, block clubs, and small businesses—in chaos. Crime and unemployment crept upward. Woodlawn, local leaders feared, was about to be annexed to the growing South Side ghetto.[17]

During and after World War II, the federal government greatly amplified the connections among race, place, and security in Chicago and other cities, embedding race ever deeper into urban geography and the social identities and perceptions surrounding it. Federal policies formulated during the 1930s, such as the Home Owners Loan Corporation (HOLC) and the Federal Housing Administration (FHA), reflected and reinforced racial segregation, encouraged whites to resist the threat of black neighbors, and accelerated the flight of capital and white families from the inner city after the war. Other federal initiatives and policies, such as public housing, urban renewal, tax incentives, and highway construction, imbricated race into the nation's social geography as well.[18]

Businessmen, clergy, and homeowners worried that Woodlawn would become a target area for urban renewal. The fear was not unwarranted; state and federal housing acts had given rise to numerous such projects in Chicago in the 1950s. Michael Reese Hospital, the Illinois Institute of Technology, and the University of Chicago all seized upon the opportunity for government funding to upgrade their surrounding neighborhoods, in the process displacing tens of thousands of black families. For residents of Woodlawn, many of whom had previously been displaced from neighborhoods to the north, city government was synonymous with the bulldozer and "Negro removal."[19] In Woodlawn and elsewhere, urban renewal would play a key role in galvanizing place-based black movements in the 1950s and 1960s. By seeking to contain areas of black residence, thereby "preserving" the viability of white middle-class neighborhoods, large institutions (universities and hospitals), and retail districts, urban renewal was very much a product of the politics of racial geography. It was also a producer of such politics by encouraging opponents to localize their analysis, interests, and attack.

In spring 1958, local Woodlawn clergy began to meet on a regular basis with public officials, community groups, and one another to discuss the social and physical deterioration of the neighborhood. Father Martin Farrell, pastor of Holy Cross Church, was the catalyst.[20] Farrell, who was white, was named pastor of Woodlawn's Holy Cross in 1956, and he began to press Saul Alinsky to initiate a project in the area. Alinsky, a Chicago native, was well-known in the city for organizing the Back of the Yards Neighborhood Council (BYNC) in the forties and for his work with the Catholic Archdiocese in the 1950s on the consequences of racial transition for parish churches. Woodlawn, Farrell wrote Alinsky, "must have a neighborhood organizer quickly. . . . [It] is the most disorganized community in the U.S." There was little in the way of local leadership in Woodlawn, he wrote, but there were "many ordinary people in the community waiting for somebody to lead them to effective democratic organization according to American and Alinsky principles."[21]

Alinsky sent his protégé, Nicholas Von Hoffman, into Woodlawn to assess the area. In March 1958, Von Hoffman sent Farrell a "Woodlawn Fact Sheet" and a proposed budget of $143,660 for a three-year organizing project. Von Hoffman agreed with Farrell's assessment of Woodlawn's predicament. Area residents suffered from increasing crime, overcrowding, and a shortage of parks and school space. The police were absent when needed and abusive when present. Woodlawn "is not a community," he wrote. Its residents are "indifferent to 'community problems' because there is nothing in Woodlawn that would attract loyalty." Unless a "People's Organization" is created, Von Hoffman wrote, "it can be said as a certainty that Woodlawn will continue to grow as a slum until conditions there will be favorable for total land clearance."[22]

Farrell recruited Charles Leber and Ulysses Blakeley, co-pastors of Woodlawn's venerable First Presbyterian Church (which many University of Chicago faculty attended), to join him. The church had undergone rapid racial change in the 1950s, and its leadership responded in 1957 by hiring co-pastors—one white (Leber) and one black (Blakeley)—to lead the new congregation.[23] Both Leber and Blakeley had read Alinsky's book *Reveille for Radicals* in seminary. They invited Arthur Brazier, the young black pastor of Woodlawn's Apostolic Church of God, to come with them to talk to Alinsky late in 1958. Alinsky told them he would only come if he was invited by a representative group of black residents and if local churches and institutions could raise enough money up front to keep the organization going for at least two years. Alinsky believed these two qualifications were crucial if he and his organizers (all of whom were white) were to be seen as legitimate and if the organization was to have community and financial support from the beginning.[24] Leber, Farrell, and Blakeley were insistent that an ecumenical alliance was essential for the success of a community organization, so Alinsky agreed to join more than thirty clergy and lay leaders at a meeting at the Union League Club on February 17, 1959.[25]

"DISSOLVING THE WALLS OF RACIAL PARTITION": ALINSKY'S VISION FOR WOODLAWN

Woodlawn, Alinsky told the gathering, "has within it representative issues that affect every community in the city of Chicago. What happens in Woodlawn would be significant for urban redevelopment in the rest of the city."[26] Alinsky outlined four goals for a community organization in Woodlawn: first, to make local churches more effective in speaking up against and correcting injustice; second, to build sufficient community strength to ensure that Woodlawn gets its share of public services; third, to provide community representation in conservation and renewal programs; and, finally, to develop a "positive climate of hope" for residents through participation.[27] As for his organizing method, Alinsky summarized it: "[T]he IAF believes in a revolutionary doctrine: given the opportunity, people in a community can work out their own problems. The issues of a community are those that the people living in the community consider to be important, not those that others may think are important for them."[28]

Alinsky had another goal in taking on the Woodlawn project: breaking down racial segregation on the South Side. Since the mid-1950s, he and his organizers had been grappling with the dilemmas of white flight and racial integration. In 1957, Alinsky received $118,800 from the Archdiocese of Chicago to study the effects of black migration and white flight on city parishes. The study provided an opportunity for Alinsky to familiarize himself with conditions in Chicago's black areas and with the larger issue of the feasibility of racial integration at the neighborhood level. As a result, he became keenly aware of the close relationship between race and place on the South Side. The city's problems (for whites and blacks) could not be solved, Alinsky argued, until "the walls of racial partition have been at least partly dissolved."[29]

He proposed the creation of two kinds of community organizations for the purpose of slowing the pace of racial change. First, the city needed interracial groups at the edge of the expanding ghetto in the midst of white neighborhoods facing change. By 1959, the IAF had begun to create such a group on the rapidly changing Southwest Side. Second, for integration to work, independent black community groups willing to negotiate with nearby white community groups to control the pace of neighborhood change would have to be organized. None existed presently, Alinsky noted.[30]

A Woodlawn organization could fit into this scheme. "One way or another the new forces and direction born in the South during the past few years will come tumbling into the northern Negro ghetto," Alinsky told the IAF Board in 1960. It could be either "a valuable tonic" that would lead to a racially integrated city or "a destructive element taking a reckless and violent course." "We hope," Alinsky wrote, "that the Woodlawn Project will bring forth the first of the two possibilities."[31]

Alinsky thus saw a Woodlawn group as a tool both for improving the lives of local residents and for furthering the larger goal of racial integration. As he told the Emil Schwarzhaupt Foundation in his ultimately successful 1960 grant application, an organization in Woodlawn had two goals: making positive changes in the lives and living standards of residents and taking "an essential step necessary for the general goal of an orderly progression toward open occupancy in Chicago."[32] Alinsky did not see these as incompatible aims, although he said little about integration publicly. Success in addressing the everyday needs of Woodlawn residents would eventually make the organization powerful enough to address the broader structures that impoverished them economically and politically. It would also help participants to draw connections between their local troubles and larger issues. Although he insisted that the citizens of Woodlawn direct the goals and methods of the group themselves, he was confident that they would move in the direction of residential integration.[33]

Residential integration was essential, Alinsky told the board. "The Negroes," he argued, "have the greatest, immediate interest in integration. They are the ones who must bring the issue to a head in Chicago, as they have already done in the Southern states." If action were not taken to "begin large-scale residential integration as rapidly as possible," Alinsky wrote, we will have to "concede the disappearance of more white communities, the marooning of more churches, and the multiplication of the economic, social and political havoc directly traceable to the Chicago segregation system." The black population must be "dispersed or integrated . . . a black and white solution is doom for cities like Chicago." A black Woodlawn organization was critical for this process, because only "a Negro organization representing immediate Negro self-interest can be the occasion by which the whites see that integration is not only in their own long range self-interest, but also in their self-interest now." Such a group would disabuse whites of the notion that blacks "run down real estate, that they prefer to live by handouts from organized charity and they cannot climb to be more than clients reliant on other people's direction." Whites would thus no longer fear the possibility of black neighbors.[34] The establishment of a large, independent black mass organization, Alinsky concluded, "will not be a step towards bolstering segregation, no matter what it may look like." Rather, it is "the weapon that Negroes and whites need to break up the racial island."[35]

"WE WILL NOT BE PLANNED FOR": BUILDING TWO

The IAF began organizing in Woodlawn in 1960. The creation of a mass base for the organization was greatly aided by the heavy-handed efforts of the University of Chicago, in neighboring Hyde Park, to acquire land to expand its campus south into Woodlawn. As would happen in countless city neighborhoods around the nation in the 1950s and 1960s, the threat of urban renewal would foster a strong sense of territorial identity among citizens in the bulldozer's path. In late 1960, the university tried to get immediate city approval to begin clearing land for its South Campus project. Von Hoffman quickly assembled forty local residents to protest the plan at a meeting of the City Planning Commission (CPC) and succeeded in getting public hearings scheduled for January 1961. Word of the university plan—and of the fledgling organization's early success—spread in Woodlawn. When the local CPC hearings were held in January, Von Hoffman had little trouble mobilizing 300 local citizens to attend. The new group, called the Temporary Woodlawn Organization (TWO), made two demands: any renewal project involving Woodlawn had to be part of an overall plan for the community and Woodlawn residents had to be involved in all planning and implementation. The CPC agreed and ordered the City Planning Department to begin putting together a proposal for the renewal of Woodlawn. As a result of this success, dozens of local groups and organizations joined TWO.

The City Planning Department issued its draft proposal for an overall renewal plan in Woodlawn in March 1962. The Woodlawn Plan, as it came to be known, was a largely uncreative mishmash of traditional expert- and agency-dominated planning, which called for large-scale demolition and the construction of high-rise public housing. The primary goal of the plan was clearly to get the University of Chicago the land it wanted—and to get the city its share of federal urban renewal money generated by the South Campus project. It had no provisions for citizen input whatsoever. The deputy commissioner of planning summed up the city's sentiments: Woodlawn residents "will be given an opportunity to react."[36]

The announcement was ill-timed, because 1,200 delegates from over 100 organizations gathered for TWO's first Community Congress one week later. Alinsky, hoping to demonstrate TWO's growing power (and anger), invited Mayor Richard Daley to address the gathering. Daley, "red-faced and apparently nervous," promised the convention that urban renewal would not touch Woodlawn "until every individual and group has had a chance to present his recommendations."[37] The skeptical crowd booed. "Self-determination" was adopted as the motto of the organization, and the delegates resolved that TWO would "fight with all its strength to win for the people of Woodlawn the deciding voice in the development of a plan for Woodlawn."[38] Asserting that "we will not be planned for as though we were children," the assembly instructed TWO to use its power to "ensure genuine citizen participation in the planning and rehabilitation of our community" by hiring its own planning consultants.[39] Urban iconoclast Jane Jacobs, who was in Chicago to cover the Woodlawn controversy for *Architectural Forum*, offered her services to TWO. "They've been calling us 'welfare chiselers' and 'dependent' and everything else in the book," a convention delegate told the *Chicago Daily News*. "Now they distrust us for trying things for ourselves."[40]

In the spring and summer of 1962, TWO began a remarkable and unprecedented exercise in citizen-based urban planning. Shortly after the March convention, TWO hired architect William Nelson to help local citizens understand the city's plan, analyze local problems, articulate community goals, and put together an alternate plan. Von Hoffman, TWO leaders, and Nelson put together study outlines that were presented and discussed at dozens of meetings around the community. They created a dictionary of city-planning terms to enable residents to understand and criticize the city's proposal and assembled slides, maps, and audiotapes documenting Woodlawn's history and present state.[41] Woodlawn was divided up into twenty geographic sections. Groups and institutions in each area sent representatives to open meetings in which the city plan was discussed, preliminary local proposals were drafted, and representatives to sit on a community-wide planning committee were elected.[42]

In July, TWO printed a "Social Policy Planning Memo" in the local newspaper, outlining the goals culled from dozens of community meetings. Woodlawn, TWO asserted, was not simply an aggregation of buildings or a group of individuals seeking greener pastures. It was a community with a representative bargaining agent—TWO—and a sense of local identity. Thus, all planning must seek to preserve Woodlawn for its residents. This was to be done by preserving and enhancing a healthy diversity of land use and economic status, constructing and protecting public spaces, and focusing on low-rise housing. "Grave questions of policy," TWO argued, "cannot be decided by experts in a democracy." All planning must "increase individual self-reliance and personal freedom" and respect self-determination of the community and the individual. Citizens must not just have veto power; they must have a role in design and implementation as well. Social and urban policy planning, TWO asserted, must enhance community power, individual responsibility, and citizen participation—otherwise it is undemocratic, and will not work.[43]

A first stab at defining self-determination, the Social Policy Planning Memo anticipated many of the ideas behind the federal Community Action Program, launched two years later. In the process, the community organization began to formulate a vision of self-determination and citizen participation that challenged not only the Daley machine but also some of the prevailing assumptions about citizenship, power, and representation that underlay the American welfare state. According to TWO, programs simply would not work if they were not embedded in local civil society and institutions—and for this to occur, local citizens had to be given the power to act responsibly. Community viability and stability were as important, if not more so, than facilitating individual mobility, because the structural causes of urban poverty were broad-based, deep-seated, and required much more in the way of solutions than just a citizenry of "clients" receiving services from the outside.

TWO's vision of black ghetto residents as citizens to be mobilized and empowered, rather than clients to be served, became widespread in the urban North by the mid-sixties. It challenged the managerial model of social change that increasingly defined liberal programs by insisting that ghetto residents suffered from a paucity of power, not just a lack of resources, skills, and opportunities. TWO's localism would be its greatest strength. As in many cities, Chicago's political system had no place for independent black community groups. TWO's outsider status and its ability to isolate identifiable targets— such as the University of Chicago, social service bureaucracies, and the Daley administration—allowed it to amass considerable power locally. At the same time, however, its localism proved to be a great weakness. The causes of black poverty in Woodlawn lay in larger structures of racial geography and political economy. Making Woodlawn a more livable place, although desirable, would not address this.

TWO had a plan and a mass base, but no authority to implement its proposals. Community opposition had effectively stalled the South Campus project and the city's plan, but nothing positive could happen in Woodlawn without federal and city money. In early July 1963, 700 TWO members staged a sit-in in Daley's office to try to push Daley and the University of Chicago to the negotiating table. It worked: twenty-five TWO members met with university and city officials on July 16 and reached an agreement. TWO would have veto power over the director of the South Campus/Woodlawn project and have a majority on all committees. Clearance was to be selected, rather than wholesale, and no clearance was to take place until housing had already been constructed in Woodlawn for those displaced. In addition, the relocation housing would not be high-rises built by the Chicago Housing Authority. Instead, TWO was to organize a nonprofit corporation to purchase vacant land and obtain federal funding to construct housing within the price range of Woodlawn residents. TWO had won an important victory.[44]

Alinsky and Von Hoffman placed strong emphasis on early victories for TWO, and its initial success in challenging the University of Chicago and the city greatly aided community confidence in its ability to deliver on its promises. The result was widespread attendance and participation at committee meetings, hearings, and rallies. By the mid-1960s, TWO, with its sixty business-related groups, fifty block clubs, and thirty churches, represented nearly 40,000 of Woodlawn's 100,000 citizens.[45] The organization ran its own newspaper, was in the process of building low-income housing, ran a federally funded job training program, and had won a significant victory for citizen participation in urban renewal two years before anyone had heard the term "maximum feasible participation." Thus, when Congress passed the Economic Opportunity Act (EOA) in 1964, TWO was organizationally and ideologically ready to push forward their program of community power and self-determination.

CIVIL RIGHTS, POVERTY, AND THE CONSTRUCTION OF A MASS BASE

Although the South Campus battle had been crucial, TWO was ready to engage these issues because the organization had succeeded in doing three important (and overlapping) things, all of which contributed to its power and local legitimacy: develop a black and locally recruited staff and leadership, connect the organization to the larger Civil Rights Movement, and reach out to Woodlawn's poorest residents. From the outset, Alinsky worried that his all-white organizing staff would make it difficult for TWO to sink deep roots in the community. Alinsky promised to quickly recruit local black staff and pull nonlocal organizers out of Woodlawn as soon as was feasible. "They knew it would be their own show," Alinsky told a reporter in 1962. By 1965, TWO's staff was all black.[46]

Alinsky initially served as the public face of TWO, but the organization was led by a series of impressive and increasingly well-known black presidents—beginning with the Rev. Arthur Brazier. Brazier was TWO's first and most influential leader. He was also the group's most important public intellectual; his 1969 book *Black Self-Determination* outlined the intellectual evolution of the organization's guiding philosophy. Born in Hyde Park in 1922, Brazier served two years in India and Burma during World War II before returning to Chicago to work as a spot welder and a letter carrier. Ordained in 1951, he was called to Woodlawn's Apostolic Church of God in 1960. With a congregation that was conservative both politically and theologically, Brazier hesitated to get involved in TWO. After hearing him preach, Von Hoffman was convinced that Brazier was a natural leader. He successfully persuaded him that ministry and community leadership were not incompatible activities.[47]

TWO's committee structure encouraged broad community participation and the development of new leadership. Above all, Alinsky's organizing approach stressed the importance of giving people something to do, however small. His belief was that this gave people a sense of efficacy and empowerment, encouraging them (with the help of the staff and a trained organizer) to draw connections between the personal and the political. At the same time, committees were supposed to provide concrete benefits to local residents, encouraging membership growth and participation. The Schools Committee worked with local PTAs whenever possible, but it also showed a willingness to challenge those that were "not willing to tackle the basic issues concerning education in the ghetto."[48] The Civil Rights Committee investigated specific cases of police brutality and handled complaints about racial and economic discrimination in South Side hospitals. As more local residents began to chair committees, and even join the paid staff, TWO became more identifiably black at the top.

In April 1963, TWO became one of the founding members of the Coordinating Council of Community Organizations (CCCO), an interracial coalition of over forty groups dedicated to eliminating school segregation in the city. Inspired by TWO's effort, CCCO organized a citywide boycott in October 1963. School boycotts to oppose racial segregation spread to other cities around the country in 1964.[49] Participation in CCCO was beneficial to both groups. TWO's activism, according to Brazier, "broadened its scope quite a bit from being a local community organization and becoming involved in much wider policies that affected black people in general."[50] Journalist Charles Silberman, writing in 1964, concluded that "the leadership and organizational strength TWO has provided is the only thing that has kept Chicago's civil rights coalition together." He also praised Brazier as the "principal spokesman on civil rights for Chicago Negroes."[51] At least through the mid-1960s, TWO attempted to parlay the moral legitimacy, spiritual energy, and protest tactics of the Civil Rights Movement into membership, power, and publicity. Its efforts to define "self-determination" intellectually and programmatically would draw upon but also seek to change the discourse of the larger movement, particularly as it moved toward issues of concern to blacks in the urban North.

Community participation in TWO, however, was waning by early 1963. Organizers and staff had difficulty translating movement energy into the nuts-and-bolts work of committee meetings and institution building. TWO's officers, Alinsky believed, were making too many decisions. He sent in Edward Chambers to replace an exhausted Nicholas Von Hoffman. Chambers quickly initiated a concentrated effort to build up the organization by taking on a series of issues central to the daily lives of Woodlawn's poorest citizens: poverty, public assistance, and the relationship between the community and social welfare agencies.

This effort would bring in new members, new voices, and new issues, moving TWO away from the more traditional civil rights focus of the previous year and toward something new: a community organization striving to bring together issues of social policy, community control, and racial pride.[52]

A two-month delay in the delivery of relief checks in spring 1963, caused by an appropriations dispute in the state legislature, prompted TWO's Social Welfare Committee to organize an emergency meeting "to prevent a wave of hunger and evictions of ADC [Aid to Dependent Children] families from ravaging Woodlawn."[53] From this point forward, TWO became increasingly focused on the issue of poverty, the paternalism and racism of social agencies, and the need for self-determination. The emergence of poverty as a national issue in 1964 only reinforced this focus.

This new priority was evident at TWO's third convention in April 1964. Resolutions passed requiring each member organization to have two representatives on call for the Social Welfare Committee and committing TWO to "investigate President Johnson's program for the war on poverty with the view toward better educational, business, and job opportunities for the people of Woodlawn."[54] The committee infused TWO with new leaders, new energy, and new goals. It worked closely with local residents on public assistance, providing information on available benefits and assistance in getting them.

In September 1966, the Social Welfare Committee transformed itself into a "welfare union" dedicated to collectively representing Woodlawn's growing population of poor citizens on public assistance.[55] The Social Welfare Union (SWU) quickly became "one of the most militant and aggressive groups" in TWO.[56] Herman Blake, who sat in on SWU meetings in 1967 while on a fact-finding visit to Woodlawn, found them to be the organization's most well-attended and energetic gatherings. Worried that he would find TWO to be a top-down group dominated by the middle class, Blake was reassured by the union meetings. Members—virtually all of them female welfare recipients—came dressed in "regular daily clothing" with their children in tow. TWO leaders "welcome[d] the welfare recipients and treat[ed] them cordially." In general, Blake found, TWO fostered a "profound respect . . . for all points of view regardless of the social and economic status of the person." SWU meetings "gave eloquent witness to the involvement of all levels of the community, and they cooperate with each other very well." TWO's program and its leadership "are both indigenous." It is, he concluded, "very much a movement of the people."[57]

TWO AND THE WAR ON POVERTY

President Johnson envisioned the War on Poverty as a program designed to help communities more effectively mobilize their own local resources in order to improve the capacities of the poor. Poor communities—and, by extension, poor people—were considered dysfunctional and in need of improvement. This improvement would come through better coordination of social services at the local level and "maximum feasible participation" of the poor in the management and distribution of those services. The 1964 EOA created a new federal agency, the Office of Economic Opportunity (OEO), which implemented a Community Action Program (CAP) to bring this vision to life in cities around the country. Community Action Agencies (CAAs) were created at the local level, with representation from the poor (at least officially) welcomed.

In an "Open Letter to Sargent Shriver" published in the *TWO Newsletter* in October 1964, TWO president Lynward Stevenson outlined the organization's plans with regard to the federal War on Poverty. The promise of "maximum feasible participation," Stevenson argued, will allow TWO "to back up our program of self-determination with deeds." The TWO president proposed a comprehensive community-run job training program, complete with health and daycare programs.[58] TWO forwarded the plan to Deton Brooks, the Daley-appointed head of Chicago's CAA, for approval. Brooks and the city stonewalled: Daley had no intention of allowing the federal government to fund any organizations that were politically independent of City Hall.[59] Brooks publicly questioned TWO's competence to run poverty programs, arguing that city experts and agencies could more efficiently and effectively spend federal money.[60]

Empowered by the participatory language of federal legislation and the OEO's early willingness to enforce it, TWO launched a public attack on Daley's interpretation of the poverty program. Stevenson issued scathing criticisms of both Daley and Brooks, accusing them of subverting the War on Poverty by using it to maintain control of the black poor and feed the patronage system. The charges were certainly accurate: Chicago's CAA had fifty-four members, none of whom represented the poor, and applications for jobs in the poverty bureaucracy were funneled through ward committee members.[61] Alinsky publicly criticized Daley's poverty program as a "prize piece of political pornography."[62] Stevenson testified before the House Committee on Labor and Education in April 1965, holding Daley up to national ridicule. In Chicago, Stevenson testified, the War on Poverty involved maximum feasible participation of the rich, the precinct captains, and the ward committee members, not the poor. Under Daley's rule, he argued, "there is no War on Poverty. There is only more of the ancient, galling war against the poor."[63]

Embarrassed and angered, Daley met with Stevenson during the summer of 1965 to discuss TWO representation on Woodlawn's local CAA. Daley agreed to allow TWO to submit a list of twenty-one names, of which he would choose at least thirteen for the twenty-five-member committee. Daley surprised TWO by accepting all of them, but then he increased the size of the board to seventy-five, with the remainder to be nominated by him. Throughout the fall and winter of 1965, TWO tried to use solid-block voting and large turnouts at meetings to gain influence on the local board, but without success. Daley was determined to shut TWO out of the poverty program.

In December 1965, TWO published a "Black Paper" titled "Poverty, Power and Race in Chicago" discussing its recent experiences and comparing the battle for self-determination with regard to urban renewal to TWO's struggle for representation in the poverty program. Experts ran both policies, "with a pittance thrown out as smokescreen to confuse the public." Federal poverty money, TWO argued, was being used to "buy off our rage against being confined in the ghetto" and to "distract black people from building enough power to break out of the ghetto." The root issue, according to the Black Paper, was "citizen participation—whether 'maximum feasible participation' of the poor means what it says, or is just a huckster's slogan . . . we insist that we be in on the decision-making of the War on Poverty . . . that is what citizen participation means to us. That is what we mean by self-determination."[64]

Daley had succeeded in blocking TWO's participation in Chicago's poverty program, but the organization remained as strong as ever. The battle with Daley kept members committed, active, and angry, and TWO used the poverty war as a pretext to organize the Social Welfare Union in 1966—expanding the membership base and providing a significant source of new militant (and often female) leadership. With the passage of the federal Model Cities Program in 1966 (which also mandated citizen participation), TWO saw an opportunity to bring its efforts of the past half-decade together.

At its March 1967 Community Congress, TWO passed a series of resolutions empowering President Stevenson to hire technical consultants to help Woodlawn residents put together the programs and ideas for reform and renewal that had emerged over the course of the decade. Interestingly, TWO also passed a resolution calling for a federally administered, guaranteed annual income for all citizens. Clearly reflecting the growing influence of the Social Welfare Union in the organization, as well as general frustration with the intrusiveness and paternalism of Chicago's social agencies, the call for a guaranteed income was a key part of TWO's evolving definition of self-determination and citizenship. Only a guaranteed income could ensure individual autonomy from economic want, from dehumanizing eligibility restrictions, and from paternalistic state agencies. Such autonomy, alongside participation in and power over those institutions governing social, political, and economic life in Woodlawn, was part of TWO's overall definition of citizenship and self-determination. Although the language of self-determination appeared to draw on Black Nationalist and Black Power ideas of the time, to TWO leaders it meant more than just community control or black control of all institutions affecting black communities. Indeed, TWO rarely expressed its vision of self-determination in racial terms. Self-determination for TWO contained within it a socially embedded notion of citizenship that valued community, public space, and the importance of civil associations over both identity politics and liberal statism.

Model Cities appeared to present an opportunity for TWO to implement its vision while solidifying its status as bargaining agent for Woodlawn. Designed to give cities an opportunity to experiment in limited target areas, it focused on "community development," unlike the Community Action Program.[65] Although inherently limited in a number of ways, Model Cities encouraged municipalities to use existing community organizations and institutions to coordinate and implement programs. TWO, Stevenson and other leaders believed, had the structure, the power, and the experience to design and implement a Woodlawn program.

The problem, of course, was that Model Cities plans had to be approved by municipal authorities—and Daley was not about to sign off on something that would render TWO the strongest independent political force in the city. Further, his disdain for citizen participation of any kind was made abundantly clear in the Model Cities plan Daley submitted to the Department of Housing and Urban Development (HUD) in spring 1968. Daley was to appoint all persons serving on citizen committees, and the city plan had no provision for technical assistance to local citizen committees. The city had chosen four target areas—including Woodlawn—but had not sought out any organized constituencies in any of the four when putting the plan together.[66]

TWO girded itself for a battle. Former president Arthur Brazier, after a disappointing meeting with Daley, told TWO's Steering Committee: "[W]e are through with plantation politics. Those days are over, but just saying so won't make it true. We must close ranks and get the kind of Model Cities program we need."[67] The Steering Committee decided that TWO needed to quickly form a community planning council, get technical help, and put together its own Model Cities plan—one that would adhere to the legislative requirement of citizen participation. TWO would then have to use all its political and persuasive powers in Chicago and Washington to argue that its plan fit federal guidelines and promised greater success than Daley's.

The TWO plan echoed many of the goals and ideas developed with William Nelson earlier in the decade. The plan was organized around three concepts: citizen responsibility, the "whole man," and "decentralized centralization." Citizen responsibility for TWO meant more than just participation in planning, as mandated by federal guidelines. It also meant the creation of a structure that would allow the community and its citizens to exercise primary responsibility for implementing and administering programs. Critics of poverty programs, TWO argued, often emphasize the lack of responsibility demanded from and exercised by the poor, but citizen responsibility ultimately must rest upon some degree of power and control through community-based organizations. Only in this way, TWO concluded, can social and urban policy improve lives and develop citizens. The second concept—treating inner-city citizens as "whole people"—was connected to the first. Community and personal problems are interrelated and cannot be split up "in terms of conventional categories of educational, medical, social welfare, or legal approaches." Poor people, TWO argued, are not simply an aggregation of personal cases, each with its own logic and self-contained causes. Poverty is experienced both individually and collectively, its causes are structural and community-wide, and thus solutions must be located at this social level as well. If problems are seen from the bottom up, from the perspective of the individual citizen and the community, TWO reasoned, then citizen control over community-generated programs makes a great deal of sense.[68]

The structure TWO proposed to implement such programs—"decentralized centralization"—called for the creation of neighborhood government, in which programs were to be carried out through community-based agencies with citizen boards. These agencies, or "pads," would each serve a limited two- or three-block area, would be staffed by local residents, and would function as outreach centers providing citizens with easy access to all manner of services in one location. Such a localized structure would allow programs to adhere closely to local needs in a nonintrusive way while embedding them into local civil society. When joined with a guaranteed annual income, TWO concluded, such a structure would truly address urban problems while respecting the dignity of citizens and communities.[69]

By early 1969, it became apparent that the new Nixon administration was not as interested in pressing HUD's citizen participation requirement as its predecessor had been. Local politicians friendly to TWO urged the organization to participate in the local Model Areas Council, in exchange for a promise from the city that TWO's plan would get a fair hearing there. In January 1969, Brazier and Stevenson sold the idea at a rowdy Steering Committee meeting, arguing that if TWO were running its own Model Cities Program, it would have all the responsibility of a government agency without any of the independence or power. The committee reluctantly agreed. Daley had gotten the better of TWO again, because the "fair hearing" never took place. HUD adopted Daley's Model Cities plan in the summer of 1969.

TWO, "SELF-DETERMINATION," AND THE POLITICS OF RACIAL GEOGRAPHY

The social programs of the 1960s offered the poor the opportunity to participate but without meaningful collective representation or power. Making sure that the poor had representation and power was an important part of Alinsky and TWO's philosophy, and it bears some discussion. Citizen responsibility for TWO meant more than just participation in planning, as mandated by federal guidelines. It also meant the creation of a structure that would allow the community and its citizens to exercise primary responsibility for implementing and administering programs. TWO took this position as early as 1962.[70] Critics of poverty programs, TWO argued, often emphasize the lack of responsibility demanded from and exercised by the poor—but citizen responsibility ultimately must rest upon some degree of power and control through community-based organizations. Only in this way, TWO concluded, can social and urban policy improve lives and develop citizens. Woodlawn residents were not just individual clients seeking services, money, and jobs. They were citizens and members of communities. Government, Brazier later argued, was not responsive to individuals, particularly if they were poor and black. Community organizations like TWO, therefore, were both legitimate and necessary. Especially for the poor, power was ultimately a collective undertaking.[71]

War on Poverty programs dealt with growing black challenges to the politics of racial geography by essentially ignoring both race and geography—and pulled black community groups like TWO into doing the same. TWO and other black community groups generally emerged in the early sixties with a focus on local issues. The almost complete exclusion of blacks as an organized force in urban politics—particularly in Chicago—virtually ensured that any kind of community mobilization would take place outside of the conventional electoral system. Often, black community groups were first formed in opposition to urban renewal or to the policies of local public service bureaucracies. These grievances, although reflective of important issues of social justice and often generative of popular mobilization, had a limited analytical reach. They provided little intellectual or political traction with regard to the economic sources of neighborhood decline.[72] Because of both these issues and Alinsky's place-based organizing philosophy, TWO struggled to move beyond the "gilding the ghetto" approach. The politics of race and community—of "self-determination," in TWO's parlance—was too limited to attack the political economy and racial geography of Chicago. Both CAP and Model Cities reinforced this localism, leaving the larger processes of neighborhood deterioration untouched.[73]

TWO's history points to a vital and still-relevant set of questions. Does localism serve the interests of racial justice when the larger structures that limit opportunity and access are far broader geographically and perhaps require coalitions that cross the boundaries of race, class, and community? If TWO focused mainly on demanding more humane, efficient, and locally responsive social services, did it not thus leave racial segregation essentially unchallenged and unchanged—including all the economic difficulties, political divisions, and inner-city disinvestment that derived from it? On the other hand, if TWO made integration and open occupancy its main goals, might this not provide the black middle class with an opportunity to flee the ghetto, thus weakening the neighborhoods and institutions left behind without addressing the desperate material conditions of most residents?

As James Wilson and Preston Smith have argued, black leadership in Chicago in the early 1960s was itself divided over this question, in terms of both class and ideology. A good portion of the South Side's black middle class had an inherent interest in stabilizing and improving places like Woodlawn. Chicago's black South Side aldermen were dependent on racial segregation for the preservation of all-black wards. Many black businesses profited from a geographically concentrated market. Black clergy relied on a steady and growing pool of potential congregants nearby. On the other hand, as upwardly mobile beneficiaries of the postwar economic boom and the opening of the housing market, many middle-class families aspired to a future outside the boundaries of the traditional Black Belt and favored whatever measures promised to make those opportunities manifest.[74]

Wilson, drawing upon interviews with dozens of black South Side political, civic, and religious leaders in the late 1950s, interpreted this dilemma as a choice between *welfare* goals and *status* goals. Those who stressed the former sought to tangibly improve the daily life of the community and its individuals through better services, enhanced living conditions, and increased political representation. Black elected officials certainly fell into this category; by seeking to build a community group through success in dealing with such issues, Alinsky inevitably did as well, even if his long-term goal was some kind of negotiated integration. "The most important thing," one black activist informed Wilson, "is to give people a roof over their heads, *not* integration . . . if in the process of putting roofs over their heads, you see that the houses are all going to one race, then you just have to live with it." Status ends, on the other hand, were at the core of postwar racial liberalism and the "black civic ideology" dominant among Chicago's black intellectuals and social reformers. It involved the integration of blacks into "all phases of community life" in accordance with their proportion of the general population on the principle of equality and color-blind opportunity. Segregation and confinement by definition entailed subordination, and any spatial strategy born of expedience that tried to turn separation to its advantage was bound to lead to deterioration, not improvement. Gains for blacks were indivisible, because the upward mobility of any black person "constituted not only racial progress but also a democratization of American social institutions." Successful instances of residential integration thus were valued as important precedents that taught white homeowners that racial propinquity was not inherently threat-ening. Arguing that black progress could only come through unwavering sup-port for legally defined civil rights and the establishment of social equality and equal access to opportunity, liberal black leaders strongly advocated the scatter-ing of racially mixed public housing projects, the integration of public schools, and the establishment of the principle of open occupancy in the private real estate market. Welfare ends, from this perspective, could only institutionalize and perpetuate racial segregation.[75]

Alinsky sought, in a sense, to use welfare means toward status ends. He hoped that a black community group would serve as the first tactical stage in the long march toward the creation and maintenance of interracial neighborhoods. Critics might accuse him of "gilding the ghetto," but he at least was attempt-ing to come up with a political technology to address the dilemmas of race and place. An Alinsky community organization in Woodlawn—or any other black area—would inevitably run into this dilemma, because it was an unavoidable part of the politics of Chicago's racial geography. The welfare state, on the other hand, seemed to offer little but co-optation, community development, and indi-vidual mobility. Black communities, especially poor urban ones, were something to be contained, bulldozed, escaped, and explained away. TWO simply did not have the power to force any other outcome.

Federal policy, and racial liberalism more generally, missed both the salience of racial segregation and the politics, identities, and interests that had grown up around it. Or more accurately, for reasons of cost and political expediency, these issues were simply elided—replaced with the old and evocative American keywords of community, neighborhood, empowerment, and individual uplift. Groups like TWO took whatever slack in the political system that was available to them and tried to use it to build opportunities for individual mobility, patron-age, and group political power. When the Vietnam conflict, the splintering of the New Deal coalition, and the economic problems of the 1970s shortened the horizons of federal urban and social policy, communities like Woodlawn were essentially left on their own. It remains so today. The situation got much worse in Woodlawn before improving somewhat in the 1990s.[76]

In the early 1970s, TWO shifted to a focus on community development, helping to launch housing and commercial projects in Woodlawn. Federal urban policy followed a similar path, from "community action" to community development. Although the names of programs and institutions have changed in the ensuing decades, the basic place-based focus of federal policy has not. Community development, in which TWO was a pioneer, essentially created public-private partnerships designed to "turn poor neighborhoods into middle-class ones."[77] These efforts provided some social and geographic mobility for local residents, but they did little to stop the rapid deterioration of Woodlawn and other black neighborhoods.

Community development assumed racial segregation as a given and sought to improve the lives of ghetto residents within the limits segregation imposed. Much like community action and Model Cities, neighborhood development tried to heal ghettos from within. It appeared to offer a way for Democrats in particular to do something about ghettos but without engaging the issues of employment, wages, open occupancy, and residential integration that by the mid-1960s were dividing the liberal wing of the party at the local level. President Johnson, for example, was forced to drop from the Model Cities bill the requirement that any new housing constructed under the program be racially integrated.[78] Although this approach may have been politically palatable to conservatives who disliked government programs; white voters who feared residential integration, job competition, and the redistribution of wealth; and black voters who valued the empowerment, patronage, and political power that community development tended to bring, it failed to understand or address the structural roots of racial inequality and metropolitan uneven development.

Alinsky was skeptical about TWO's tactical shift. "It is ironic," he told *Harper's Magazine* in the early seventies, "that the blacks themselves are pushing now for apartheid. This makes the racist whites very comfortable."[79] The black push for community development ("apartheid," to Alinsky) was a reaction to the limitations imposed both by Chicago's racial geopolitics and by government programs unwilling to challenge the assumptions, interests, and identities that had grown up around those geopolitics. As Thomas Sugrue and others have argued, it is historically inaccurate to see the "white backlash" against racial liberalism as a phenomenon prompted by the increasingly radical demands of urban blacks in the mid- to late 1960s. That backlash was in fact an integral part of the politics of racial geography in Chicago and other cities well before "maximum feasible participation," TWO, the Watts riots, and "black power." Federal policy, by not challenging the relationship between race and place in cities like Chicago, offered groups like TWO little more than the opportunity to contend over the terms of their participation in programs with limited budgets, narrow mandates, and toothless analyses of the origins of ghetto poverty.

It is a classic progressive dilemma to wonder and theorize about the proper level of focus, when there seems so much to do and all problems seem connected. TWO's story doesn't tell us that local means for addressing the issues of segregation, racial inequality, and urban disinvestment are a dead end. What it may tell us instead is that neighborhood organizing must be ultimately directed toward changes in the law and in the distribution of political power and toward the creation of multi-racial geographically broad coalitions. To build effective democratic organizations capable of exercising power and mobilizing people, local action is a necessity, as Alinsky argued. But his story must also make us aware of the dangers of place-based organizing—and especially of similarly structured federal urban policy—when the ways in which people, institutions, and governments think about social geography are so tightly connected to race even now.

Racial segregation matters and the small victories of empowerment zones and community development corporations (CDCs) will not change that fact. The persistent American belief in and practice of neighborhood-based approaches as an end in themselves—the Community Action Program, Model Cities, Empowerment Zones, and even CDCs—accept racial segregation as a given and thus reproduce the politics, interests, and identities that have created racial inequality and urban decline in the first place and resist broader solutions. Especially in recent decades, when a diminishing federal interest in and commitment to cities and the urban poor have taken the form of increasingly modest and private interventions into deep-seated and regional problems, place-based policy seems to ask the victims to deal with the effects of a racial geopolitics over which they have little power. The idea that urban neighborhoods can and should regenerate themselves naturalizes racial segregation, delegitimizes the proper role of the state in addressing inequalities, and allows white suburbanites to rest comfortably with the belief that their wealth is unrelated to the deprivation in nearby cities. It confirms the assumptions of racial geopolitics while removing the underlying problems of our society further and further from daily experience and daily consciousness.

This criticism should not minimize TWO's accomplishments or its importance. The organization, in the words of Edward Chambers, "became the teacher of how one functions in society." Committee members had to master the intricacies of property law, mortgage financing, landlord-tenant relations, building codes, zoning, and federal programs, among other things. They had to do research, keep track of hearings, and mobilize turnout at protests and meetings. As Carl Tjerandsen, president of a foundation that provided funding for TWO, later remarked: "[A]lmost no individual would ever be likely to acquire the range and depth of knowledge indicated above . . . in short, it was the group, the organization which made it possible to assemble the information and through discussion achieve an understanding of it. The group was essential to the motivation to undertake the task because it was the power of TWO to make a difference, to solve a problem, that encouraged its members to begin so arduous a task."[80] Lynward Stevenson's stirring speech at TWO's 1966 convention sums up the impact of the group best:

I cannot describe to you what it means to negotiate with people like Sargent Shriver and Richard Daley and not be alone. For, when the president of TWO goes anywhere to bargain, he has a collective leadership beside him and huge numbers of people behind him. He goes into battle with a real weapon, the weapon of the poor—their numbers. What does it mean to a man to have that kind of support? It means that he and those that support him are free men in every sense of the word. We have paid heavily over the past five years for our self-determination . . . you have made me proud to be a part of TWO. You have made me proud to be a member of the Woodlawn community. You have made me proud—more than I can say—to be a Negro. And finally, you have made me proud to be a man.[81]

NOTES

1. The phrase "Chicago's Great Question" comes from M. W. Newman, "South Side Neighborhood Works for Racial Peace," *Chicago Daily News*, September 9, 1960.

2. For works that examine the transition and disappearance of white ethnic city neighborhoods and their effects on identity and politics, see Ray Suarez, *The Old Neighborhood* (New York: Free Press, 1999); Gerald Gamm, *Urban Exodus: Why the Jews Left Boston and the Catholics Stayed* (Cambridge, MA: Harvard University Press, 1999); Louis Rosen, *South Side: The Racial Transformation of an American Neighborhood* (New York: Ivan Dee Publishing, 1998); Tom Sugrue, *Origins of the Urban Crisis* (Princeton, NJ: Princeton University Press, 1996); Alan Ehrenhalt, *Lost City: Discovering the Forgotten Virtues of Community in the Chicago of the 1950s* (New York: HarperCollins, 1995); Alexander Von Hoffman, *Local Attachments: The Making of an American Neighborhood, 1850–1920* (Baltimore: Johns Hopkins University Press, 1994); Hillel Levine and Lawrence Harmon, *The Death of an American Jewish Community: A Tragedy of Good Intentions* (New York: Touchstone, 1992); Jonathan Reider, *Canarsie: The Jews and Italians of Brooklyn Against Liberalism* (Cambridge, MA: Harvard University Press, 1985); Arnold Hirsch, *Making the Second Ghetto* (Chicago: University of Chicago Press, 1983); Vincent Giese, *Revolution in the City* (Notre Dame, IN: Fides Publishers, 1961).

3. On Woodlawn and TWO, see Nicholas Lemann, *The Promised Land: The Great Black Migration and How It Changed America* (New York: Knopf, 1991); Sanford Horwitt, *Let Them Call Me Rebel* (New York: Alfred A. Knopf, 1989); John Hall Fish, *Black Power / White Control* (Princeton, NJ: Princeton University Press, 1973); Arthur Brazier, *Black Self-Determination: The Story of the Woodlawn Organization* (Grand Rapids, MI: Eerdmans, 1969). On the Civil Rights Movement in Chicago, see Roger Biles, *Richard J. Daley: Politics, Race, and the Governing of Chicago* (Chicago: Northern Illinois University Press, 1995); James Ralph, *Northern Protest: Martin Luther King, Jr., Chicago, and the Civil Rights Movement* (Cambridge, MA: Harvard University Press, 1993); Arnold Hirsch, "The Cook County Democratic Organization and the Dilemma of Race, 1931–1987," *Snowbelt Cities: Metropolitan Politics in the Northeast and Midwest Since World War II*, ed. Richard Bernard (Bloomington: Indiana University Press, 1990), 63–90; David Garrow, ed., *Chicago 1966: Open Housing Marches, Summit Negotiations, and Operation Breadbasket* (Brooklyn, NY: Carlson Publishing, 1989); Alan Anderson and George Pickering, *Confronting the Color*

Line: The Broken Promise of the Civil Rights Movement in Chicago (Athens: University of Georgia Press, 1986).

4. Douglas Massey and Nancy Denton define the term "ghetto" as "a set of neighborhoods that are exclusively inhabited by members of one group, within which virtually all members of that group live." I use it in the same manner. Douglas Massey and Nancy Denton, *American Apartheid: Segregation and the Making of the Underclass* (Cambridge, MA: Harvard University Press, 1993), 18–19.

5. On whiteness and property, see Mark Santow, "Saul Alinsky and the Dilemmas of Race in the Post-war City," Ph.D. diss., University of Pennsylvania, 2000; George Lipsitz, *The Possessive Investment in Whiteness* (Philadelphia: Temple University Press, 1998); Cheryl Harris, "Whiteness as Property," *Harvard Law Review* 106 (1993): 1707–1791.

6. David Delaney, *Race, Place and the Law: 1836–1948* (Austin: University of Texas Press, 1998), 7, 9, 103–104.

7. Ibid., 6–7, 9, 103–104.

8. Ibid., 13.

9. Ibid., 96; See Thomas Jackson, "The State, the Movement, and the Urban Poor: The War on Poverty and Political Mobilization in the 1960s," in *The Underclass Debate: Views from History,* ed. Michael Katz (Princeton, NJ: Princeton University Press, 1993), 403–439.

10. Philip Hauser and Evelyn Kitagawa, *Local Community Fact Book, 1950* (Chicago: Chicago Community Inventory, University of Chicago Press, 1953).

11. Memo from Von Hoffman to Farrell, March 17, 1958, Saul Alinsky Papers, Special Collections, University of Illinois–Chicago (hereafter cited as UIC). Woodlawn's business district was fourth among retail trade centers outside the Loop in 1948. The quote is Von Hoffman's.

12. Brazier, *Black Self-Determination,* 25.

13. From "Population and Housing Data for the Woodlawn Community," May 1960, assembled by Nicholas Von Hoffman from preliminary census reports, Alinsky Papers, UIC. See also Evelyn Kitagawa and Karl Taeuber, *Local Community Fact Book: Chicago Metropolitan Area, 1960* (Chicago: Chicago Community Inventory, University of Chicago Press, 1963).

14. Herman Blake, "Report on TWO" (1967), 88, in the Emil Schwarzhaupt Foundation Papers, Special Collections, University of Chicago.

15. Carl Tjerandsen, *Education for Citizenship: A Foundation's Experience* (Santa Cruz, CA: Emil Schwarzhaupt Foundation, 1980), 236.

16. Data from Research Department, Welfare Council of Metropolitan Chicago, November 3, 1967, Welfare Council Papers, Chicago Historical Society (hereafter cited as CHS).

17. See "Population and Housing Data for the Woodlawn Community"; Kitagawa and Taeuber, *Local Community Fact Book.*

18. On the role of the federal government and its programs in shaping the relationship between race and geography, see John Bauman et al., *From Tenements to the Taylor Homes: In Search of an Urban Housing Policy in Twentieth-Century America* (University Park: Pennsylvania State University Press, 2000); Sugrue, *Origins of the Urban Crisis*; Ronald Tobey et al., "Moving Out and Settling In: Residential Mobility, Home Ownership, and the

Public Enframing of Citizenship, 1921–1950," *American Historical Review* 95 (December 1990): 1395–1422; Kenneth Jackson, *Crabgrass Frontier: The Suburbanization of the United States* (New York: Oxford University Press, 1985); Hirsch, *Making the Second Ghetto*.

19. James Briggs Murray interview with the Rev. Arthur Brazier, June 7, 1991, 8–9; Hirsch, *Making the Second Ghetto*.

20. Farrell had heard Alinsky speak at meetings of Cardinal Samuel Stritch's Conservation Council back in 1952, when Stritch had called together over 150 pastors from Catholic parishes across the city and advised them to resist efforts by some of their parishioners to keep certain groups out of their neighborhoods. Alinsky had outlined a plan for a citywide network of neighborhood organizations, and Farrell was impressed. See Cardinal Stritch, "Speech to Chicago Pastors," November 26, 1952, Msgr. John O'Grady Papers, Catholic University; and Alinsky, "Speech at National Conference of Catholic Charities Annual Meeting," September 29, 1953, Alinsky Papers, UIC.

21. Letter from Martin Farrell to Alinsky, February 22, 1958, Alinsky Papers, UIC.

22. Memo from Von Hoffman to Farrell, March 17, 1958, Alinsky Papers, UIC.

23. See Leber and Blakeley, "The Great Debate in Chicago," *Presbyterian Life*, June 15, 1961; and David Finks, *The Radical Vision of Saul Alinsky* (Mahwah, NJ: Paulist Press, 1984), 137. The Sixth United Presbyterian Church is emblematic: in May 1956, the congregation had 165 members—all white. By February 1961, 86 percent of its 250-member congregation was black. Floyd Mulkey, "Historical Sketches of Woodlawn Organizations," October 8, 1962, TWO File, CHS.

24. Finks, *Radical Vision of Saul Alinsky*.

25. See Brazier, *Black Self-Determination*, 16; and Letter from Archbishop Meyer to Martin Farrell, September 25, 1959, Folder 43, Alinsky Papers, UIC.

26. Georgie Geyer, "Woodlawn: A Community in Revolt," *Chicago Scene*, June 7, 1962.

27. Alinsky, "Sixteen Questions," March 1959, Alinsky Papers, UIC. See also Tjerandsen, *Education for Citizenship*, 239.

28. Geyer, *Chicago Scene*, June 7, 1962.

29. Alinsky et al., *General Report of the Industrial Areas Foundation for the Archdiocese: Part I, Chapter II, Section C* (1957), 36, Alinsky Papers, UIC.

30. Alinsky et al., *General Report: Part I, Chapter IV: Summary of Recommendations* (1957), 68, Alinsky Papers, UIC.

31. Alinsky, *IAF Annual Report 1960*, 12, Alinsky Papers, UIC.

32. Blake, "Report on TWO," 97. Alinsky received a three-year grant of just under $70,000 in November 1960.

33. Ernestine Cofield, "Found: A General to Lead a Slum Army," *Chicago Defender Magazine* (November 20, 1962): 7–8, 16.

34. *IAF Annual Report 1960*, 7–8, 16.

35. *General Report: Part 1, Chapter 1* (1957), 7.

36. Jane Jacobs, "Chicago's Woodlawn—Renewal by Whom?" *Architectural Forum* (May 1962): 122.

37. Georgie Anne Geyer, "Woodlawn: A Community in Revolt," *Chicago Scene*, June 7, 1962.

38. *Woodlawn Booster*, March 21, 1962.

39. *IAF Annual Report 1960*, 16.

40. Charles Silberman, *Crisis in Black and White* (New York: Random House, 1964), 345.

41. "Study Outline: Preliminary Phase of 'Woodlawn Plan' Discussion," Alinsky Papers, UIC.

42. Letter from Nicholas Von Hoffman to William Nelson, April 10, 1962, Alinsky Papers, UIC.

43. "Social Policy Planning Memo," *Woodlawn Booster*, July 25, 1962; Georgie Anne Geyer, "Woodlawn: A Community in Revolt," *Chicago Scene*, June 7, 1962. See also Ernestine Cofield, "A Blueprint to Secure Community's Future," *Chicago Defender Magazine* (December 3, 1962).

44. "Agreement Reached Between Mayor Daley and TWO on 7/16/63," Alinsky Papers, UIC.

45. Silberman, *Crisis in Black and White*.

46. Cofield, "Found"; "TWO Evaluation," June 24, 1964, Church Federation of Greater Chicago Records, box 52, file 1, CHS.

47. Sanford Horwitt, *Let Them Call Me Rebel: Saul Alinsky, His Life and Legacy* (New York: Vintage, 1992), 418.

48. Brazier, *Black Self-Determination*, 35.

49. Adam Fairclough, *To Redeem the Soul of America: The SCLC and Martin Luther King, Jr.* (Athens: University of Georgia Press, 1987); Lois Wille, "Mayor Daley Meets the Movement," *The Nation* (September 30, 1965): 92; Ralph, *Northern Protest*, 20–23; Anderson and Pickering (1986), 90, 99.

50. Transcript of James B. Murray interview with Arthur Brazier, June 7, 1991, Schaumburg Center, New York.

51. Silberman, *Crisis in Black and White*, 346.

52. Joan Lancourt, *Confront or Concede: The Alinsky Citizen-Action Organizations* (Lexington, MA: Lexington Books, 1979), 116; Tjerandsen, *Education for Citizenship*, 253.

53. *Woodlawn Booster*, May 1, 1963.

54. *TWO Newsletter*, April 17, 1964.

55. "Hyde Park Voices, November 1967," Leon Despres Papers, box 181, file 4, CHS; "TWO Evaluation," June 24, 1964, Church Federation of Greater Chicago Records, box 52, file 1, CHS; *Woodlawn Booster*, May 1, 1963; *TWO Newsletter*, April 17, 1964; Brazier, *Black Self-Determination*, 35; William Swenson, "The Continuing Colloquium on University of Chicago Demonstration Projects in Woodlawn," Center for Urban Studies, University of Chicago, November 1968.

56. Blake, "Report on TWO," 114.

57. Ibid., 114, 139–140.

58. "Open Letter to Sargent Shriver," *TWO Newsletter*, October 21, 1964.

59. Lois Wille, "TWO Wants to Know: Will We Share in Poverty Funds?" *Chicago Daily News*, April 7, 1965.

60. Ibid.

61. Wille, *Chicago Daily News*, April 5–April 9, 1965.

62. Saul Alinsky, "The War on Poverty—Political Pornography," *Journal of Social Issues* 11, no. 1 (Summer 1965): 41–47.

63. Congressional testimony of Lynward Stevenson before the House Committee on Labor and Education, Examination of the War on Poverty, printed in *TWO Newsletter*, April 14, 1965.

64. "TWO Black Paper Number Two: Poverty, Power and Race in Chicago," *TWO Newsletter*, December 9, 1965, 14–16.

65. U.S. Department of Housing and Urban Development, *Program Guide: Model Neighborhoods in Demonstration Cities HUD PG-47* (Washington, DC: Government Printing Office, December 1967), 3.

66. Community Legal Council, "Citizen Participation in Chicago's Model Cities Program: A Critical Analysis," May 15, 1968, Chicago, IL.

67. Fish, *Black Power / White Control*.

68. The Woodlawn Organization, *Woodlawn's Model Cities Plan* (Chicago: Whitehall Company, 1970), 26.

69. Ibid.; Eddie Williams, "The Model Cities Plan of TWO—An Abstract," in *Delivery Systems for Model Cities: New Concepts in Serving the Urban Community* (Chicago: University of Chicago Center for Policy Study, 1969).

70. At its first convention in 1962, TWO resolved that "the best programs are the ones that we develop, pay for and direct ourselves . . . our aim is to lessen the burdens of members in practical ways, but in ways that also guarantee we will keep our personal and community independence." George Geyer, "Woodlawn: A Community Revolt," *Chicago Scene*, June 7, 1962.

71. James B. Murray interview with Arthur Brazier, June 7, 1991, Schomburg Center, New York Public Library.

72. T. Jackson (1993), "The State, the Movement," 424–425.

73. Ibid., 424–429.

74. James Wilson, *Negro Politics: The Search for Leadership* (New York: Simon and Schuster, 1960); Preston Smith II, "The Quest for Racial Democracy: Black Civic Ideology and Housing Interests in Postwar Chicago," *Journal of Urban History* 26, no. 2 (January 2000): 131–157.

75. Wilson, *Negro Politics*, 185–186, 195; Smith, "Quest for Racial Democracy," 136.

76. On recent improvements in Woodlawn, see Celeste Garrett, "Woodlawn Has a Bold Vision: Renewal Already Making Its Mark," *Chicago Tribune*, December 22, 2002.

77. Lemann, *Promised Land*, 193.

78. Ibid., 199.

79. Marion K. Sanders, *The Professional Radical: Conversations with Saul Alinsky* (New York: Harper & Row, 1970).

80. Tjerandsen, *Education for Citizenship*, 257, 665.

81. Blake, "Report on TWO," 34.

PART II

Intellectual and Political Space

Michael Dennis

A Recess from Jim Crow

Luther P. Jackson, the Teachers, and the Movement for Racial Justice

Professor and historian Luther P. Jackson was convinced that African Americans had to change the political culture of southern life before they could achieve racial equality. Modifying that collection of assumptions about the exercise of power depended on a fundamental alteration of the African American worldview. More astutely than most, this obscure but dynamic professor understood that the public forum had to be cleansed of the noxious belief that blacks did not belong in political life. As he told readers of the *Norfolk Journal and Guide* in 1946,

> In my classes in history at Virginia State College we are saying more and
> more that when the year 1865 rolled around the Negro did not pass from
> slavery to freedom but from slavery to segregation. Thus from 1619 to the
> present he has never enjoyed genuine democracy because of the operation of
> these two restraining forces. Slavery lasted for almost 250 years. Will segrega-
> tion last that long? It will not if Negroes can shake off the spurious doctrine
> taught them by the white man that they belong to an inferior race.[1]

The conviction that blacks had to create an intellectual space for imagining equality as well as a public space in which they could act on a sense of citizenship governed his civil rights strategy. It also exemplified the attitudes of a generation of middle-class activists. More than piecemeal litigation, bold claims for racial inclusion grounded in the universal principles of the American creed characterized the New Deal years. Fully aware of the responsibility that southern whites bore for black subjugation, Jackson was certain that African Americans had it within their power to alter the status quo. That required a dual strategy of forging a space of independent thought in which blacks could revise the doctrines of racial inferiority absorbed since slavery, thereby opening a seam in a public arena that had been controlled by whites since the 1890s.

For Jackson, a history professor at Virginia State College in Petersburg, Virginia, education was the medium for pursuing this dual strategy. Committed to historical inquiry and devoted to teaching, he operated with the belief that scholarship and pedagogy could dissolve the most destructive misconceptions supporting black political subservience. He believed that by teaching black students the rubrics of political participation, teachers could demystify the political process and reclaim it from white control. The streets, the union hall, the courtroom, and the church provided the physical spaces in which some black activists forged new conceptions of black freedom, but Jackson turned to the school and its network of teachers as vehicles of racial advancement. In large part, this reflected the growing recognition that the high school had become a vital instrument of social advancement. African Americans understood that they were losing out on economic opportunities because of the inadequacy of their educational facilities.[2]

Yet Jackson and a coterie of teachers like him also believed that education offered the most promising forum for political rehabilitation. After all, it was in the school that students directly confronted the intellectual heritage of America's revolutionary origins. Steeped in Enlightenment ideals of equality and self-determination, those revolutionary principles diametrically opposed the irrational customs and myths that supported white supremacy. From the college where he spent the better part of his career, Jackson launched into political activism that focused on the revitalization of the public sphere through African American voting.

His experience underlines the importance of black colleges and schools in the movement for racial equality. Although historians have begun to devote sustained attention to the role of schools in fostering civil rights consciousness, little attention has been paid to the place of black colleges in the freedom struggle. More than this, historians have yet to investigate the synergies that activist professors like Jackson forged between schools and black colleges.[3] As a training ground for black teachers, colleges provided conduits to the minds and hearts of future educators. Relatively more independent from white control than the black elementary or high school, the black college offered a haven for critical thought about racial inequality. Staffed by African Americans with advanced degrees from northern universities and some of the best schools in the South, it provided a seedbed for black intellectual and political development.

For African Americans schooled in the logic of accommodation, Jackson and his associated teachers offered a lesson in political equality grounded in American constitutional principles. In the years before the Montgomery bus boycott, African American colleges, schools, voting groups, and professional associations provided the spatial coordinates for mobilizing black political involvement. Before the church meetings that spawned the sit-ins and the freedom marches, professional teachers' associations and classrooms offered the most important sites of black political engagement.

A native of Kentucky and the son of former slaves, Luther Porter Jackson exceeded his mother's ambitions that he receive an education.[4] After graduating from Fisk University in 1914, he continued there in graduate studies, acquiring a Master of Arts in 1916. Following a teaching appointment at the Voorhees Industrial School in Denmark, South Carolina, and at the Topeka Industrial Institute in Topeka, Kansas, he enrolled at the University of Kansas. It was a short interlude before he left to breathe the more liberal air at City College of New York. Jackson then completed a master's degree at Columbia University Teachers College, a popular destination for African Americans in search of teaching credentials. At Fisk University, he had met Johnella Frazer, a music aficionado who shared Jackson's lifelong passion for the jubilees. They had corresponded since graduation and kept in contact throughout Jackson's New York sojourn. Frazer, in the meantime, had landed a job teaching music at Virginia State Normal and Industrial Institute in Petersburg, Virginia. Frazer was instrumental in securing Jackson a teaching position, and Virginia Normal became home to both after they married in September 1922. Jackson remained at Virginia Normal (later Virginia State College) until his death in 1950.[5]

The ambitious historian had already published in the *Journal of Negro History* when he entered the Ph.D. program at the University of Chicago in 1929. After hundreds of hours researching property and tax records at Virginia's courthouses, he finished his dissertation on antebellum free blacks and graduated in 1937. He eventually published his meticulously researched work as *Free Negro Labor and Property Holding in Virginia, 1830–1860* in 1942.

By that time, the professor had become a political activist. Working through local chapters of the NAACP, the Petersburg Negro Business Association, the Association for the Study of Negro Life and History, the all-black Virginia

Teachers Association (VTA), and the Virginia Voters League (VVL), Professor Jackson promoted black political engagement. Through these organizations, Jackson was able to foster historical consciousness, which had been so critical to his own political development. These organizations became mechanisms of political action and spaces for independent black thought. As early as 1929, the gregarious and amiable professor had decided that "the most effective way to educate one's self and to educate others is to mingle with the people beyond the college campus and to promote among [them] such organizations as will lead to their advancement."[6] Linking the schools and the public sphere, Jackson became a conduit of political awareness. Furthermore, he methodically fostered organizations that bound those spheres together. In his view, schools were not simply vocational academies or avenues of social mobility but sites of citizenship training.

The *Norfolk Journal and Guide* gave Jackson an ideal platform for pursuing the dual strategy of carving out black organizational and intellectual space. In 1942, he began publishing "Rights and Duties in a Democracy," a weekly column that advocated political activity. His articles expressed the rising optimism about achieving racial justice in the New Deal era. In 1942, for example, as the ranks of the NAACP grew and as wartime industry created unprecedented opportunities for black Americans, Jackson assailed Virginia's black leadership for failing to mobilize the vote. Despite Virginia court decisions permitting black voting in Democratic primaries and prohibiting registrars from disqualifying applicants through arbitrary questions, black leaders failed to mobilize their followers. "Because of this situation it is safe to say that the school and church, the so-called democratic school and democratic church, are failing to promote the political democracy for which we are now fighting."[7] Here, the professor reminded his readers of the public and ultimately political character of spaces that figured so prominently in African American communities. Those institutions took on a deeper ideological significance as they became tied in wartime propaganda to the anti-fascist crusade abroad. By 1945, Jackson was applauding the teachers for "converting" to the gospel of political action by voting in strength in the last presidential election.[8] In both cases, Jackson was eager to impress upon the *Journal and Guide*'s black readers that the war had become the anvil on which they could forge their claims of racial equality.

The column provided the forum in which Jackson could draw the connections among history, education, and racial equality. Underlying his constant appeals for political involvement was the theme of citizenship, the democratic inheritance denied blacks since the founding of the republic. As one reader of the *Journal and Guide* put it, Jackson was "rendering a distinct service to the full-fledged Negro citizens of Virginia, as well as helping those who have not yet placed themselves in the full-fledged class, to do so."[9] In the pages of the *Journal and Guide*, the professor crafted his message that politically engaged teachers were the vanguard of racial justice.

Historical consciousness was the Archimedean point of racial equality. The Association for the Study of Negro Life and History (ASNLH), which scholar and activist Carter G. Woodson established in 1915, became the institutional embodiment of this insight. From a primarily academic enterprise the association developed into a popular vehicle for disseminating black historical contributions. Through Negro History Week celebrations, pageants, correspondence courses, lectures, pamphlets, and annual meetings, teachers and middle-class activists generated interest in the neglected chronicle of African American accomplishments. Although the association never reached far beyond urban settings and never achieved the influence that its architects had hoped, it left its mark on African American life. It fostered the awareness that blacks did in fact have a history, one in which they were not simply victims. By presenting historical narratives that highlighted black accomplishments, the association's literature challenged the racial mythologies that were deeply embedded in American culture.[10] The schools provided the physical coordinates in which association-affiliated teachers could sketch a completely new image of the black American. In that image, the accumulated detritus of racial stereotyping was stripped away, creating the mental space in which blacks could entertain the concepts of citizenship and electoral participation.

Jackson quickly became a leading force in the association, taking over its Virginia branch and initiating a statewide fund-raising campaign that generated almost $500 a year in the hardscrabble 1930s. By creating a network of committed school principals, he ensured contributions from almost every African American schoolteacher and college professor.[11] Since Virginia Normal and Industrial Institute hosted summer school sessions for teachers, Jackson was able to use the school as a recruiting ground for the association. He coordinated the distribution of kits for use during Negro History Week, sent information to students and teachers seeking insight into their past, and contributed booklets on African American soldiers in the American Revolution. He published extensively in the association's *Journal of Negro History* and joined academics such as Rayford W. Logan, Lorenzo Greene, and Charles Wesley in delivering addresses to Negro History Week audiences.[12] The college and the association became key public spaces for breaking down the isolation that prevented black political activity. They provided the environments in which educated African Americans could address the issues that the white South had simply erased from public consciousness. In those physical spaces, Jackson and the association fostered the intellectual connections among the black historical experience, a tradition of American egalitarianism, and contemporary realities.

His indefatigable efforts on multiple civil rights fronts paid off. After enlisting the support of Jeanes school supervisors to survey the observance of Negro History Week in 1935, Jackson was proud to report that the association had moved beyond the urban areas and into the schools and churches of rural Virginia. As one respondent from Surry County reported, "Five years ago the schools of the county were not so well informed as to the necessity of acquainting the pupils with great men, women, and deeds of the Negro race. But now every school in the county [twenty-two] observes Negro History Week. . . . This year we gave a county wide program at the largest church in our county to which all school communities were invited."[13] Through his peripatetic voting rights work, he expanded the reach of the association in Virginia, and in the process, he transformed it into a public space in which African Americans grafted their own meaning onto the American past. Again, the physical and the intellectual intersected. Schoolrooms, church basements, and fraternity lodges were transformed into places where association members could cultivate black dignity and political will. In those spaces, black Virginians could transcend a universe seemingly defined by the white mind.

The association uncritically celebrated black achievements and often presented an idealized, heroic image of black leaders that did not stand up to historical scrutiny. In focusing on the great men of the black American past, it neglected the experience of average people, which was defined more by exploitation than by rugged individualism. Negro history, as it was known, did not challenge class divisions or break out of the confines of what some of its critics described as narrow Black Nationalism.[14] Even so, the association's historians challenged the racist assumptions that permeated the dominant treatments of the nation's past. Jackson understood the association's larger significance: "They [teachers] have responded because they believe in the cause; and because they realize that the inculcation of race pride and loyalty in the Negro youth serves as one of the main solutions to the so-called race problem. . . . It is an effort to have him shake off his racial inferiority complex."[15] Commenting on the ASNLH's campaign for black historical awareness, Jackson observed: "This swing to Negro History Week simply means that Negroes in America have at last become historical minded and they have become race conscious. The two forces combined to produce race pride."[16] For Jackson and other civil rights activists, restoring blacks to the historical record meant more than stimulating a sense of racial identity: "The observance of Negro History Week and the promotion of other forms of historical activity constitute one phase of our rights and duties in a democracy." Situating African Americans in the sweep of American history was "an aid in the preservation of the democratic ideal for which we are now fighting."[17] Despite the shortcomings of Jackson's later work on black Revolutionary War soldiers and Reconstruction leaders, his insights on the larger significance of bringing alive the African Americans were astute. American history offered a foundation for claiming black inclusion in contemporary society. It also provided a rational foundation for overturning the racial stereotypes that had achieved the authority of timeless absolutes.

The impulse to establish a place for independent black thought and action also animated his involvement in the Virginia Voters League. Formed in 1941 as a federation of voter organizations for the entire state, it became a clearinghouse of information and ideas. Equally important, the VVL developed into an organizing vehicle for black political action. Paralleling his activity in the ASNLH, Jackson established county chairpersons to collect data, gather information about local registrars, report on political attitudes, and mobilize the black electorate. He also started publishing *The Voting Status of Negroes in Virginia*, an annual study of poll tax payment, registration, and voting rates throughout the state. The studies provided an indispensable gauge of black political activity and a spur to electoral participation. The Virginia State professor kept up a deluge of correspondence with local leaders and individual citizens. Cajoling people to register, appealing to people to pay the poll tax, alerting citizens to recalcitrant registrars, and imploring the reluctant to abandon timeworn assumptions about the futility or illegitimacy of black voting, Jackson and the Virginia Voters League expanded black political consciousness.

Black and white elites took notice. Political scientist V. O. Key believed that Jackson had "been doing an extremely useful service in pulling together the facts on a subject in the discussion of which facts are usually ignored."[18] Historian and journalist Douglas Southall Freeman agreed, attributing the growth of black voting to Jackson's "calm but vigorous leadership."[19] A. A. Taylor, dean of Fisk University and fellow disciple of Carter Woodson, believed that Jackson's *Voting Status* illustrated the "democratic processes" at work in the South as well as Jackson's "distinctive, practical and worthwhile contribution on behalf of the people of the South and America."[20] Jackson's appeal extended beyond the state. According to R. G. Higgins of the Agricultural and Technical College in Greensboro, North Carolina, Jackson was a "pioneer" and "trailblazer." As Higgins confessed, "Your work has been most stimulating in stirring within me a greater desire to uncover and destroy the cantankerous growths that impedes [*sic*] the progress toward democracy which the American people have chosen for their goal."[21] And although *Journal and Guide* publisher P. B. Young could no longer afford to keep Jackson on the payroll, he credited the Virginia State scholar with having made a "definitive contribution to the more active participation of Negroes in southern elections."[22] Through overlapping networks of political activism that included the VVL and the ASNLH,

Jackson solidified the growing sense of black political confidence in the New Deal era.[23]

The most important of these events was World War II. The conflict accelerated the hopes for racial change stirred by the economic upheavals and class militancy of the 1930s. Although African Americans benefited unevenly from New Deal programs, they began to expect a sympathetic hearing from a federal government that had provided timely assistance during those desperate years. Drawn by wartime employment opportunities, over a million blacks migrated to northern urban centers burgeoning with wartime manufacturing contracts. Black migrants increased the political strength of the Democratic Party and augmented their influence in the Roosevelt administration. The president's support for economically vulnerable blacks stimulated African American interest in voting. The war then quickened the pace of NAACP registration and spawned community organizations committed to mobilizing black voters.[24]

Black militancy also grew, illustrated dramatically by A. Philip Randolph's threatened mass march on Washington to protest racial discrimination in federal defense contracts. Flummoxed by the prospect of African American activism in his own backyard, Roosevelt blinked. He struck the Fair Employment Practices Committee to investigate charges of racial prejudice in defense employment. Black newspapers and social leaders sounded the call for the "double V," a crusade against fascism abroad and segregation at home. African American soldiers poured into a segregated military that nevertheless promised opportunities for those who did their country's bidding. The NAACP's legal campaign to equalize institutions of higher education, which had produced the momentous 1938 *Gaines* decision ordering Missouri to fund a law school for African Americans or admit them to the University of Missouri, increased the movement's momentum. In the 1940s, the NAACP and several black teachers' associations launched successful litigation against inequitable teachers' salaries in the South. The social forces unleashed by the war seemed to promise substantial change in race relations. Those changes depended, however, on the successful utilization of black space, both physical and intellectual.[25]

It was in this whirlwind of social and political change that Luther P. Jackson sought to convert the Virginia Teachers Association into an agency of political reform. His enthusiasm for activating the teachers developed out of his belief that teachers were responsible for transforming indifferent students into active citizens. If teachers failed to vote and instruct their students in the rubrics of government, young people would never be able to influence the world in which they lived: "They may never attain decent wages by associating with the organized labor movement, they may never save on their low incomes by joining consumer cooperatives, and they may never lobby, vote, send telegrams, or lay any pressure on office holders to influence legislation affecting their jobs and their social security. Justice may be forever denied them, for they may never sue in the courts."[26] Influenced by the Popular Front ethic of the 1930s, which shaped the labor movement as well as the black freedom struggle, Jackson believed that political participation was indispensable for achieving any measure of economic democracy in the United States. For civil rights activists in the 1940s, the movement for black freedom and labor rights intersected in the drive to liberalize the South, the greatest threat to the achievement of New Deal reform.[27]

The African American teachers' organization had been tied to Virginia State College since its origins as a "reading circle" in 1887. Until the 1930s, it functioned primarily as a teacher and school improvement organization. In the 1930s, it evolved into an advocacy group that stressed professional advancement through salary equalization with white educators and political reform through black voting.[28] It also became an important network for promoting the ASNLH and black history in the classrooms. Several of Virginia State's faculty members contributed time and expertise to the VTA. It was Luther P. Jackson, however, who transformed its Speakers Bureau, which was designed as a platform for education experts, into an instrument for political and historical consciousness raising. Acknowledging the professor's leadership in social outreach, the VTA made him secretary of civic education. Jackson also orchestrated an affiliation between the Virginia Voters League and the Virginia Teachers Association, cementing the connection between the teachers' fight for equal salaries and the larger cause of black political mobilization.[29]

More than any other professional group, teachers offered the medium for civil rights leaders to influence the political views of young African Americans. Based on this insight, Jackson fashioned the civic education office into a tool for political action. Unlike the Virginia Voters League and the ASNLH, the VTA was composed exclusively of educators, the most respected professional strata in the black middle class. Unlike business owners, blue-collar workers, and professionals, teachers worked in institutions that simultaneously symbolized the promise of class mobility and the degradation of racial inequality. Teachers occupied the unique position of being able to influence youthful expectations about what the world would offer them and its susceptibility to change. They could perpetuate black subservience or attack it at its roots. As Jackson explained to the state's high school principals, the objective was to "produce a body of vote conscious young people who may face the future determined to participate in the affairs of government in contrast to the non-participation of our people during the past generation."[30] Appealing first to the Jeanes supervisors and high school principals to register, Jackson planned to extend the campaign to all of Virginia's African American educators.[31]

The civic education program paralleled Jackson's strategy for the Virginia Voters League. Like the VVL, one of several statewide voters' clubs that sprang up in the South during the war years, the secretary's office recruited a "talented tenth" of political leaders by highlighting the benefits of voting while simultaneously shaming the "voteless." Typical of most civil rights leaders before the 1950s, Jackson believed that racial progress required elite leadership that respected American institutions and abided by the protocol of Jim Crow.

What he and other voting rights activists grasped years before the sit-ins at Greensboro and the Freedom Rides was that racial change required a fundamental change in the worldview of young African Americans. As Jackson wrote to attorney Moss Plunkett, chairperson of the Virginia Electoral Reform League and perennial white liberal, "You recognize that in the final analysis our growth is dependent on the school room."[32] The "shame of the race," Jackson announced in the pages of his weekly column in the *Norfolk Journal and Guide*, was that "[v]oteless professors and voteless teachers make voteless pupils who finish school only to swell the number of non-voters."[33] Teaching political action in the classrooms was not simply a matter of drumming up support for equal educational facilities but of preparing students for citizenship.

Jackson outlined his tactics for the state's high school principals and Jeanes supervisors. The Office of Civic Education would collect data on teachers' registration and voting activity. It would then publish the findings in handbooks that included instructions on voting procedures. Mirroring the tactics of the ASNLH, the secretary's office would support a statewide voting week for teachers and students, featuring instruction on electoral rubrics. In addition, it would coordinate with the Virginia Voters League in promoting voter registration.[34] Operating openly, the secretary of civic education would cooperate with school authorities in registering black teachers to vote. Just as the voters' leagues and the history association designated areas in which civil rights activists could address racial inequality, the Office of Civic Education became a staging ground for political activism among black teachers. Largely through Jackson's efforts, the Virginia Teachers Association became a shifting geographical locus of black political reform. At the same time, it fostered the intellectual space that was critical to democratizing southern political culture.

The new secretary was convinced that quantitative data and persistent appeals could overcome political indifference. He dispatched over 200 copies of his voting instruction handbooks to Jeanes supervisors, school superintendents, high school principals, college professors, and "influential white citizens." The booklets testified to voting progress, documented the limits of black political activity, and provided a tool for political education in the classroom. He wrote to administrators of historically black colleges and appealed to them to promote faculty registration and voting.[35] He also spread the voting message in the pages of the VTA *Bulletin* and the *Norfolk Journal and Guide*. Addressing local teachers' associations and the faculty of Virginia State College, he entreated them to set an example of political involvement.[36]

Many teachers grasped quite clearly the connection between education and political participation. Well before the Office of Civic Education was established, principal James Spencer of Richmond admitted to Jackson that he had discerned "a close correlation between good teaching and voting. The teacher who is interested in getting close to the community needs and serves well in the community votes." Along with Jackson, Spencer believed that school officials would not punish the teacher who voted. "One told me once to drop my garden hoe and go out and scare up some votes for good county officials who were up for election." One can only wonder what, according to the school administrator, constituted a "good" county official. In any case, Spencer reported that twenty-eight out of forty-five teachers in the county had voted, an indication that the voting message was hitting the mark, particularly in the urban centers.[37]

Spencer's report on teacher voting raises two issues. First, teachers lagged in voting not simply because of political indifference but because of persistent fear that political activity might get them fired. As public servants of a system controlled by whites, teachers felt particularly vulnerable to reprisals. In addition, the ideological sanction against black voting fell particularly heavily on teachers, since schools had the unique potential to subvert the social order. Jackson understood the source of teacher anxiety about voting: "Hanging over the heads of multitudes of teachers is the fear of losing their jobs. Living as they do in a society and under officials who have professed one principle about democracy and have practiced another, these teachers seek to conform to what they believe to be the wishes of their superintendents and to prevailing custom." At the same time, he worked assiduously to quell these fears. Having conferred with a "high official" in the state school system in 1947, Jackson reassured the teachers that not a single county or city superintendent would retaliate against a teacher for voting.[38]

Although many could not find solace in Jackson's assurances, the ranks of voting teachers did increase. In the presidential election of 1944, 75 percent of the 1,269 teachers in city schools cast ballots, whereas 39 percent of the 911 teachers in the county schools voted that year. Considering the institutional and cultural impediments on voting, Jackson believed that the numbers for 1944 signaled impressive progress.[39] Jackson's own numbers point out the second issue: the lower rate of voting among rural teachers in Virginia. There are several factors that explain higher political participation in urban areas, including stronger networks of political mobilization, dynamic middle-class leadership, concentrated

African American populations, cross-fertilization between the labor movement and black civil rights, and greater economic resources for voting rights groups. Yet no less important is the persistence of personal forms of racial paternalism in the rural South. In voting, rural teachers struggled with the same inhibitions that prevented most African American country dwellers from voting: the problem of registering in person at a white official's home. When white registrars compounded the problem by deliberately being unavailable or losing the registration ledger, the prospects of African Americans voting in the rural South declined even more.[40]

Despite the difficulties facing teacher mobilization, Spencer continued to champion racial advancement through education. He consistently replied to Jackson's queries, updating him on the status of teacher voting and the progress of civic education in his school. In 1949, he discussed voting with his five teachers and determined the voting status of their parents. He sponsored mock elections and civic programs in the school. He also drove students to the polls to witness electoral participation in action. As a leading member of the Virginia Voters League and an NAACP stalwart, Spencer traveled throughout the state, "spreading civic information" through speeches, addresses, and lectures.[41] Like Jackson's, Spencer's editorials and political education were part of a "civic crusade to arouse the so-called sons and daughters of Ham to become vote-conscious in our local and State communities."[42]

Principal Ethel Thompson Overby of the Elba Elementary School in Richmond rivaled Spencer's commitment to political mobilization. Throughout the 1940s, Overby had been active in local politics. She persuaded 150 blacks to register to vote, recruited members for the interracial and progressive Richmond Citizens Association, and encouraged schoolteachers and parents to cast a ballot on a proposed charter for the city of Richmond. Overby was diligent in promoting black history in the school and supported the ASNLH's program through regular contributions to Jackson's office at Virginia State College. In both, Overby challenged the idea that the school was an instrument of racial control. As Jackson noted, "Her activity is civic and likewise highly racial. She wants to instill pride of race in the pupils of Elba." The principal also used the school as a democratic space for community meetings. One fortuitous consequence was the creation of a citizenship loan fund that paid the poll taxes for those in attendance. Overby was not alone: she and a group of "progressive and cooperative teachers" were creating a "community school" that redefined the meaning of education. The community school was becoming a center for democratic training, a forum for black self-determination and political revitalization. With the shift from white to black principals, Richmond's schools became something more than institutional reminders of racial discrimination. Activist teachers transformed some of these schools into community centers for articulating grievances and hopes that southern whites contemptuously dismissed. As Jackson explained, "From institutions which were completely cut off from the Richmond Negro public and where nothing inspirational was offered to the pupils, they have now become workshops for the training of the children in the needs of society and of their race."[43] In urban areas where African Americans enjoyed greater resources and overlapping networks of support, educators provided valuable leadership in the movement toward racial equality.

Jackson knew that the civic education program was challenging hallowed social conventions. Discussing inhibitions about registering to vote in rural Virginia and North Carolina, Jackson observed that to many blacks it seemed "forbidding" since "it involves a social relationship which Negroes have always been taught never to infringe." Since registration was often conducted in a private home rather than a public office, the process violated "the unwritten laws of racial etiquette," which prohibited an African American person from visiting a white person's home "except as a servant or on business."[44] According to Jackson, black leaders since the 1890s had only reinforced the prohibition on voting by insisting that politics was a dangerous activity best left to whites.[45] By voting and training students in the mechanics of democracy, teachers broke down the inhibitions that had been as effective at disfranchising blacks as the poll tax and the white primary.[46]

Spencer and Overby were by no means the only high school principals to support voting instruction. Lutrelle Palmer agreed that Jackson's initiative would reinforce existing programs of political instruction. As principal of Huntington High School in Norfolk, Palmer assured him that a school-wide program of instruction on the requirements and rubrics of voting had been in place for several years. The students applied their knowledge in annual elections for student council representatives, paying poll taxes and registering to vote in polling booths supervised by judges and clerks.[47] George Binford, principal of Central High School in Charlotte, notified Jackson that social science teachers had instructed students on voting and persuaded some of their parents to vote as well. In schools relatively insulated from white intrusion, students received training in the electoral process, which reduced the mystery and inhibitions that had surrounded voting. In staging elections supervised by judges and clerks, civics teachers also exposed African American children to the idea that voting was not a privilege of political white paternalism but an exercise of civil rights under the authority of national law. Classroom instruction on voting, government, and the implications of political involvement accelerated the process through which young African Americans detached themselves from a segregated worldview, one that automatically conferred power and authority on whites. And yet, teachers offering civic instruction were in the minority. For the most part, voting teachers could only be found in urban centers, not in the countryside, where traditional structures of white authority were strongest.[48]

The civic education program contributed to the political awakening of Virginia's rural teachers. Mary Carr Greer, principal of the Albemarle County Training School, held a faculty conference soon after receiving Jackson's appeal to vote and teach politics. Greer reported that the faculty would now cooperate "100% with you in your effort to get all the teachers in the Counties and Cities of Virginia to pay poll taxes, register, and vote." Greer became Jackson's steadfast ally and a proponent of political activity. In the coveted position of school principal, she expressed the political sensitivities that African American women had cultivated since the Reconstruction period. In response to Jackson's annual call for teacher registration in 1944, Carr reported that political posters from the *Journal and Guide* had been distributed throughout the school and that the social studies classes had examined the question of black voting. "Several members of the classes were interested and promised to persuade their parents to register. As a result, many actually registered."[49]

By 1946, the teachers of the Albemarle school had extended the voter mobilization program into the community. Jackson's teacher registration drive had become another channel for catalyzing political awareness in Virginia. The immediate incentive for voting in Charlottesville was the question of a bond issue to support local school improvement. "As you know," Greer confided to Jackson, "the Negroes are the ones who will profit most by the program because we have the poorest school." Beginning as a drive for teacher registration, the suffrage movement spilled over the walls of the training school and into the community, sparking a political campaign that featured nightly meetings and teacher involvement in voter recruitment. In Albemarle as well as in other communities, the school became a conduit of democratic thinking, and women played a key role in promoting it. By 1947, Greer could confidently report that all of her teachers had registered and were prepared to vote in an approaching election.[50]

Women figured prominently in the movement to expand voter registration and advance civil rights. Eunice D. Bundy, principal of Hanover County Training School, announced that her school had conducted "an effective mock campaign and election," with each civics class going through the steps of poll tax paying, registering, and voting. Janie Sims wrote to thank Jackson for the voting information he had sent her, adding perceptively that "[i]f children become interested parents will be influenced." Sims was a vigilant proponent of voting. She consistently used her classes to stress the idea that to be "worthy" of citizenship, African Americans had to register to vote. Echoing Jackson's convictions, Sims argued that "there are many rights the Negro could demand if he voted or more negroes voted." Detailing the electoral procedures taught in her social studies classes, Sims signed her letter "your teacher for better citizenship." Marie Hubbard, a Jeanes supervisor in Amelia County, informed Jackson that a woman in Amelia County not only chaired the NAACP committee in charge of voter mobilization but also functioned as president of the local teachers' association. Hubbard revealed that Jackson's relentless effort to expose the political lassitude of Virginia's black educators through registration and poll-tax-paying surveys was paying off. "I think that your survey will make more vote the next time because some seemed ashamed of not having voted when the question was asked." In fact, out of thirty-six teachers in Amelia County, only six had voted in the presidential election of 1944.[51]

Some teachers wrote to report their voting status and express their gratitude to Jackson for waking them from political somnolence. Letters such as the one from Rosa Carter must have been gratifying. With none of the dramatic flair of Janie Sims, Carter notified Jackson that she was "now a qualified voter because of your letter."[52] Maud Valentine informed the professor that, although the teachers in her school had qualified to vote, it was the *students* who had taken responsibility for interesting their parents in electoral matters. School supervisor T. A. Randolph declared that he held Jackson's program "in high esteem" and said, "I shall contact every teacher under my supervision to become a qualified voter." Eunice Bundy assured Jackson that his investment of time and energy in *The Voting Status of the Negro in Virginia* was paying off. "The handbooks are proving helpful," Bundy wrote, "not only individually but they are very valuable in connection with our civic classes and our voters league." As tools of political instruction and a touchstone for several community action groups, Jackson's handbooks served the larger purpose of political mobilization.

Jackson became the lightning rod for the teachers' political enthusiasm. They turned to him for information, for statistics on the voting patterns of teachers, or to invite him to address a group of teachers or the local voters' league. Catherine Holmes of Emporia, Virginia, wrote to request information on "citizenship," adding that "[w]e have heard quite a bit about your interest in the Negro in Virginia. We read your article in the *Journal and Guide* every week and enjoy it very much." A former student also found in Jackson's newspaper articles a source of information and guidance for conducting registration and voting programs for sixth- and seventh-grade history students. As Jackson promoted the civic education program and integrated it into the Virginia Teachers Association, educators made him the natural choice to lead local teachers' political action meetings. The VTA Speakers Bureau had given Jackson the vehicle to disseminate the voting message, but as secretary of civic education, he refined his message and expanded his political network. His activity in the VTA only strengthened the reputation he had gained as a popular college educator and architect of the ASNLH. Mary Thompson certainly encapsulated the views of a majority of teachers who had weathered the salary disputes and internalized the connection between educational improvement and black political activity when she said, "I think you are doing a wonderful job in trying to get our people to vote."[53]

Jackson's requests for information on the voting behavior of teachers afforded African American women the opportunity to profile their own political odyssey. Offering insight into the political enthusiasm generated by wartime economic gains, favorable Supreme Court decisions, the liberal hopes stirred by the Henry Wallace campaign, and no doubt Jackson's own efforts, Margarette Brooks wrote excitedly that she had received Jackson's inquiry and felt it "much to [sic] important to sleep over tonight." Proudly, she informed Jackson that she was a qualified voter who had cast a ballot in 1947. Brooks not only voted but also did so at an advanced polling booth "in Lawrenceville Va. a month before the election in Mr. Elmores [sic] office before him and two other persons in there at that time, as I was going away for the summer." It required considerable fortitude to pay the required tax six months in advance, register to vote, and then cast a ballot in the presence of a white male official representing a state that had spent the previous forty-five years policing the ballot box against African American influence. Conscious of her accomplishment, she shared it with Jackson, reviewed the candidates for state office, and announced that she had been the "third person to vote by marking the ballot in present [sic] of the county clerk." For Brooks and others like her, voting was not an empty formality. It exemplified self-determination, the moment when African Americans exercised the moral imperative behind racial equality. Whites might hope to neutralize black demands for equality by improving separate facilities and cordoning off access to power, but the electoral process threatened to become the public area where whites could not impose segregation or channel black expectations into safe waters. By voting, Brooks exercised the social equality denied by the southern caste system.[54]

Although Brooks absorbed the racial optimism of the Truman era, she made it clear that political consciousness was nothing new. Brooks had been voting in Maryland "since Harding elections"; she understood the "importance" of voting for herself and to "all who cast the ballot." Thanking him for his interest in her "personal civic welfare," she added eagerly that she had "used all the influence to bring many peoples with [sic] their civic duty and shall continue as long as I can for a better country state and nation." In the case of many African American women, particularly teachers who regularly confronted the consequences of political exclusion in the form of inadequate schools and inequitable pay, political involvement reflected circumstances, not will. Given the chance to vote in

Maryland, Margarette Brooks cast a ballot; permitted to vote in Virginia, she exercised the franchise there, negotiating the racial barriers that kept so many others away. Yet the theme that dominates Brooks's letter is not individual courage but a sense of "civic duty" motivated by the recognition of "its importance." Jackson's civic education campaign must have encouraged Brooks, but Brooks traveled to the voting booth alone on July 3, 1947, casting a ballot "before him [the registrar] and two other persons."[55]

The teachers' movement toward political involvement was in no small part a function of Jackson's civic education office. In November 1944, Jackson informed VTA president C. W. Seay that "three fourths or more" of black teachers had voted in the presidential election of 1944. Jackson was slightly more modest in the pages of the *Journal and Guide*, claiming that "more than two thousand" out of approximately 4,000 teachers voted in the 1944 presidential election, a remarkable improvement, nonetheless, over 1936, when fewer than 500 teachers went to the polls.[56] The response to Jackson's program offers a barometer of political awareness among black teachers. It also offers insight into the political expectations of African Americans in the wake of the precedent-setting teacher salary equalization cases, the Supreme Court rulings against the white primary, an emerging liberal labor coalition that supported black voting rights, and a social climate favorable to racial amelioration.

Jackson accelerated the teachers' movement by expanding the civic education program. His efforts invariably drew the "voteless" teachers into the glare of public scrutiny. Examining the "non-voting tradition" among teachers, Jackson claimed that politically disengaged educators were "non-reading teachers" who failed to inform themselves about current events and politics. He acknowledged the teachers' fears of retaliation from school supervisors, but he stubbornly reiterated his familiar mantra that things had changed. The activist professor insisted that "not to vote is not to appreciate full-fledged American citizenship" or to "appreciate the contribution that the individual's race has made to his country." Voting and teaching civic participation was as much an exercise in nationalism as a demonstration of racial pride. Spurred on by increasing black voting strength and the Truman administration's support for desegregation, he became increasingly militant about "voteless" teachers. In circular letters of 1948, he chided them for claiming nonresidency as an excuse for nonvoting, announcing that "[w]e accept no such point of view." If teachers earning a living in Virginia did not register and vote in the state, "[they] should no longer accept employment in this state."[57]

The salary equalization cases of 1939 and 1940 testified to the growth of the Virginia Teachers Association as a vehicle of racial protest. During the protracted court proceedings that finally established the principle of equal salaries for black and white teachers, the VTA mobilized popular support for the litigating teachers. It also marshaled financial resources for the lawyers and petitioned school boards and public officials to restore the jobs of teachers fired for participating in the movement. Despite the divisions that plagued the teachers, particularly after the firing of association leaders Lutrelle Palmer and J. Rupert Picott, two teachers involved in the Newport News case of 1943, the VTA emerged as a vehicle of racial protest. Reviewing the momentous developments of the past four years, Jackson exulted in the "brilliant success of the Virginia Teachers Association" in the salary dispute cases. Working alongside the NAACP, the VTA developed from an exclusively professional affair into a forum for addressing the racial injustices that plagued all African Americans:

> The great influence and the great importance of the Virginia State Teachers Association is to be noted in this governmental program—government with respect to the suffrage, with respect to petition, and with respect to the courts. In making its bows to the public in these fields the Association has naturally met with criticism and opposition from both white school officials and Negro school patrons, but in years to come the pioneering of the organization in these fields will be recognized by all as one of the most constructive forces in building a better democracy in our Southland.[58]

The movement to radicalize Virginia's teachers reacted symbiotically with other forces in fostering black middle-class impatience with the racial status quo.

Reaching beyond the elementary and high schools, Jackson appealed to college professors to register and instruct their students in the rubrics of voting. Criticizing the common assertion that college instructors had no business in politics, Jackson argued that the same logic required black institutions of higher education to abnegate responsibility for "any of the crying needs of Negroes" throughout American society. Jackson also targeted college summer school students, most of whom were teachers upgrading their qualifications. Since many of the summer school students were away from their voting precinct, Jackson sent them detailed information on how to submit an absentee ballot in the upcoming gubernatorial election, which pitted the liberal Moss Plunkett against William M. Tuck. In addition to relentless appeals for registration and poll tax payment, Jackson called on high school principals to rally teachers for the referendums on the poll tax. He also called on principals to mobilize the teachers to vote against the Campbell suffrage amendments, which proposed to replace the poll tax with annual registration four months prior to any election. The amendments also imposed literacy tests but left the General Assembly discretion to apply additional suffrage conditions. Together with the Virginia Voters League, the NAACP, and the Civil Rights Organization, Jackson's voting teachers defeated the discriminatory amendments.[59]

In addition to pressuring teachers to vote, he encouraged Virginia's black teachers to conduct political instruction in their classrooms. Shortly after appealing to the Jeanes supervisors, he called on school principals to adopt voting exercises in their history, civics, and social studies classes. His reasoning underscores the psychological dimensions of racial exclusion and the physical strategies that were necessary to challenge it at its roots. He believed that "mere book instruction" on social questions would never generate political engagement. Just as activists in Montgomery and other communities would discover, political change required collective rituals of defiance, self-confidence, and democratic participation. These actions graphically countered the customary subservience expected of African Americans. They delineated the schoolroom as a space in which blacks anticipated full political participation. They also encouraged the second component of Jackson's strategy, the cultivation of intellectual independence. As Jackson explained, "In order to get action and instill a voting consciousness in our youth they should go through some form of dramatization." Just as Virginia State College had provided space in which the VTA could become a vehicle of political action, the classrooms of segregated schools became the loci of democratic training for young blacks.[60]

What Jackson planned was a mock primary election in which students paid the poll tax, registered to vote, and cast a ballot. The mock elections would give students the opportunity to imagine themselves in the role of active citizens. The mock elections offered political instruction in schools designed to prepare African Americans for a world circumscribed by racial boundaries. Since the Reconstruction period, parents and teachers had challenged the logic of Jim Crow at the center of the social order, that is, at the schools that were designed to ensure black subordination. They could not insulate children entirely from the social conditioning of segregation, but they did create places that permitted black autonomy. Now, Jackson and his educational allies expanded the significance of that space by injecting into the curriculum an explicitly political dimension. Classrooms would not reinforce racial subjugation but instead teach students to conceive of themselves as rights-bearing individuals. By instructing students in the rubrics and importance of political participation, the civic education exercises started the process through which young people would make a legitimate claim on the public sphere.

Significant though Jackson's campaign was, he soon found out that some teachers were already offering political instruction in the classroom. For James Spencer, Jackson's mail-out campaign was a "timely civic recommendation" to promote voting among students. Even before Jackson's program, however, Spencer's school had been conducting classroom instruction and field trips to the General Assembly. Students also visited the polls to witness the unusual spectacle of teachers casting the ballot. Moving beyond Jackson's recommendations, Spencer planned to contact students who had graduated in the last seven years to determine their voting status and remind them of their civic obligations. His local voters' league appealed to area ministers to preach the benefits of poll tax paying and voting, whereas the county teachers' association printed circulars and posters for distribution to black business establishments. For Spencer and the teachers of south Richmond, inculcating political consciousness in the classroom was part of a wider program of social activism.[61]

The changes were modest, but Jackson interpreted them as a sign of political awakening. In a December column of the *Journal and Guide*, he celebrated "some very effective civic training" that had accompanied the Roosevelt and Dewey campaign of 1944. He congratulated the students and teachers who had sponsored mock elections, campaigned, and then cast ballots for their preferred nominees. In one case, a principal arranged a bus trip for his senior class to witness African Americans voting—a pilgrimage of sorts filled with overtones of civic ritual. Not surprisingly, the students at Virginia State College gave Roosevelt a landslide victory over Thomas E. Dewey. For Jackson, the school exercises suggested that educators could begin to dismantle racial inequality by teaching and exemplifying political inclusion.[62]

A core of school principals provided indispensable support for Jackson's civic education program. This pedagogical cadre encouraged civic education, supplied Jackson with information on teacher voting and poll tax paying, and offered a window on teacher involvement as well as student response to political instruction.[63] Principal Clyde Scott of Campbell County adopted the civic education department's political instruction program, an undertaking that proved "very beneficial to the citizens of this county." Scott and Lutrelle Palmer were among the few principals able to report mock elections during the war years. With the expansion of the NAACP and the political excitement of the third-party initiatives in 1948, mock elections became a standard feature of civic instruction. In Charlotte, Virginia, principal George Binford presided over a mock election in 1948 involving all teachers and students. Female teachers took a leading role in the exercise, but they benefited from the active support of interested students. A. M. Binford, his wife, and Eugene Wells, president of the student council, directed the project as part of a class on government. Encouraged by the exercise in civic equality, one of the teachers drove eighty-five miles to Richmond after school to cast his ballot. That year, principal W. E. Friend of S. C. Abrams High School reported that Truman won the school's mock election. Spurred by newfound political consciousness, a group of students commandeered their families' cars to transport eligible African American voters to the polls. In a scene probably played out in countless rural villages throughout Virginia, a teacher from Friend's school traveled from "Fluvanna to Culpepper to cast her vote—a distance of 50 miles." But Friend would not be outdone: he drove eighty miles from Fluvanna to Chesterfield to cast his ballot.[64]

As a growing number of teachers registered and taught their students to vote, they made the transition from individual to community action. Students in the government and sociology classes at principal Caleb Gregory Brown's school conducted surveys "to make the community vote conscious." Learning the theory of democratic participation in schools that connected black history and social issues, young African Americans translated their knowledge into community activism, raising political awareness and setting an example of social concern. Citizens of Alleghany County subsequently organized a political club. Reform energies also radiated from the Augusta County Training School. In 1948, most of the teachers were busy recruiting voters through the Staunton-Augusta County Civic League. Political enthusiasm followed principal A. N. Jackson's efforts to encourage teachers "to emphasize the value of the ballot" and the responsibilities of citizens. Teachers at the Henry County Training School also transferred the ideological momentum generated in the classroom to the larger public sphere by forming a committee to canvas the community and publishing an honor roll of registered voters.[65]

In some schools, students internalized developments in national politics. In response to Jackson's inquiries about civic education at the Buckingham County Training School, principal G. F. Harris notified him that his students had conducted a "real election" for the student council. The elections, "patterned after that of our national and local governments," were particularly elaborate. Each class elected representatives for a planning convention and organized precincts in which students registered to vote once they had paid a six-cent poll tax. Harris was particularly pleased that, in the election year of 1948, several students followed the national campaigns and "injected much of what went on throughout the country in their little campaign here."[66]

Although challenging racial exclusion, the elections transmitted contradictory messages about political reform. Although students "kept up with the national campaign," the election featured only the two major parties, not the Progressive Party, which unequivocally opposed racial discrimination. Presumably, the teachers considered Henry Wallace's party too dangerous for young minds and public schools. Students also learned to qualify by paying a poll tax in the one election where it could have been avoided. Teachers encouraged children "to be good citizens," an image simultaneously suggesting compliance and full participation. Teachers operated on the assumption that change had to come from within the system, even if that included paying a poll tax and limiting the electoral playing field to mainstream political parties. Although the student elections encouraged political involvement, they also suggested that political liberation might coexist with racial and class control.[67]

Despite the moderate subtext, the voting exercises challenged the political culture of black subordination and encouraged the students to make a public commitment to racial equality. The mock elections, poll tax exercises, field excursions to Washington to observe government in action, and trips to the polls became a powerful solvent against the rust of political indifference. They forged links between political education in the schools and social action in the community. In addition, they vividly demonstrated their own commitment to political participation. By casting ballots as students looked out, pressuring teachers to register, and encouraging teachers to apply the lessons they taught, activist teachers set a convincing example of political commitment. Operating as a shifting site of political engagement, the Virginia Teachers Association had generated spaces of democratic revitalization at the very core of the Jim Crow system. In those classrooms where students engaged in the seemingly innocuous activity of registering to vote, mental spaces were created in the void of racial exclusion. In those spaces, students perhaps for the first time addressed the contradiction between American ideals and the black experience.

When the VTA founded the office of secretary of civic education, Jackson asserted that its main objective was to produce "vote conscious young people" who would participate in government affairs. In 1943, Jackson underscored the democratic and nationalistic implications of voting. By 1948, he was placing the teachers' crusade in the larger context of southern race relations. By voting, teachers would "inspire pupils," but they would also "influence all teachers in the states to the south of us." Once Virginia's teachers could "announce to our fellow teachers in the Southern states that all or nearly all" had registered to vote, "then they too will awaken from their slumbers." Politically active teachers were involved in issues that extended beyond the Old Dominion: "The task in which we are engaged, then, is one of seeking to bring about reform in a whole region of our nation." By participating in a movement that had ramifications for all southern blacks, teachers promoted "political democracy."[68]

In the era before direct action protests, Jackson's strategy of relying on African American educators made perfect sense. Before the emergence of region-wide civil rights groups, these educators were uniquely situated to reach students and mold their thinking about racial issues. Since Supreme Court decisions had produced change and political influence within the Democratic Party had produced results, Jackson and the VTA were right to believe that a strategy of black voting and litigation could eliminate black proscription. Certainly, the Student Non-Violent Coordinating Committee and the Congress of Racial Equality thought so. Both promoted ventures such as the Mississippi Freedom Democratic Party, black voter registration, political education, and voting rights legislation. Where Jackson and others miscalculated was in believing that gradual improvement through conventional channels would spark a civil rights revolution.

But his efforts did more than reflect the gradualist mood of the period; they also advanced the movement for black civil rights. Along with key members of the VTA, he transformed black colleges, schools, and professional associations into seedbeds of democratic thought. Utilizing Virginia State College and the teachers' association, he supported citizenship initiatives throughout the state's segregated schools. The teachers' association and the civic education office allowed Jackson to construct what sociologist Doug McAdam refers to as an "associational network" that eventually stimulated "social insurgency" and created the conditions for "mass political action." Through annual conventions, extension lectures, and school improvement programs, the VTA forged an organizational nexus between education and civil rights. Jackson strengthened those ties by making political involvement the litmus test of teacher professionalism. The teachers' association, Jackson's Speakers Bureau lectures, his newspaper editorials, seminars on civic education, voting surveys, correspondence, and the association's *Bulletin* became channels of communication binding teachers together in the movement toward fundamental change.[69]

By creating locations hospitable to racial dignity and visions of freedom, Luther P. Jackson played a critical role in what McAdam refers to as "cognitive liberation." This is the significance of his mountainous correspondence with principals and teachers, of the frequently emotional letters written by teachers recently "converted" to voting or those eager to share their revitalized political convictions. More than the empirical data he collected, Jackson's efforts to connect teachers to political groups outside the schools, infuse political instruction in the classroom, and excite students about political solutions to racial inequality opened the door to "cognitive liberation." Relying on the VTA and Virginia State College, this struggle to create independent space galvanized the *idea* of political self-determination. Through community action, students and teachers began the process of transmitting a revitalized political perspective to those steeped in the tradition of racial subjugation.[70]

Although Jackson admitted that it was "practically impossible" to determine how many teachers had registered to vote, he tried to gauge the impact of his campaign in quantitative terms. In 1948, he claimed that "more than one-half of the 4,500 public school teachers in Virginia are qualified voters," whereas a "fair proportion" offered instruction on voting procedures, parties, and elections. In "Race and Race Suffrage in the South since 1940," he concluded that teacher registration rates in Virginia and Texas stood at "fifty percent or more" but noted disappointedly that "in the South as a whole the number drops to less than twenty percent." Depending on his audience, he either applauded vote-conscious teachers or stressed their political torpor. He was probably the most forthcoming in his reports to the Virginia Teachers Association executive committee, since they not only sponsored his office but also had a ground-level perspective on Virginia's black teachers. In 1948, he reported that "a growing number of teachers are becoming vote conscious [and] are giving instruction in suffrage and the affairs of government in their schools [while] a few are participating on a wider front by teaching voting requirements to adults in their communities." Clearly, then, a majority of teachers had to one degree or another become politically active.[71]

The civic training that flourished in Virginia's black schools anticipated the Freedom Schools of the Student Non-Violent Coordinating Committee's 1964 Mississippi campaign. In adopting Jackson's civic education program, the teachers and students of the 1940s foreshadowed the Mississippi Freedom Vote initiative of 1963, in which African Americans voted in a mock election supervised by the Student Non-Violent Coordinating Committee and the Council of Federated Organizations. As Student Non-Violent Coordinating Committee activists would do in the Magnolia State, Jackson and the teachers created the conditions in which, as one historian of the Freedom Schools of the 1960s put it, southern blacks could grasp "the intersection of education and political action" and contemplate even briefly "a life unmarked by racial oppression."[72] Under Jackson's leadership, Virginia's politically minded teachers created spheres of racial self-determination at segregated schools, which lay at the heart of Jim Crow. That did not make them utopias of independent thought; it certainly did not relieve them of the economic inequalities of segregation or the negative consequences of southern racism. Yet it did promise change and, in the years before Martin Luther King, that mattered enormously. Through community action, voters' league meetings, and Negro History Week celebrations, Jackson and others created spaces of political independence that supported the classroom project. Together, these intersecting spaces departed dramatically from the Washingtonian tradition of political neutrality. Like the activists who would endure the sweltering heat of racial oppression in Mississippi in 1964, they understood that the ballot was essential to any civil rights protest.

Throughout his public career, Jackson believed that African Americans had to create an intellectual space in which they might conceive of themselves as citizens. The Association for the Study of Negro Life and History, the Virginia Voters League, and the Virginia Teachers Association provided the organizational framework that allowed blacks to foster intellectual autonomy. Like the colonists' Committees of Correspondence, the abolitionists' church meetings, and the black Republicans' Union League, the civil rights activists of the 1940s grasped the connection between collective action and intellectual liberation. By promoting collective solutions to social problems, they went against the grain of an American society that increasingly championed individualism as the antidote to the alleged virus of communist influence. Jackson and others crafted associations such as the VTA that fostered a common language of reform and a set of galvanizing ideals, the most important of which was citizenship. They then used these organizations to forge links between important community institutions that could potentially challenge the dominant norms of racial submission. The two-pronged strategy of creating independent physical space and intellectual autonomy was not unprecedented, but it was essential for the success of civil rights reform.

The significance of schools as sites of political awakening became clear in the early 1950s, when the NAACP relinquished the frustrating effort to equalize school facilities and confronted segregation as a violation of constitutional principle. Under the leadership of Barbara Johns, students at Robert Moton High School in Prince Edward County, a district that Jackson had canvassed often in his efforts to promote the ASNLH and voting rights, went on strike against the abysmal school they attended courtesy of Jim Crow. A delegation of students contacted the NAACP in Richmond to support a suit against the school board for better facilities. The lawyers offered their assistance on one condition: that the students and their parents be prepared for a direct assault on segregation.[73] When the students agreed, they triggered a series of events that led to the inclusion of the Prince Edward County suit in the *Brown v. Board of Education* case of 1954. Of course, Jackson was not directly responsible for the student strike. Yet in prodding teachers to take up their political responsibilities, urging them to indoctrinate students in the principles of democratic governance, and building overlapping networks of political and historical consciousness, Luther P. Jackson fostered the atmosphere that made the developments at Robert Moton High School possible. Lacking spaces for independent thought and action, the progress of the Civil Rights Movement might have been entirely different. One might also wonder whether it could have happened at all.

NOTES

1. Luther P. Jackson, "Segregation—Will It Last Always?" *Norfolk Journal and Guide*, July 20, 1946.

2. James D. Anderson, "On the Meaning of Reform: African American Education in the Twentieth-Century South," in *The American South in the Twentieth Century*, ed. Craig S. Pascoe et al. (Athens: University of Georgia Press, 2005), 272–273.

3. See, for example, Adam Fairclough, "Being in the Field of Education and Also Being a Negro . . . Seems . . . Tragic": Black Teachers in the Jim Crow South," *Journal of American History* 87 (June 2000): 65–91; Adam Fairclough, *Teaching Equality: Black Teachers in the Era of Jim Crow* (Athens: University of Georgia Press, 2001); Michael Fultz,

"African American Teachers in the South: Powerlessness and the Ironies of Expectation and Protest," *History of Education Quarterly* 35 (Winter 1995): 401–422; Michael Fultz, "African American Teachers in the South, 1890–1940: Growth, Feminization, and Salary Discrimination," *Teachers College Record* 96 (Spring 1995): 544–568; Michael Fultz, "Teacher Training and African American Education in the South, 1900–1940," *Journal of Negro Education* 64 (Spring 1995): 196–210; Vanessa Siddle Walker, *Their Highest Potential: An African American School Community in the Segregated South* (Chapel Hill: University of North Carolina Press, 1996).

4. Thomas D. Pawley, "Jackson, Luther Porter: Educator, Historian, Virginia Civic Leader," 1–2, box 1, folder 1, Jackson Papers, Johnston Memorial Library, Virginia State University, Petersburg, Virginia (hereafter cited as Jackson Papers).

5. "Biographical Sketch of Luther Porter Jackson, Professor of History, Virginia State College, Ettrick, Virginia," *Virginia Teachers Bulletin* 20 (May 1943): 3–4, 8; Wilhelmina Hamlin, "Luther P. Jackson—Historian," *Negro History Bulletin* 6 (November 1942): 34–35, 46–47.

6. Quoted in Thomas D. Pawley, "Jackson, Luther Porter," 3.

7. Luther P. Jackson, "Failing to Embrace Political Opportunities," *Norfolk Journal and Guide*, November 14, 1942.

8. Jackson, "Honor to the Teachers of Virginia," *Norfolk Journal and Guide,* May 12, 1945.

9. Grover C. Grant, "Says Dr. Jackson Is a Real Leader," *Norfolk Journal and Guide*, February 20, 1943.

10. On the importance of Woodson and the association in discrediting historical scholarship dominated by racist assumptions and fostering an alternative interpretation of the black experience, see "Countering White Racist Scholarship: Carter G. Woodson and *The Journal of Negro History." Journal of Negro History* 68 (Autumn 1983): 355–375.

11. L. F. Palmer, "He Left a Lonesome Place," *Negro History Bulletin* 13 (June 1950): 198, 214.

12. Jackson to Carter G. Woodson, June 26, 1944, folder 990, box 35, Jackson Papers; Janette Hoston Harris, "Woodson and Wesley: A Partnership in Building the Association for the Study of Afro-American Life and History," *Journal of Negro History* 83 (Spring 1998): 111–112. Jackson also addressed the annual meeting of the ASNLH in Petersburg in 1937 and almost certainly played a part in organizing the meeting. Interestingly, the evening's proceedings included a dramatic presentation on the African experience in America. Felicia D. Anderson of Virginia State College directed the presentation, which covered events from the slave trade to the Reconstruction era and played to a crowd of more than 2,000 local residents, students, and faculty. Clearly, the college had become a space in which African Americans enacted their freedom, recollected an often-distorted and misrepresented history, and anticipated greater freedom. See Luther P. Jackson, "Proceedings of the Annual Meeting of the Association for the Study of Negro Life and History," *Journal of Negro History* 22 (January 1937): 1–16.

13. Quoted in Luther P. Jackson, "The Work of the Association and the People," *Journal of Negro History* 20 (October 1935): 391–392.

14. On the significance and ideological limitations of the Negro History movement, see W. Fitzhugh Brundage, *The Southern Past: A Clash of Race and Memory* (Cambridge:

Belknap Press of Harvard University Press, 2005), 178–182; and "'To Turn as on a Pivot': Writing African Americans into a History of Overlapping Diasporas," *American Historical Review* 100 (June 1995): 765–787.

15. Jackson, "The Annual Negro History Drive in Va.," *Virginia Teachers Bulletin* 16 (April 1939): 13.

16. Jackson, "The History of Negro History," *Norfolk Journal and Guide*, February 9, 1944, box 64, folder 1614, Jackson Papers. (Date is from original manuscript—Jackson's articles were published a week later in the newspaper.) Jackson's dissertation on free black property owners of the antebellum period was published as *Free Negro Labor and Property Holding in Virginia, 1830–1860* (New York: Appleton Century, 1942). As he explained in an article for the college journal, the study aimed to challenge stereotypes about indolent free blacks: "The damaging statements of contemporaries have influenced most of our present day writing on the subject. Some writers . . . take the view that after the passing of the reactionary legislation of 1831–32, this class was bound to enter into a period of decline. . . . He therefore became helpless and the ward of society." Plowing through census data and county tax records, Jackson discovered that by 1860, one in every five African American families were property owners. Rather than indigent loafers, manumitted African Americans became skilled mechanics and agricultural laborers, earning economic autonomy in the process. See *Virginia State College Gazette* 33 (March 1938): 43–48, quote on 43. For more on Carter Woodson and the Association for the Study of Negro Life and History, see Jacqueline Goggin, *Carter G. Woodson: A Life in Black History* (Baton Rouge: Louisiana State University Press, 1993). For a consideration of Jackson's place in the wider spectrum of civil rights activism before the 1950s, see Raymond Gavins, "Hancock, Jackson, and Young: Virginia's Black Triumvirate, 1930–1945," *Virginia Magazine of History and Biography* 85 (1977): 470–486.

17. Jackson, "Negro History Week," *Norfolk Journal and Guide*, February 13, 1943.

18. V. O. Key to Jackson, September 14, 1948, folder 239, box 12, Jackson Papers.

19. Douglas Southall Freeman to Jackson, July 1948, folder 237, box 12, Jackson Papers.

20. A. A. Taylor to Jackson, July 27, 1948, folder 237, box 12, Jackson Papers.

21. R. G. Higgins to Jackson, April 18, 1941, folder 138, box 6, Jackson Papers.

22. P. B. Young to Jackson, July 20, 1948, folder 237, box 12, Jackson Papers.

23. As a sample of the range and energy of Jackson's voting rights activism, see Jackson to the One Hundred Chairmen of the Virginia Voters League, December 16, 1941, and Jackson form letter to the county leaders of the VVL, August 4, 1941, both in the folder titled "Virginia Voters League Main Office 1940–1941," box 18, Jackson Papers. On the Virginia Voters League, see Marva Curtis, "Luther P. Jackson and the Virginia Voters League," master's thesis, Virginia State University, 1979; on Jackson's successful efforts to coordinate with the NAACP, see Larissa Smith, "Where the South Begins: Black Politics and Civil Rights Activism in Virginia, 1930–1951," Ph.D. diss., Emory University, 2001, 186–192; on the multi-faceted struggle of Richmond's African Americans against the Virginia tradition of racial paternalism and the ideological contradictions of white liberalism, see J. Douglas Smith, *Managing White Supremacy: Race, Politics, and Citizenship in Jim Crow Virginia* (Chapel Hill: University of North Carolina Press, 2002), particularly chapter 9 and epilogue.

24. On the significance of the war for promoting NAACP membership and crystallizing its commitment to economic reform, see August Meier and John H. Bracey, "The NAACP as a Reform Movement, 1900–1965: 'To Reach the Conscience of America,'" *Journal of Southern History* 59 (February 1993): 20–22; and Steven Lawson, *Running for Freedom: Civil Rights and Black Politics in America Since 1941*, 2nd ed. (New York: McGraw-Hill, 1991; reprint, 1997). On the war as a stimulus to black hope about the possibility of change, a mood that often coexisted with black skepticism about racial improvement, as well as the ideological significance of the war for the early Civil Rights Movement, see Richard M. Dalfiume, "The 'Forgotten Years' of the Negro Revolution," in *Journal of American History* 55, no. 1 (June 1968): 90–106; George B. Tindall, *The Emergence of the New South, 1913–1945* (Baton Rouge: Louisiana State University Press, 1967), 711–721; Robert Weisbrot, *Freedom Bound: A History of America's Civil Rights Movement* (New York: Plume Books, 1991), 9–11. For contrasting views of the impact of the war on the South, see James Cobb, "World War II and the Mind of the Modern South," in *Remaking Dixie: The Impact of World War Two on the American South*, ed. Neil R. McMillen (Jackson: University of Mississippi Press, 1997), 3–20, which stresses the war as a stimulus to racial liberalism and favorable economic changes; and Harvard Sitkoff, "African American Militancy in the World War II South: Another Perspective," ibid., 70–92, which emphasizes the support that blacks gave to the national military effort and the corresponding drop in militant protest.

25. Adam Fairclough, *Better Day Coming: Blacks and Equality, 1890–2000* (New York: Viking Press, 2001), 186–187, 196–197; David R. Goldfield, *Black, White and Southern: Race Relations and Southern Culture, 1940 to the Present* (Baton Rouge: Louisiana State University, 1990), 25–28; David M. Kennedy, *Freedom from Fear: The American People in Depression and War, 1929–1945* (New York: Oxford University Press, 1999), 208–210; Patricia Sullivan, *Days of Hope: Race and Democracy in the New Deal Era* (Chapel Hill: University of North Carolina Press, 1996), 3–5, 177–178. For a study of the social and intellectual ferment that produced the Black Freedom Struggle, see John Egerton, *Speak Now Against the Day: The Generation Before the Civil Rights Movement in the South* (Chapel Hill: University of North Carolina, 1994). Not all African American southerners embraced the move toward desegregation, at least not before 1954. Many, including local NAACP members, were concerned about the impact of segregation on African American cultural autonomy and the prospect that black students would suffer discrimination in integrated schools. African American schoolteachers were naturally worried about losing their incomes. See James T. Patterson, *Brown v. Board of Education: A Civil Rights Milestone and Its Troubled Legacy* (New York: Oxford University Press, 2001), 6–12.

26. Jackson, "The Voteless School Teachers of Virginia," *Virginia Teachers Bulletin* 18 (November 1941): 13.

27. The importance of this Popular Front coalition in advancing black civil rights as part of a larger program of social democratic reform has been developed most recently by Jacquelyn Dowd Hall in "The Long Civil Rights Movement and the Political Uses of the Past," *Journal of American History* 91 (March 2005): 1233–1263. On the importance of black equality in the Popular Front ethos, which included but was not dominated by or limited to the agenda of the Communist Party, see Michael Denning, *The Cultural Front: The Laboring of American Culture in the Twentieth Century* (New York: Verso, 1996).

28. Discussing the importance of professional black legal and medical associations in the advancement of civil rights, historian Darlene Clark Hine makes a similar point: "Black professionals identified the Achilles' heel of white supremacy: Segregation provided blacks the chance, indeed, the imperative, to develop a range of distinct institutions that they controlled. . . . I argue that parallel institutions offered black Americans not only private space to buttress battered dignity, nurture positive self-images, sharpen skills, and demonstrate expertise. These safe havens sustained relationships and wove networks across communities served." Teachers' organizations and the Association for the Study of Negro Life and History performed similar functions. At once, they cultivated a corps of articulate intellectuals engaged in the political issues of their time. They also gave middle-class blacks the institutions they needed to forge relationships that were indispensable to civil rights reform. At the same time, they encouraged members to realize that separate but equal was no longer morally or constitutionally defensible. See Darlene Clark Hine, "Black Professionals and Race Consciousness: Origins of the Civil Rights Movement, 1890–1950," *Journal of American History* 89 (March 2003): 1279–1280.

29. Alfred Kenneth Talbot, "History of the Virginia Teachers Association, 1940–1965," Ph.D. diss., College of William and Mary, 1981, 12–33. Jackson, *A History of the Virginia State Teachers Association* (Norfolk: Guide Publishing Company, 1937), chapters 1 and 5; J. Rupert Picott, *History of the Virginia Teachers Association* (Washington, DC: National Education Association, 1975), 96–102, 106–120; Lutrelle Palmer to Jackson, October 10, 1941, folder 140, box 6; William Cooper to Jackson, October 13, folder 140, box 6; Jackson to the Jeanes Supervisors and High School Principals in Virginia, February 2, 1942, folder 705, box 28, Jackson Papers.

30. Jackson to the Jeanes Supervisors and High School Principals in Virginia, February 2, 1942, box 28, folder 705; Jackson to Speakers on Speakers Bureau, February 14, 1942, box 28, folder 705, Jackson Papers.

31. On the importance of African American teachers' organizations as instruments of professional advocacy and educational reform, see Gerald L. Smith, *A Black Educator in the Segregated South: Kentucky's Rufus B. Atwood* (Lexington: University Press of Kentucky, 1994), 88–96; Fultz, "Teacher Training," 104–106; and Jackson, "Work of the Association and the People," 391–392.

32. Jackson to the Jeanes Supervisors and High School Principals in Virginia, February 2, 1942, box 28, folder 705; Jackson to Speakers on Speakers Bureau, February 14, 1942, box 28, folder 705; Jackson to Moss Plunkett, July 7, 1942, box 6, folder 147, Jackson Papers. Writing to a voting activist in 1943, Jackson once again exhibited his elitist strategy for political action. "In order that we may stir up Accomac somewhat kindly furnish me the names and addresses of fifteen or twenty of your leading citizens." In Jackson's view, political mobilization would start with the elite and trickle down to masses. Jackson to D. C. Rawley, May 6, 1943, box 6, folder 160; quote from Jackson to Plunkett, October 2, 1942, box 6, folder 150, Jackson Papers.

33. Jackson, "The Shame of the Race," September 19, 1945, box 64, folder 1609, Jackson Papers. African Americans in general understood the importance of education as a vehicle of social mobility and the inculcation of cultural values. As social analyst Gunnar Myrdal observed: "They feel that education should not only be accepted passively but should be used as a tool of concerted action to gain the equal status they

are seeking. For this reason, many, if not most, Negro leaders desire that Negro students should get special training in Negro problems." See Gunnar Myrdal, *An American Dilemma: The Negro Problem and Modern Democracy* (New York: Harper and Row, 1944 [twentieth anniversary edition, 2 vols., New York: McGraw Hill, 1964]), 901.

34. Jackson actively encouraged chairpersons of the Virginia Voters League to coordinate with Jeanes supervisors in promoting suffrage qualification. He also emphasized the importance of placing "special stress on voting in class room instruction." See Jackson to One Hundred Chairmen of the Virginia Voters League, April 19, 1942, box 18, folder titled "Virginia Voters League, Main Office 1942–43," Jackson Papers.

35. Jackson to J. M. Ellison, President of Virginia Union University, March 19, 1942, folder 729, box 28; Jackson to "certain members of the Staff of Virginia State College," December 4, 1944, box 28, folder 707, Jackson Papers.

36. "Report of the Secretary of Civic Education at the Delegate Assembly," November 17, 1943, box 28, folder 706; Jackson to Principals of Virginia High Schools, March 23, 1943, box 28, folder 706, Jackson Papers.

37. Spencer to Jackson, December 20, 1940, box 29, folder 750; see also Spencer to Jackson, November 9, 1944, box 29, folder 750, Jackson Papers.

38. Jackson, "The False Belief of Most Teachers About Voting," *Norfolk Journal and Guide*, July 12, 1947.

39. Jackson, "Honor to the Teachers of Virginia."

40. Jackson, "Race and Suffrage in the South Since 1940," *New South* (June–July 1948): 9–12; Smith, "Where the South Begins," 237–238.

41. Spencer to Jackson, June 13, 1949, box 29, folder 750; in addition to applauding Jackson's confrontational letter to school superintendent Greene, Spencer thanked Jackson for "the splendid [word indecipherable] job that [you] are putting over in our Virginia. Let me say 'Carry On.'" Spencer to Jackson, June 14, 1948, box 29, folder 750, Jackson Papers.

42. Spencer to Jackson, June 13, 1949, box 29, folder 750, Jackson Papers. Following the *Gaines* decision, the NAACP began to challenge salary disparities between black and white teachers. After a precedent-setting decision in Maryland in 1939, the NAACP began to challenge salary discrimination in each state in the South with the exception of North Carolina and Mississippi. Teachers often paid the price when school boards dismissed them for participating in the cases. Despite official retaliation, the court cases had effectively eliminated salary discrepancies by the end of the war. For NAACP's salary equalization campaign in Virginia, see Mark Tushnet, *The NAACP's Legal Strategy Against Segregated Education, 1929–1950* (Chapel Hill: University of North Carolina Press, 1987), 79–80; for the NAACP's campaign against racial exclusion in the 1930s and 1940s, see Fairclough, *Better Day Coming*, 181–201.

43. Jackson, "Mrs. Ethel Thompson Overby, Principal of Elba School, Richmond, Praised for Civic Activities," *Norfolk Journal and Guide*, May 31, 1947.

44. Jackson, "Race and Suffrage," 9.

45. Jackson, "Reason for the Inactivity of Negroes in Political Affairs," *Norfolk Journal and Guide*, June 15, 1946.

46. As Jackson described in 1944, "That the schools should serve as centers for civic training is an idea which was grasped and is now enthusiastically promoted by a group

of leaders in education in one state—namely, Virginia, through the agency of its Virginia State Teachers Association." The association had evolved into a political action committee that pressured teachers to vote and to instruct their students in the fundamentals of democracy. See "Civic Training in the Schools of Virginia," *Norfolk Journal and Guide*, December 23, 1944.

47. Palmer to Jackson, April 24, 1942, box 28, folder 712, Jackson Papers.

48. Binford to Jackson, June 2, 1942, box 29 (folder number unavailable), Jackson Papers. For additional evidence of voting instruction prior to Jackson's efforts as well as expressions of support for his civic education program, see G. B. Ruffin to Jackson, May 21, 1942, box 29, folder 746, and M. H. Watson to Jackson, February 16, 1942, box 29, folder 762; Mayme H. Coleman to Jackson, April 1, 1942, box 29, folder 746, Jackson Papers.

49. Greer to Jackson, October 13, 1944, box 29, folder 733, Jackson Papers.

50. Greer to Jackson, April 30, 1946, box 29, folder 733; ibid., June 4, 1947, box 29, folder 733; ibid., December 1, 1948, box 29, folder 733, Jackson Papers.

51. Bundy to Jackson, December 6, 1948, box 29, folder 770; Sims to Jackson, May 1, 1948, box 28, folder 735; Hubbard to Jackson, January 29, 1945, box 29, folder 735, Jackson Papers. African American women did not discover politics in the 1930s but directed the political energies they had channeled into voluntary associations in the late nineteenth century back into the "formal" arena of voting and parties. In this political tradition, churches had offered the public space in which African American men and women elaborated a community-based rather than individualistic, masculine conception of freedom. See Elsa Barkley Brown, "Negotiating and Transforming the Public Sphere: African American Life in the Transition from Slavery to Freedom," *Public Culture* 7 (1994): 107–146. Women dominated the black teaching profession, and their dedication to improving education and lifting the prospects of their students easily blossomed into support for the Civil Rights Movement. See Fairclough, *Teaching Equality*, 52–55 and chapter 3.

52. Rosa Carter to Jackson, May 10, 1948, box 29, folder 760, Jackson Papers.

53. Valentine to Jackson, June 12, 1948, box 29, folder 768; Randolph to Jackson, February 25, 1942, box 29, folder 773; Holmes to Jackson, February 12, 1943, box 29, folder 769; for invitations from teachers' groups stemming from his work as secretary of civic education, see M. J. Spriggs to Jackson, October 9, 1946, box 29, folder 772, C.W. Seay to Jackson, February 25, 1942, box 28, folder 725; quote from Mary E. Thompson to Jackson, May 11, 1948, box 29, folder 760, Jackson Papers.

54. Brooks to Jackson, April 26, 1948, box 29, folder 742, Jackson Papers.

55. Ibid.

56. Jackson to Seay, November 13, 1944, box 28, folder 723; Jackson, "Civic Training in the Schools of Virginia," *Norfolk Journal and Guide*, December 23, 1944, box 64, folder 1624, Jackson Papers.

57. Jackson, "The Non-Voting Tradition Among School Teachers," *Norfolk Journal and Guide*, March 13, 1944, box 64, folder 1603. Jackson used every source of information and influence he could to promote the civic education agenda. In 1944, Jackson appealed to executive secretary Rupert Picott to identify the number of teachers qualified to vote in any given town or city. Further adding to Picott's task, Jackson asked that he determine

whether teachers understood the Virginia voting requirements, if they studied his hand-book on voting, and that he educate any teachers he met in the mechanics of voting. Jackson also asked Picott to proselytize for civic education among teachers by suggesting "some of the exercises you had in your own school at Newport News." Jackson to Picott, April 16, 1944, box 28, folder 715; Jackson to "Mrs. Gaskins," April 21, 1948, box 28, folder 731 (final quote); see also Jackson to "Miss Graves," ibid., and Jackson to "the Principals of High Schools in Virginia," April 28, 1947, box 28, folder 708, all in Jackson Papers.

58. Jackson, "The Virginia State Teachers Association," *Norfolk Journal and Guide*, June 3, 1944; see also Jackson, "The State Teachers Association and the General Assembly," ibid., April 27, 1946. On the significance of the teachers' salary issue as a wedge for expanding black freedom and a precedent for further reforms, see "The Teachers Salary Fight—the Hope for the Future," ibid., January 13, 1945.

59. Jackson, "Non-Voting Among College Teachers and Workers," *Norfolk Journal and Guide*, March 20, 1944, box 64, folder 1603; Jackson to "the Summer School Students and Members of the Staffs of Virginia State College, Virginia Union University, and Hampton Institute," July 24, 1945, box 28, folder 707; Jackson to "the High School Principals and certain Jeanes Supervisors," March 1, 1945, box 28, folder 707; Jackson to "the High School Principals in Virginia," November 1, 1949, box 28, folder 709, Jackson Papers; Andrew Buni, *The Negro in Virginia Politics, 1902–1965* (Charlottesville: University of Virginia Press, 1967), 138–141. For one of several appeals to teachers to register and vote, see Jackson to "the Teachers in the Schools of Virginia," April 30, 1946, box 28, folder 708, Jackson Papers.

60. "A Proposal to High School Principals for Class Instruction in Voting," Department of Civic Education, State Teachers Association, April 3, 1942, box 28, folder 705, Jackson Papers.

61. Spencer to Jackson, April 7, 1942, box 29, folder 750, Jackson Papers.

62. Jackson, "Civic Training in the Schools of Virginia," *Norfolk Journal and Guide*, December 23, 1944, box 64, folder 1624, Jackson Papers. The principal that Jackson referred to was none other than James F. Spencer, Jackson's loyal ally. As Spencer wrote in the letter that Jackson quoted, he arranged for students to visit the polls "whenever an election is held." Spencer to Jackson, November 9, 1944, box 29, folder 750, Jackson Papers. In another gloss on teacher voting activity, Jackson wrote, "[A]t long last a majority of our 4,000 public school teachers have awakened to the fact that the salvation of any people rests partly on their attitude toward elections and the affairs of government." Jackson to S. H. Clarke, J. H. Carey, and W. H. Willis, December 2, 1944, Jackson Papers.

63. Jackson made a direct connection between increased teacher voting and the activity of supportive school principals. "More than half the public school teachers in Virginia participated in the recent election partly because their principals urged them to do so." Jackson to "certain members of the Staff of the Virginia State College," December 4, 1944, box 28, folder 707, Jackson Papers.

64. Clyde Scott to Jackson, May 28, 1942, box 29, folder 745; Binford to Jackson, December 17, 1948, box 29, folder 749, Jackson Papers; W. L. Johns of the Academy High School also informed Jackson that his school had held mock elections that were "carried out with a good deal of interest, with all high school pupils taking an active part." Johns to Jackson, January 12, 1949, box 29, folder 741, Jackson Papers.

65. Caleb Gregory Brown to Jackson, June 11, 1948, box 29, folder 734; A. N. Jackson to Jackson, December 3, 1948; ibid., June 8, 1948 (second quote), both in box 29, folder 738, Jackson Papers. A. N. Jackson had already written to Jackson, asking for assistance in developing a program for Staunton's civic association, which the former had hoped would be patterned after the program "outlined by the State Civic Organization of the Virginia Education Association." See A. N. Jackson to Jackson, May 13, 1946, and Jackson to A. N. Jackson, May 15, 1946, both in box 29, folder 739; S. S. Trott to Jackson, April 30, 1948, box 29, folder 773, Jackson Papers.

66. Harris to Jackson, November 23, 1948, box 29, folder 744, Jackson Papers.

67. Ibid.

68. Jackson to "the Principals of High Schools in Virginia," April 28, 1947, box 28, folder 708, Jackson Papers.

69. Doug McAdam, *Political Process and the Development of Black Insurgency* (Chicago: University of Chicago Press, 1982), 43–48.

70. Ibid., 108.

71. Jackson, untitled report on teacher voting behavior, 1948, box 18, folder 529; Jackson, "Race and Suffrage," 17; Annual Report, Secretary of Civic Education, Virginia Teachers Association, 1947–1948, box 28, folder 719, Jackson Papers.

72. Daniel Perlstein, "Teaching Freedom: SNCC and the Creation of the Mississippi Freedom Schools," *History of Education Quarterly* 30 (Fall 1990): 301. As he had explained in correspondence through the Virginia Voters League office, Jackson expected civic instruction to stimulate student awareness as well as electoral participation on the part of reluctant parents. Classroom instruction would become an instrument of political education for an entire community.

73. Smith, "Where the South Begins," 297–298.

Scott Hancock

Claiming the Courtroom

Space, Race, and Law, 1808–1856

During a cold Boston January in 1824, Venus Synix, a black woman, charged a white woman, Patty Rouse, with being a common drunkard. Boston's Police Court found Rouse guilty and sent her to jail for four months.[1] This was not the first time Synix, a widow, had entered a courtroom to clear out someone who violated her sense of what was acceptable public conduct. Several years previously, she dragged a black man, John Bowers, before the local justice of the peace for keeping a "bad noisy house." Synix was not just complaining about late-night parties. The case eventually landed in the Municipal Court, which found that Bowers "with force and arms [maintained] a certain common ill governed and disorderly house . . . for his own wicked gain, [permitting] diverse people of evil name and fame and dishonest conversation, both black and white, to frequent and come together . . . there Whoring and otherwise misbehaving themselves . . . to the common nuisance of all the good citizens." The court declared Bowers guilty, fined him $100, and ordered him to post another $100 to ensure good behavior for six months.

Although the several references to the "good citizens of the commonwealth" were standard language in the court records, they nonetheless carried some meaning by casting behavior like Bowers's as antithetical to good citizenship. Furthermore, cases of this sort were of particular importance to legal and political officials of the town government, who sharpened their perennial focus on organized vice in the first decades of the new century. Synix's use of these lower courts affirmed her status as a "good citizen," and her success in punishing a neighborhood nuisance expressed her attempt—backed by the power of the legal system—to maintain some amount of control over her daily life. Her legal actions, as did the actions of many African Americans in Boston, marked out a place for herself in a key public space of the legal system by tapping into the law's multiple ideologies about order, citizenship, and equality.[2]

Space, as modern geographers conceive of it, is not defined simply as a specific physical area in which things or people are located. Although a precise definition is elusive, a general consensus includes understanding space as an area that is defined by relationships and interactions occurring within it. And because relationships and interactions are fluid and dynamic, space is defined and redefined as it undergoes "continual construction . . . through the agency of things encountering each other in more or less organized circulations."[3] Like virtually every city, Boston had particular spaces designated for the administration of the law in which some of the central ideals of the relatively young nation were expressed and carried out: the courtrooms of Boston's Beacon Hill. The interactions and relationships of ideals, individuals, and institutions defined these public spaces.

Courts and courtrooms, terms often used synonymously, often carried differing yet linked spatial meanings. "Courts" frequently signified a conceptual space involving the interactions and relationships of the law and signified order, justice, and power. People then and now, for instance, complain about how the courts fail to live up to expectations of controlling crime or express disappointment when the courts seem to punish the poor harshly and the rich mildly. Bound up in the signification of courts were national ideals of egalitarianism, rights, and equality, all of which were central to the fashioning of American identity. "Courtrooms" identified a specific physical space within which individuals encountered one another in "more or less organized circulations." Individuals, whether judges, constables, litigants, or witnesses, performed in the courtroom in ways that participated in the defining, creating, reinforcement, or challenging of national ideals signified by law and courts. This was one way in which "society and space [were] simultaneously produced."[4]

In 1812, Bostonians had a new building near the top of Beacon Hill in which the ideals of the nation, the power of the law, and the needs and desires of

FIGURE 5.1.
Suffolk County Court House, ca. 1860. The courthouse was torn down in 1862 and replaced by a more elaborate structure. (Philip Bergen, *Old Boston in Early Photographs, 1850–1918*. Used by permission of Dover Publications)

FIGURE 5.2.
Tudor building, ca. 1870. The Tudor building is on the left.
Stephen Gorham, the justice of the peace with whom
African American litigants interacted most frequently before
1822, had his offices on the ground floor. The rear of the
Suffolk County Court House would have been on the right,
where the courthouse built in 1862 stood at the time of
this photo. (Philip Bergen, *Old Boston in Early Photographs,
1850–1918*. Used by permission of Dover Publications)

individual citizens would all intersect. The Suffolk County Court House was a
rather imposing granite structure with a front lawn in the heart of the city and
space and style that communicated power and authority. But Venus Synix, like
hundreds of other black and white litigants, made her initial complaint to Justice
of the Peace Stephen Gorham in his office in the Tudor building, at the end of
a row of buildings facing the back of the courthouse. The Tudor building spoke
less of power and more of the ordinary daily affairs of a growing city.[5] This
dichotomy epitomized the justice of the peace: his position in the judicial hierarchy reconciled what was intended to meld an image of the power and majesty of
the law with an image of egalitarian justice and accessibility in the early republic.

African Americans successfully wedged themselves into this union of ideals as they began their cases with the justice of the peace in the Tudor building and finished in the courthouse.

Although justice-of-the-peace courtrooms predated the early republic, they were not immune to the nineteenth-century transformation of what public space meant. Early on in the nineteenth century, public spaces began to be more specifically defined and therefore infused with purpose and meaning tied to what it meant to be an American, to the country's present and future prosperity, and to the emerging moral and social order. As William Novak points out, there was "nothing *inherently public*" about certain geographic areas that would come to be understood as public space. "'Publicness' had to be constructed and defended," and judges, lawyers, selectmen, and legislators began to successfully define, create, expand, and protect public space early in the nineteenth century. Local, state, and federal governments steadily removed riverways, bridges, roadways, and other spaces deemed necessary for the expansion of commerce and for the public good from control of private property owners.[6] Commerce and transportation have frequently been common rationales for making a space public; other spaces can be created for government functions but necessarily involve public use as a part of their normal operation, such as a town hall or a courtroom. All of these spaces were intended to help the relatively young country survive and prosper, whether by assisting moral and social order, such as a town hall might do, or by supporting the individual decisions of autonomous self-interested beings, such as facilitating commerce by making a bridge open to public traffic. And these spaces were typically construed as geographic areas equally available to the entire public. Public space is often loaded with histories of culture, ideologies, power, and struggle; American notions that it was supposedly available to all the public bespoke the republic's egalitarian ideals.[7]

But scholars such as Donald S. Moore and David Delaney argue that a public space is frequently an area in which power works to inscribe social inequities onto spatial categories. A simple example would be segregationist practices that designated certain spaces for whites. Public space, then, not only is an expression of social (and in this case racial) inequity—that is, it does not simply reflect it—but also has potential to mold and further particular relations of power. Those spaces can also become sites of struggle to challenge how power works and who holds it, whether in polite negotiations, adversarial yet peaceful litigation, physical demonstrations, or violent confrontations. Public spaces can even be used for their intended purposes by those with little power to increase their power. The power ordinary folks gain may not be the kinds of power that usurp social, political, or economic order, but it may grant them greater control over their immediate circumstances.[8]

Subaltern groups and individuals at times participate in the construction of publicness and, in some respects, benefit from the result. Holders of power are often not alone in the construction of public space and subaltern groups do not necessarily resist those constructions and uses. When public officials in the nineteenth-century United States limited the rights of private property owners in order to maintain public access to a roadway, their decision had been pushed by the cumulative effect of thousands of individual decisions made over previous decades. If, for instance, a farmer had been in the habit of letting individuals use a strip of his land as a throughway for years and then suddenly decided to deny permission and obstruct what had become a roadway for carts and carriages, a court case would likely ensue. And in the nineteenth century, the property owner would likely lose. These kinds of cases have been rightly read by Novak and others as the expansion of regulatory and government powers, an expansion inseparable from the maturing ideologies of the early republic that connected commerce, citizenship, individual autonomy, and the future of the nation.[9] But these cases were only made possible because of the actions of ordinary people—not those who typically constitute the human element of what scholars label "power." Furthermore, those ordinary people did not necessarily oppose power being wielded when it meant they could continue with what had become habit.

In other situations, people may not help in the construction but rather participate in the functioning of public space. Justice-of-the-peace courtrooms were public spaces in ways that other courts were not. Higher courts may be understood as public but only in contrast to standard definitions of what constitutes "private." Whereas few people experienced litigation in the space of a higher court, far more people gained access to the lower courts as litigants, witnesses, or simply as spectators. Additionally, although African Americans in Massachusetts had the ability to function in the legal polity through property ownership, marriage, and even voting, the use of the lower courts afforded the most regular, repeatable, and proactive forum for flexing their legal rights. The justice-of-the-peace court was the lowest of the lower courts, and black Bostonians stepped often into this specific spatial entry point of the broader public space of the court.

Venus Synix joined hundreds of other African Americans in Boston who lived out the benefits and consequences of a liberal legal rights ideology that made courtrooms remarkably accessible to citizens rich and poor, black and white, female and male during the early republic era. Consisting of only one-twentieth of Boston's adult population, African Americans appeared in over one-fourth of all cases from 1818 to 1820, when their involvement in the most centrally located justice-of-the-peace court peaked. In 1822, the town consolidated the justice-of-the-peace courts into an ostensibly more manageable Boston Police Court, but the trend of disproportionate black participation in this lower court remained unabated throughout the decade and likely continued throughout the antebellum era.[10] By becoming a persistent presence, black Bostonians staked out a public place within the law, perhaps the central institution of a nation in which, as Tom Paine had declared decades before, the law was king.[11] African Americans were often proactive; they appeared as plaintiffs just as frequently as defendants, and the majority of the defendants, like John Bowers, were brought to courtrooms by other black Bostonians—especially black women like Venus Synix.

Black Bostonians resorted increasingly to the lower courts in the early decades of the nineteenth century for several reasons. They had never been strangers to the courtroom; black men and women had been plaintiffs, defendants, and witnesses for over 150 years. In 1663, Zippora, a slave accused of murdering her baby, was exonerated primarily due to testimony from herself and two other black female laborers. In 1701, a slave named Adam commenced a two-year courtroom battle and ultimately won his own freedom. A litany of cases continued throughout the eighteenth century. Black plaintiffs were not unheard of but nor were they common, in part because slave and free blacks often used extralegal forums to resolve their own disputes. For instance, Election Day and Pinkster festivals in New England appointed black governors and kings who crowned an "informal system of black government." Whites had sanctioned their power to adjudicate disputes among slaves throughout the year. After emancipation, however, this system gradually disappeared. Historian Shane White noted that by 1820, black festivals occurred only sporadically, and African Americans in the North developed more public and political means, such as parades, of displaying themselves "as both African Americans and citizens of the new nation." However, lower courts, especially the justice-of-the-peace court, did have certain advantages over parades as a vehicle for displaying oneself as an active citizen. Courtrooms, unlike parades, were not occasional but open daily, and women, typically not permitted leading roles in parades or festivals, could use them with ease.

Finally, the trend toward using the lower courts coincided with the trend toward formalizing popular political participation. In Revolutionary America, mob action often functioned as one means of political expression by ordinary people. On several occasions, when a protest expressed shared values, these mobs were interracial—black and white urbanites, for instance, at times joined forces against neighborhood brothels. Although some mob actions continued into the nineteenth century, voting and office-holding opened up new and safer avenues for ordinary white men to participate in politics. But African Americans were increasingly marginalized in political affairs as northern states persistently sought to remove or limit black voting rights. At the same time, mobs in the North took on an ominous character that excluded black involvement. Although nineteenth-century interracial mobs were not unheard of, they typically consisted of the white working class and more frequently targeted black neighborhoods. In 1823, when Boston's Mayor Quincy led raids against brothels, he focused on the black section of Beacon Hill and targeted the area for a "renovation" in which several houses were destroyed three years later. Squeezed out of traditional modes of public expression against undesirable neighborhood elements, many black men and women like Venus Synix appear to have increasingly turned to the lower courts to reinforce order and shared values.[12]

Black Bostonians were far from alone in taking advantage of lower courts' accessibility. In New York City, enslaved and free blacks appeared in thousands of cases, many instigated by African Americans. In Philadelphia, African Americans regularly initiated and prosecuted cases in the lower courts and were even chastised for rushing to courtrooms in large numbers as spectators of cases involving black litigants. During the antebellum era, they landed in court because "they often invoked the law against each other, or indeed anyone, when they felt they had been wronged."[13] Whether Boston's high percentage of black plaintiffs typified northern cities requires further research, but given the ease of access to courts typical throughout the North, it would not be surprising to find similar patterns.

Black courtroom activity, whether as plaintiffs, witnesses, or even defendants, was a form of popular participation in the polity. Through parades, speeches, commemorations of the 1808 abolition of the slave trade, *Freedom's Journal*, and other means, free blacks in the North constructed ways of publicly claiming their place in the polity and presenting themselves "as both African American and citizens of the new nation." Although black citizens of all ranks participated, the leaders of these events were typically male and belonged to what has been called the "black elite." But in the courts, black women led, and virtually all female and male litigants occupied the lower rungs of the economic ladder, as did most black northerners. These litigants, then, typified the black populace to a greater extent than did the key participants of better-known black public expressions.[14] These ordinary black folks made a place for themselves in the public space of the courtroom, a physical space heavily freighted with maturing American ideologies of egalitarianism and individual rights. When black litigants hacked out room within that space, regardless of their motives, which varied from personal safety to vengeance, their routine exercise of legal rights was a means of claiming a place within the polity.

Racially charged changes in mob action and political efforts to deny black suffrage were only a few manifestations of the trend toward squeezing African Americans out of the polity. Along with notions of rights, egalitarianism, equality, and independence, race was rapidly becoming another important component defining what it meant to be an American in the early republic era. African Americans possessed only one of these components with any certainty—race—and in that they possessed the wrong kind in the eyes of most Americans. American identity, pregnant with possibilities of inclusiveness after the American Revolution, was quickly barring nonwhites from consideration in the eyes of most white Americans.[15] African Americans resisted exclusion, but there were few public spaces, intellectual or physical, in which African Americans of all classes could consistently make a claim to possess the other necessary qualities defining American citizenship. Courtrooms were one space they could enter and claim that they, too, belonged on equal terms with any other American.

Attributing agency to black litigants in making a place for themselves in courtrooms is entirely appropriate. Making one's way to the courthouse and walking into the courtroom to pursue justice, vengeance, or some control over one's neighbors meant claiming a physical and intellectual space within the legal system. Furthermore, a system of private prosecution remained in place; the victim-turned-plaintiff opened the case by stipulating the charge, offering proof, and having any witnesses testify. The defendant then cross-examined the plaintiff and witnesses, after which the plaintiff could question the defendant. Each was allowed a final rebuttal. The justice then rendered his decision.[16] Many of these women and men demonstrated that they were comfortable operating in court: that is, they were not out of place. When Betsey Green dragged another black woman, Lucretia Hunt, into court in January 1814, she charged her with "profane swearing" and "threatening." Green had no witnesses. Of the other sixteen cases of profane swearing in this court that involved black litigants, the only others without witnesses against the defendant were one in which the defendant pled guilty and another in which the constable, George Reed, was the plaintiff. Absent witnesses, the case between Green and Hunt would have to be decided by whom the justice believed. Green had already established her credibility in this courtroom, however. In 1811 she brought four witnesses and successfully prosecuted two white males for assault; six months later she brought another witness while successfully prosecuting a black woman for assault; six months after that, she brought yet one more witness when she won a case against a black married couple for threatening her. The lack of a witness did not prevent her from getting Hunt fined when she appeared for the fourth time before the same justice. Green's actions had claimed a place for her in this courtroom, a place that she capitalized on at Hunt's expense.[17]

In early nineteenth-century Boston, the path to justice had few obstacles. For those who perceived themselves as a victim of an alleged crime, the first step was getting a constable to arrest the perpetrator. George Reed, the constable who served from around 1810 through the 1830s and made the arrests in many of the cases involving African Americans, was an easily identifiable and familiar figure for black Bostonians. Standing six feet tall, wearing a "broad brimmed high crowned felt hat, [and] a bright spotted red bandana," Reed conducted a daily patrol through the streets of Boston's Sixth Ward, which had the highest proportion of black residents. Called "Old Land Shark," he became so familiar that one chronicler of Boston remembered black mothers invoking the specter of "Old Reed comin' to gobble yis up" to keep their children in line. One account demonstrated how easy it was to engage Reed's services. Around 1830, a customer passed counterfeit money to a boy working as a clerk in a shoe store. The boy showed the storeowner the counterfeits, who asked his young clerk if he knew "Old Reed." The clerk, thinking "what manner of boy did not know him," ran to the old courthouse in the center of Boston and found Reed, who immediately followed the boy back to the shoe store. The suspect was eventually caught. Justice lay close at hand: common folk knew the constable, knew where to find him, and knew that his response was likely to be immediate. In the same way, they knew the justice of the peace.[18]

The people of Massachusetts had long been in the habit of turning to the justice of the peace to resolve disputes. In keeping with English law and custom, "Puritan leaders placed great responsibility on the justice of the peace." In the antebellum era, Bostonians still looked to the justice of the peace as an integral part of maintaining order; in the anti-Catholic Charlestown riots of 1834, Boston's sheriff asked "where were the Justices of the Peace?" Black Bostonians, who had managed to use the justice-of-the-peace court and its successor, the Police Court, with significant success in the first three decades of the nineteenth century, likely also placed responsibility on the justices to act as an aid in maintaining a semblance of order in their communities. This had been the expectation of people in Massachusetts for over 150 years. Africans and African Americans in New England, whose incorporation into white families exposed them to "Yankee" habits of mind and work, shared whites' familiarity with the legal system as well as expectations of what was supposed to work—along with recognition that it did not always fulfill those expectations.[19]

During the latter half of the seventeenth century, as the church and the town meeting proved to be inadequate venues to handle the wide range of disputes cropping up in a society transitioning to new social and economic environments, the courts "helped establish and enforce a 'totality of norms' to regulate the relationships of private individuals."[20] Many New Englanders became accustomed to using the courts to manage their conflicts, making litigation and the law an integral part of maintaining and interpreting social order as "standards of neighborliness had to be demanded and asserted in court." Although the law could specify what constituted a crime, it "could not set standards of daily interpersonal activity which had to be tested and established in court." People expected each other to conform to what the court affirmed as normative behavior; those who did not could expect to find themselves in front of a justice of the peace.[21]

The accessibility of justices of the peace had been the intent of the English court system. More serious crimes were generally dealt with by higher courts, whereas the justices of the peace were expected to handle the sort of persistent disruptions that might regularly plague a community. Justice needed to be easily available on a local basis in order to ensure social order. Hence, justices of the peace could hear cases and deliver verdicts individually in their own homes or as a group during one of the quarterly sessions in their own county. They were given the authority to punish through corporal punishment, imprisonment, or fines and sureties. They had the authority to act as a constable, accusing and arresting suspected violators. Conviction in a justice-of-the-peace court was meant to be "an easy prompt matter upon the testimony of one or two witnesses."[22] They were protected in English, and later in American, law against countersuits—for instance, from being accused of trespassing if they had gone on another's property to order an arrest. The authority and duties of the justice of the peace remained fairly consistent throughout the eighteenth century and into the nineteenth. Late in the eighteenth century, the jurisdiction of justices of the peace actually expanded somewhat, as postrevolutionary reformers sought to make the judicial system even more accessible and efficient. During the first two decades of the nineteenth century, as Massachusetts bounced judicial responsibilities from one court to another in a spasm of attempted reforms, one constant was the continued jurisdiction of the justice-of-the-peace court over daily neighborhood civil and criminal conflicts.[23]

That steady connection with the life of the neighborhood meant the courtroom of the justice of the peace was often the best recourse for managing conflict. Once a plaintiff lodged a charge with either the justice or the constable, the constable apprehended the accused and escorted him or her into the courtroom, where the defendant's name was called and charges read aloud. For those new to the court, it could be an intimidating experience; one white defendant charged with stealing molasses remembered the command to plead guilty or not guilty "came forth in a nerve destroying voice."[24] Part of the intimidation must have stemmed from the relative power held by the justice of the peace. Although a minor judicial figure, he had a fair amount of autonomy in early nineteenth-century Boston—enough autonomy, in fact, to worry the selectmen, who expressed concern that too much power was concentrated in the justices of the peace and that the office could be easily abused. The long-standing practice of providing the justices' salaries from the fines and court fees imposed by the justices themselves was a primary reason for the selectmen's fears. In an attempt to "give the justices of the peace an opportunity to exercise their offices in a manner more publick and responsible," the selectmen proposed establishing a Police Court, composed of three justices of the peace with fixed salaries. It was not until 1822, seven years after the selectmen's proposal and the same year that Boston moved from the status of town to incorporation as a city, that the Police Court began functioning. A significant amount of power remained in the hands of the justices, who could still dispatch the accused to jail on the spot or levy fines that demanded immediate payment. Recognizing this, black Bostonians used this power as a tool in managing conflicts across and within racial boundaries.[25]

The justice-of-the-peace court also wielded power because of the unique space it occupied in the legal system. Barbara Yngvesson and Lynn Mather have described how even in "simple" or "tribal" societies, institutions devised for dispute resolution may be characterized by restricted participation, specialized language and procedures, and several layers of organization for dispute resolution. More complex or modern societies nearly always exhibit these characteristics in their court systems. In both types of societies, "these contextual features often allow for those of higher social status to dominate in the handling of individual disputes and, in so doing, to reinforce broader patterns of social order." Similarly, the development of an "official language of law increases the power of certain political interests by restricting access to the disputing forum, by defining the kinds of disputes which can be placed on the agenda of the forum."[26] The court system in Boston, a focus of reform during the first few decades of the nineteenth century, exhibited these characteristics to varying degrees, especially the higher courts. The lowest court, however, was not highly specialized, and although it may have reinforced the basic power structure, the justice-of-the-peace court remained highly accessible and minimized those "contextual features" that facilitated domination by litigants of higher status. This unique space within what would be an increasingly centralized legal system provided a unique opportunity for African Americans in the early republic.

Black plaintiffs took advantage of that opportunity and placed themselves firmly within that legal space in increasing numbers through the second decade of the nineteenth century. Free men of color used the courtroom as plaintiffs against their fellow black Bostonians about twice as frequently as they did against whites. Free women of color, however, demonstrated a proclivity to pursue justice almost exclusively against other blacks. Rebecca Freeman appeared before Justice of the Peace Stephen Gorham on thirteen occasions, five times as a plaintiff, five as a defendant, and three times as a witness. All of the cases but one were against other African Americans. In Gorham's courtroom, 86 percent of all black female plaintiffs charged other African Americans. The number of black defendants brought by whites remained fairly constant over a thirteen-year span, but the total number of black defendants rose due to black prosecution of other African Americans. From 1808 to 1810, 65 black plaintiffs and 168 black defendants came to court; just under 24 percent (39) of those defendants were brought by black plaintiffs. Ten years later, 247 plaintiffs and 261 defendants appeared over a two-year span; 71 percent (185) of those defendants were brought by black plaintiffs. In the earlier period, only 15 percent of black defendants appeared because they had been charged by a black woman; in the later period, that proportion rose to 52 percent.[27]

A combination of factors likely contributed to the increase in African American women using the court proactively. Many of the cases suggest an "intricate network of exchange" of information and savvy regarding how the justice of the peace could be used as a weapon against neighborhood antagonists and how to best defend oneself when charged. Freeman, for instance, brought several black female witnesses to the courtroom, many of whom appear later as plaintiffs. And since this knowledge was used most frequently against other people of color, the sphere of learning expanded to the defendants. Christine Stansell notes that within female relationships there were "structured expectations of reciprocal help" but that this "cooperation did not automatically engender harmony" as quarrels were common, resulting at times in fighting, cursing, or other manifestations of dissatisfaction.[28] The justice-of-the-peace courtroom provided a stage upon which the conflicts of the neighborhood were acted out, but it also displayed the interconnectedness of the black community, particularly for black women. Furthermore, in an era of increasing racial antipathy, black women may have been more constricted than any other social group as far as utilizing formal systems of power such as government and law to effect immediate change in their neighborhoods.

Using the justice-of-the-peace courtroom gave black Bostonians opportunity to exercise some influence over the circumstances of their often difficult lives. When faced with the possibility of raising a child out of wedlock, Elizabeth Fitch charged her black lover with bastardy in 1808. Edward Bishop initially pled not guilty, but the court, whether motivated by a lack of faith in his assertion of innocence or by a desire to target a source of financial support other than the meager government charities, ordered him to pay a surety. Bishop had no means to pay, so the court ordered him to jail, standard treatment for those unable to provide a surety. Whether it took a brief spell in jail or merely the threat of such to prompt Bishop's sense of responsibility is uncertain, but sometime after pronouncing sentence, the court noted that "the parties having agreed and settled, Bishop is discharged."[29] Fitch got at least a part of what she wanted—financial help—by accessing the power this public space wielded.

Table 1.1. Success rates in interracial court cases, 1818–1820

	# of cases	Charge proved	Not proved	Conviction rate
Black plaintiff–white defendant	68	40	28	59%
White plaintiff–black defendant	75	60	15	80%
Conviction rate, all cases				70%[30]

Fitch epitomized many black litigants. They entered the courtroom not to explicitly resist power but to access the power that this particular space expressed and wielded. By marking out a place, black litigants participated in the maintenance of this holdover from the colonial era as an egalitarian institution in the early republic. And the justice-of-the-peace court appears to have come close to realizing those ideals. This does not mean the significance of status or race was entirely mitigated; a higher proportion of black defendants were penalized when prosecuted by white plaintiffs than were white defendants prosecuted by black plaintiffs. Also, a black defendant stood a greater chance of being convicted when the plaintiff was white than when the plaintiff was black. Here the justice-of-the-peace court, at the bottom of the court hierarchy, did indeed act to reinforce one of the most fundamental patterns of social order—white over black.

Race, then, may have been a factor. But the "haves" do better in court for a number of reasons, and the higher conviction rate that white plaintiffs attained against black defendants could be explained by a number of factors in addition to race.[31] When black defendants were brought to court by white plaintiffs, it was for theft more than any other charge, and these plaintiffs tended to be merchants or other men with occupations of potentially middle-class status. Combined with the U.S. legal system's tendency to protect property, class, although not a huge advantage, appears to have worked to some degree in merchants' favor: between 1808 and 1820, against black defendants, white merchants won 85 percent of their cases, whereas white traders and laborers won 75 percent. This would also account for some of the discrepancy in conviction rates, as black plaintiffs rarely charged anyone, black or white, with crimes against property. More importantly, it is doubtful that black Bostonians were acutely aware of any statistical bias. Some black defendants did succeed in obtaining judgments of "charges not proven"—Lucretia Hunt did so in 1818 despite being charged with theft by a jeweler and a cooper who each had witnesses. Twenty percent of black defendants charged by white plaintiffs were acquitted—and the general acquittal rate was 30 percent, not such a huge disparity that people at that time, from their more limited perspective without the benefit of statistical analysis, would have necessarily perceived as a glaring inequity or felt they had no place in court. And they did, after all, experience more success than failure against white defendants.[32]

Sketching a picture of how black women and men in Boston made a place for themselves in the courtroom while attempting to govern their circumstances does not necessarily create a portrayal of triumph over adversity. Too much weight can be given to the small victories and the minor power black litigants managed to achieve—at the end of the day, the economic and political vulnerability of a victorious black plaintiff or defendant remained unchanged. And many of those small triumphs came at the expense of other African Americans, like Edward Bishop, sometimes resulting not only in financial loss but in days, weeks, or even months in jail for the loser. But it is important, as Nell Painter pointed out some time ago, to "transcend the weight of stereotype and to bravely investigate black life fully, even when the evidence shows angry, violent, disorderly black people. After all, anger, violence, and disorder are thoroughly human emotions and actions. By sanitizing blacks who lived in the past, historians make them *less* complete human beings."[33]

Black Bostonians knew how completely human they could be and often used their place in the courtroom to try to manage the ugly side of their humanity; at times they used the courtroom to express that ugliness when petty vengeance became the overriding motive. But a wide range of motives likely explained the degree to which black Bostonians used the lower courts. The courts provided a relatively simple and cheap way to resolve disputes with black and white residents that could not be contained within the sphere of individual relationships. For some black litigants, like Venus Synix, there appears to have also been concern with maintaining a moral community. Black churches began laying physical and spiritual foundations in Boston in the 1810s, and the African Humane Society began operating in 1818. Some members of each appeared as plaintiffs, perhaps in part because of growing concern about building and sustaining a healthy black community.

Regardless of the motives, African American usage of lower courts also had weighty unpleasant consequences. Black prisoners were disproportionately represented in area jails in part as a result of litigation initiated by other African Americans. As they came to occupy a regular place in the courtroom, they increasingly occupied a place in the prisons. In 1822 the town of Boston was incorporated into a city, and the newly created Boston Police Court, which was a kind of centralized justice-of-the-peace court, supposedly regulated the type of cases each court heard and imposed some sense of order on the legal system. Contrary to the spasmodic changes of the first two decades of the nineteenth century, these changes endured throughout the antebellum period. Composed of three justices of the peace, who rotated periodically and were paid a regular salary, the Police Court ended the practice whereby justices of the peace were paid by fines and court fees.[34]

Initially, the Police Court handled a half dozen or so cases a day. The caseload gradually increased, and by the 1850s one observer put the average number of daily cases at thirty-five and described days of fifty to sixty cases as nothing out of the ordinary.[35] Since individual justices, who continued to carry out other functions, took turns sitting on the Police Court, many black Bostonians would have been familiar with some of the Police Court justices. The constable system also remained in place—Constable George Reed remained at his post at least into the mid-1830s. As they had done before, plaintiffs typically lodged a complaint with a justice of the peace or a constable. Courtroom procedure remained somewhat similar to what African Americans had known in justice-of-the-peace courtrooms, and cases were frequently argued by the litigants themselves.

Yet changes did occur. The criminal justice system became more codified, and the courts more streamlined. The attorney general gained authority at the expense of individual justices of the peace, and the courts became a more useful tool for men like Josiah Quincy, who wished to secure an orderly society during a period of economic and urban growth. Michael Hindus notes that "the same values that the legal system endorsed for the sake of economic growth—certainty, predictability, and rationality—can be found in the criminal justice system of Massachusetts."[36] But change was layered. Even though legislators and court officials were in the midst of attempting to reorganize the criminal justice system and make it more professional and predictable through centralization, the substance of the Police Court's day-to-day activities was not altered dramatically in the antebellum era. The system of private prosecution remained largely intact. The personal, face-to-face nature of adjudication, where litigants appeared before neighborhood justices of the peace, began to erode, but since those same justices sat on the Police Court, some element of familiarity lingered. Probably because of these similarities, the creation of the Police Court appears to have had little effect on African Americans' efforts at managing conflicts through litigation—black litigants, who made up one-fourth of all litigants in Justice of the Peace Stephen Gorham's courtroom from 1818 to 1820, still made up between 20 and 25 percent of all litigants in the Police Court at least through the 1820s.

In at least one instance, an African American made a different kind of place for himself in the evolving legal system in an informal yet effective role. Richard Cephas—also known as Richard Crafus, King Richard, and Big Dick—procured an unofficial position with the Boston police during the 1820s until his death in 1831. Cephas, a veteran sailor of the War of 1812 who had served time in Britain's Dartmoor Prison, stood well over six feet tall and may have weighed as much as 300 pounds. By all accounts, he was extraordinarily strong, although he commanded attention and allegiance as much by his personality as by his strength. The local newspaper *Boston Patriot* described him as an enforcer of basic justice and "a man of good understanding, and he exercises it to a good purpose. If any one of his color cheats, defrauds, or steals from his comrades, he is sure to be punished for it." Many years later, Cephas was memorialized as "always advocating the cause of right, preventing the strong from triumphing upon the weak."[37] As one of the last governors for Boston's black community, Cephas held a prominent position among African Americans. Boston's developing police force, themselves carving out space in the evolving urban administrative world, took note and offered Cephas a role in helping to maintain order in the black community. This served law enforcement and governmental interest as well as Cephas's interest in further enhancing his status. He probably kept many people out of court but also contributed to the flow of black litigants into the courtroom by bringing suit against other African Americans, perhaps individuals who resisted his extralegal efforts for adjudication. Cephas kept busy, fulfilling his role, and knew the courtroom well: he appeared several times in the Boston Police Court over the years, sometimes probably in connection with his de facto constable position and at other times because his own exuberance made for an active social life not always in harmony with legal norms.[38]

Although the power of black governors diminished in the early decades of the nineteenth century, it did not disappear entirely. Part of their power had always rested on whites' acquiescence in allowing festivals and black courts to be conducted. In the 1820s and 1830s, at least in Boston, some of the remnants of their power seem to have been maintained by an informal connection with the legal system. Job Riggins, Boston's black governor in the early 1830s and likely Cephas's successor, used the court on at least one occasion to teach one of his "subjects" a lesson and reinforce his own power when he publicly rebuked one of his subordinates, William Patterson. Patterson had bought some unlicensed liquor for a group of African Americans who probably sought momentary escape from the travails of a sometimes difficult existence. Making up only about 5 percent of the population and living in a growing metropolis during an era of diminishing opportunity for and increased antipathy toward free people of color, black Bostonians had good reason to desire escape, even if only temporary. But Patterson's mistake was not buying unlicensed liquor. He had acted outside of the governor's authority and made his purchase on a Sunday—Riggins reminded him the practice was to get "a *gallon* of good spirit on Saturday night"—and thus drew the ire of reform-minded city authorities. Riggins washed his hands of Patterson, publicly supporting his prosecution in the Police Court and declaring "the law will make you smart."[39]

Riggins spoke as a man firmly ensconced in black culture and community. He also spoke as a man well aware of the law's utility and power, and his public chastisement of Patterson in the courtroom suggests his ability to work within the system. Riggins was probably the one who charged Patterson; he definitely appeared as a witness. Riggins managed to use the law to cast himself as a black man who supported the law's function of maintaining certain moral codes while reminding his subordinate of the price for overstepping his authority. That recasting of self in relation to the law likely had implications for Riggins's identity; it held the potential to reinforce an image of himself as a black man who could sometimes use white institutions to his advantage.

The place that African Americans claimed in the courtroom and in the law, however, did not always work to strengthen individual identity. As African Americans continued to make use of their place in the courtroom, the consequences began to attract unwelcome attention. In 1821, a state congressional committee, concerned about the "increase of a species of population, which threatens to be both injurious and burthensome," reported a ratio of 1 black convict out of every 146 African Americans in Massachusetts, whereas for whites the ratio was 1 to 2,140. George Levesque has documented the significant fluctuations in these ratios up to the Civil War, with black Bostonians being eight times more likely to be incarcerated than whites in 1833, to a low of less than twice as likely in 1837. Overall, between 1823 and 1843, the average proportion of black convicts was five times greater than that of white convicts. The report of the state congressional committee indicates that this disproportion did not go unnoticed by white citizens.[40]

Breaking those numbers down a bit further for one year reveals a gendered pattern of incarceration. In 1835 the total number of incarcerations made by the Municipal and Police Courts by the end of November was 253 men and 151 women. Twenty-four of the men and 34 of the women were black. Of the male convicts, then, black men comprised 9.5 percent of male convicts, or about twice their proportion of the population, whereas black women made up 22.5 percent of female convicts, five times their proportion of the population. Multiple factors produced disproportionate rates; poverty spurring some black women into prostitution and intensifying racism no doubt played a major role. But it must also be noted that from 1810 into the 1820s, the most aggressive prosecutors of black women were other black women. Court records stopped consistently identifying plaintiffs by race in the 1830s, making it more difficult to determine if this pattern persisted. But if it did, and there is little reason to suppose the pattern changed suddenly, it would partly explain the higher proportion of black female convicts.[41]

During the 1830s, the black presence in the courtroom also began to attract the attention of newspapers. Thomas Gill, a court reporter, related the foibles of white as well as black litigants, but the cultural context made black litigants public fodder for evolving racist ideologies. One observer who wrote a kind of exposé of the lower courts in 1856 described the omnipresent court reporters as "fellows of infinite jest." African Americans in particular attracted their attention: "when a colored individual is arraigned for some minor offence, they always seemed determined to have a little sport among themselves." One young biracial woman with dark blue eyes, arrested during a raid on a brothel, had been seen earlier by a reporter when she sang at "a negro concert." The reporter knew she had a "sweet and melodious voice" and he knew the clerk of the court had a fondness for music. Taking the young lady aside before her arraignment, the reporter told her to enter her plea in song. She complied, singing a line from "a well-known German song, 'Thou, thou, know'st that I love thee.'" The judge, clerk, and officers sat in stunned silence. Recomposing themselves and asking again for her plea, she answered not guilty and then sang "Let me go where fate may lead me, Let me cross yon troubled deep; Where no strange ear shall greet me, Where no eye for me shall weep." The officers gave minimal testimony: the clerk declared, "That woman can't be guilty of any *crime!*"; and the judge discharged her.[42]

Throughout the antebellum era, newspapers in Boston and other northern cities ran court reports as regular features for their readers. The courtrooms became, in some respects, a kind of free public theater, epitomized by the unnamed singer. Centralizing the lowest rung of the criminal justice system into the Police Court no doubt spurred on the theatrical aspect by giving spectators and reporters a predictable performance. Justice-of-the-peace offices had been scattered about the city, and complainants could show up at any one of their offices with no warning and at all hours. The Police Court provided a forum with regular hours, and the courtroom in the Suffolk County Court House was more accessible and roomy for reporters and spectators. Some of the spectators would have been litigants waiting their turn on the docket. Boston's lower courts likely mirrored Philadelphia's courts, described by Allen Steinberg as a "free popular theater, with friends and neighbors as the performers."[43] The place that African Americans had made for themselves in the lower courts took on an added meaning they had never intended.

African Americans appearing as "performers" in courtrooms, unwittingly or not, fit within a broader antebellum context of public "black" performance for white entertainment. African Americans attracted attention in Boston, sometimes in unusual ways. In the mid-1830s, the Lafayette Guards, a New York military unit, camped out on the Washington Hotel grounds for a week, feasting and drinking. One of the highlights of the week was entertainment provided by some of the regiment's black servants, in particular one "round, bullet-headed little fellow." The officers wagered on his butting ability, and one witness remembered seeing him "dive through the panel of a stout door, disappearing bodily into the room . . . without displaying the slightest sign of mental or bodily perturbation." This act so impressed local boys that they attempted to imitate him, only to acquire many sore heads. The black servant's feat actually had deep African cultural roots, and identical scenes of African Americans impressing whites persisted at least through the Civil War.[44]

The singer and servant exemplify the battleground that African American expression became in the antebellum era. The "bullet-headed" servant's cultural expression likely helped sustain his own unique identity; regardless of the white soldiers' ignorance, the servant likely understood at least in part that this was the cultural provenance of men of African descent. The fact that some soldiers unsuccessfully attempted to imitate him probably further buttressed a sense of pride in his culturally acquired talent. Likewise, the singer's ability to use her talent, perhaps a mix of European lyrics and African American style, to win her acquittal may have buoyed her sense of identity. In addition, the singer, entering the law's most public space, used her talent and blending of cultures to her advantage.

It would be a mistake, however, to cast these stories simply as triumphs for the individuals involved. Black public performance had a long history, beginning with eighteenth-century slaves in the Boston area and other northern towns who adapted white election holidays into distinctly African American celebrations. Although some whites disapproved of the noise, drinking, and general revelry, others enjoyed and participated in the weeklong festivals that included different forms of combat, footraces, and dancing. In Boston, the tradition continued at least sporadically into the nineteenth century. Historians have noted the cultural significance of these festivals but have perhaps overlooked the significance of the festivals as performances in public spaces before white observers. At least up to 1831, in Boston the black parades, led by the legendary "King Richard" Cephas and composed of a "squad of colored brethren of all sizes and costumes," marched around and through Boston Common "amid the shouts and laughter of the assembled crowd who came to witness." That whites gained something from watching is apparent; it was the only time of public gathering or celebration that white men did not chase black Bostonians off the Commons.[45]

Although the laughter may have had moments of genuine innocence, much of it was no doubt a part of the heightening public denigration of African Americans throughout the North. Black balls and parades also elicited derision from white observers; in 1828 *Freedom's Journal* reprinted a story from the *Pennsylvania Gazette* on an alleged disturbance at what the *Gazette* claimed was a "fancy ball." Supposedly a group of white boys attempted to break up the ball by scaring carriage horses and insulting the women. *Freedom's Journal* claimed the ball had been a "plain" one, that no disturbance had taken place, and that actually a white ball on the same night had degenerated into an unruly affair. Regardless of which report was correct, the *Gazette*'s portrayal of the black celebrants as pretentious buffoons epitomized many public renderings of African Americans.[46]

Court reports did likewise. When Rosanna Turney prosecuted Samuel Wallace, she was labeled a "dandizette." The *Boston Morning Post* described one of her witnesses as "a real grandee—of middling stature, but magnificent breadth of beam, and would come to a good round penny if bought by weight. She was a first-chop pattern for an empress of Morocco . . . the expanding skirt of her figured calico gown, diverging equi-distant from her sable and stable ankles, in branching out in picturesque folds of light and shade, covered an immense area, like a field-marshal's marquee." The depiction concluded by comparing her to "the cloud-capped dome of the State House."[47]

In the nineteenth century, what white readers and observers of African Americans' place in court gained beyond simple entertainment was probably similar to what David Roediger argues white audiences of blackface minstrel shows gained: defining whiteness against the outlandish behavior of blacks. And, as Eric Lott has argued was true of most white Americans' enthusiastic support for minstrel shows, white Bostonians were probably simultaneously attracted and repulsed by black public displays in court. Robert C. Toll places the beginning of the touring minstrel shows around 1830, about the same time they first showed up in Boston. Shortly after the demise of Negro Election Day on the Commons in 1831, a well-known nineteenth-century chronicler of Boston's police force made a note of "Jim Crow Rice *jumping* at Tremont Theatre" in 1833. The *Boston Morning Post* began publishing court reports the next year. Minstrel shows and court reporters continued to construe African Americans as the "other" in Boston; Ordway's Aeolian Vocalists had a ten-year run into the 1850s.[48]

Minstrel shows and court reports both served to crystallize ideas about race that were still forming in antebellum America. African Americans had no control over whites' appropriation and uses of black culture in the minstrel shows. The tragic irony of the court reports was that the propensity of African Americans to use the courts, a propensity fostered in part by the courts' intentional accessibility and attempted impartiality, provided material for the court reporters. When African Americans used the law to gain control over circumstances important in their own lives, they often did so because they believed the law could provide useful remedies. And it often did. The very nature of the law in the American polity and ideology mandated the utility of the law for African Americans. During the colonial era, law as carried out in the lower courts had been a public process, and as long as it continued to be understood as a public process, the spaces within which it functioned had to be accessible. The justice-of-the-peace courtroom, and later the Police Court, were perhaps the most apt physical expression of the publicness of the law. To deny access to a group of citizens who had been able to use it for nearly 200 years would have shredded the idea of the law as fair, egalitarian, and open. The idea of the law as such was a necessary construction in order for it to maintain legitimacy, and in order to maintain the idea, the law had to fulfill those ideals to some degree. And it was important that this be done publicly, so that the rich and poor alike subscribed, to an extent, to the legitimacy of the rule of law. Otherwise, Tom Paine would be wrong—law would not be king.[49]

Furthermore, barring the court to black citizens would have been an onerous legal process and perhaps counterproductive, since black plaintiffs were using the courts to prosecute some of the problem types that Mayor Quincy and other reformers wanted off the streets. Whites had sometimes used black governors and their de facto courts in the colonial era to help maintain order among slaves and free blacks; white leaders in the era of growing urbanization and professionalization preferred more formal methods of social order in the North. For the black community, black governors and their courts receded while the dominant legal order's courts ascended, although black leaders like King Richard still had connections to white power structures, like the budding police force. In sum, black access to courtrooms served multiple interests.

Cutting off African Americans from the courts was never seriously proposed. Instead, the natural response was to mitigate the little power African Americans flexed in courtrooms through other means, such as the court reports that attempted to transform black litigants' use of public legal space into public performances. When one black man named White brought an action of trover to recover what he believed was his parrot from a white man, he judged the matter important enough to bring witnesses and a lawyer. White's case may have been solid. But under the hand of the court reporter, White became a dim-witted and petty fool pursuing a trivial matter. The report mocked White for bringing the case to court and then for filing an appeal of the Police Court's acquittal of the white defendant, when at most "the value of the parrot was estimated at *five dollars.*"[50]

Unlike the "black" performers in minstrel shows, though, White and the "real grandee" who came as a witness for Rosanna Turney did have some control over their representations of blackness. Whether the grandee struck spectators in the courtroom in the same way as the court reporter intended his description to strike readers cannot be ascertained. But the description of clothing suggests that this black woman had taken some pains to make her body respectable and visually pleasurable, in contrast to popular perceptions of the black body as useful primarily for labor or ridicule. White, regardless of the reporters' mocking tone, demonstrated some legal savvy in pursuing his action for trover. Whether or not he won his appeal is uncertain; in either case, he knew how to use the law to attempt to retrieve something that was important to him. But again, like the cases of the singer and the servant, the stories of the witness and White are complicated by the multiple meanings they acquired.

Court reports at times closely mimicked the kind of depictions the minstrel shows perfected. One court report mocked a nineteenth-century black man's attempt to elude prosecution by his own "cleverness." Robert Gardner came to court charged by the city marshal for smoking a cigar in a fire-conscious tinderbox part of the city. Gardner, however, pointed out that he had actually been smoking a pipe, and since he was specifically charged with smoking a cigar, he should be acquitted. The court promptly dispatched a messenger to get the city marshal to amend the charge. The newspaper described Gardner as greatly amused by all the trouble the court was going through—for a moment, it appeared that this poor bootblack held the upper hand. But the court report quickly restored the proper hierarchy by turning Gardner into a smug fool, concentrating in particular on prominent physical racial markers. Gardner, "whose face shone like his customers' polished boots," had been "licking his purple lips with his poppy-red tongue" when he believed he had trumped the court, and "didst look blue . . . as blue as a black-a-moor could look" when the court fined him five dollars, while his "twine eyeballs glistened, and shot their quick gleams crosswise over [his] unpretending nose" as he pressed his "broad heel" into the carpet—implying that Gardner had come to court barefoot. The court report painted a blackface performer for the newspaper's readers, many of whom had no doubt been to a minstrel show.[51] In general, court reports depicted black litigants as pretentious, deceptive, violent, or bumbling, and at best naïve; the reports frequently focused on physical attributes, describing William Weevis's hair as "mongrel" and his wife as having a complexion "one shade darker than a lump of coal in a cloudy day." Another man's skin was "some shades darker—say the color of a dun cow."[52]

Humor and ridicule were the usual methods for making black litigants into public spectacles. One black man, who successfully prosecuted two sailors for assault in the Police Court, became a different kind of victim in the newspaper report. The paper reported that sailors "licked a nigger in Ann street. It might have been supposed that such an abolition taste carried its own penalty with it; but our courts will not allow any such public indulgence of the licking propensity. Therefore they had to pay for their peculiar gratification." The black victim, who became the protagonist in court, was slapped down again as the public recounting made him an object of ridicule and identified the white assailants as objects of favorable humor. Nonetheless, the public ridicule could not alter this black man's successful exploitation of the law's need to maintain some degree of impartiality—he did, after all, get some measure of justice in the end.

Southern immigrants, particularly "a genuine African, or one of African descent, who knows nothing of our courts of law," provided especially rich material. Characterized as polite but ignorant, they supposedly called the judge "General" and the clerk "Yer Honor." One recently freed slave was cast as a "comical negro witness" who, when asked of his past, said he was a slave in Virginia, but "I'se my own nigger now! The free darkey shook his sides with laughter . . . many of the court officers and spectators involuntarily joined him."[53] What the court officials, spectators, and court reporter missed, however, was the import of this former slave's public declaration: a person whose place in society had been rigidly defined now stood in a place that represented the law, which enabled him to declare he was indeed his own person.

The reaction of the court officials and spectators to the freedman's assertion that he was now his own man spoke to the uneasiness many whites felt about free people of color asserting rights and citizenship—claiming a place in the polity. Because whites were not willing to undermine the law by denying this man the right to testify, laughing at the "free darkey" served to assuage, but not erase, discomfort with African Americans' ability to make a place within such an important social institution as the law.[54]

In the antebellum era, entering the courtroom to manage daily life sometimes became something of a two-edged sword. The black man attacked on Ann Street benefited from being able to punish his assailants, but he and other African Americans who came to court—which was intended to be accessible—attracted unwanted attention that contributed to the construction of whiteness through the continued stereotyping of black men and women.

Space and place in a society are rarely disconnected from expressions of power. At the same time African Americans settled in the space they had worked themselves into, a response to black participation in the social, economic, and political life of the polity developed. Northern antebellum society as a whole steadily rearranged what David Delaney calls "spatial configurations" in ways that constructed and buttressed developing notions of race and racial hierarchy. African Americans in northern states faced early attempts to erect de facto and de jure forerunners to Jim Crow. Since "spatial configurations are not incidental to power relations such as those predicated on race but are integral to them," it is not surprising that when African Americans became a significant presence in the courtroom, the place they had made eventually fell under assault.[55] Reconstructing the courtroom and legal system in such a way that denied African

Americans access would have been too blatant a violation of fundamental under-standings of the alleged impartiality of the law—that very impartiality helped maintain order through its assurance that reasonable prospects of justice existed for everyone.[56] The place that African Americans made in the courtroom could not be lost, but ability to use that space to resist power could itself be resisted through the inscription of racist meaning onto black court activity, thus rein-forcing the racial relations of power. Cultural tools like the court reports could be brought to bear, tools that never questioned African Americans' place in the courtroom but tried to render the place they claimed a laughable, ridiculous, and hopefully harmless site of black activity. Nonetheless, for African Americans, especially the non-elite, courtrooms continued to be a place in which they could at least attempt to ease the difficult circumstances facing black women and men in the urban North.

NOTES

1. *Synix v. Rouse,* January 6, 1824, Boston Police Court Docket books. Located in the office of the Clerk of Criminal Courts for Suffolk County. Venus Synix's last name is vari-ously spelled as Synex and Sinex.

2. *Synix v. Bowers,* August 31, 1819, in *Criminal Actions from June 3 1819 to November 6 1820*, from the record book of Justice of the Peace Stephen Gorham (located in the Rare Books Room of the Boston Public Library). This book and eight others, documenting cases from April 1806 to November 1820 (except for one missing book covering October 1816 through January 1818), are part of the Addlow Collection in the Rare Books Room of the Boston Public Library. The statistical analysis of African Americans' court appear-ances in the Gorham record books is presented in much greater detail in Scott Hancock, "'The Law Will Make You Smart': Legal Consciousness, Rights Rhetoric, and African American Identity Formation in Massachusetts, 1641–1855," Ph.D. diss., University of New Hampshire, 1999. There is no pagination of these record books, therefore all refer-ences will be according to date. *Synix v. Bowers,* September 9, 1919, 129, *Boston Municipal Court Record Books* (located at the Massachusetts State Archives). On the courts' focus on vice, see Theodore Ferdinand, *Boston's Lower Criminal Courts, 1814–1850* (Newark: University of Delaware Press, 1992), 23; William J. Novak, *The People's Welfare: Law and Regulation in Nineteenth-Century America* (Chapel Hill: University of North Carolina Press, 1996), 149–189. Novak argues for greater continuity in the policing and governance of public morality from the colonial era through the early republic era instead of seeing the efforts of Boston mayor Josiah Quincy and others as an era of new reforms.

3. Nigel Thrift, "Space: The Fundamental Stuff of Human Geography," in *Key Concepts in Geography*, ed. Sarah L. Holloway, Stephen P. Rice, and Gill Valentine (Thousand Oaks, CA: Sage Publications, 2003), 96.

4. Cindi Katz, "Social Formations: Thinking About Society, Identity, Power, and Resistance," in *Key Concepts in Geography*, 252.

5. Photographs of the courthouse and the Tudor building are in *Old Boston in Early Photographs, 1850–1918: 174 Prints from the Collection of the Bostonian Society* (New York:

Dover Publications, 1990), 11, 37. According to an 1821 tax list, Stephen Gorham's office was at the courthouse on Court Street. Likewise, the Boston Directory lists his office at 6 Court Street until 1809. The 1813 directory, however, has Gorham's office in the Tudor building. It makes sense that he would have relocated to be immediately adjacent to the new courthouse. The tax list may have been noting the general location, whereas his office is recorded as being in the Tudor building in the 1813, 1816, 1818, and 1820 directories. Tax list in *At a Legal Meeting of Freeholders and Other Inhabitants of the Town of Boston . . . a correct list stating the amount of Real and Personal Estate on which the Inhabitants of the Town have been valued, doomed, assessed and taxed for the year 1821 . . .* (Boston: True & Greene, 1822). Locations of the courthouse and jail were also determined from John G. Hales's 1814 map of Boston, which, along with the tax list and Boston Directory, is in the Massachusetts State House Library.

6. Novak, *The People's Welfare*, 117.

7. Ibid., 117; David Delaney, *Race, Place, and the Law, 1836–1948* (Austin: University of Texas Press, 1998); Steve Pile and Michael Keith, eds., *Geographies of Resistance* (New York: Routledge, 1997).

8. Donald S. Moore, "Remapping Resistance: 'Ground for Struggle' and the Politics of Place," in *Geographies of Resistance*, 87–106; Delaney, *Race, Place, and the Law*.

9. See Joyce Appleby, *Capitalism and a New Social Order: The Republican Vision of the 1790s* (New York: New York University Press, 1984); Morton J. Horwitz, *The Transformation of American Law, 1780–1860* (Cambridge, MA: Harvard University Press, 1977); James Willard Hurst, *The Law and Conditions of Freedom in the Nineteenth-Century United States* (Madison: University of Wisconsin Press, 1956).

10. The justice-of-the-peace record books and the Boston Police Court record books noted African Americans as black, colored, or mulatto. During the 1830s, however, the Police Court gradually stopped consistently noting the race of litigants, which makes it virtually impossible to calculate the percentage of black litigants. Anecdotal information from newspaper accounts (see later discussion) and other sources indicates that black litigants remained common. Courts stopped noting race probably because the overall volume of cases began increasing markedly, and the court recorders began putting as little information as possible in the dockets.

11. Thomas Paine, *Common Sense*, ed. Isaac Kramnick (New York: Penguin, 1986), 98.

12. Zippora's case is in Suffolk Court Files v. 5, Reel 3, case 605; Adam's case is in Suffolk Court Files, v. 55, Reel 30, File 5542, and v. 59, Reel 31, File 5941; all housed at the Massachusetts State Archives. For more on both cases as well as many others, see Hancock, "'The Law Will Make You Smart,'" chapter 1; William D. Piersen, *Black Yankees: The Development of an Afro-American Subculture in Eighteenth Century New England* (Amherst: University of Massachusetts Press, 1988), 134–135; Shane White, "'It Was a Proud Day': African Americans, Festivals, and Parades in the North, 1741–1834," *Journal of American History* 81 (June 1994): 13–50. On popular political expression, see Gordon Wood, *The Radicalism of the American Revolution* (New York: Vintage Books, 1991), 287–305; James Oliver Horton and Lois E. Horton, *In Hope of Liberty: Culture, Community, and Protest Among Northern Free Blacks, 1700–1860* (New York: Oxford University Press, 1997), 162–170; Paul A. Gilje, *The Road to Mobocracy: Popular Disorder in New York City, 1763–1834* (Chapel Hill: University of North Carolina Press, 1987). On disturbances and reform tar-

geting Boston's black areas, see Edward H. Savage, *Boston Events: A Brief Mention and the Dates of More Than 5,000 Events That Transpired in Boston from 1630 to 1880* (Boston: Tolman & White, 1884), 131.

13. Shane White, *Stories of Freedom in Black New York* (Cambridge, MA: Harvard University Press, 2002), 10–24; Allen Steinberg, *The Transformation of Criminal Justice: Philadelphia, 1800–1880* (Chapel Hill: University of North Carolina Press, 1989), 21, 258; quotation from Roger Lane, *The Roots of Violence in Black Philadelphia, 1860–1900* (Cambridge, MA: Harvard University Press, 1986), 87.

14. White, "'It Was a Proud Day,'" 15–16. On African Americans using parades and other means to claim a place in the polity, David Waldstreicher makes an argument similar to White's; see Waldstreicher, *In the Midst of Perpetual Fetes: The Making of American Nationalism, 1776–1820* (Chapel Hill: University of North Carolina Press, 1997), 294–348.

15. For an excellent collection of essays on the connections between race, identity, and nationality in the United States during this era, see Michael A. Morrison and James Brewer Stewart, eds., *Race and the Early Republic: Racial Consciousness and Nation-building in the Early Republic* (Lanham, MD: Rowman & Littlefield, 2002).

16. John C. Davis, *The Massachusetts Justice: A Treatise upon the Powers and Duties of Justices of the Peace, with Copious forms* (Worcester, MA: W. Lazell, 1847), 69; similar descriptions are given in Samuel Freeman, *The Massachusetts Justice: Being a Collection of the Laws of the Commonwealth of Massachusetts, Relative to the Power and Duty of Justices of the Peace* (Boston: I. Thomas and E. T. Andrews, 1802); Rodolphus Dickinson, *A Digest of the Common Law, the Statute Laws of Massachusetts, and of the United States, and the Decisions of the Supreme Judicial Court of Massachusetts, Relative to the Powers and Duties of Justices of the Peace, to which is subjoined an extensive Appendix of Forms* (Deerfield, MA: John Wilson, 1818).

17. *Green v. Pendleton* and *Green v. Clayton*, October 9, 1811, and *Green v. Nickelson*, April 23, 1812, in Gorham, *Criminal Actions from August 11 1810 to July 18 1812*; *Green v. Porter Tidd* and *Green v. Betsey Tidd*, October 8, 1812, in Gorham, *Criminal Actions from July 19 1812 to November 24 1813*; *Green v. Hunt*, January 25, 1814, in Gorham, *Criminal Actions from November 24 1813 to June 28 1815*.

18. George Hugh Crichton, *Old Boston and Its Once Familiar Faces: Sketches of Some Odd Characters Who Have Flourished in Boston During the Past Fifty Years* (unpublished manuscript, 1881, located at the Boston Athenæum); Savage, *Boston Events*, 39. The first record I have found of George Reed arresting a black defendant is dated 1812, and in 1838 Charles Pinckney Sumner, Boston's sheriff, instructed Reed to select three other constables to staff the session of the Municipal Court. Charles Pinckney Sumner Papers, box 3, Letterbox, March 3, 1838.

19. David Thomas Konig, *Law and Society in Puritan Massachusetts: Essex County, 1629–1692* (Chapel Hill: University of North Carolina Press, 1979), 5; Charles Pinckney Sumner Papers, box 1, "Miscellany," Massachusetts Historical Society; Piersen, *Black Yankees*.

20. Konig, *Law and Society in Puritan Massachusetts*, 69.

21. Ibid., xiv–xv. William Nelson also notes that the courts became the primary method of dispute resolution. See William E. Nelson, *Dispute and Conflict Resolution in Plymouth County, Massachusetts, 1725–1825* (Chapel Hill: University of North Carolina Press, 1981).

22. Konig, *Law and Society in Puritan Massachusetts*, 16; William E. Nelson, *Americanization of the Common Law: The Impact of Legal Change on Massachusetts Society, 1760–1830* (Athens: University of Georgia Press, 1994), 15.

23. Michael Stephen Hindus, *Prison and Plantation: Crime, Justice, and Authority in Massachusetts and South Carolina, 1767–1878* (Chapel Hill: University of North Carolina Press, 1980); Nelson, *Americanization of the Common Law*, 166. Comparison of three manuals written as guidebooks for justices of the peace indicates that even as late as 1847, the justice was expected to fulfill virtually the same function. Although these manuals give no suggestion as to how the types of cases brought to a justice of the peace may have changed over time, the justice-of-the-peace records that I use here clearly indicate a pattern consistent with this description of the justice's intended function of dealing with day-to-day disputes ranging from forgery to assault to AWOL sailors. The manuals are Freeman, *The Massachusetts Justice*; Dickinson, *A Digest of the Common Law*; Davis, *The Massachusetts Justice*.

24. Crichton, *Old Boston and Its Once Familiar Faces*, n.p.

25. *A Volume of Records Relating to the Early History of Boston Containing Boston Town Records, 1814–1822* (Boston: Municipal Printing Office, 1906), 40–41; Theodore Ferdinand, *Boston's Lower Criminal Courts, 1814–1850* (Newark: University of Delaware Press, 1992), 34.

26. Barbara Yngvesson and Lynn Mather, "Courts, Moots, and the Disputing Process," in *Empirical Theories About Courts*, ed. Keith Boyum and Lynn Mather (New York: Longman, 1983), 51–83, 73; and Yngvesson and Mather, "Language, Audience, and the Transformation of Disputes," *Law and Society Review* 15 (1980–1981): 775–821, 796.

27. Gorham, *Criminal Actions from April 11 1806 to July 15 1807*; *Criminal Actions from July 16 1807 to November 18 1808*; *Criminal Actions from November 19 1808 to August 10 1810*; *Criminal Actions from August 11 1810 to July 18 1812*; *Criminal Actions from July 19 1812 to November 24 1813*; *Criminal Actions from November 24 1813 to June 28 1815*; *Criminal Actions from June 28 1815 to September 2 1816*; *Criminal Actions from February 2 1818 to June 2 1819*; *Criminal Actions from June 3 1819 to November 6 1820*.

28. Christine Stansell, *City of Women: Sex and Class in New York, 1789–1860* (New York: Alfred A. Knopf, 1986), 41, 57–58. "Community," as I use it here, is clearly not synonymous with harmony but connotes multiple and continuing layers of relationships.

29. *Fitch v. Bishop*, August 11, 1806, in Gorham, *Criminal Actions from April 11 1806 to July 15 1807*.

30. "Conviction" may not be the most accurate term. Included in this category in this table are all adverse verdicts against a defendant. Certain charges, such as threatening, apparently fell into a different category, as Gorham did not fine defendants he deemed guilty but ordered defendants to provide a surety, ostensibly for the purpose of keeping the peace for an unstated period. When defendants could not or would not provide this surety, however, they went to jail, as did defendants who did not pay fines when other types of charges, such as assault, were "proved."

31. Marc Galanter, "Why the 'Haves' Come Out Ahead: Speculations on the Limits of Legal Change," *Law and Society Review* 9 (Fall 1974): 95–148.

32. *Hutchinson v. Hunt* and *Clapp v. Hunt*, February 26, 1818, in Gorham, *Criminal Actions from February 2 1818 to June 2 1819*.

33. Nell Irvin Painter, "Comment," in *The State of Afro-American History: Past, Present, and Future* (Baton Rouge: Louisiana State University Press, 1986), 88. Painter's "Comment" was in response to an essay in the same volume by Armstead L. Robinson, "The Difference Freedom Made: The Emancipation of Afro-Americans," 51–74 (emphasis in original). For similar arguments, see also Clarence Walker, *Deromanticizing Black History: Critical Essays and Reappraisals* (Knoxville: University of Tennessee Press, 1991); Evelyn Brooks Higginbotham, "African-American Women's History and the Metalanguage of Race," *Signs* 17 (Winter 1992): 251–274; James Oliver Horton and Lois E. Horton, *Free People of Color: Inside the African American Community* (Washington, DC: Smithsonian Institution Press, 1993); on not overestimating African Americans' successes, see Patrick Rael, *Black Identity and Black Protest in the Antebellum North* (Chapel Hill: University of North Carolina Press, 2002), 21.

34. *A Volume of Records Relating to the Early History of Boston*, 40–41. The selectmen proposed a Police Court for this reason in 1815. Also see chapter 2 of Hancock, "'The Law Will Make You Smart,'" 17.

35. Ferdinand, *Boston's Lower Criminal Courts*, 9–17; Ball Fenner, *Raising the Veil; or Scenes in the Courts* (Boston: J. French, 1856), 26–28.

36. Michael Stephen Hindus, *Prison and Plantation: Crime, Justice, and Authority in Massachusetts and South Carolina, 1767–1878* (Chapel Hill: University of North Carolina Press, 1980), xxii; on Quincy and others who viewed Boston's courts as a useful tool for social reform, see Ferdinand, *Boston's Lower Criminal Courts*.

37. Quote from the *Boston Patriot* appeared in *The Liberator*, February 26, 1831; Crichton, "Big Dick, King of Darkies," in *Old Boston and Its Once Familiar Faces*.

38. In 1825 alone, Cephas appeared eleven times in court. See Boston Police Court Dockets, located at the Massachusetts Supreme Judicial Court Archives.

39. *Selections from the Court Reports Originally Published in the* Boston Morning Post, *from 1834 to 1837* (Boston: Otis, Broaders, & Co., 1837), 173–174.

40. "Free Negroes and Mulattoes," *Massachusetts Legislative Documents 1817–1822*, House No. 46 (located at the Massachusetts State House Library, Special Collections); George Levesque, *Black Boston: African American Life and Culture in Urban America, 1750–1860* (New York: Garland, 1994), 384.

41. *Boston Municipal Court Record Books*, November 1835.

42. Fenner, *Raising the Veil*, 121–122.

43. Steinberg, *The Transformation of Criminal Justice*, 18. Ball Fenner mentions spectators in Boston's courtrooms in *Raising the Veil*.

44. Crichton, *Old Boston and Its Once Familiar Faces*, chapter 1. W. Jeffrey Bolster describes head-butting among black sailors from New England to Brazil in *Black Jacks: African American Seamen in the Age of Sail* (Cambridge, MA: Harvard University Press, 1997), 119–120; also, David A. Cercere has documented white Union soldiers from New England being entertained by head-butting black soldiers during the Civil War. See Cercere, "Carrying the Home Front to War: Soldiers, Race, and New England Culture During the Civil War," in *Union Soldiers and the Northern Home Front: Wartime Experiences, Postwar Adjustments* (New York: Fordham University Press, 2002).

45. Piersen, *Black Yankees*, 122–123; Joseph P. Reidy, "'Negro Election Day' and Black Community Life in New England, 1750–1860," *Marxist Perspectives* 1 (Fall 1978): 102–117;

Crichton, "Big Dick, King of Darkies"; David Roediger, *The Wages of Whiteness: Race and the Making of the American Working Class* (New York: Verso, 1991), 101; White, " 'It Was a Proud Day,' " 17.

46. *Freedom's Journal,* March 14, 1828; Gary Nash, *Forging Freedom: The Formation of Philadelphia's Black Community, 1720–1840* (Cambridge, MA: Harvard University Press, 1988), 253–259.

47. *Selections from the Court Reports,* 135–137.

48. Robert C. Toll, *Blacking Up: The Minstrel Show in Nineteenth-Century America* (New York: Oxford University Press, 1974), 27–32, 68; Eric Lott, *Love and Theft: Blackface Minstrelsy and the American Working Class* (New York: Oxford University Press, 1993), 20–21; Edward H. Savage, *A Chronological History of the Boston Watch and Police, from 1631 to 1865; Together with the Recollections of a Boston Police Officer, or Boston by Daylight and Gaslight* (Boston: Edward H. Savage, 1865), 73 (emphasis in original); Crichton, "Old Province House," *Old Boston and Its Once Familiar Faces.* The "Jim Crow Rice" that Savage mentioned was undoubtedly Thomas D. Rice, whom Toll credits with creating and popularizing "jump Jim Crow."

49. I adapt the concept of law as public process and the resulting need for public access from Susan Silbey and Patricia Ewick, "The Architecture of Authority: The Place of Law in the Space of Science," in *The Place of Law,* ed. Austin Sarat, Lawrence Douglas, and Martha Merrill Umphrey (Ann Arbor: University of Michigan Press, 2003), 87; on the law's need to render real justice as a part of maintaining legal hegemony, see Douglas Hay, "Property, Authority, and the Criminal Law," in *Albion's Fatal Tree: Crime and Society in Eighteenth-Century England* (New York: Pantheon, 1975), 3–64; and E. P. Thompson, *Whigs and Hunters: The Origin of the Black Act* (New York: Pantheon, 1975).

50. *Selections from the Court Reports,* 25 (emphasis in original); on the ongoing racial formation in the North, see George M. Fredrickson, *The Black Image in the White Mind: The Debate on Afro-American Character and Destiny, 1817–1914* (New York: Harper & Row, 1971), especially 97–129; on the role of minstrel shows in racial formation, see Lott, *Love and Theft,* and Roediger, *The Wages of Whiteness.*

51. *Selections from the Court Reports,* 92–93.

52. Ibid., 158.

53. Ibid., 87 (emphasis in original); Fenner, *Raising the Veil,* 238.

54. Lott, *Love and Theft,* 6.

55. Delaney, *Race, Place, and the Law,* 7.

56. Hay, "Property, Authority, and the Criminal Law"; Thompson, *Whigs and Hunters.*

Derrick E. White

"Liberated Grounds"

The Institute of the Black World and Black Intellectual Space

> An embattled, colonized people need liberated grounds on which to
> gather, to reflect, to learn, to publish, to move towards self-definition
> and self-determination.
>
> VINCENT HARDING[1]

In the last decade, Black academics have been increasingly visible in the public
arena. Black scholars, both liberal and conservative, have made regular appear-
ances in the op-ed sections of major newspapers and on talk shows and have
recently produced a rap CD. The public activism of Black intellectuals is by no
means a new phenomenon; Ida B. Wells-Barnett, Mary Church Terrell, and Anna
J. Cooper helped to found the National Association of Colored Women (NACW)
in 1896; Alexander Crummell established the American Negro Academy in
1897; and W.E.B. Du Bois helped to found the National Association for the
Advancement of Colored People in 1909. The complex relationship between
political activism and scholarly and artistic production demonstrated by Black
intellectuals represents the two antagonistic poles of Black intellectual life:
hyperpoliticalization and depoliticization. Although both characterizations are
extremes, they represent an agonizing attempt of intellectuals to deal with their
social marginality. Finding creative methods of overcoming this marginality has

been a central goal in creating Black intellectual space. As exemplified by the legacies of Wells-Barnett, Terrell, Crummell, Du Bois, and others, Black intellectual work more often than not took place outside the university.[2]

In the post–civil rights era, Black intellectuals' ties to academia have complicated the development of intellectual space and raised serious critiques about the effectiveness of this relationship. Public intellectuals, both Black and White, have been the subjects of serious scholarly debate in the last two decades. Although most of the scholarship focuses on White public intellectuals, most can be applied to Black intellectuals, as the debates revolve around the quality of their intellectual production. Russell Jacoby argues that academia has reduced the independence of earlier nonacademic scholars who educated the public on complex issues. More recently, Richard Posner argues the lures of celebrity undermine the intellectual integrity and quality of a new generation of public intellectuals. The commentary on Black scholars, from both the left and the right, uses similar terms, as seen in the 2002 controversy surrounding Cornel West. Conservatives have referred to West as a "clownish minstrel" who wallows in victimization, and radicals worry that public intellectuals, such as West, have avoided both rigorous intellectual scholarship and "committed political action."[3]

Princeton University's hiring of Cornel West from Harvard University underscores the desirability of many Black public intellectuals. The circumstances surrounding West's departure, however, raise questions about the viability of the university setting for politicized Black intellectuals. While at Harvard, West had a public feud with Harvard University president Lawrence Summers, much of which played out in the pages of the *New York Times*. During a private meeting between the two, Summers criticized West for his public actions, grade inflation, and a lack of scholarly production, citing his rap CD. West felt "disrespected" and eventually accepted a position in Princeton University's African American Studies program in 2002. The criticism by Summers and the movement of West, Michael Eric Dyson, and other Black intellectuals to various universities suggest a social marginality between Black intellectuals and the predominately White universities that house them. Black scholars at elite universities have done little to create a space outside of the university to conduct their politicized intellectual activities and promote their independent thoughts. They have yet to use their success or publicity as a basis to launch an independent institution in search of new ideas and perspectives that would reduce their marginality to the Black community.[4]

Black public intellectuals' politicized activities reflect a desire to reduce the space between themselves and the Black community. The failure to create an independent space, however, has had profound political consequences. Black progressives have been losing the war of ideas with the conservative ideologues. One cause is the lack of independent liberal think tanks, Black or otherwise.

Conservatives, on the other hand, have funneled millions of dollars into independent think tanks, such as the Heritage Foundation. These conservative think tanks attempt to shape the perception of issues to fit within a mold. The books produced and supported by these think tanks, according to an article in the *Nation*, were "directed at a mass audience and received funding and support from conservative sources that understood the fundamental importance of the battle of ideas." Considering the importance of the dissemination of ideas, the question that remains is, where are the Black think tanks? Where are the locations in which independent Black thought and discourse can come together and continue the task left by the Black Power era to shape the world anew? A model for independent Black thought outside the university was the Institute of the Black World (IBW). This organization created a Black intellectual space removed from the day-to-day rigors of the movement and various ideological strains that characterized Black radicalism in the late 1960s and early 1970s. It provided space for activists from across the diaspora to explore and analyze the Black experience and, most importantly, prescribe solutions to these problems. More importantly, the Institute of the Black World represented the importance of ideas in the Black Power era; this is reflected in IBW's origins with the "Black University" project at historically Black colleges, its separation from the King Center, and its accomplishments as an independent organization during the 1970s.[5]

THE IMPORTANCE OF IDEAS DURING THE BLACK POWER ERA

A key but often-overlooked component of the Black Power era was a search for new ideas. Historians of the era have focused on the development of Black Nationalism and racial separatism, the organizations, conflicts between cultural nationalists and political nationalists, and the idea of violence, in terms of both self-defense and liberatory violence. As a result, little attention has been paid to the ideas of Black Power aside from the debate between the cultural and political nationalist. However, guiding figures of the era, including Malcolm X, Frantz Fanon, and Kwame Ture (Stokely Carmichael), all promoted their ideas within a framework of searching for new interpretations.[6]

Malcolm X's complexity has led scholars and activists to promote a variety of interpretations of the importance and meaning of his life.[7] Malcolm X even understood his complexity, stating his life was "a chronology of—*changes*."[8] As he made the transition from hustler to Nation of Islam minister to revolutionary nationalist, he was searching for ideas and new interpretations that best describe reality. In Malcolm X's 1964 "Ballot or the Bullet" speech, he makes this point:

> The entire civil-rights struggle needs a new interpretation, a broader interpretation. We need to look at this civil-rights thing from another angle—from the

inside as well as from the outside. To those of us whose philosophy is black nationalism, the only way you can get involved in the civil-rights struggle is to give it a new interpretation. That old interpretation excluded us. It kept us out. So, we're giving a new interpretation that will enable us to come into it, take part in it.[9]

If Malcolm X is the paradigm for Black Power, as suggested by historian William Van DeBurg, then it is in terms of a search for new interpretations of reality and the importance of those interpretations in social action. The call for new interpretations during the 1960s also emanated from across the African diaspora.[10]

Martinican psychiatrist and Algerian revolutionary Frantz Fanon emphasized new interpretations, and his perspective lends credence to a need to understand Black Power as a search for new ideas. Scholars have placed considerable focus on Fanon's discussion of the emancipatory and therapeutic potential of violence and its impact on the Black Power era.[11] However, Fanon concluded *The Wretched of the Earth* by demanding a new interpretation history, turning "over a new leaf," and working out "new concepts."[12] Although some Black Power advocates during the 1960s used Fanon's philosophy on violence, others also took up his challenge to create new concepts.

Kwame Ture and Charles V. Hamilton's *Black Power: The Politics of Liberation* epitomized Black Power's concern with new interpretations. According to the authors, the book offers "no pat formulas . . . for ending racism," nor does it present a timetable for freedom. The book reinterpreted the civil rights era, as suggested by Malcolm X and Fanon. They introduced institutionalized racism into the discourse on racism, as an attempt to move beyond overt racist acts and to discuss the de jure segregation that continued after the 1964 Civil Rights Act. Moreover, they believed that Black people must "redefine" themselves. According to Ture and Hamilton, Black Power "is a call for black people to begin to define their own goals, to lead their own organizations and to support those organizations. It is a call to reject the racist institutions and values of the society." A new interpretation of Black life would then, as suggested by Malcolm, Fanon, and Ture, lead to new political understanding. The essential piece in Black Power is not only Black Nationalism, but also the process of developing new ideas.[13]

The call for new ideas and new interpretations by leading advocates of Black Power was predicated on an understanding between ideas and action. These intellectuals understood that the dominant interpretations of Blacks shaped perceptions and subsequently shaped actions toward the Black community. Historian Richard Waswo locates the importance of an interpretive frame that marginalizes Black and indigenous peoples by arguing that the founding historical interpretation of Western civilization—the descent from Troy—"shaped the actual behavior of Europeans and Americans in their subsequent contact with other, newly 'discovered' cultures" as the historical narrative determined consciousness and controlled perception. The Black intellectual tradition acknowledged this relationship, which was articulated most clearly by Carter G. Woodson. He stated in his classic, *The Mis-Education of the Negro*:

> No systematic effort toward change has been possible, for, taught the same economics, history, philosophy, literature and religion which have established the present code of morals, the Negro's mind has been brought under the control of his oppressor. The problem of holding the Negro down, therefore, is easily solved. When you control a man's thinking you do not have to worry about his actions. You do not have to tell him to stand here or go yonder. He will find his "proper place" and will stay in it. He will go without being told. In fact, if there is no back door, he will cut one for his special benefit. His education makes it necessary.

Therefore, this search for new ideas would work to subvert those existing ideologies that had perpetuated the subordinate position of African descendants in the world.[14]

It is no shock that the demand for new interpretations looked at the university system as an essential location for debate. According to Black Power theorists, developing and disseminating the new interpretation were the responsibility of intellectuals. Ture and Hamilton argued that Blacks were to "raise hard questions" and intellectuals were to challenge "long-standing values, beliefs and institutions." Moreover, Black intellectuals had a responsibility to lead the process of redefinition and uproot the "cultural terrorism" of whites. Black Power intellectuals were determined to attack the distorted scholarship of White imperialism, challenge the social myths, and argue for the Black intellectual to attach himself to the Black community.[15]

FOUNDING INSTITUTE OF THE BLACK WORLD

The process of redefining the Black experience was clearly articulated at historically Black colleges and universities in their demands for a "Black University." A series of protests in 1967–1968 at Howard University led to students demanding that the university redefine its curriculum to promote a positive Black identity, which would lead to Black liberation.[16] Leading scholars on the Black experience held a conference, "Toward the Black University," in fall 1968 at Howard University. In a 1968 issue of *Negro Digest*, scholars debated the attributes, feasibility, and purpose of the Black University. Sociologist Gerald McWorter (later Abdul Alkalimat) declared that the concept of Blackness itself forces the university to make the Afro-American community the focus of its endeavors. The goal of the Black University, according to McWorter, "must be one of service to the community." Historian Vincent Harding and literary critic Stephen Henderson reiterated this idea with Harding adding that any proposed Black University must address the Black diaspora and Stephen Henderson suggesting that a Black University be established in highly Black-populated areas, such as Atlanta, Washington, DC/Baltimore, and Durham/Raleigh, to address the concerns of the local Black communities.[17]

Black University supporters wanted to create a new perception or consciousness with a Black-centered curriculum or a field of Black Studies that provided a different interpretive framework on the United States and the world. The Black University and Black Studies programs sought to put the category of race at the center of research as the catalyst for policy and as the central mechanism in identity formation. Those demanding Black Studies proposed a separate or alternative academic interpretation, claiming the dominant mode of analyses reflected institutionalized racism. As sociologist St. Clair Drake suggested, Black Studies was a "counterideology." For Vincent Harding and Stephen Henderson, the "Toward the Black University" conference and development of Black Studies represented a continuation of ideas they had begun to develop since Martin Luther King's assassination in April 1968.[18]

King's assassination set forth a sequence of events that allowed Harding and Henderson to begin to institutionalize the ideas that grew out of their conversations and the Howard University conference. They had held many personal discussions about the direction of the Black Freedom Struggle and purpose of Black intellectuals as colleagues in the Atlanta University Center. Harding recalled the flood of Black consciousness that led to Henderson and him "having these long, long conversations about what it might be to develop something that we were then calling an Institute for Advanced African American Studies in the AU [Atlanta University] Center."[19] Harding, Henderson, and other faculty members at the Atlanta University Center proposed the W.E.B. Du Bois Institute for Advanced Afro-American Studies. The planned institute pushed

> toward the goals of assembling beneath one roof the most creative scholars, writers, and artists in all of the fields of Afro-American Studies in order that they may uncover and review neglected or unknown data on the Afro-American experience, created through their research, writing and performances new knowledge and works, and disseminated these materials to the Atlanta University Center Institutions, to adjacent communities and other educational institutions.[20]

After King's death, his family developed plans for the Martin Luther King Center, which would be a memorial, library, and archive of the Civil Rights Movement. Coretta Scott King named Vincent Harding to direct the center, and he believed that his idea for an institute on Black Studies would complement the plans.[21] After several discussions, the organizers decided to rename the W.E.B.

Du Bois Institute the Institute of the Black World because it was "more descriptive of [the] purpose."[22] Stephen Henderson remembered the initial objective of the institute was "to shape and give direction . . . to the Black Studies Movement."[23] Following the insights of Fanon, who viewed the native intellectual as a servant of the masses, IBW was "a gathering of black intellectuals who are convinced that the gifts of their minds are meant to be fully used in the service of the black community. It was therefore an experiment with scholarship in the context of struggle."[24]

The Institute of the Black World's connection with the King Center and location outside of the university system allowed it to lead a critical review of developing Black Studies programs. In summer 1969, IBW organized a Black Studies Directors Seminar, in which a task force of Black students, faculty, and others conducted interviews and examined documents from over 200 Black Studies programs. In November 1969, over thirty-five Department of Black Studies directors, along with IBW associates and several students, analyzed the results of the research and "attempted to identify that very small segment which seemed to hold some clear promise as possible models on which the thousands of Black students in northern schools could build in their movements toward an education appropriate to our struggle."[25] IBW associate, sociologist Joyce Ladner understood the significance of the space provided by the institute and Black Studies seminar. She declared:

> I think it is very important that you understand why we are here. Each of us could be any place else in these United States, but we are here because we intend to build an Institution that does not exist any place today. We are committed to building that Institution almost at all costs. I think the thing that distinguishes us from groups of black people who are scattered about elsewhere . . . is that as a group of black scholars, . . . we are building that Institution *together* even if we have to take care of ourselves, even if we have to experiment with various forms of communal living.[26]

In the conference's keynote address, *Ebony* magazine's Lerone Bennett captured the tone and gravity of the directors seminar. In his speech, "The Challenge of Blackness," Bennett envisioned IBW as "a center for defining, defending, and illustrating blackness." He also outlined how the institute would meet the challenge of Blackness through at least six different activities. First, IBW would begin the process of creating and collecting the data that formed the foundation of Black Studies, collecting items such as bibliographies, card indexes, books, and documents. Second, IBW would generate new concepts because Black researchers' eyes have been "clouded by the concepts of white supremacy." Bennett recognized that the concept of Blackness specifically questioned the values of American society. Out of these new concepts developed by the institute would emerge a new philosophy of education, which was the third level of the institute's challenge. Fourth, IBW would facilitate the creations of new "organic" intellectuals, "who would live and think within a perspective of blood and pain and want." The fifth activity was for emergent intellectuals to help institutionalize the Black experience, not only in the university but also in society in general. Last, the challenge of Blackness would lead the Institute of the Black World to redefine the American experience "in order to remake American society." Through these actions, the Black Studies Directors Seminar would establish the institute as a location for independent thought.[27]

After officially opening its doors in January 1970, the institute hosted intellectuals from across the diaspora. As Vincent Harding recalled, "[O]ne of the most important things . . . was trying to bring some of the elders out of, in many cases, their almost anonymity."[28] Black intellectuals such as Horace Cayton, St. Clair Drake, Sylvia Wynter, Walter Rodney, and C.L.R. James all spent time developing and analyzing the ideas and directions of the movement.[29]

To understand the significance of the coming together of this diverse group of intellectuals, one must remember that many of the individuals hosted by IBW came out of the Marxist tradition. During the post–World War II period and developing Cold War, the United States repressed many Blacks for their left-leaning views. Under the auspices of the House Un-American Activities Committee, Senator Joseph McCarthy destroyed the diaspora-based strategies developed out of the Ethiopian crisis and the Spanish Civil War by organizations such as the Council of African Affairs led by Paul Robeson. Historian Penny Von Eschen has pointed out that the Cold War created a new political language on civil rights, which "left no room for the internationalism that had characterized black American politics through the mid-1940s."[30] As a result of this shift in focus, domestic civil rights became the primary objective, forcing pan-Africanists such as Paul Robeson, W.E.B. Du Bois, and C.L.R. James out of the country or into isolation.[31] The space provided by the Institute of the Black World reconnected the pan-Africanist network that once dominated the intellectual horizons during the 1940s and connected the institute directly to the Black radical tradition.[32]

Cedric Robinson's *Black Marxism* identifies a Black radical tradition in which many Black intellectuals in the early twentieth century used Marxism as a "staging area" or a conduit into this tradition. Intellectuals such as Du Bois, James, and Drake recognized the limitations of Marxism, and as Robinson stated, "Marxism, the dominant form of the critique of capitalism in Western thought, incorporated theoretical and ideological weaknesses that stemmed from the same social forces that provided the bases of capitalist formation."[33] And Michel Foucault would observe, "Marxism introduced no real discontinuity; it found its place without difficulty. . . . Marxism exists in nineteenth-century thought like a fish in water: that is, it is unable to breathe anywhere else."[34] The Black radical tradition started with the critique of capitalism; however, it recognized that production was not the organizing principle of society; rather race and racial ideology were the mode of inclusion and exclusion and were mapped onto a capitalist structure. As Robinson states, the Black radical tradition was "the continuing development of a collective consciousness informed by the historical struggles for liberation and motivated by the shared sense of obligation to preserve the collective being, the ontological totality."[35] IBW embodied this tradition.

Even in the earliest conceptions of the institute, its founders believed the organization would analyze the direction of the Black Freedom Struggle as it sought an identity after the assassinations of Malcolm X in 1965 and Martin Luther King in 1968. The sanctuary for Black intellectuals and ideas provided by the IBW allowed for the exchange of ideas among intellectuals, activists, the university, and the community. The unique international and intergenerational combination can be seen in the institute's *Education and Black Struggle*, which included essays by Vincent Harding, C.L.R. James, St. Clair Drake, Grace Lee Boggs, Black prisoners, and Julius Nyerere.[36]

IBW'S SEPARATION FROM THE MARTIN LUTHER KING CENTER

The conglomeration of Black intellectuals from across the diaspora and from across the political spectrum caused friction with the newly founded Martin Luther King Center. In the wake of the assassination of Martin Luther King Jr., the nation, his family, and the Southern Christian Leadership Conference focused on his philosophy of nonviolence rather than on his biting criticism of the American social system and the Vietnam War.[37] Michael Eric Dyson points out that "when King began to say that racism was deeply rooted in our society and that only a structural change would remove it, he alienated key segments of the liberal establishment."[38] Therefore, the "I Have a Dream" speech became his lasting image, whereas King's marching with striking garbage workers in Memphis and organizing the Poor People's Campaign were relegated to the margins of his legacy. The sole focus on the philosophy of nonviolence contrasted sharply with the Institute of the Black World. Although IBW never advocated violence, it did support a variety of radical scholars whose commitment to nonviolence was at best strategic. Vincent Harding recalled years later, "[T]here was a tension because so much of the public image of King and the family's image of King, and some of his support's image, was King as the major integrationist and we were sounding non-integrationist by our Black World kind of thing."[39]

Almost from the very beginning, associates of the institute were worried about the connection with the King Center. William Strickland remarked on rumors that IBW was "a front for the man" because of the King Center board's ties to "the establishment." In addition, a financial crisis heightened the tension between IBW and the King family because both sides believed there would be an outpouring of financial support for the center after King's death. When only a fraction of the money materialized, both sides began to struggle for survival.[40]

Less than a year after the January 17, 1970, official opening of the institute, the King Center board formed an investigative committee and articulated their major concerns with the institute. The King Center board identified three fundamental issues in their complaints about IBW. First, the work and life of Martin Luther King Jr. were not a priority at the institute. Second, the institute made no public or overt commitment to nonviolence. Finally, the institute prohibited White scholars. These three issues led to the conclusion that "the Institute's purpose was not in harmony with the one adopted by the Center's Board."[41]

The Institute of the Black World analyzed and responded to each of the major critiques leveled by the committee appointed by the King Center, reflecting IBW's commitment to independent thought and ideas. IBW responded to the charge that King was not the focus of its work by pointing out that their "primary commitment and first priority must be to record, analyze, and forward the larger struggles of African peoples."[42] The pan-African perspective of IBW was beyond the King Center's narrow conception of hero worship. The institute emphasized the relationship between scholarship and politics, whereas the King Center wanted scholarship that honored the greatness of King and announced the successful conclusion of the Civil Rights Movement. To the second accusation, regarding a lack of commitment to King's philosophy of nonviolence, IBW responded by pointing out their commitment to the liberation of Blacks globally and stating that it could not "base its work on and demand loyalty to any one exclusive philosophy or strategy."[43] The interactions with scholars across the diaspora reiterated to the institute that no one philosophy or strategy can accurately describe or analyze the variety of situations facing the diaspora. The final accusation by the King Center committee against IBW was its exclusion of White scholars.[44] Yet, the Institute of the Black World believed that Black people must control and define their experience.[45] Overall, IBW challenged the liberal integrationists' image of King and the position of traditional civil rights organizations, which had shied away from the burgeoning Black Power and Black Consciousness Movements. The King Center board concluded that "the members of the panel have no doubt in their minds that the final authority to determine" the affairs of the institute, including staff, "must reside in the hands of the Board of Directors of the Martin Luther King, Jr. Center."[46] Thus, the Institute of the Black World lost its independence to the liberalism of the Martin Luther King Center. The only choice was separation from the King Center, which officially occurred on September 1, 1970.

The official separation from the King Center allowed the Institute of the Black World to accomplish its objectives. The independent infrastructure permitted the organization to become the "obstetrician" to Black Studies and the ideas of the Black Consciousness Movement.[47] Vincent Harding understood the importance of higher education to the entire social structure:

> Because the walls of the academy are, on the whole, merely more tastefully, delicately wrought extensions of the walls of the government, industry, and the military . . . it is not surprising that they too should now encompass part of the national army of cynical, despairing, increasingly frightened men and women. Indeed . . . these places reveal more vividly than ever the band of intellectual seekers who have forgotten their vocation.[48]

Building on this theme, the institute organized a Research Consortium on the Black Experience with Howard and Fisk Universities in late 1971. In addition, associates of IBW continued to make their presence felt at various conferences on Black Studies, and various Black Studies Departments continued to send students to Atlanta to study at the institute.[49] More importantly, the institute questioned the makeshift Black Studies programs that began across the country. Stephen Henderson recognized this, stating, "the notion of 'blackening' or 'blackenizing' courses . . . may mean as little as using 'black' examples to illustrate concepts irrelevant or inimical to black life to using traditional courses as a vehicle for black liberation."[50]

Although Black Studies remained a major focus, the organization began to move beyond the concerns of the university and to situate itself in the broader concerns of the "masses," eliminating the marginalization many Black academics faced. Black Studies was never the sole focus of the institute; however, the other objectives of the organization were underdeveloped in its first year of existence. The crisis and eventual separation from the King Center allowed IBW to improve its relationship to the community. William Strickland made this point clear in the internal reorganization document, arguing that IBW "has erred in restricting itself to academic education." Furthermore, he believed that revolutionary intellectuals must use their abilities in conjunction with the masses; they must become, in Walter Rodney's terms, "guerilla intellectuals."[51]

The Institute of the Black World began to "marry their thought" to the masses in various ways.[52] First, IBW created a bimonthly syndicated news column in over twenty Black newspapers. This column provided the institute's view on historic figures and contemporary events. The first column was on Malcolm X, whom the institute held as a model of transformation—a "New Black Man." The column was not about a specific political viewpoint that Malcolm had, an idea stressed by the institute, but "on a[n] overriding, powerful, personal and political methodology for change."[53] Malcolm modeled this methodology for change through self-criticism and self-education, which led to an embattled humanism.[54] Another column was on the rebellion at Attica State Prison in New York. The institute countered the dominant interpretation of the retaking of the prison by focusing on how the prisoners transformed their consciousness.[55] These columns began to establish the institute outside the walls of academia.

In addition to the newspaper columns, IBW was influential in drafting the introduction to the 1972 Gary Convention, which scholars and participants view as a monumental event in Black politics. For many activists, including Vincent Harding, the founding of the National Black Political Assembly was an event built on the legacies of the Civil Rights Movement and the subsequent calls for Black Power and Black Consciousness.[56] Vincent Harding, William Strickland, and Lerone Bennett created a draft for the introduction to the Gary Convention, which was based on the premise that "[t]he American system does not work for the masses of our people, and it cannot be made to work without radical fundamental change."[57] Associates of the Institute of the Black World used their expertise to articulate the position of transformation at the Gary Convention. The convention will be remembered for its Black Nationalist leaning, especially the dominant role of Amiri Baraka, but the introduction recognized "social transformation or social destruction" as the only choice.[58]

The institute continued its mission well into the 1970s; however, the economic and political realities of the decade made it extremely hard to maintain its influence. The decline of Black Studies, the political advancement of Black elected officials, and the economic crisis facing America reduced IBW to a shell of its former self. Vincent Harding noted that Black Studies had failed to continue to critique and analyze the American system; it failed to "press the critical issue of the relationship between Black people inside the university and those who will never make it; and many faculty were incorporated into the university politics of tenure and advancement."[59] As Jason Glenn recently pointed out, "Black Studies has become a quest for middle-class status without any questions of global politics that make the collective over-consumptive, resource wasting habits of the middle-class possible."[60]

Although the Gary Convention represented the high point of Black independent politics, its aftermath was the rise of Black elected officials. These officials often used the support of Black grassroots activists to win elections but when in office enacted moderate and sometimes damaging policies toward the Black community.[61] Moreover, the Gary Convention signaled the shift from the politics of mass demonstrations to electoral politics.[62] These elected officials played within the confines of legitimate electoral politics, which had little sociopolitical impact on Blacks in America's cities.[63]

The economic crisis of the 1970s put an extreme burden on Black America. Although the state institutionalized the social and economic position of the Black middle class throughout the decade with affirmative action, a majority of the Black population was hit hard by deindustrialization, the oil crisis, and high inflation. For the Institute of the Black World this meant their precarious financial situation worsened as the decade progressed. The institute had continued to ask for funds in their newsletter but, by May 1974, made a massive front-page appeal in *The Monthly Report*.[64] As it became clear the institute was pursuing transformative analysis and research, grant money, which had been sparse, all but dried up. To compensate for the lack of funds, the senior associates, such as Stephen Henderson, Vincent Harding, Robert Hill, and William Strickland, eventually took jobs in academia to alleviate the financial burden.[65] Their lack of permanent residence at the institute in Atlanta ended the collective scholarship that had made the institute a vibrant location for intellectual production. The lack of funds meant that the intellectual space was eventually lost. Vincent Harding remembered that the Institute of the Black World "became less and less a center for people who were in residence there and working and struggling with concepts, and became more of a resource center."[66]

The eventual closing of the Institute of the Black World in the early 1980s meant the total loss of an intellectual space in which scholars from across the diaspora could research, analyze, and create in an independent and collective environment. IBW's existence points to the importance Black activists placed in developing ideas. The institute and its personnel represented the Black radical tradition as intellectually it began to move beyond the confines of Black Nationalism and Marxism and tried to forge a new analytical perspective. In light of the successes of IBW, one is left to wonder why leading Black public intellectuals, such as Cornel West, Michael Eric Dyson, and bell hooks, do not try to create a location outside of the university structure. An independent Black organization could accomplish two major goals. First, it could reduce Black intellectual social marginality to the Black community. Second, it could begin to counter conservative ideas that have gained increasing strength in the last three decades. Any independent Black organizations will face an uphill battle, but the Institute of the Black World's history points to the possibilities, many of which cannot be found even in the Black Studies programs of elite universities.

NOTES

1. Vincent Harding, "Vocation of the Black Scholar," in *Education and Black Struggle: Notes from the Colonized World*, ed. Institute of the Black World (Cambridge, MA: Harvard Educational Review, 1974), 25.

2. Jerry Gafio Watts, *Heroism and the Black Intellectual: Ralph Ellison, Politics, and Afro-American Intellectual Life* (Chapel Hill: University of North Carolina Press, 1994), 11, 15.

3. Russell Jacoby, *The Last Intellectuals: American Culture in the Age of Academe* (New York: Basic Books, 1987); Richard Posner, *Public Intellectuals: A Study in Decline* (Cambridge, MA: Harvard University Press, 2001); John Donatich, Russell Jacoby, Jean Bethke Elshtain, Stephen Carter, Herbert Gans, Steven Johnson, and Christopher Hitchens, "The Future of the Public Intellectual: A Forum," *The Nation* 272, no. 6 (February 12, 2001): 25–35; William M. Banks, *Black Intellectuals: Race and Responsibility in American Life* (New York: W. W. Norton, 1995); Rod Dreher, "Harvard's Rapper: Cornel West Hits Bottom," *National Review Online,* January 4, 2002, http://www.nationalreview.com/dreher/dreher-print010402.html; Adolph Reed Jr., "What Are the Drums Saying, Booker?" *Village Voice*, April 11, 1995, 31–36.

4. David Abel, "Harvard 'Dream Team' Roiled: Black Scholars, Summers in Rift," *Boston Globe*, December 22, 2001, Metro A1; Jacques Steinberg, "At Odds with Harvard President, Black Studies Stars Eye Princeton," *New York Times*, December 29, 2001, A1; Kate Zernike, "Black Scholars Mending a Rift with Harvard," *New York Times,* January 4, 2002, A1; Pam Belluck, "Black Scholar Looks Beyond Mended Fence and Harvard," *New York Times*, January 10, 2002, A18; Kate Zernike, "Can Crying Race Be Crying Wolf?" *New York Times,* January 13, 2002, 4, 6; Michael Eric Dyson, "Ivy League Shuffle," *Savoy* 2, no. 7 (September 2002): 50; Tatsha Robertson, "Harvard Exodus," *The New Crisis* 109, no. 3 (May/June 2002): 23–27; Rosemary Cowan, "Cornel West and the Tempest in the Ivory Tower," *Politics* 24, no. 1 (February 2004): 72–78; Cornel West, *Democracy Matters: Winning the Fight Against Imperialism* (New York: Penguin, 2004), 190–200.

5. Manning Marable, "Knowledge, Power, and Black America," *The Columbus Free Press* (July 17, 1996); Manning Marable, "The Battle for Ideas," September 18, 1999, http://www.zmag.org/sustainers/content/1999-09/18marable.htm; Eric Alterman, "The 'Right' Books and Big Ideas," *The Nation* 269, no. 17 (November 22, 1999): 17; David Callahan, "$1 Billion for Conservative Ideas," *The Nation* 268, no. 15 (April 26, 1999): 21–23.

6. Clayborne Carson, *In Struggle: SNCC and the Black Awakening of the 1960s* (Cambridge, MA: Harvard University Press, 1981, 1996), 191–305; August Meier and Elliot Rudwick, *CORE: A Study in the Civil Rights Movement, 1942–1968* (New York: Oxford University Press, 1973); William Van DeBurg, *A New Day in Babylon: The Black Power Movement and American Culture, 1965–1975* (Chicago: University of Chicago Press, 1992); Komozi Woodard, *A Nation Within a Nation: Amiri Baraka (LeRoi Jones) and Black Power Politics* (Chapel Hill: University of North Carolina Press, 1999); Scot Brown, *Fighting for US: Maulana Karenga, the US Organization, and Black Cultural Nationalism* (New York: New York University Press, 2003); John T. McCartney, *Black Power Ideologies: An Essay in African-American Political Thought* (Philadelphia: Temple University Press, 1992), 116–121; Richard H. King, *Civil Rights and the Idea of Freedom* (New York: Oxford University Press, 1992), 172–200.

7. See Michael Eric Dyson, *Making Malcolm: The Myth and Meaning of Malcolm X* (New York: Oxford University Press, 1995), for a discussion of the variety of interpretations of Malcolm.

8. Malcolm X and Alex Haley, *The Autobiography of Malcolm X* (New York: Ballantine Books, 1965, 1992), 390.

9. Malcolm X, "The Ballot or the Bullet," in *Malcolm X Speaks: Selected Speeches and Statements*, ed. George Breitman (New York: Grove Press, 1966, 1990), 31.

10. William Van DeBurg, *New Day in Babylon*, 1–10.

11. See King, "Violence and Self-Respect: Fanon and Black Radicalism," in *Civil Rights and the Idea of Freedom*, 172–200.

12. Frantz Fanon, *The Wretched of the Earth* (New York: Grove Press, 1963), 315–316.

13. Stokely Carmichael and Charles V. Hamilton, *Black Power: The Politics of Liberation in America* (New York: Vintage Books, 1967, 1992), xv, 5, 44.

14. Richard Waswo, "The History That Literature Makes," *New Literary History* 19, no. 3 (Spring 1988): 541; Carter G. Woodson, *Mis-Education of the Negro* (Trenton, NJ: African World Press, 1933, 1993), xiii. See also Michael Allen Gillespie, *Hegel, Heidegger, and the Ground of History* (Chicago: University of Chicago Press, 1984), 1–24; Charles W. Mills, *The Racial Contract* (Ithaca, NY: Cornell University Press, 1997); Sylvia Wynter, "1492: A New World View," *Race, Discourse, and the Origin of the Americas*, ed. Vera Lawrence Hyatt and Rex Nettleford (Washington, DC: Smithsonian Institution Press, 1995), 5–57; Richard Waswo, *The Founding Legend of Western Civilization: From Virgil to Vietnam* (Middleton, CT: Wesleyan University Press, 1997).

15. Walter Rodney, *Groundings with My Brothers* (London: Bogle-L'Ouverture, 1975), 32.

16. Robert A. Malson, "The Black Power Rebellion at Howard University," *Negro Digest* (December 1967): 21–30; Rayford W. Logan, *Howard University: The First Hundred Years, 1867–1967* (New York: New York University Press, 1969), 509–511.

17. Gerald McWorter, "The Nature and Needs of the Black University," *Negro Digest* (March 1968): 9; Vincent Harding, "For Our People Everywhere: Some International Implications of the Black University," *Negro Digest* (March 1968): 36; Stephen Henderson, "The Black University: Towards Its Realization," *Negro Digest* (March 1968): 21–26.

18. St. Clair Drake, "Black Studies: Toward an Intellectual Framework," address delivered at Brooklyn College, September 23, 1969, quoted in Ronald Bailey, "Black Studies in Historical Perspective," *Social Issues* 29, no. 1 (1973): 104. See Kwame Ture and Charles V. Hamilton, *Black Power: The Politics of Liberation* (New York: Vintage, 1992), 4–5, for a discussion of institutionalized racism. Vincent Harding worked in the South as a part of the Mennonite Church and was a neighbor of Martin Luther King Jr. It was Harding who encouraged King to speak against the Vietnam War and even drafted King's first antiwar speech. Stephen Henderson attended Morehouse College in the 1940s and was a classmate of *Ebony* magazine editor Lerone Bennett. Gerald McWorter, now Abdul Alkalimat, was finishing his Ph.D. in sociology from the University of Chicago. At the time, all three men were teaching at the Atlanta University Center (AUC) and were active in trying to establish a Black Studies program at the center, which included Atlanta University, Clark College, Morehouse College, Spelman College, Morris Brown College, and the Interdenominational Theological Center. Derrick E. White, "New Concepts for the New Man: The Institute of the Black World and the Incomplete Victory of the Second Reconstruction," Ph.D. diss., Ohio State University, 2004, 52–100.

19. Rachel E. Harding, "Biography, Democracy and Spirit: An Interview with Vincent Harding," *Callaloo* 20, no. 3 (Summer 1997): 691.

20. Vincent Harding, Stephen Henderson et al., "To Fill This Immense Void: Proposal for the Creation of The W.E.B. Du Bois Institute for Advanced Afro-American Studies,

October 1968, 3, Institute of Black World Papers, Schomburg Center for Research in Black Culture (hereafter cited as IBW Papers). The Institute of the Black World Papers are not completely cataloged at the present time. I give special thanks to Andre Elizee for allowing me access to the papers.

21. Vincent Harding, "Introduction," in *IBW and Education for Liberation* (Chicago: Third World Press, 1973), v; E. Ethelbert Miller, "Stephen E. Henderson: A Conversation with a Literary Critic," in *A Howard Reader: An Intellectual and Cultural Quilt of the African American Experience*, ed. Paul E. Logan (Boston: Houghton Mifflin, 1997), 320.

22. The organizers were the Institute of the Black World Governing Council, which included Margaret Walker Alexander, Walter F. Anderson, Lerone Bennett, Horace Mann Bond, Robert Browne, John Henrik Clarke, Dorothy Cotton, Ossie Davis, St. Clair Drake, Katherine Dunham, Freddye Henderson, Vivian Henderson, Tobe Johnson, Julius Lester, Frances Lucas, Jesse Noel, Rene Piquion, Eleo Pomare, Pearl Primus, Benjamin Quarles, Bernice Reagon, William Strickland, Councill Taylor, E. U. Essien-Udom, C. T. Vivian, Charles White, and Hosea Williams. V. Harding, "Introduction," vi. The institute was not founded at the AUC because, like many Black colleges and universities, AUC believed they did not need a Black Studies program. They believed their Black faculty and expanded course offerings sufficed. See White, "New Concepts for the New Man," 76–92.

23. Miller, "Stephen E. Henderson," 320.

24. Institute of the Black World Statement of Purpose, *Negro Digest*, March 1970, 20; Frantz Fanon, *The Wretched of the Earth* (New York: Grove Press, 1963).

25. V. Harding, "Introduction," iii. Some attendees were Vincent Harding (IBW), Lerone Bennett (IBW and *Ebony*), Joyce Ladner (IBW and University of Southern Illinois), Chester Davis (IBW), William Strickland (IBW), Stephen Henderson (IBW), Sterling Stuckey (IBW), Robert Johnson (University of Indiana), Michael Thelwell (University of Massachusetts–Amherst), Robert S. Browne (IBW and Black Economics Research Center), Kwame McDonald (Livingstone College), and Boniface Obichere (University of Southern California). Alex Poinsett, "Think Tank for Black Scholars: Institute of the Black World Serves Liberation Movement," *Ebony* 25, no. 4 (February 1970): 46–54.

26. Institute of the Black World, "Introduction of Senior Research Fellows," *Institute of the Black World Directors Seminar* (Atlanta: Institute of the Black World, 1969), 7 (emphasis in original).

27. Lerone Bennett Jr., "The Challenge of Blackness," in *IBW and Education for Liberation*, 1, 2–8.

28. R. Harding, "Biography, Democracy, and Spirit."

29. Ibid., 692; V. Harding, "Vocation of the Black Scholar," 23–24.

30. Penny Von Eschen, *Race Against Empire: Black Americans and Anticolonialism, 1937–1957* (Ithaca, NY: Cornell University Press, 1997), 112.

31. Ibid., 167–184; Grace Lee Boggs, "C.L.R. James: Organizing in the U.S., 1938–1952," in *C.L.R. James: His Intellectual Legacies,* ed. Selwyn Cudjoe and William E. Cain (Amherst: University of Massachusetts Press, 1995), 163–172; C.L.R. James, *C.L.R. James on the "Negro Question,"* ed. Scott McLemee (Jackson: University Press of Mississippi, 1996).

32. Here I somewhat disagree with Von Eschen, who argues that activists of the 1960s were cut off from earlier generations and forced to "reinvent the wheel" in devel-

oping their own critique of capitalism and imperialism. I think that IBW modifies her conclusion, believing that the interactions among James, Cayton, and Drake nurtured the analysis of young activists such as Rodney, Hill, Wynter, and Harding. Although there was indeed some reinventing, there was a great deal of sharing among activists of different generations.

33. Cedric J. Robinson, *Black Marxism: The Making of the Black Radical Tradition* (Chapel Hill: University of North Carolina Press, 1983, 2000), 10.

34. Michel Foucault, *The Order of Things: An Archaeology of the Human Sciences* (New York: Vintage Press, 1970), 261–262.

35. Robinson, *Black Marxism*, 171.

36. Institute of the Black World, ed., *Education and Black Struggle: Notes from the Colonized World* (Cambridge, MA: Harvard Educational Review, 1974).

37. Michael Eric Dyson, *I May Not Get There with You: The True Martin Luther King, Jr.* (New York: Free Press, 2000).

38. Ibid., 32.

39. R. Harding, "Biography, Democracy and Spirit," 692.

40. Letter from William Strickland to Vincent Harding, July 16, 1969, IBW Papers.

41. "Report of the Staff of the Institute of the Black World," 7–9; "Report of the Committee Appointed to Evaluate the Institute of the Black World," 1, IBW Papers.

42. "To Our Friends, Associates and Companions in the Struggle: A Letter on Behalf of the Institute of the Black World Regarding the Current Crisis in the Martin Luther King, Jr. Memorial Center," 2, IBW Papers.

43. Ibid.

44. "Report of the Committee Appointed to Evaluate the Institute of the Black World," 5, IBW Papers.

45. V. Harding, "Vocation of the Black Scholar," 10.

46. "Report of the Committee Appointed to Evaluate the Institute of the Black World," 4–5, IBW Papers.

47. Miller, "Stephen E. Henderson," 320.

48. V. Harding, "Vocation of the Black Scholar," 4.

49. Institute of the Black World, *Inside the Black World: Newsletter of the Institute of the Black World* 1, no. 1 (April 1971), IBW Papers.

50. Stephen E. Henderson, "Toward a Black University," *Ebony* (September 1970): 21–26.

51. William Strickland, "Towards a Theory of a Scientific Direction," 6, 7, IBW Papers; Walter Rodney, *Walter Rodney Speaks: The Making of an African Intellectual* (Trenton, NJ: Africa World Press, 1990), 111–114.

52. Zygmunt Bauman, *Legislators and Interpreters* (Ithaca, NY: Cornell University Press, 1987), 179. Bauman states, "[T]he present day poor, who are not embourgeoisied, privatized or incorporated, are not trusted with the inheritance of historical agency; indeed they have not been offered one." This was recognized during the Black Power era and was reflected in the focus on the Black masses.

53. Institute of the Black World, "A New Black Man: The Meaning of Malcolm for the 70s," 2, 3, Hoyt Fuller Collection, Atlanta University Center Woodruff Library, Box 21, Folder 17.

54. David Scott uses the phrase "embattled humanism" in an interview with Sylvia Wynter. In referring to the *experience* of blackness, or colonialism, one begins to understand the dialectical nature of the European enterprise of humanism. Wynter responds: "And why I like that phrase [embattled humanism] is that, as Aimé Césaire says in his *Discourse on Colonialism*, 'They say I'm the enemy of Europe; where ever have I said that there can be any going back to *before* Europe?' So your idea of an embattled humanism precisely identifies the dilemma . . . you know that you cannot turn your back on that which the West has brought in since the fifteenth century. It's transformed the world, and central to that has been humanism. . . . So it is that embattled [humanism], one which challenges itself at the same time you're using it to think with." David Scott, "The Re-Enchantment of Humanism: An Interview with Sylvia Wynter," *Small Axe* 8 (September 2000): 153–154.

55. *IBW Monthly Report*, September 1971, University of Michigan Urban Affairs Vertical Files.

56. Manning Marable, *Race, Reform, and Rebellion: The Second Reconstruction in Black America, 1945–1990* (Jackson: University Press of Mississippi, 1991), 132.

57. *National Black Political Agenda: The Gary Declaration: Black Politics at the Crossroads*, "Introduction" (Washington, DC: National Black Political Convention, 1972), 2.

58. Ibid., 3.

59. Vincent Harding, "'A Long Hard Winter to Endure': Reflections of the Meaning of the 1970s," *The Black Collegian* 10, no. 2 (December 1979 / January 1980): 96–97.

60. Jason Glenn, "A Second Failed Reconstruction," *Journal of West Indian Literature* 10, nos. 1–2 (November 2001): 147.

61. Komozi Woodard, *A Nation Within a Nation: Amiri Baraka (Leroi Jones) and Black Power Politics* (Chapel Hill: University of North Carolina Press, 1999).

62. Darlene Clark Hine et al., *The African American Odyssey*, vol. 2 (Upper Saddle River, NJ: Prentice Hall, 2000), 546.

63. One can point to the continued deterioration of inner-city schools, as well as the persistence of poverty, although it has declined since the 1960s. In 2006, 13 percent of people were in poverty. Eighteen percent of related children under 18 were below the poverty level, compared with 10 percent of people 65 years old and over. Ten percent of all families and 29 percent of families with a female householder and no husband present had incomes below the poverty level. Using statistical measures and anecdotal evidence, one can see that the success of the Civil Rights Movement has allowed only a portion of the African American population to achieve the American Dream. http://www.census.gov/hhes/poverty/poverty01/table2.pdf.

64. *IBW Monthly Report*, May 1974, University of Michigan Urban Affairs Vertical Files.

65. Stephen Henderson went to Howard University, Vincent Harding went to the University of Pennsylvania, Robert Hill went to UCLA, and William Strickland relocated to the University of Massachusetts at Amherst. Howard Dodson handled the day-to-day operations of IBW.

66. Hazel Carby and Don Edwards, "Vincent Harding," in *Visions of History*, ed. Henry Abelove and E. P. Thompson (New York: Pantheon Books, 1984), 232.

PART III

Segregated Spaces

Ann Denkler

Subverting Heritage and Memory

Investigating Luray's "Ol' Slave Auction Block"

In June 1998, the Page County Heritage Association (PCHA), headquartered in Luray, Virginia, a small rural town almost two hours west of Washington, DC, held a rededication of the Confederate "Barbee" monument, a single soldier memorial named after its sculptor, Herbert Barbee.[1] This event, held 100 years after the statue's initial unveiling, was as grand an affair as the original ceremony in 1898, featuring reenactors, parades, and community singing. Located on a grassy circle on the eastern end of the town's Main Street, the soldier statue stands tall and proud on a granite square base inscribed with a relief of the quintessential southern heritage figure, General Robert E. Lee.

Near the center of town, farther west and just off Main Street, another commemoration was taking place: a counterdedication to a purported slave auction block sponsored by a local African American citizen (Fig. 7.1). His ceremony consisted of a few supporters, a wreath laying, and a plaque bearing the inscription "In memory of the Black men, women, and children who were put upon

FIGURE 7.1.
Luray's "Ol' Slave Auction Block," Luray, Virginia, 1999.
Behind the block is the back of the town's train depot,
undergoing renovation. The Blue Ridge Mountains are
in far background, to the right. (Photograph by author)

this 'Slave Auction Block' to be displayed and sold. May we remember, too, the social system that placed them there." The citizen's agitprop action gained significant press coverage in the local paper.

This essay explores this extremely complex and important public history site that embodies, echoes, and reflects African American history and memory and the contemporary racial tensions that underlie it. Resolutions focused on coming to terms with slavery, including dedicating the auction block, are made especially difficult as any criticism expressed against Confederate heritage is seen as an *attack* relying on an ideology of "northern aggression" and victimization. This perspective sets African Americans, who do not support Confederate heritage, on the offensive. In the face of this adversity, some white and African American citizens, most notably the dedicator of the auction block, have sought to reclaim heritage, history, and equitable treatment by formally organizing into the citizens' group Concerned Citizens for Equality (CCE) and by drawing attention to Luray's "Ol' Slave Auction Block."

Because African American history and public history revolve around a strong oral tradition, they often are not readily revealed on the landscape and are, in the case of Luray, overlooked because they lack "factual" or written documentation. This refusal to recognize oral tradition as "real" history is not simply limited to Luray: consider the guidelines for historic designation at the local, state, and national levels. Most of these standards require *written documentation* of the site's historical importance, leaving out the possibility that its history and significance were not written down and exist only in an oral realm. New methodologies and perspectives are needed for unearthing African American history, and new considerations need to be addressed, including the idea that African American commemorative activities and celebrations of heritage should be considered with an emphasis on churches and other venues and events that have been important to African American culture over time.

Although public displays of Confederate heritage are vital to private and public identity in Luray, Confederate memory is founded on beliefs that exclude African Americans and their history. The auction block, the only publicly commemorated African American history site, has been criticized and defaced by a white citizen who was determined not to allow a public commemoration in honor of African American history. This individual could have been working alone and has angered other white citizens, but support for African American history on the landscape has not been taken up by the PCHA or other southern heritage groups in the Shenandoah Valley. Thus, hegemonic white Confederate memory has not allowed room on the commemorative landscape for African American expressions of heritage.

Some current academic theories claim that the practice of heritage is false, misguided, and saturated in nostalgia. Yet, this block is proof that notions of heritage are paramount to personal and community identity, and that African American public history and material culture have the power to subvert the status quo by their very presence.

HISTORY OF THE BLOCK

The slave block, prior to its dedication, remained a historical enigma. According to a 1961 historical account, the stone lay at a corner on Main Street in downtown Luray for fifty years.[2] When Main Street was widened that year, the block was placed inside a nearby building. The white mayor of Luray at that time asked that the block be moved to Inn Lawn Park, a small park a few blocks away, adjacent to the public library, where he wanted it recognized with a brass plaque. This was never done, however, possibly because the stone's authenticity could not be determined. The stone then sat unmarked next to the library where it has stood for the last forty years. Frank, the African American responsible for dedicating the block, first learned of the stone's history as a slave block from an African American citizen whom he was driving around town one day.[3] Shocked by her claim, he forged his journey to explore the block's history, culminating in the dedication in July 1998.

One of the strangest elements in the story of the slave block is that it sat in its current location unmarked for forty years. Some older residents remember the block and its near-dedication in 1961, but others who had been told about the legend simply disbelieved that the stone was an auction block and instead thought that it was a stepping block used to mount horses.[4] Thus, counterarguments against the stone being a slave auction block are also a part of this monument's history. In 1961, the *Page News and Courier* claimed that it was "a mount for horseback riders."[5] Many of my white informants told me that it was highly unlikely slaves in Luray were auctioned off since there were probably no full-fledged auctions in this area of Virginia, unlike in Richmond or Alexandria.[6] And verification of the block's existence on Main Street is not mentioned in either *Page: County of Plenty* (1976) or *A Short History of Page County* (1952), two of the principal historical narratives of the town.[7] Certainly, there is credence in the reasons why the stone is believed to be a slave auction block, but the exclusion of the stone in the two written narratives should be viewed with caution because these works glorify the founding white fathers of the town and lack a comprehensive history of African Americans in Luray.

A more detailed look at the African American presence in Page County, however, reveals the contributions made by slaves, especially in the ironmaking industry, possibly providing the initial impetus for Black settlement in this region. In the late eighteenth century, ambitious ironmasters constructed ironworks run by enslaved African Americans brought in as "rented" slaves from eastern Virginia.[8]

This block, either on its side or standing upright, could have been a slave auction block. According to my informants who believe it was only a stepping-stone, the fact that a stepping-stone could also have been an auction block is not considered. Notably, the location of the block on a corner on Main Street (although it is not known how long it stood there) was, at one time, the home of Nicholas Yager, a slave owner whose slaves lived in the basement of the building. Contrary to popular conceptions of slave auctions being held in public spaces and only in geographical areas with large numbers of slaves, written evidence suggests that slave buying and selling did occur in more private settings—like the doorways of individual homes—in the Shenandoah Valley, if not elsewhere in the United States.

In spring 1999, a distinguished forensic anthropologist from George Washington University, Dr. James Starrs, agreed to come to Luray to test some dark stains on the block's surface without remuneration, and in September of that year, Starrs brought a team of experts to Luray. The event received front-page coverage in the "Page County Plus" section of the *Page News and Courier* with photographs of the team in action.[9]

It was not until early in 2000 that the forensic report was passed on to Frank. According to the results, the maroon stain "is most consistent with a possible blood splatter, noting the darker lichen growth in the sunken contours and cracks of the stone."[10] Intriguingly, the report also claims that the stain was "most likely spilled or dripped from about 4 feet above the top horizontal surface."[11] Even if it were proven that the stain was blood, it is not known whether the blood was white or African American. The investigative team could not, therefore, truly authenticate the stone as a slave auction block.

After all of the press about the events of the previous two years—the counterdedication and the visit by the forensic experts—stories about the block seemed to vanish from the pages of the *Page News and Courier*. Instead, the newest preservation project, the renovation of the train depot (which is just across the railroad tracks from the block and is visible from its location), has taken the historical spotlight. The Page County Civil War Commission (PCCWC), a group organized in 1999, discussed the possibility of acknowledging the stone as a *symbol* of an auction block in February 2000. As proposed by the PCCWC, the block would be moved next to a new Civil War kiosk devoted to telling the history of the Civil War in Page County. But the new president of the PCCWC has given no indication that he is interested in the slave block as part of Civil War history. In fact, he is more interested in pursuing the history of African Americans who fought for the Confederacy, arguing that the number of those who fought "not necessarily under duress" is drastically higher than history books and popular culture would have the public believe.[12]

A CATALYZING EVENT

CCE, a Luray-based organization of approximately twenty individuals comprising whites, African Americans, and Hispanics, meets informally and irregularly to discuss issues of racial inequality in the community. One member, a white minister, agreed to talk with me and explained what prompted the start of this group. Once again I was referred to the news coverage of an event that occurred in 1997, which she identified as the "catalyzing incident" that brought CCE together.[13] What is notable about the formation of CCE is how the group, at first galvanized by racially offensive remarks made at a joint Page County Board of Supervisors and School Board meeting, also became involved in a fight over injustice in the heritage arena when members of CCE assisted Frank with the wreath-laying ceremony for the slave auction block.

The catalyzing incident took place in late March 1997, during a discussion about consolidating the county's two public high schools, when a supervisor made disparaging comments about U.S. immigration policy. The controversy was recounted in the *Page News and Courier*:

> "In 1965," Cubbage said at one point, "Washington D.C. was a city full of problems. Today it's a city in chaos. You know why? We failed to consider the people who didn't live in the same place we did. . . . We shot a lot of money at the black folks and what did it do for them?" Cubbage continued, "Nothing. I don't want to see Page County ghettoes in 20 years."[14]

Cubbage later apologized to the community, but only after citizens decided to meet to discuss the issue and how it could be resolved. From this meeting, the CCE was born.[15]

Cubbage's divisive words about a white "us" and a Black "them" reflects, of course, the segregated physical and cultural landscape of the town and the exclusion of the African American community in general as active historical agents. Both white and African American citizens were moved not to retaliate but to figure out how to deal with this public official.

Before its involvement in the slave block dedication, CCE was responsible for new displays in one of the most central and often ignored public history sites—the glass case in the public library. According to an informant, CCE has "broken the chain of library displays" to include African American history.[16] An exhibition devoted to Martin Luther King Jr. in celebration of his birthday in January is now a part of the local revolving exhibitions. Since January 2000, students from the county's public schools have participated in King celebrations. According to a member, "The celebration [of 2000] was bigger than last year, and I hope it will be even bigger next year. . . . It very clearly is well-supported by the whole county."[17] Thus, CCE turned a devastating political and racial attack into a mission to support African American history and heritage, as it continued to promote political forums, study circles, and picnics.[18] It may also have been because of CCE efforts that Christmas wreaths, which are hung on streetlights on the eastern side of Main Street, were put up for the first time on West Main Street, considered the "Black" section of the street, for Christmas 1998. An individual noted to me, however, that the wreaths put up on "The Hill" (one of the nicknames for the Black neighborhood) were old ones.[19]

Frank's initial letter in the *Page News and Courier*, appearing a little over a month before the "Barbee" Confederate statue dedication, warned that the upcoming event was going to be a celebration of the "darkest period in American history":

> While the bands are playing "Dixie" and the Confederate Stars & Bars "yet wave," an urgent occasion presents itself for all of the county's black churches to come together and give thanks unto God for his deliverance of our race

from the depths of slavery and the subsequent decades of beatings, burnings, lynchings, and racial repression that was and is [sic] our black "Confederate heritage."[20]

In the following two weeks, the editorial section was filled with responses to Frank's letter:

It is unlikely Barbee had the ideological, cultural, and economic causes of the war in mind as he labored on his masterpiece.[21]

It was myth that Confederates went to the battlefield to perpetuate slavery. They fought and died because their homeland was invaded and their natural instinct was to protect home and hearth.[22]

The statue is of a man who fought for his state like many did and for no more reason than that.[23]

If anything undoes advances blacks have made, it won't be a Confederate gala held once every hundred years. It will be something else that trips them up.[24]

Frank's letter unlocked the floodgate of issues related to Confederate heritage and race relations that have plagued southern communities for well over 100 years. The range of comments suggests that heritage and public history in the South are divided along racial lines. Sanford Levinson writes:

Sacred grounds characteristically serve as venues for public art, including monuments to social heroes. Yet a sometimes better reality about life within truly multicultural societies is that the very notion of a unified public is up for grabs. As already suggested, one aspect of multiculturalism is precisely that different cultures are likely to have disparate—and even conflicting—notions of who counts as heroes or villains.[25]

Notions of heritage differ not just from group to group or race to race but from person to person. In the first editorial, the Barbee statue is simply a work of art, removed from any political implications. The second and third writers, like many supporters of Confederate heritage, use the argument that slavery was not why ordinary soldiers fought in the Civil War. The last writer uses the controversy of the slave block to make a more general comment on race in American history. This episode, then, speaks not just of feuds over ownership of history and heritage, or over debates of who are the heroes and who are the villains, but how race relations and tensions define American history and public history.

THE BLOCK AS A TOOL OF SUBVERSION

The fact that a slave block was dedicated as a piece of public history in a town devoted to Confederate memory is significant, of course, but the date on which it occurred, the day of the rededication of the Herbert Barbee Confederate soldier statue, is perhaps even more significant. This block stood in direct opposition to the Confederate heritage that was being celebrated on a large scale that day, with the racial and political resonances taking on even greater importance. According to Frank, he placed the wreath on the block the morning of the Confederate celebration and remained next to the block and wreath during the course of the event. People who attended the Confederate ceremony discussed the possibility of the block being used to sell slaves but also told him it was most likely a stepping-stone for mounting horses or climbing into carriages.

Even though the block has been neglected throughout its history, it still subverted dominant notions of heritage on its dedication day and even today. David Lowenthal argues, "Heritage exaggerates and omits, candidly invents and frankly forgets, and thrives on ignorance and error."[26] But heritage, as demonstrated through the auction block, can also serve to candidly reinvent and frankly remember marginalized cultures.

The heritage embodied in the slave block is a necessary and vital way to challenge dominant notions of memory and heritage, just as the early nineteenth-century African American heritage celebrations sought to assert emerging African American notions of memory. In their provocative article, "Artifacts as Expressions of Society and Culture: Subversive Genealogy and the Value of History," Mark Leone and Barbara Little suggest that "self-justifying genealogies" are tools by which an individual or state asserts certain ideologies that appear to be "natural" or historically inevitable. In their study, they examine Charles Wilson Peale's natural history museum and the Maryland State House, two works of the Federal era.[27] They illuminate their claim:

> Knowledge of history provides the power to create genealogy, and such power is the key to control. Genealogy here is to be seen as the version of history that suggests the inevitability of the present social order. Thus genealogy becomes a political necessity because it legitimizes the tie between the present and the past. . . . Connections between past and present are inevitable, determined, or epigenetic, implying that the present could not be other than it is.[28]

One of the genealogies at work in Luray is the Confederate history of the Civil War, and the artifacts, statues, road signs, and celebrations all serve to make these historical moments the most important in the town's history. This commemorative hegemony leaves no room for alternative, or subversive, genealogies, unless they happen to be discovered on the landscape. In Luray, the dedication of the slave auction block provided this subversive story, revealing how material culture can illuminate the study of history and memory.

The auction block can also represent how one artifact can elicit perspectives and emotions based on race and individual and communal notions of heritage and reveal the profound differences in these perspectives derived from objects on the American landscape. Certainly one of the most contested history sites revolving around the differences between black and white perspectives on slavery is the John Brown Fort, the site of the unsuccessful slave revolt in 1859 in Harper's Ferry, West Virginia. After Reconstruction and during the Jim Crow era, the site became one of the few where African Americans could visit an actual *place* devoted to their years of horrific servitude and celebrate John Brown's determination to abolish slavery.[29]

Thus, the block and an interrogation of the controversy surrounding it can yield a plethora of information on larger issues, including the subversive potential of artifacts in recapturing heritage, differences in white and African American history and memory, the invisibility of African American public history on the American landscape, issues involving race and public history, and race as a factor in the ethnographic equation of "us" and "them." Perhaps most importantly, the slave auction block also demonstrates that heritage—here the acceptance of an alternative history—can be a necessary and dynamic part of gaining agency in the historic process if its goal is cultural inclusion. Possibly inauthentic and ensconced in power relationships, the block still can serve to liberate.

THE FUTURE OF RACE AND PUBLIC HISTORY IN LURAY

In October 2000, in an unprovoked action, an "antiwreath" and handmade plaque were placed at the slave auction block.[30] The commemorator wrote:

> In Memory . . . Of days by-gone, days of grace and Manners in the Southland
> Represented by this symbol called a CARRIAGE STEPPING STONE
> Which assisted men, women and children to enter and exit a Horse-drawn vehicle.
>
> May this rock find peace back in the Quarry. (emphasis in original)

The dedicator left his name, apparently wanting to claim responsibility for his actions. A couple of weeks after the random placing of the "antiwreath," a popular valley historian wrote an article on the role of African Americans in the Confederacy. Arguing that a "significant number" of African Americans fought willingly for the Confederacy, the historian hit a nerve with Frank. He, in turn, wrote an editorial in the following week's *Page News and Courier*: "Suppose that for the sake of discussion that hundreds of blacks did flock to the Confederate cause. . . . Suppose they fought for the denial of the most basic human rights for themselves. . . . How, then, were those 'good Negroes' and their progeny rewarded? Through continued and often brutal disenfranchisement in every aspect of Southern society."[31]

Once again, a rebuttal written by a white informant accused Frank of aggression: "He [Frank] has attacked Southern heritage and attempted to demonize the entire white population of Page County repeatedly—and seemingly there will be no end to these attacks."[32] Coincidently, in the same issue, a historian wrote of slavery in the valley.

The following week, Frank once again had a letter printed, this one noting again the inhumane ways the stories of slaves in the valley are told. He writes: "There are interesting references to factual statistics regarding the number of slaves and slave owners in Page County before the war. The terms 'slave' and 'slavery' appear here, like in other Confederate publications and literature, as objective, abstract and statistical terms—inconsequential things, primarily devoid of full human value or consideration."[33] Frank continues that he would like to know more about the lives and emotions of the slaves—how they felt as they were auctioned: "Did he have to leave his wife and children behind? Was he sold on the block at public auction?"[34]

Frank's goal of seeing the block and African American history recognized in Luray was realized in November 2005. He spent over five years working with town officials in pursuit of his dream, and today one can read the following words on a plaque in front of the slave block:

> This native sandstone block, which stood at the corner of Main and Court Streets at the Chamber of Commerce building, was used as a perch for slaves about to be sold at auction. The stone is said to be one of the few now in existence. It is similar to many which existed in the South prior to the Civil War. As a part of everyday life, black men, women and children would be displayed and examined on slave blocks and sold for the highest bid. Family groups were frequently sold apart: husbands from wives, mothers from children, etc. This block is an historic symbol of a dark past of man's inhumanity toward his fellow man. It is also a symbol of how far we have come in learning to respect its victims and in resolving to go forward into the future with mutual respect and understanding.

Sadly, Frank passed away suddenly only two weeks after the sign's placement. At the ceremony celebrating his life, I was struck by the racial diversity of the audience, and I am certain this crowd would have pleased him. But his battle may not be over: letters of outrage over the new sign appeared in the local paper, and there exists the possibility that the sign could be defaced or, worse, removed.

What cannot be disputed is Frank's ambitious journey to see African American history represented on the landscape and his drive to pursue racial reconciliation. He strove, as we should all continue to strive, to recognize our shared heritage and shared public landscapes and to seek out fresh perspectives on African American conceptions of history, memory, and public history in Luray and in the United States.

NOTES

1. Luray lies within Page County, Virginia.

2. Robert H. Moore II, "Looking for Information About Luray's Mysterious Slave Block," *Page News and Courier*, August 13, 1998.

3. "Frank" is a pseudonym.

4. The only other image of a slave block that I have been able to locate is of one that sits at Green Hill Plantation in Campbell County, Virginia. From photographs, the block in Luray appears to have possibly been part of a larger structure used to sell slaves.

5. "Looking for Information," *Page News and Courier*, August 13, 1998.

6. Charlie Thomas, interview by the author, July 1999.

7. Harry Strickler, *A Short History of Page County, Virginia* (Richmond: Dietz Press, 1952); Page County Bicentennial Commission, *Page: The County of Plenty* (Page County, VA: The Commission, 1976).

8. Charles Ballard, "The Impact of Slavery on Page County, Part II," *Page News and Courier*, February 14, 2002. According to Dr. Ballard, slaves were probably preferred over day laborers since the cost of maintaining a slave was considerably less than that of a day laborer.

9. "High-Tech Sleuths Study 'Slave Block,'" *Page News and Courier*, September 23, 1999, Page County Public Library, Luray, Virginia.

10. Dr. James Starrs et al., "The Slave Auction Block of Luray, Virginia: A Report on the September 18, 1999 Investigation," George Washington University, Department of Forensic Anthropology, Washington, DC.

11. Ibid.

12. Robert H. Moore II, "Did Page County African-Americans Serve for the Confederacy?" *Page News and Courier*, November 2, 2000.

13. Gale Curtis, interview by the author, June 22, 1999.

14. "Cubbage's Words Cause Outrage," *Page News and Courier*, March 29, 1997.

15. Ibid.

16. Gale Curtis, interview by the author, June 22, 1999.

17. "Students Celebrate Dr. King's Life," *Page News and Courier*, January 20, 2000, Page County Public Library, Luray, Virginia.

18. Meeting Notes, Concerned Citizens for Equality, July 8, 1999. According to the notes, it was suggested that members of the group "approach . . . the Page County School Board about inviting School Board and/or school personnel to a mini presentation regarding issues of concern, i.e. violence, peer counseling, etc."

19. Gale Curtis, interview by the author, June 22, 1999.

20. "Celebration of Confederate Statue Hurts Racial Harmony," *Page News and Courier*, June 18, 1998, editorial.

21. "Heritage Event Not a 'Cause,'" *Page News and Courier*, June 25, 1998, editorial.

22. "Myths About Civil War Are Many," *Page News and Courier*, July 2, 1998, editorial.

23. "Statue Not About White Supremacy," *Page News and Courier*, July 2, 1998, editorial.

24. Ibid.

25. Sanford Levinson, *Written in Stone: Public Monuments in Changing Societies* (Durham, NC: Duke University Press, 1998), 37.

26. David Lowenthal, *Possessed by the Past: The Heritage Crusade and the Spoils of History* (New York: Free Press, 1996), 121.

27. Mark P. Leone and Barbara J. Little, "Artifacts as Expressions of Society and Culture: Subversive Genealogy and the Value of History," in *History from Things: Essays on Material Culture*, ed. Steven Lubar and W. David Kingery (Washington, DC: Smithsonian Institution Press, 1993), 160–181.

28. Ibid., 173.

29. Paul A. Shackel, *Memory in Black and White: Race, Commemoration, and the Post-Bellum Landscape* (Lanham, MD: AltaMira Press, 2003), 73.

30. My informant Frank and I gave this name to the wreath.

31. "Black Confederates Never Included in Southern Society," *Page News and Courier*, November 9, 2000.

32. "— Writes with a One-Track Mind," *Page News and Courier*, November 16, 2000.

33. "History Dehumanizes Slaves," *Page News and Courier*, November 22, 2000.

34. Ibid.

Kevin M. Kruse

"Going Colored"

The Struggle over Race and Residence in the Urban South

Normally, licensing renewals for real estate agents attract little interest. But as John C. Calhoun stood before the Georgia Real Estate Commission (GREC), he knew he had attracted a great deal of attention. Atlanta's newspapers had been giving front-page coverage to his case throughout the spring of 1949. During that time, the governor of Georgia, the mayor of Atlanta, the chief of police, and most members of the city council had been following the proceedings closely. They were not alone. So many spectators showed up for the hearing that it had to be relocated to the main chamber in the State Capitol, a space usually reserved for gatherings of the full legislature.[1] The high level of interest stemmed from the fact that Calhoun's case involved "blockbusting," one of the most hotly contested issues of the postwar era. This was a charge commonly leveled against black real estate agents, like Calhoun, who had supposedly plotted to undermine the security and stability of white neighborhoods by infiltrating black buyers into the area and thereby making trouble for others and profit for

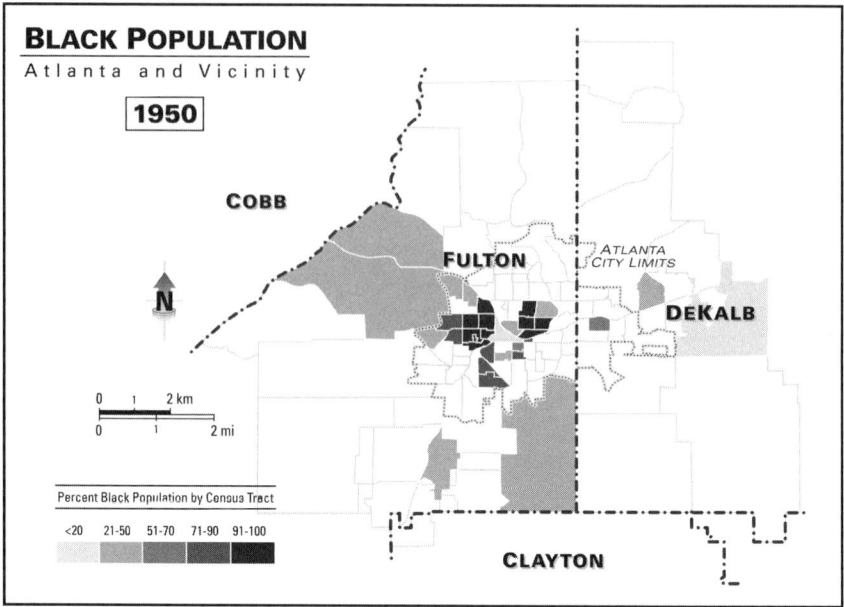

FIGURE 8.1.
Black population of Atlanta in 1950.
(Map courtesy of David Deis)

themselves. Officially, "blockbusting" was not the charge. Instead, Calhoun was accused of "misrepresentation" for claiming that a white neighborhood in which he had a home listed was "going colored."[2]

Hoping to send a warning to all others who might follow in his wake, the state waged a strong case against John Calhoun. Even though the issue at hand was ostensibly a single, simple real estate license, the state assigned not one but two assistant attorneys general to take charge of the case. One of them, Robert Addleton, set the mood for the Calhoun hearing with his first words, a crisp request that the witnesses be segregated. He then pressed the state's case quickly. To prove the charges of "misrepresentation," he trotted out the black buyers, Geneva and Wesley Allen. They had purchased the home only to find that it made them the focal point of a statewide controversy, chanting mobs, and threats of arson and violence. On the stand, a frightened Geneva Allen claimed she had been misled. "Calhoun told me that that street was going colored," she swore. "I asked if [it] had been agreed upon for colored people to move in there and he told me yes." Throughout the proceedings, the prosecutors placed all blame for the racial trouble on his shoulders. "The whole truth about the thing," Addleton charged while examining Calhoun, "was you were maneuvering around and pussyfooting around there by yourself trying to develop a white section into a Negro section, isn't that true?" Calhoun shot back, "It is not true." By this denial, John Calhoun meant that he had not made any misrepresentations in handling the property. In this sense, he was right. But he was right in another sense, too. John Calhoun alone did not change this neighborhood from white to black.[3]

Many observers of the time and since have placed great emphasis on the role of real estate agents like John Calhoun, but the true story of racial residential change is much more complicated. In recent years, urban historians have done much to improve our understanding of the complex processes of African American place making in the urban environment.[4] Although such studies have done a great deal to dispel the old myths and misconceptions about racial change, they have tended to portray the phenomenon in broad strokes. The study of an individual city makes for a coherent account, of course. The processes of racial change and resistance, however, were experienced not in generalized terms across a metropolitan area but rather at more intimate levels inside individual neighborhoods. By tracing residential racial transition in this more immediate sense, this study seeks to understand the phenomenon's dynamics as the participants themselves understood them. To do so, this essay focuses on a singularly important neighborhood in a singularly important southern city. The city—Atlanta, Georgia—was long heralded as the model metropolis of the New South. Seen as an "oasis" in a desert of southern segregation, Atlanta self-consciously styled itself "the city too busy to hate." To be sure, inside the city's limits, African Americans carved out a strong place for themselves. That struggle, however, was fiercely contested, especially when that space was understood in a literal sense as the search for housing and land.[5]

The complexities of the struggle for urban space were perhaps clearest in the racial transition of the neighborhood at the center of the Calhoun case—Mozley Park. The racial transition of that residential section, largely unfolding between 1949 and 1954, had an enormous impact on the course of residential desegregation elsewhere in the city. "Of the postwar tension areas, perhaps the most crucial for Negroes and whites was Mozley Park," reflected Robert Thompson of the Atlanta Urban League, "not only because it illustrates some of the problems which arise when Negroes move into a 'restricted' area in Atlanta, but because it has had a continuing effect on the thinking and the activities of buyers, sellers, builders, financing agents, and city officials involved in similar situations in other parts of Atlanta." Indeed, the example of Mozley Park demonstrates that the dynamics of African American place making were infinitely complex and constantly in flux. Black leaders shaped and reshaped their approach to residential desegregation before, during, and after the Mozley Park transition. At times, they forged cautious compromises with moderate city officials and, at other times, they moved boldly ahead on their own. After years of struggle, they succeeded in securing new homes for themselves in Mozley Park. Their victory was a pyrrhic one, however, for the battle over the neighborhood had changed it significantly. As white residents fled from Mozley Park, they staged a bitter, scorched-earth retreat that brought social turmoil and physical damage to the once-peaceful neighborhood. City officials, meanwhile, only made matters worse by relaxing zoning standards for the region and ushering in new waves of public housing, industrial development, and highway construction. In the eyes of African Americans, as soon as they succeeded in making a place for themselves in the city, the city set out to ruin it.[6]

Although segregationists often claimed that blacks who sought homes in white neighborhoods were simply looking for trouble, the truth was that they really had nowhere else to turn. In postwar Atlanta, for instance, black housing was in a disastrous state. The prewar years had been marked by widespread overcrowding, disproportionately high rents, and generally substandard construction. These conditions had only grown worse during World War II. "This problem, like a cancer, had not only grown during the war years," recalled Grace Towns Hamilton of the Atlanta Urban League, "but had reached such proportions until the peace and harmony of the entire community was seriously threatened." Indeed, as soldiers returned home from the war, confrontations over race and residence spread throughout Atlanta. One black serviceman, for example, used funding from the GI Bill to make the down payment on a home in a white neighborhood near the black enclave in the West End. Before he could move in, nearby whites peppered the front door with shotgun blasts, threw a brick through his living room window, and set fire to his back porch. In the end, the veteran decided he had to abandon his new home. Countless other incidents like this one played out across Atlanta in the postwar years. As Robert Thompson put it, "the town was about to explode."[7]

Realizing black movement into white neighborhoods could lead to widespread violence, the Atlanta Urban League channeled its energies in another direction. Instead of acquiring secondhand homes inside Atlanta, the organization hoped to find vacant land outside the city limits for purchase, development, and occupation by blacks. To reach that end, the organization called together the representatives of financial and real estate companies, social agencies, and related governmental agencies in late 1946 for a meeting at the offices of a local black contractor, Walter H. Aiken. There, they established the Temporary Coordinating Committee on Housing (TCCH), with Aiken as chairman. As its first order of business, the TCCH set out to determine the number of homes needed and discovered that, for black veterans alone, the figure was 4,500. The

TCCH next created three committees to help the housing program: first, a land committee "to investigate further the possibilities of getting out-let areas for Negro expansion"; second, a planning committee to secure information from county and city officials about the sites; and, third, a corporation committee to formulate plans for a corporation that might construct new homes on those sites.[8]

The TCCH's Land Committee, under the leadership of real estate broker T. M. Alexander and the Urban League's Robert Thompson, succeeded in finding suitable sites on the outskirts of town. "See, at that time, Atlanta only had 26 square miles of ground," Thompson recalled later. "And we saw—at least I saw—an opportunity for blacks to get out of the 26 square mile area by finding land outside of the old city limits and having it pinned down or publicized that these were what we called expansion areas." To enhance its effectiveness, the Land Committee expanded its membership to include representatives from the Atlanta Housing Authority, the Community Planning Council, the black Empire Real Estate Board, and the local Federal Housing Administration office. Now known as the Atlanta Housing Council, the group issued a report detailing six areas outside Atlanta into which blacks might expand without controversy or confrontation. "In each of these areas," Thompson noted, "some Negroes were living, and land, much of it owned by Negroes, was available for good residential quarters." According to the council's own analysis of the areas, two sites seemed ideal—to the west, blacks owned fifty-seven acres adjacent to the city's new park for African Americans and, to the south, the Methodist Church had eighty-one acres available for black use. These two sites quickly gained priority for the council as "Expansion Areas Nos. 1 and 2."[9]

Meanwhile, the TCCH's Corporation Committee, led by J. P. Whittaker of the black-operated Atlanta Mutual Building and Loan Association, decided to push ahead with plans to form a construction corporation. Expectations were high. "I believe," Aiken remarked at the time, "that the proposed corporation will be the most significant and worthwhile adventure ever undertaken by Negroes in Atlanta." Those outside the black community agreed. The Atlanta B'nai B'rith chapter hoped the expansion program "would tend to eliminate friction over the housing problem whereas such friction is often detected in those areas where white and Negro families tend to overlap." Likewise, the head of the Atlanta Chamber of Commerce hailed the plan as "a first step in solving one of Atlanta's major problems." To underscore the project's importance, Whittaker enlisted two distinguished black Atlantans, Bishop W. R. Wilkes and the Rev. Martin Luther King Sr., to join him in creating the Community Housing Corporation in late 1947. The following spring, they attempted to purchase forty-five acres of "Expansion Area No. 1." Although it could not meet the price of the land, the corporation convinced the property owners to form their own corporation for the purpose of building low-cost homes for blacks. Sponsoring the project, the Atlanta Urban League took bids from engineers, consulted architects, and helped coordinate the activities of the property owners, lending institutions, and the Federal Housing Administration (FHA). The result of these efforts, a community of 153 single-family homes, called "Fairhaven," gave hope that the solution to the housing crisis was indeed expansion outside the city limits.[10]

That hope, however, was dashed in the struggle to develop "Expansion Area No. 2." The project began ambitiously in late 1949. The Atlanta Urban League convinced two prominent whites, Morris Abram and Hugh Howell, to sponsor the development under the guise of Housing, Inc. After purchasing the land from the Methodist Church, they staked out an unprecedented plan for a self-contained community of 1,400 apartments, complete with shopping centers, playgrounds, and a gymnasium-auditorium. But the plan was confronted by countless problems. "Before ground could be broken," a contemporary recalled, "the developers had to argue, plead, sometimes fight their way through a wilderness of difficulties." Soon after announcing the apartment project was intended for black occupants, for example, Abram and Howell discovered that a proposed expressway was being rerouted onto the Highpoint property. Accusing white real estate developers of pushing for the change, the Highpoint officials had to lobby all the way to Washington, on two separate occasions, before the highway was restored to its original location.[11]

More problematically, the developers had to secure rezoning of the area for apartments. Since black colleges and neighborhoods surrounded the site on three sides, its planners had not anticipated any controversy. In fact, Robert Thompson applauded Abram and Howell for their "foresight and courage in developing vacant property which does not, in any measure, inconvenience either white or colored residents on the adjoining tracts of land." Likewise, the *Atlanta Journal* judged that "the land in question falls naturally and logically within the Negro residential orbit." Neighboring whites disagreed, however, and staged protests by the hundreds. Even after the Fulton County commissioners assured whites that the nonaccess expressway would separate their neighborhood from the black development, with walls forty feet high in some places, whites remained violently opposed. They argued that the "boundary to further Negro developments" should be pushed eastward, farther from their homes. Only after the Highpoint developers agreed to cut twenty-seven acres of land off the project for the creation of a "buffer zone" between the black and white communities did the objections die down. This concession, however, meant that the project— already scaled down from the original 1,400 apartments to a more manageable 800—could now contain only 500 units at the very most.[12]

Next, the developers had to convince the Federal Housing Administration to provide mortgage insurance. Given the site's proximity to white-owned property, this would not be an easy task. As housing expert Charles Abrams observed, the FHA followed "a racial policy that could well have been culled from the Nuremberg laws." Its official *Underwriting Manual* encouraged racism, warning agents that "if a neighborhood is to retain stability it is necessary that properties shall continue to be occupied by the same social and racial classes." To prevent any possible mixture of "inharmonious races and classes," the organization encouraged use of racial restrictions, racial covenants, racial zoning, and even physical barriers to segregate blacks from white property. Bankers and builders who dared to finance and construct black housing were strongly discouraged by its officials. Whatever its objections to black housing in general, the FHA had even stronger objections to Highpoint Apartments in particular. Having thus far covered only two dozen units for blacks in Atlanta, the agency was loathe to lend its support for a project of over 500. Furthermore, FHA officials argued that blacks would not be able to afford the estimated mid-range rents and would not be attracted to the project since, in their opinion, blacks traditionally preferred substandard housing. Again, Abram and Howell had to argue their case before officials in Washington before they could obtain the necessary coverage. Even then, the agencies agreed to issue insurance for only 452 units.[13]

Confronted by such obstacles, the expansion plans of the Atlanta Urban League ultimately did little to alleviate the chronic overcrowding of the inner city. Worse, at the same time their expansion efforts were being frustrated, black communities across the city were being destroyed. In the upscale Buckhead area, for example, there had long stood Bagley Park, a community of 200 black families. For fifty years, Fulton County commissioners refused to provide its residents with paved streets, running water, and sewage systems. "While the Negro residents have lacked these basic essentials of living," noted one observer, "all around them white residents have all necessary elements of sanitation and security." As those whites moved closer around Bagley Park, they pressed for the eviction of its black residents. "The white people in Buckhead wanted them cleared out," the mayor recalled later. "So the County Commission said they would turn it into a park. This gave them the excuse to condemn the property and run the negroes out." In April 1948, the Fulton County Commission pushed through a program whereby the black homes would be systematically condemned, purchased, and emptied of their occupants. The only white objections came from those who complained they would be inconvenienced by the removal of their cooks, chauffeurs, yardmen, and maids. The black residents of Bagley Park, however, certainly objected—to the "pittance" the county was offering them, to the rush to have them evicted, to their general inability to find new homes—but they were no match for the pressure of neighboring whites and the power of county officials. Those who refused to accept the proffered price were evicted by the sheriff's office that October and, as one reporter put it, "unceremoniously dumped into the streets." No plans were made for their relocation. Across Atlanta, similar developments pushed more and more black families from their homes. In 1949, for instance, Fulton County condemned nearly 200 more parcels of property—almost all of which housed black Atlantans—to make room for the North-South Expressway. Another thirty-four families were evicted from their homes when the Atlantic Coast Line Railroad began construction for a warehouse. "Instead of the condition being improved by new housing being added to the existing supply," W. H. Aiken warned, "the picture is growing steadily worse."[14]

With the supply of housing inside the city limits shrinking and the hopes for expansion outside the city limits dashed, blacks had only one option. "Following the pressure of increased population," Atlanta's Metropolitan Planning Commission conceded, "their only avenue for expansion has been 'encroachment' into white neighborhoods adjoining their own areas of concentration." As the white neighborhood nearest to the largest "concentration" of black Atlantans, Mozley Park thus found itself at the forefront of residential racial change. Located three miles west of downtown, along what were then the city limits, it stood as a small community of working-class and lower-middle-class whites living in single-story homes on narrow streets. Although a small neighborhood, its attractiveness was enhanced by a semicircle of park-like public spaces surrounding it. In the northwest corner stood Mozley Park itself, a whites-only civic space that boasted thirty-eight acres of land with a large swimming pool, natatorium, and clubhouse. Along the southwest stretched Westview Cemetery, with nearly 600 more acres of landscaped lawns and a requirement that all who came there—both visitors and permanent residents—be white. Last, overlooking the park from the west stood the three-story Frank L. Stanton Elementary School for white children. And just as these civic spaces barred blacks, so too did the neighborhood surrounded by them. The region lay immediately west of one of Atlanta's most overcrowded black enclaves, but for much of the twentieth century, whites there had held blacks out through a familiar combination of racial covenants and intimidation. After World War II, however, the structural bulwarks of residential segregation began to crumble and a new generation of African Americans emerged to challenge the status quo.[15]

For whites in Mozley Park, the first sign of "trouble" appeared on Mozley Place. William A. Scott Jr., whose father had founded the city's black-owned daily newspaper, had returned in 1946 from overseas service to help his uncle run the business. Unable to find a home in a tight real estate market, Scott decided to build one himself, on two lots he had inherited at the corner of Mozley Place and Chappell Road. Although the section along Mozley was completely white, blacks occupied all but two homes along the rest of the block and owned virtually everything to the east. White residents had seemingly accepted this state of things, although in a less than neighborly manner. When blacks began "taking over" blocks of Hunter Street to the east, for instance, whites convinced the city to change the name of their part of Hunter to "Mozley Drive," so they could avoid the stigma of having an address on a "black" street. The exact dividing line was Chappell Road.[16] Building a home at the corner of Chappell and Mozley Place, near white homes but still on the "black" side, must have seemed entirely rational to Scott.[17]

The white stretch of Mozley Place near Scott's site was composed mostly of small land lots and single-story frame houses. Much of the housing had been built before the Depression, but it was still of a higher stock than blacks' homes to the east. Unlike most of those shotgun shacks, all the homes along Mozley Place had running water and just about all had private baths.[18] Furthermore, most residents owned their homes. Much as in the rest of the neighborhood, those homeowners along Mozley Place were a mix of working-class and lower-middle-class whites. Two or three held white-collar positions as clerks or claims agents. Some served as foremen or managers at small businesses, like drapery shops and tire companies, whereas others worked as salesmen on the road or at retail stores like Sears, Roebuck and Company. But the majority worked as skilled and semi-skilled craftsmen, holding jobs as seamstresses, plumbers, bricklayers, mechanics, machine operators, servicemen, welders, or pipe coverers. Their homes were their largest investment, their neighborhood a prized possession.[19]

Upon discovering Scott's plans to make Mozley Place his home, these whites gathered at Stanton Elementary and hastily formed a committee to stop him. First, they tried to have his building permit revoked but found no support at City Hall. They next pled with Scott through the minister of a large local church, who begged him to build elsewhere or, at the very least, kindly turn his home around so it would not face theirs. When that approach failed, fifty residents banded together to repurchase the lot in order "to keep them off the street." In the end, the negotiations fell through, but they did have a significant result. Scott told his white neighbors that "Negroes would pay much more for these lots than the whites thought they were worth." Thus, unable to remove Scott, some whites decided to remove themselves instead. The first homes listed for black buyers were those nearest Scott's site. Ed Turner, a plumber, and his wife, Maybelle, lived in a small single-story house at 1400 Mozley Place, about 100 feet across the street. Watching the black veteran lay his home's foundation, Maybelle Turner decided he was there to stay. "I feel like [they] have a right, that this is a free country," she later explained. But she asserted her own "right" to sell and leave. "I did not feel like I wanted to be there and be a fence to protect other people," she stated. Soon thereafter, in 1948, the Turners listed their home with a black realtist,* starting a domino effect along Mozley Place. The couple next door at 1406 Mozley, salesman John Ogletree and his wife, Ethel, quickly listed their house with a black broker; Margaret Hall of 1416 soon followed suit. "Mrs. Turner and Mrs. Ogletree were selling their houses to colored people," she later reflected. "I knew no white person would buy mine." Whites farther down the street understood what was happening, especially after John Calhoun made visits to the Turner and Ogletree homes. "He was going back and forward to their houses just like an ant, two or three times a day," recalled one neighbor. "We would catch him in there, see him in there, and at night." In response, some tried to keep their neighbors from selling. "They said they didn't blame me," recalled Maybelle Turner, but "they wished that I wouldn't sell, being down there, and stay and protect them." The Turners realized, however, that their neighbors were worried not about the Turners' plight but rather about blacks becoming their next-door neighbors. "I told them that if they objected so much to me selling," Ed Turner scoffed, "they could move on down there to my place, but they didn't want to do that."[20]

Unable to prevent whites from selling their homes, residents of Mozley Park set out to persuade the new black buyers that buying those homes had been a mistake. Suddenly the center of a coordinated campaign of public protests and private pressure, the black buyers of 1400 and 1406 Mozley Place soon decided to abandon their homes. The new owners of 1416 Mozley Place, Geneva and Wesley Allen, likewise wanted to get out of the neighborhood but found the white woman who sold them their new home unwilling to break the contract. Accordingly, local whites tried to nullify the agreement—and get a little revenge as well—by bringing in the Georgia Real Estate Commission to revoke John Calhoun's license. In the end, not only did the commission refuse renewal of his license but local prosecutors brought criminal charges of "cheating and swindling" against him as well. The message to others involved in "Negro encroachments" in Mozley Park and the rest of the city was abundantly clear.[21]

When the state and county finished their cases against John Calhoun, locals in Mozley Park tried to correct the "damages" he had wrought. In April 1949, more than 100 concerned whites met at a neighborhood school to form a new "defensive organization," the Mozley Park Home Owners' Protective Association. Its

---

* The term "realtor" was the copyrighted property of the National Association of Real Estate Boards, which banned the admission of blacks. Therefore, black real estate agents generally used the term "realtist."

president, Arnold Kennedy, soon sketched out a plan for the "protection" of their neighborhood from further racial change. The key, he said, would be raising enough money to buy back the homes and then establishing a "voluntary boundary line for Negro expansion." There was no question that the blacks who were already there wanted out after all that had unfolded. Working in pairs, the group visited every house around Mozley Place and quickly raised the needed funds. Within a month, 1400 and 1406 Mozley Place were "safely" in the hands of two white veterans. When their fellow veteran William Scott finally finished his home across the street, he was the only black owner on the block.[22]

This stabilization proved temporary, however. Taking stock of the situation, some whites realized that, by selling to black buyers, their former neighbors had turned a tremendous profit. The Turners, for instance, had originally spent $3,750 for their home but resold it, after years of wear and tear, for $9,050. For some whites, the possibility of tripling their most serious investment proved to be too strong a temptation. In October 1949, eight homeowners along Adele Avenue and Mozley Drive decided to list their homes on the black realty market. To their surprise, most realtists refused to handle the sales. The largest and most reputable firms belonged to the Empire Real Estate Board (EREB), Atlanta's association for black brokers. Their representatives had agreed to a "voluntary boundary line for Negro expansion" that spring, and the members promised to abide by that agreement. There were, however, several unaffiliated black brokers who had no qualms about handling the hot properties. By early spring, all eight homes—plus two more—had been sold to black buyers. The panic was on again.[23]

The Mozley Park Home Owners' Protective Association tried to fight the new "invasion" as it had the first. In March 1950, Arnold Kennedy sketched out an ambitious plan, calling for local businessmen to "purchase or resell to Whites" all the recently transferred property: the five homes on Mozley Drive, the three on Adele Avenue, a number of empty lots on various streets, and even the Scott residence on Mozley Place. In addition, he advocated closing virtually every street connecting to Mozley Place and Westview Drive to isolate the neighborhood. In April, the Mozley Park representatives met with thirty leading white citizens—including the mayor, their ward's entire delegation to the city council and aldermanic board, and even local officials from the Lions, Optimist, Kiwanis, and Civitan Clubs—in an attempt to "work out amicably" a solution to the "new housing encroachments" in Mozley Park. A group from that meeting in turn met with black leaders, setting forth a much less ambitious plan than that called for by Arnold Kennedy. Having made what they thought to be a civil request, the white representatives reported to the mayor that "real progress was made."[24]

This time, however, the black realtists refused to go along. The original agreement had been easily circumvented by other real estate agents, they pointed out. And, in any case, they never enjoyed endorsing a system of segregation that held them in check, both personally and professionally. The entire rationale behind the "defense" of white neighborhoods was preposterous, noted members of the Atlanta Urban League. "Negroes have legally purchased property or moved into homes adjacent to or near white sections, and such actions cannot be considered as 'encroachment,'" they asserted. "It is inconceivable to believe that Negroes have gradually or silently infringed upon the rights of the white citizens in the Mozley Park Section of Atlanta, especially when the white residents of the area made overtures [to sell] first." With all the black realty firms in agreement, the Empire Real Estate Board decided to abandon their "gentleman's agreement" accepting residential segregation in Mozley Park. Realtists began to collect listings in Mozley Park quietly, each according to his own rules. Some refused to take a house unless every other one on the block was also listed, therefore ensuring "a complete transition from white to Negro occupancy." Others agreed to individual sales but with the explicit agreement that the white seller would remain in the residence "until conditions permitted the Negro to move in." To prevent a broader panic of whites, the realtists decided to concentrate solely on blocks north of Westview Drive. And as an added safeguard, they agreed to contribute a 5 percent commission from each sale to "a separate fund for [an] emergency," such as another lawsuit or licensing trial.[25]

The realtists stuck together through the spring and summer of 1951, holding their prized listings back until they had secured a majority of the listings along Mozley Place and its surrounding streets. At that point, the EREB gave the "go sign." On the first Sunday of September 1951, black brokers suddenly announced a staggering number of Mozley Park properties. Each realtist had his own block of land—J. R. Wilson displayed a whole block on Mozley Place, Caldwell Realty had eight homes on nearby Browning Street, and the offices of J. L. Wolfe Realty bragged of fourteen more on Mozley Drive. The next week, the pages of the *Atlanta Daily World* were nearly filled with listings. In two-column photo spreads with half-inch banners, the Alexander-Calloway Real Estate Company urged readers to "LET US HELP YOU PURCHASE A BEAUTIFUL HOME IN THE MOZLEY PARK SECTION." Other agents encouraged all of black Atlanta to drive through the neighborhood, browse its streets, and attend open houses. "These Home Owners Want to Sell," assured Caldwell Realty. "They Are Friendly People Who Want You to Stop, Look, and Call Us for an Appointment." The whole region was up for grabs, they promised. "If you see a house anywhere in this section you want," urged another ad, "call us." An already heavy load of listings grew heavier, as white homeowners farther south rushed to put their property up for sale. "Whites panicked and many became anxious to sell to get the top dollar while the getting was good," remembered T. M. Alexander, then president of the Empire Real Estate Board and an active realtist himself. "One Sunday, while driving a Black client around, a White lady stood out motioning to us excitedly to, 'Come look at our house!'" By October, entire rows on Mims Street and Westview Drive were likewise listed for black buyers.[26]

Purchasing the homes, however, depended on finding financing. Already scarce for black homeowners in general, loans were especially rare for those wanting homes in "transitional" areas. "In my humble opinion, it is not altogether the Government that is keeping Negroes and other minority groups confined to the central sections of our metropolitan areas," Robert Thompson reported to the Urban League's national offices. "The groups that keep us hemmed in are the officials of banks, building and loan associations, life insurance companies and other approved lending institutions." Although most banks refused to make such loans in general, some had an added incentive in the case of Mozley Park, since the Protective Association persuaded at least one white institution not to loan money to blacks there. To whites' astonishment, however, black financiers quickly filled the void. In late 1951, the black-owned Citizens Trust Company began working with two black-owned insurance companies to provide mortgage money for black buyers in the area. "Some of these loans," Thompson later acknowledged, "made possible the 'breaking' of the Mozley Park bottleneck." But the bank did more than assist black buyers. It also worked the other end, helping white sellers settle outstanding loans, so they could get their finances in order and get out. By the end of the year, the realtists and bankers had secured the sales of most of the property around Mozley Place. Finally, on January 2, 1952, all the black buyers arrived together, to take possession of their new homes.[27]

As this large section of Mozley Park transferred from white to black ownership, alarmed whites in neighborhoods nearby demanded the city government step in and stop the processes of residential transition. In a move that was unusual for that time and place, Mayor William Hartsfield made a personal trip to the black-owned restaurant where the Empire Real Estate Board held its monthly meetings. Before the assembled brokers, the mayor asked them to let "Westview Drive serve as a dividing line of houses for whites and colored in the area." His suggestion struck the realtists as a mixed proposition. On one hand, the proposal would open the rest of Mozley Park for blacks; on the other, it would signal acceptance of residential segregation. In the end, the brokers decided to strike a delicate balance—they would go along with the mayor's plan, for the time being, but "would not make any boundary line" that might legitimize segregation.

In a public letter, they announced their withdrawal from all business south of Westview Drive. All outstanding listings would be turned over to Councilman Milton Farris, who would contact white sellers and ask "them to withdraw their property from the market."[28]

The white residents below Westview Drive, however, were unwilling to trust the realtists. As other whites had done, they again decided to unite in "defense" of their neighborhoods through a new group, the Southwest Citizens Association. Practically speaking, the new organization and its predecessor in Mozley Park were virtually identical. The only real difference was that Southwest Citizens embraced a much larger region of the city and therefore could count on a much larger membership. In spite of this larger scope, Southwest Citizens remained focused on Mozley Park. Its president, Sid Avery, a transportation engineer with General Electric, lived there on Mathewson Place. Meanwhile, the group's rank and file, living both inside and outside Mozley Park, believed that the line had to be drawn there to prevent further "Negro encroachments." Naturally, they welcomed word of the Westview Drive agreement. Whether black brokers were calling it a "boundary" or not, that was exactly what the street was becoming, as the realtists removed themselves and their signs from the streets south of Westview.

In order to cement the dividing line, Southwest Citizens worked behind the scenes with Mayor Hartsfield and the ward's councilmen, eventually coming up with a foolproof plan. On the evening of October 13, 1952, in the Brown High School gym, a crowd of over 1,500 whites gathered to hear about some "startling progress." On behalf of Southwest Citizens, Richard Florrid gave them the good news, announcing there would soon be a permanent "barrier" between the blacks to the north and the whites to the south. The mayor, he explained over the cheers, had agreed to build a six-lane highway along Westview Drive, running from far to their east all the way over to Westview Cemetery.[29] Alongside the highway, residential lands would be rezoned for light industry and warehouses. Furthermore, the Atlanta Housing Authority promised to build a 500-unit housing project, for whites only, to their southeast. Ordinarily, middle-class homeowners would not have welcomed news that their neighborhood would soon be filled with factories, industrial warehouses, and public housing, but the white residents of Mozley Park considered these things a small nuisance compared to the "threat" of black homeowners. Together, they hoped, this unbroken line of barriers, coupled with the existing public spaces of the cemetery and park, would provide an unprecedented "buffer zone" between blacks and whites stretching for miles along Atlanta's West End.[30]

Immediately, black leaders attacked the "buffer plan." Although they found the whole scheme reprehensible, critics were particularly incensed by the proposal to create a housing project merely "as the east anchor of a so-called racial 'buffer.'" Public housing was desperately needed in other "slum areas," the *Atlanta Daily World* editorialized. To waste the Housing Authority's time and resources to prevent black Atlantans from securing homes—instead of helping them—seemed a cruel joke. Despite the protests, the Housing Authority pushed ahead with the project, completing it in late 1955 and naming it after Joel Chandler Harris, the Atlantan who had authored the Uncle Remus tales. Underscoring the "racial buffer" aspect of the Harris Homes, the city constructed high-strength cyclone fences between the whites-only project and the black neighborhood to the north. Although black real estate agents resented the "buffer plan," they grudgingly went along with it. Practically speaking, they knew, the acquisition of a large residential section outweighed the stigma. And so, after three years of bitterness, the Mozley Park "problem" had found a solution.[31]

But the neighborhood's transition was still incomplete. Black residents had moved into more than 700 homes in Mozley Park and had even spilled over into blocks to the north. By early 1953, the new residents had "encircled" both the park and school. But in spite of the neighborhood's residential changes, the mayor refused to change the racial designation of these spaces. Running for reelection, Hartsfield worried about the political fallout. The "loss" of individual homes had given the mayor enough headaches; he refused to fuel whites' resentment by pushing for the transfer of the prized park and school as well. Indeed, some in his campaign thought the mayor might be able to use the situation to his advantage by claiming his opponent would "on a population basis give Moseley Park and Stanton School" to blacks. Hartsfield simply decided to wait the campaign out, promising to do something once the election was won.[32]

Only then did the city start the transition of the neighborhood's facilities. The Board of Education, as expected, announced that Frank L. Stanton Elementary School would be used for black students that fall. For black children in the neighborhood, such as Charlayne Hunter at 1306 Mozley Place, the thought of taking over the "white" school atop Mozley Drive was a daunting one. "Of course," she later recalled, "once I had climbed the hill and walked through the doors for the first time, there was nothing white in sight—only the ghost-whites that I conjured up as I climbed the stairs to my classroom and as I sat down in one of 'their' seats for the first time. It was a strange experience, being in one of 'their' schools." After the school changed hands, black leaders called for the city to follow suit with the pool and park. Indeed, the Metropolitan Planning Commission warned in June 1953 that "pressure was very strong in some quarters for the immediate transfer of Mozley Park to the Negroes." But Hartsfield still wanted to wait. Until "a comparable facility for whites" was constructed on the west side as a replacement, Mozley Park would remain all white. Ultimately, the park changed hands in April 1954, finally completing the transfer of the Mozley Park neighborhood from white to black after nearly five years of animosity and negotiations.[33]

Throughout the transition tensions, the whites of Mozley Park assumed that the "invading" blacks were of a lower class and a cruder background. In truth, the initial black residents were very much like their white counterparts, at least in class terms. The stretch of Mozley Place from Ed and Maybelle Turner's home down to Mathewson Place was a prime example. When whites fled, their homes were inherited by a similar cross-section of blacks. As with the whites, a few were middle class, such as the principal of an elementary school and an office clerk at Clark College, but the vast majority held working-class positions as painters, bakers, maids, day laborers, laundry machinists, freight handlers, loaders for a trucking firm, and janitors at Georgia Tech. Once the neighborhood had settled down, however, many more professionals moved into the area—including several ministers, some faculty members from nearby Atlanta University, and even some of the real estate agents who had secured the neighborhood's "transition" in the first place. In a 1957 study, Carson Lee of Atlanta University's sociology department compared the new residents of Mozley Park with the whites they had replaced. In general, he found that the new black homeowners generally had higher levels of education, income, property ownership, political activity, and civic involvement than their white predecessors. Two-thirds of them had picked Mozley Park because it had a "better location" or was "less crowded" than older black enclaves. Indeed, in contrast to where they had once been, the neighborhood seemed a paradise. "The house my mother bought was on Mozley Place," remembered Charlayne Hunter. "It was twice as big as our house in Covington, with beautiful grassy lawns in the front and back. The streets were paved, just like the white folks' streets."[34]

Accordingly, the new occupants wanted to keep those streets just as they had inherited them. The main problem with this was, of course, the scorched-earth retreat of whites. The "buffer plan" had clumsily scattered two areas of light industry, a center of industrial warehouses, and a housing project around the neighborhood. With those aspects of the "no-man's-land" taking shape, Mayor Hartsfield pressed for the buffer highway as well. "There is a very delicate racial situation along this highway which we are anxious to aid," he wrote his chief of construction in 1954, "and the people out there are going to expect action." The highway project stalled when bonds could not be secured, but later in the decade the city ensured that a stretch of the new interstate highway took its place. To make way for the project, the state and county condemned much of the black-owned land in 1959, offering "extremely low" sums in compensation. The Rev.

William Holmes Borders, for instance, was offered $992 for his lot, even though homes on that block had been going for nearly ten times that amount. Over strong protests, the city bulldozed the whole southwestern section of Mozley Park.[35]

Although the freeway was an obvious case, public incursions came in subtler ways as well. Typically, once an Atlanta neighborhood had "gone colored," public officials automatically assumed it would become a slum. Accordingly, city planners and zoning committees lowered their standards for the region and began approving projects they would have routinely rejected if the residents were still white. After fighting for a neighborhood of single-family homes, black residents often found cramped apartment complexes and commercial projects springing up nearby. "It's awfully disgusting to pay inflated prices for homes in a residential section and as soon as you begin to get settled, here comes white 'investors' throwing up anything that will get by the inspectors," complained one black man. "Juke joints and pool rooms will probably be next. Can't we expect any type of protection from our city government?"[36]

Not surprisingly, blacks found this pattern playing out in Mozley Park soon after they arrived. In December 1952, for instance, they discovered that a white landlord on Penelope Road, just two blocks on the other side of the park and school, planned to construct a 200-unit apartment complex for whites. Mozley Park residents protested not merely because the project would present another "buffer" to the west but because it would mean more overcrowding. Austin Walden wrote a letter to the Municipal Planning Board, sounding quite like white residents protesting black "encroachments." "The Atlanta Urban League has worked hard and long to provide decent housing in desirable locations for Negroes, and we are naturally opposed to any efforts to destroy the investments of the property owners," he argued. "To permit the re-zoning . . . is tantamount to admitting that Negroes do not have the same right to protection of their neighborhoods as do citizens of white residential sections." In a coordinated protest, busloads of homeowners were shuttled to City Hall, where they presented city planners with a petition. "The fifteen acre tract of land is in the heart of a brand new Negro residential community," they noted. Construction of such a large project "would tend to lower property values of the existing home owners" and "would increase the population density, a major factor in the development of a slum." On this one occasion, their protests succeeded.[37]

Although black residents fought to maintain their high standards for the neighborhood, the city rarely followed suit. This was best seen in the decline of the city park. Prior to the "racial transfer" of Mozley Park, black Atlantans had only three underfunded sites in the city, compared with twenty-two for whites. Even with the new site, Atlanta still fell short of meeting the needs of its black population because of its segregation policies. "If all park areas were equally open to all Atlanta citizens, our city would provide one acre of public recreational land per 200 people," the Atlanta Urban League calculated in 1954. "Under the present arrangements which limit the use of public recreational space and facilities to separate racial groups, there is one acre for every 155 white citizens and one for every 1020 Negro citizens." Although all black parks suffered from overcrowding, Mozley Park received the most visitors of all. Built with white patrons in mind, it was by far the best-equipped and most attractive spot. "Because there was no other facility like it anywhere in Atlanta," one patron remembered, "it drew crowds of young Black people." Those crowds took a toll. After the first summer of black use, the *Atlanta Daily World* complained that the lack of other recreational spots created "the necessary overuse of the Mozley Park" pool and recreation center. "Overcrowding of Negro parks has long been a sore spot," the reporter noted, adding that surrounding "residential sections suffer." The city ignored their pleas; thus, Mozley Park remained underfunded and overused. Just a decade later, the decline was striking. In 1964, the *Atlanta Inquirer* ticked off a litany of problems at Mozley Park—windows broken for years, boards on the pool's deck completely rotten, and grounds so untended as to "evoke a feeling of disgust." "The general run-down conditions," the paper noted, "make it hard for a person to believe that this is the same recreational facility that existed when it was tabbed 'For White Only.'"[38]

The decline of the Mozley Park neighborhood after its "racial transition" served as a warning sign to other white homeowners. In truth, the steady decay there had been brought on by city planners who lowered zoning standards, park officials who allowed overuse, private companies who slighted the needs of black residents, and the fundamental economic exhaustion of black buyers who bought secondhand housing at highly inflated prices and thus had limited funds for repairs or refurnishings. But these causes were hidden to white eyes. For them, the reason was simpler—blacks moved into Mozley Park and the neighborhood immediately started to decline. As blacks moved into other "white" neighborhoods around Atlanta, the specter of Mozley Park was, to them, a warning of what black homeowners would bring in their wake.

The struggle over space in Mozley Park carried other lessons as well. For African Americans, the larger lessons over the strategies and structures of place making were perhaps even more important than the places that had been made. Black leaders emerged from this specific struggle against residential segregation with a broader understanding of the price of place making in the urban South. Sensing the stakes of the game, they now realized the degree to which black expansion would be bitterly resented and resisted by local whites. Accordingly, they adopted a stronger determination to fight for their rightful places—physical, political, social, and legal—in southern society. As their struggle for civic space expanded into the movement for civil rights, southern blacks would apply those lessons well.

NOTES

1. *Atlanta Constitution*, March 10, 1949.

2. Of course, the "misrepresentation" charge held a double appeal for segregationists. Internally, it reinforced a fundamental pillar of segregation, the belief that blacks consented to racial separation and would never knowingly purchase a home in a whites-only neighborhood. Externally, it let them circumvent recent court rulings against racial covenants. Instead of outlawing residential desegregation, the state simply made outlaws of those who helped such residential desegregation. There was just a slight difference between the two tactics, but the end result was the same, with white neighborhoods "protected" and an intimidated black population kept at bay.

3. Georgia Real Estate Commission Hearing, March 10, 1949, 1, 10, 77, located in *E. M. Smith, Investigator, Georgia Real Estate Commission, v. J. H. Calhoun*, Civil Case No. A-12007, Fulton County Superior Court, Atlanta (hereafter cited as GREC Hearing).

4. For two exemplary works in urban race history, see Arnold R. Hirsch, *Making the Second Ghetto: Race and Housing in Chicago, 1940–1960* (Chicago: University of Chicago Press, 1983), and Thomas J. Sugrue, *The Origins of the Urban Crisis: Race and Inequality in Postwar Detroit* (Princeton, NJ: Princeton University Press, 1996).

5. Among other things, Atlantans have disagreed on the correct spelling of Mozley, writing it out as "Mozely," "Mosley," "Moseley," and "Mosely" from time to time. (Even a map of the city today still spells the park "Mozley" and the street running alongside it "Mozely.") In this study, "Mozley" will be used, although alternative spellings will be presented in quotations according to the speaker's choice.

6. Robert A. Thompson, Hylan Lewis, and Davis McEntire, "Atlanta and Birmingham: A Comparative Study in Negro Housing," in *Studies in Housing and Minority Groups*, ed. Nathan Glazer and Davis McEntire (Berkeley: University of California Press, 1960), 27.

7. Rommel Benjamin, "The Non-White Population of Atlanta, Georgia, 1940–1950," Master's thesis, Atlanta University, 1961, 31–35; "A Report of the Activities of the Atlanta Urban League," November 28, 1951, Box 5, Grace Towns Hamilton Papers, Atlanta Historical Society, Atlanta History Center (hereafter cited as GTH); *Atlanta Daily World*, October 25, 1947; Herbert T. Jenkins, *Keeping the Peace: A Police Chief Looks at His Job* (New York: Harper, 1970), 17–18; Ronald H. Bayor, "Roads to Racial Segregation: Atlanta in the Twentieth Century," *Journal of Urban History* 15, no. 1 (November 1988): 7.

8. Robert J. Alexander, "Negro Business in Atlanta," *Southern Economic Journal* (Winter 1951): 460; Thompson, Lewis, and McEntire, "Atlanta and Birmingham," 22; Minutes and Committees Roster, Temporary Coordinating Committee on Housing, December 4, 1946, Box 254, Atlanta Urban League Papers, Special Collections, Woodruff Library, Clark Atlanta University (hereafter cited as AUL).

9. W. H. Aiken to TCCH Members, June 9, 1947, Box 254, AUL; Robert Thompson, interview by Duane Stewart, transcript, June 5, 1989, Georgia Government Documentation

Project, Georgia State University; W. H. Aiken, "Report of the Committee on Housing for Negroes," February 15, 1949, Box 254, AUL; Thompson, Lewis, and McEntire, "Atlanta and Birmingham," 23; "A Report of the Activities of the Atlanta Urban League," November 28, 1951, Box 5, GTH.

10. Minutes of the Corporation Committee of the Temporary Coordinating Committee on Housing, October 9, 1947, Box 254, AUL; W. H. Aiken to TCCH Members, June 9, 1947, Box 254, AUL; Alexander F. Miller, President, Gate City Lodge No. 144, B'nai B'rith, to Atlanta Housing Council, Atlanta, June 19, 1947, Box 238, AUL; *Atlanta Journal*, March 29, 1949; Community Housing Corporation, Petition for Incorporation, Fulton County Superior Court, [1947], Box 254, AUL; Minutes of the Corporation Committee of the Temporary Coordinating Committee on Housing, March 23, 1948, Box 254, AUL; "A Report of the Activities of the Atlanta Urban League," November 28, 1951, Box 5, GTH; Thompson, Lewis, and McEntire, "Atlanta and Birmingham," 23–24. For an excellent study of African American suburbanization in Atlanta and the nation as a whole, see Andrew Wiese, *Places of Their Own: African American Suburbanization in the Twentieth Century* (Chicago: University of Chicago Press, 2004).

11. Morris B. Abram, *The Day Is Short: An Autobiography* (New York: Harcourt Brace Jovanovich, 1982), 96; [Robert Thompson] to Housing, Incorporated, c/o Morris Abram, January 9, 1950, Box 234, AUL; *Atlanta Daily World*, February 9, 1950; *Atlanta Journal-Constitution*, July 30, 1950; Thompson, Lewis, and McEntire, "Atlanta and Birmingham," 24.

12. [Robert Thompson] to Housing, Incorporated, c/o Morris Abram, January 9, 1950, Box 234, AUL; *Atlanta Journal*, January 31, 1950; Thompson, Lewis, and McEntire, "Atlanta and Birmingham," 25; *Atlanta Constitution*, February 2, 1950; *Atlanta Daily World*, February 9, 1950.

13. Charles Abrams, *Forbidden Neighbors: A Study of Prejudice in Housing* (New York: Harper, 1955), 162, 229–230; Federal Housing Administration, *Underwriting Manual*, 1938, Sec. 937, cited in Luigi Laurenti, *Property Values and Race: Studies in Seven Cities* (Berkeley: University of California Press, 1960), 24–25; Kenneth T. Jackson, "Race, Ethnicity, and Real Estate Appraisal: The Home Owners Loan Corporation and the Federal Housing Administration," *Journal of Urban History* 6, no. 4 (August 1980): 430–447; Charles S. Johnson and Herman H. Long, *People vs. Property: Race Restrictive Covenants in Housing* (Nashville: Fisk University Press, 1947), 71; Harold C. Fleming, "Housing for a New Middle Class," *The Survey* 87, no. 9 (September 1951): 384; Thompson, Lewis, and McEntire, "Atlanta and Birmingham," 25.

14. *Atlanta Daily World*, April 11, October 22, 1948; William B. Hartsfield, Press Announcement, [1949], Box 10, William Berry Hartsfield Papers, Special Collections Department, Woodruff Library, Emory University (hereafter cited as WBH); *Northside News*, April 2, 1948; "Bagley Park," typewritten manuscript, April 21, 1947, Box 257, AUL; Petition to Commissioners of Roads and Revenue, Fulton County, Georgia, April 6, 1949, Box 257, AUL; Report of the Committee on Housing for Negroes to Atlanta Advisory Committee, Economy Housing Program, from W. H. Aiken, Chairman of the Committee on Housing for Negroes, February 15, 1949, Box 254, AUL.

15. Atlanta Metropolitan Planning Commission, *A Factual Inventory: A Report Containing Texts and Maps on Georgia's Capital City* (Atlanta: Metropolitan Planning

Commission, 1950), 40; Gail Anne D'Avino, "Atlanta Municipal Parks, 1882–1917: Urban Boosterism, Urban Reform in a New South City," Ph.D. diss., Emory University, 1988, 148–150; Charlayne Hunter-Gault, *In My Place* (New York: Farrar, Straus & Giroux, 1992), 82; Dana F. White, "Landscaped Atlanta: The Romantic Tradition in Cemetery, Park, and Suburban Development," *Atlanta Historical Journal* 26 (Summer/Fall 1982): 102; Franklin M. Garrett, *Atlanta and Environs: A Chronicle of Its People and Events*, vol. 2 (New York: Lewis Historical Publishing Company, 1954), 71–72; Timothy J. Crimmins, "West End: Metamorphosis from Suburban Town to Intown Neighborhood," *Atlanta Historical Journal* 26 (Summer/Fall 1982): 41.

16. Samuel Adams, "Blueprint for Segregation: A Survey of Atlanta Housing," *New South* 22 (Spring 1967): 76, 80; Thompson, Lewis, and McEntire, "Atlanta and Birmingham," 28; U.S. Bureau of the Census, *U.S. Census of Housing: 1950*, vol. 5, *Block Statistics*, Pt. 9 (Washington, DC: U.S. Government Printing Office, 1952), table 3.

17. Other observers apparently agreed. The Atlanta Urban League, for instance, assumed in 1947 that an area bound by "Mosely Drive (to Chappell Road) and the A.B. and C. Railroad (to Gordon Road) and Gordon Road on the South . . . may be thought of as the main area for Negro expansion in the City of Atlanta." See Report, "Proposed Expansion Areas for Negroes in Atlanta, Georgia," [n.d., 1947,] Box 243, AUL.

18. Report, "Historical Trends in Negro Population Areas," Box 1, Atlanta Bureau of Planning Papers, Archives, Atlanta Historical Society, Atlanta (hereafter cited as ABP); U.S. Bureau of the Census, *U.S. Census of Housing: 1940*, vol. 3, *Supplement to the First Series: Housing Bulletin for Georgia: Atlanta: Block Statistics* (Washington, DC: U.S. Government Printing Office, 1942), table 3, Census Tract F-40, Blocks 18, 28, 29; U.S. Bureau of the Census, *U.S. Census of Housing: 1950*, vol. 5, *Block Statistics*, Pt. 9 (Washington, DC: U.S. Government Printing Office, 1952), table 3, Census Tract F-40, Blocks 8, 24, 25.

19. Of forty-six homes along Mozley Place, forty were owner-occupied when racial transition began. *City Directory, 1948–1949* (Atlanta: Atlanta City Directory Company Publishing, 1948).

20. Testimonies, GREC Hearing, 22, 30, 36, 89–90, 95, 103, 109–110; Thompson, Lewis, and McEntire, "Atlanta and Birmingham," 28; [Robert Thompson,] "Fr Chn Hearing," March 10, 1949, Box 246, AUL.

21. Andrew Jackson, "The Case of J. H. Calhoun, Atlanta, Georgia Real-Estate Agent," Box 255, AUL; Testimony, GREC Hearing, 10, 178–180; *Atlanta Constitution*, February 15–16, March 11, 18, 1949; [Robert A. Thompson,] "Fr Chn Hearing," Notes on GREC Hearing, March 10, 1949, Box 246, AUL; Thompson, Lewis, and McEntire, "Atlanta and Birmingham," 29.

22. *Atlanta Journal*, April 22, May 20, 1949; *West End Eagle*, April 8, 1949; *Atlanta Daily World*, May 11, 1949; Adams, "Blueprint for Segregation," 76.

23. [Robert A. Thompson,] "Fr Chn Hearing," Notes on GREC Hearing, March 10, 1949, Box 246, AUL; J. R. Wilson to Jack Dilliard, 1484 Adele Avenue, November 23, 1949, Box 240, AUL; Empire Real Estate Board, "History," *Annual Banquet Program*, 1955, Box 6, ABP; Minutes, Empire Real Estate Board, January 18, 1950, Box 254, AUL; Memorandum, West End Business Man's Association, May 31, 1950, Box 8, Long-Rucker-Aiken Family Papers, Archives, Atlanta Historical Society, Atlanta (hereafter cited as LRA).

24. Report, "Recommendation: Mozley Park Home Owners Protective Association," [March 1950,] Box 8, LRA; *Atlanta Constitution*, April 28, 1950; West End Business Man's Association to Hartsfield, May 31, 1950, Box 8, LRA.

25. R. A. Thompson and A. T. Walden to T. M. Alexander, June 6, 1950, Box 234, AUL; Minutes, Empire Real Estate Board, June 21, 1950, Box 254, AUL; Minutes, Empire Real Estate Board, March 13, 1950, September 22, December 19, 1951, Box 254, AUL; Thompson, Lewis, and McEntire, "Atlanta and Birmingham," 29.

26. *Atlanta Daily World*, August 19, 26, September 2, 9, 16, October 7, 1951; Theodore Martin Alexander Sr., *Beyond the Timberline: The Trials and Triumphs of a Black Entrepreneur* (Edgewood, MD: M. E. Duncan Publishers, 1992), 161.

27. R. A. Thompson to Lester Granger, Executive Director, National Urban League, July 19, 1954, Box 236, AUL; Thompson, Lewis, and McEntire, "Atlanta and Birmingham," 29; Minutes, Empire Real Estate Board, September 19, December 19, 1951, January 16, 1952, Box 254, AUL; Notes, "Sutton," [Robert Thompson interview with R.O. Sutton], [August 1956,] Box 246, AUL.

28. Minutes, Empire Real Estate Board, August 20, September 8, 1952, and Copy of EREB Statement, September 9, 1952, Box 254, AUL.

29. Earlier in the decade, whites had tried unsuccessfully to have a highway barrier constructed. Plans for a "Westview Parkway" called for two lanes of traffic with a "greenbelt" of trees and tall cyclone fences to separate the races. See Howard L. Preston, *Automobile Age Atlanta: The Making of a Southern Metropolis, 1900–1935* (Athens: University of Georgia Press, 1979), 102–103; Ronald H. Bayor, *Race and the Shaping of Twentieth-Century Atlanta* (Chapel Hill: University of North Carolina Press, 1996), 58.

30. *Atlanta Daily World*, October 14, 1952; *Atlanta Journal*, October 13, 1952; *Atlanta Constitution*, October 14, 1952.

31. *Atlanta Daily World*, September 7, 18, December 10, 1952; T. M. Alexander to Housing Committee Members, September 10, 1952, Box 243, AUL; Robert A. Thompson, Draft, Statement Before United States Commission on Civil Rights, [1959,] Box 244, AUL; Thompson, Lewis, and McEntire, "Atlanta and Birmingham," 30.

32. Visitors Log, Hartsfield Campaign Headquarters, [May 8, 1953 Entry,] Box 12, WBH.

33. *Atlanta Daily World*, May 31, June 7, 1953; Hunter-Gault, *In My Place*, 83; Robert C. Stuart to S. B. Avery, June 10, 1953, Box 3, ABP; Stuart to Hartsfield, August 7, 1953, Box 3, ABP; *Atlanta Constitution*, February 17, 1954.

34. *City Directory, 1953* (Atlanta: Atlanta City Directory Co., 1953); Membership List, Mozley Park Civic Association, 1954–1955, Box 224, AUL; Carson Lee, "Social Characteristics of Negroes Who Invaded a White Residential Area in the City of Atlanta," Master's thesis, Atlanta University, 1957, 24–30; Hunter-Gault, *In My Place*, 74.

35. Hartsfield to Clarke Donaldson, August 6, 1954, Box 3, ABP; John Calhoun and Charles Bell to William Holmes Borders, October 9, 1959, Box 2, Austin T. Walden Papers, Archives, Atlanta Historical Society, Atlanta (hereafter cited as ATW). Borders eventually secured a total compensation of $1,560. See Judgment in Fulton Superior Court, Civil Case No. A-76053, and Edwin L. Sterne to Walden, March 24, 1961, Box 2, ATW. On the value of similar homes, see U.S. Bureau of the Census, *U.S. Census of Housing: 1950*, vol.

5, *Block Statistics*, Pt. 9 (Washington, DC: U.S. Government Printing Office, 1952), table 3, Census Tract F-40, Block 38.

36. C. Adams, Letter to the Editor, *Atlanta Constitution*, June 12, 1949.

37. A. T. Walden to Wyont Bean, December 12, 1952, Box 240; R. A. Thompson to "Mr. and Mrs. Home Owner," December 15, 1952, Box 243; Petition to the Members of the Municipal Planning Board and Board of Adjustment, December 1952, Box 243, AUL.

38. *Atlanta Daily World*, June 5, 1952, October 21, 1954; Atlanta Urban League, "A Report on Parks and Public Recreational Facilities for the Negro Population of Atlanta, Georgia," [1954,] Box 5, GTH; Hunter-Gault, *In My Place*, 82; *Atlanta Inquirer*, May 23, August 3, 8, 1964.

Andrew Wiese

The Other Suburbanites

African American Suburbanization in the North Before 1950

In 1959, a writer from the Cleveland *Plain Dealer* visited a small African American community near Cleveland called Chagrin Falls Park. He described a landscape of small houses, large gardens, frame churches, and cinder-block stores, as well as overgrown lots and cannibalized automobiles. To the reporter's eye, the 900 inhabitants of Chagrin Falls Park lived in a "shanty town." But among those he interviewed were men and women who described "the Park" as a community where they had built better lives for themselves. Representative of these was Magnolia Strickland, a native of Georgia, who praised the community for its open space, fresh air, gardens, and the opportunity to own a home. "I think I bettered my condition," Strickland said. I got five rooms; they all got heat from an oil furnace. I got an electric stove and hot and cold running water from my well—and it's all paid for. . . . I couldn't have done all that in Cleveland."[1]

The divergent views of Strickland and the white reporter illustrate common reactions to the phenomenon of early black suburbanization. To outsiders—journalists, city planners, white neighbors, and many middle-class blacks— these places were "slums" or, in the case of Chagrin Falls Park, "a curse." To scholars, too, these communities often seemed little more than "rural slums" or "little ghettoes" that belonged outside the legitimate suburbanization process.[2] To residents, however, these communities represented something altogether different: they were home, places where people had bought land, built houses, nurtured families, and created community. Moreover, the comments of Magnolia Strickland and her neighbors suggest that residents of these suburbs wanted many of the same things as other suburbanites, including homes of their own, a bucolic landscape, and family-centered community life. Slums to some, these places were also suburbs, and they were suburbs shaped by the experience, aspirations, and income of the black families who made them home.

Although scholars have paid little attention to such suburbs until recently, early black suburbanites formed an important component of the Great Migration—the movement of more than a million African Americans out of the South in the 1910s and 1920s. The great majority of these migrants settled in central cities, but suburbs accounted for approximately 15 percent of black population growth in metropolitan areas outside the South between 1910 and 1940, or about 285,000 people. By 1940, approximately 500,000 African Americans lived in suburbs north of the Mason-Dixon Line, a number that represented almost one-fifth (19 percent) of the African Americans in metropolitan areas of the North and West.[3] Socially, these suburbanites were similar to migrants who settled in cities. Most were southern-born, low-skilled, and poorly paid, and they shared like patterns of migration and family structure. At the same time, they made choices that distinguished them from their central-city counterparts. They were more likely to be home owners, and they pursued different patterns of economic survival, including distinctive uses of property and wider variation in the proportion of women who worked outside the home.[4] Many of them also avoided cities explicitly, and, like other suburbanites, they created suburban landscapes that mixed elements of urban and rural living.

These differences raise interesting questions for the study of African American and suburban history. The fact that as many as one in six black migrants to the North before World War II settled in suburbs suggests that a wider range of options was available to working-class migrants than studies of central-city communities have suggested. Moreover, the diversity of black urban and suburban neighborhoods illustrates that migrant community members voiced a range of opinions about what constituted better places to live and work. At the same time, similarities among black suburbs suggest that early suburbanites—and perhaps southern migrants in general—shared values regarding housing and home ownership, as well as aesthetic preferences for landscape, that have been largely ignored by historians.[5]

Early black suburbs are also important to the history of American suburbanization. Although African Americans never constituted more than 5 percent of the U.S. suburban population before 1960, they were part of a much larger group of blue-collar suburbanites who formed the majority in many suburbs before 1940.[6] Working-class families often moved to suburbs for employment, but the suburbs appear to have been as attractive to workers as they were to middle-class Americans. The precise features of suburban landscape and life-style, however, differed with each group. For historians, the presence of several hundred thousand African American suburbanites in northern suburbs, as well as millions of other working-class suburbanites, poses a challenge to write suburban histories that include the range of Americans who lived on the city's edge, and it suggests that we need to reconceptualize suburbanization to mean the *whole* expansion of American cities beyond their bounds, not just the celebrated decentralization of the white middle class.[7]

Through a case study of one early black suburb, Chagrin Falls Park, Ohio, this essay will place early black suburbanization within the context of U.S. suburban history, and it will offer tentative conclusions about the motivations and values of early black suburbanites. First, early black suburbanites appear to have moved to the suburbs for many of the same reasons as non-blacks did. Many of the normative values associated with middle-class suburbanization ("the suburban dream") were widely shared among Americans in the early twentieth century. Black suburbanites also responded to many of the structural forces that encouraged urban decentralization generally. At the same time, race and class influenced the patterns of the suburban life they created. Like other Americans, early black suburbanites internalized images of ideal places to live, drawing upon their southern history and culture, as well as their experience and aspirations as black migrants in northern cities. They desired home ownership in fulfillment of long-held dreams in the black South. They preferred living in family-based communities, more often structured around extended rather than nuclear families. They rejected city living, and they re-created rustic landscapes reminiscent of the region from which most had come.

Finally, many early black suburbanites, like many working-class whites, settled at the edge of town as a means of adapting to urban industrial life. Faced with low incomes and unstable employment, blue-collar workers used suburban property in similar ways, regardless of race. Before the advent of the welfare state, they sought economic security through various forms of domestic production and thrift. They grew extensive gardens, took in work, kept livestock, rented rooms to newcomers, and delayed costly services such as water and electricity.

Many even built their own homes, substituting "sweat equity" for the largest cash expense they faced.[8] Racism contributed to these patterns by limiting black access to credit and skilled labor. Thus, even as working-class white suburbs moved closer to middle-class norms over time, early black suburbs lagged in income, housing quality, and public improvements. In these ways, race, as well as class, shaped the process of African American suburbanization before 1950.

Although Chagrin Falls Park was a small place, it is an apt choice for a case study. As a residential "all-black" subdivision, it represented a whole category of early black suburbs. Moreover, a growing body of literature suggests that patterns characteristic of Chagrin Falls Park were common in black suburbs of all kinds.[9] Because Chagrin Falls Park was a suburb developed from scratch by working-class black families, it reveals migrant values and aesthetics with a minimum of external influence. These values and the domestic life that nourished them suggest that early suburbanites shared a coherent vision of better living in the urban North—what we might call a working-class African American suburban dream.

RESIDENTIAL BLACK SUBURB: CHAGRIN FALLS PARK, OHIO

During spring 1921, an agent of the Home Guardian Corporation of New York approached Samuel Rocker, publisher of the *Jewish World*, a Yiddish-language newspaper in Cleveland. Home Guardian had recently subdivided an eighty-one-acre suburban tract southeast of the city called Chagrin Falls Park. The agent proposed to Rocker that the *Jewish World* offer lots in Chagrin Falls Park as subscription premiums. Home Guardian would sell lots, and Rocker would sell papers. By June 1921, full-page advertisements in the *World* announced the premiums, and readers began buying the 20-by-100-foot lots in the subdivision. Developed with a minimum of investment and no building restrictions, the subdivision had no sewers, water mains, or electricity, and its streets were crude dirt lanes. Perhaps because of poor services, the buoyant expectations of Rocker and Home Guardian went unfulfilled. Lots sold slowly, and in 1924, Home Guardian sold the remainder of its lots to real estate agents Grover and Florence Brow (also white), who began a thirty-year career selling Chagrin Falls Park lots—most of them to African Americans in the city of Cleveland.[10]

In marketing rustic building lots to African Americans, the Brows replicated the decision of real estate agents in dozens of American cities. Throughout the 1910s and 1920s, black newspapers routinely advertised lot subdivisions like Chagrin Falls Park. The *New York Age* and the *Amsterdam News*, for instance, advertised subdivisions in no less than thirteen suburbs between 1921 and 1927. The *Chicago Defender, California Eagle, Pittsburgh Courier, Cleveland Gazette*, and *Baltimore Afro-American* similarly published advertisements for local subdivisions, as well as faraway developments in Egg Harbor and New Brunswick, New Jersey; Gainesville, Florida; Washington, DC; and other cities.[11]

Regardless of region or the race of the subdivider, sales pitches for these allotments were remarkably similar, reflecting agents' best understanding of their market. Insofar as families bought, these ads offer clues to the desires of black suburbanites during the Great Migration. Appealing to migrants' rural southern origins, ad after ad offered a slice of country life: open space for fruit trees, garden plots, and chickens and other small livestock. Further, they promised the country in combination with urban amenities: proximity to urban employment, convenient transportation, and community facilities such as churches, schools, and stores. In a few cases, agents appealed to race pride overtly, encouraging readers to "join hands with your own people" by buying lots in a black subdivision. More often, they linked suburbanization to race uplift by naming streets and subdivisions after heroes in the freedom struggle, such as Booker T. Washington, Frederick Douglass, and Abraham Lincoln. Promoting a borderland between urban and rural living with the image of racial progress at center stage, agents, above all, promised the opportunity "for colored people to own a home."[12]

Although the Brows' sales pitch is not recorded, they made inexpensive suburban land available to working-class black Clevelanders. Prices of a Chagrin Falls Park lot fluctuated during the 1920s from $60 to $200—two weeks' to two months' salary for the average black factory worker in Cleveland. By contrast, similar parcels in the city ran to several hundreds of dollars, and house prices reached into the thousands. African Americans began purchasing lots from the Brows after 1924, and a small number began to build houses in this semi-rural subdivision. Ironically, lot sales picked up after 1929 as real estate prices collapsed during the Great Depression. By the mid-1930s, Florence Brow sold lots in the park for as little as $25, and black families who had managed to save money were able to purchase at a bargain. Even more important, many early white purchasers let their taxes fall delinquent during the 1930s, and scores of black Clevelanders purchased lots at the county sheriff's auction, some for as little as two dollars apiece.[13]

The people who bought lots and built homes in Chagrin Falls Park were primarily working-class black Clevelanders who had migrated from the South (predominantly Georgia, Alabama, and Tennessee). Of household heads who settled in the park between 1924 and 1945, 60 percent had worked in unskilled labor or personal service in Cleveland before moving there. Fully a third had been common laborers. Most settlers relocated to the park as mature married couples—most were in their late thirties or forties—having lived in Cleveland for a number of years before moving to the suburbs. Just 5 percent owned homes before moving to the park, a home-ownership rate less than half the average in the neighborhoods from which they moved. On the whole, then, original park residents represented a cross-section of black Cleveland weighted toward the lower end of the economic ladder.[14]

Having purchased bare lots in Chagrin Falls Park, black families built homes and community institutions in a fashion similar to that of immigrant workers in cities such as Detroit, Chicago, Milwaukee, Toronto, and Los Angeles.[15] Clara Adams described her husband's efforts:

> When they had the sheriff's sale, he went up there and bought these three lots. He built on two lots a little three-room house. He had friends to help him. The funny part about it, he was on WPA at that time and he was talking about building a house. I said, "How you gonna build a house? You haven't got any money." And he said, "I got $50." And I said, "$50?" Cause that tickled me, him talking about building a house on $50. But he said, "Well, if you never start anything, you never get anything."[16]

Buyers with greater resources hired builders, and a few rented or bought houses vacated by early white residents, but most newcomers, like Adams, came out on the weekends or evenings and built their own homes.[17] To cut costs, many used scrap lumber, and they extended construction over long periods, building what they could afford and then waiting until the next few paychecks to proceed. Where family labor or carpentry skills proved insufficient, many builders employed the muscle and abilities of friends and neighbors. An ethic of neighborly aid pervaded the community during the early years of building. Essie Kirklen, whose mother built her own house, remarked that "most everybody could do some kind of fixing, and everybody kind of helped everybody." Ruby Hall, who was a young adult when her father built in the park, remembered: "The neighbors dug the basement by hand, and my father and another man that lived down the street built the house. Everything was done as we went. We paid for the stuff as we went along."[18] In some cases, the products of these labors were little more than tar-paper shelters or rickety "nautilus houses" that expanded each year as a family's needs and income grew.

In spite of primitive conditions and the challenge of owner building, Chagrin Falls Park gained population. The 1930 census enumerated just 57 African American residents, who were interspersed with a smaller number of whites. By 1940, the census tallied 200 African Americans in the park (most whites had moved on), but World War II spurred a period of rapid growth that marked the community's heyday. After the war, Chagrin Falls Park was a bustling settlement with four churches; numerous social clubs; several small night spots, beauty parlors, and stores; and an automobile service station. The community's most notable public buildings were a two-room elementary school, a cinder-block firehouse, and a brand new community center, built with local donations and volunteer labor. By

1950, Chagrin Falls Park was home to approximately 650 black residents, and the community boasted a home-ownership rate of 70 percent, considerably higher than the 52 percent recorded in neighboring Chagrin Falls, where many park residents worked as domestic servants.[19]

Owner building was just one factor that reduced the cost of a suburban home for residents of the park. Living at the margins of their income, residents avoided the cost of utilities by doing without. Like many such communities, Chagrin Falls Park had no paved streets, electricity, gas, water lines, sewers, garbage collection, or local fire protection throughout its early years. Residents lit with kerosene, they dug wells and backyard privies, and they cooked over coal or wood stoves. Families burned or hauled their own garbage (or fed it to the pigs that many kept), and they struggled frantically when a home or church caught fire. Electricity arrived in the park in 1936, when the Bainbridge Township school board built a new (and de facto segregated) elementary school in the community, although it would be decades before some residents connected. The school board also drilled the first deep well in the community, and some residents relied on the schoolhouse pump for water. Other services followed slowly. In 1946, the park welcomed its first paved street, and by that time, a group of local men had established a volunteer fire company. A survey that year revealed that 40 percent of local wells faced imminent danger of seepage from septic tanks and outdoor toilets, but families were left to respond to the problem on an individual basis. Sanitary conditions in the park remained a recurrent problem until the township government laid sewers and storm drains in 1974, but even then a substantial number of residents opposed construction for fear that the tax assessment would price them out of their homes. As late as the 1980s, there were still a few older residents in Chagrin Falls Park who lived in homes without running water.[20]

Although the longevity of primitive services in Chagrin Falls Park represented an extreme, limited public service and regulation were characteristic of working-class suburbanization before 1945. In fact, as Marc A. Weiss and Robert Fishman have noted, the ubiquity of unrestricted development was one of the reasons that cities and suburbs enacted land-use planning in the first place. Still, most suburbs did not enact zoning laws until the 1940s, and even those that did had no influence over development outside their boundaries. Hence, the unincorporated fringe was the native environment of working-class suburbia.[21]

In African American suburbs, however, race often acted as a brake on future improvements. Discrimination in employment and lending kept black suburbs poor and poorly housed, even as working-class white suburbs installed public improvements, upgraded housing, and rose in income after World War II. Racism also made it unlikely that neighboring suburbs would annex, extend utilities, or share schools with these communities. Where black neighborhoods were located within larger suburbs, poor services expressed municipal bias as much as African American thrift, serving as a clear means to mark the color line. Either way, the rustic environment of many black suburbs served to reinforce white racism over time, solidifying in white opinion an equation between black people, poverty, and substandard housing. Poor conditions became the rationale for redlining, municipal avoidance, and inattention. As a result, rudimentary services persisted for much longer in early black suburbs than in most comparable white communities.[22]

In addition to doing without services, residents of Chagrin Falls Park and other suburbs extended their incomes by growing fruit and vegetables and raising small livestock. Ruby Hall recalled that her father "wanted a place where he could have a garden to help with the food, and he got him hogs and killed them in the winter time. A lot of people was doing the same. So people had them a lot of chickens and gardens. A lot of people had been farmers, so they knew how to farm." Throughout the early years of community growth, residents relied on gardens to supply fresh food in the summer and to produce surplus for the winter. Like Mrs. Hall's father, many residents supplemented their diets with animal produce as well. Chickens were abundant, but residents also kept geese and ducks and occasionally a pig or two. A few residents, like Horace Lumpkin, raised animals to sell (or turned corn into alcohol), and others sold garden produce in small stores that dotted the community.[23] Residents also put the nearby landscape to economic use, cutting wood for fuel, picking fruit, and hunting. Essie Kirklen remarked, "[A]ll this was woods back up in here, and people didn't care whose woods it was, and they thinned that woods out and burned it up."[24] Although urban African Americans of the same income level suffered during years of economic hardship, residents of suburbs such as Chagrin Falls Park at least had the cushion of home produce to keep starvation from the door.

Even in prosperous times, though, the challenge of making a living in a community distant from city employment placed a burden on families in Chagrin Falls Park. As low-skilled and low-paid workers, residents acutely felt fluctuations in the business cycle. Most residents held blue-collar jobs, and men often commuted to work in Cleveland or nearby suburbs. Stephen Hall noted: "[W]e went through a whole lot . . . just to be out here . . . [but] there wasn't no thought of us not staying, of this not being home. This was home. Once we got here, this was it. Whatever it took to get back here, that's what we did." Trolley service from Cleveland to Chagrin Falls ceased in 1924, but workers could catch a bus to the city from several neighboring suburbs. Some men drove or carpooled, whereas other men spent the week in the city and weekends in the park with their families. Luke Walker, for example, worked at American Steel and Wire in Cleveland and drove himself and several other park men to and from the city each day. Henry MacMiller and his brother-in-law, Frank Young, were among several park men who worked for the Cleveland Department of Sanitation and who carpooled in MacMiller's auto. Al Turner, on the other hand, worked with his wife as caretaker for a whites-only social club in a nearby suburb.[25] Facing a restrictive job market, limited incomes, and a commute of more than fifteen miles to the most reliable sources of employment, black men in the park risked a great deal more for a home in the suburbs than did their middle-class white counterparts.

Given the insecurity of male employment, women's wage work was vital to the survival of Chagrin Falls Park and suburbs like it. Middle-class white suburbanites could generally afford to live on the salary of a male breadwinner alone, and research on working-class white suburbanites suggests that most married women did not work outside the home.[26] In contrast, working-class black families who aspired to a home in the suburbs often relied on the income of both parents. Whereas men typically commuted to distant jobs, many women found work as domestic servants for white families just a mile away in the village of Chagrin Falls. The 1940 census reported 29 percent of park women employed outside the home, but other sources suggest that women's wage labor played an even more important role than this figure implies. All twelve of the early female settlers of the park interviewed in 1986 reported having worked as domestic servants, cooks, or laundresses at one time or another during their years in Chagrin Falls Park. Moreover, service was the occupation of their mothers, aunts, and sisters in the park. Women who worked exclusively as housewives were identified prominently as such. One elderly man proudly noted that his wife had not had to work outside the home. A 1983 community survey supported this conclusion; when asked to list their occupation, 79 percent of female seniors who had lived in the community for longer than thirty years listed a current occupation or reported the category "retired" as opposed to that of "housewife."[27] Even if the census revealed that less than a third of women were in the labor force at enumeration time, a higher percentage appear to have been employed at crucial times during their lives—periods of male unemployment, for example, or during periods of property accumulation and home building.

In other suburbs, women's participation in the paid labor force varied greatly depending on local economic opportunities, as well as individual choices. In industrial suburbs, where relatively high-paying industrial jobs were available to black men, typically fewer black women worked outside the home than in central cities or other suburbs. In Lackawanna, New York, near Buffalo, just 12 percent of black women were in the paid labor force in 1940. Proportions were almost as low in River Rouge and Ecorse, Michigan, south of Detroit. In these suburbs, there were usually fewer opportunities for working women, but the numbers suggest that black couples also made conscious choices to rely on one income. For these families, suburban factory work was the foundation for a family pattern otherwise common only at the top echelons of black society. By contrast, other suburbs attracted large numbers of black women who needed, or wanted, to work for wages. In leafy suburbs such as Mount Vernon and New Rochelle, New York, where white elites hired domestic laborers, more than 60 percent of black women worked outside the home in 1940, and a proportion above 50 percent was normal in similar suburbs. Black women were often the first migrants in a family to move to domestic service suburbs, and they routinely outnumbered men in the local population by large margins. As in Chagrin Falls Park, women's wage work in a racially segmented labor market was instrumental in establishing these black communities, and women's earnings formed a basis for institution building, home ownership, and family mobility.[28]

In addition to working for wages, black women in all kinds of suburbs stretched incomes through production at home. In Chagrin Falls Park, for example, women took in laundry or sewing from Chagrin Falls, and several daughters remember their mothers rendering soap from lard and selling the product to neighbors or families in Chagrin Falls. Several women in the park also operated small stores. Nellie May Lawrence, who was the local midwife, opened a store in a tar-paper structure in the 1940s from which she sold products ranging from coal oil to candy and fresh produce from her garden. Lottie Lewis and Estella Jackson ran small canteens with jukeboxes and space for dancing. Thursday afternoon, the domestics' day off, was the liveliest time of the week. In addition to increasing women's influence within the community, women's work provided a vital source of income for black families who wanted to purchase land, build homes, and relocate from the city.[29] In contrast to the emphasis on suburban homes as sites of consumption, property in working-class suburbs was the locale of essential domestic production—much of it by women.

Women in Chagrin Falls Park also appear to have played broader public roles than women in white suburbs—regardless of class.[30] That role often included employment outside the home, as well as active participation, if not leadership, in local politics and public affairs. During the 1940s, residents of the park organized a number of campaigns for local improvement, including the establishment of a political organization, a move for municipal incorporation, a desegregation suit against the township school board, and efforts to construct a local community center and a fire station. Women took leading roles in all but the last effort.

The surviving minutes of the Geauga County Negro Republican Club (May 1940–April 1941) offer several examples of women's public roles in Chagrin Falls Park. Established in 1940, the Republican Club rallied voters, secured patronage jobs through the county Republican Party, and transported voters to the polls on election day, as well as sponsoring the local baseball team and other social activities. Within the club, women fulfilled a variety of "traditional" gender roles. For example, women chaired the sick committee and the social committee, they performed the musical numbers that opened and closed each meeting (a man always led the opening prayer), and their comments tended to emphasize social service, health, education, and children. Even before the war began to siphon young men from the community (although most of the club's members were above draft age), women filled three of the five positions on the club's executive committee. Women were nearly equal contributors to the club's frequent collections. Finally, when the club appointed official delegations—to visit the offices of the county Republican chair or the editor of the Cleveland *Call and Post*, the city's black newspaper, for example—women shared these responsibilities.[31] Although women in many suburbs participated in child- and family-related service activities, women's political participation in Chagrin Falls Park suggests an even broader latitude for public action in early African American suburbs.

This same pattern was evident after the war. When residents petitioned Bainbridge Township for incorporation as a village in 1946, a woman led the initiative, and two women served on the three-person committee that presented the case to the township's board of trustees. That same year, a delegation from Chagrin Falls Park addressed the Cleveland Branch of the National Association for the Advancement of Colored People to press for desegregation of the park's elementary school; eleven of the fourteen representatives from the park were women. Two years later, when residents established a local community center, half of the founders were women.[32]

The activities of the irrepressible Essie Kirklen suggest the range of women's roles in Chagrin Falls Park. In the years before 1945, Mrs. Kirklen not only taught Sunday school at the Church of God, but she helped lay the church's foundation and swung a hammer in the church rafters.[33] She raised a son and the children of relatives, and she earned an income for a time through day work in white homes. She purchased building lots at the county sheriff's auction, rented property, and lent a hand while neighbors built homes. She kept minutes for the Republican Club and pushed for the establishment of the community center, and, in 1946, Kirklen led the failed campaign for municipal incorporation. Kirklen was an extraordinary individual, but her vita suggests that there was space in communities such as Chagrin Falls Park for women to play broader public roles than in suburbs of either middle-class or working-class whites. In a suburb with limited economic resources in which men earned uncertain incomes at distant jobs, the needs of community building itself may have challenged gender roles within African American families and offered assertive women the opportunity to shoulder responsibilities that were less available elsewhere.

TOWARD A WORKING-CLASS AFRICAN AMERICAN SUBURBAN VISION

The most important reason early residents gave for settling in Chagrin Falls Park was the desire to own a house and property. Among early settlers, the value for property ownership ran so deep that it needed almost no explanation. Ruby Hall, for example, noted that families like hers moved to the park because "wasn't nobody could buy in the city." Others seemed to take it for granted that working-class people would buy property when the chance presented itself. Describing the events that led to her move in 1940, Clara Adams recalled:

> I had a couple of days [of work] per week out in Euclid [another suburb], and I met Mrs. Love who was living out here. She was telling me about the lots and how you would get them for four and five dollars. . . . I told my husband about this, and so he wanted to meet her. She told him about how he could go to the sheriff's sale in Chardon and get these lots. So when they had the sheriff's sale, he went up there and bought three lots.

To Ruby Hall, the reason people struggled to build a community in an isolated section of suburban Cleveland was simple. "Everybody at that time," she said, "wanted a little place of their own."[34]

The desire for "a place of one's own," historians have shown, has been a central feature of American suburbanization since the nineteenth century. Exactly what different groups wanted and why, however, remain subjects for debate. Middle-class whites, for example, often invested home ownership with images of masculine independence, female domesticity, and idealized nuclear families (not to mention long-term capital appreciation). Working-class whites, on the other hand, more often valued home ownership for its everyday economic usefulness, as well as for economic security over the long run.[35] Among African Americans in Chagrin Falls Park, too, the desire for home ownership reflected several interrelated values that included strategies of economic subsistence. A closer look at the meaning of home ownership and the broader pattern of settlement and community life in Chagrin Falls Park and other suburbs suggests the outlines of a working-class African American suburban vision rooted in settlers' experience in the rural South as well as their expectations for life in the northern metropolis.

As black southerners, Chagrin Falls Park residents' value for property ownership had a long history. In the aftermath of the Civil War, property ownership was closely related to freedom in the aspirations of former slaves. Throughout the late nineteenth and early twentieth centuries, property ownership persisted among the chief objectives of blacks in the rural South.[36] Proprietorship symbolized hard work and ambition in a way evident to every member of the community. It provided a basis for upward mobility, shelter for immediate and extended families, and a footing in a society that systematically marginalized African Americans. Last, it meant a greater degree of independence, which is to say freedom, than any form of tenancy. Although historians such as James Grossman have suggested that the ideal of upward mobility through urban industrial labor gradually supplanted the value of independent landownership among African Americans as the Great Migration progressed, rural southerners who boarded trains for northern cities did not discard older values easily. Peter Gottlieb suggests as much in his study of black migrants to Pittsburgh, adding that the difficulty most blacks faced in finding and purchasing housing contributed to a lasting ambivalence about northern life. Even more recently, anthropologist Carol Stack has revealed that the desire to own or protect family property, even at the cost of modern utilities, is among the values that have drawn many African Americans back to the rural South since 1970.[37]

Despite limited means, thousands of African Americans in Cleveland and other cities jumped at the chance to buy property. Although some may have relinquished this dream over time, others clearly did not. Early park resident Nellie May Lawrence was a case in point. As her daughter explained, Mrs. Lawrence had been a sharecropper all her life—"did all the work, give 'em half the profits." Consequently, she "always wanted to be in a home of her own."[38] For migrants like Mrs. Lawrence, communities like Chagrin Falls Park offered the prospect of upward mobility through urban labor without the sacrifice of long-held desires for independent property ownership. Hence, for a significant group of African American migrants before World War II, suburbanization combined the best of both worlds.

In addition to fulfilling historic desires for property ownership, a house of one's own represented an economic strategy for many early suburbanites. Here, however, African American values merged with those of working-class whites. As Richard Harris and Becky Nicolaides demonstrate, owner building and other economic uses of housing were widespread among working-class suburbanites in the early twentieth century. Gardens and livestock helped families economize. Proprietorship allowed them to escape central-city rents, and home ownership occasionally provided income that supported economic mobility and helped families weather hard times. Regardless of race or ethnicity, domestic production was a characteristic feature of working-class suburbia.[39]

This was particularly true of black suburbs, where sources offer abundant evidence of self-provisioning and other economic uses of property across the range of suburban types. In Homestead, Pennsylvania, for instance, Margaret Byington reported in 1910 that African American and white immigrant steelworkers used yards for gardening and raising small livestock whenever they could. Similarly, Gretchen Lemke-Santangelo reveals that black women in wartime Richmond, California, almost uniformly kept kitchen gardens where they grew okra, collards, butter beans, sweet potatoes, and other vegetables. By growing familiar foods, they not only supplemented their income and diet but also reinforced community bonds through exchange and preserved direct links to their heritage as African American southerners.[40]

Black suburbanites not only grew food in their backyards but also used interior spaces as a source of income. Women took in laundry, sewing, or piecework, and, as one New York suburbanite noted, "There were rooms in the house, which could be rented to get extra money."[41] In some suburbs, builders inscribed the practice into the landscape by constructing or converting houses for two or more families.[42] In Chagrin Falls Park, Estella Jackson not only ran a small canteen in her house but she and her husband also built an addition to their home that they rented to recent arrivals. Essie Kirklen initially rented space from another family when she moved to Chagrin Falls Park, and once she became settled, she, too, occasionally took in boarders to supplement her family's income. Clara Adams's husband built their own home as well as three additional houses, which the Adamses kept as rentals. Socially and economically, then, home ownership in suburbs like Chagrin Falls Park supported upward mobility for many African American families. Magnolia Strickland's comments that open this essay support precisely this point. Looking back from 1959, Strickland remembered that her twenty years in Chagrin Falls Park had not been easy, but they had been worth the struggle. Measuring the distance she had traveled from the rural South by the amenities of her Chagrin Falls Park home, she concluded, "I couldn't have done all that in Cleveland."[43]

In addition to supporting upward mobility, home ownership in a suburb like Chagrin Falls Park reflected migrants' insecurity regarding the urban economy. Although wage relations had expanded in the South during the late nineteenth and early twentieth centuries, millions of southern blacks worked as tenant farmers at the margins of the cash economy. With expanding industrial job opportunities during World War I, thousands of young southerners left this life behind—often moving to nearby towns or cities before making the leap north. High wages promised access to a world of new consumer goods, but the transition to a cash economy could also be traumatic. As wage workers at the bottom of the metropolitan labor market, African American migrants suffered greatly during slumps in the economy. Dependence on an urban wage alone could spell disaster in the event of unemployment, sickness, or injury. Hence, like many European immigrants, as well as native-born whites, some black migrants responded to "proletarianization" by holding on to familiar patterns of economic survival.[44] Household production in the suburbs was a cushion against the market and a middle ground between rural and urban life.

A number of contemporary observers drew this same connection, often contrasting suburbanites' "rural" strategies with "progressive" or "modern" city life. For example, a black social worker argued critically in 1926 that residents of black suburbs often "slip into old southern rural ways of doing things." A black real estate agent in the same study agreed, noting that in the suburbs, "there is no opportunity for a type of development which would enable them to adjust to an urban environment."[45] To the contrary, it appears that many early suburbanites were doing just that. For laboring families who understood privation firsthand, these strategies were not backward; they were adaptive and practical. Several residents of Chagrin Falls Park remarked pointedly that they had seen hard times, but they had never gone hungry. Although many southern migrants embraced the market—perhaps, as Lizabeth Cohen argues, more avidly than their working-class white counterparts—others were clearly chastened by the experience, and some sought a life-style in the suburbs that gave them access to urban opportunities without requiring complete dependence on the market.[46] Evidence from black suburbs suggests that migrants brought with them diverse ideas about survival and mobility in the northern metropolis as well as considerable ambivalence about the urban economy.

In other ways, too, black suburbanites adapted to life in the North by bringing parts of the South with them. Like migrants to central cities, early black suburbanites followed intricate migration chains to the suburbs.[47] The kinship network of Chagrin Falls Park resident Sallie Denson suggests the ways that extended family supported the development of suburban communities. Mrs. Denson, a widow, moved to the park in the late 1920s and built a cinder-block house on Geneva Street with the help of her grown children. By the early 1930s, five of those children, Essie, Edith, Cornelia, Letha, and Pete, had relocated from Cleveland to Chagrin Falls Park with their spouses. Two other sons, John and Willie, lived in the park with their wives for a short time before returning to Cleveland. By 1940, Essie's sister-in-law and her husband had also settled there, as had two of Mrs. Denson's nephews and their wives. Those wives, Annie and Mattie Pounds, attracted cousins, Shepherd Beck and Nellie May Lawrence, to settle with their families in Chagrin Falls Park during the early 1940s. The Denson family had among the most extensive kin relations in the park, but other early residents followed a similar pattern, settling with or joining family already living in the park. Henry MacMiller and his sister, Josephine Young, for example, settled with their spouses in the late 1920s. Josephine's brother-in-law, Eugene Young, and his wife also settled in the park in the early 1930s. In 1936,

Mr. MacMiller's adult daughter, Ruby Hall, moved to Chagrin Falls Park with her husband.[48] By the 1940s, a strong network of kin-based suburbanization had created a web of familial relationships that bound residents to one another as a community. In a suburb where incomes and jobs were insecure, transportation inconvenient, and voluntary cooperation important for survival, extended families were a bulwark against hardship and a foundation for upward mobility. In contrast to the middle-class suburban model of this era, which was characterized by child-centered nuclear families, suburbanization for African Americans in Chagrin Falls Park strengthened the bonds of extended family and friendships that stretched through Cleveland to roots in the South.[49]

Finally, in addition to visions of home and family, residents expressed normative ideas about landscape that reflected their experience in the South and shaped the community they built in the suburbs. "My family heard about a place where they could buy them some land which reminded them of home," Ruby Hall said. "They all came from the South, and they had lived in Cleveland for many years, but they never forgot their home. They wanted a little place where they could have chickens and different little things and a little farm life and gardens." Weighing the sacrifice of city services against the benefits of country living, Clara Adams, who relocated with her husband in 1940, claimed:

> I didn't mind it [giving up a modern apartment in Cleveland]. When we came out here it was just so nice and quiet. You didn't hear nothing but the birds in the morning singing nice. It was where I could have a garden, and I liked that. So it wasn't hard at all. Plus, I was used to the country. That's where I was raised up, so it didn't bother me at all. I didn't like [life] in the city—too congested. I liked out. I like the fresh air, and it's nice and quiet.[50]

Magnolia Strickland echoed these sentiments, noting, "I think I bettered my conditions. I had a nice new house to live in. I had nice, fresh air, and you could have vegetables and a garden."[51] Based on preferences such as these, residents let side lots grow thick, they cultivated extensive gardens, and they planted fruit trees and even familiar pine trees from "down home." In the evenings, they sat on front porches they had built and surveyed the quiet. Like middle-class suburbanites, they created a bucolic landscape of residence in union with nature, but with a difference. For early park settlers, the prospect of fresh air, birdsong, open space, and "a little farm life and gardens" outweighed the desire for modern conveniences that were fundamental to middle-class suburbanization. Their landscape was more rustic, but it was no less suburban.[52]

Coupled with the attractions of country living, many park settlers also explained their relocation in terms of repulsion from the city. "I was determined not to live in Cleveland," said Fanny Detwyler. Mrs. Detwyler brought her mistrust of urban living directly from the North Carolina countryside, and she avoided the city altogether in her journey to Chagrin Falls Park. Other early residents, however, sought upward mobility through migration to Cleveland and other cities, and they found the experience wanting. Congestion, poverty—especially during the Depression—and what some perceived as the atmosphere of immorality that plagued certain city neighborhoods spurred many early park residents to seek a better place to live. Magnolia Strickland remarked, "I wanted to move out here, I wanted to move anywhere, because East 61st and Thackery was no good."[53] Ruby Hall stressed that many people like herself came because of rum running and rent parties in Cleveland's crowded east side—"especially a person that had a family and they didn't believe in none of that stuff."[54] Truck driver Shepherd Beck explained his decision in terms of sleep. "I was working the road, and I'd come home and all the children from the neighborhood was playing ball in my yard and yelling. How am I gonna sleep? I said, 'I'm gonna find me some place quiet.'"[55] The place he found was Chagrin Falls Park.

Beyond the environmental influence of southern roots, race and the shared culture of African Americans shaped the process of early black suburbanization. External pressures, as well as internal cohesion, ensured that most black suburbanites lived in a segregated world. Racism limited black incomes and prevented black families from buying property in all but a few areas of the metropolis—often marginal land with few services. Similarly, bias in mortgage lending encouraged working-class black families to build their own homes and to use property to supplement income. Although informal home building was common among working-class whites, it was a choice that African Americans made from even fewer options. Race also shaped early black suburbanization from the inside. Suburbanites' passion for home ownership sprang from a venerable black tradition in the South. Patterns of family migration and settlement followed lines that were common among African American migrants in general, and women's economic activity in many suburbs reflected the wider economic participation of black women in the wage economy. Here again, the distinction between externally imposed necessity and internal choice is difficult to discern, but clearly some black women chose to settle in suburbs because they were good places to work as well as to live.

If race and racism shaped early black suburbanization, suburban life itself tended to reinforce migrants' racial identities.[56] Held at arm's length by white suburbanites, African Americans relied on their own resources. They established separate institutions, worshiped in separate churches, and socialized in a predominantly black milieu. In Chagrin Falls Park, black men rode to work together and labored with other blacks in segmented occupations—in the foundry at American Steel and Wire, for example, or at the back of a garbage truck with the Department of Sanitation. Women who worked as domestic servants had closer connections with local whites, but at best these relationships left racism unchallenged. Religious groups from the park visited black churches in nearby suburbs such as Twinsburg and Miles Heights, and ministers from these communities, as well as Cleveland, preached guest sermons in local churches. The park baseball team played black "nines" from all over northeastern Ohio, and when the Republican Club hosted an August fish fry, black families from Cleveland and its suburbs crowded Woodland Avenue with their automobiles and "walked in that dust like it was gold dust."[57] Encouraged by persisting white racism as well as their own sense of accomplishment, residents of such places as Chagrin Falls Park forged a distinct sense of themselves as both African Americans and suburbanites.

Although early African American suburbanites confronted the challenge of urbanization as black people with a unique history and culture, they also followed patterns that were common among working-class suburbanites generally, and they shaped a landscape that shared many features with a wider working-class suburbia. Faced with similar economic circumstances, they responded to urban industrial capitalism in part by withdrawing from it. They valued home ownership for many of the same economic reasons, and they pursued similar strategies of economic subsistence: owner building, home gardening, and other productive uses of domestic space. Working-class suburbanites responded to the urban economy in similar ways, whether they were Mexican immigrants in East Los Angeles; Polish workers in Milwaukee or Detroit; blue-collar emigrants from the British Isles in Toronto or Hamilton, Ontario; or African Americans in Chagrin Falls Park.[58]

Even as suburbs like Chagrin Falls Park peaked in population after World War II, conditions that had nurtured early working-class suburbanization began to change. Rapid white suburbanization led to the adoption of land-use controls in formerly unregulated areas. Zoning and building codes curtailed informal home building and raised the price of a suburban home for working-class and poor families. Racist application of these regulations, too, closed the door on development for blacks, and the enforcement of sanitary regulations led to the demolition of existing black housing and restrictions on domestic production. A number of suburbs also resorted to urban renewal as a means of isolating, or even expelling, suburban black communities.[59]

At the same time, federal intervention in the housing market and the development of a welfare state undercut some of the economic insecurity that had shaped early working-class suburbanization. This was especially true for working-class whites, but the same trends also affected African Americans. The extension of social security and unemployment insurance to a growing number of black workers, as well as black entrance into unions in the 1940s, promised the kinds of economic security that suburban home ownership had provided before the war. Further, the establishment of federal mortgage programs accommodated the dreams of home ownership for millions of blue-collar families without the hardships of owner building. Comparatively few blacks and other minorities participated in these programs. Even so, tens of thousands of modestly priced new homes were constructed for African Americans during the late 1940s and 1950s, and FHA (Federal Housing Administration) insistence on racial segregation ensured that most were built within existing black areas—usually older black suburbs.[60] Although home ownership became marginally more available to middle-income black families and black home-ownership rates inched upward, poor families were increasingly priced out of the market. Within a decade of the war, regulation of the suburbs had foreclosed a wide range of working-class suburban outlets, and federal subsidies limited the number who were willing or able to make the move out from the city. By the mid-1950s, the stream of new black suburbanites had shifted measurably toward the middle class.[61]

Semi-rural suburbs like Chagrin Falls Park weathered these changes poorly. The park tripled in population during the 1940s, and it reached a peak of nearly 900 in 1960 as a new wave of black southerners hit the city. However, population dwindled thereafter. As African American living standards improved nationally during the 1950s and 1960s, black expectations for life in an "affluent society" expanded. Strategies of working-class subsistence that had served early suburbanites failed to support a standard of living that was satisfactory to most urban-born African Americans. Whereas pioneer suburbanites preferred a life-style reminiscent of the rural South, their children and grandchildren often saw these places as "the boondocks." Moreover, they had a greater number of options. By the 1990s, population in Chagrin Falls Park had shrunk to less than 500, and average incomes remained the lowest in Geauga County.[62] Even so, dozens of long-term families and elderly singles lived independently in homes that they owned.

Even though many African American suburbs suffered depopulation and chronic poverty, their history belies the mystique of suburbia as the preserve of elite and middle-class whites. In the years before 1950, thousands of central-city blacks moved to suburbs. Long ridiculed as "poverty pockets" and "suburban slums," the communities where they settled were poor, but they were fully part of the national trend toward urban decentralization known as suburbanization. At the same time, they reflected a vision of residential, family, and community life that was at once suburban, working-class, and African American. This vision, as much as economic necessity, shaped the landscape of American suburbia in the same fashion as the well-documented dreams of middle-class whites.

Early residents of Chagrin Falls Park valued home ownership less as a long-term capital investment or as shelter for an idealized nuclear family than for its usefulness in cutting costs, providing supplemental income, and limiting dependence on a fragile wage. Equally important, home ownership was a basic symbol of status in African American communities of the South and a marker by which to measure upward mobility in the North. To the southerners who settled in Chagrin Falls Park, home ownership was a long-deferred dream, and they were willing to sacrifice urban services and modern conveniences in order to achieve it.

Like other suburbanites, residents of Chagrin Falls Park expressed preferences for a bucolic landscape, but their ideal included unrefined open space, an elaborate garden, small livestock, and the familiar food and routine that these implied. In these suburbs, the cackle of chickens was more common than the sound of a lawn mower. Women's participation in the economic and civic life of Chagrin Falls Park also distinguished it from white suburbs of the era, and the family ideal that encouraged settlement in Chagrin Falls Park placed higher value on kinship networks than on nuclear family. Extended families allowed women to work outside the home without worrying about the care of their children. They provided conduits for information about employment and economic support during times of need. Last, the complex networks of family and friendship that characterized Chagrin Falls Park laid a foundation for an intimate, stable, and controllable community life that differed from both central-city black neighborhoods and the highly mobile, individualistic, and nuclear-family-based society of middle-class white suburbia. To a greater or lesser extent, similar patterns can be discerned in early black suburbs of all kinds.

Finally, early black suburbanites shared a common displeasure with the quality of life in many city neighborhoods. They desired an atmosphere reminiscent of the small towns and countryside from which most had come. Low incomes and white racism often thwarted these designs, but where they could, early black suburbanites shaped the landscape to suit their preferences as well as their needs. Like white suburbanites, they settled in places that combined country pleasures with proximity to urban jobs and the cultural and social opportunities of the city. In short, they built suburbs.

NOTES

An earlier version of this essay appeared as "The Other Suburbanites: African American Suburbanization in the North Before 1950," *Journal of American History* 85 (March 1999): 1495–1524.

1. Quoted in "Negroes Fight for Better Life in Chagrin Park Shantytown," Cleveland *Plain Dealer*, February 2, 1959, 1.

2. Marvel Daines, *Be It Ever So Tumbled: The Story of a Suburban Slum* (Detroit: Marvel Daines, 1940); Greg Stricharchuk, "The Secret Chagrin Falls," *Cleveland Magazine* 10 (February 1981): 49–51, 122–127, 134; Harold M. Rose, "The All-Black Town: Suburban Prototype or Rural Slum?" *Urban Affairs Annual Reviews* 6 (1972): 407; Leonard Blumberg and Michael Lalli, "Little Ghettoes: A Study of Negroes in the Suburbs," *Phylon* 27 (Summer 1966): 117–131; Harold M. Rose, *Black Suburbanization: Access to Improved Quality of Life or Maintenance of the Status Quo?* (Cambridge: Ballinger Publishing, 1976).

3. In 1940, the U.S. Census defined suburbs as "thickly settled" districts adjacent to a central city; however, it drew metropolitan limits using county boundaries. By this definition, there were 468,000 African Americans in northern suburbs and 32,000 in suburbs in the West in 1940 (compared with 208,000 and 7,000, respectively, in 1910). In the North and West, most black suburbanites were recent migrants who held urban jobs. In the South, there were 982,000 African Americans in "suburbs" in 1940; many of them, however, were actually farmers. Eighteenth Census of the U.S.: 1960, *Population*, vol. 2, pt. 1 D: *Selected Area Reports, Standard Metropolitan Statistical Areas* (Washington, DC: U.S. Government Printing Office, 1963), 2–5.

4. Nonwhite home ownership, 1940 (city vs. suburban ring): Chicago, 7 percent vs. 25 percent; Kansas City, 15:49; St. Louis, 7:43; Los Angeles, 24:34; Detroit, 15:49; Newark (Essex County), 3:17; Philadelphia, 10:28; Pittsburgh, 13:19. Sixteenth Census of the United States: 1940, *Housing*, vol. 2, *General Characteristics*, pt. 2: *Alabama–Indiana* (Washington, DC: U.S. Government Printing Office, 1943), 213, 763; pt. 3: *Iowa–Montana*, 575, 869; pt. 4: *Nebraska–Pennsylvania*, 145, 859, 176.

5. For the ways in which migrants refreshed and reconstructed southern values in northern cities, see Darlene Clark Hine, "Black Migration in the Urban Midwest: The Gender Dimension, 1915–1945," in *The Great Migration in Historical Perspective: New Dimensions of Race, Class, and Gender*, ed. Joe William Trotter Jr. (Bloomington: Indiana University Press, 1991), 134. See also James Borchert, *Alley Life in Washington: Family, Community, Religion, and Folklife in the City, 1850–1970* (Urbana: University of Illinois Press, 1980), 100–142.

6. Reynolds Farley, "The Changing Distribution of Negroes Within Metropolitan Areas: The Emergence of Black Suburbs," *American Journal of Sociology* 75 (January 1970): 333–351; Richard Harris, "Working Class Home Ownership in the American Metropolis," *Journal of Urban History* 17 (November 1990): 46–69.

7. Classic studies of U.S. suburbanization include Sam Bass Warner Jr., *Streetcar Suburbs: The Process of Growth in Boston, 1870–1900* (Cambridge, MA: Harvard University Press, 1962); Kenneth T. Jackson, *Crabgrass Frontier: The Suburbanization of the United States* (New York: Oxford University Press, 1985); Henry Binford, *The First Suburbs* (Chicago: University of Chicago Press, 1985); Robert Fishman, *Bourgeois Utopias: The Rise and Fall of Suburbia* (New York: Basic Books, 1987); John Stilgoe, *Borderland: Origins of the American Suburb, 1820–1939* (New Haven, CT: Yale University Press, 1988); Margaret Marsh, *Suburban Lives* (New Brunswick, NJ: Rutgers University Press, 1990). Recent scholarship has begun to encompass the diversity of population on the urban rim. See Rosalyn Baxandall and Elizabeth Ewen, *Picture Windows: How the Suburbs Happened* (New York: Basic Books, 2000); Dolores Hayden, *Building Suburbia: Green Fields and Urban Growth, 1820–2000* (New York: Vintage, 2003); Richard Harris, *Unplanned Suburbs: Toronto's American Tragedy, 1900*

to 1950 (Baltimore: Johns Hopkins University Press, 1996); Becky M. Nicolaides, *My Blue Heaven: Life and Politics in the Working-Class Suburbs of Los Angeles, 1920–1965* (Chicago: University of Chicago Press, 2002).

8. On working-class suburbanization, see Harris, "Working Class Home Ownership," 56, 58, 62; Richard Harris, "The Unplanned Blue-Collar Suburb in Its Heyday, 1900–1940," in *Geographical Snapshots of North America*, ed. Donald G. Janelle (New York: Guilford Press, 1992), 94–98; Harris, *Unplanned Suburbs*; Becky Nicolaides, "'Where the Working Man Is Welcomed': Working-Class Suburbia in Los Angeles, 1900–1940," *Pacific Historical Review* 68, no. 4 (November 1999): 517–559; Nicolaides, *My Blue Heaven*; also Stephan Thernstrom, *Poverty and Progress: Social Mobility in a Nineteenth Century City* (Cambridge, MA: Harvard University Press, 1964), 117–122, 135–137, 155–157; Roger Simon, "Housing and Services in an Immigrant Neighborhood: Milwaukee's 14th Ward," *Journal of Urban History* 2 (August 1976): 435–458; Olivier Zunz, *The Changing Face of Inequality: Urbanization, Industrial Development, and Immigrants in Detroit, 1880–1920* (Chicago: University of Chicago Press, 1982), 152–153.

9. On African American suburbanization, see Harold M. Rose, "The All-Negro Town: Its Evolution and Function," *Geographical Review* 55 (July 1965): 362–381; Bruce B. Williams, *Black Workers in an Industrial Suburb* (New Brunswick, NJ: Rutgers University Press, 1987); Ann Morris and Henrietta Ambrose, *North Webster: A Photographic History of a Black Community* (Bloomington: Indiana University Press, 1993); Henry L. Taylor Jr., "City Building, Public Policy, the Rise of the Industrial City, and Black Ghetto-Slum Formation in Cincinnati, 1850–1940," in *Race and the City: Work, Community, and Protest in Cincinnati, 1820–1970*, ed. Henry L. Taylor Jr. (Urbana: University of Illinois Press, 1993); Andrew Wiese, "Places of Our Own: Suburban Black Towns Before 1960," *Journal of Urban History* 19 (May 1993): 30–54; Thomas J. Sugrue, *Origins of the Urban Crisis: Race and Inequality in Post War Detroit* (Princeton, NJ: Princeton University Press, 1996), 39–41; Shirley Ann Wilson Moore, *To Place Our Deeds: The African American Community in Richmond, California, 1910–1963* (Los Angeles: University of California Press, 2000); Bruce D. Haynes, *Red Lines, Black Spaces: The Politics of Race and Space in a Black Middle Class Suburb* (New Haven, CT: Yale University Press, 2001), 18–52. The first synthetic work is Leslie Wilson, "Dark Spaces: An Account of Afro-American Suburbanization," Ph.D. diss., City University of New York, 1991. For a survey, see Andrew Wiese, *Places of Their Own: African American Suburbanization in the 20th Century* (Chicago: University of Chicago Press, 2004).

10. Judge Manuel Rocker (grandson of Samuel Rocker) interview by Andrew Wiese, July 1986; Geauga County Torrens Record Docket, no. 1, Geauga County Recorder (Courthouse Annex, Chardon, Ohio); "For This We Waited," *Jewish World*, June 14, 1921, 1; "New Allotment Is Started," *Chagrin Falls Exponent*, June 23, 1921.

11. Ads appeared for subdivisions in Amityville, Deer Park, Yonkers, Croton, and Jamaica (Queens), New York; and New Brunswick, Asbury Park, Hackensack, Plainfield, Westwood, Coytesville, Reevytown, Potter's Station, Rahway, and Fanwood, New Jersey. *New York Age*, April 16, 1921, July 30, 1921; *Amsterdam News*, November 29, 1922; *Chicago Defender*, January 17, 1920, February 24, 1923. *The Gazette* advertised lots in Oakwood and Miles Heights as well as in Oberlin, Ohio; Douglass Park, near Washington; and Egg Harbor, New Jersey. *Cleveland Gazette*, April 5, 1924; *Cleveland Gazette*, March 26,

1921. "High Ridge Park, the Land of Promise," *Baltimore Afro American*, August 15, 1925; "Oakdale Park . . . Florida's Greatest Colored Addition," *Pittsburgh Courier*, March 13, 1926; "$1 a Week Pays for a Crestas Lot," ibid., May 7, 1927. For the *California Eagle*, see Wilson, "Dark Spaces," 76–79.

12. "$5 per Month Buys You a Lot near Hackensack," *Amsterdam News*, November 29, 1922, 8; "Stop Paying Rent," *Cleveland Gazette*, June 14, 1924, 1; for Shrewsbury Manor and Reevytown, New Jersey, see "Join Hands with Your Own People," *Amsterdam News*, October 17, 1923, 11; for New Brunswick, New Jersey, see "Plenty of Work at a High Wage Scale," *Chicago Defender*, January 17, 1920, 3; for Jamaica, New York, see "Opportunity for Colored People to Own a Home," ibid., July 7, 1917, 3. Subdivisions intended for blacks often had race-coded names, such as Booker Terrace (Amityville, New York) (Subdivision Registrations, Babylon Town Assessor, Babylon Town Hall, Lindenhurst, NY), Douglass Park (near Washington, DC) (*Cleveland Gazette*, April 5, 1924, 2), and Lincoln Heights (Oakwood, Ohio) (ibid., May 31, 1924, 1).

13. For advertised real estate prices in Cleveland, see *Cleveland Gazette*, 1921–1927; Essie Kirklen interview by Wiese, July 16, 1986; William Hagler interview by Wiese, August 11, 1986; *Geauga County Common Pleas Court Appearance and Execution Docket*, nos. 1–7, 1929–1941, Common Pleas Court of Geauga County (Geauga County Courthouse, Chardon, Ohio).

14. Using deed records, membership rosters, and other local sources, I compiled a list of 150 adults who lived in Chagrin Falls Park before 1945. Using Cleveland city directories, I verified a last place of residence in Cleveland for 93 household heads, occupations for 73, and housing tenure for 66. Fifty-three percent of men who moved to Chagrin Falls held unskilled jobs before their move, compared with 45 percent of black men in Cleveland in 1930. Another 9 percent worked in domestic or personal service, compared with 16 percent of black men in Cleveland. Kenneth Kusmer, *A Ghetto Takes Shape: Black Cleveland 1870–1930* (Urbana: University of Illinois Press, 1976), 201; Andrew Wiese, "A Place of Our Own: The Chagrin Falls Park from 1921 through 1950," Senior honors thesis, University of Iowa, 1987, appendix, 4–9. Evidence for nativity is anecdotal. Thirteen of fifteen early residents interviewed for this project were born in the South, as were their spouses and extended families. Because of the role of family ties in peopling the park, this sample provided information for several dozen families who moved to Chagrin Falls before 1950. By all reports, southerners were the great majority.

15. See Richard Harris, "Self Building and the Social Geography of Toronto, 1901–1913: A Challenge for Urban Theory," *Transactions, Institute of British Geographers, New Series* 15 (1990): 387–402; Richard Harris, "Self-Building in the Urban Housing Market," *Economic Geography* 67 (January 1991): 1–21; Richard Harris, "The Unplanned Blue-Collar Suburb in Its Heyday, 1900–1940," in *Geographical Snapshots of North America*, 94–98; Simon, "Housing and Services in an Immigrant Neighborhood"; Zunz, *The Changing Face of Inequality*, 152–153; and Nicolaides, "'Where the Workingman Is Welcomed.'"

16. Clara Adams interview by Wiese, July 29, 1986.

17. Essie Kirklen interview by Wiese, August 15, 1986; Shepherd Beck interview by Wiese, August 18, 1986; Lula Hitchcock interview by Wiese, July 31, 1986.

18. Kirklen interview, July 16, 1986; Ruby Hall interview by Wiese, July 7, 1986.

19. Totals for 1930 and 1940 are for Bainbridge Township. The total for 1950 is esti-mated from the "Negro" population of Geauga County (758). Fifteenth Census of the United States: 1930, *Population*, vol. 3, pt. 2: *Montana–Wyoming* (Washington, DC: U.S. Government Printing Office, 1932), 521; Sixteenth Census of the United States: 1940, *Population*, vol. 2, *Characteristics of the Population*, pt. 5: *New York–Oregon* (Washington, DC: U.S. Government Printing Office, 1943), 628; Seventeenth Census of the United States: 1950, *Population*, vol. 2, *Characteristics of the Population*, pt. 35: *Ohio* (Washington, DC: U.S. Government Printing Office, 1952), 183. Rural, non-farm home ownership by blacks in Geauga County (the category that comprised the park) was 73 percent; Sixteenth Census of the United States: 1940, *Housing*, vol. 2, pt. 4: *Nebraska–Pennsylvania* (Washington, DC: U.S. Government Printing Office, 1943), 609, 613.

20. "Chagrin Falls Park Plans to Revitalize," *Cleveland Call and Post*, December 21, 1974, 3; Mary E. Crawford, "Bainbridge School Investigation," March 15, 1946, Chagrin Falls Park School File, Papers of the National Association for the Advancement of Colored People (NAACP), Cleveland Branch (Western Reserve Historical Society, Cleveland, Ohio); "Re *Lois Wilson v. Chagrin Board of Education, Geauga County*," August 2, 1945, ibid.; "Park School Origins," October 1963, Kenston School Board Records (Kenston School District Offices, Bainbridge, Ohio); Raymond J. Walsh, "Exclusionary Housing Practices in Bainbridge Township, Geauga County, Ohio," typescript, May 31, 1972, 3. Rustic conditions characterized many black suburbs through the 1960s. Farley, "Changing Distribution of Negroes," 340; see also David Kenneth Bruner, "A General Survey of the Negro Population of Evanston," Senior thesis, Northwestern University, 1924, 34.

21. Marc A. Weiss, *Rise of the Community Builders: The American Real Estate Industry and Urban Land Planning* (New York: Columbia University Press, 1987), 68–72; Robert Fishman, "Comment," panel "The Other Suburbanites," Organization of American Historians meeting, April 1992; see also J. C. Nichols, "When You Buy a Home Site You Make an Investment, Try to Make It a Safe One," *Good Housekeeping* 76 (February 1923): 38–39. On uneven land-use restrictions in incorporated suburbs, see Harris, *Unplanned Suburbs*, 147–160; Becky M. Nicolaides, "In Search of the Good Life: Community and Politics in Working Class Los Angeles, 1922–1955," Ph.D. diss., Columbia University, 1993, 47–48, 54–62, 65, 247–285; Andrew Wiese, "Black Housing, White Finance: African American Housing and Home Ownership in Evanston, Illinois, Before 1940," *Journal of Social History* 33 (Winter 1999): 429–459; Blumberg and Lalli, "Little Ghettoes," 117.

22. Rose, "All-Black Town," 398–399, 418; Wiese, "Struggle for the Suburban Dream," 211–212.

23. Ruby and Stephen Hall interview by Wiese, July 20, 1986. See also Hitchcock interview; Fannie Derwyler interview by Wiese, August 19, 1986; Clydie Smith interview by Wiese, July 29, 1986; Estella Jackson interview by Wiese, August 18, 1986; Lumpkin divorce, Case 8934, November 19, 1937, Geauga County Common Pleas Court (Geauga County Courthouse, Chardon, Ohio).

24. Kirklen interview, July 16, 1986.

25. Ruby and Stephen Hall interview by Wiese, August 22, 1986; Hitchcock inter-view; Ruby and Stephen Hall interview, August 22, 1986; Essie Kirklen interview by Wiese, August 11, 1986; "Summary of the Chagrin Falls Park School Case," typescript, January 11, 1946, 2 (Cleveland NAACP Papers).

26. Nicolaides, *My Blue Heaven*, 51; Richard Harris and Robert Lewis, "The Geography of North American Cities and Suburbs, 1900–1950: A New Synthesis," *Journal of Urban History* 27 (March 2001): 279.

27. Census of Population, 1940, vol. 2, pt. 5: *New York–Oregon* (Washington, 1943), 593; Beck interview; Chagrin Falls Park Community Center, "Residents' Roster," 1983.

28. Rates of black female employment in domestic service suburbs, 1940: Evanston, Illinois (56%); Mount Vernon (65%), New Rochelle (62%), and White Plains (60%), New York; Montclair (62%), East Orange (54%), and Englewood (50%), New Jersey; Webster Groves, Missouri (54%); and Pasadena, California (41%). Female paid labor-force participation in central cities ranged from one-third to one-half: Chicago (35%), Cleveland (35%), St. Louis (37%), Newark (40%), Los Angeles (42%), and New York (51%). Census of Population: 1940, vol. 2, pt. 1: *Alabama–District of Columbia*, 617, 633; ibid., pt. 2: *Florida–Iowa*, 631, 643; pt. 4: *Minnesota–New Mexico*, 445, 459, 893, 896, 928; pt. 5: *New York–Oklahoma*, 132, 135, 160.

29. Alma Walker interview with Wiese, August 12, 1986; Hitchcock interview; Derwyler interview.

30. Marsh, *Suburban Lives*, 100–101, 109–111, 174–179; David Contosta, *Suburb in the City: Chestnut Hill, Philadelphia, 1850–1990* (Columbus: Ohio State University Press, 1992), 175–189; Nicolaides, *My Blue Heaven*, 102–104.

31. Minutes Book, May 1, 1940, to April 25, 1941, Geauga County Negro Republican Club.

32. "Minutes of Special Meeting," November 6, 1946, Bainbridge Township Board of Commissioners (Bainbridge Township Hall, Bainbridge, Ohio); "Education Committee Minutes," April 3, 1946, Cleveland NAACP Papers.

33. Essie Kirken, "The History of the Origin of the Church of God," typescript, n.d.

34. Ruby and Stephen Hall interview, July 20, 1986; Adams interview.

35. Warner, *Streetcar Suburbs*, 120, 131, 157; Jackson, *Crabgrass Frontier*, 45–72; John Bodnar, Roger Simon, and Michael R. Weber, *Lives of Their Own: Blacks, Italians, and Poles in Pittsburgh, 1900–1930* (Urbana: University of Illinois Press, 1982), 153–180.

36. Eric Foner, *Reconstruction: America's Unfinished Revolution, 1863–1877* (New York: Harper & Row, 1988), 104–106, 374–377; Leon E. Litwak, *Been in the Storm So Long: The Aftermath of Slavery* (New York: Vintage, 1979), 398–407; Theodore Rosengarten, *All God's Dangers: The Life of Nate Shaw* (New York: Alfred A. Knopf, 1974), 236–237, 537–538.

37. James R. Grossman, *Land of Hope: Chicago, Black Southerners, and the Great Migration* (Chicago: University of Chicago Press, 1989), 36; Peter Gottlieb, *Making Their Own Way: Southern Blacks' Migration to Pittsburgh, 1916–1930* (Urbana: University of Illinois Press, 1987), 76, 183, 209–210; Carol Stack, *Call to Home: African Americans Reclaim the Rural South* (New York: Basic Books, 1996), 17–44.

38. Detwyler interview.

39. Harris, *Unplanned Suburbs*, 109–135; Nicolaides, *My Blue Heaven*, 29–35.

40. Margaret E. Byington, *Homestead: The Households of a Mill Town* (New York: Charities Publication Committee, 1910), 46–49; Gretchen Lemke-Santangelo, *Abiding Courage: African American Migrant Women and the East Bay Community* (Chapel Hill: University of North Carolina Press, 1996), 139–141. For self-provisioning in other suburbs, see Alice Bugg interview by Nettie Simons, October 8, 1984 (Pasadena Public

Library, Pasadena, California), 10; City of Pasadena to owner of 523 Pepper Street, April 4, 1952, Building Permit Files (Hale Municipal Building, Pasadena, California); Wilson, "Dark Spaces," 349; Armstrong Association of Philadelphia, *A Study of Living Conditions Among Colored People in Towns in the Outer Part of Philadelphia and in Other Suburbs Both in Pennsylvania and New Jersey* (Philadelphia: Armstrong Association of Philadelphia, 1915), 11–12, 22, 30, 32, 35, 51, 54; Walter G. Clerk, *North Amityville: A History* (North Amityville: Walter G. Clerk, 1976); Henry L. Taylor Jr., "The Building of a Black Industrial Suburb: The Lincoln Heights, Ohio, Story," Ph.D. diss., State University of New York at Buffalo, 1979; Grace E. Richmond, "Housing Conditions in the Outlying Districts of Columbus," M.A. thesis, Ohio State University, 1926, 11–12, 18, 37; Ann Morris and Henrietta Ambrose, *North Webster: A Photographic History of a Black Community* (Bloomington: Indiana University Press, 1993), 9, 17.

41. Mary Ann Courtney interview by Elizabeth Langley, October 26, 1979 (Mount Vernon, New York, Public Library).

42. Bruner, "General Survey," 35–36; City of Evanston, Building Permits for 1919, 1921, and 1937 Grey Avenue, Building Permit Files (Evanston Historical Society, Evanston, Illinois); U.S. Census of Housing: 1940, vol. 1, *Block Statistics, Evanston, Illinois* (Washington, DC: U.S. Government Printing Office, 1942), 6–12. For white workers, see Simon, "Housing and Services in an Immigrant Neighborhood," 448–449.

43. Jackson interview; Kirklen interview, July 16, 1986; Adams interview; Strickland quoted in "Negroes Fight for Better Life," 1.

44. Joe William Trotter Jr., *Black Milwaukee: The Making of an Industrial Proletariat* (Urbana: University of Illinois Press, 1985). For self-provisioning and other economic uses of housing among black coal-mining families, see Trotter, "Race, Class, and Industrial Change: Black Migration to Southern West Virginia, 1915–1932," in *Great Migration in Historical Perspective*, 60, 62. For home production among whites, see Lizabeth Cohen, *Making a New Deal: Industrial Workers in Chicago, 1919–1939* (New York: Cambridge University Press, 1990), 11; Jack Temple Kirby, *Rural Worlds Lost: The American South, 1920–1960* (Baton Rouge: Louisiana State University Press, 1987), 115–133, 298–300.

45. Mayor's Interracial Committee, *Negro in Detroit*, 58–59; Wilfred S. Lewin, "A Study of the Negro Population of Mount Vernon," typescript, 1935 (Mount Vernon Public Library, Mount Vernon, NY).

46. Cohen, *Making a New Deal*, 147–157.

47. Gottlieb, *Making Their Own Way*, 49–52; Kimberley L. Phillips, "'But It Is a Fine Place to Make Money': Migration and African American Families in Cleveland, 1915–1929," *Journal of Social History* 30 (Winter 1996): 393–413. For kinship and migration to industrial suburbs, see Shirley Ann Moore, "Getting There, Being There: African-American Migration to Richmond, California, 1910–1940," in *Great Migration in Historical Perspective*, 108.

48. Kirklen interview, August 15, 1986; Detwyler interview; Beck interview; Mr. and Mrs. Noah Pounds interview by Wiese, July 15, 1986; Walker interview; Geauga County Torrens Record Docket, no. 1; Ruby and Stephen Hall interview, August 22, 1986.

49. Marsh, *Suburban Lives*, 173–179; Barbara Kelly, *Expanding the American Dream: Building and Rebuilding Levittown* (Albany: State University of New York Press, 1993), 106–110. Samples of black households in eleven suburbs revealed similar extended family

patterns. Fourteenth Census of the United States: 1920, *Census Schedules*, Freeport, NY, Enumeration Districts (ED) 13–15 (Washington, DC: U.S. Government Printing Office, 1922); ibid., Mt. Vernon, NY, ED 76–87; ibid., Montclair, NJ, ED 74–90; ibid., Englewood, NJ, ED 22–27; ibid., Evanston, IL, ED 68–89; ibid., Glencoe Village, IL, ED 119; ibid., Harvey, IL, ED 215–219; ibid., Robbins Village, IL, ED 25; ibid., Maywood, IL, ED 194–195; ibid., River Rouge, MI, ED 679; see also *Evanston Review*, Obituaries, 1950–1990; Oral History Collection (Evanston Historical Society, Evanston, IL); Pasadena Oral History Project (Pasadena History Museum, Pasadena, CA); Langley Oral Histories (Mount Vernon Public Library, Mount Vernon, NY).

50. Ruby and Stephen Hall interview, August 22, 1986; Adams interview; Strickland quoted in "Negroes Fight for Better Life."

51. Adams interview.

52. Warner, *Streetcar Suburbs*, 29–31; Jackson, *Crabgrass Frontier*, 103–137.

53. Detwyler interview; Strickland quoted in "Negroes Fight for Better Life."

54. Ruby and Stephen Hall interview, August 22, 1986. The city's principal black newspaper, the *Cleveland Gazette*, regularly decried crime and vice on the east side; see, for example, *Gazette*, April 21, 1923, 3; August 23, 1923, 3.

55. Beck interview. For urban antipathies in other suburbs, see Cora Warson interview by S. F. Patton, May 24, 1974, transcript (Evanston Historical Society, Evanston, IL); Wilson, "Dark Spaces"; Morris and Ambrose, *North Webster*, 17; Lewin, "Study of the Negro Population"; and "Official History of River Rouge, Michigan," Minutes, River Rouge City Council, March 23, 1971 (River Rouge Public Library, River Rouge, MI).

56. For race and identity in white suburbs, see Nicolaides, *My Blue Heaven*, 120–121, 156–168, 186–196, 272–327.

57. Kirklen interview, August 11, 1986.

58. George J. Sanchez, *Becoming Mexican American: Ethnicity, Culture, and Identity in Chicano Los Angeles, 1910–1945* (New York: Oxford University Press, 1993), 198–201; Simon, "Housing and Services in an Immigrant Neighborhood," 447–450; Zunz, *Changing Face of Inequality*, 170–174; Harris, *Unplanned Suburbs*, 109–135; Richard Harris and Matt Sendbuhler, "The Making of a Working Class Suburb in Hamilton's East End, 1900–1945," *Journal of Urban History* 20 (August 1994): 486–511.

59. On land-use controls and working-class suburbanization, see Harris, *Unplanned Suburbs*, 233–263; Henry L. Taylor Jr., "City Building, Public Policy: The Rise of the Industrial City and Black Ghetto-Slum Formation in Cincinnati, 1850–1940," in *Race and the City: Work, Community, and Protest in Cincinnati, 1820–1970*, ed. Henry L. Taylor Jr. (Urbana: University of Illinois Press, 1993), 176. After World War II, see Wiese, *Places of Their Own*, 94–109.

60. Jackson, *Crabgrass Frontier*, 203–218; see also Davis McEntire, *Residence and Race: Final and Comprehensive Report to the Commission on Race and Housing* (Berkeley: University of California Press, 1960), 291–314; Charles Abrams, *Forbidden Neighbors: A Study of Prejudice in Housing* (New York: Associated Faculty Press, 1955). On new housing for African Americans, see Wiese, *Places of Their Own*, 110–142, 164–208; Roland Sawyer, "FHA Program Aids Minorities," *Insured Mortgage Portfolio*, 16 (4th Q., 1951), 6–9; William H. Wilson, *Hamilton Park: A Planned Black Community in Dallas* (Baltimore: Johns Hopkins University Press, 1998).

61. Farley, "Changing Distribution of Negroes," 344.

62. In 1960, the African American population of Bainbridge Township peaked at 892. By 1990, it had slipped to 507, although not all African Americans in the township lived in Chagrin Falls Park. Eighteenth Census of the United States: 1960, *Population*, vol. 1, *General Population Characteristics*, pt. 37: *Ohio* (Washington, DC: U.S. Government Printing Office, 1961), 135; Twenty-first Census of the United States: 1990, *Population*, vol. 1, *General Population Characteristics*, pt. 37: *Ohio* (Washington, DC: U.S. Government Printing Office, 1992), 572; "Building a Proud Future," *Chagrin Valley News-Herald*, April 19, 1998, A8.

Megan Kate Nelson

Hidden Away in the Woods and Swamps

Slavery, Fugitive Slaves, and Swamplands in the Southeastern
Borderlands, 1739–1845

When the British actress and author Frances Anne (Fanny) Kemble visited her husband's St. Simons Island rice plantation in February 1839, she admired the riot of growth on the margins of the fields: "[T]hickets of the most beautiful and various evergreen growth, . . . beckoned my inexperience most irresistibly" and "the wood paths are as tempting as paths into Paradise."[1] A St. Simons slave named Jack, upon hearing Kemble's exultations, warned her against venturing into the wooded swamps. Rattlesnakes, bottomless sandpits, and various other untold horrors awaited her there, he argued. But Jack could have had more than his mistress's safety in mind, for the swamps surrounding the rice fields were the provinces of fugitives and slaves during the antebellum era. In "scaring" Kemble away from the plantation hinterlands, Jack may have been preventing her from trespassing upon his community's property.

Swamplands are both land and water, fertile and barren, peculiar ecologies that seemed to observers to grow and decay at an alarmingly rapid pace. These forested lowlands are more prevalent in the American Southeast than in any other region of the continent and were even more numerous during the eighteenth and nineteenth centuries. In response to encounters with swamps, communities in the area developed an ecolocal culture: constellations of ideas about and images of local inundated lowlands that shaped community identity and action. Between 1739 and 1845, European and European American communities saw swamplands in the southeastern borderlands—an area politically identified as southern Georgia and northern Florida, and geographically delineated as the Lower Coastal Plain, stretching from the Savannah River to Lake George and westward to the Flint River—as sites in which they could exercise control over nature and power over other people. Africans and African Americans, forcibly transported to the southeastern borderlands to work as slaves on rice plantations, saw swamps quite differently. They thought of and used them as sites of refuge, places where they could potentially lead independent lives.

Africans first came to the swamps of the southeastern borderlands because European colonists in Georgia used theories connecting race, disease, and environment to establish and bolster slavery in the early eighteenth century. But as slaves labored in southeastern rice fields and the swamps that surrounded them, they developed their own ecolocal culture and often subverted European American desires, most significantly by using swamplands to run away. An investigation of reasons European planters placed African slaves in swamps and the ways these slaves used lowland landscapes to assert their independence reveals the ways that ideas about race and environment have been linked in American culture. This study also illuminates murky landscapes that were sites of fierce struggles over social power, community identity, and individual self-determination between 1739 and 1845.

SLAVERY AND ECOLOCAL THEORIES OF RACE, DISEASE, AND ENVIRONMENT

In the early eighteenth century, English colonists reacted to the lands of Georgia's Lower Coastal Plain with shock and horror. They faced a fifty-mile-wide swath of swampland and pine forests, interlocked and fed by the region's plentiful rivers. In the southeastern part of the colony sat the largest freshwater swamp in North America: the Okefenokee (a Creek name meaning "trembling earth"), a 660-square-mile inundated forest. This swamp is "an ecological mosaic; it contains six kinds of swamp ecosystems, each defined and differentiated by its tree growth."[2] Its waterways, like those of other southeastern swamplands, were shallow and stained by the tannin of cypress trees to a dark amber color; the water's opacity made cypress stumps, mounds of peat, and alligators difficult to see. The Georgia Trustees had advertised a lush, fertile landscape ripe for cultivation, but what the colonists found in 1733 were miles and miles of cypress trees and saw palmettos firmly rooted in mucky soil that swallowed people, cattle, and equipment.

Within months of the initial clearing and building of Savannah, the colonists were already grumbling.[3] A group of "Mutinous Malcontents," as the trustees deemed them, voiced their discontent through petitions and pamphlets beginning in December 1738, calling for a restructuring of land policies and the use of African slaves in the colony. In a satirical protest booklet called *A True and Historical Narrative of the Colony of Georgia in America*, published in 1741, Malcontents Patrick Tailfer, Hugh Anderson, and David Douglas mobilized long-accepted ideas about the connections among race, climate, and illness and manipulated the image of Georgia's swamplands in order to bolster their arguments for the introduction of slavery to the colony. They complained that the extreme preponderance of sickness in the European community during the summer months demonstrated the inability of European laborers to work in Georgia's topography; attempts to cultivate the lowlands with white servants, they argued, had proven "vain and fruitless."[4] The Malcontents depicted swamplands as a source of pestilence; this belief was long-standing in medical theory and practice. The Greek physician Hippocrates had noted in the fifth century BC that inundated landscapes were poisonous and that strangers to lowland areas should avoid them at all costs.[5] By the eighteenth century, doctors in Europe and in the Americas agreed that both endemic and epidemic diseases emerged from a combination of "insalubrious conditions of the atmosphere," high humidity, strong winds, hot temperatures, and a preponderance of landscapes dominated by standing water.[6] These conditions created miasmas—pockets of poisoned air that caused a range of illnesses, from mild recurrent bilious fevers to fatal epidemic attacks of typhoid and yellow fever. The Malcontents, informed by long-held beliefs in the pestilent nature of swamps and in response to the high mortality rates among European colonists, argued that these lands were, literally, killing them.

The medical theories that connected swamps and disease also made links between a person's native latitudes and the ability to withstand the effects of swamp miasmas. Africans, eighteenth-century physicians argued, were acclimatized to the epidemic atmospheres created by lowlands of West and Central Africa. In North America, Africans seemed almost immune to endemic fevers like malaria and survived yellow fever epidemics at a much higher rate than Europeans. Although doctors acknowledged that these perceived immunities were not absolute, they argued that Africans were ideal sources of labor in the swampy lands of colonial Georgia because they seemed to be impervious to miasmatic illnesses. John Brickell, a natural historian who wrote about the landscapes and peoples of the American Southeast, noted in 1737 that Africans could labor even in the warmest and wettest months, "being better able to undergo fatigues in the extremity of the hot Weather than any *Europeans*."[7]

This theory of African resistance to miasmatic diseases like malaria and yellow fever was, for the most part, correct. Efficient resistance to yellow fever among Africans and African Americans was due to a combination of genetic traits, acquired immunities, and geographic circumstances. A large number of Africans and African Americans lacked the Duffy antigen (or enzyme glucose-6-phosphate dehydrogenase), which rendered them less susceptible to the milder *vivax* malaria strain. Others also had a hemoglobin condition, a form of anemia (sickle cell disease), that provided some measure of resistance to the more virulent *falciparum* malaria strain in addition to yellow fever. Medical historian Todd Savitt has suggested that roughly 30 to 40 percent of the enslaved and free African and African American population in nineteenth-century America expressed one or more of these genetic conditions and passed them on to their children.[8]

In addition to some genetic protections against malaria and yellow fever, those Africans and their descendents who were forced to labor in the southeastern borderlands had also acquired immunities to miasmatic diseases during their lifetimes. In West Africa, malarial diseases were endemic and adults were a population of survivors. Where populations were stable and families lived in one area for several years consecutively, chances were good that children, who usually survived first attacks of yellow fever, would grow into immune adults. Communities in western Africa, which tended to be more stable than others, were also more likely to be raided by slave traders; immunities thus crossed the Atlantic with African captives.

The Malcontents had noted miasmatic disease resistance among African slaves working on South Carolina rice plantations and promoted the association of swamps, rice, and black labor in a defense of slavery: "If they had swamp that would bear rice, white people are unable to clear them if they are covered with trees. . . . [I]t were simply impossible to manufacture the rice by white men."[9] The introduction of slavery as a system of labor in Georgia, according to the Malcontents, would prevent white mortality, attract European and European American migrants, and increase rice production and profits. Black labor "would both occasion great numbers of white people to come here, and also render us capable to subsist ourselves, by raising provisions upon our lands, until we could make sure produce fit for export."[10]

Although the Malcontents' arguments provoked some resistance among inhabitants of the most southern reaches of the colony (who had to contend with Spanish offers of freedom for British slaves; see below), they nonetheless ultimately succeeded in their quest.[11] Ecolocal ideas promoting the close relationship between Africans and swamps ultimately wore down trustee resistance on the subject of slave labor. Shortly before they surrendered their dominion over Georgia to the British Crown in 1750, the trustees repealed their prohibition on slavery.[12] The repeal provoked a population explosion in the colony and dramatically altered the borderland landscape. Within three years, the number of Europeans in Georgia increased by 23 percent. The transformation of lowlands from mucky forests to bounded rectangular rice grids, as Joyce Chaplin has argued, gave the borderlands distinctive physical features and entrenched slavery deeper into the area.[13] Within months of the repeal, 1,000 African and African American slaves had been forcefully relocated to Georgia. By 1776, their numbers had grown to 16,000, 48 percent of the total population of the colony.[14] Between 1750 and 1790, the borderlands morphed into a region of sculpted rice plantations and hinterland swamps worked intensively by Africans and African Americans.[15]

SLAVES IN THE RICE KINGDOM

Ironically, by building rice plantations and relegating slaves to swamplands, planters supplied the source of plantation society's instability in the southeastern borderlands. Planters were dependent on large numbers of slaves to cultivate their fields; the rice belt averaged 226 slaves per plantation between 1750 and 1860.[16] Consequently, a black majority characterized much of the southeastern borderlands. This majority was often the context for an emergent creolized slave culture on large rice plantations that adapted African styles of dress, food, religion, music, and oral narration to life in the slave quarters.[17] Slaves also brought African methods in agriculture to the borderland landscape and, in so doing, developed their own ecolocal culture.

As Peter Wood, Daniel Littlefield, and Judith Carney have pointed out, Africans who inhabited the Upper Guinea Coast of West Africa (from Senegal to Liberia) were rice farmers. The rich soils and large floodplains of the western coast provided several kinds of sites suitable to rice agriculture: floodplains, coastal estuaries, and mangrove swamps. The Upper Guinea region also included several coastal port cities in which African farmers bought and sold rice. This proximity to the coast and its ports made Upper Guinea rice farmers successful but also made them more visible to European slave traders; they were thus primary targets for the transatlantic slave trade.[18] These Africans brought both disease immunities and rice culture—a sophisticated "underlying knowledge system" that shaped the cultivation, milling, and preparation of rice—across the Atlantic with them.[19]

There is abundant evidence that South Carolina and Georgia planters knew of the rice expertise of certain African ethnic groups and that they deliberately purchased slaves from these groups in order to exploit their experience. On plantations in the American southeastern borderlands, both before and after the cessation of the Atlantic slave trade in 1808, large numbers of slaves not only applied their knowledge to shaping rice fields but also recognized and used their hinterlands—forested, swampy lowlands—as sites of cultural formation and resistance against slavery.[20] Familiarity with the ecology of inundated lands (although West African swamplands are significantly more saline than North American swamps—the growth of mangrove trees is indicative of this salinity), in addition to the prevalence of the task system on rice plantations, gave many southeastern slaves opportunities for independence that may not have been available to slaves residing and working on plantations in more northern climes.

African and African American slaves "provided critical expertise in exchange for a labor regime that would improve the conditions of their bondage," shaping a task system (which Carney argues is of African origin) through arbitration with their owners.[21] This negotiated labor system offered a more technical, varied, and flexible work schedule. Overseers or drivers assigned individual slaves tasks, usually measured spatially: anywhere from a quarter acre to a full acre of tilling, planting, or hoeing to be completed. When the slaves finished their tasks, they could spend the rest of the day in their houses or gardens. Slaves shaped the task system to suit their needs, using their post-task time to develop other skills and, often, individual garden plots that augmented diets and created a local provision economy in the slave quarters.[22]

This is not to say that life on a rice plantation was pleasant or enjoyable. Hours were long, sickness prevalent, and the labor arduous. Mortality rates, as William Dusinberre has shown, were horrifyingly high.[23] But the presence of swamplands and many slaves' familiarity with them, in addition to the sporadic free time that they carved out for themselves, prompted many slaves to use the plantation hinterlands for their own benefit. Use of the swamps that surrounded rice fields provided many slaves with better diets and a sense of independence. It also assisted flight from slavery, either for short periods or permanently. In coastal plain swamps, slaves and fugitive slaves found a refuge from the horrors of slavery; the European American ecolocal culture that propagated enslavement in the southeastern borderlands put African and African American slaves into contact with an environment that increased their chances for freedom between 1750 and 1845.

SLAVES IN HINTERLAND SWAMPS

Plantations were meant to discipline both slaves and the environment, but black labor created plantations out of the southeastern lowlands and slaves knew more about rice production than most owners or overseers. Clearing swamplands and constructing the plantation grid out of the muck brought slaves into contact with swamplands and their peculiar ecologies. The theory of race, labor, and environment had become a reality: as slaves, African and African American men and women came to know borderland swamplands intimately. Their knowledge of these ecosystems allowed slaves to pass through them with greater ease and within these places they procured animals and plants to supplement their diet or to sell for profit.

Although Fanny Kemble reported that St. Simons slaves "seem to me to have a holy horror of ever setting their foot near either tree or bush, or anywhere but on the open road and the fields where they labor," many enslaved men and women came to the plantation infirmary with rattlesnake bites during the year, indicating that such fears were either exaggerated or were not enough of a deterrent to keep slaves out of the swamps.[24] Slaves entered these areas to gather herbs and edible plants; they also hunted wild game that supplemented their meager diets. Although Kemble's husband, Pierce Butler, did not allow his slaves to carry firearms, other planters did and expected their slaves to hunt for birds and other wild game in the lowland forests surrounding the plantation. When Frederick Law Olmsted traveled through Georgia in 1853, he stayed with "Mr. X," a planter who allowed his slaves to store guns and ammunition in their own cabins. Mr. X expected that slaves would hunt "for their own sport."[25] Some slaves procured as much as half the meat in their diet from hinterland hunting excursions, whereas the other half came from fishing, plantation provisions, or domesticated animals (fowl, cattle, hogs) that some slaves kept on the edges of the plantation.[26] Wood was also plentiful on the margins, and slaves cut firewood for their own use or for sale and felled cypress trees (which are water-resistant) to shape into canoes they would then use to navigate the intricate waterways of lowland swamps. In addition, slaves made use of products unique to the swamp environment. As Fanny Kemble reported, "the people collect moss from the trees and sell it to the shopkeepers in Darien for the purpose of stuffing furniture."[27]

It is clear from the architecture of southeastern borderland plantations that planters themselves expected slaves to be "closer" to the surrounding swamplands than to white residents. Planters usually arranged slave quarters in a block pattern away from the Big House, sometimes far beyond eye- or earshot. Such physical distance from the seat of white control allowed slaves to exert domestic control and take possession of lands for their own benefit. As John Michael Vlach has shown, slaves laid claim to portions of the plantation landscape—some of those spaces were ceded to them and others were not. Forest paths and trails, like those that appealed to Fanny Kemble on St. Simons, were central elements of the slave landscape that provided them with a means to escape their masters' control, if but briefly. The slave environment, as Vlach has argued, was "marked by few overt boundaries and fixed sites, an environment open to and characterized by movement."[28] Swamps were such open, poorly marked landscapes; varying water levels and rapid vegetative growth meant that boundaries shifted constantly and offered both concealment and abundant resources.

Plantations were places of work, as were the hinterlands, but slave appropriation of surrounding swamplands was a direct material expression of their desire for power over their own lives.[29] Slaves were, as Mart Stewart has put it, "the nexus of social and environmental relationships" on southeastern plantations—their relationship with both plantation lands and hinterlands was socially prescribed through European ecolocal theories of race, labor, and environment yet it was also socially destabilizing.[30] By harvesting the products of the swamplands surrounding plantations, borderland slaves created some measure of independence for themselves in these spaces. But no act was more subversive in this landscape of slaves than flight. Fugitives fled southeastern rice plantations in large numbers between 1750 and 1845 and they used the Okefenokee and other borderland swamps as pathways to freedom.

FUGITIVES IN SWAMPS

Slaves were both human and property; this unique doubleness meant they could use their status as chattel as a weapon against their masters. Resistance reduced the fugitive's worth and robbed his master of labor and resultant revenue. Also, owners forced to advertise for their runaways acknowledged publicly that they were not in control of their laborers. Slave resistance challenged the controlled social, economic, and environmental world rice planters attempted to shape and had both political and environmental implications.[31] Planters desired control over their property while slaves desired freedom; these conflicting aims clashed within the fluctuating boundaries of southeastern borderland swamps in the eighteenth and nineteenth centuries.

MAROON COMMUNITIES

Most runaways did not flee to established maroon communities in nearby swamplands, however. While maroons inhabited every slave society in which mountains, swamps, or other difficult terrain provided places of refuge, few viable maroon groups emerged in the American southeastern borderlands. Those that did exist emerged in the eighteenth century and were small and fragmented communities based on agricultural subsistence, hunting, and theft.[32] In October 1786, the Charleston *Morning Post* reported that over 100 South Carolina runaways established a camp on a swampy island seventeen miles up the Savannah River "and for some time past committed robberies on the neighboring Planters. . . . [I]t was found necessary to attempt to dislodge them."[33] The attempt succeeded, but only after a bloody battle between the Savannah Light Infantry and South Carolinian militia and the maroons.

The outskirts of Savannah were a popular gathering place for fugitive slaves. During the late eighteenth century, the area was still sparsely populated but, most importantly, the "Forest City" was surrounded on three sides by forested lowlands during this time.[34] These river swamps were not viable for maroon use, however, because aggressive drainage projects initiated during the early nineteenth century eradicated them and brought white settlers to the area. Also, it was difficult for gangs of runaways to subsist for long periods of time in swampy places, particularly if they had not yet obtained guns for hunting the abundant game that roamed the lowlands. The Seminole towns of central and northern Florida were more successful sites of maroon community formation; fugitive slaves and Seminoles lived in towns within the Okefenokee Swamp and ventured out to raid Spanish and Anglo American plantations and homesteads during the eighteenth and early nineteenth centuries.[35] But after the First Seminole War (1817–1818), these groups were scattered and mobile, and the Second Seminole War (1835–1842) resulted in the evacuation of Seminoles from the Okefenokee Swamp permanently. Maroon communities were rare in North America, but those few that did exist reveal the importance of environment in resistance to slavery. Running away was an act of environmental knowledge and use.

LYING OUT

Fugitives who took advantage of the protection that swamps offered most often used them as havens for a short period (the practice of *petit marronage*, or lying out) or as conduits to other counties, states, or territories (to remain undetected or to shake off dogs and hunters in pursuit). Those slaves engaging in *petit marronage* stayed away from the plantation for weeks or even months but remained in the neighborhood, harboring in swamps and often participating in the pillaging or looting of local plantations. Many slave owners saw this fugitive behavior as acceptable and different from actually running away; some owners did not advertise for a runaway until he or she had been gone for more than a month. Roderick McIver, a planter from Pedee Island, South Carolina, advertised four fugitive slaves on September 1, 1763, and noted that three of the four (Whan, Isaac, and Christopher) had fled almost two months before while Jack, presumably the ringleader, had been gone for three years.[36] Some slaves experimented with lying out before attempting permanent escape. A slave named Sampson, who escaped from his Georgia plantation in 1844, had run away earlier that year when "his master undertook to whip him." He stayed in the area and "no one knew where he was, except for a trusted few of his faithful companions. He kept hid during the day, only venturing out at night, in order to procure necessary supplies." Sampson lay out for about three months before he approached Lewis Paine, a northern white factory manager, to help him get to Alabama.[37]

John Brown, a Georgia slave who escaped to Ohio and then to England in the 1840s, also had a past of *petit marronage* in borderland swamps:

> During my old master's lifetime, I had frequently hidden away in the woods and swamps; sometimes for a few days only; at others for a fortnight at a stretch; and once for a whole month. I used to sneak out at night from my hiding-place to steal corn, fruit and such like. As long as it lasted, the release from the severe labour put upon me was quite grateful; and though I always got cruelly flogged on my return, the temptation to get rest this way was too great to be resisted.[38]

The presence of slaves lying out tried masters' patience and disconcerted the white southern community. Swamps were dark, mysterious, dangerous places and the fugitives within them challenged white assumptions about their slaves' "happy" dispositions and racial inferiority—the foundations upon which southern slavery rested. Also, fugitives in the swamps served as a reminder to their owners that their ecolocal theories of race and labor had been undermined. Slaves used their relationship with swamplands to escape from, not to bolster, slavery in the southeastern borderlands.[39] Fugitive slaves created chaos as they claimed southeastern swamps as sites of freedom.

FUGITIVE SLAVERY AND BORDERLAND GEOPOLITICS

Runaways who were neither hiding out in groups nor lying out but who were seeking permanent freedom were likely to use the Okefenokee and other southeastern swamps to elude pursuers and provide shelter while they were on the move. They were aided in their quest for personal liberty by the unstable geopolitical situation in the southeastern borderlands between 1750 and 1821. Most Georgia slaves lived within 150 miles of the Florida border, and the Spanish presence in Florida (until 1821) offered southeastern slaves unique opportunities. During these years, the borderlands were tumultuous and many slaves took advantage of geopolitical tensions evolving between Spain and Britain and between the United States and Spain to achieve freedom.

In 1739, a group of Scots-Irish farmers who disagreed with the Malcontents' call for slavery in Georgia wrote a petition from Darien, Georgia, arguing that the "Liberty of having Slaves" would be "dangerous" and lead to "bad Consequence." The petitioners listed five reasons for these dangers; the first of these was even more persuasive in light of the commencement of the War of Jenkin's Ear later that year, which pitted England against Spain in North America: "The Nearness of the Spaniards, who have proclaimed Freedom to all Slaves who run away from their Masters, makes it impossible for us to keep them without more Labour in guarding them, that what we would be at to do their Work."[40] The Darien petitioners were justified in their fears; the Spanish Crown had granted freedom to all runaways in 1693 and reiterated the offer in 1739. That year Spanish colonists also began construction on Fort Mose, which would house runaways and provide a defensive Spanish outpost in northeastern Florida. English general James Oglethorpe understood the point of these actions, writing to the trustees from Frederica (an island off the St. Marys River) on June 19, 1741:

> The Spanish Emissarys are very busy in stirring up Discontents amongst the People hence their Principal Point is Negroes since as many Slaves as there are, are so many Enemys to the Government, and consequently Friends to the Spaniards. Another great Point is to Discourage the Planters, since they think if planting don't go forward England will grow tired of supporting the Colony & then of course the Spaniards will gain their ends.[41]

Oglethorpe clearly linked Spanish seductions to both slave escape and rebellion; he argued in 1742 that the Spanish had undoubtedly encouraged the Stono Rebellion in South Carolina three years earlier. Spain offered slaves freedom, homesteads, and the opportunity to take up arms against their former owners. Their offers of sanctuary spread to Anglo American plantations mostly through the channels of conversation; some literate slaves may also have read of Spain's policies as borderland editors excoriated them in local newspapers. Whatever the route of information, print culture produced on both sides of the international border attests to the fact that hundreds of slaves living in the southeastern borderlands heard of Spain's amnesty proclamation and used the Okefenokee and other swamplands in order to gain personal liberty in Spanish Florida.

Britain's brief tenure in Florida (1763–1784), as Jane Landers has noted, temporarily eradicated the international border, and subsequently, black freedom in Florida became only a remote possibility.[42] With the restoration of Spanish rule in Florida in 1784, however, the borderlands again became a site of American slave society's instability. The Spanish Crown repeated its offer of sanctuary to runaway slaves, enticing them with land grants, royal subsidies, tax relief, and other privileges and exemptions.[43] But Georgia planters complained loudly to the U.S. government, and in 1790, Spain capitulated and abrogated its sanctuary policy. The Spanish governors insisted, however, that all fugitives who had already reached Florida remained free.[44]

Even without a sanctuary policy, slaves still ran. They crossed the border in family groups or by themselves, but they continued to seek freedom in Florida until its annexation to the United States in 1821. The Spanish governors of Florida did what they could to stave off slave-catchers and angry owners and provided some measure of protection for those runaways arriving in St. Augustine after the sanctuary abrogation. For over a century, many Georgia slaves took advantage of Anglo-Spanish tensions and used the dark and tangled passageways of borderland swamps, particularly the Okefenokee, to escape from and thus undermine slavery.

RUNNING SOUTH TO FREEDOM

Those runaways with an eye toward permanent self-determination most likely used the Okefenokee and other southeastern swamplands to mask their movements, but definitive evidence of their use of these ecosystems is sparse. Maroon activity was only sporadic and only one or two slave narratives illuminate the multiple roles that swamps played in runaways' struggle for freedom. But newspaper advertisements for runaway slaves and the letters sent between Georgia and St. Augustine reveal that substantial numbers of slaves fled from South Carolina and Georgia plantations in a southerly direction, and that the Okefenokee Swamp especially was in the perfect geographical position to provide shelter, food, and protection for those fugitives who fled southward to freedom.

Investigations of runaway slave advertisements and Brought to Jail notices in the *Georgia Gazette*, the Milledgeville *Recorder*, and the Milledgeville *Federal Union* between 1763 and 1845 and runaways discussed in letters between Georgia officials and governors of East Florida between 1784 and 1821 reveal that of the 349 runaway slaves advertised as heading southward from middle or southern Georgia, 83 percent were men and 57 percent of all runaways traveled in groups.[45] Spanish policies were a powerful impetus to flight: 140 (40 percent—the largest percentage) ran south into East and West Florida when Spain offered sanctuary between 1784 and 1821.

A precise count of fugitive slaves is, of course, impossible to achieve. The 349 southbound slaves advertised in these three newspapers between 1763 and 1845 are only a small percentage of the total advertised runaways in the state of Georgia. And, as Philip Morgan has put it, "advertised runaways represent only the most visible tip of an otherwise indeterminate iceberg."[46] Some owners did not advertise at all for many reasons: they thought the slave would return of his or her own accord; they could not afford to place an ad; their distance from a city center or access to mails to place the ad presented an obstacle; embarrassment about their failure to control their slaves deterred them. And even if they did manage to advertise, owners or overseers could have also made many misjudgments about their slaves. But most historians agree that it was in the owner's best interest to be honest about his runaways. Otherwise, the advertisement was misleading to readers, and the chances of catching the runaway would decrease significantly.[47]

Although newspaper advertisements might be a bit vague, the letters that darted over the border between Georgia officials and slave owners and the Spanish governors of East Florida between 1784 and 1821 are clear and specific. They detail the numbers and names of those fugitives who fled from slavery in Georgia and crossed into Spanish Florida in order to claim sanctuary. These slaves must have encountered the swamps of the southeastern borderlands, especially the Okefenokee (which crosses the Georgia/Florida border) at some point during their travels, and it is probable that they used these ecosystems as paths to freedom.

Runaways to East Florida during these years took minimal possessions with them and traveled by canoe, by horse, or on foot—sometimes by all three. The most striking fact gleaned from runaway-slave advertisements, Brought to Jail notices, and international letters is that, of the 140 fugitives known to have crossed the border into East Florida between 1783 and 1821, when Spanish sanctuary was their goal, 109 (78 percent) traveled in groups. In comparison, between 1763 and 1770, during part of the British occupation of Florida, 56 percent of runaways ran in groups through southern Georgia; after annexation, between 1830 and 1845, only 35 percent of fugitives ran together. This decrease in the numbers of groups traveling southward after annexation suggests that the Seminoles may not have offered opportunities for families as much as for individuals. Most runaways heading for Spanish sanctuary ran with family; many groups consisted of two to four members—including men, women, and their children.

One fugitive family from South Carolina, the Wittens, took advantage of wartime chaos and the reversion of East Florida to Spanish possession in 1783. Sometime during the Revolutionary War, British soldiers plundered Prince Witten, his wife Judy, and their children Glasgow and Polly from their proprietor's estate in South Carolina. American troops then recaptured the family, but they ran away from these U.S. soldiers in June or July 1785, making their way across the border and requesting sanctuary in St. Augustine in 1786. They ultimately became property holders, were baptized into the Catholic Church, and took Spanish names.[48] Like the Wittens, the Blackwood family ran to St. Augustine in the 1780s, although their fate is not so clear. According to their former owner John Blackwood, Amos Blackwood and his wife, Silvia, and their two children, Aron and Dolley, were stolen from his southern Georgia plantation and taken to St. Augustine. John Blackwood spent much of the year 1792 trying to track down this family. Their labor meant a good deal to him and his finances were suffering in their absence; in August 1792, John Blackwood could not afford to hire a lawyer or travel to St. Augustine to file the appropriate paperwork and claim his property. In a letter to Captain Howard, the fort captain on Amelia

Island, John Blackwood worried that "unless I do Something Shortly I Should Loose them." Although a Spanish government agent wrote to Blackwood and assured him that "Justice would be done," it is unclear whether John Blackwood was ever successful in recapturing Amos, Silvia, or their children.[49]

Groups of runaways to East Florida were not always composed of family members, however. In May 1797, southern Georgia slave owners compiled a list of runaway slaves that included twelve fugitives who escaped together: Titus, Tice, Jeffry, John, Summer, Lester, Sue, Beck, Beck's child, D., Rose, and Rose's child. It is possible that two of the men in the group were the fathers of Beck's and Rose's children, but the list did not make note of any other familial relationships.[50] Some groups formed and re-formed over the border; in 1797, a fugitive named Titus (a different man from the Titus mentioned above) gathered a band of other runaways together in Florida and traveled northward to wreak havoc on their former owners. The band made their way along the seacoast until they reached Savannah, where they absorbed some fugitive slaves hiding out in the surrounding swamps. They "became very troublesome to the people," as James Seagrove (the commissioner of Indian Affairs in Georgia) put it, while they traveled up and down the coastal plain, plundering neighborhood plantations. Titus's band was then outlawed, and a party of armed men went after them in the swamps. "It being a very thick Swamp, most of them escaped," but rumors of some deaths (because of the amount of blood on the ground) circulated. Seagrove was unsettled but not too disturbed at Titus's getaway: "Parties are constantly after them," he wrote, "and there is little doubt they will be taken or killed."[51]

Fugitives running to East Florida most likely made the trip in large numbers because it was feasible to move larger groups the relatively short distance between southeastern Georgia plantations and the St. Marys River. Group running provided safety, more numbers for hunting and provision gathering, and sociability in a time of great stress. The dense vegetation and multiple waterways in the Okefenokee and other swamps would have provided abundant shelter for larger groups, unlike more thinly forested areas or riverbanks. Fugitives probably also considered that the Spanish Crown would grant them land, and greater numbers meant more labor to develop such land grants in addition to an instant community providing psychological and emotional support during the transition to a life of freedom in Florida. But perhaps the most meaningful suggestion that these data provide is that fugitives in groups were planning for long-term freedom—they cultivated a vision of the future that included family members and friends.

Several slaves did strike out for freedom alone, however, and most were young men. Of the thirty-one individual runaways known to have crossed into

East Florida between 1783 and 1819, 84 percent were male. One such runaway was Emanuel McGillis, who "eloped" from his master's service in July 1803. Emanuel had been captured by the British during the Revolutionary War and changed hands several times in the postwar years. When he made his escape from the St. Marys district, he passed into Florida "under a pretence he is not the property of Mr. McGillis." Emanuel may have not remembered his former master's name; most likely, he lied to gain admittance to Florida. The guards at Amelia Island allowed him to cross the border; James Seagrove subsequently petitioned Governor White of St. Augustine to return the fugitive to the United States so his owner could retrieve him. It is unknown whether White or Seagrove was ever successful in capturing Emanuel.[52]

Only one female fugitive is known to have run alone between 1783 and 1817: Nelly Pooler appeared on the list of forty-three slaves that Georgia slave owners compiled for claiming purposes in 1797. But more women took advantage of the chaos in the borderlands during the First Seminole War of 1817–1818. Of the six women who were advertised as running southward alone from South Georgia in 1817, one was advertised as a runaway (Priss Spradlin). The other five were brought to jails in Savannah, Augusta, and in Jacksonborough and Baldwin Counties, all having been headed in a southerly direction. Individual fugitives traveling southward were not as numerous as runaways in groups, but most runaways were likely to have traversed or taken refuge in the Okefenokee and other borderland swamps in their travels to Florida. The landscape of slaves became an environment of fugitives in these cases.

As slaves ran through swamps, their former owners and public officials bickered over their capture. Seagrove and the slave owners in southern Georgia expected their slaves to be returned to them; a treaty between the United States and Spain, signed in May 1797, stipulated that

> all Fugitive Slaves, who have taken shelter in his Catholic Majesty's province of East Florida, since the Second day of September, in the year one thousand Seven hundred & Ninety, belonging to Citizens or Inhabitants of the United States (those belonging to His Catholic Majesty's Rebellious subjects excepted) shall without delay be delivered to the said Commissioner to be by him convey'd into the United States, in order to be delivered, to their respective owners—or in the case of failure in delivery of any part of such fugitives, that the Government of Spain pay a reasonable price for the same.[53]

The Spanish governors of St. Augustine were, again, polite but uncooperative when faced with the return of runaway slaves to the United States. The Treaty of 1797 was meant to codify custom, but Spanish landowners and Seminole communities were more than happy to welcome new workers, warriors, and soldiers to their communities. The attempts of Georgia slave owners to retrieve runaways, therefore, were most often frustrated. James Spalding, a Georgian who owned a plantation on the St. Marys River and lost ten slaves to East Florida from 1789 to 1794, was particularly chagrined. Not only did he and his family suffer from the lack of labor—he claimed that "their detention is a greater loss than their death on my plantation would be"—but the fugitives' success damaged his hopes of keeping his other slaves in line: "[I]t shows the slaves yet remaining with me that they can change their situation when they please and as this knowledge spreads amongst the slaves of my neighbours many of whome they have already lost and if you shall persist in retaining our slaves no doubt many now will be lost."[54]

Hundreds of slaves took advantage of the geopolitical chaos and the presence of the Okefenokee and other interlocked swamplands in the southeastern borderlands in order to flee to Spanish Florida between 1750 and 1821. Many owners reported the theft of canoes at the same time as runaways; those slaves working on rice plantations on the coast or inland had knowledge of the multiple serpentine waterways in the region and the skills to navigate them. It is difficult to determine precise routes, for as Frederick Douglass, John Brown, and many other fugitives-turned-writers have argued, silence kept anyone who aided in the escape alive and cleared the path for those who would subsequently run. Silence also served to obfuscate the path to freedom itself; Georgia officials suspected that fugitives utilized swamplands as escape routes, but without concrete information, they could not possibly pinpoint particular swamplands and thus could not hope to prevent their appropriation by runaways. Within swamps, fugitive slaves not only represented a loss of labor and capital but also became a threat to the South's carefully constructed social and racial hierarchy. Like swamplands, which are neither entirely water nor entirely land, fugitive slaves led a murky, twilight kind of existence. Neither enslaved nor truly free until they reached a destination that would grant them permanent freedom, fugitives on the run were unsettling symbols of liberty in the southeastern borderlands between 1750 and 1845.

PLACES OF BECOMING

The Malcontents and Carolina rice planters who supported the introduction of slavery into Georgia envisioned the swamps, when cultivated, as sites of European American profit and social power. In order to justify the use of slave labor, planters promoted an ecolocal theory of race, disease, and environment that closely associated Africans and African Americans with swamp ecologies. However, by using swamplands for hunting or gathering and inhabiting or traversing them on a journey to personal liberty in Florida, slaves undermined European American ecolocal culture while creating their own. The knowledge of swamplands that slaves gained and the skills runaways honed in order to exploit these ecosystems reminded their owners that their carefully ordered society was built upon the unstable foundation of swamp muck.

Many fugitives were successful in their quest for freedom in Florida between 1750 and 1845, and those who were used swamplands to their advantage. Fugitive actions within these environments, however transient and murky, reveal that Africans and African Americans perceived swamps as places of refuge. Swamplands are "edge" landscapes, as writer Barbara Hurd has called them, "places of transition and diversity and abundance," of overlap, blurred lines, and ambiguity. As such, swamps have seemed to promise change to those communities that encountered them: "[T]hings in the margins, including humans who wander there, are often on the brink of becoming something else, or someone else."[55] This promise of alteration, of "becoming," is what Africans and African Americans embraced in their interaction with southeastern swamplands. These edge places offered slaves blank spaces in which they could inscribe their own identities and determine their futures.

NOTES

A version of Chapter 10 appears as "A Path to Freedom: Slavery and Resistance," in *Trembling Earth: A Cultural History of the Okefenokee Swamp*, by Megan Kate Nelson (Athens: University of Georgia Press, 2005), © 2005 by Megan Kate Nelson.

1. Frances Anne Kemble, *Journal of a Residence on a Georgian Plantation in 1838–1839*, ed. John A. Scott (Athens: University of Georgia Press, Brown Thrasher Books, 1984), 200, 241.

2. Megan Kate Nelson, *Trembling Earth: A Cultural History of the Okefenokee Swamp* (Athens: University of Georgia Press, 2005), 2.

3. Mart A. Stewart, *"What Nature Suffers to Groe": Life, Labor, and Landscape on the Georgia Coast, 1680–1920* (Athens: University of Georgia Press, 1996), 30, 54–59.

4. Patrick Tailfer, Hugh Anderson, and David Douglas, *A True and Historical Narrative of the Colony of Georgia in America* (1741; reprint, Athens: University of Georgia Press, 1960), 51, 58–59.

5. Rene LaRoche, *Yellow Fever, Considered in Its Historical, Pathological, Etiological, Therapeutical Relations . . .* , vol. 2 (Philadelphia: Blanchard and Lea, 1855), 18 (Rare Books and Special Collections, Francis A. Countway Library of Medicine, Harvard University).

6. Ibid., 268–562.

7. Brickell, *Natural History of North Carolina* (1737), as quoted in Peter H. Wood, *Black Majority: Negroes in Colonial South Carolina from 1670 Through the Stono Rebellion* (New York: W. W. Norton and Co., 1974), 84 (emphasis in original).

8. Todd L. Savitt, "Black Health on the Plantation: Masters, Slaves, and Physicians," in *Sickness and Health in America: Readings in the History of Medicine and Public Health,* 2nd ed., ed. Judith Walzer Leavitt and Ronald L. Numbers (Madison: University of Wisconsin Press, 1985), 314–316; LaRoche, *Yellow Fever*, 2:66; Kenneth F. Kiple and Virginia H. Kiple,

"Black Yellow Fever Immunities, Innate and Acquired, as Revealed in the American South," *Social Science History* 1, no. 4 (Summer 1997): 420–421, 422, 424–425; Wood, *Black Majority*, 76–85; John S. Haller, "The Negro and the Southern Physician: A Study of Medical and Racial Attitudes, 1800–1860," *Medical History* 16, no. 3 (1972): 238–253.

9. Tailfer et al., *True and Historical Narrative*, 139.

10. Ibid., 94.

11. Allen D. Candler, ed., *The Colonial Records of the State of Georgia*, vol. 3 (Atlanta: Franklin-Turner Co., 1907), 394–395.

12. Kenneth Coleman, *Colonial Georgia: A History* (New York: Charles Scribner's Sons, 1976); Coleman, *Georgia History in Outline*, rev. ed. (Athens: University of Georgia Press, 1978); Phinizy Spalding, "Colonial Period," in *A History of Georgia*, 2nd ed., ed. Kenneth Coleman (Athens: University of Georgia Press, 1991): 9–70; Betty Wood, *Slavery in Colonial Georgia, 1730–1775* (Athens: University of Georgia Press, 1984). The trustees repealed the prohibition of slavery on August 8, 1750.

13. Joyce Chaplin, *An Anxious Pursuit: Agricultural Innovation and Modernity in the Lower South, 1730–1815* (Chapel Hill: University of North Carolina Press, 1993), 227–228.

14. In 1750, 4,200 whites and 1,000 blacks lived in Georgia; in 1760, 6,000 whites and 3,578 blacks; in 1770, 12,750 whites and 10,625 blacks; in 1776, 17,000 whites and 16,000 blacks. Julia Floyd Smith, *Slavery and Rice Culture in Low Country Georgia, 1750–1860* (Knoxville: University of Tennessee Press, 1985), 22.

15. Hugh Fraser Grant, *Planter Management and Capitalism in Antebellum Georgia: The Journal of Hugh Fraser Grant, Ricegrower*, ed. Albert Virgil House (New York: Columbia University Press, 1954), 23–24.

16. Smith, *Slavery and Rice Culture in Low Country Georgia*, 9.

17. Wood, *Black Majority*; Philip D. Morgan, "Black Society in the Lowcountry, 1760–1810," in *Slavery and Freedom in the Age of the American Revolution*, ed. Ira Berlin and Ronald Hoffman (Charlottesville: University Press of Virginia, 1983); John W. Blassingame, *The Slave Community: Plantation Life in the Antebellum South* (Oxford: Oxford University Press, 1972, 1979); Charles Joyner, *Down by the Riverside: A South Carolina Slave Community* (Urbana: University of Illinois Press, 1984).

18. Judith A. Carney, *Black Rice: The African Origins of Rice Cultivation in the Americas* (Cambridge, MA: Harvard University Press, 2001), 11, 13, 16–18, 29.

19. Ibid., 81, 31.

20. Ibid., 81; Daniel Littlefield, *Rice and Slaves: Ethnicity and the Slave Trade in Colonial South Carolina* (Baton Rouge: Louisiana State University Press, 1981).

21. Carney, *Black Rice*, 100.

22. Ira Berlin, "Introduction," in *Slavery and Freedom in the Age of the American Revolution*, xix; Morgan, "Black Society in the Lowcountry, 1760–1810," in ibid., 105.

23. William Dusinberre argues that slaves' daily lives were marked by the physical and emotional impact of sickness and the death of family and community members in *Them Dark Days: Slavery in the American Rice Swamps* (New York: Oxford University Press, 1996). See also Jeffrey R. Young, "Ideology and Death on a Savannah River Rice Plantation, 1833–1867: Paternalism Amongst 'a Good Supply of Disease and Pain,'" *Journal of Southern History* 59, no. 4 (November 1993): 673–706; Smith, *Slavery and Rice Culture in Low Country Georgia*, 49–50. John Brown, a slave who escaped from a Georgia

rice plantation in the 1840s, noted in his autobiography that "it is not an uncommon thing, by any means, for the task to be doubled, for it is always 'staving times' with them; they are always in a hurry to get the crops in, and always in a hurry to get them out." He also argued in his narrative that rice cultivation was much more trying for laborers than either cotton or tobacco, and that Georgia rice plantations were especially dangerous to the health of slaves: "The growing crop remained under water three or four days, during which time the slaves are obliged to go into these swamps, grubbing up the grass between the rows. It is awful work. Men, women, and children are all employed incessantly, for it is a busy time. They work naked, or nearly so, and contract all sorts of maladies. There is muddy soil into which you sink knee-deep, and which sends up the foulest smell and vapour, causing fever and sickness. The heat, too, from the sun over-head, reflected back into your face from the water, is intolerably painful, frequently bringing on giddiness and sunstroke. Then the feet get water-poisoned, or you take the toe or ground-itch, when the flesh cracks and cankers. . . . You have also run the risk of getting bitten by all kinds of water-reptiles, and are sure to have some sickness or another." John Brown, *Slave Life in Georgia: A Narrative of the Life, Sufferings, and Escape of John Brown, a Fugitive Slave* (London, 1855; Savannah: Beehive Press, 1991), 154–155.

24. Kemble, *Journal*, 208.

25. Frederick Law Olmsted, *A Journey in the Seaboard Slave States* (New York: Dix and Edwards, 1856), 484–485.

26. Stewart, *"What Nature Suffers to Groe,"* 135–136.

27. Kemble, *Journal*, 276.

28. John Michael Vlach, *Back of the Big House: The Architecture of Plantation Slavery* (Chapel Hill: University of North Carolina Press, 1993), 14.

29. Ibid., 183, 228.

30. Stewart, *"What Nature Suffers to Groe,"* 126.

31. Marvin L. Michael Kay and Lorin Lee Cary, "'They Are Indeed the Constant Plague of Their Tyrants': Slave Defence of a Moral Economy in Colonial North Carolina, 1748–1772," in *Out of the House of Bondage: Runaways, Resistance, and Marronage in Africa and the New World*, ed. Gad Heuman (London: Frank Cass & Co., 1986), 39.

32. Richard Price, ed., *Maroon Societies: Rebel Slave Communities in the Americas* (Garden City, NY: Anchor Press, 1973); Eugene D. Genovese, *From Rebellion to Revolution: Afro-American Slave Revolts in the Making of the Modern World* (Baton Rouge: Louisiana State University Press, 1979).

33. Charleston *Morning Post*, October 26, 1786, as quoted in Morgan, "Black Society in the Lowcountry, 1760–1810," in Berlin and Hoffman, eds., *Slavery and Freedom in the Age of the American Revolution*, 138–139.

34. Herbert Aptheker, "Maroons Within the Present Limits of the United States," *Journal of Negro History* 24 (April 1939): 170–171, as quoted in John Hope Franklin and Loren Schweninger, eds., *Runaway Slaves: Rebels on the Plantation* (New York: Oxford University Press, 1999), 86. Virtually every state assembly reported outlying gangs of ten or twenty fugitives, but the largest body of runaways lived in the Great Dismal Swamp (in southern Virginia and northern North Carolina). This maroon community was rumored to number in the thousands, and J.F.D. Smyth noted in 1784 that the runaways deep in the Great Dismal's watery depths "were perfectly safe, and with the greatest fac-

ulty elude the most diligent search of their pursuers." Over seventy years later, Elkanah Watson wrote that the fugitives, even if apprehended, "could not be approached with safety" because of their violent propensities. White anxiety about the Great Dismal and its inhabitants reached a fevered pitch in Virginia and North Carolina as it became known that Nat Turner had planned to ensconce his victorious clan in its depths after the rebellion of 1831. J.F.D. Smyth, *Tour of the United States of America*, vol. 1 (London: Printed for G. Robinson, 1784), 101–102, and Elkanah Watson, *Men and the Times of the Revolution* (New York: Dana and Company, 1856), 51–52, both as quoted in Kay and Cary, " 'They Are Indeed the Constant Plague of Their Tyrants,' " 40–41; Nat Turner, *The Confession of Nat Turner* (1832; reprint, Boston: St. Martin's Press, 1996); Stephen B. Oates, *The Fires of Jubilee: Nat Turner's Fierce Rebellion* (New York: Harper and Row, 1975).

35. For years, fugitive slaves from the Carolinas and Georgia had been running southward through the borderlands of southern Georgia and northern Florida, and many found sanctuary with the Cherokees and Creeks in western Georgia and, later, the Seminoles along the border. After 1750, many southeastern rice plantation runaways joined Seminole-owned black slaves in Indian towns but most established separate communities that closely resembled maroon communities around the world. The largest concentrations of maroons gathered around Alligator's Town, Suwannee Old Town, Charley Emathla's Town, and Coe Hadjo's Town in north-central Florida. Both maroons and their Seminole allies struggled to maintain their autonomy in the borderlands, independent of both the Spanish and the newly created United States government. They contended with both of these powers for seventy years, and their alliance with one another and with southeastern swamplands was the white southerner's worst nightmare. Kevin Mulroy, *Freedom on the Border: The Seminole Maroons in Florida and the Indian Territory, Coahuila, and Texas* (Lubbock: Texas Tech University Press, 1993), 1–2, 12; Kenneth Porter, *The Black Seminoles: History of a Freedom-Seeking People* (Gainesville: University Press of Florida, 1996), 11, 66; Jane L. Landers, "A Separate Nation: Free Blacks and Indians on the Florida Frontier," paper delivered at the Annual Meeting of the Society for Historians of the Early American Republic, July 1999 (courtesy of the author), 11.

36. *Georgia Gazette*, vol. 22, September 1, 1763, *Early American Newspapers*, microfilm reel 425.

37. Paine was caught aiding Sampson and spent six years in one of Georgia's prisons for helping a fugitive slave. Lewis W. Paine, *Six Years in a Georgia Prison: Narrative of Lewis W. Paine, Who Suffered Imprisonment Six Years in Georgia, for the Crime of Aiding the Escape of a Fellow-Man from That State, After He Had Fled from Slavery* (New York: Printed for the Author, 1851), 28 (Rare Books Collection, Georgia Historical Society).

38. Brown, *Slave Life in Georgia*, 61–62.

39. There is an argument to be made that, through acts of *petit marronage*, runaways were provided a "safety valve" within the plantation—preventing rebellion through small acts of resistance that gave slaves a sense of freedom and thus the ability to return to slavery. Slave use of swamplands and the continued availability of these environments reveal, however, that such spaces constantly destabilized the plantation order in ways that did not serve to bolster the institution of slavery.

40. "Petition Against the Introduction of Slaves," in Candler, ed., *Colonial Records*, 3:427.

41. James Oglethorpe to the Trustees, Frederica, June 29, 1741, in Candler, ed., *Colonial Records*, 23:51–52.

42. Jane L. Landers, *Black Society in Spanish Florida* (Urbana: University of Illinois Press, 1999), 1–2.

43. Ibid., 86.

44. Jane L. Landers, "Traditions of African American Freedom in Spanish Colonial Florida," in *The African American Heritage of Florida*, ed. David R. Colburn and Jane L. Landers (Gainesville: University Press of Florida, 1995), 29.

45. The *Georgia Gazette*, Georgia's first newspaper, was founded in Savannah and provided runaway-slave documentation for the years 1763 through 1770. The Milledgeville *Recorder* provided information on runaways from 1817 to 1818, years important because of the existence of East Florida as a Spanish territory in the borderlands and the context of the First Seminole War. The Milledgeville *Federal Union* provided information on post-annexation runaways between 1830 and 1845. All of these newspapers were published weekly and offered advertising space for a small fee. To determine the direction the slave was running, I considered the following: regarding runaway-slave advertisements, I considered the owner's guess as to where the slave was headed and the location of the owner's plantation in relation to the location of the newspaper in which he was advertising. For Brought to Jail advertisements, I considered the location of the jail and the information provided about the owners' location, assuming that the runaway was apprehended in flight away from the plantation. There is evidence that some runaways may have lied to jailors about their owner's names and whereabouts, using intentionally vague names to prolong their stay and increase their chance for escape—some owners who advertised for their slaves noted that "she probably won't tell her master's name." However, I have gone forward on the assumption that those fugitives brought to jail or taken up did not lie, as a consequence of whipping or other methods jailors may have used to get information out of their charges.

46. Philip D. Morgan, "Colonial South Carolina Runaways: Their Significance for Slave Culture," in Heuman, ed., *Out of the House of Bondage*, 57.

47. Ibid., 66.

48. Alexander Temple to Captain McTernan, December 16, 1786, bundle 108D9, East Florida Papers (hereafter cited as EFP); Jane L. Landers, "Acquisition and Loss on a Spanish Frontier: The Free Black Homesteaders of Florida, 1784–1821," in *Against the Odds: Free Blacks in the Slave Societies of the Americas*, ed. Landers (London: Frank Cass & Co., 1996), 91; Landers, *Black Society in Spanish Florida*.

49. John Blackwood to Captain Howard, St. Marys, summer 1792; John Blackwood to Captain Howard, August 15, 1792; and unknown Spanish official to John Blackwood, St. Augustine, August 20, 1792, bundle 108D9, EFP.

50. List of forty-three slaves, May 4, 1797, bundle 108D9, EFP.

51. James Seagrove to Henry White, Governor of East Florida, Point Peter, July 4, 1797, bundle 109E9, EFP.

52. James Seagrove to Henry White, Governor of St. Augustine and East Florida, July 26, 1803, bundle 109E9, EFP.

53. "Articles entered into by the Honorable Henry White, Governor and Commandant General of the City of Saint Augustine, and Province of East Florida, on the part of

His Most Catholic Majesty; and James Seagrove Esq. Commissioner on the part of the United States of America, May 19, 1797," bundle 109E9, EFP.

54. James Spalding to the Governor of St. Augustine, May 20, 1794, bundle 108D9, EFP.

55. Barbara Hurd, *Stirring the Mud: On Swamps, Bogs, and the Human Imagination* (Boston: Beacon Press, 2001), 4, 7.

PART IV

Schools and Educational Spaces

Mary S. Hoffschwelle

Rosenwald Schools in the Southern Landscape

In the early years of the twentieth century, the Rosenwald school building program brought together philanthropists, educators, architects, and Black and white citizens, creating new educational space for Black children in fifteen southern states. The children who attended what came to be known as "Rosenwald schools" learned in structures that transformed the material culture of schools and communities. By requiring the active participation of Black citizens in school construction—in essence, following Booker T. Washington's doctrine of self-help—the Rosenwald school program gave southern African Americans access to public space even as it buttressed Jim Crow boundaries. African Americans built Rosenwald schools as visible community institutions that expanded Black public space in the southern landscape and stood in silent reproof of the racism around them.

Booker T. Washington, principal of the Tuskegee Normal and Industrial Institute in Alabama, collaborated with Julius Rosenwald, president of Sears,

FIGURE 11.1.
Lincoln School. (Photograph by author)

Roebuck and Company, to establish the school building program.[1] Tuskegee extension department staff had already organized school building campaigns in nearby rural communities with financial assistance from northern benefactors, including former Standard Oil executive Henry Huttleston Rogers and Anna T. Jeanes, a Philadelphia Quaker who had contributed large sums to both Tuskegee and Hampton Institute and endowed the Jeanes Fund in 1907. After Rogers's death in 1909, Washington needed a new patron to underwrite these projects. He met Julius Rosenwald in spring 1911, when Rosenwald hosted a dinner in Chicago during Washington's visit to that city. Rosenwald, who had masterminded Sears, Roebuck's phenomenal success at the turn of the century, was already an active supporter of Jewish causes and Jane Addams's Hull House settlement in Chicago.[2] Rosenwald expanded his philanthropic efforts to African American needs after reading a biography of railroad executive William H. Baldwin Jr., who had chaired the boards of trustees for both Tuskegee Institute and the General Education Board. In 1910, Rosenwald had offered $25,000 for the construction of a YMCA facility for African Americans in any city where citizens raised an additional $75,000, inaugurating a challenge-grant program that eventually aided twenty-six African American YMCA and YWCA buildings. After accepting Washington's invitation to visit Tuskegee Institute, Rosenwald joined its board of trustees in 1912 and became one of Washington's and the institute's strongest allies.[3]

Booker T. Washington and Julius Rosenwald quickly realized that they shared two key beliefs: first, in the power of self-help, and second, in the value of public spaces as demonstrations of how Black and white Americans could prosper side by side.[4] Rosenwald immediately approved Washington's request to use part of a 1912 donation he had made to Tuskegee Institute as matching grants for six new one-room schools. Within two years, this small, localized initiative grew into a regional program administered by Tuskegee's Extension Department, led by Clinton J. Calloway.[5] Calloway had been involved in Tuskegee's school building campaigns from the start and, especially after Booker T. Washington's death in 1915, shouldered an ever-increasing administrative burden as Rosenwald made repeated donations for school projects. He coordinated the building program with the state agents for Negro schools at southern departments of education. State Negro school agents were white men who supervised all aspects of Black education in their states, their salaries subsidized by the leading philanthropic foundation in southern education, John D. Rockefeller's General Education Board.[6] Calloway and the state Negro school agents identified building projects that qualified for aid, distributed building plans prepared at Tuskegee by architect Robert R. Taylor and published in 1915 in *The Negro Rural School and Its Relation to the Community*, and coordinated the flow of grant funds.[7] In nine states, African American Rosenwald building agents worked with communities desiring Rosenwald schools, with salary support from Julius Rosenwald.

By the end of the decade, the program had overwhelmed all of its principal administrators. Tuskegee staff could barely keep up with the paperwork and bookkeeping of a rapidly expanding regional program, and the very success of the program brought in participants with different expectations. Some local and state white school officials resented having to submit to Tuskegee's authority. Others, especially some of the white men who served as state agents for Negro schools, grew impatient with Tuskegee's increasing administrative difficulties and haphazard supervision of construction practices. In 1919, Rosenwald commissioned a study of the schools by rural school architecture expert Fletcher B. Dresslar and an audit of Tuskegee's financial records.[8] The audit documented slipshod accounting methods, but Rosenwald was more concerned by Dresslar's findings. Dresslar not only criticized Tuskegee school designs as not being completely up-to-date in their provisions for lighting and ventilation but indicted the Tuskegee staff for inadequate supervision of building projects and local school officials and builders for using their own inferior designs and poor construction methods. Rosenwald removed the building program from Tuskegee in 1920 to an independent office in Nashville, Tennessee, headed by one of Dresslar's former students, Samuel L. Smith. The Nashville office operated as the southern branch of the Chicago-based Julius Rosenwald Fund, which Rosenwald had established in 1917. Smith directed the school building program, still working through the state Negro school agents and Rosenwald building agents, and issued the first of a new series of architectural plans and specifications titled *Community School Plans*. By the end of the 1920s, the Rosenwald Fund had expanded the building program beyond its initial focus on small, rural Black schools to include larger consolidated schools in towns and cities and a plethora of auxiliary programs ranging from library collections to school transportation.

Changing philanthropic objectives promoted by Rosenwald Fund director Edwin R. Embree, financial losses because of the stock market crash and ensuing Great Depression, and Julius Rosenwald's death in 1932 combined to close down the school building program in 1932. The Rosenwald school building program in twenty years had contributed to the construction of 5,357 schools, vocational buildings, and teachers' homes in the South valued at $28,408,520.[9] Rosenwald School Days, community events that featured friendly competitions in repairing and improving school buildings and grounds, reached out to all African American public schools. Meanwhile, the *Community School Plans*, distributed free of charge and reprinted in other school architecture books, set new standards for white school buildings as well. Portraits of Julius Rosenwald remained hanging in many schools, where teachers and parents taught children to consider themselves privileged to learn in a Rosenwald school.

The Julius Rosenwald school building program required a diverse coalition of people to cross Jim Crow's invisible lines in a united effort to build decent, modern spaces for a positive Black future.[10] The most important element in that coalition was African American activism and self-help, mandatory components of the building program that Black southerners seized upon to make these schools their own. Closer examination of the key participants, how they used the Rosenwald program to establish modern public educational facilities in their communities, and the ways in which both Blacks and whites recognized the meaning of those new features in their landscapes reveal how African Americans claimed a better place within the prescribed racial boundaries of the Jim Crow South.

This essay considers space in two ways. One is as a physical place that includes a site, the structures on that site, and the rooms with them. Space is also a setting or stage for human activity, the interactions that define the meaning of the place where they gather. The process of building a Rosenwald school was as important as the building itself. A Rosenwald school building was a new structure on a local landscape, usually quite small and modest in comparison with the facilities being constructed for white schoolchildren. Yet it spoke with many voices. The building's design echoed the calls of Progressive-era school architects and educators, northern philanthropists, and southern white school officials. Its walls reverberated with the voices of the Black school patrons, teachers, and students who clamored for a new school to continue their community's quest for learning, who got the school built, and who put its vision into practice.

A Rosenwald school began in a series of spaces—offices, school and church buildings, and outdoor locales—where Rosenwald school campaigners declared their intention to build a school and committed their time and treasure toward that goal. The momentum built at these spaces kept community members focused on their campaign and pushed local and state school authorities to complete the construction project. As the Rosenwald school went up in a community, its physical structure created another and more lasting space shaped by professional architects' and educators' ideas about the health and educational needs of all schoolchildren and the value of industrial education for Black children. Consequently, a Rosenwald school looked quite different from its predecessors or the churches, lodge halls, and other community spaces that had previously doubled as schools. Its construction reconfigured the existing community landscape by giving the school a separate physical location and a structural appearance imposed by outsiders. Finally, community members incorporated that new space into their landscape by investing it with the legacy of their continuous efforts to claim the right to an education, a process that continues today in community heritage and preservation projects.

The Rosenwald school building program began at the all-Black Tuskegee Institute, and even after Julius Rosenwald removed his project to an all-white office in Nashville, it offered Black southerners positive public roles on local, state, and regional stages. Program administrators' insistence that white and Black people collaborate on Rosenwald schools transformed the image of public education by representing African Americans as professional educators and committed school patrons backed by the power of the state and outside experts. Most whites involved in school reform, however, began their work under the assumption that African Americans needed white guidance.[11] Thus, Louisiana's state Negro school agents wrote a speech for an "advanced pupil" to declaim at Rosenwald School Day events that asserted, "It is good for the colored people to work in cooperation with their white neighbors. It is good for the colored people to be made aware of the interest of these white friends, and to receive their guidance, advice, and contributions. It is good for the colored people to realize that they have a friend [Rosenwald] in a distant state."[12] When outside philanthropies intervened on behalf of Black schools, they moved carefully to avoid white backlash by maintaining white control. The General Education Board paid the salaries of the state agents for Negro schools for state education departments, and the Anna T. Jeanes Fund distributed salary support for Black industrial supervising teachers (Jeanes supervisors) through those Negro school agents and white county school superintendents.[13] The removal of the Rosenwald building program from Tuskegee to Nashville had the same effect of centralizing white control over a program for Blacks.

The Rosenwald school building program depended on white state Negro school agents and county superintendents, to be sure, but it also opened up space for Black leadership within the South's educational hierarchy by funding Rosenwald building agents, one of the first state positions for African Americans in state departments of education.[14] A Rosenwald building agent provided the Rosenwald Fund and state departments of education with a direct link to Black southerners. For example, Booker T. Washington Jr. had his father's name and the prestige of Tuskegee Institute behind him when he entered the field in 1915; more commonly, Rosenwald agents had been teachers and principals or faculty at Black colleges and held office in Black state teachers' associations.[15]

Rosenwald building agents generally accepted segregation and believed in interracial cooperation, Black self-help, and the power of industrial education to advance the material and moral conditions of African Americans' lives. Like Booker T. Washington, they placed Black educational and economic rights ahead of—but not necessarily as substitutes for—social and political rights. Their brand of activism certainly accommodated Jim Crow's discrimination and disfranchisement, and sought to blunt the lynch mob's ugly violence with deference. Yet they asserted their own and southern Blacks' rights as citizens by using professional associations and public-private partnerships, such as the Rosenwald school building program, to leverage more of the benefits of citizenship from local and state governments.[16]

Rosenwald building agents usually made their initial visits to communities at the invitation of school principals and teachers, school patrons, and county superintendents. They helped to coordinate community efforts with local and state education officials. Rosenwald agents visited communities repeatedly to check on the progress of fund-raising efforts, the selection of the school site, and construction standards. Their final inspections assessed whether the state agent should release the Rosenwald grant to the county superintendent.[17]

Rosenwald building agents traversed spaces of white and Black, state and local authority. As Black representatives of the state, they entered white local authorities' offices and invited them into Black communities. Successful agents worked hard "to make the approach to the white people in creating a favorable sentiment" themselves and to show Black school patrons how to do the same.[18] A Rosenwald agent's skill as a mediator endured many challenges from within Black communities as well. Schools were valuable community institutions that Black southerners had already made places for in their community landscapes, and a new school building sometimes disrupted those familiar spaces and the community hierarchies and values they represented. Denominational loyalties could threaten a building campaign that would remove a school from the control of a particular church or minister. Consolidation of one-teacher schools into larger, centrally located facilities pitted rural communities against each other over whether they would lose their school or become the new focal point of a larger school neighborhood.[19] When a factional dispute erupted, a Rosenwald agent returned to hammer out a compromise and save the building campaign.[20] The Rosenwald school building program tapped into grassroots Black activism. Very quickly, word spread across the South that a man from Chicago was giving money for Black schools. The June 25, 1914, issue of the *New York Age* announced to the larger public that Booker T. Washington had convinced Julius Rosenwald to expand his support of new schools for Black children across the American South.

Prominent members of Black communities most often started the process of building a Rosenwald school. Principals and teachers had a professional and personal stake in a Rosenwald school building. They provided leadership in racial uplift campaigns, as many scholars have demonstrated, out of their own and their communities' expectations about the proper roles of educated Black men and women. Ministers, some of whom were either teachers or the leaders of congregations that sheltered schools, also took the lead in Black communities where the church and religious life were central to citizens' daily lives and aspirations.[21] Community leaders quickly stepped forward as the Rosenwald building program spread across the South.

Accustomed to official neglect, African Americans often started working on a Rosenwald campaign on their own and then invited the Negro school agent or Rosenwald building agent to join in their effort. A Rev. R. B. Angel wrote a May 1919 letter to Alabama Negro school agent J. S. Lambert for more information: "[D]ear Sir we ar try to bild a School on your plan here at Zin [Zion] Rest 3 ½ mils east of wedowee ala as you ar the proper one for it to come throw we want to know just how to get at this. we have a little one room bilding cost us about $700 but we want to get on your plan plese write me at once the detail of your plan ples rite me by return mail as ar goin to have a school meeting tusday night."[22] F. H. Edwards, who had heard about the Rosenwald program from his wife, a Jeanes teacher, wrote North Carolina's state agent for Negro schools for a Rosenwald grant, informing him that school patrons in Everetts had cut 7,000 feet of timber and hauled it to their building site.[23] Even in the last years of the building program, local initiative remained a critical element of every school project. In 1929, M. M. Leak wrote from his school in Tippo, Mississippi, to the State Board of Education because "we have been ask[ed] to built a consolidated

Rosen Wall School at this place which is very much needed." Vincent Harris, Georgia's Rosenwald building agent, reported in 1931, "I often find a small community raising money that there is no record on file for them, but they understand about the Rosenwald school."[24]

With the building campaign under way, participants had to meet specific requirements for Rosenwald aid that Black activists found problematic yet valuable for their claim to public space: the school building and its site had to be deeded to the local board of education or the state; the building design had to meet modern standards of school construction and include provisions for industrial education; and Black school patrons had to contribute materially to the new school.[25] Requiring that a Rosenwald school become the property of the public school system reflected the desire of Booker T. Washington, Julius Rosenwald, and the building program's staff to increase public support of Black schools. They believed in the social and personal value of universal education and wanted white southerners to accept that Black education was a public responsibility. Although they deliberately stopped short of demanding equal funding for completely equal educational programs and facilities, Rosenwald school program officers believed that they could move white southerners in that direction. At the same time, these requirements set Rosenwald schools apart as spaces for Black education. The schools had to be new structures—no more sending white children off to new and better facilities and turning over the worn-out, outmoded ones to Black children. Rosenwald program officials also insisted that Rosenwald schools be public schools on public property—no more housing schools in churches or lodge halls, or setting up private schools that allowed white local authorities to ignore their responsibilities to Black schoolchildren.[26]

At the local level, a Rosenwald building redefined Black education from a private value to a public right. Scholars such as James D. Anderson have documented Black southerners' historic commitment to education, and indeed many Rosenwald structures housed schools that traced their roots back to the 1860s and 1870s. Some originated as Freedmen's Bureau and missionary schools during and soon after the Civil War, or as public schools established by Reconstruction state governments; others had denominational associations.[27] Because southern states and counties refused to appropriate any meaningful funds for Black education, most early twentieth-century Black schools remained housed in churches, fraternal lodges, stores, abandoned white schools, private homes, and farm buildings.[28] These facilities tied the schools tightly to Black southerners by locating them within existing community spaces. But, as revealed when church congregations complained about teachers and pupils disrupting their sacred spaces, Black children were being crowded into spaces never intended as formal learning environments, hidden from public view and public responsibility.

A Rosenwald school immediately moved those children and their teachers into a public space that offered a new focal point for the community, even when it still stood next to a church or within an established Black neighborhood. The new structure was visibly not a church, lodge, house, or anything else but a school. Rosenwald schools did not necessarily look alike: they varied from small one-teacher structures to multistory facilities with more than twenty classrooms, from frame to brick to concrete construction, and from the plainest boxes to striking Spanish Revival styles. Yet they all shared the same approach to building design. From the outset, the building program's administrators required the use of a building plan that they had approved. In practice, that plan could come from an architect specially commissioned for the project, which was the case only in the largest Rosenwald schools; but more commonly building plans came either from the building program staff or from state departments of education. Both Tuskegee Institute and the Julius Rosenwald Fund's Nashville office sent out their own plans free of charge. These standardized plans, which building program staff periodically revised and updated, embodied the newest concepts of progressive rural school architecture.[29]

Schools that followed designs from the successive editions of the Rosenwald Fund's *Community School Plans* of the 1920s and early 1930s visually represented those concepts and repeated them across the southern landscape (Fig. 11.1). Several features contributed to a *Community School Plan*: a Rosenwald school's distinctive appearance and command of the community landscape around it, most notably its fenestration, the plainness of the façade, and the integration of industrial training spaces.[30] School architects of the early twentieth century, including Fletcher B. Dresslar, forged a Progressive school architecture aesthetic that integrated a stylistic preference for symmetry and simplicity with scientific measures to promote public health and learning that ensured the efficient use of building space and materials. They were obsessed with window size and location to provide the necessary illumination for instruction and protect children's eyesight.[31] Unilateral lighting was essential so that neither teachers nor students looked directly into a light source or constantly refocused their eyes because of uneven or cross lighting. Rosenwald *Community School Plans* oriented the building so that classroom windows faced east or west and permitted windows on only one classroom wall. Window needs dictated the floor plan of the school as well, requiring blocks of classrooms in rectangles or H-shaped forms. Each classroom's windows stretched from about four feet above the floor up close to the ceiling to meet the prescribed 5:1 ratio between floor and window surface areas. Adjustable shades inside softened the glare of early morning or late afternoon sun. Grouped in "batteries" of tall slender sashes encased by narrow mullions, these windows provided a virtually unbroken stream of light from left to right across every student's desk and the blackboard. Unilateral lighting by battery windows signaled a modern school to educational reformers and allowed the most casual viewer to distinguish Rosenwald schools from their predecessors.

Window batteries dominated the façades of Rosenwald *Community School Plans* not just because of their size but because the exterior design was so plain. Most plans limited stylistic details to overhanging eaves that hinted at the Arts and Crafts style or gabled porches over doorways that suggested Colonial Revival design. Otherwise, only paint or a simple brickwork pattern adorned a Rosenwald school.[32] The lack of decorative detailing blended aesthetic and professional judgments with the realities of segregation. At the inception of the building program, Booker T. Washington had demanded that the schools be as modest as possible in their appearance to preclude white backlash and to keep them as cost-efficient as possible to appeal to Julius Rosenwald.[33] Even after the Rosenwald Fund revamped its designs to emphasize model school architecture and larger consolidated school structures, cost—what Black patrons could donate and white school authorities would appropriate—lurked at the back of everyone's minds. Equally important were design considerations. Architects had long argued that country schools should reflect the simplicity of rural life and thus reject decorative excess. Rosenwald Fund staff added a modernist sensibility to this, stripping away anything from the building's form that did not serve its function. Rosenwald staff also preferred one-story schools for safety and cost, which automatically differentiated their Black schools from the traditional two-story Black fraternal lodge. Even when they introduced larger school plans with overt Colonial Revival styling, Rosenwald staff avoided adding cupolas that might suggest a church steeple or belfry.[34] This aesthetic visually removed the school from the lodge hall and church and set it beside them as a dedicated space for the education of Black children.

Modest and modern, most Rosenwald schools stood just off the road in the Black sections of towns or in Black enclaves in the countryside. Professional observers often singled them out from the "shabbiest and shoddiest types of cabins, churches, and halls" endemic in Black education.[35] Thus, the caption beneath a photograph of a two-teacher Rosenwald school in the 1919 U.S. Bureau of Education survey of Alabama's public schools identified it as "A Colored School Unusually Well Constructed." In a later survey of Florida's Black schools, educational experts complained that "when one gets out into the county districts . . . one finds few, if any, buildings that would be rated as high or fair, with the exception of the schools that have been built with the assistance of the Rosenwald Fund." In East Texas, Rosenwald schools were "the only Negro school buildings . . . that might be considered adequate for school purposes."[36]

Spaces for industrial education in Rosenwald facilities tempered the buildings' up-to-date appearance. Historians have often characterized the conflict over industrial education for African Americans as a debate between Booker T. Washington and vocational training for second-class citizenship versus W.E.B. Du Bois and academic education for a Black leadership cadre. Yet the two forms of education were not mutually exclusive, and the argument centered on the relative power of northern-based philanthropies, southern white educators, and Black southerners to define the scope, content, and purpose of Black education. Officials of the Rosenwald school building program clearly sided with the vocational camp, not only to assuage southern white fears but also as a tangible expression of Washington's demand that whites recognize Blacks' economic citizenship and, after the 1917 Smith-Hughes Act, to secure the federal and state funding for vocational training that otherwise flowed exclusively into white schools. State agents for Negro schools and Rosenwald building agents agreed in 1919 that "especially is it absolutely necessary that an Industrial Room be provided in every plan submitted before the plan is approved, and that in order to carry out the Rosenwald idea the school building including the Industrial Room be properly equipped."[37] Like Louisiana Rosenwald building agent J. S. Jones, they praised schools for "living up to the Rosenwald idea" of integrating industrial education into the building's physical space: the Prairieville, Louisiana, school was excellent because it had a "kitchen equipped with necessary utensils" as well as a "full set of dining room dishes" and a sewing machine. Photographs of Rosenwald schools intended for white viewers reinforced such images by showing the kitchen equipment or students working on farm projects at the school site.[38]

Yet the vocational education meant to assuage white fears proved elusive, as the state agents for Negro schools recognized when they complained about finding children in Rosenwald schools who spent little or no time on vocational projects.[39] Demands for agricultural training precipitated conflict with teachers who espoused a different philosophy. One African American teacher, Elias J. Murdock, reportedly informed his Black school trustees that "if they expected him to go on the farm and plow and hoe they were craze, that he didn't come here for that purpose."[40] When teachers and patrons preferred academic instruction to vocational subjects for their children, they simply ignored the industrial curriculum. Everyday realities limited industrial education just as effectively. Equipment expenses and the lack of trained vocational teachers hampered some schools; in others, the opening of a decent school building attracted so many new students that the industrial room had to be converted into a regular classroom.

Even with their modest façades and industrial rooms, some whites thought these schools were too good for the Black landscape. As happened to many

African American schools for decades before and since, Rosenwald schools fell victim to other southerners' attempts to squash Black initiative and prevent the modernization of African American education embodied in Rosenwald structures. In 1916, Louisiana Negro school agent Leo M. Favrot lamented: "I have just lost my most interesting parish training school. It was burned down Saturday night by a low class of prejudiced whites. . . . We are doing all we can to try to run down the incendiaries, but we understand that the parish authorities are not with us, and it is going to be a hard job."[41] Black residents of Wilson, Arkansas, recalled the destruction of their Rosenwald school, a prepossessing two-story brick structure, in 1924: "It was so much like the white school that it is believed the community radicals burned it" almost immediately after its completion.[42] Sometimes whites who rejected the implicit message of the Rosenwald school invaded that space to bring it down to the level they believed more appropriate for African Americans or to reassert white power in Black spaces. E. A. McGruder took the folding doors out of the Wedgeworth, Alabama, school for use in his new house. When David Miller removed the new patent desks from the Loam Land School and installed them in the school on his own plantation in Tensas Parish, Louisiana, he acted on his power as the chair of the board of education and as a planter to control the distribution of resources to Black tenants.[43]

Yet the balance of power had slightly shifted. In communities that had Rosenwald schools, citizens could call upon Rosenwald staff and state departments of education to force the return or replacement of stolen items and rebuild burned schools. They did so not simply as supplicants to a higher—and outside—authority but as citizens who had acted in good faith to raise their required self-help contribution to match the Rosenwald grant and now could reasonably expect school authorities to honor their requests. Booker T. Washington had built self-help and community participation into the program from his first approach to Julius Rosenwald. In September 1912, he wrote Julius Rosenwald: "One thing I am convinced of and that is that it is the best thing to have the people themselves build houses in their own community. I have found by investigation that many people who cannot give money, would give a half day or a day's work and others would give material in the way of nails, brick, lime, etc."[44]

Washington's self-help philosophy, which Rosenwald shared and the two men made a centerpiece of the school building program, demanded sacrifices from Black school patrons. As has been pointed out, self-help in reality meant that African Americans paid their taxes and then voluntarily taxed themselves a second time to build and maintain Rosenwald schools.[45] Given that many southern counties diverted state and local tax revenues for Black schools to pay for white schools, superintendents' repeated demands that African Americans make additional contributions to finish and furnish Rosenwald schools can seem punitive. Indeed, the self-help requirement also set a standard that allowed outsiders to blame Black communities that could not meet this test.[46]

Nevertheless, Black southerners incorporated Rosenwald schools into a tradition of self-help in education extending from the antebellum period, when free Blacks had been excluded from the limited public school systems in southern states and slaves were expressly denied any right to formal education. Rosenwald building agents, principals, and Jeanes supervisors orchestrated the many individual contributions necessary to raise the required local contribution, which varied according to the type and size of building planned. The most common fund-raising strategy was the rally, which typically featured speeches, reports on the status of fund-raising and construction, requests for additional contributions from the audience, food, and entertainment. Lottie Q. Beadle advertised her rally at the Gurley, Alabama, Christian Methodist Episcopal (CME) church as a "Union Thanksgiving Service and Dinner" where, for twenty-five cents one could enjoy "roast turkey and pork, rabbit salad, bread and jelly, mashed potatoes, pumpkin pie, sweet potato pie, ice cream and cake" prepared by the school girls' club.[47] Audience members in turn signed their names to the pledge list or handed over money; they might later see a list of contributors and their donations in the local newspaper.[48] These events created temporary stages for demonstrations of community identity and values. At school rallies, Black leaders such as teachers, principals, and ministers who spearheaded Rosenwald campaigns and the Black school patrons whose self-help would make the school possible celebrated each other's contributions to the community project. When whites were in attendance, most often the state agent for Negro schools and county superintendent but sometimes also white school board members and business leaders, rallies became interracial stages on which Black southerners articulated what they expected of white local and state officials and from their white neighbors.[49]

Self-help for the sake of a Rosenwald school brought into public view the Black men and women who made short-term sacrifices for the promise of long-term improvements for their students and children. Their sacrifices were not new, but the Rosenwald building program required an official accounting of black self-help measures, which ensured that white school authorities at least had to acknowledge those efforts as meaningful. Rosenwald school campaigns also offered public recognition of the legions of anonymous Black southerners who performed the labor that brought forth a new school. Rosenwald program staff, from the Rosenwald building agents in the field to program headquarters at Tuskegee Institute and Nashville and the Julius Rosenwald Fund office in Chicago, broadcast news of Black self-help efforts to their peers in other philanthropic and educational organizations and the general public. Their reports were generally paternalistic and often condescending, but they nevertheless document how African Americans created spaces for themselves in the South, and the ways that they used Rosenwald school campaigns for that purpose. Official reports by Rosenwald building agents, state Negro school agents, and state superintendents of education often noted that Black landowners donated the school site or patrons raised the funds for land purchases.[50] "Hustling" members of school committees knocked on the doors of their neighbors and the whites who employed them or with whom they traded in town.[51] Black southerners' daily labor also provided school funds. Frequently men cut the timber and hauled it from the forest to the sawmill and then to the school site; they hauled bricks, lumber, roofing materials, and equipment as well. In the early years of the program, male patrons might build and paint the school as well. Women prepared the food served at rallies or sold at countless picnics, suppers, and cake walks. Patrons of a Rosenwald school in Tennessee accumulated their contribution by marketing farm products ranging from eggs to cotton.[52] Other cotton-producing communities set aside the proceeds from selected portions of their acreage to benefit the school. Industrial workers donated a day's pay.[53] Members of the community institutions that had long sheltered schools redirected their activities toward new facilities. Churches like the Israel CME Church in Jackson, Georgia, provided meeting spaces for building committees and took up collections during services, as did fraternal lodges.[54]

Cornerstone ceremonies by Black masons and special dedication events celebrated the community's achievement in visible signs of local identity and pride.[55] This pattern of Black agency, repeated thousands of times across fifteen states, broadened local African Americans' initiative and influence. The self-help measures that brought forth Rosenwald schools signified the value that Black southerners gave to community institutions, yet when put before white eyes, seemed also to signal an acceptable deference to Jim Crow. This seeming contradiction made Rosenwald schools safe places for Blacks to voice their aspirations and put the burden on whites to recognize African Americans' educational needs and goals as legitimate.[56]

Rosenwald buildings gave African Americans much-needed leverage with white school leaders, just as Washington and Rosenwald had hoped. Local white authorities typically ignored or refused Black requests for their schools. But when Black school patrons appeared in the superintendent's office and offered to combine Rosenwald assistance with their own contributions, buttressed by resolutions from their school rally, they were much harder to resist. The added inspiration of a Rosenwald grant also spurred school patrons to renew their demands on local school authorities. For example, in Hawthorne, Florida, Chester Shell was one of nine Black men who had unsuccessfully petitioned the Alachua

County Board of Education for a school between 1922 and 1925. Armed with information about the Rosenwald program and a network of contacts with affluent whites that Shell had met in his career as railroad porter and sports guide, Shell raised $11,000 and won approval for the school in 1926.[57]

African Americans could use their connections to the program and state officials to force recalcitrant whites to respect Black spaces. Rosenwald building agents performed this duty constantly, reminding superintendents of their obligations concerning building plans, construction practices, equipment purchases, and sanitary toilets and reporting their faults to the state department of education. Principals, teachers, and ministers could do the same. Harvey Foster requested that W. F. Credle, who administered North Carolina's Rosenwald building program, to intervene with a superintendent who was content to leave the lumber sitting on the ground at the Tucker's Grove school site, just as Charles N. Hunter asked Credle not to pay out the grant for the Manchester school because local authorities had not provided toilets or suitable blackboards and desks.[58]

With the completion of a Rosenwald school, Black southerners transferred the energies and sentiment generated by their school campaign to a lasting physical structure surrounded by several acres of playgrounds and gardens. Local people had little, if any, control over the appearance of their school, which the Rosenwald building program kept in the hands of its own officials and the state agents for Negro schools. But the purpose of the building campaign, after all, had been to secure a modern school facility, which meant accepting outside expertise. Black southerners integrated the new structure into their landscape in other ways, such as by naming the school.

The Rosenwald program's summary lists of its schools identified them by county, and then by a mixture of place-names and given names or district numbers. Some took the name "Rosenwald" or those of Booker T. Washington, Paul Laurence Dunbar, and the state Negro school agents and Rosenwald building agents. More common, however, were familiar country place-names, such as Shady Grove, Cedar Grove, and Pleasant Grove. Names like Mount Olive, Shiloh, and Mount Zion reflected many schools' previous identification with a church. Even when white authorities designated one name for the Rosenwald school, local people might prefer another: for example, the Rosenwald school in South Carolina officially identified as Prosperity and later the Howard School was the Shiloh School to those it served because it stood next to the Shiloh AME Church that had sponsored it.[59] Marianna, Florida, residents called the Jackson County Training School "Gilmore Academy" in honor of the man who led its building campaign. Names also provided continuity by tying the modern structure to a community's tradition of education, as with Tallahassee's Lincoln School, which dated to 1869. Thus, Black southerners used school names both to acknowledge that a Rosenwald project had reorganized community space by creating a separate modern structure for learning and simultaneously to locate that new space in the ongoing evolution of a community's landscape.

"Rosenwald School" also became a signifier, using "Rosenwald" as an adjective to distinguish it from other "colored" schools. "Rosenwald School" came to define a building constructed specifically for African American children according to modern architectural and educational standards by activist community members and leaders. Supporters consistently identified the presence of a Rosenwald school as a marker of personal success and community pride. One man from Prosperity, South Carolina, ran for office in the African Methodist Episcopal Church on his record of establishing and teaching in Rosenwald schools. Teachers and principals across the South sought acclaim by reporting on successful Rosenwald building campaigns in the pages of their professional journals. Even in retirement, Mississippian Eva Lois Gordon recalled how she inaugurated her successful career with a Rosenwald school: "[I]n 1919 I was elected principal of the school and began immediately working with the community people to raise money to qualify for a Rosenwald Fund Grant to build a much-needed school. . . . [W]e entered the Pike County Training School, January, 1921. . . . In later years, the Pike County Training School became the Pike County Agricultural High School, and in 1963 a large modern plant was built and named in my honor, the Eva Gordon Attendance Center."[60]

Rosenwald schools also became symbols of collective achievement. The Colored Public School Trustees Association of Prince George's County, Maryland, used Rosenwald schools as barometers of the communities they surveyed in 1924, praising those that had completed Rosenwald projects and chiding school patrons and staff who had not yet taken action to replace their shabby facilities.[61] A Black minister who had spearheaded the campaign for a two-teacher Rosenwald school in Virginia told Jackson Davis, "Now we know that we can build schoolhouses and do any other good thing that we make up our minds to do."[62]

White observers also correlated successful Rosenwald campaigns with broader improvements in educational standards, living conditions, and white public opinion. Their commentaries bespeak the multiple meanings of Rosenwald school spaces, as whites interpreted these schools both as symbols of successful interracial cooperation under white supervision and as Black vehicles of educational and community progress. Reflecting on the meaning of a Rosenwald school in 1923, Louisiana Negro school agent Leo Favrot opined, "[T]here is no doubt that the building of Rosenwald schools has stimulated a greater interest in Negro education on the part of both white and colored, has helped to make terms longer, to create a desire for better teachers, and a greater respect for the

Negro school on the part of all concerned."[63] South Carolina's Joseph B. Felton declared, "In every community, without exception, all the people both white and colored, have pointed with pride to these [Rosenwald] buildings and to what they stand for in the community." And in 1931, he asserted that Rosenwald schools are "a credit to the communities in which they are located."[64] These state agents for Negro schools shaped their reports to emphasize interracial support for their intended white audiences, yet, as Felton's words suggest, they also recognized African American activism and the value of Rosenwald spaces.

A few years earlier, Felton had pushed to the very boundaries of the Rosenwald school's potential meaning for the southern social landscape. In "The Attitude of the White People," Felton praised whites for their support of Black education, adding, "it is not an unusual sight to see two school buildings erected in the same district of exactly the same type and structure, one for the white children and the other for the colored children. Thinking people realize that it is an economic asset to have good school buildings and good school advantages for all of the children of the community."[65] The same could have been true in many other communities, as state departments of education often distributed the Rosenwald Fund's *Community School Plans* for use in constructing white schools or, as in Alabama, published almost identical designs without the Rosenwald name or "industrial" notations on floor plans that would identify the buildings with African Americans.[66] Indeed, one of the Rosenwald Fund's ulterior motives was to build schools for Black children that would serve as models for all schools and thus prod southern school boards at least to live up to their obligations under the *Plessy v. Ferguson* U.S. Supreme Court decision and Booker T. Washington's "Atlanta Compromise."

For at least a decade after the demise of the building program, Rosenwald schools retained their special place in Black education. A 1939 article on southern schools for African Americans noted, "[S]o strong is the tradition that good schools are Rosenwald schools," some constructed after the program's demise appropriated the name for themselves.[67] Perhaps these were some of the schools still being constructed according to *Community School Plans* but by New Deal agencies such as the Works Projects Administration.[68] Nonetheless, by the later 1940s, Rosenwald schools had obviously fallen short of their promise. State and county education officials, supported by white voters, continued shortchanging Black public schools, and Rosenwald schools fell victim to insufficient maintenance and operational funds. Self-help could not keep up with the need, or bring about all the changes needed for full equality, and so the teachers, patrons, and children at Rosenwald schools increasingly joined with other Black southerners and the National Association for the Advancement of Colored People for direct challenges to legal segregation and discrimination.[69]

FIGURE 11.2.
Rosenwald–St. David Elementary School.
(Photograph by author)

As southern states have come to terms with the U.S. Supreme Court's decisions mandating school desegregation and integration, Rosenwald schools have become links between the way that past and present generations assigned racial identity to community spaces. Schools bearing the Rosenwald name are still scattered across southern states, but many others lost their "Rosenwald" or community-based name when consolidated with white schools. Florida's Rosenwald Center in Altamonte Springs still operates in its original building whereas the Rosenwald school in Society Hill, South Carolina, is a later twentieth-century building (Fig. 11.2). But the Brevard Rosenwald School in North Carolina received a new name after school integration.[70] Street signs still bear the Rosenwald name even when the schools have moved, as in Society Hill; have been rebuilt and then renamed, as in Brevard; or have been demolished, as in Perry, Georgia.

Alumni and former teachers preserve their connections to the Rosenwald school building program. Like their forebears who wrote to educational officials based on scraps of information about the Rosenwald program, some recall only bits and pieces of their schools' history: the connection to Sears, Roebuck and Company or Chicago, the standardized appearance of *Community School Plan* structures, or the division between Black and white worlds that automatically defined Rosenwald schools as African American.[71] Others, like Eva Gordon, proudly assign the school a key place in their personal and professional land-scapes.[72] Reunions of Rosenwald school alumni reenact their youthful claim to the communities' landscape and reaffirm decades of continuous use of the school as a physical assertion of vibrant African American community identity.[73] Monuments in front of surviving Rosenwald-funded schools honor the memo-ries of teachers and students in the segregation era, as do others that mark the location of schools demolished in the wake of school integration and new build-ing standards. Signs, stone markers, plaques, and flagpoles compel the viewer to recognize that earlier generations of the community's Black citizens had carved out this space for themselves and that their descendants have a prior claim on its meaning within the present landscape.[74]

Heritage programs perpetuate the tradition of marking Rosenwald schools as African American places in the South's public landscape.[75] Preservation and community activists have erected markers and nominated surviving schools to the National Register of Historic Places, designated them on state historic place listings, and undertaken publicity and cleanup campaigns.[76] Several former Rosenwald schools now serve as museums, with restored classrooms and exhib-its about African American history.[77] Public programs at these museums and in Rosenwald school communities reaffirm their connections with the Rosenwald school program and with Julius Rosenwald.[78] Looking outward, heritage tour-ism publications tout the presence of Rosenwald schools to visitors interested in Black history and historic sites.[79] In 2002, the National Trust for Historic Preservation named Rosenwald schools one of America's most endangered his-toric sites. The National Trust's Rosenwald School Initiative, headquartered at its regional office in Charleston, South Carolina, brings together community activists and preservationists from all fifteen states with Rosenwald schools and sponsors special sessions during the trust's annual meeting. The trust also orga-nized a regional conference on Rosenwald schools in the summer of 2004 at Fisk University, where the Special Collections department of the John Hope and Aurelia Elizabeth Franklin Library holds the Julius Rosenwald Fund Archives.[80]

In addition to the trust's expanding Web site devoted to Rosenwald schools and historian Thomas W. Hanchett's Web site, which includes the *Community School Plans*, Rosenwald schools are appearing with greater frequency in elec-tronic media. The proliferation of school Web sites allows a new generation to employ Rosenwald schools to claim space simultaneously in physical and virtual landscapes. Regardless of whether the original Rosenwald structures or names survive, these schools use their space on the World Wide Web to celebrate their origins in a Rosenwald school project. School history Web pages dutifully note their origins as all-Black institutions, celebrate the initiative and sacrifices of school founders who led the building campaigns, and explain the Rosenwald building program. Just as in the years of Rosenwald construction campaigns, congratulatory electronic texts and images suggest that local Blacks who participated in the Rosenwald school program possessed special merits that allowed them to prevail within and despite segregation and racism. The Rosenwald school, they imply, has bequeathed a better life to all of the students who now mingle in hallways, classrooms, and playing grounds.[81]

Building a Rosenwald school required Black and white people to cross into each other's physical, professional, and social spaces to create a distinctive African American place of pride and achievement. Whether it stood in an open country of fields and country lanes or on the busy streets of an urban neighborhood, a Rosenwald school made a permanent place in the southern landscape worthy of the African Americans who joined forces with Julius Rosenwald in "building an ideal."[82]

NOTES

The author thanks the Department of History, the Faculty Research and Creative Activity Committee, and the Non-Instructional Assignment Committee at Middle Tennessee State University and the John Hope Franklin Center at Duke University for supporting this research. This essay includes material from *The Rosenwald Schools of the American South* (Gainesville: University Press of Florida, 2006).

1. General histories of the Rosenwald school building program can be found in Edwin R. Embree and Julia Waxman, *Investment in People: The Story of the Julius Rosenwald Fund* (New York: Harper and Brothers, 1949); S. L. Smith, *Builders of Goodwill* (Nashville: Tennessee Book Company, 1950); Louis R. Harlan, *Booker T. Washington: The Wizard of Tuskegee, 1901–1915* (New York: Oxford University Press, 1983); James D. Anderson, *The Education of Blacks in the South, 1865–1935* (Chapel Hill: University of North Carolina Press, 1988); Thomas W. Hanchett, "The Rosenwald Schools and Black Education in North Carolina," *North Carolina Historical Review* 65 (October 1988): 387–444; James L. Leloudis, *Schooling the New South: Pedagogy, Self, and Society in North Carolina, 1880–1920* (Chapel Hill: University of North Carolina Press, 1996); Mary S. Hoffschwelle, *Rebuilding the Rural Southern Community: Reformers, Schools and Homes in Tennessee, 1900–1930* (Knoxville: University of Tennessee Press, 1998); and Eric Anderson and Alfred A. Moss Jr., *Dangerous Donations: Northern Philanthropy and Southern Education, 1902–1930* (Columbia: University of Missouri Press, 1999).

2. On Rosenwald's place among Jewish philanthropists and the broader network of northern business leaders, see Peter M. Ascoli, *Julius Rosenwald: The Man Who Built Sears, Roebuck and Advanced the Cause of Black Education in the American South* (Bloomington: Indiana University Press, 2006); Morris R. Werner, *Julius Rosenwald: The Life of a Practical Humanitarian* (New York: Harper & Brothers, 1939); and Jayne R. Beilke, "'Partners in Distress': Jewish Philanthropy and Black Education During the Progressive Era," *American Educational History Journal* 29, no. 1 (2002): 26–34.

3. Rosenwald remained a trustee and generous contributor to Tuskegee Institute the rest of his life. He supported other Black causes as well, including the NAACP. See Ascoli,

Julius Rosenwald, 87–92, 135–158; Werner, *Julius Rosenwald*, 3–30; as well as Harlan, *The Wizard of Tuskegee*.

4. Washington and Rosenwald did not compare their school project to Andrew Carnegie's library program, which preceded theirs by several decades. Rather, their school building initiative emerged out of Washington and Tuskegee staff's commitment to create successful black community institutions through a combination of self-help, outside philanthropy, and interracial effort. Yet the two endeavors share some similarities. Carnegie sought to reform philanthropy by turning to a corporate model, as historian Abigail Van Slyck has shown; Julius Rosenwald attempted to reform philanthropy by rejecting perpetual endowments in favor of self-extinguishing foundations like his own Julius Rosenwald Fund. Both programs relied on a single philanthropic benefactor who turned over the program to professional administrators and set out strict guidelines for community involvement and support for their buildings, although Carnegie's donations to individual libraries dwarfed Rosenwald's matching grants. The Carnegie library program did not prepare its own building plans as the Rosenwald program did, but administrator James Bertram took a keen interest in the design and both programs had a significant impact on contemporary standards for their building types. Abigail A. Van Slyke analyzes Carnegie's philanthropic evolution, his program's influence on library architecture and the library profession, and the social and cultural context for Carnegie library projects in *Free to All: Carnegie Libraries and American Culture, 1890–1920* (Chicago: University of Chicago Press, 1995). Thomas W. Hanchett also notes the Carnegie library program as a possible model for Booker T. Washington and Julius Rosenwald in "The Rosenwald Schools and Black Education in North Carolina," 387–427.

5. Clinton J. Calloway, A.B., and Clinton J. Calloway, "Co-Operative School Building," in *The National Cyclopedia of the Colored Race*, vol. 1, ed. Clement Richardson (Montgomery, AL: National Publishing Company, 1919), 25, 569–572.

6. In this essay, I also refer to the state agents for Negro schools as Negro school agents and identify the African American building agents variously as Rosenwald building agents or Rosenwald agents. On the state agents for Negro schools, see Smith, *Builders of Goodwill*; Anderson, *Education of Blacks in the South*; and Leloudis, *Schooling the New South*.

7. On Robert R. Taylor, see Ellen Weiss, "Robert R. Taylor of Tuskegee: An Early Black American Architect," *ARRIS: Journal of the Southeast Chapter of the Society of Architectural Historians* 2 (1991): 3–19; ibid., "Tuskegee: Landscape in Black and White," *Winterthur Portfolio* 36, no. 1 (Spring 2001): 19–37; Clarence G. Williams, "From 'Tech' to Tuskegee: The Life of Robert Robinson Taylor, 1868–1942," *MIT Archives and Special Collections*, http://libraries.mit.edu/archives/mithistory/blacks-at-mit/taylor.html (accessed January 6, 2004); Angel David Nieves, "'We Gave Our Hearts and Lives to It': African-American Women Reformers, Industrial Education, and the Monuments of Nation-Building in the Post-Reconstruction South, 1877–1938," Ph.D. diss., Cornell University, 2001, 189–190, 222–232.

8. Fletcher B. Dresslar, *Report on the Rosenwald School Buildings* (Nashville, TN: Julius Rosenwald Fund, 1920); Arthur Young & Co., "Mr. Julius Rosenwald, Aid for Colored Schools, Report on Audit of Accounts, January 1, 1915, to June 30, 1919," box 51, General Correspondence, Robert Russa Moton Papers, Tuskegee University Archives, Tuskegee, Alabama.

9. African Americans had contributed $4,725,891, Rosenwald $4,364,869, and whites $1,211,975; the remaining $18,105,805 came from public revenues. Anderson, *Education of Blacks*, table 5.2, 155.

10. An address to the 1947 North Carolina Conference of Superintendents, presumably written by Negro school agent Nathan Carter Newbold, emphasized this point, concluding that "thousands" of Black and white North Carolinians "participated actively, whole heartedly in the planning and building of Rosenwald schools. It was a magnificent experiment in cooperative interracial endeavor." "Today, Yesterday, and Tomorrow," box 4, Special Subject File, Division of Negro Education, Department of Public Instruction Records, North Carolina Division of Archives and History, Raleigh, North Carolina. See also Alicestyne Turley-Adams, *Rosenwald Schools in Kentucky* (Lexington: Kentucky Heritage Council and Kentucky African American Heritage Commission, 1997), 1; and James C. Carbaugh, "The Philanthropic Confluence of the General Education Board and the Jeanes, Slater, and Rosenwald Funds: African-American Education in South Carolina, 1900–1930," Ph.D. diss., Clemson University, 1997, 76.

11. William A. Link, *The Paradox of Southern Progressivism, 1880–1930* (Chapel Hill: University of North Carolina Press, 1992).

12. A. C. Lewis and J. W. Bateman, *Rosenwald-Day Program*, Bulletin 102 (Baton Rouge: Louisiana State Department of Education, 1927), 8.

13. Raymond B. Fosdick, *Adventure in Giving: The Story of the General Education Board* (New York: Harper and Row, 1971); Mildred M. Williams, Kara Vaughn Jackson, Madie A. Kiney, Susie W. Wheeler, Rebecca Davis, Rebecca A. Crawford, Maggie Forte, and Ethel Bell, *The Jeanes Story: A Chapter in the History of American Education* (Jackson, MS: Southern Education Foundation, 1979); and Smith, *Builders of Goodwill*. Many Rosenwald-aided schools also received support from these foundations and, if they served as county training schools, from the John F. Slater Fund. Edward E. Redcay, *County Training Schools and Public Secondary Education for Negroes in the South* (Washington, DC: John F. Slater Fund, 1935).

14. Alabama, Arkansas, Georgia, Kentucky, Louisiana, Mississippi, North Carolina, Tennessee, and Virginia had Rosenwald building agents. These men had state positions but not necessarily office space in the education department offices. Reports by Rosenwald building agents are scattered among the records of state departments of education; the Moton Papers; the Julius Rosenwald Fund Archives; Fisk University Special Collections, Nashville, Tennessee; and the records of the General Education Board at the Rockefeller Foundation Archives, Rockefeller Archive Center, Sleepy Hollow, New York.

15. Louisiana building agents O. W. Gray and John Sebastian Jones held joint appointments with the state department of education and Southern University; M. H. Griffin supervised teacher training at Alabama State Teachers College; and Robert E. Clay worked out of Tennessee Agricultural and Industrial College.

16. See also Hanchett, "The Rosenwald Schools"; David Strong et al., "Leveraging the State: Private Money and the Development of Public Education for Blacks," *American Sociological Review* 65 (October 2000): 658–681; V. P. Franklin, "Introduction," xi–xv, and the essays in *Cultural Capital and Black Education: African American Communities and the Funding of Black Schooling, 1865 to the Present*, ed. V. P. Franklin and Carter Julian Savage (Greenwich, CT: Information Age Publishing, 2004).

17. "Minutes of the Meeting of the Rosenwald Schoolhouse Building Agents," January 15–16, 1923, box 187, Julius Rosenwald Fund Archives; "Negro Rural Schoolhouse Building," *Field Force Reports* (Baton Rouge: Louisiana Department of Education, December 1917), 76–78; and "Report[s] of M. H. Griffin, State Supervisor Teacher-Training and Rosenwald Fund Agent for Alabama," 1922, SG 15466, Rural School Agent Correspondence, Department of Education Records, Alabama Department of Archives and History, Montgomery, Alabama.

18. R. E. Clay to Dudley Tanner, October 31, 1929, box 269, Tennessee Commissioner of Education Records, Tennessee State Library and Archives, Nashville, Tennessee.

19. P. L. Dorman, "Report, Rosenwald Schoolhouse Building for Arkansas," February 1919, box 51, General Correspondence, Moton Papers; G. E. Davis to N. C. Newbold, November 14, 1922, box 6, General Correspondence of the Director, Division of Negro Education, North Carolina Department of Public Instruction Records; and A. C. Lewis to S. L. Smith, March 17, 1928, box 339, Julius Rosenwald Fund Archives.

20. R. E. Clay to O. H. Bernard, May 1, 1926, and May 31, 1926, box 270, Tennessee Commissioner of Education Records.

21. Elisabeth Lasch-Quinn, *Black Neighbors: Race and the Limits of Reform in the American Settlement House Movement, 1890–1945* (Chapel Hill: University of North Carolina Press, 1993); Kevin K. Gaines, *Uplifting the Race: Black Leadership, Politics, and Culture in the Twentieth Century* (Chapel Hill: University of North Carolina Press, 1996); Stephanie J. Shaw, *What a Woman Ought to Be and to Do: Black Professional Women Workers During the Jim Crow Era* (Chicago: University of Chicago Press, 1996); Nieves, "'We Gave Our Hearts and Lives to It'"; ibid., "'We Are Too Busy Making History . . . to Write History': African American Women, Constructions of Nation, and the Built Environment in the New South, 1892–1968," in this volume, Chapter 12; Carroll Van West, "Sacred Spaces of Faith, Community, and Resistance: Rural African American Churches in Jim Crow Tennessee," also in this volume, Chapter 18.

22. Rev. R. B. Angel to J. S. Lambert, May 24, 1919, SG 15452, Rural School Agent Correspondence, Alabama Department of Education Records.

23. F. H. Edwards to N. C. Newbold, February 14, 1916, box 2, General Correspondence of the Director, Division of Negro Education, North Carolina Department of Public Instruction Records.

24. M. M. Leak to State Board of Education, February 26, 1929, vol. 141, Department of Education Records, Mississippi Department of Archives and History, Jackson, Mississippi, and Vincent Harris, "Monthly Report of Rosenwald Building Agent," March 1931, Box 1, Division of Negro Education, Department of Education Records, Georgia Department of Archives and History, Atlanta, Georgia.

25. Rosenwald program staff issued annual versions of the "Plan for Distribution of Aid," outlining the requirements for participants; one example can be found in box 51, General Correspondence, Moton Papers.

26. As an Atlanta University writer observed, out of sight was out of mind: "It does not appear that the colored schools enter definitely into the minds of those who are charged with common school education. This is borne out by the fact that more than half of the schools for the colored children are taught in churches, lodge halls, and dwellings." *Negro Education in Georgia*, Atlanta University Bulletin, series 2, no. 67 (February 1927): 10.

27. A North Carolina teacher described the Jones Rosenwald School's history: "It is said that the Jones School had its origin as far back as the eighties. The first schools were taught in the church on the same plot of ground that present church and school now stand." Susan G. Pearl, *African-American Heritage Survey, 1996* (Upper Marlboro: Maryland–National Capital Park & Planning Commission, Prince George's County Planning Department, 1996), 94–95; Debra Herman and Althemese Barnes, *African-American Education in Leon County, Florida: Emancipation Through Desegregation, 1863–1968* (Tallahassee, FL: John G. Riley Research Center and Museum of African-American History, 1997), 105–107; Lisa B. Randle, "Mt. Zion Rosenwald School," National Register of Historic Places Nomination Form (U.S. Department of the Interior, 2001), 16–17; unidentified teacher, "Jones School," box 12, Hunter Papers. See also Henry Allen Bullock, *A History of Negro Education in the South* (Cambridge, MA: Harvard University Press, 1967); James D. Anderson, "Ex-Slaves and the Rise of Universal Education in the New South, 1860–1880," in *Education and the Rise of the New South*, ed. Ronald K. Goodenow and Arthur O. White (Boston: G. K. Hall and Co., 1981), 1–25; Harry Morgan, *Historical Perspectives on the Education of Black Children* (Westport, CT: Praeger, 1995).

28. Even after construction of the Sanibel Island, Florida, Rosenwald school allowed teachers and children to move out of a packinghouse, they continued joint use of their building with a Baptist congregation. Personal communications to the author from Francis Bailey, March 23, 2002, and Margaret White, March 23, 2002. My thanks to Jerry Kearns, who took me to this school and introduced me to Mr. Bailey.

29. Fletcher B. Dresslar, whom Rosenwald had tapped for an evaluation of the Rosenwald schools built under Tuskegee's administration, was the leading authority in rural school architecture at this time. Samuel L. Smith and many state Negro school agents studied under Dresslar at George Peabody College for Teachers in Nashville. Dresslar's works include *American Schoolhouses*, U.S. Bureau of Education Bulletin 5 (Washington, DC: Government Printing Office, 1911); *Rural Schoolhouses and Grounds*, U.S. Bureau of Education Bulletin 12 (Washington, DC: Government Printing Office, 1914); *School Hygiene* (New York: Macmillan, 1925); and, with Haskell Pruett, *Rural School-houses, School Grounds, and Their Equipment*, U.S. Office of Education Bulletin 21 (Washington, DC: Government Printing Office, 1930). For examples of early twentieth-century discussions of school design, see "Standardization of the Rural School Plant," *School and Society* 1 (February 13, 1915): 222–225, and "Standardized School House Design," Parts 1 and 2, *American Architect* 114 (November 6, 13, 1918): 559–564, 598–691.

30. *The Negro Rural School and Its Relation to the Community* (Tuskegee, AL: Tuskegee Normal and Industrial Institute, 1915), and Julius Rosenwald Fund, *Community School Plans* (Nashville, TN: The Fund, 1921, 1924, 1927, 1931).

31. Dresslar made fenestration a top priority in his evaluation of Rosenwald schools. Dresslar, *Report on the Rosenwald School Buildings*, 9–22.

32. *Paint Colors and Directions for Painting*, Community Schools Pamphlet No. 14 (Nashville, TN: Julius Rosenwald Fund, 1922).

33. Booker T. Washington to J. L. Sibley, January 5, 1915, and May 26, 1915, SG15443, Rural School Agent Correspondence, Alabama Department of Education Records.

34. In 1931, Walter R. McCornack and J. E. Crain drafted plans for larger schools with eight, ten, and twelve classrooms, following the principles of earlier and smaller designs

but adding slightly more "Georgian-Colonial" detailing and cupolas. Rosenwald officials had the "belfries" removed from their designs. Bessie W. Carney to Alfred K. Stern, March 12, 1931, box 128, and "Community School Plans," box 331, Julius Rosenwald Fund Archives, and *Community School Plans* (1931).

35. Leo M. Favrot, "The Service of a Rosenwald Building Agent Is Greatly Needed in Several States," 1928, box 202, Julius Rosenwald Fund Archives.

36. *An Educational Study of Alabama*, U.S. Bureau of Education Bulletin no. 41 (Washington, DC: Government Printing Office, 1919), plate 4; *Official Report of Educational Survey Commission on the Education of Negroes in Florida* (Tallahassee: Florida State Department of Education, [1929?]), 7; and William R. Davis, *The Development and Present Status of Negro Education in East Texas* (New York: Bureau of Publications, Teachers College, Columbia University, 1934; reprint, New York: AMS Press, 1972), 59–60.

37. Recommendations from the Conference of Rural School Agents for Negroes in the South and Rosenwald Schoolbuilding Agents, July 17, 1919, box 51, General Correspondence, Moton Papers.

38. J. S. Jones, "Report, Rosenwald Schoolhouse Building for Louisiana," April 1919, March 1920, box 50, General Correspondence, Moton Papers. For examples of photographs documenting industrial work at Rosenwald schools, see "Interior View of the Arcadia Schoolhouse, Built with Aid from the Rosenwald Fund," which shows a woodstove and rack of dishes like those praised by J. S. Jones, and "One Acre of Cabbage and Tomatoes, Tallulah Colored School Garden, Madison Parish," *Field Force Reports* (Baton Rouge: Louisiana Department of Education, May 1917), 47, 48.

39. "Report, Rosenwald Schoolhouse Building for Louisiana," April 1920, October 1919, and January 1920, box 51, General Correspondence, Moton Papers. State education officials and school staff and patrons often disagreed about priorities: "The Winterville Rosenwald school, one of the first Rosenwald schools erected in [Louisiana], is a modern two-teacher building. The outside of this building presents a pleasing appearance, but the mistake of placing a valuable piano, instead of painting the interior and installing the necessary equipment, was made by the teachers and community people." The writer also complained that they had neglected their school garden. Maggie Nance Ringgold, "Report of Visit to Negro Schools of West Baton Rouge Parish, Louisiana," box 1, Miscellaneous Records, Department of Education Records, Louisiana State Archives, Baton Rouge, Louisiana. See also "Minutes of the Meeting of the Rosenwald Schoolhouse Building Agents," 1923, and "Conference of State Agents for Negro Rural Schools" 1923, box 188, Julius Rosenwald Fund Archives.

40. Murdock had been very accommodating in his letters to the Negro school agent but his patrons complained about his actions at the school. E. J. Murdock to J. L. Sibley, December 23, 1923, and Harris Oden to J. L. Sibley, May 8, 1914, SG 15443, Rural School Agent Correspondence, Alabama Department of Education Records.

41. Leo M. Favrot to James L. Sibley, April 23, 1916, SG15450, Rural School Agent Correspondence, Alabama Department of Education Records. Such actions support Grace Elizabeth Hale's argument that whites used segregation to relocate white supremacy and Black inferiority from persons to places. *Making Whiteness: The Culture of Segregation in the South, 1890–1940* (New York: Vintage Books, 1999), 129–138.

42. The Rosenwald Fund made a second grant for a replacement building. *Blytheville/ Mississippi County Black Culture Sesquicentennial Scrapbook* (n.p., 1986), 57, in Black History and Culture Collection, box 2, Arkansas Historical Commission, Little Rock, Arkansas.

43. S. L. Smith to Clark Foreman, May 18, 1931, box 339, Julius Rosenwald Fund Archives, and C. J. Calloway to J. S. Lambert, September 3, 1919, and Clarence Wilburn to J. S. Lambert, September 6, 1919, SG 15452, Rural School Agent Correspondence, Alabama Department of Education Records.

44. Booker T. Washington to Julius Rosenwald, September 12, 1912, box 336, Julius Rosenwald Fund Archives.

45. Anderson, *Education of Blacks*, 171–173, 176–179.

46. W. C. Graves to R. R. Moton, December 5, 1917, box 52, General Correspondence, Moton Papers. During World War I, Clinton J. Calloway complained about Dallas County, Alabama, African Americans who had given more to the war effort than to their school buildings. C. J. Calloway to J. S. Lambert, February 18, 1919, SG 15453, Rural School Agent Correspondence, Alabama Department of Education Records.

47. Lottie Q. Beadle to J. Sibley, November 27, 1916, SG 15448, Rural School Agent Correspondence, Alabama Department of Education Records. J.R.E. Lee, president of Florida Agricultural and Mechanical College, made FAMC musicians available for Rosenwald school rallies. When whites were present, schoolchildren often sang spirituals. School rallies were also staples of the school improvement leagues organized among white school patrons, as shown by James L. Leloudis, "School Reform in the New South: The Woman's Association for the Betterment of Public School Houses in North Carolina, 1902–1919," *Journal of American History* 69 (March 1983): 886–909. Tuskegee Institute included suggestions for organizing improvement leagues and fund-raising events in its 1915 Rosenwald school publication, *The Negro Rural School*, 70–78.

48. "Loachapoka, Lee County, Ala. $68.49 Raised in Last Rally. New Schoolhouse in Course of Erection," *Tuskegee Messenger*, January 10, 1913, set the precedent for publishing individual contributions to one of the South's first Rosenwald building campaigns; see also "Money Is Raised for Negro School," *Yazoo Herald*, January 23, 1925, and "Roxboro Negroes Are Raising Sum," *Durham Herald*, April 26, 1926, Tuskegee Clippings Files, and the unidentified newspaper clipping included in A. Wells Henderson to J. S. Lambert, January 4, 1919, SG 15453, Rural School Agent Correspondence, Alabama Department of Education Records. Unpublished lists can be found attached to L. N. Hickerson to N. C. Newbold, March 28, 1916, box 2, General Correspondence of the Director, Division of Negro Education, North Carolina Department of Public Instruction Records, and in the 1917 files of James Sibley, SG15463, Rural School Agent Correspondence, Alabama Department of Education Records.

49. For descriptions of rallies, see Leo M. Favrot, "Report of State Agent of Rural Schools for Negroes," *Field Force Reports* (Baton Rouge: Louisiana Department of Education, April 1917), 104, as well as reports by the Rosenwald building agents. On the importance of these public meetings, see "Minutes of the Meeting of the Rosenwald Schoolhouse Building Agents," 1923.

50. For example, "one colored farmer donated a splendid ten-acre tract for the school site" at King's Welcome, Florida. *Biennial Report of the Superintendent of Public Instruction of the State of Florida for the Two Years Ending June 30, 1922* (Tallahassee: T. J.

Appleyard, Printer, [1922]), 332. Rosenwald and state Negro school agent reports constantly mentioned that Blacks had paid for the school site, such as F. M. Wood's notations that patrons at Adairsville bought three and a half acres of land valued at about $800 and those at Mayslick had expended $1,450 for their three acres. "Report, Rosenwald Schoolhouse Building for Kentucky," February 1920 and March 1920, box 51, General Correspondence, Moton Papers.

51. George T. Rouson to W. F. Credle, December 22, 1925, box 2, Correspondence of the Supervisor of the Rosenwald Fund, Division of Negro Education, North Carolina Department of Public Instruction Records, and R. E. Clay to O. H. Bernard, January 30, 1926, box 270, Tennessee Commissioner of Education Records.

52. Samuel L. Smith, "A Story of the Julius Rosenwald Fund in Tenn. from the Beginning to July 1, 1920," box 76, Julius Rosenwald Fund Archives.

53. P. L. Dorman reported that Caledonia farmers each had donated from fifty to one hundred pounds of cotton to make up a bale that they sold for the school's benefit, and sawmill workers arranged to have contributions deducted from their pay to purchase the lumber from their employer. "Report, Rosenwald Schoolhouse Building for Arkansas," October 1919, box 51, General Correspondence, Moton Papers.

54. "Move to Obtain a Model School," *Jackson Progress-Argus*, December 24, 1926, and "Jackson Negroes Start Movement to Obtain Industrial School," *Atlanta Constitution*, December 25, 1926, Tuskegee Clippings Files.

55. Photographs of the cornerstone ceremony at the Conecuh County Training School, box 1, Rural School Photograph Collection, State Agent for Negro Rural Schools, 1915–1917, Alabama Department of Education Records.

56. O. H. Bernard, "The Julius Rosenwald Fund in Tennessee," box 76, Julius Rosenwald Fund Archives, and "Negro Education," *Biennial Report of the Superintendent of Public Instruction of the State of Florida for the Two Years Ending June 30, 1926* (Tallahassee: T. J. Appleyard, Printer, [1926]), 224.

57. "Chester Shell," http://www.sbac.edu/~shell/mrchestershell.html (accessed November 18, 2004).

58. Foster and Credle corresponded in July and August 1925, and Hunter and Credle from October to December 1926, boxes 2 and 3, Correspondence of the Supervisor, Division of Negro Education, North Carolina Department of Public Instruction Records.

59. Andy Hawkins, "The Rosenwald Schools: The Chicago Connection," *Mid-Carolina Journal* 1 (Winter 1988–1989): 20–21. My thanks to Erin Shaw, formerly of the South Carolina State Historic Preservation Office, for a copy of this article with me, and to the Rev. Dr. Bruce Jackson and the members of the Shiloh AME congregation for allowing me to visit with them and see the Shiloh school.

60. Carbaugh, "Philanthropic Confluence," 96; "Progress of Negro Education in Montgomery County," "Report of Mrs. Mary F. Mitchell, Jeanes Agent of Halifax County, South Boston, Virginia," and "Henry County Shows Commendable Progress," in *Virginia Teachers' Bulletin* 6 (March 1929): 18; 7 (February 1931): 8; 9 (May 1932): 13, respectively; and Eva Lois Gordon, "Fifty-Two Years of Public Service," in *Bells Are Ringing,* Mississippi Retired Teachers Association (Jackson, MS: Jackson Public Schools Print Shop, 1976), 1927.

61. Thomas J. Calloway, George D. Brown, Ignatius Mitchell, and Isaiah Gray, *A Survey of Colored Public Schools of Prince George's County, Maryland* (Colored Public School Trustees Association, 1924). Susan G. Pearl kindly provided this reference.

62. Jackson Davis to S. L. Smith, March 24, 1927, box 331, Julius Rosenwald Fund Archives.

63. L. M. Favrot to J. S. Jones, March 19, 1923, Superintendent's Records, 1904–1923, Department of Education Records, Louisiana State Archives, Baton Rouge, Louisiana.

64. "Annual Report of the State Superintendent of the State of South Carolina," 1922, *Reports and Resolutions of the General Assembly of the State of South Carolina* (Columbia, SC: Gonzales and Bryan, State Printers, 1923), 176, and "Annual Report of the State Superintendent of the State of South Carolina," 1930, *Reports and Resolutions of the General Assembly of the State of South Carolina* (Columbia, SC: n.p., 1931), 3. Similarly, in her survey of public schools in Columbia, South Carolina, Janet Leake noted: "[T]here are three Rosenwald schools in District No 1. This means that in three sections removed from the city schools, the people of the community were so interested in having their children attend a standard [graded] school that they were willing to raise a large sum of money to put with that received from the Rosenwald Foundation to build such a school." Janet Scott Leake, "Survey of the Negro Public Schools of Columbia, South Carolina," M.A. thesis, University of South Carolina, 1932, 67.

65. "Annual Report of the State Superintendent of the State of South Carolina," 1926, *Reports and Resolutions of the General Assembly of the State of South Carolina* (Columbia, SC: State Budget and Control Board, 1927), 33.

66. Plans 1-C and 3-1-F, SG 13206, State Publications, Alabama Department of Education Records. Rosenwald plans became an integral part of the design vocabulary of American schools, thanks to Dresslar's students who cooperated in the Interstate School Building Service, headquartered at George Peabody College for Teachers in Nashville, and publications such as *For Better Schoolhouses* (Nashville, TN: Interstate School Building Service, 1929).

67. Gould Beech, "Schools for a Minority," *Survey Graphic* 28 (October 1939): 615.

68. Robert L. Cousins to S. L. Smith, August 30, 1933, and September 10, 1938, Unit 1, Division of Negro Education Correspondence Relating to Funding Programs, Georgia Department of Education Records.

69. Images of deteriorated Rosenwald schools appear in a photographic survey conducted prior to a major building campaign intended to forestall desegregation. Statewide School Facilities Photographs, 1946–1960, and School Building Photographs, Mississippi Department of Education Records. For an example of a teacher who had been a student and teacher in Florida Rosenwald schools and went on to become "a sacrificial lamb" in a teacher pay equity suit, see Hazel and Frederick Leeks's account of Sadye Colbert Leeks in Lake County Retired Teachers Association, *Through Schoolhouse Doors: A History of Lake County Schools* (n.p., 1982), 372–374.

70. Betty Jamerson Reed, "The Brevard Rosenwald School: An Historical Case Study," Ed.D. diss., Western Carolina University, 2000, 149–151; ibid., *The Brevard Rosenwald School: Black Education and Community Building in a Southern Appalachian Town, 1920–1966*, Contributions to Southern Appalachian Studies, 11 (Jefferson, NC: McFarland & Company, 2004).

71. Jewel McCalla, interviewed by Tracy Caradine, June 13, 2001, in *Parallel and Crossover Lives: Texas Before and After Desegregation*, Texas Council for the Humanities, http://www.public-humanities.org/crossoversite/NEW%HTML/JHTML/McCalla.html (accessed April 15, 2002) (recalling the Fouke-Hawkins Rosenwald School in Texas); Morris B. Abram, "A House Divided Can't Stand; a House United Will Stand," October 1999 speech to the Atlanta Anti-Defamation League, http://www.unwatch.org/speeches/housediv.html (accessed November 18, 2004) (recalling the segregated schools of Fitzgerald, Georgia).

72. For example, Alfred Q. Jarrette was a student at the school, his father had participated in its construction, two of his uncles had taught there, and his stepmother's father had donated the land. Alfred Q. Jarrette, *Julius Rosenwald: Benefactor of Mankind* (Greenville, SC: Southeastern University Press, [1975]), 22–23. Internet searches will locate obituaries in which family members follow the tradition of describing attendance or teaching at a Rosenwald school as a personal achievement.

73. The Fairmont Chapter of Rosenwald Alumni meets monthly in Fairmont, North Carolina. My thanks to Robert Delane Shaw for the chapter's 2002 calendar.

74. Inscribed stone markers stand before the Lincoln School in Forrest City and the Osceola Rosenwald School, both in Arkansas, and the site of Gilmore Academy in Marianna, Florida. The Rev. Shirley Palmer spearheads a campaign to mark the sites of Rosenwald schools in Sumter County, South Carolina, with flagpoles, benches, and small markers. Generally such monuments commemorate teachers, students, and alumni from the date of the school's construction through its desegregation.

75. One example is the marker for "Julius Rosenwald High School," Northumberland County, Virginia, Department of Historic Resources, 2000. See Phyllis McClure, "Rosenwald Schools in the Northern Neck," *Virginia Magazine of History and Biography* 113, no. 2 (2005): 114–145.

76. "'Little Red' School House," http://drew-ms.netfirms.com/Little%20Red.htm (accessed March 10, 2002) documents the community effort to restore the Rosenwald school in Drew, Mississippi; perhaps the most extensive campaign to document Rosenwald school histories and make them available electronically has come from Charlotte and Mecklenburg County, North Carolina, with sites featuring preservation surveys, cultural and heritage tourism information, and African American history resources. Current information about Rosenwald schools on the National Register of Historic Places can be obtained from the National Register program of the National Park Service and state historic preservation offices; they also have featured such schools in their newsletters and Web sites. Southern state preservation offices have increased attention to Rosenwald schools as key indicators of African American history and culture in their architectural surveys. Examples include "Three Surviving Rosenwald Schools: The Georgia Inventory," *Reflections* (newsletter of the Georgia African American Historic Preservation Network, published by the Historic Preservation Division of the Georgia Department of Natural Resources) (September 30, 2004): 1–2; and the Maryland Commission on African American History and Culture's "Sailor: Inventory of African American Historical and Cultural Resources," http://www.sailor.lib.md.us/docs/af_am/af_am.html (accessed April 15, 2002). African American preservation organizations have targeted Rosenwald schools as well; for example, see the minutes of the Southeast Regional African American

Preservation Alliance Annual Meeting, March 24–25, 2000, http://www.sraapa.org/events/March%202000%20Annual%20Meeting.doc (accessed January 4, 2002).

77. Noble Hill–Wheeler Memorial Center, Cassville, Georgia; Allen Grove Rosenwald School, Halifax County Agricultural Museum, North Carolina; "Duncan Signs Deed Transferring Ownership of Former 'Smithville Colored School' Site to Alpha Phi Alpha for Reuse as Museum," Montgomery County, Maryland, News Release, June 2, 1999, http://www.co.mo.md.us/news/press/99-207.html (accessed March 10, 2002).

78. See, for example, a newspaper story announcing Dr. Peter Ascoli's presentation on Julius Rosenwald to a reunion of Rosenwald school alumni in Aiken County, Georgia: Betsy Gilliland, "Historic Schools Recalled," *Augusta* [Georgia] *Chronicle*, January 17, 2006, http://chat.augustachronicle.com/stories/011806/aik_school.shtml (accessed December 6, 2006).

79. An example of complementary public and private heritage tourism initiatives comes from the Division of Historical Resources of the Florida Department of State, which has published the *Florida Heritage Trail* in printed and electronic forms, and "Lift Ev'ry Voice," a theme of the FLAUSA Web site *Culturally Florida* at http://www.culturallyflorida.com/voice/ (accessed November 18, 2004).

80. The Archives and Museums Division of Tuskegee University holds many other important records of the Rosenwald building program in the Robert Russa Moton Papers and the Clinton J. Calloway Papers; the Special Collections Research Center of the Joseph Regenstein Library at the University of Chicago holds the Julius Rosenwald Papers.

81. Examples include the biography of Charles W. Rankin, former principal of Scotts Rosenwald Elementary School in Scotts, North Carolina, http://www.iss.k12.nc.us/schools/nihs/archives/stories/blksch/cwrankin.htm (accessed November 18, 2004), and Kelly Edwards Elementary School's "School History," http://www.williston.k12.sc.us/kees/schoolhistory.html (accessed November 18, 2004).

82. S. L. Smith to Julius Rosenwald, December 26, 1921, box 127, Julius Rosenwald Fund Archives.

Angel David Nieves

"We Are Too Busy Making History . . . to Write History"

African American Women, Constructions of Nation, and the
Built Environment in the New South, 1892–1968

> There is material in them well worth your while, the hope in germ of a staunch,
> helpful, regenerating womanhood on which, primarily rests the foundation
> stones of our future as a race.
>
> ANNA JULIA COOPER[1]

Racial uplift became an acceptable forum for African American women's activism at the end of the nineteenth century only after such women had endured for years the dual biases of racial and gender discrimination, both from within the Black community and from without. Since the founding of early literary and mutual aid societies in the 1830s, Black women reformers had long been concerned with the issue of "race uplift," involving as it did a sense of duty and obligation to the race. African American women's educational reform efforts were a primary force in creating a Black nationalist forum. Although no sustained analysis of the spatial practices of Black women reformers active between the collapse of Reconstruction politics and the outbreak of World War I currently exists, the race work of such women—their experiments in nation building—is the focus of the research upon which much of this essay draws. Understanding that a segregated landscape engenders subversive spatial practice that often remains buried or hidden to the "trained historian" requires our theorizing differently about landscape and the ideological significance of place for African Americans.[2] Those hidden traces, when coupled with a more thorough analysis of the cultural meanings these sites held for African Americans, illustrate how women reformers reinforced their own social constructions of race betterment and progress through the built environment. I contend that these women reformers were in fact modeling a kind of "political architecture" through the building of these race-based vernacular landscapes. In many ways these physical environments became a reflection of their own solutions for social justice.[3] Two contested landscapes that aided African American reformers in articulating new spatial paradigms for collective action are the World's Columbian Exposition of 1893 and the American campus of the nineteenth century.

At the close of the Civil War, African American women were faced not only with the unique challenges of emancipation but with the dual tasks of rebuilding their lives and that of the larger community as a newly freed African people. Such women remained insistent in helping to rebuild their race through higher education and used school reform as a vehicle for establishing a spatialized social countermovement. Many believed that the industrial education model was the very best solution for African Americans who were still suffering from the ravages of decades of enforced slavery and the many newly legislated Jim Crow laws. Through an examination of African American industrial education, school building, and social welfare activism, the assumption that African American women were not purposefully invested in the physical design of their many community-based institutions for race uplift can be disproved. On the contrary, African American women were uniquely aware of the spatial power their social welfare institutions had in the making of what were radical agendas for social change and race-based advancement. African American women were not simply the clients of a burgeoning architectural profession in the late nineteenth century but were very much acting as designers, although lacking formal education in architecture or its allied arts.

To understand our assumptions about the differences between the "official" and vernacular landscapes, we should examine those theories related to the field of cultural landscape studies. For landscape historian J. B. Jackson, official or political landscapes foster the order, security, and continuity of society by reminding people of their rights, their obligations, and the history of the nation or state.[4] Vernacular landscapes, however, reinforce individual decisions, traditions, customs, personal relationships, and utility by illustrating "how individuals or groups within a society organize local spaces."[5] Efforts to memorialize the Confederate past by white southerners can be seen as the expressions of an "official" culture since they sought to maintain social order and reinforce existing institutions by discouraging disorder and radical change. These displays of official white culture stress the duties of citizens to the state or nation above their individual rights. A vernacular culture is a local, grassroots expression of diverse interests based on individuals whose reality reflects their personal experience within the local community.[6] Since white southerners maintained their own "official" culture through acts of racial violence, African Americans responded by continuing to develop a nationalist culture with strong ties to the built environment.

For African Americans, the built environment provided them with the opportunity to physically "celebrate or perpetuate the memory of particular events, ideals, individuals, or groups of persons."[7] Black women reformers constructed their own models for race uplift as "imagined communities" through the cultural production of textual race narratives (or "race literature") in the pages of popular literary magazines of the 1890s.[8] Literature would play a critical role in women's self-help strategies, particularly throughout the 1890s, in the descriptions of the physical Black landscape for "race uplift." "Race women"[9] like Pauline Hopkins, Frances Ellen Watkins Harper, Victoria Earle Matthews, and Anna Julia Cooper—all race leaders and journalists of the woman's era— used literature as a vehicle for advancing their approaches to "race uplift." By examining their literary works, it is possible to see how women reformers took up the cause for Black education. All of these race women believed that fiction "was of great historical and political significance."[10] As Hazel Carby has argued, these novels are "testaments to the racist practices of the suffrage and temperance movements and indictments of the ways in which white women allied themselves not with black women but with a racist patriarchal order against all black people."[11] These novels and serialized fictional works provided a site for the formation of a gendered discourse of uplift that often revolved around the founding of industrial schools as well as new models for civic reform. As novels they were written to promote social change and also to question Jim Crow practices that threatened the last hopes for Black political self-empowerment in the South.[12] Descriptions of boarding homes, lyceums, churches, convents, and homes are found throughout these novels and provide us with the physical elements of a Black nationalist landscape.

Cultural theorist Benedict Anderson in *Imagined Communities* (1983) has effectively argued that nationalism can be seen and understood as a kind of cultural artifact.[13] Anderson maintains that a nation is a cultural artifact because it is constructed through buildings, monuments, common customs, and political rhetoric in order to align its citizens in a common project. For Anderson, nationalism is itself defined by both paradox and contradiction:[14] "[I]t is an imagined political community—and imagined as both inherently limited and sovereign. It is imagined because the members of even the smallest nation will never know most of their fellow-members, meet them or even hear of them, yet in the minds of each lives the image of their communion."[15] In attempting to examine nations/nationhood as imagined communities in some manner, Anderson suggests that national identities are fictional and "constituted in and through a vernacular language."[16] Anderson seemingly does not understand the complexity of gender and its impact on national identity—almost failing to see gender's role in image making.

Architectural historian Catherine Bishir also interestingly posits that,

> in 1893, the World's Columbian Exposition in Chicago presented a spectacular display of a set of official American ideals. An ensemble of heroic sculpture and classical architecture, laid out in the formal plan and rationally divided sectors promoted by the City Beautiful movement, offered an image of a unified, stable, hierarchical Anglo-Saxon nation asserting its place in the world, an image that soon reached into communities of the North and South.[17]

For African Americans, the "White City" became a site of political contest over their rights to speak out against lynching, mob violence, and civil disorder throughout the South.[18] The exposition was, as was the earlier 1876 fair in Philadelphia, a major venue for the promotion of the Colonial Revival style through its architecture, interior decoration, historical exhibitions, and commemorative activities.[19] The Colonial Revival style was a reflection of the growing nostalgia for America's colonial history and a desire to strengthen connections to the past. Further study might reveal the cultural impact of the Colonial Revival style on African Americans in their later adoption of the style for many campus projects, but by reappropriating the style of the "master class," African Americans were again pressing their rights to their own national identity and citizenship. Many African American reformers of the period no longer advocated an equal place in the larger nation's narrative, as in their belief in the Great Tradition[20] of the earlier antebellum era. The narrative of the new Black "nation" was now fully under way and made up of self-help institutions that were often the target of white racist attacks. A central question to consider throughout this essay is how African American women used the built environment as an effective and integral part of their nationalist agenda for institution building. As Neil Harris has suggested, "examining buildings through their [many] life stages and modes of representation [only] encourages us to conceive of them not simply as places but as sets of events."[21] African Americans understood the value of normal and industrial schools as an important part of a larger racial project in promoting a Black civic discourse whose ultimate goal was providing new forms of power and control over the production of cultural capital[22]—quite literally through the founding, establishment, and building of these racialized landscapes in the "New South."[23] Harris argues that architectural meaning often "reflects and legitimates power relationships and hegemonic patterns."[24] These educational landscapes legitimated African American attempts at redefining a new public order in the American landscape. The buildings themselves act as sites of "racially inflected national identities"[25] and memory making.

Drawing on the work of anthropologist James C. Scott, historian Robin D.G. Kelley maintains that oppressed groups, like African Americans in the Jim Crow South, challenged the dominant power structure by creating a "hidden transcript" of resistance and communal self-empowerment. Kelley urges us to reexamine Black resistance to white power in public space and to view public space as a site of conflict over issues surrounding race, class, and gender. Kelley writes: "[S]egregation facilitated the creation and maintenance of the unmonitored, unauthorized social sites in which black workers could freely articulate the hidden transcript. Jim Crow ordinances ensured that churches, bars, social clubs, barbershops, beauty salons, even alleys, remained 'black' space."[26] African Americans were constructing autonomous "Black space," or what David Harvey might call "spaces of hope," in response to the racial violence and political exclusion they continued to face. Blacks knew that acquiring land was not simply symbolic of freedom and citizenship but the only assured way of garnering independence and social mobility despite massive Jim Crow covenants. In acquiring land, African Americans understood that by establishing their own public spaces/sphere, they could foster new forms of self-respect, group identity, and Black civic pride. African Americans developed Black institutional landscapes while redefining citizenship on their own terms and promoting their own vision of a more inclusive nationalist struggle.[27]

The struggle over public space, or "the parallel polis," has focused much scholarly attention on acts of resistance among the disenfranchised. The works of several leading historians of the American South have revealed modes of underground resistance employed by enslaved Africans. Historian Jane Dailey reveals how the struggle over civil rights in Danville, South Carolina, in 1883 resulted in the deaths of countless numbers of African American men, women, and children. Dailey maintains that "the appropriation of public space was an important way for African Americans in this period to assert their humanity, demonstrate their political rights, and stake their claim to equal citizenship."[28] The fight over public space extended beyond the streetscape of the southern landscape and became for Blacks a way of testing the boundaries of their rights under emancipation. In proposing a new polis, or civic realm, African Americans were in effect destroying previous understandings of the landscape and refashioning for themselves a new spatialized ordering device based on social justice.[29]

By the 1890s, attempts to control public space could only be achieved if African Americans constructed this new civic order through the founding of their own all-Black-based institutions for race uplift and nation making.

For African American women social reformers, the construction of an "imagined community" took on actual physical characteristics and formal shape in the many descriptions found in examples of "race literature" that emerged throughout the decades of the late nineteenth century. For cultural critic Homi Bhabha, the "nation's narrative" involves actively forgetting as well as actively remembering. For Bhabha, men and women are not just historical objects or passive participants of the body politic but also subjects of "a process of signification that must erase any prior or original presence of the [larger] nation-people to demonstrate the prodigious, living principle of the people as that continual process by which the national life is redeemed and signified as a repeating and reproductive process."[30] Those narratives often helped articulate the complexities involved in rebuilding a nation after decades of enforced slavery. As some scholars have noted, the very means for imagining nationhood are often at odds with the kinds of actualized images, or buildings, that are reproduced.[31] The "nation's narrative" is only understood when we characterize these buildings and school sites as monuments for race-based institution building. Historian Marvin Trachtenberg suggests that monuments "function as social magnets, crystallizations of social energy, one of the means civilization has devised to reinforce its cohesiveness and to give meaning and structure to life. Monuments are a way men transmit communal emotions, a medium of continuity and interaction between generations, not only in space but across time, for to be monumental is to be permanent."[32]

African American involvement in the planning and building of the South is complex and difficult to reconstruct because much of their work went unrecorded. Enslaved Africans arrived in America skilled in traditional crafts such as woodcarving, building, and ironmaking. Their skills were employed on southern plantations in the construction of manor houses and their many associated outbuildings. Enslaved and free Blacks, as master carpenters, also constructed the furniture found in many of these homes. As historians James E. Newton and Ronald L. Lewis have argued, "if slave occupational categories were given modern terminology, many bondsmen would have such titles as architect, industrial engineer, graphic artist, landscaper, and other titles representing highly skilled fields associated with the visual arts."[33] Slaves also constructed their own dwellings, typically one-room cabins made of clay, thatched roofs, dirt floors, and fireplaces, all clear evidence of West African building traditions. On many plantations, "[a] considerable number of Negroes uniting the function of both the architect and the builder led almost free and independent careers although nominally held as slaves."[34] For example, when John Sims's house at Gippy Plantation in South Carolina was destroyed by a massive fire, it was later rebuilt by slave artisans. In accounts of his thirty years spent under enslavement, Louis Hughes tells of how slaves were sent ahead to make bricks for their master's new mansion, which they later built. A school of the manual arts for skilled slaves was established in Alabama.[35] James Weldon Johnson, referring to his early years in Florida after the Civil War, writes: "All the most interesting things that came under my observation were being done by colored men. . . . [T]hey built houses, they laid the brick, they painted the buildings. . . . When I was a child, I did not even know that there existed such a thing as a white carpenter or bricklayer."[36] Unforeseen was the rapid decline in the number of Black craftsmen used in antebellum southern cities—especially for fear of uprisings. The legacy of Denmark Vesey's failed 1822 insurrection in Charleston helped to label the artisan class as untrustworthy and politically volatile to many whites across the South. Vesey, a free Black carpenter, attempted to launch a slave rebellion and sail to freedom in Haiti with his followers—leaving much of white Charleston in constant fear that their skilled craftsmen might be involved in the murderous plot.[37] As historian John W. Blassingame has argued, "Southern whites not only adapted their language and religion to that of the slaves but also adapted agricultural practices, sexual attitudes, rhythm of life, architecture, food and social relations to African patterns."[38] Other reasons for a decline in available Black artisans was the steady stream of newly arriving immigrant craftsmen from Europe who worked for less than minimum wages and stringent legal restrictions preventing African Americans from working.[39]

Any discussion of developing a civic realm among African Americans in the late nineteenth century cannot ignore the contributions of religion and Africanity in shaping political enfranchisement. Most significant are the ways in which African Americans continued to envision their liberation struggle, even in the 1880s and 1890s, as a reenactment of the Bible's Exodus account. Commemorative activity like freedom celebrations openly challenged white collective memory of the Civil War, the "Lost Cause" movement, and their significance in the construction of a reunified American nation. Marches, parades, and the use of public ceremonial places in cities across the country, like New York, Atlanta, Chicago, and Richmond, helped African Americans reclaim and honor their role in American civic life.[40] Under enslavement, Blacks believed they were the children of God and like the Israelites would leave Egypt behind and escape to freedom.[41] Writer and social reformer Anna Julia Cooper uses the Exodus tale in her work *A Voice from the South* (1892); she writes: "We look within that we may gather together once more practical methods, address ourselves to the tasks before us. We look forward with hope and trust that the same God whose guiding hand led our fathers through and out of the gall and bitterness of oppression, will still lead and direct their children, to the honor of His name, and for their ultimate salvation."[42] Race women often evoked the Exodus tale in their literary works (such as novels and newspapers) to contest the prevailing narrative of white supremacy and the racial purity of the American nation by helping to redefine the prevailing civic discourse. Their stories often provided a "countermemory" or "countermonument" to the master narrative of the white nation.[43] As we reexamine the role of the slave quarter or church in shaping political consciousness we might also understand the long-standing ideology of forging an ideal democratic community. Historian Sterling Stuckey argues that "[w]hen one considers that the most important ceremonies occurred in the slave quarters, where the children were found as well, the transmission of culture from the old to the young seems inevitable, a development that could not be prevented."[44] For Stuckey, the space of the quarter provided those enslaved children who later became reformers with a model of community building that they followed in the founding of their own schools. They must have felt that the strong network of relations established in the quarter could easily be replicated in the school as a site for rebuilding the Black family and community. The school site also helped to maintain a sense of tradition and folk heritage as a center for community life. Several historians strongly maintain that the idea of a nation was not often conceived specific to any geographical territory or even as an independent nation-state but rather articulated only within the confines of a "race language" based solely on patriarchal oppression. Black Nationalism for other scholars is the expression of racial solidarity on issues impacting the larger African community. Some have even suggested that "[i]t generally has no ideological or programmatic implications beyond the desire that black people organize themselves on the basis of their common color and oppressed condition."[45] Black Nationalism therefore requires African Americans to take full responsibility of their own liberation and the maintenance of their own culturally specific institutions. Black Nationalism, according to some scholars, often falls short of advocating for the absolute and total control of a geographic or spatial territory alone.[46] Certain ideals, although presumably utopian, are, however, upheld that will one day advance the collective cause of self-determination. I argue that Black Nationalism does occupy a spatialized or "geographic territory," a physical ideal, that moves us well beyond the limited conceptualization of a "race language" used only in literary forms of cultural production. That spatialized or geographic territory appears prominently in the founding of institutions built by African American women and designed by Black architects and building craftsmen. Race literature also helps us document those civic ideals of a Black public realm. The nationalist landscapes often constructed in these race uplift texts are replete with multiple self-help institutions. Black women reformers organized around two basic tenets, theology and community, which allowed local churches to erect church buildings and schools, provide food and clothing for the poor, and help "spread a gospel of self-help, self-discipline and self-determination."[47] The church provided a sphere in which African American women could publicly deliberate and debate over current social concerns, apart from the Victorian ideals of true womanhood, and propose new institutional models for race-based advancement by women. The home was no longer the only acknowledged space for women in the Victorian era, especially among African American women.

Anna Julia Cooper best describes the role of women in developing new institutional models for the race. She writes:

> As far as my experience goes the average man of our race is less frequently ready to admit the actual need among the sturdier forces of the world for woman's help or influence. That great social and economic questions await her interference, that she could throw any light on problems of national import, that her intermeddling could improve the management of school systems, or elevate the tone of public institutions . . . that she has a word worth hearing on mooted questions in political economy, that she could contribute a suggestion on the relations of labor and capital.[48]

For Cooper, Black Nationalism meant that women must help to redefine their role in the public and civic realms for race betterment. Black women, like herself, argues Cooper, are uniquely suited to redefine American civilization because of their former enslavement. She writes, "[T]o be a woman of the Negro race in America, and to be able to grasp the deep significance of the possibilities of the crisis, is to *have a heritage*" (emphasis added).[49] She also contends that

> [n]o plan for renovating society, no scheme for purifying politics, no reform in church or in state, no moral, social, or economic question, no movement upward or downward in the human plane is lost on her. . . . All departments in the new era are to be hers, in the sense that her interests are in all and through all; and it is incumbent on her to keep intelligently and sympathetically *en rapport* with all the great movements of her time, that she may know on which side to throw the weight of her influence. She stands now at the gateway of this new era of American civilization. In her hands must be moulded the strength, the wit, the statesmanship, the morality, all the psychic force, the social and economic intercourse of that era. To be alive at such an epoch is a privilege, to be a woman then is sublime.[50]

The formation of a new civic order was predicated in a belief that freedom was not a guarantee unless African Americans worked collectively to enact the racialized landscape for their collective self-benefit. The construction of a physical, social, and morally just national identity was based largely on the biblical

Exodus tale as a way of imagining a Black "New South." Undertaking the challenges of a Black Nationalist agenda meant that African American women would respond to "their second enslavement," in the post-Reconstruction South, in ways that might have included the implementation of multiple racial projects at any one given time. The first in a long series of racialized projects was developing a way that African Americans might "bear witness" to their collective past under enslavement and express a now growing political consciousness despite attempts to thwart their advances by angry white supremacists. Departing from Benedict Anderson's definition of nationalism as an "imagined community" (one that is both limited and sovereign), we can better understand how national belonging is imagined, remembered, and recorded among African American women reformers. As I have already suggested, Anderson does not consider the complexity of gender and its impact on national identity formation. Women reformers understood the importance of commemorative narratives that provided African Americans with a story of the nation's origin. Women's literary works and the built environment could now be seen as a series of race-history texts.[51] National self-determination among Blacks, especially in the late nineteenth century, was evident in the spaces fashioned by female reformers trained at schools like Tuskegee Institute.[52] Women believed strongly that by the 1890s, "the fundamental agency under God in the regeneration, the retraining of the race, as well as the ground work and starting point of its progress upward, must be the *black woman*."[53]

Black schooling, as historian James D. Anderson has argued, emerged at a time when American popular education was being transformed into a critical and highly formal endeavor. Black southerners had already been freed by this time and enjoyed limited privileges as free laborers, citizens, and actual voters. The failure of Reconstruction to secure their rights left them disenfranchised and politically segregated by virtue of legal statutes.[54] The challenges of their second enslavement at the hands of former masters made for the development of educational institutions that, many have argued, were ill-equipped for any social reform. I would maintain that these former slaves turned educators effectively brought national attention to their causes and succeeded in providing the Black community with an institutional base for massive social reform. Booker T. Washington, founder and principal of Tuskegee, best describes the struggle freed men and women experienced: "Few people who were not right in the midst of the scenes can form any exact idea of the intense desire which the people of my race showed for education. It was a whole race trying to go to school. Few were too young, and none too old, to make the attempt to learn. As fast as any kind of teachers could be secured, not only were day-schools filled, but night-schools as well."[55]

White resistance to Black educational achievement was based primarily on the belief that it undermined the economy of the South by endangering the supply of cheap agricultural labor. An educated and informed Black working class would further threaten the already unstable white power structure. Although Booker T. Washington was considered a moderate among many whites because he publicly advocated vocational training over a more classically based education for African Americans, many of his students understood how a more radical social agenda could be achieved by establishing other schools modeled after Tuskegee. The study of architectural and mechanical drawing for male students became an important part of the all-Black racial project of uplift and nation making—with its earliest beginnings as a course of study in the Negro State Normal School in Montgomery, Alabama, and Claflin University in Orangeburg, South Carolina.[56]

In Washington's autobiography, *Up from Slavery*, he writes, "When it is considered that the laying of this corner-stone took place in the heart of the South, in the 'Black Belt,' in the centre part of our country that was most devoted to slavery . . . I believe that there are few places in the world where it could have taken place."[57] Washington felt that having his students participate in the construction of Tuskegee's campus was a key component of their educational and moral training. He suggested, "I knew that our first buildings would [not] be [as] comfortable or complete in their finish as buildings erected by the experienced hands of outside workmen, but that in the teaching of civilization, self-help, and self reliance, the erection of the buildings by the students themselves would more than compensate for any lack of comfort or finish."[58]

The campus quadrangle for African American architects and reformers provided a physical, social, and metaphorical space for exploring issues of self-governance, identity, and citizenship. Unfortunately, the voices of those students, faculty, and staff who have occupied those spaces is particularly difficult to recover because of a lack of primary documentation. Any aesthetic and/or macropolitical readings of that space are not enough to consider when those individuals who used the campus quadrangle have somehow been left out of the larger narrative. As anthropologist Setha M. Low has argued, "these [kinds of] perspectives exclude the indigenous archaeological and ethnohistorical past, as well as the memories, stories, and conversations that create the myths and meanings" of the space's life.[59] I maintain that despite a lack of these primary sources, the race literature of the 1890s provides a way of understanding why the public space of the campus is so culturally and politically important to African Americans as they redefine the civic realm. The quadrangle remains a dominant public space and a source of symbolic civic power—a constructed cultural center for communal self-expression. As I have argued, significant for this study is conceptualizing the built environment as a space rather than a collection of pieces and parts. Assembled together, these buildings tell us more about the social and economic relations of the era than the reading of just one building alone. By "spatializing culture,"[60] we can begin to see the processes by which African Americans redefined the southern landscape, their contributions to American history, and their impact on architectural expressions of a redefined republican democracy. For African American women, the campus was a site in which they could address changing gender roles and assume the primary responsibility of shaping Black civic life.

Interestingly, historian Louis R. Harlan, Washington's biographer, critically questioned Tuskegee's educational approach and its effectiveness in promoting self-help strategies. Harlan writes, "Was it [Tuskegee] the instrument for achieving a black man's dream of self-sufficiency through a marketable skill, or was it a white man's dream of preparing black people to fill the subordinate places, the only ones available to them in the new order of white supremacy?"[61] Harlan does not see how Washington operated on a number of different levels in order to shape the Black nation-state. The space-making agenda of Black Nationalism attempted to effectively counteract white social dominance. The dream of building a model institution of self-sufficiency was not Washington's alone—African American women who worked to found industrial schools understood how they would simultaneously impact the social, economic, and political structures of the New South.

Literacy can be seen as a strategy of engagement that addressed the most pressing social issue for African Americans—educational advancement. As one element within a Black Nationalist agenda, literacy acted as a kind of utopian project that enabled educators (and their students) to reject the dominant order of the South. For African American educators, particularly those in architecture, I would argue that "the utopianism of ongoing democratic projects consists of both criticizing the existing order of things and using the terrain of culture and education to actually intervene in the world, to struggle to change the current configurations of power in society."[62] I maintain that architectural education became an expression of utopianism for African Americans and allowed its practitioners and clients alike to transform structures of oppression long in place since the earliest days of enslavement.[63] Progressive political and educational work, I argue, only begins at the margins or intersections of institutional sites like these industrial schools, where people not only live their daily lives but are active members in a participatory democracy. As cultural critic Henry Giroux has argued, "Such a project uses theory to understand such contexts as lived relations of power while pedagogically fashioning new and imagined possibilities through art and other cultural practices in order to bear witness . . . [and]

animate both the specificity of such contexts and their connection to the larger social landscape."[64] Ultimately, these democratic spaces provided educators, particularly women, with the public forums or civic spaces, normally unavailable to them, to participate actively in decision-making processes for their community.

African Americans as early as 1865 were beginning to build model utopias in the "Black or Negro towns" spread throughout the South as experiments in "race planning." Some of the most significant settlements included Cedarlake, Greenwood Village, Plateau, and Shepherdsville, all in Alabama; Biscoe, Edmonson, and Thomasville in Arkansas; Eatonville and New Monrovia in Florida; Archery, Burroughs, Cannonville, Grenough, and Leroy in Georgia; and Expose, Renova, and Mound Bayou in Mississippi. The state of Oklahoma had the largest number of Black towns, including Boley, Bookertee, Clearview, Porter, Grayson, Lima, Mantu, Redbird, Rentiesville, Taft, Tatums, Tullahassee, and Vernon.[65] Black towns in the South were more substantial than those established in northern or western states; although smaller in size, southern settlements developed their own resources for self-improvement and support. "School settlements," founded by African American organizations such as Wilberforce in Ohio, the Institute in West Virginia, and Langston in Oklahoma, were developed as a result of establishing large institutions for race betterment.[66] Sites like Mound Bayou, Mississippi, began as one way of refuting claims that once "removed from under the immediate restraint of the white governing hand we start on the path of retrogression and revert back to the original condition from whence we have come only by difficult slow steps. Any considerable number of Negroes left entirely to themselves, it was said, would inevitably drift in the direction of their own mutual debasement and destruction."[67] Tuskegee also experimented with town planning in its designs for Greenwood, the community immediately surrounding the school. The development began with the school's founding in 1881 and Washington's belief that every teacher and worker should own a home. Washington had the institute purchase as much of its adjacent property as possible to then allow easy terms for teachers and workers to obtain homes. At its height, the community boasted some 175 homes with 1,500 residents living and working in close proximity.[68] Greenwood became a prime example of Washington's self-help communal model and an easily adaptable prototype for modern living throughout the South. By 1901, some 200 acres were purchased and subdivided by forty wide streets and forty-five wide avenues at Greenwood.[69] Washington used all the available resources of the architecture department to help design affordable model cottages for Greenwood. The town was described as "A Progressive Village Adjoining the Tuskegee Normal and Industrial Center for Colored People in the South." The model school building originally located on campus, as well as the Mount Olive Baptist Church, was moved to Greenwood. Washington's village was self-supporting with its own industries, retail stores, and local shops.[70] Washington biographer Louis Harlan suggests that Greenwood, like Tuskegee, "was a preparation for life, and for assimilation into the mainstream of American life, as Washington strongly believed, [and] Greenwood was that life in miniature."[71] Were Washington and his Tuskegee architects truly advocating eventual assimilation into dominant culture by promoting Greenwood as a model community for African Americans? I would maintain that Greenwood, like Tuskegee, is just another example of Washington's race uplift project expressed in the built domain. The Black nation would not only be made up of institutions like the industrial school but also transform the domestic and communal realms as sites of Black self-expression and autonomy. Constructing homes of brick and mortar, only some thirty years after enslavement, suggested a form of radicalism that soon was spread throughout the South by Tuskegee graduates, men and women committed to social, economic, political, and spatial self-empowerment. J. B. Jackson contends that these vernacular landscapes are "the image of our common humanity—hard work, stubborn hope, and mutual forbearance."[72] Greenwood as a cultural landscape reflects the struggle of African Americans to survive economically and participate in community life. White responses to Tuskegee initiatives suggest the delicate balance that Washington was able to achieve between campus and town. School administrators cautioned its students to avoid the hostility of local townspeople, even asking them not to carry too many books while walking around town. For many school leaders it was important to show that "Tuskegee was training the intellect rather than the heart and hands."[73]

Among African Americans, the impact of gender on identity formation is clearly evident in the narratives of remembrance and oppression written by race women in the 1890s and in the building of all-Black institutions, like the industrial school complex, as an archive to the brutality of bondage and eventual freedom. Women like Frances Ellen Watkins Harper made clear that "no nation can gain its full measure of enlightenment and happiness if one-half of it is free and the other half is fettered." Race women maintained that the social and political emancipation of all women was essential in reconstructing American democracy. Harper knew that if a radical transformation was to occur, women must spearhead massive social reform efforts. At the World's Congress of Representative Women she declared just what those efforts should be: "O women of America! . . . to create a healthy public sentiment; to demand justice, simple justice, as the right of every race; to brand with everlasting infamy the lawless and brutal cowardice that lynches, burns, and tortures your own countrymen."[74]

As has been argued, the closing decades of the nineteenth century were impacted by neocolonial enthusiasm, anti-immigrationism, and a commitment to the Colonial Revival and American Renaissance styles by an emerging architectural profession. The World's Columbian Exposition clearly reflects the kind of racialized discourse pervasive in American consumer culture, particularly in its adoption of the "White City" or "City Beautiful" ideal. The relationship between race and architecture is clearly evident in the novels of women reformers like Frances Ellen Watkins Harper. These race-uplift texts show how African Americans have been shaping, transforming, and rebuilding the American cultural landscape since slavery—even questioning the values of American republicanism and democracy. The texts themselves bring together aspects of cultural memory and place making that are clearly evident in the genre of race literature as never discussed by previous literary historians of the Black experience.[75] As historian Michael Kammen has made clear, African Americans at the close of the nineteenth century chose to perpetuate "their own distinctive traditions and memories."[76] Arguably, African Americans were committed to refuting the Lost Cause movement and effectively assisted whites in curing their cultural amnesia regarding the innumerable decades of chattel slavery and establishing new symbolic forms of Black self-determination as seen in the founding of race-based institutions. In describing spaces like the church or school within the novel, Black women writers also engaged with the actual sites of schools such as Tuskegee. As sites of memory, the industrial school complexes help to establish a countertradition that reframes white perceptions of race and the built environment. The schools not only threaten white social control and the national myth of white superiority but also help commemorate the lived experiences of countless enslaved Africans. The history of slavery and segregation is recast at industrial school sites, reflecting a vernacular literary and architectural tradition espoused not only by men but most significantly by race women.

NOTES

The quotation in the title comes from Anna Julia Cooper, *A Voice from the South* (Xenia: Aldine Printing House, 1892), 165. This chapter is adapted from a chapter in the author's book *"We Gave Our Hearts and Lives to It": Black Women, Industrial Schools, and Nation-Building in the New South* (Durham, NC: Duke University Press, forthcoming).

1. Anna Julia Cooper, *A Voice from the South* (Xenia: Aldine Printing House, 1892), 25.

2. Don Mitchell, "Cultural Landscapes: Just Landscapes or Landscapes of Justice?" *Progress in Human Geography* 27, no. 6 (2003): 790. Mitchell argues that "landscape may demand a theory of landscape, but it also demands that theories of capital circulation and crisis, of race and gender, and of geopolitics and power be built right into it." Three important essays that have already begun this important work are Mary Corbin Sies, "Toward a Performance Theory of the Suburban Ideal, 1877–1917," in *Perspectives in Vernacular Architecture IV*, ed. Thomas Carter and Bernard Herman (St. Louis: University

of Missouri Press, 1991); Elsa Barkley Brown and Gregg D. Kimball, "Mapping the Terrain of Black Richmond," *Journal of Urban History* 21, no. 3 (March 1995): 296–346; and Denis R. Byrne, "Nervous Landscapes: Race and Space in Australia," *Journal of Social Archaeology* 3, no. 2 (2003): 169–193.

3. Ibid., 788. For a discussion of "political architecture" in the context of colonialism, see Thomas R. Metcalf, *An Imperial Vision: Indian Architecture and Britain's Raj* (New York: Oxford University Press, 1989).

4. J. B. Jackson, *Discovering the Vernacular Landscape* (New Haven, CT: Yale University Press, 1984), 12, 149–150.

5. H. E. Gulley, "Women and the Lost Cause: Preserving a Confederate Identity in the American Deep South," *Journal of Historical Geography* 19, no. 2 (1993): 125.

6. Ibid., 125–126.

7. Ibid., 126.

8. Benedict Anderson, *Imagined Communities: Reflections on the Origin and Spread of Nationalism* (New York: Verso, 1983). Although Benedict Anderson has been lauded for his concept of "imagined communities," it must be noted that two important pieces of scholarship predate his study of nationalism and the imaginary. See John K. Wright, "Terrae Incognitae: The Place of the Imagination in Geography," *Annals of the Association of American Geographers* 37, no. 1 (1947): 546–562; and David Lowenthal, "Geography, Experience, and Imagination: Towards a Geographical Epistemology," *Annals of the Association of American Geographers* 51, no. 3 (1961): 241–260.

9. See Gerald Horne, *Race Woman: The Lives of Shirley Graham Du Bois* (New York: New York University Press, 2000).

10. Hazel Carby, *Reconstructing Womanhood: The Emergence of the Afro-American Woman Novelist* (New York: Oxford University Press, 1987), 128.

11. Ibid., 6.

12. Ibid., 64.

13. Anderson, *Imagined Communities*. See also Vincente L. Rafael, "Nationalism, Imagery, and the Filipino Intelligentsia in the Nineteenth Century," *Critical Inquiry* 16 (Spring 1990): 591; and Anthony Molho and Gordon S. Wood, eds., *Imagined Histories: American Historians Interpret the Past* (Princeton, NJ: Princeton University Press, 1998).

14. Rafael, "Nationalism, Imagery, and the Filipino Intelligentsia," 591.

15. Anderson, *Imagined Communities*, 5–6.

16. Rafael, "Nationalism, Imagery, and the Filipino Intelligentsia," 593.

17. Catherine W. Bishir, "Landmarks of Power: Building a Southern Past, 1885–1915," *Southern Cultures* (Inaugural Issue, 1993): 7.

18. See W. Fitzhugh Brundage, ed., *Under Sentence of Death: Lynching in the South* (Chapel Hill: University of North Carolina Press, 1997).

19. Susan Prendergast Schoelwer, "Curious Relics and Quaint Scenes: The Colonial Revival at Chicago's Great Fair," in *The Colonial Revival in America*, ed. Alan Axelrod, 184–214 (New York: W. W. Norton & Company, 1985), 184–185.

20. W. Stuart Towns, "Honoring the Confederacy in Northwest Florida: The Confederate Monument Ritual," *Florida Historical Quarterly* 57, no. 2 (1978): 205.

21. Neil Harris, *Building Lives: Constructing Rites and Passages* (New Haven, CT: Yale University Press, 1999), 163–164.

22. Robin Bachin, "Cultural Boundaries: Constructing Urban Space and Civic Culture on Chicago's South Side, 1890–1919," Ph.D. diss., University of Michigan, 1996, 6.

23. For a discussion on the term "New South," see Leon F. Litwack, *Trouble in Mind: Black Southerners in the Age of Jim Crow* (New York: Alfred A. Knopf, 1998), 184–189.

24. Harris, *Building Lives*, 165.

25. Shawn Michelle Smith, "Photographing the 'American Negro': Nation, Race, and Photography at the Paris Exposition of 1900," in *With Other Eyes: Looking at Race and Gender in Visual Culture*, ed. Lisa Bloom, 58–87 (Minneapolis: University of Minnesota Press, 1999), 86.

26. Robin D.G. Kelley, "'We Are Not What We Seem': Rethinking Black Working-Class Opposition in the Jim Crow South," *Journal of American History* 80, no. 1 (1993): 77.

27. For a discussion similar to Robin D.G. Kelley's, see Sara M. Evans and Harry C. Boyte, *Free Spaces: The Sources of Democratic Change in America* (New York: Harper & Row Publishers, 1986), 17, and especially 18. Evans and Boyte contend that "a focus on free spaces at the heart of democratic movements aids in the resolution of polarities that have long and bitterly divided modern observers and critics—expressive individualism versus ties of community; modernity versus tradition; public and private values, and so forth—by highlighting the living environments where people draw upon both 'oppositions' to create new experiments." For a compelling look at utopian movements and their failures, see David Harvey, *Spaces of Hope* (Berkeley: University of California Press, 2000).

28. Jane Dailey, "Deference and Violence in the Postbellum South: Manners and Massacres in Danville, Virginia," *Journal of Southern History* 58, no. 3 (1997): 557–558.

29. Mitchell, "Cultural Landscapes," 788.

30. Homi Bhabha, *Nation and Narration* (London, England: Routledge, 1990), 297.

31. Ibid., 593.

32. Marvin Trachtenberg, *The Statue of Liberty* (New York: Viking, 1976), 15. Also see Alan Trachtenberg, *Brooklyn Bridge: Fact and Symbol* (Chicago: University of Chicago Press, 1979).

33. James E. Newton and Ronald L. Lewis, eds., *The Other Slaves: Mechanics, Artisans, and Craftsmen* (Boston: G. K. Hall & Co., 1978), xiv. See also Tia Marie Blassingame, "Breaking Through a 'Thunderous Silence': The African American in the Evolution of American Architecture," Senior thesis, Princeton University, n.d., American Institute of Architects (AIA) Archives, Washington, DC.

34. "Architecture Among Negroes in America," *The Negro History Bulletin* (April 1940): 99.

35. Richard K. Dozier, "A Historical Survey: Black Architects and Craftsmen," *Black World* (May 1974): 5–6.

36. Ibid., 7.

37. Douglas R. Egerton, *He Shall Go out Free: The Lives of Denmark Vesey* (Madison, WI: Madison House, 1999), xiii–xvi, 203–205. See also David Robertson, *Denmark Vesey: The Buried History of America's Largest Slave Rebellion and the Man Who Led It* (New York: Alfred A. Knopf, 1999).

38. John W. Blassingame, *The Slave Community: Plantation Life in the Antebellum South* (New York: Oxford University Press, 1972), 101–104.

39. Mary N. Woods, *From Craft to Profession: The Practice of Architecture in Nineteenth-Century America* (Berkeley: University of California Press, 1999), 100.

40. For a discussion of freedom celebrations, see Alessandra Lorini, *Rituals of Race: American Public Culture and the Search for Racial Democracy* (Charlottesville: University of Virginia Press, 1999), 28–32, 209–256. See also Geneviève Fabre, "African-American Commemorative Celebrations in the Nineteenth Century," in *History & Memory in African-American Culture*, ed. Geneviève Fabre and Robert O'Meally (New York: Oxford University Press, 1994), 72–91.

41. Eddie S. Glaude Jr., *Exodus! Religion, Race, and Nation in Early Nineteenth-Century Black America* (Chicago: University of Chicago Press, 2000), 3–5, 84.

42. Cooper, *Voice from the South*, 27.

43. Glaude, *Exodus!* 83–84; John Gillis, ed., *Commemorations: The Politics of National Identity* (Princeton, NJ: Princeton University Press, 1994); and Yael Zerubavel, *Recovered Roots: Collective Memory and the Making of the Israeli National Tradition* (Chicago: University of Chicago Press, 1995).

44. Sterling Stuckey, *Slave Culture: Nationalist Theory & the Foundations of Black America* (New York: Oxford University Press, 1987), 73.

45. Glaude, *Exodus!* 10.

46. Ibid., 10–11.

47. Cedric J. Robinson, *Black Movements in America* (New York: Routledge, 1997), 101.

48. Cooper, *Voice from the South*, 135.

49. Ibid., 144.

50. Ibid., 143.

51. Joanne P. Sharp, "Gendering Nationhood": A Feminist Engagement with National Identity," in *BodySpace*, ed. Nancy Duncan (New York: Routledge, 1996), 97.

52. Ibid., 97.

53. Cooper, *Voice from the South*, 28 (emphasis added).

54. James D. Anderson, *The Education of Blacks in the South, 1860–1935* (Chapel Hill: University of North Carolina Press, 1988), 2.

55. Washington as quoted in W.E.B. Du Bois, *Black Reconstruction in America* (New York: Touchstone, 1992), 641–642.

56. Ibid., 49–50. See also Blinzy L. Gore, *"On a Hilltop High": The Origin and History of Claflin College to 1984* (Spartanburg, SC: The Reprint Company, 1994).

57. Booker T. Washington, *Up from Slavery* (New York: Oxford University Press, 1901), 84.

58. Washington as quoted in Dozier, "Tuskegee," 41.

59. Setha M. Low, *On the Plaza: The Politics of Public Space and Culture* (Austin: University of Texas Press, 2000), 33.

60. Ibid., 36. For theoretical approaches to space, see also Pierre Bourdieu, *Outline of a Theory of Practice* (New York: Cambridge University Press, 1977); Michel De Certeau, *The Practice of Everyday Life* (Berkeley: University of California Press, 1984); Anthony D. King, *Buildings and Society* (London: Routledge, 1976); and Henri Lefebvre, *The Production of Space* (Oxford: Basil Blackwell, 1991). Most recently, historian Sarah Deutsch has looked to women's impact on the social production of space in Boston. See Sarah Deutsch, *Women and the City: Gender, Space, and Power in Boston, 1870–1940* (New York: Oxford

University Press, 2000). An earlier work is Mary P. Ryan's *Women in Public: Between Banners and Ballots, 1825–1880* (Baltimore: Johns Hopkins University Press, 1990).

61. Louis R. Harlan, *Booker T. Washington: The Wizard of Tuskegee, 1901–1915* (New York: Oxford University Press, 1983), 144.

62. Henry A. Giroux, *Impure Acts: The Practical Politics of Cultural Studies* (New York: Routledge, 2000).

63. For an examination of Black experiments in building utopias, see William Pease and Jane Pease, *Black Utopia: Negro Communal Experiments in America* (Madison: State Historical Society of Wisconsin, 1972).

64. Giroux, *Impure Acts*, 130. See also Robert W. McChesney's introduction to Noam Chomsky's *Profit over People* (New York: Seven Stories Press, 1999), 9.

65. "Architecture Among Negroes in America," 99–100.

66. Ibid., 100.

67. Aurelius P. Hood, *The Negro at Mound Bayou: Being an Authentic Story of the Founding, Growth and Development of the "Most Celebrated Town in the South"* (Mound Bayou, MS: A. P. Hood, 1909), 9; Towns and Settlements, Booker T. Washington Collection, Tuskegee University Archives, Tuskegee, Alabama; and "Mound Bayou—Past and Present," *The Negro History Bulletin* (April 1940): 105, 107, 109. For other works on Black towns, see Nell Irvine Painter, *Exodusters: Black Migration to Kansas After Reconstruction* (New York: Knopf, 1977); and Elizabeth Rauh Bethel, *Promiseland: A Century of Life in a Negro Community* (Philadelphia: Temple University Press, 1981).

68. O. A. Stewart, "Greenwood: A Dream Come True," *Tuskegee Messenger* 10 (July 1934).

69. Dozier, "Tuskegee," 132–133.

70. Ibid., 134–137.

71. Harlan, *Booker T. Washington*, 171.

72. Jackson, *Discovering the Vernacular Landscape*, xii.

73. Kenrick Ian Grandison, "Beyond Buildings: Landscape as Cultural History in Constructing the Historical Significance of Place," in *Preservation of What, for Whom? A Critical Look at Historical Significance*, ed. Michael A. Tomlan (Ithaca: National Council for Preservation Education, 1998), 162. See also Raymond Wolters, *New Negro on Campus: Black College Rebellion of the 1920s* (Princeton, NJ: Princeton University Press, 1975), 144. The only recorded incident of racial violence in the early decades of the school's founding happened in 1923 when the federal government decided it would build a hospital for Black World War I veterans on the Tuskegee campus. Local whites were demanding that the segregated hospital be managed by whites only. Tuskegee's principal Robert Moton refused their demands. See K. Ian Grandison, "Negotiated Space: Historically Black College Campuses as Spatial Records of the Postbellum South," Sites of Memory Symposium, Conference Paper, School of Architecture, University of Virginia, 1999.

74. Frances Ellen Watkins Harper, "Woman's Political Future," in *World's Congress of Representative Women*, ed. May Wright Sewall (Chicago: Rand McNally, 1894), 433–437; and Manning Marable, "Introduction," *Souls* (Fall 2000): 6.

75. William Gleason, "Chestnutt's Piazza Tales: Architecture, Race, and Memory in the Conjure Stories," *American Quarterly* 51, no. 1 (1999): 37.

76. Michael Kammen as quoted by Gleason, "Chestnutt's Piazza Tales," 37.

Stefan Bradley

Gym Crow Must Go

The 1960s Struggle Between Columbia University and
Its New York City Neighbors

> They own you. They build a gymnasium for you, and then they take it away
> from you anytime they want. Then they have control of that area.
>
> DANIEL DOUGLAS, 1997[1]

Race, power, and space are key elements in the narrative of American history, and they are even more important to the story of Columbia University's relationship to its black and Puerto Rican neighbors during the 1950s and 1960s. In April 1968, that story came to a head during one of the most influential student demonstrations of the decade.[2] The predominantly white Ivy League school in the Morningside Heights neighborhood of New York City functioned, as did many white institutions in the 1960s, as one that would impose its will on the seemingly defenseless black communities of neighboring Harlem and Morningside Heights, in this case by building a ten-story gymnasium in the precious recreational space of Morningside Park.

In the 1950s, university officials made plans to build a new gymnasium in the park for three reasons. First, the university had already constructed softball fields in the park earlier in the decade, so officials wanted a field house to go along with the ball fields. Second, university officials believed they had the right to use whatever land the institution could afford to improve the aesthetic appeal of the school to potential and current students. Third, university officials seemed to assume that, because of financial backing from philanthropic groups like the Ford Foundation, as well as contractual agreements that the university maintained with the city and builders, the mostly black and Puerto Rican neighboring communities could not prevent the university from building the gym. This last belief was based, in part, on premises of paternalism, white privilege, and class privilege.

In April 1968, following the lead of Harlem and Morningside Heights community members, student protesters from the university attempted to halt the construction of the gymnasium in the nearby park, asserting that Columbia University, as an imposing white institution, was using its affluence and power to build the structure against the will of the neighboring black community. Many students learned of the controversy over the gym through various community groups and student organizations that had been protesting the proposed gym since the early 1960s. Specifically, two groups—the Students' Afro-American Society (SAS), headed by Cicero Wilson, and the Columbia branch of the nationwide organization Students for a Democratic Society (SDS)—strongly opposed the raising of the gym on the basis that Columbia acted on racist motives. The groups believed that the university did not need to build a new gymnasium in the mostly black neighboring community's park, where the residents were already short of parkland.

After consulting with various members of the Harlem community, SAS saw the proposed gym as a symbol of racism and a struggle for control over land in the adjacent neighborhoods. By constructing the gym in Morningside Park, many Harlem residents believed that the university was trying to take even more land from the community, and, to some extent, they were correct. Not only did Columbia own many buildings and much land in Harlem but it had also leased several acres of land in the park in the late 1950s. The proposed ten-story gymnasium, although open to community residents, only allocated the community a small percentage of actual floor space and forced non-Columbia affiliates to enter through a different set of doors. In fact, during the protest, the critics of the proposed structure cleverly referred to it as "Gym Crow."[3]

This essay will offer a short history of the citizens who initiated the protest against the university's proposal for the gym in Morningside Park. Benefiting from a large cache of archived material and numerous oral history interviews, this essay also attempts to provide a new perspective on the conflict concerning the park by placing race, black residents, black politicians, and black students at the forefront of the controversy. Previous accounts of Columbia in the 1950s and 1960s focused on the university's ties to the war in Vietnam, the plight of the campus chapter of the mostly white Students for a Democratic Society (SDS) to achieve student power, and SDS's push to end the school's complicity with the war effort. These accounts place the conflict over the gym as a sidebar to the antiwar movement that spilled onto Columbia's campus. In this essay, the efforts of the residents of the neighborhoods that surround the Ivy League institution are particularly important, as those efforts speak to the assertion of power against an overbearing opponent. The role of city officials is also important to the background of this drama because the community's issues became much more than just complaints; they became a political debate with municipal consequences. This debate over the possibility of a gymnasium in the park points to the competition that occurred among the city, the university, and the local Harlem and Morningside Heights communities.

Columbia University, in spite of claims of wanting to cooperate with the Harlem and Morningside Heights communities on matters such as the gymnasium, was using its power to expand into black neighborhoods that could rarely resist the large white institution's efforts to encroach onto land that the residents considered their own. Because of the university's power and prestige in American society, many university officials seemed not to respect the ideas of ownership that black people in the nearby neighborhoods believed were so important to their survival and advancement in the United States.[4]

As industry burgeoned in cities like New York in the late 1800s and early 1900s, city officials began to note the need to section off green park areas as enclaves from the degradation that they felt came along with urbanization. In New York City, American landscape architect Frederick Law Olmsted was placed in charge of designing several of the major parks in the city, including Central, Riverside, Prospect, and Morningside Parks. City planners and the architects the planners employed initially believed that these parks could foster the coexistence of the industrial city and nature.[5] As the years passed, the city grew but the amount of available park space did not. Often, the city, universities, high schools, and community residents were in competition for the same parkland, and that was the case in 1968 when that competition for the coveted green parcels of land came to a head over Columbia's attempt to build a large gymnasium in Morningside Park.

The resentment Harlem's black residents felt toward Columbia University developed mostly in the 1950s and 1960s. Located amid the nation's largest urban population, Columbia's main campus is adjacent to the lower west side of New York City's Harlem section. Riverside Park is on the western side of the university, and on the eastern side is Morningside Park, which constituted the only barrier between the richly endowed, elite educational center and Harlem, where many working-class and poor blacks and Puerto Ricans resided.

Originally, the university had not been located in Morningside Heights. In 1775, the institution, then known as King's College, sat on the land of the Trinity Episcopal Church. Later, in 1897, it moved to Morningside Heights because, according to Robert E. Price in *The University and the City: Eight Cases of Involvement*, Columbia University was attempting to "escape" the encroachment of the city onto the campus.[6]

To be sure, Columbia wanted to integrate with certain sections of the city. In the late 1800s, after moving to Morningside Heights, the school's president, Seth Low, authorized Charles Follen McKim to design the new campus. The master plan for the new university site indicated that Columbia not only would be a part of the city but through its grand architecture and intellectual stature would shine as an example of virtue, knowledge, and endurance as both the campus and the city grew. Low explained his vision well: "[T]he city may be made[,] to a considerable extent, a part of the university."[7] It was at this point that Columbia's name changed from Columbia College to Columbia University in the City of New York, symbolizing its relationship to the metropolis.[8]

The Morningside Heights section of Manhattan stretches from 110th to 125th Streets on its western side and from Morningside Park to the Hudson River on the eastern side. Within the heights is the very strange-shaped Morningside Park that Frederick Law Olmsted and Calvert Vaux designed in the early 1870s. There are cliffs and ledges within the park itself with very few flat areas available for practical use. Olmsted commented on its terrain in an 1873 preliminary report to the New York Department of Public Parks: "The only surfaces within it not sharply inclined are two small patches lying widely apart, against the northeast and southeast corners respectively."[9] Harlem begins from the flats of the park and extends eastward and northward. So, above the park on the heights, is the Ivy League center of higher education, and below and adjacent to the park are the slums and poorer neighborhoods of Harlem. Morningside Park provides the buffer zone between the two very different environments.

Just before World War II, no black families could be found on most blocks of Morningside Heights. Early on, many of the faculty members from Columbia resided in the then-comely apartments on Riverside Drive and Claremont Avenue. During World War II, blacks began moving into many of the once-exclusive white neighborhoods. Concurrently, the construction of the elevated transit lines out of 120th Street brought property values down and contributed to the deterioration of the area. As Melvin Webber put it in the book *Urban Planning and Social Policy*, "Highway and transit facilities . . . are now treated as both servers and shapers of the larger land-use and accessibility relationships." This comment spoke directly to the fact that city planners were most interested in getting those who worked in the city but lived in the suburbs directly in contact with the city through transportation. Unfortunately for many of the blacks and other minorities who had moved closer to jobs in the city, this meant that the lines of transportation would cut through their neighborhoods.[10]

At about the same time that the black population was growing in Morningside Heights, the black population in Harlem skyrocketed, creating a somewhat homogeneous community that dealt daily with racism and segregation. Because of the first and second Great Migrations, as well as the Harlem Renaissance, the enclave swelled with various types of black immigrants. Describing Harlem, historian Roi Ottley wrote that "it [Harlem] is the fountainhead of mass movements. From it flows the progressive vitality of Negro life."[11]

That statement in itself described the history of social protest in Harlem. Residents of Harlem had rioted in 1935 in part because of the economic effects of the Great Depression and partly because of the frustration of blacks with local white shop owners. Protesters pointed to the fact that although mostly blacks lived in Harlem, whites owned a majority of the businesses, leaving the residents feeling economically exploited.[12] Rioters destroyed the shops of those owners who would sell to blacks but would not hire them.

One mass protest in particular, the Harlem Riot of 1943, signified a difference in the way blacks in Harlem viewed themselves and how whites in America viewed the residents of the New York enclave. In the midst of World War II, blacks in Harlem questioned the country's allegiance to democracy for all when a white police officer shot a black uniformed soldier in a local hotel. The soldier, who had allegedly engaged the officer in a scuffle after the officer placed an elderly woman under arrest for disturbing the peace, attempted to run from the altercation. When news of the arrest and shooting traveled, Harlem blacks filled the streets to vent their frustration with housing and employment discrimination, as well as with police brutality. By the end of the riot, 6 blacks had died and over 500 had been arrested.[13] This disturbing scene set the stage for many others in the decades to come. It also showed that race relations would continue to be unstable unless discrimination faded.

Columbia University sat in the midst of this burgeoning black community. Between 1950 and 1960, the black population in the Morningside Heights neighborhood alone grew by 700 percent, from 470 to 3,133.[14] Socially, things changed rapidly and the living conditions in Morningside Heights and Harlem deteriorated considerably. As the black and Puerto Rican populations increased, corporate and municipal support in the area declined, and many parts of those communities turned into ghettos, bringing a mix of problems.

This shift, along with myriad urban problems, eventually led to the rise of the single-room-occupancy (SRO) buildings, which further destabilized the neighborhoods in those areas where many minorities lived during the 1960s.

These edifices were once apartment buildings, but because of the weakness of the market, they were separated and rented out as rooms.[15] Initially, students used these SROs as their dwellings. Later, poorer and more elderly people took over the residences because of the inexpensive rent. Some of the tenants, however, were those who had troubles with the law, such as prostitutes and various roguish types. Harlem, once the home of a renaissance, was rapidly withering. In this declining economy, inexpensive land provided an impetus for Columbia University to expand its domain.

After the rise of the ghetto, the concept of urban renewal became popular. The idea was that in order to alleviate the unsightliness, vice, and waste of the ghetto, institutions and businesses would have to invest in the inexpensive land and property of the ghettos to revitalize the economy. Superficially, the concept of urban renewal seemed like a positive act; however, its underside dealt with the displacement of residents who might not be able to afford to move anywhere else. For institutions like Columbia University, the removal of tenants was more an impediment to progress than a problem that needed resolution.[16]

The university, in a sense, attempted to deal with the problem of the ghetto by taking it over before it overran the Morningside Heights campus, as reflected by Robert Price's comment concerning Columbia University's attempt to "escape" the city.[17] One might have asked what exactly about New York City was the university trying to escape. Although it would have been impossible for Columbia to literally escape the growth of the city by buying the land surrounding the university, the school attempted to insulate itself from certain segments of the city by purchasing buildings in the areas closest to the campus.

Along these lines, Jacques Barzun, Columbia university provost in 1967, believed that the neighborhoods that surrounded the university in the Heights and Harlem were becoming "uninviting, abnormal, sinister, and dangerous."[18] The Faculty Civil Rights Group of Columbia University, which did a study on the university's policy in regard to the Morningside Heights neighborhood, quoted one of the university planners as stating: "We are looking for a community where the faculty can talk to people like themselves. We don't want a dirty group."[19] It is unclear what the planner meant by "people like themselves," but more than likely he was not referring to the mostly black and Puerto Rican residents of Morningside Heights. When he stated the desire for a group of "people like themselves," he was undoubtedly speaking of people who were white like the faculty members, which speaks to the ideas of whiteness that he and possibly his colleagues maintained. If Columbia were to become the civic leader that early officials had envisioned it would be, it must set itself apart from those it would lead.[20] Columbia, then, could be like the puritan "city on the hill."

Between 1961 and 1967, a great deal happened throughout the world and within the neighborhoods of Morningside Heights and Harlem. The influx of heroin, lack of job opportunities, slum living, and racial injustice infused the residents of these areas with a feeling of resentment for white America that made the residents prime candidates for civil rights and protest movements. Tired of second-class citizenship, many Harlem blacks decided to change their fate by following the leadership of black leaders like Martin Luther King Jr. and Malcolm X and by joining organizations like the Congress of Racial Equality (CORE). The followers of King advocated nonviolent change in the still-segregated and unjust society of America. In August 1963, King preached the message of nonviolence and racial equality to the thousands who heard, watched, or attended his "I Have a Dream" speech at the March on Washington.

King's painstaking position on nonviolence in the struggle for racial equality did not appeal to every black person during the Civil Rights Movement. Many of the black residents in Harlem endorsed a different, more aggressive push for civil rights. Agreeing with King's goal of racial justice but not with his tactics was Malcolm X, a leader of the Nation of Islam, who did not care to integrate, associate, or negotiate with whites about the civil rights of blacks. Many of the Harlem blacks welcomed and embraced his words. Unlike King, Malcolm X, a northerner, advocated self-defense and did not refer to whites as his "brothers and sisters" but rather as "devils." He asserted that blacks could fight back against white America by unifying economically through purchasing businesses in their communities and taking pride in their neighborhoods as well as their heritage.[21] To the residents of Harlem, that advice meant buying into their community and not allowing outsiders to purchase large parcels of land within its boundaries, like Morningside Park.

At a time when the nation was supposedly celebrating over 100 years of racial progress, Harlem blacks watched southern whites sic dogs on black protesters while police turned water hoses on black women and youth. After 1965, groups like the Student Non-Violent Coordinating Committee (SNCC) abandoned King's nonviolence stance and took up the more aggressive approach to civil rights that Malcolm X had advocated earlier. By 1966, SNCC had become one of the main proponents of the new philosophy that stopped advocating the struggle to attain freedom and started advocating the attainment of "Black Power."

According to the tenets of Black Power, as noted by Kwame Ture (also known as Stokely Carmichael), former president of SNCC, and the economist Charles V. Hamilton (who would later become a professor at Columbia University), black people must go through several processes to reach a position of power in the United States. One of these was self-definition, which involved the reclamation of the history of black people and black people defining themselves by showing pride in their culture. Another process was that of political modernization, which included three steps: "(1) questioning old values and institutions of society; (2) searching for new and different forms of political structure to solve political and economic problems; and (3) broadening the base of political participation to include more people in the decision-making process."[22] Appealing to the resentment and frustration that festered in black communities like Harlem, SNCC, with its new Black Power motto, urged working-class and lower-class blacks "to get some guns, . . . don't be trying to love that honky to death. Shoot him to death."[23] An institution like Columbia could easily become the target of such resentment, especially considering the university's proximity to the Harlem community.

COLUMBIA'S EXPANSION

In 1968, Roger Kahn, a critic of Columbia and an observer throughout the Morningside Park controversy, claimed that the university represented one of "the largest and most aggressive landlords on earth" and that more than half of its assets ($280 million) were in land, buildings, and mortgages.[24] Unfortunately for its dislocated residents, Harlem and Morningside Heights provided prime locations for many of Columbia's ventures. The *New York Times* recorded that "resentment, some of it justified, has built up over the years at Columbia's acquisition of many buildings on Morningside Heights."[25] Dr. Robert S. Liebert, instructor of psychiatry at Columbia, noted that in the 1960s alone, the university purchased 150 housing units previously used mostly by blacks and Puerto Ricans. During that period, the university facilitated the displacement of 7,500 people, approximately 85 percent of whom were black and Puerto Rican.[26] Undoubtedly, rancor for the university arose from its efforts to expand at the neighborhood's expense.

A headline in the May 1968 communist publication called *The Worker* (which succeeded the *Daily Worker*) read: "Columbia Crushing Tenants" and showed a picture of Columbia University's president, Grayson Kirk, above the caption "Kirk—Ruthless Landlord."[27] The paper affirmed Liebert's contention by claiming that a majority of the people affected by the university's housing policies were black and Puerto Rican, as well as poor whites who resided within the Morningside district. Holding that the trustees were the invaders, *The Worker* alleged that "Columbia made war on its Harlem neighbors" without regard for their need for shelter and homes.[28] Kahn agreed with *The Worker* and added that "in . . . human terms, the story becomes an assault of Columbia, the immense institution, on underprivileged human beings living in Manhattan's SROs."[29]

The SRO buildings represented the essence of the New York slum. Expressing his disdain for the university's treatment of the tenants, Kahn suggested that "eight derelicts pay more rent than a single family," and by most accounts, he was correct.[30]

Roger Starr, who in 1968 was the executive director of the Citizens' Housing and Planning Council of New York, Inc., noted that Columbia, as an Ivy League college, needed to keep up with the rest of the schools in its class. Universities like Harvard and Dartmouth had beautiful field houses and fields for their students to use, but Columbia, mostly because of its location in the city, did not have that luxury. Columbia University, if it wished to uphold its classification as Ivy League, really needed to have recreational facilities that matched the standards of the other schools in its class. Regardless of its intentions, the fact was clear that Columbia, as with much of New York City, needed recreational space. That need for recreational space brought Columbia in direct conflict with its Harlem neighbors.[31]

Unfortunately for the school, the rich, predominantly white university had not fostered the most positive relationship with its neighbors. In his testimony to the Cox Commission of Investigation that the university established in April 1968, vice-chairman of the board of trustees and chairman of the University Gymnasium Committee Harold McGuire explained: "Columbia wants to be a friend . . . of the community, . . . [but] we must do it in such a fashion as to be dealing not as Lady Bountiful, but as one who is genuinely interested in and wishes to co-operate with the community."[32] After hearing testimony from university officials, the Cox Committee asserted that by buying those buildings and removing the residents from the SROs, Columbia had tried to find a way to get rid of the "undesirables" of society. The commission presented, as evidence, a Columbia publication that read: "Morningside Heights has been cleaned up. . . . All but two of the worst SRO houses have been eliminated, and nobody really regrets their passing."[33] Certainly someone regretted their passing. Aware of this, McGuire exclaimed: "I can't blame them [those evicted]. I am not being at all critical of them. All I'm saying is that since they wish to stay, and since the only manner in which the University can expand is to acquire additional property . . . there is this inevitable and necessary conflict of interest."[34]

Although, by the late 1960s, many Harlem residents were complaining about Columbia's tenant-removal program, a decade earlier there were some positive aspects to the university's relationship with the community. For example, in spite of previous objections to its expansion policies into the Harlem neighborhoods, school officials constructed two softball fields on the southeast corner of Morningside Park, one of the only flat areas in the park.[35] Because the university had the fields built on public land, the city parks department made arrangements with the school to allow non-students to use the fields on weekends and during school breaks. Early on, the university and the community of Harlem cooperatively hosted Little League baseball and football teams.

University officials believed that the school's purchase of buildings, leasing of land, and construction of fields satisfied their community-service duty as leaders of an institution so close in proximity to Harlem and Morningside Heights.[36] McGuire recalled a conversation he had with Jim Young, the director of the Columbia-Community Athletic Field Program. With a sense of pride, McGuire touted that the program "can field a team with a Chinese boy on first base and a Puerto Rican boy on second base, and a Negro lad at shortstop, and a white boy at third base, but they can all make the double play."[37] McGuire assessed the university's community service youth program, testifying that "[a] terribly important aspect of this program, we feel, is the fact that it has really been an experiment, and a successful experiment in harmonious living."[38] He claimed that this "harmonious living" strategy took place in a very diverse urban area, yet it still succeeded. A critic might have asked what the university meant by success. If it meant that many young people involved themselves in the program, then the university would have been correct in stating that it had succeeded, in some sense, with its program. If, however, it meant that the university was living harmoniously with its neighbors and they enjoyed the university's looming presence, then that success might have been less substantiated.

Until the mid-1960s, when Columbia incrementally cut off community access to the park, many residents enjoyed and supported this arrangement. Accordingly, even up until the late 1960s, the university was spending $25,000 a year to fund the program, and all was relatively well. Soon, however, the residents of Harlem noticed that the gate that surrounded the fields stayed locked more than it stayed open. Dwight C. Smith, chairman of the Morningside Renewal Council, which was interested in improving the appearance of Morningside Heights, wrote to the editor of the *New York Times*: "As the neighbors look at the locked fence around the ball field on what was one of the most available play areas in Morningside Park, they seldom see it occupied by other than Columbia students."[39] The residents feared that further university acquisition of parkland to build another structure would end with similar results.

ENTER GYM CROW

In February 1960, two years after Columbia University president Grayson Kirk accepted then New York City parks commissioner Robert Moses's offer to rent a portion of the land from the city, state senator James L. Watson, a black man who represented Morningside Heights and West Harlem in the upper house of the state legislature, proposed a bill that allowed the school to lease a "specified" amount of land from the city.[40] Assemblyman Percy Sutton, also black, voted for the bill.[41] On April 14, 1961, Governor Nelson Rockefeller signed a measure allocating the university 2.1 acres in the park to use for the purpose of building a gymnasium. The next year, when the university started making its payments of $3,000 per month to the city, the matter stirred little controversy.

The initial outline of the gymnasium stipulated that the city had "exclusive rights" to the gym. That meant that the university could not require that only its staff could be used. The agreement also stipulated that the university had to submit a second set of "intermediate" plans within nine months of the initial submission. After receipt and acceptance of those designs, the university would have no more than five and a half years to complete final design plans. The city also stipulated that construction on the gym must begin no later than August 29, 1967, and once started, it must be completed within five years of the day of commencement. As of 1961, the estimated cost of the gymnasium was $6 million.[42]

At this point, the school's relationship with the adjacent neighborhood remained relatively stable. By 1961, the Columbia-Community Athletic Program was doing well and most area residents appreciated the opportunity for their children to participate. Community members found that as long as the fields stayed open, there was no problem. So when Columbia initially put forth plans for a gym in the park, they seemed acceptable to many in the community. The planners of the gym, in turn, believed that they had avoided a sore spot with the community by using parkland instead of buying up more buildings and evicting tenants. In this way, "no Morningside residents would be displaced," claimed the planners.[43] Columbia, again, attempted to promote goodwill in the community, announcing plans to allot two of the ten floors of gymnasium for public use.[44] Better yet, though, the university publication *Columbia College Today* noted that the gym would affect "the park, by becoming an interracial meeting place full of activity, [and] would become a safe place in which to play again."[45]

Some critics wondered if the park "would become a safe place to play again" only because it would be an "interracial meeting place," as if the publication inferred that as long as it was mainly black and Puerto Rican people who used the park, the park was unsafe. Only when the university added the idea of an "interracial meeting place" to the functions of the park did the concept of safety play a role.

In its attempt to sustain a healthy relationship with its neighbors, the university may have caused more harm than good. Many questioned the sincerity of the large, white institution on the hill and wanted to know who would benefit most from the proposed structure in the park that separated Harlem from Columbia. Author of *Crisis in Black and White* Charles E. Silberman has made general observations of the relationship between large white institutions and their urban neighbors. He noted that often, institutions erred when they did not involve those in the community who were to be the most affected by future plans: "Public officials, civic leaders, [in this case university officials], and foundation executives frequently draw up and publicize new programs for the downtrodden Negroes without bothering to consult those who are to be 'uplifted.' "[46] Silberman's observation was also true of Columbia's proposed gymnasium in Morningside Park.

At a hearing on July 27, 1961, several groups voiced concern for the new edifice. Most of those organizations were against the proposal on the grounds that it would be a private building in a public space, thereby taking advantage of public domain. Those such as the Citizens Union, the Municipal Art Society, St. Luke's Hospital, and the Cathedral of St. John the Divine resisted the construction of the gymnasium along those lines. Most of those people and other groups who were present at the hearing advocated its construction. These were members of the Adult-Youth Association, the Grant-Morningside Neighborhood Group, and the Morningside Citizens Committee.[47]

In late 1965 and early 1966, opposition to the gym grew even further when Mayor John Lindsay and Thomas Hoving, the newly appointed New York City parks commissioner, asserted that Columbia had attempted to fool Harlem and Morningside Heights community members in its offer to share two of the ten floors in the proposed gym. The city officials examined the actual floor space of the proposed structure and found that the two floors that the community would use made up only 12.5 percent of the total floor space area rather than the assumed 20 percent.

Hoving and Lindsay raised this concern at meetings, at conferences, and in the press. Lindsay, who used opposition to the gym as part of his mayoral campaign in 1965, asserted that "park property should not fall to private builders," particularly Columbia University.[48] Hoving held that "if we are going to have to live with this big ugly structure, built on community land, then the community and not Columbia should get most [of the] benefit."[49] He vowed, "I am dead set against this gymnasium and I will fight as hard as I can to stop it."[50]

Parks Commissioner Hoving presented a special obstacle to the university's plans for the gym. He, like many New Yorkers, was a staunch supporter of recreational park space. In his opinion, one of the most detestable acts possible was placing a large cement building in a green park, and that was exactly what Columbia University, the private owner, intended to do. Hoving was such a protector of park space that he forced the withdrawal of a donated cafeteria restaurant planned to be built in Central Park. In the same manner, he went so far as to demand that only "moveable," not permanent, refreshment kiosks be allowed in Central Park. More than most, he did not appreciate the school's attempt to place the gym in the park regardless of the goodwill that it was supposed to promote in the community.[51]

The parks commissioner and mayor were only part of a growing group of concerned citizens. On February 1, 1966, Richard Hatch, the executive director of the Architects' Renewal Commission in Harlem (ARCH), also protested to the editor of the *New York Times* about the plan to build the gymnasium at the Morningside Park site.[52] He pledged ARCH's support to Hoving and claimed that the gym would turn out like the school's previous projects, in which the community received little attention. Another opponent, M. M. Graff, sent a letter (which was subsequently not published) to the editor as well. He dramatically announced that "the rape of Morningside Park has been carried out with arrogant disregard of the public will."[53] Criticizing the school for its attempt to use public land for private use, Graff continued, "Parks are publicly owned land, held in trust for the people, and not to be parceled out for restricted use by any institution, commercial firm, or private egoist."[54]

Soon, because of the proposed gymnasium, ARCH became a politicized organization. With the rise of Black Power and its focus on black ownership and neighborhood control tied to the resentment of poor black and Puerto Rican residents near the university, ARCH's ranks swelled in the late 1960s.[55] One of the issues that ARCH took up regarded "outsiders" acquiring property in Harlem. According to an article, Columbia University was part of a growing contingent of those who could change the makeup and character of Harlem. An article describing ARCH's role in the community claimed that "in ARCH's view, most of new [renewal] projects do not keep with the ethnic orientation of Harlem." The ability of ARCH to recognize the phenomenon endeared the organization to many poor black and Puerto Rican members.[56]

Agreeing with ARCH's complaints against the school, some Harlem residents opposed the raising of the gym for other reasons. Years later, Daniel Douglas pointed out that Columbia's gym would have represented yet another attempt of a white institution to own Harlem. He explained what institutions like Columbia did: "They own you. They build a gymnasium for you, and then they take it away from you anytime they want. Then they have control of that area. . . . If they build a gym on public land, then they have control over the public and private." Besides, Douglas added, "If that school wanted to help Harlem, then there were more vital things the community needed."[57] Another resident of Harlem, who referred to himself as Reverend Sam, later recalled that at the time, his feeling was that "[i]f you don't give our people a fair share of the responsibility in running this facility, then you can't come in our community. They [institutions like Columbia University] are trying to whiten Harlem."[58]

Whether the university was really trying to "whiten" Harlem was debatable, but what was interesting about the two Harlem residents' statements were the ideas of ownership and space. They both insisted that the mostly black and Puerto Rican dwellers of Harlem should own the land and buildings in that particular enclave, but instead, Columbia was trying to own not only the buildings and land in Harlem but also the people. This point was one that psychologists, sociologists, and economists had been toiling with for some time. Ture and Hamilton believed that the black communities in America were colonies that institutional white America controlled, and to a degree, Ture and Hamilton were correct. As had been the case since before the 1935 and 1943 riots, most of the businesses and buildings in Harlem belonged to whites. What is more, the urban renewal projects that the city undertook during the early 1960s further "whitened" (to use the Reverend Sam's term) Harlem by making it possible for companies and institutions (nearly all white) to purchase land for fairly inexpensive prices. In that sense, the larger institutions of America would literally own places like Harlem, without their executives and main employees ever having to live there. This situation, understandably, made some residents of the area feel like colonists.

Representing the black community in politics, state senator Basil A. Paterson and Assemblyman Sutton, both black Democrats, put forth a bill in each house to invalidate the city's 1960 grant giving Columbia the right to lease the land at Morningside Park.[59] Paterson could not understand why Columbia should be able to control eight of the ten floors of the edifice, especially when one observed the populations of the students on campus and the residents of West Harlem. According to an article in *The Morningside Citizen*, a newsletter of the Morningside Citizens Committee, Paterson compared "the number of students at Columbia, 26,000, to the number of people living in a three-block area of West Harlem, 80,000."[60] "Columbia shall not build a gym in this park," Paterson indignantly proclaimed on April 28, 1966, at an outdoor rally at Morningside Park. In clarifying his statement, he warned, "Let the first bulldozers come here and you'll know what we mean."[61] In a published statement, Paterson and Sutton asked, "Why must the university's obligation to educate its students be fulfilled at the expense of communities hungry for park space?"[62]

When Columbia's President Kirk became aware of the opposition, he proclaimed that if the bills passed, the university would sue the state. Kirk noted that "Columbia has two legally binding contracts: one with the city of New York, which if we withdrew would expose us [Columbia] to suit, and the other . . . with the builders."[63] So with legal contracts binding Columbia to the gym, he announced firmly, "Groundbreaking will occur in October." He estimated the gym would cost $9 million.[64]

A separate article in *The Morningside Citizen* deftly explained the situation. "Above and beyond the legal intricacies of whether or not the gym will be built in the park," the columnist noted, "the controversy reflects several large issues common to most large cities: the complications and inconsistencies created by administrative changes, the shortage of city land, a university's crucial need to expand . . . , and the disruption of a neighborhood caused by the spatial needs of a large institution."[65] The Morningside Heights and Harlem communities would have to deal directly with this controversy over space.

On November 1, 1966, a *New York Times* headline read: "Columbia Starts 3-Year Campaign for $200-Million." A major contributor to the fund, the Ford Foundation, approved its donation of $35 million to the school on the condition that it "work with the Negro population on Morningside Heights."[66] Implying that the university could improve on its relationship with that community, the president of the Ford Foundation and former national security adviser McGeorge Bundy added explicitly that he and his corporation were "not talking about doing things to the city or *to* the minorities" but that Columbia and the foundation "will concern [themselves] *with* 'the city and the Negro' . . . by cooperation rather than imposed action."[67]

With the university enjoying the funding and advocacy of contributors like the Ford Foundation, the people of Harlem realized that the university had more than enough power to build its gym. Keeping that in mind, the people decided to act. The long hot summer of 1966 was long and hot in more ways than one. Black Power fostered a strong resentment against powerful white institutions. In many large cities across the United States, blacks were fighting back against racial and economic oppression in ways that forced white America to hear their grievances. Columbia University, which was directly adjacent to one of the main black metropolises in the country, began to reconsider its community relations after observing some of the destructive and violent rhetoric that was common to Black Power advocates. The thought of Columbia actually being damaged or destroyed scared university trustees so much that they urged McGuire to authorize the local community's use of a larger share of the gym "by invitation," of course.[68] The university also offered to add a swimming pool and locker room to the plans for the community portion of the gym. Percy Sutton, who had since become Manhattan Borough president, accepted the offer, but not wholeheartedly.

Although the addition of a swimming pool might have been useful to the residents of Harlem, a pool could not possibly satisfy the resentments of many inhabitants.[69] Although moderate leaders like Sutton thought that the addition of the pool and locker room facilities might help the situation, more militant leaders like Rap Brown, who represented SNCC, and Victor Solomon of the Harlem chapter of CORE, opposed the "racist gym" in its entirety. Solomon, agreeing with earlier ideas of Ture and Hamilton, contended that "Harlem is a colony and is being treated like one" and that the community should impede the progress of the imperialist (Columbia).[70] In a February 1967 meeting, Brown, nearly at the pinnacle of his influence with the Black Power movement, encouraged his audience to protest: "If they build the first story[,] blow it up. If they sneak back at night and build three stories[,] burn it down. And if they get nine stories built, its yours. Take it over, and maybe we'll let them in on the weekends."[71]

Ironically, the gym issue brought together militant and moderate black leaders. For instance, state senator Paterson, usually a moderate in the struggle for civil rights, disagreed with Brown's destructive rhetoric but shared Rap Brown's sentiments about the gym. In December 1967, Paterson contended that he "would stand with anyone [including Brown] against the racist gym."[72] Reminding Harlem blacks of the discrimination of previous times, Brown, Paterson, and other black leaders referred to the building as "Gym Crow." The term grew from the notion that the university was forcing the community to submit to acts like those that had taken place in the Jim Crow South. Following the lead of William H. Booth, head of the Human Rights Commission, black leaders pointed out that the community section of the proposed building was separate from the portion the university members would use. Moreover, Booth showed that community residents had to enter through the basement of the structure, just as blacks had to enter through basements and back doors during the Jim Crow era.[73] In defense of the university, the gymnasium was to be built on a ledge, and geographically, the entrance that might have been most convenient for Harlem residents would have been at the bottom of the ledge. That does not, however, dismiss the fact that community dwellers could not explore the other floors of the structure. In spite of that, after being allotted only 15 percent of the proposed structure that Columbia University would still control and being forced to use a different entrance, many blacks in the community saw that things were once more separate but hardly equal.

Indeed, physically, the gymnasium that Columbia planned to build was very intimidating. According to the designs, it appeared as though the structure would provide a wall of sorts between the campus community and Harlem. Furthermore, representatives of ARCH noted that the size of the proposed gym was also imposing for a park that was only 2.1 square acres.[74]

1968: AMERICA'S RECKONING

In the United States, the year 1968 touched down like a whirlwind, creating chaos and drama for all those in its path. One author, Jules Witcover, described 1968 as "the year the dream died,"[75] and in many ways, the author's description was accurate. The dream Witcover was referring to was the hope that leaders like Martin Luther King Jr. and Robert Kennedy provided to the optimistic generation of the 1960s. The author of this essay, however, sees 1968 somewhat differently. The year 1968 could be better termed as the year of "America's reckoning." That year, the United States was forced to deal with race, class, and other domestic issues that the nation had not dealt with directly since the Civil War. America faced black citizens vehemently demanding their civil rights, young people fighting for a say in society, the assassination of viable leadership, and the ever-looming conflict in Vietnam that was continually escalating. As fate would have it, in April 1968, Columbia University's Morningside Heights campus found itself also in the middle of controversy over the gym issue.

On campus, two groups took up the protest against the gym. The first group had a special relationship with the neighboring working-class black residents. The Students' Afro-American Society (SAS) adopted the gym as an issue after sending representatives to join Harlem community organizations. Throughout the campus controversy, the members of SAS acted as representatives of the community, which was rare in the history of student/community relations. Typically, students from universities and local residents have had tense relationships, but Columbia's black student protesters viewed themselves as activists for the Black Freedom Struggle, and demonstrating against the gym provided them with a way to further that cause. Leadership in the campus movement also came from the Columbia chapter of the mostly white national organization Students for a Democratic Society (SDS). During the 1960s, the radical group's goal was to change the authoritative nature of society by way of the American university.

The main goal of SDS during the protest became the radicalization of the mostly white general population of the school. For the black students of SAS, halting construction on the gymnasium on behalf of the black community was their primary issue. The fact that SDS used the gymnasium issue, which directly affected the black community in the city, as a means to an end (i.e., the radicalization of students) in the end contributed to the break along racial lines of the protesting student groups.

The start of the protest occurred on April 23, almost three weeks after the death of civil rights leader Martin Luther King Jr., at the sundial in the middle of Columbia's campus. After protests throughout the day, the two campus organizations led students to take over Hamilton Hall, a classroom building. In the process, the racially mixed group of nearly 500 intensified the demonstration by cornering a dean in his office and placing guards outside of his door.

By evening, the demonstration switched tones. At about 7:00 PM, H. Rap Brown, a man described as "Amerika's baddest, meanest, most violent nigger,"[76] showed up with an entourage of black men from Harlem, coolly announcing:

"I'd like to tell you that the Harlem community is now here and we want to thank you for taking the first steps in this struggle. . . . The black community is taking over."[77] Fearful for the dean's safety, pro-gym white athletes stood guard outside his door. At 2:00 AM, SAS, with the backing of Rap Brown and his following of community members, instructed the white followers of SDS to leave because of irreconcilable differences regarding the occupation of the building. The leadership of SAS suggested, however, that if the white radicals of SDS wanted to help the Harlem community, then the radicals should take some buildings of their own.

Taking the advice of the SAS leadership and using the black militants as a model, the followers of SDS left Hamilton Hall and eventually took over and occupied four other campus buildings during the course of the week.[78] By the end of the week long demonstration, the mass removal of these SDS-led students and various onlookers gained national attention, which eventually helped the cause of the students and community.

"The fact that a group of black students were in sole occupancy of one of our buildings did complicate the matter," university president Grayson Kirk admitted.[79] By this comment, it was possible that the president meant that the concept of a race riot like the one that had occurred in Harlem just weeks before was frightening to him and the rest of the school officials. The president, as well as the black militants of SAS, understood that when both the white and the black protesters were occupying the building, it was an issue of student protest. When SAS asked the white students to leave, however, it was no longer simply a student protest but rather a *black* student and community protest. The black student group used the threat of community backlash as a weapon against the university to gain its demand. The community used the students to strengthen its position against the gym.

Fear provided the motivation behind the university officials' actions to quell the disturbance in Hamilton. The president seriously worried about the potential arrival of a massive group of outside black protesters on Columbia's campus. He believed that "it was quite clear that the people of City Hall would not be happy about responding very positively [to a request for the police] . . . until they made an assessment of the attitudes in Harlem. . . . They were still feeling the effects of the very serious riots in Harlem upon the assassination of Martin Luther King, Jr."[80]

Most of the black students in Hamilton recognized their collective position of power. One maintained that "they [university officials] weren't that worried about a handful of black students at Columbia, but when Harlem protesters arrived, the mood certainly changed."[81] Gaining the assistance of Harlem residents who had been protesting against the gym would not be difficult. In fact, in the first few hours of their sole occupation of the building, emissaries from Hamilton Hall had raised $125 in local bars in Harlem.[82] Similarly, most of the food they were eating had come from the homes of Harlem anti-gym advocates. As one Harlem mother, who stood outside of Hamilton Hall in the rain, indicated: "Rain or no rain, I don't care. We must support these young people. They went out on a limb for us. . . . I for one am coming back and bringing them hot, nourishing food."[83]

It was like "the invasion of the ivory tower," claimed the Reverend Sam of Harlem when he recalled the demonstration against the gym. The Harlem community enveloped the black student protesters with support. Community organizations such as the NAACP, CORE, the United Black Front, and the Mau Maus offered support to the struggle.[84] National leaders like Stokely Carmichael showed up on campus to oppose the gym and aid SAS.[85] Black high school students marched to campus with bats and sticks in protest.[86] The *Amsterdam News*, a black New York news organ, showed its dismay with the university by featuring articles and editorials opposing the gym. One headline read: "Harlem Backed Columbia Students."[87]

One member of the United Black Front of Harlem stated that "Kirk is the biggest slumlord in Harlem," revealing some of the resentment that community members had because of the school's earlier landownership policies.[88] With that in mind, many of the community members did not see too many positive aspects of the university's gymnasium venture. Blyden Jackson, from the Peace and Freedom Party, suggested that the crowd that had gathered on campus for a rally against the gym go to the site "with buckets and shovels and fill that damned hole [where builders had begun to dig] up." To some of the people at the rally, however, the university's policy regarding the proposed gymnasium was not their only concern.

The night of April 26 presented a time for the black residents of Morningside Heights and Harlem to air their grievances against the university in a way that forced the school to listen. With the black students independently holding a building on campus and black protesters coming from the community onto campus to support them, black people were placing a great amount of pressure on Columbia to back away from the gym project. Furthermore, the situation gave the community a clearer voice in matters of white institutional and black community relations.

The results of the demonstration were violence, validation, and victory. To remove the students, the university employed over 1,000 city and state police officers, who at times were heavy-handed with the demonstrators. That police action led to a six-week strike at Columbia. As the university reeled from the controversy, at last it had to validate the serious concerns of Harlem residents with regard to space, particularly space in Morningside Park. Finally, the community and students won victories in forcing the university to change how it dealt with students and to scrap its plans to build the gym in Morningside Park.

Most important was the change that occurred in the way university officials considered the community of Harlem and Morningside Heights. Together, the local community and students demanded that "Gym Crow Must Go!" and indeed it did. Because the community, with the help of Columbia students, exerted its collective power, the university never built the gymnasium in Morningside Park. What remains, however, is a scar in the area where the builders first began to excavate and vivid memories of the "battle for Morningside Heights."[89] Although Columbia University continues to expand, its officials realize that they cannot afford to approach the local community as the school did before 1968. As Steven V. Roberts, a reporter for the *New York Times*, correctly wrote in a 1968 article for *Commonweal* magazine, "now Columbia knows that almost anybody—students and faculty as well as poor people—will 'cause disturbances' if pushed far enough."[90]

Although those disturbances were enough to prevent Columbia from building a gym in Morningside Park, the disturbances were not enough to end the conflict over space between Columbia and city residents. In 2003, New York residents again criticized Columbia for "land grabbing," when the university announced a proposal to acquire more than seventeen acres in West Harlem.[91] School officials quickly formed a task force consisting of local leaders and organizations to discuss concerns with the proposal. In 2006, Columbia hired a consulting firm to advise the university in regard to expansion and marketing. The firm bore a group called the Coalition for the Future of Manhattanville. The coalition, which ostensibly includes community members, businesses, and politicians who have an interest in the area, backs Columbia's plan to redevelop Manhattanville. In direct contrast to the coalition and Columbia is the Community Board #9 (CB9). When Columbia recently submitted a 197-c plan of redevelopment for community review, the CB9 rejected the school's plan and instead submitted its own 197-a plan for redevelopment. One of the major concerns of the CB9 is the potential of Columbia's use of eminent domain laws as a tool to expand. Many in the West Harlem community worry that Columbia's redevelopment will lead to the displacement of residents as the school acquires new buildings and an increase in rent will occur with the creation of new structures. Further, opponents charge that Columbia has made no proposal to create affordable moderate- to low-income housing that reflects the economic status of many of Manhattanville's residents.[92]

The current scenario is in stark contrast to that of forty years earlier, when the Ivy League institution attempted to force its expansion plans on the community without prior consideration of the community's desires. After learning a hard lesson about the volatility of the Harlem and Morningside Heights community, Columbia is currently "treading lightly," according to the executive director of West Harlem Environmental Action. Undoubtedly, not far from the community residents and school officials' minds is the 1968 controversy over "Gym Crow."

NOTES

1. In an 1997 interview, Douglas commented on the intentions of Columbia University concerning the proposed gymnasium of the 1960s. Daniel Douglas, interview by author, November 22, 1997, New York, handwritten notes, the "Pan Pan" restaurant, Harlem, New York (hereafter cited as Douglas interview).

2. Derrick Bell, *Faces at the Bottom of the Well: The Permanence of Racism* (New York: Basic Books, 1992); Frantz Fanon, *The Wretched of the Earth: A Negro Psychoanalyst's Study of the Problems of Racism and Colonialism in the World Today* (New York: Grove Press, 1966); Andrew Hacker, *Two Nations: Black and White, Separate, Hostile, Unequal* (New York: Ballantine Books, 1995); Robin Kelley, *Race Rebels: Culture, Politics, and the Black Working Class* (New York: Free Press, 1996); Melvin Oliver and Thomas Shapiro, *Black Wealth / White Wealth: A New Perspective on Racial Inequality* (New York: Routledge, 1997); Michael Omi and Howard Winant, *Racial Formation in the United States from the 1960s to the 1990s* (New York: Routledge, 1994); Kwame Ture and Charles V. Hamilton, *Black Power: The Politics of Liberation* (New York: Vintage Books, 1992); Cornel West, *Race Matters* (New York: Vintage Books, 1994).

3. Roger Starr, "The Case of the Columbia Gym," *The Public Interest* (May 1968): 105.

4. Fact-Finding Commission on Columbia Disturbances, *Crisis at Columbia: Report of the Fact-Finding Commission Appointed to Investigate the Disturbances at Columbia University in April and May 1968* (New York: Random House, 1968), 39 (hereafter cited as Fact-Finding Commission, *Crisis at Columbia*).

5. Frederic Law Olmsted Jr. and Theodore Kimball, *Frederick Law Olmsted: Landscape Architect, 1822–1903* (New York: G. P. Putnam, 1922); S. B. Sutton, *Civilizing American Cities: A Selection of Frederick Law Olmsted's Writing on City Landscapes* (Cambridge, MA: MIT Press, 1971).

6. George Nash, *The University and the City: Eight Cases of Involvement* (New York: McGraw-Hill, 1973), 95.

7. Thomas Bender, *New York Intellect: A History of New York Intellectual Life, from 1750 to the Beginnings of Our Time* (New York: Alfred A. Knopf, 1987), 282.

8. Barry Bergdoll, *Mastering McKim's Plan: Columbia's First Century on Morningside Heights* (New York: Columbia University Press, 1997), 20–21.

9. Frederick Law Olmsted and Calvert Vaux, *Preliminary Study of a Design for the Laying Out of Morningside Park* (New York: Board of the Department of Public Parks, Document 50, October 11, 1873), 334–335; Frederick Law Olmsted and Albert Fein, eds., *Landscape into Cityscape* (Ithaca: Cornell University Press, 1968), 334.

10. Bernard Frieden and Robert Morris, eds., *Urban Planning and Social Policy* (New York: Basic Books, 1968), 18.

11. John Henrik Clarke, *Harlem: A Community in Transition* (New York: Citadel Press, 1964), 3.

12. John Hope Franklin and Alfred Moss, *From Slavery to Freedom: A History of African Americans*, 7th ed. (New York: McGraw Hill, 1994), 400.

13. Dominic Capeci Jr., *The Harlem Riot of 1943* (Philadelphia: Temple University Press, 1977).

14. Roger Kahn, *The Battle for Morningside Heights: Why Students Rebel* (New York: William Morrow and Company, 1970), 84.

15. Daniel Bell and Irving Kristol, eds., *Confrontation: The Student Rebellion and the Universities* (New York: Basic Books, 1968), 110.

16. Frieden and Morris, *Urban Planning and Social Policy*, 321.

17. Nash, *The University and the City*, 95.

18. Ibid., 97.

19. Ibid.

20. Bergdoll, *Mastering McKim's Plan*, 20.

21. Betty Shabazz, *Malcolm X Speaks Out* (Indianapolis: Curtis Management, 1992).

22. Kwame Ture and Charles V. Hamilton, *Black Power: The Politics of Liberation* (New York: Vintage Books, 1967, 1992), 34–39.

23. Douglas T. Miller, *On Our Own: Americans in the Sixties* (Lexington: D. C. Heath and Company, 1996), 142.

24. Kahn, *The Battle for Morningside Heights*, 82–83.

25. *New York Times*, April 26, 1968, 50.

26. Robert S. Liebert, *Radical and Militant Youth: A Psychoanalytic Inquiry* (New York: Praeger Press, 1971), 36.

27. *The Worker* (New York), May 17, 1968.

28. Ibid.; Massey and Denton, *American Apartheid*, 187; Frieden and Morris, *Urban Planning and Social Policy*; Lynne Sharon Schwartz, *We Are Talking About Homes: A Great University and Its Neighbors* (New York: Harper and Row, 1985).

29. Kahn, *The Battle for Morningside Heights*, 86.

30. Ibid.

31. Bell and Kristol, *Confrontation*, 111–112.

32. Testimony of Harold McGuire, *Cox Commission Columbia University, Fact Finding Commission Proceedings*, Archibald Cox, chairman (Ann Arbor: University Microfilms, a Xerox Company, 1972), text-microfilm, 428.

33. Fact-Finding Commission, *Crisis at Columbia*, 39.

34. Testimony of Harold McGuire, *Cox Commission Columbia University*, 433.

35. Starr, *Public Interest*, 107.

36. *Partners in the Park* (New York), March 1968.

37. Testimony of Harold McGuire, *Cox Commission Columbia University*, 402.

38. Ibid., 401.

39. *New York Times*, May 20, 1966, 46.

40. McGuire testified that it was important that the "mayor and city council . . . send a home rule message to the state legislature for authorizing the carrying out of this proj-

ect [the gym]." He also made it clear that the legislature should approve of the measure by two-thirds vote, the governor should concur, and so should all "cognizant municipal departments." Testimony of Harold McGuire, *Cox Commission Columbia University,* 407.

41. George Keller, "Six Weeks That Shook Morningside: A Special Report," *Columbia College Today,* Spring 1968, 31.

42. Bell and Kristol, *Confrontation,* 118.

43. Keller, "Six Weeks That Shook Morningside," 31.

44. Kahn, *Battle for Morningside Heights,* 93.

45. Keller, "Six Weeks That Shook Morningside," 31.

46. Frieden and Morris, *Urban Planning and Social Policy,* ed. Charles Silberman (New York: Basic Books, 1968), 185.

47. Bell and Kristol, *Confrontation,* 118.

48. Kahn, *Battle for Morningside Heights,* 93.

49. Ibid., 94.

50. Starr, "The Case of the Columbia Gym," 116.

51. Bell and Kristol, *Confrontation,* 120.

52. *New York Times,* February 1, 1966, 34.

53. M. M. Graff to the editor of the *New York Times,* April 25, 1968, Collins Collection, Schomburg Center for Research in Black Culture, New York Public Library, New York.

54. Ibid.

55. *Advocacy Planning,* September 1968, 109.

56. Ibid., 110.

57. Douglas interview.

58. Rev. Samuel N. Brown, interview by author, November 22, 1997, New York, handwritten notes, the "Pan Pan" restaurant, Harlem, New York.

59. *New York Times,* May 17, 1966, 49.

60. *The Morningside Citizen,* May 6, 1966, 3.

61. Starr, "Case of the Columbia Gym," 116.

62. *New York Times,* May 17, 1966, 49.

63. Administration version of events file, 1968, Columbiana Collection, Columbia University, New York.

64. *New York Times,* February 24, 1966, 21.

65. D.W.C., *The Morningside Citizen,* October 14, 1966, 4.

66. Ibid., November 1, 1967, 1.

67. Miller, *On Our Own,* 80, 157. His statement about Columbia came from *New York Times,* February 24, 1966, 27.

68. Fact-Finding Commission, *Crisis at Columbia,* 95.

69. Louis Lusky and Mary H. Lusky, "Columbia 1968: The Wound Unhealed," *Political Science Quarterly* 84, no. 2 (June 1969): 169–288.

70. *Amsterdam News* (New York), April 27, 1968, 37.

71. Jerry Avorn, *Up Against the Ivy Wall: A History of the Columbia Crisis* (New York: Atheneum, 1969), 20.

72. *Battle for Morningside Heights,* 96.

73. Starr, *Public Interest,* 118.

74. Bergdoll, *Mastering McKim's Plan,* 116.

75. Jules Witcover, *The Year the Dream Died: Revisiting 1968 in America* (New York: Warner Books, 1997).

76. Todd Gitlin, *The Sixties: Years of Hope, Days of Rage* (Toronto: Bantam Books, 1987), 234.

77. Avorn, *Up Against the Ivy Wall,* 58.

78. Students of Columbia, directors and producers, *Columbia Revolt* (New York: Third World Newsreel, 1968), videocassette.

79. Ibid.

80. Ibid.

81. Ibid.

82. Joanne Grant, *Confrontation on Campus: The Columbia Pattern for the New Protest* (New York: Signet Books, 1969), 77.

83. Allon Schroener, ed., *Harlem on My Mind: Cultural Capital of Black America, 1900–1968* (New York: Random House, 1968), 238.

84. *New York Times*, April 24, 1968, 1, 30.

85. Columbia *Daily Spectator*, April 27, 1968, 1.

86. Ibid.

87. Sara Slack, "Harlem Backed Columbia Students," *Amsterdam News* (New York), May 4, 1968, 1.

88. "Brown Speaks Before 500 at Hamilton Rally," Columbia *Daily Spectator* (New York), April 27, 1968, 4.

89. Kahn, *Battle for Morningside Heights.*

90. Steven Roberts, "The Debacle at Columbia," *America*, May 18, 1968, 287.

91. Charles V. Bagli, "Columbia, in a Growth Spurt, Is Buying Swath of Harlem," *New York Times*, July 30, 2003, A1.

92. A log of events can be found at a blog spot operated by the CB9 chairman, Jordi Reyes-Montblanc, http://cb9m.blogspot.com (accessed December 17, 2007).

PART V

Urban Space and Leisure

Robin F. Bachin

Mapping out Spaces of Race Pride

The Social Geography of Leisure on the
South Side of Chicago, 1900–1919

In 1918, black author and poet Langston Hughes arrived in Chicago for the first time. In his autobiographical novel *The Big Sea*, he described the thrill of experiencing the Stroll, the section of State Street on the South Side of Chicago that formed the heart of the Black Belt, the rigidly defined area where most African Americans lived by World War I. "South State Street was in its glory then," he wrote, "a teeming Negro Street with crowded theaters, restaurants, and cabarets. And excitement from noon to noon. Midnight was like day. The street was full of workers and gamblers, prostitutes and pimps, church folks and sinners."[1] The *Chicago Defender* touted the Stroll as "the popular promenade for the masses and classes." It claimed that even the thrill of amusements parks, "with their narrow ideas in the treatment afforded various races," could be ignored when one experienced the Stroll. This "poor man's paradise" was a "Mecca for Pleasure" for local residents as well as visitors, blacks as well as whites.[2]

The excitement Hughes and the *Defender* conveyed in their descriptions of the Stroll is a testament to the role the district played in shaping ideas about identity, freedom, and race pride in the urban North. It was in this rigidly defined space that blacks could carve out a cultural identity that wedded the traditions of their southern heritage with their hopes and ambitions in industrialized cities of the North. For many African Americans in Chicago, especially the new migrants just making their way from the South in the first decades of the twentieth century, civic pride and community identity could be found in the emerging commercial leisure district centered on South State Street. This district included both the respectable businesses of "Old Settlers" and the new sites of commercial amusement that began to proliferate by 1910 in cities throughout America.

William Everett Samuels, one of the leaders of the Black Musicians' Union 208, described how the Stroll provided blacks a place to exhibit a sense of pride and even flamboyance that was off limits to them in other parts of the city. He explained: "You see, you could go from 31st to 35th Street. . . . The stores were open twenty-four hours a day—the barber shops, the haberdasheries, the restaurants; and people would come from all over the world. You could stand at 35th Street and see people from any place you wanted to see because they came here to go—just like Times Square."[3] Samuels's comments illustrate the importance for blacks of claiming urban spaces as their own in order to create a sense of community and belonging. It was here, on the Stroll, that blacks met friends and relatives, caught up on the day's news, and established communal ties. This was a site of local knowledge, a gathering place, where community concerns could be discussed, debated, and negotiated. The fact that these activities took place on street corners and sidewalks, in front of saloons and dance halls, attests to the lack of public recreational facilities like parks and field houses in Black Belt neighborhoods. It also highlights the difficulties and dangers blacks faced when they attempted to use these so-called public spaces.[4]

It was no surprise, then, that the race riot of 1919 began at a public beach. On a steamy July afternoon, two African American boys enjoyed a swim in Lake Michigan at the black Twenty-sixth Street beach. But when Eugene Williams drifted past the invisible barrier separating the black beach from the white one farther south, he ignited a violent and deadly battle that would have an enduring legacy in structuring race relations in Chicago for decades to come. His drowning death that resulted from whites stoning him set off the fury, as did the fact that white police officers nearby did nothing to apprehend the perpetrators of the crime. By the end of nearly a week of rioting, 38 people were dead and over 500 injured.[5]

A close examination of the social geography of the Black Belt illustrates both the physical and cultural proximity of spaces of respectability and areas of "vice." Race leaders, like white reformers, often decried the rise of commercial-ized leisure for its role in promoting vice. Yet efforts at eradicating vice in white areas, and the simultaneous rigidification of the Black Belt during the first Great Migration at the time of World War I, meant that the segregation of vice went hand in hand with racial segregation, with "licit" and "illicit" economies and leisure sites moving in closer and closer proximity.[6] The formal and informal economies of the Black Belt often intermingled and made definitions of respect-ability more permeable than those in white communities. This is not to suggest that race leaders promoting respectability accepted the presence of so-called vice activities in their community. Rather, the process of urban segregation made the sharp lines leaders hoped to draw between licit and illicit spaces in the Black Belt more difficult to maintain, particularly with the increasing importance of com-mercialized leisure in structuring urban life, both black and white.

THE RACIALIZATION OF SPACE IN CHICAGO

The racial boundaries shaping the South Side of Chicago became increasingly sharp in the years leading up to and following World War I. Between 1890 and 1915, the African American population of Chicago grew from less than 15,000, or a little over 1 percent of the city's population, to over 50,000, or over 2 per-cent. After the Great Migration of black southerners to Chicago during World War I, the number increased to over 100,000, with the black population rising 148.5 percent between 1910 and 1920 while the white population increased by 21 percent.[7] This influx of blacks from the South contributed to the solidifica-tion of racial boundaries in the city, as the areas available to blacks for housing became increasingly circumscribed. Restrictive covenants played a central role in securing these borders. As a result of these efforts to stem the tide of "Negro invasion," the boundaries of the Black Belt, between Twelfth and Thirty-ninth Streets, State and Lake Michigan, were drawn by 1915. These boundaries would expand southward to Fifty-fifth Street by 1919. At the time of the riot, over 90 percent of Chicago's African American population lived in the South Side Black Belt.[8]

One of the factors fueling the expansion of the Black Belt was the avail-ability of less expensive housing in bordering areas like Hyde Park, Kenwood, and Woodlawn prior to World War I. Many of the hotels and apartment build-ings constructed for the 1893 World's Columbian Exposition now were vacant, and owners were turning them into rooming houses to try to keep them profit-able. Many whites in the area also began moving to the North and South Shore regions, farther from downtown, in areas that were more suburban in charac-ter. At a time when more blacks were coming to Chicago from the South and the Black Belt was increasingly overcrowded, these neighborhoods provided the cheaper housing necessary to help supply the growing population. Both white and black real estate agents rented property to the black migrants in large part because blacks were the only takers. Yet as the boundaries of the Black Belt expanded during and after the war, racial tensions were fueled. The greatest hostility was in contested neighborhoods that still were predominantly white, like Hyde Park and Kenwood.[9]

Restrictive covenants were not the only tactics whites used to keep blacks within the confines of the Black Belt. Some residents resorted to violence. Between July 1917 and March 1921, fifty-eight black homes were bombed in Chicago, most of them on the South Side. Victims of the bombings were blacks who had moved into white neighborhoods and both black and white real estate agents who sold property to blacks in predominantly white areas. These bombing incidents attest to the central role of territoriality and the racialization of urban space in shaping white response to black settlement patterns. As the commission appointed to investigate the race riot explained, "Bombing of real estate men's properties appears to have been part of a general scheme to close the channels through which the ['Negro'] invasion proceeded rather than a protest of neighbors."[10] Bombings, like restrictive covenants, served as a means to maintain the color line in housing and neighborhood composition.

REFORMING THE "SOCIAL EVIL" IN CHICAGO

The issues that shaped the racial segregation of housing also structured leisure relations between the races in Chicago. Twentieth-century efforts to promote a culture of respectability and eradicate vice exposed the ways in which race, space, and vice came to be intimately connected during the period of the Great Migration. These efforts also highlighted the extent to which it was the intermingling of the races in brothels, saloons, and dance halls that prompted widespread concern among urban reformers about the need to police the boundaries of these districts, so that by the postwar period, vice, and explicitly prostitution, were relocated to African American neighborhoods.

The emerging field of sociology—shaped largely by University of Chicago faculty, including Albion Small, William I. Thomas, Ernest Burgess, and Robert Park—provided the foundation for these studies of urban vice. These sociologists posited a spatial view of social pathology and its links to urban growth and used a variety of firsthand accounts to study these conditions. Sociologists, along with many urban reformers, believed that by observing urban life through the process of "scientific" investigation, they could understand the social, economic, and cultural factors shaping society and formulate methods for social improvement.[11] Most often these ideas for improvement involved reshaping the spatial geography of the city. Utilizing mapmaking as the basis of social investigation, the sociologists collected data on poverty, vice, delinquency, and ethnicity to formulate a comprehensive picture of city life. They worked closely with settlement house workers, such as Jane Addams at Hull House and Mary McDowell at the University of Chicago Settlement, to link social scientific inquiry with urban reform. These processes of investigation became the basis for vice reform.

The use of the term "vice" was widespread in reformist rhetoric at the turn of the century and often encompassed a variety of activities, both legal and illegal. Reformers lumped gambling, prostitution, petty theft, the sale of alcohol from unlicensed distributors, "lewd" dancing, and racial mixing together under the term "vice." The conflation of illegal activities with legal ones attests to the central role urban space played in structuring ideas about licit and illicit activity. Reformers looked to the physical landscape, and especially commercial leisure districts, for ways to "purify" the city. They argued that controlling, containing, and regulating spaces of commercial leisure would aid in eradicating vice. Moreover, even though legal definitions characterized activities like gambling and prostitution as illegal, these activities played an important role in structuring economic relations in black neighborhoods, where participation in the "formal" economy often was tenuous and unstable. Thus, as recent scholars of prostitution have shown, the distinction between formal and informal economies in black urban communities was ambiguous because the two were interwoven and dependent upon one another for creating employment opportunities and shaping economic exchange.[12]

Noted British journalist and reformer William T. Stead's analysis of the so-called Levee district on the near South Side pointed to the mixture of black and white "vice" and prostitution that intermingled to make this district so notorious and "depraved." He described the parlor houses, brothels, and saloons that gave the area its character and noted that black "houses of assignation" existed right alongside more elite white establishments.[13] According to police detective Clifton Woolridge, "Here at all hours of the day and night women could be seen at the doors and windows, frequently half-clad, making an exhibition of themselves and using vulgar and obscene language. . . . The habitués of this place embraced every nationality, both black and white, their ages ranging from eighteen to fifty."[14] What struck many observers like Stead was that the culture of the sex trade was not confined to the interior spaces of the brothel or parlor house but instead made its way into the street. As historian Cynthia Blair explains, "[T]he streets themselves were drawn quite aggressively into the sex economy." Indeed, it was the "very publicness of late nineteenth-century sexual commerce" that concerned most reformers.[15]

Efforts to address the "vicious elements" that existed in the Levee emerged by the late 1890s. Mayor Carter Harrison ordered police to force brothel owners to move their enterprises to other parts of the city. This effort reflected Harrison's concern that the presence of the Levee so close to the Central Business District would prevent that district from being able to expand.[16] It was noteworthy that Harrison's move to clean up the area resulted in having the vice district moved farther south but not eradicated entirely. At least initially, economic and political decisions, rather than concerns about the moral geography of the city, prompted reform. As a result, the location of the Levee simply shifted, moving south to Twenty-second Street and closer to the expanding Black Belt.[17]

Lingering concern among reformers about the continued existence of the vice district fueled the creation of the Chicago Vice Commission in 1910. Religious and civic leaders met at the Central YMCA Building to discuss "the social evil problem in Chicago." At the conclusion of the meeting, the attendants passed a resolution that the mayor be asked to appoint a commission "made up of men and women who command the respect and confidence of the public at large . . . to investigate thoroughly the conditions that exist. With such knowledge obtained, let it map out such a course, as in its judgment, will bring about some relief from the frightful conditions that surround us."[18] This emphasis on "mapping out" the course of action is significant, for it highlights the ways in which reformers understood vice spatially and foreshadows the geographic approach taken to eradicate it.[19]

The result of the Vice Commission investigation was a campaign to clean up vice districts, especially the Levee. In 1912, investigators descended upon the district to arrest offenders and shut down the flats and saloons associated with prostitution. The raids led to the demise of many of the sites, but others simply scattered to nearby neighborhoods. The simultaneous growth of the Black Belt and the anti-vice crusade in the Levee meant that, increasingly, both white and black prostitution moved deeper into African American neighborhoods.

Leaders in the black community expressed their outrage that the result of the vice campaign was the scattering of brothels, gambling dens, and "sporting taverns" into the Black Belt. The *Chicago Defender* stated, "The present vice crusade in this city is of considerable moment to Negro citizens." The paper chided black religious and business leaders for not playing a greater role in seeking to control vice. The *Defender* explained that the efforts of anti-vice crusaders resulted in "scattering the denizens of the red light district and menacing the residence districts of the race." Interestingly, the paper did not call for the eradication of vice. Like reformers on the Vice Commission, the *Defender* suggested that vice be segregated so that it would not take over the residential districts of the South Side. "Keep them from roaming" was the advice of the *Defender*, so that vice areas may be properly regulated.[20]

With the movement of vice out of more visible white districts and largely dispersed throughout the Black Belt, race and vice were even further conflated. Black race leaders recognized the dangers this association held for images of blacks in general. Numerous religious and civic organizations instructed residents and new migrants in appropriate dress and decorum, both in order to stave off discrimination and in order to promote a public culture of respectability that would counter the association with vice. The Chicago League on Urban Conditions Among Negroes (what would become the Urban League) instructed blacks on how to behave once they arrived in northern cities. Hard work, industriousness, sobriety, and cleanliness would lead to useful employment, their brochures explained. Members argued that instruction in public deportment was essential for instilling race pride, for "bad action and conduct are embarrassing to members of the race and reflect not only upon the individual, but react upon the masses." The league warned against overcrowding in housing because of its associations with immorality and highlighted the importance of living among respectable neighbors so that no possibility of illicit activity might be suspected.[21]

These ideals of self-help and race uplift shaped the black reform organizations in the city. Many "Old Settlers" looked to the black church as well as to new civic organizations to provide vehicles for promoting respectability within the black community. Like their white counterparts, these reform organizations searched for ways to promote respectability and industriousness among new migrants to the city. Yet unlike settlement houses, community centers, and other aid societies serving whites, the black organizations often struggled for funds and, at least initially, received little financial backing either from wealthy white philanthropists or from municipal government. That meant the ideology of self-help was particularly important in the black community and shaped ideas about the meaning of race pride.[22]

Black women led the way in establishing a number of organizations to aid blacks in finding housing, securing jobs, and adapting to urban life.[23] Ida B. Wells-Barnett's efforts at creating clubs to promote respectability for blacks in Chicago highlighted how these efforts increasingly were intertwined with calls for racial justice. Her marriage to prominent black Chicago publisher Ferdinand Barnett made her an even more important leader of efforts at race uplift in the city. The Negro Fellowship League was founded in 1910 by Wells-Barnett, the leading anti-lynching crusader who moved to Chicago after being driven out of Memphis as a result of her exposés of lynching and demands for justice. The league was devoted to providing housing for men and helping them attain employment. She pointed to "the problem of the boys" and argued that aiding black men in finding employment was one of the most important factors in shaping family stability and community advancement. The league maintained a reading room to provide wholesome recreation so that young men would not be "idling away their time at saloons or pool rooms."[24] Through her role in founding the league as well as other clubs, Wells worked closely with white reformers like Jane Addams and Mary McDowell to press for a variety of reforms, including an end to police brutality against blacks, reform of the court system, the promotion of women's suffrage, and, of course, the passage of anti-lynching legislation.[25]

In addition, black women helped lead programs at several settlements for blacks, including the Frederick Douglass Center and the Emanuel Settlement on the South Side. Both of these settlements included day nurseries and kinder-gartens for children, as well as reading rooms, athletic equipment, and training in domestic arts for young women. Wells-Barnett worked closely with Bethel AME reverend Reverdy Ranson and his new Institutional Church and Settlement on State Street near Thirty-fifth, which included a library, day nursery, music and business classes, as well as welfare, employment, and educational services.[26] Like their white counterparts, black women sought wholesome spaces of rec-reation that could counter the lure of commercial leisure and vice. This need for alternative spaces of leisure was even more pressing in black communities precisely because of the increasing ties between the geographies of race and vice in the city. Yet black settlements still could not offer the same level of support for "wholesome" recreation that white neighborhoods enjoyed. Black club woman Irene McCoy-Gaines lamented the inadequacy of facilities available for blacks in contrast to "the cozy clubrooms, well-equipped gyms, and swimming pools" of white neighborhoods.[27]

Black reformers received a boost in their efforts to provide wholesome rec-reation to counter the lure of commercial amusement and illicit activity with the opening of the Wabash YMCA. In 1913, this branch of the YMCA opened explicitly for use by African Americans. It was located at 3743 Wabash Avenue, in the heart of the Black Belt. The movement for a YMCA in the Black Belt began after a 1909 speech by Wells-Barnett to members of the Congregational Church in Chicago. Wells-Barnett stated that African Americans were denied access to the major sources of wholesome recreation in the city, including YMCAs and other sites of social uplift. Following the talk, Victor Lawson, the publisher of the *Chicago Daily News*, approached Wells-Barnett and offered to fund the read-ing room at the Negro Fellowship League until a black YMCA was established on the South Side.[28] In 1911, Julius Rosenwald of Sears, Roebuck and Company launched a fund-raising campaign to establish a black YMCA. He offered to pro-vide $25,000 if other Chicago philanthropists would make contributions as well. Several followed suit, including Cyrus McCormick, Mrs. Charles F. Swift, and the George Pullman Company. An additional $20,000 was raised from blacks within the Douglas community where the building was to be located.[29]

The establishment of the Chicago branch of the Urban League provided additional services to South Side blacks, both in terms of recreational facilities and with regard to aid in securing housing and employment. The Chicago chapter was founded in 1917 and served as the vehicle for promoting interracial reform efforts for the black community. Its focus was on the "adjustment or assimilation" of recent black migrants to Chicago.[30] The league sponsored programs in urban etiquette and helped new migrants find employment and housing. It also provided reading rooms and club spaces for meetings. According to historian Christopher Robert Reed, its board comprised many of the founders of the NAACP in Chicago in 1910. Members serving on both boards included Jane Addams, Mrs. Emmons Blaine, Sophonisba Breckinridge, Oscar C. Brown, Dr. George Cleveland Hall, Julius Rosenwald, and Celia Parker Woolley. Woolley, head of the Frederick Douglass Center, offered to allow the league to set up its headquarters there until its permanent office was built. Julius Rosenwald was one of the principal funders of the Chicago branch of the Urban League, which led to his increasingly prominent role as a philanthropist of black causes.[31]

One of the central goals of the Urban League, both in Chicago and nationwide, was to promote respectability among new migrants. The *Chicago Defender* published lists of do's and don't's put forward by the league. Some of the don't's included "Don't use vile language; Don't make yourself a public nuisance; Don't congregate with crowds on the streets . . . ; Don't encourage gamblers, disreputable women or men to ply their business any time or place; Don't leave your job when you have a few dollars in your pocket."[32] The last two warnings were particularly significant, for one of the greatest worries of middle-class black leaders was that new migrants would be drawn into the world of disreputable dance halls, saloons, and gambling dens increasingly structuring urban nightlife on the South Side. The Urban League encouraged new migrants to avoid places like the Stroll altogether and instead seek out places of wholesome recreation, such as the settlement reading rooms, church facilities, and recreational spaces included in the Wabash YMCA and the Urban League. The Chicago Urban League soon sponsored dances, socials, and athletic teams to counter the attractions of commercialized leisure.[33]

SPORT AND COMMERCIAL LEISURE IN BLACK CHICAGO

This emphasis on wholesomeness and respectability belied the intimate connections between licit and illicit recreation in the cultural geography of the Black Belt. The economics of black baseball in Chicago highlighted the increasingly ill-defined boundaries between legal and illegal economies, respectability and vice. Many black civic leaders touted black sports heroes and team owners as symbols of race pride and entrepreneurial success. At the same time, though, these proprietors of athletic teams and sporting venues often maintained closer connections to the "sporting world" than many black leaders wanted to admit. The narrowly confined borders of the Black Belt and the limited financial resources for black business success meant that licit and illicit enterprises often existed side by side and were operated by the same entrepreneurs.

In Chicago and other northern cities, baseball played an increasingly large role in the social and economic life of black communities. The *Defender* featured regular stories covering games between clubs in the black church league. Black teams also played in the Chicago City Semi-Pro League, competing against white teams throughout the city. More significant, however, were the phenomenal professional teams that graced Chicago parks. As early as 1900, there were five black teams in the city with paid players. Fans flocked to the games, and the *Defender* urged African Americans to support these teams as an expression of race pride.[34]

The *Defender* touted the expansion of professional black baseball in Chicago as a symbol of black entrepreneurial success. In 1910, Rube Foster's success as manager of the Leland Giants prompted him to break from team owner Frank Leland and form his own competing team. In 1911, Foster established a partnership with white tavern owner John Schorling and founded the Chicago American Giants. After the Chicago White Sox moved out of their South Side park at Thirty-ninth and Wentworth, Schorling bought the land and refurbished the grounds to house Foster's new team. According to the *Defender*, the rival team meant that black Chicagoans now had more opportunities to express their sense of race pride. "Now, with two splendid teams playing at the same hour, on the same day, the all-absorbing question is, 'What game shall I go to?'" The *Defender* answered the question by explaining that there were more than enough fans to support each team, and having the option of more than one game to attend should be seen as a source of pride.[35]

Frank Leland sought to keep fans coming to his park by highlighting its role in promoting race pride. After Foster established his team, Leland changed his ads to emphasize the black ownership of the team. His new ads read: "Upon the success of the Leland Giants this year depends the Negro's continuance as a factor in the baseball arena. The Park is the only Park in the city operated and controlled by Negroes. This should be sufficient for every Negro to attend the games at this Park." The ad also explained that the Leland Giants played "Genteel, Scientific, and Gentlemanly Ball," suggesting that the ballpark was a space of respectability and decorum for all classes of the race. That the sporting arena became such a charged space of demonstrations of race loyalty suggests the central role commercial leisure played in structuring the social and economic life of the Black Belt.[36]

THE STROLL AND THE CONSTRUCTION OF BLACK COMMERCIAL LEISURE

Frank Leland's mass amusement enterprise symbolizes the increasingly dramatic role played by commercial leisure spaces in structuring African American community life during and after World War I. Like white middle-class promoters of wholesome recreation, Leland touted baseball parks as appropriate sites for family entertainment. He also promoted his skating rink and dance hall, at Fifty-third and State Streets, as a source of family entertainment. The Chateau de la Plaisance, first opened by black businessmen Beauregard Mosely and Robert Jackson in 1907, featured roller skating from seven to ten-thirty at night and dancing from ten-thirty to midnight. By 1910, the Chateau was under the proprietorship of the Leland Giants Baseball and Amusement Association. Ads for the Chateau exclaimed: "Go where you will. Pay what you may, but the Chateau leads in wholesome, health-giving entertainment." The text went on to say, "Come away from the stuffy, tubercular, 5¢ death-giving, cheap theater and enjoy the invigorating, health-giving atmosphere of the Chateau." Admission to the Chateau was ten cents, making it accessible for all classes.[37]

Although Leland's Chateau represented only the most "wholesome entertainment," other attempts by blacks involved in the sporting world highlighted the difficulties in creating boundaries between respectable and illicit enterprises in the commercial leisure district of the Black Belt. The case of black prizefighter and world champion Jack Johnson is instructive, for it illustrates the precarious nature of the recreation business on the South Side.

After Johnson's victory over white fighter James J. Jeffries to secure the title of world heavyweight champion, he came back to Chicago amidst great fanfare and celebration. Moreover, he vowed to stay in Chicago and contribute to the life of the community by establishing a cabaret on the South Side. As early as December 1910, Johnson secured an option on a property on State Street near Thirty-first, the South Side Turner Hall. The property reportedly was worth $60,000, and there was some question about whether the association of German Turners that owned the property would lease it to Johnson.[38] The deal fell through, although the site later became home to the grandiose Vendome Theater in 1919, one of the largest theaters on the South Side. Johnson instead bought the property at 41 West Thirty-first Street and on July 12, 1912, opened the Café de Champion. The grand opening was a huge affair for the South Side. Crowds packed Thirty-first Street for blocks, waiting for a chance to view the elaborate interior of the club. The cabaret featured three stories, with the first floor devoted to a large barroom as well as the main cabaret where large orchestras, singers, and dancers performed. The second floor housed a café for private dining and drinking and featured a piano bar, whereas the top floor was reserved for Johnson's own apartment. Patrons flocking to the club on opening night marveled at the "delicately tinted walls and ceiling, the brilliant chandeliers," as well as the life-sized oil paintings of Johnson himself that adorned the walls.[39]

Still, Johnson faced repeated harassment from local and national authorities as a result of his very public liaisons with white women and his eventual marriage to a white woman. As a result, Justice Department officials sent investigators into the Café de Champion to drum up charges against Johnson and undermine his activities. Investigators made note of black and white prostitutes who worked in his club in various capacities, including as waitresses and entertainers. Johnson acknowledged that these women did serve as employees in his club, but he claimed that he did not in any way profit from their involvement in the illegal sex trade.[40] Johnson's 1913 prosecution on charges of violating the Mann Act, the law forbidding white slavery, led to the closing of the club and Johnson's exile from the United States.

Efforts to open a black-owned theater catering to blacks illustrated the important role of saloon and gambling interests in promoting black entrepreneurship. In 1901, several prominent South Side blacks, including physician George C. Hall (one of the founders of the Urban League), planned to open a theater at Thirty-first and State Streets called Havlin's Theater. Hall agreed to invest $20,000 in the theater. Since there were no licensed black architects in Chicago, he hired Saint Shuttle, a cakewalk artist, and "Billy" Caldwell, a vaudeville performer, to draw up plans. Yet the venture fell through for unknown reasons, so the dream of creating a black-owned theater catering to black audiences was put on hold.[41]

The promise of a black-owned theater in Chicago was realized in 1905, when Robert T. Motts opened the Pekin Theater. The theater grew out of Motts's popular beer garden and gambling house, the Pekin Inn, opened in 1900 at 2700 South State, in which Motts invested his earnings from his years in the gambling trade. Motts's role in creating the first theater featuring black performance and catering to interracial audiences highlights the intimate connections among legitimate business, "illicit" activity, and race pride on the South Side. Motts first came to Chicago in 1881 and made his money working with John "Mushmouth" Johnson, the leader of black gambling and prostitution in Chicago at the turn of the century. Johnson had worked for several years as a porter in a white gambling house and then used his money to open his own saloon and gambling house at 464 South State Street. One description of Johnson's gambling den said it was "ornate in the Gay Nineties style," with "glittering incandescent bulbs in rococo chandeliers." It went on to marvel at the "illuminated bar made of polished Honduran mahogany" and the "varicolored cut glassware and many brands of wine, liquor, and cigars."[42] Johnson's establishment attracted black and white clientele, rich and poor, who came to his resort to partake in all levels of gambling, from roulette to five-card poker. He also ran policy games, a form of lottery

FIGURE 14.1.
Pekin Theater, Chicago, Illinois. (Courtesy
of Hogan Jazz Archive, Howard-Tilton
Memorial Library, Tulane University)

in which numbers would be drawn randomly and people would place bets on the draw. Johnson's gambling house, along with his interests in crap games and policy throughout the South Side, made his one of the largest gambling syndicates in the city.[43]

Johnson's success helped set a foundation for Robert Motts as well. The money he made working with Johnson allowed Motts first to buy the beer garden and then to refurbish it into a legitimate theater. In 1905, Motts retooled the Pekin Inn and established the Pekin Temple of Music, featuring sentimental musical performances as well as ragtime, vaudeville, acts with popular comedic actors like Bert Williams, and stock theatrical productions. The Pekin was an immediate success, and black newspapers touted it as a symbol of pride for the entire race. The *Chicago Broad Ax* called Motts "the new Moses of the Negro race in the theater world." The article compared him to "those great race heroes" Benjamin Banneker, Toussaint L'Ouverture, and Booker T. Washington. In a July 1910 article, the newspaper identified Motts as "full of race pride."[44] Ida B. Wells-Barnett later said, "The race owed Mr. Motts a debt of gratitude for giving us a theater in which we could sit anywhere we chose without any restriction."[45]

The Pekin became a fixture in the black community and served both black and white audiences. The theater's larger civic role became clear in 1906, after Motts yet again revamped the theater and added more seating and additional ornamentation. That year, Motts offered to host a charity ball to raise funds for the Frederick Douglass Center. Ida B. Wells-Barnett coordinated the plans for the event and thanked Motts for offering the services of his "little gem of a theater" to the center. Over 100 patrons of the center were invited to the ball, which promised to be a success. Among the attendees were several prominent reformers in the city, both black and white. Jane Addams was joined in her box by leading African American club women, including Wells-Barnett, Mrs. George Hall (wife of the physician), and black physician Fannie Emanuel.[46]

Reformers such as Addams and Wells-Barnett recognized the central role commercial leisure sites could play in the civic life of the community even as they tried to encourage alternative forms of recreation for the city's population. Their support for Motts illustrated the recognition that "illicit" activities, business success, and civic responsibility could all be intertwined. The financially precarious position of the Pekin after Motts's death in 1911 also illustrated the importance of the theater as a symbol of black accomplishment. Motts was mourned by prominent business and civic leaders, both black and white, and banker Jessie Binga was an honorary pallbearer at his funeral. Following Motts's death, his sister Lucy ran the theater along with her husband, Dan Jackson. Jackson was the proprietor of an undertaking business located next door to the theater and eventually created the Metropolitan Funeral Systems Association, one of the most important black businesses on the South Side. He also was a prominent Second Ward politician and leading gambler in the city. Jackson used his gambling money to help the Pekin remain viable.[47]

The Pekin set the stage for the development of the Stroll on South State Street as the "great light way," the centerpiece of black life in Chicago, and the breeding ground for jazz. Following the success of the Pekin, several white theater owners who had establishments in the downtown Loop and on the North Side saw how lucrative the Black Belt could be. They opened clubs and theaters including the Monogram Theater, the Pompeii, and the Panama, which would become incubators for Chicago jazz. Black entrepreneurs also established cabarets, dance halls, and theaters on State Street, leading to competition for control of the South Side leisure market. Mushmouth Johnson's fortune played a role in the success of this market. On November 6, 1912, Johnson's brother, who inherited part of his estate, leased the property directly across the street from Binga's bank and built the Dreamland Ballroom.[48] The Dreamland, at 3518 South State Street, became the hub of black music in the 1910s and 1920s. It hosted some of the leading jazz performers of the day, including pianist Lil Hardin, cornetist Louis Armstrong (who married Hardin), singer Alberta Hunter, clarinetist Johnny "Baby" Dodds, and Joe "King" Oliver.

Blues singer Alberta Hunter recalled her days at the Dreamland: "That Dreamland was really some place. It was *big* and always packed. And you had to be a singer then—there were no microphones and those bands were marvelous. . . . There were no such things as intermissions and there was never a quiet moment. When you worked at the Dreamland, you worked from about seven thirty in the evening to three or four in the morning—and you didn't move out of there."[49]

The arrival of the Original Creole Jazz Orchestra in Chicago in 1911 signaled the beginning of Chicago's emergence as the capital of jazz. The band, led by Bill Johnson and cornetist Eddie Keppard, immediately secured a spot at the Big Grand Theater at Thirty-first and State Streets. Other New Orleans musicians had played in Chicago before, including pianists Ferd "Jelly Roll" Morton and Tony Jackson, who got their start in Chicago, playing at the bawdy houses of the Levee prior to vice reform.[50] Yet the Creole Jazz Orchestra's arrival precipitated the migration of jazz musicians to Chicago, including Joe Oliver and Louis Armstrong, and fueled the transition from the black southern musical tradition of ragtime to the jazz of the urban North.[51]

Black businessmen began opening additional cabarets along the Stroll, and this endeavor further attested to the strong connections between commercial leisure and the underworld in structuring urban nightlife. Henry "Teenan" Jones got his start in the cabaret business when he ran the Senate Buffet and Lakeside Club in Hyde Park before being forced out after efforts to make the area an all-

FIGURE 14.2.
King Oliver's Creole Jazz Band. (Courtesy
of Hogan Jazz Archive, Howard-Tilton
Memorial Library, Tulane University)

white residential neighborhood. Jones then moved farther north and joined with white businessmen Art Codozoe and J. H. "Lovie Joe" Whitson to own and run the Elite Café at 3030 South State Street, next door to the Monogram Theater. The Elite was a small music hall, with space for dancing, and featured such performers as pianists Tony Jackson and Earl Hines. In 1915, Jones opened his own club, the Elite No. 2, at 3445 South State Street. The club featured a white-tiled façade and was advertised as the "most elaborate emporium of the Stroll. Fine wines, liquors, and cigars; café and cabaret in connection." The *Chicago Defender* stated, thanks to Jones and his role in opening Elite No. 2, "[T]he race will have a . . . Mecca for High-Class Amusement."[52] Despite this praise, Jones was best known for his role as the "colored ruler of the underworld district," who, after the death of Johnson, controlled much of the gambling and prostitution that took place in cabarets throughout the South Side.[53]

By the time of World War I, South State Street was transformed into a mecca of dance halls, theaters, and nightclubs dominated by black musicians and interracial crowds. Black owners opened the DeLuxe Café, the Sunset Café, and the Royal Gardens along State Street, adding to this glorious space of leisure and musical entertainment. The innovation of the musicians, the lure of "suggestive songs," and the thrill of experiencing "indecent" dancing led white customers to frequent these places, contributing to the charged atmosphere of the Stroll. As jazz historian William Howard Kenney explains, "Black-and-tan cabarets sold not vice but suggestive African-American musical entertainment which helped customers create an atmosphere of inter-racial 'sensuality.' "[54]

The black-and-tans along the Stroll contributed to a sense of raw excitement and sensuality in part because of all the activity taking place, as Langston Hughes recalled, "from noon to noon." Despite dance hall regulations that required the establishments to close at one o'clock in the morning, musicians regularly played through the night and into the morning. According to Earl Hines, musicians on the South Side "worked seven days a week. There was so much going on that nobody paid any attention to the time of day. You'd go to work, get on the stand, play, come off the stand, go outside, get into all sorts of arguments, go back, play again, and so on like that through the night."[55] Trumpeter Joe "King" Oliver, who arrived in Chicago in 1918 to join the Creole Jazz Band, regularly played at both the Royal Gardens Café and the Dreamland Café. Other musicians regularly played at the DeLuxe and the Dreamland, which were right across State Street from one another. The Elite No. 2 fast became known as an after-hours club, with musicians playing their main jobs at clubs like the Dreamland and then moving on to the Elite or the Pekin. The *Defender* claimed that going to the Pekin for dancing was better than going to the Loop, for "dancers leave that section and go to the Pekin. . . . Refreshments are served and public dancing is from 11:00 to 5:00 a.m."[56]

The all-night activity contributed to the sense of risk and lasciviousness along the Stroll. The pervasive presence of so-called illicit activities within the confines of the dance halls further promoted this atmosphere. Alberta Hunter recounted her experiences in the early days of Chicago jazz and pointed to the variety of performances that took place at the Panama, at Thirty-sixth and State Streets. "Now the downstairs at the Panama was more of a quiet reserved type of entertainment. But upstairs it was rougher. Upstairs, we had Mamie Carter, a dancer, the 'shake' kind, and Twinkle Davis who danced and sang. . . . There, I would really lay the blues on. In fact, it was at the Panama that I introduced the *St. Louis Blues*. Oh yes, I was there a long time and people like Bert Williams and Al Jolson would come to hear me sing."[57] Other musicians recalled how pervasive policy and gambling were in the back rooms of the clubs. Earl Hines, for example, remembered being "sucked into" the gaming room at the Elite No. 2 on numerous occasions. According to musician Scoville Brown, backstage gambling in South Side clubs "was a ritual. This was part of the night's activities, to have a few games going on."[58]

The proximity between licit and illicit activity in the world of urban nightlife extended out into the street and suggested how definitions of respectability were fluid and permeable and also often were spatially determined. Alberta Hunter, for example, argued that she tried to maintain a sense of respectability even as she sang the blues and established a "rough and ready" reputation. She looked down on women who "get on the street and sell [their] wares right out on the corner . . . where's the refinement?" She explained that being on stage meant that "you had to enter properly and exit properly," with the theatricality of the performance lending an air of respectability.[59] The *Defender*, at the same time that it praised establishments like the Elite and the Pekin, decried the pool halls that existed along State Street in the heart of the Stroll. It argued: "Nightly crowds of men and half-grown boys sit in unsightly positions in front of the [pool hall] or line up along the curb and walls. . . . Vulgarity of the worst is freely used as peaceful women wend their way past the low dives." The article went on to claim that "no section of South State Street is exempt. Around 31st Street people to and fro from the various churches and patrons of the theaters are constantly thrown into consternation by these conditions and these dives and their attendant mob of loungers." The *Defender* urged the police to "close up the dives and lock up the loafers."[60]

It is interesting to note that the *Defender* placed churchgoers in the same company as theatergoers. Indeed, the quote highlights how the respectable and "illicit" elements of cultural life in the Black Belt rubbed against one another cheek by jowl. A survey of the establishments that existed along the Stroll further suggests how the boundaries between legal and illegal business enterprise were difficult to maintain, contributing to shifting notions of respectability. *Esquire* magazine's map of jazz spots on the South Side illustrates the multiplicity of spaces that structured the everyday lives of black Chicagoans in this district. It gives visual evidence of the proximity of spaces of leisure and labor, licit and illicit activity, private and public life. There were enough varied spaces at Thirty-first and State Streets, for example, that one would not have to leave that corner to have all of life's necessities met. Rooming houses and apartments were nestled between a music shop and utensil manufacturing company. A few storefronts away were drugstores, restaurants, a shoeshine parlor, a barbershop, and a bank. Interspersed throughout these spaces were the cabarets and theaters, including the Big Grand Theater and the Vendome Theater, one of the most grandiose theaters on the South Side, which housed Erskine Tate's Orchestra, featuring Louis Armstrong.[61]

The map highlights the specificity of place that animated life in the Black Belt. Each storefront represented a different feature of the South Side economy and was juxtaposed with those that seemingly had little relationship to it in terms of function. What united these spaces was the central role each played in structuring the quotidian lives of black Chicagoans. Unable to find basic services like barbershops, restaurants, and theaters that catered to them in other parts of the city, blacks on the South Side made these businesses along the Stroll into symbols of race pride and entrepreneurial success. They served as the fabric of a rich community life, and the interior as well as the exterior spaces of these stores, rooming houses, and cabarets became critical components shaping that community. The *Esquire* map highlights the people who made up this district and showcases the variety of places people interacted with in the course of their daily lives.

If leisure spaces of urban nightlife were places where many of the codes of decorum could be relaxed and rewritten, they also were places where racial divisions that structured other phases of life in the city could be transcended. The dance halls and cabarets of the South Side were places that increasingly brought the races together during a time of heightened racial tension. Where public parks and beaches posed grave danger for blacks, as the 1919 riot signifies, the clubs in the Black Belt were havens, leisure spaces shaped by blacks. Following World War I, with the advent of the Vitaphone and jazz recording, more white audiences were introduced to South Side jazz. Many white youth, especially young musicians, began making excursions into the Black Belt to experience firsthand the thrill of the new music they heard on their radios and record players. The most famous of these white interlopers was the Austin High Gang, a group of musicians including trumpeter Jimmy McPartland, saxophonist Bud Freeman, and clarinetist Frank Teschemacher. They grew up in the Austin neighborhood west of Chicago and forged close relationships with Chicago's black jazz impresarios. By the interwar period, white musicians had adapted many of the musical styles and improvisational techniques of black jazz musicians and, together with black orchestras, helped cultivate the big band sound.[62]

While white reformers continued their efforts to eradicate vice and to equate vice with black jazz, the white musicians who ventured into the Black Belt forged a new sense of connection to black culture. According to Bud Freeman, hearing black jazz musicians on the South Side "was the greatest education in music I've ever had. I was not only hearing a new form of music but was experiencing a whole new way of life."[63] The dance halls and jazz clubs of the South Side, then, became important sites for developing and promoting interracial exchange.

In addition, the relative freedom that spaces along the Stroll provided blacks allowed for the establishment of new black identities. The luxurious theaters and dance halls, the sophisticated dress of the musicians, and the excitement of urban nightlife created a new subjectivity for blacks, one shaped by their encounters with this variegated urban landscape. Claiming these spaces as their own, infusing them with race pride, and celebrating their role in fostering the entrepreneurial spirit highlighted the role of culture in shaping notions of citizenship and community. The Stroll offered a chance to express oneself in public through dress, speech, and performance that contributed to an emerging sense of racial autonomy that eventually would be translated into political power. Identity, power, and new ideas about citizenship were enacted and displayed in the process of engaging with sites of commercial leisure.[64]

Examining the history of leisure sites such as ballparks, dance halls, and cabarets exposes the role of a commercial leisure economy in breaking down some of the barriers between respectability and vice. This was especially true in African American communities like Chicago's Black Belt. The desire to promote black entrepreneurship and the importance of business leaders supporting more traditional sites of race uplift—including churches and civic organizations—helped redefine the meaning of race uplift and make it more expansive. At the same time, leisure sites, perhaps more than sites of work or housing, helped blur the lines of segregation in urban America. Within leisure spaces like ballparks, saloons, and dance halls, blacks and whites could cross the boundaries that divided the races, thereby at least temporarily redrawing the mental maps that delimited community and neighborhood.

NOTES

An earlier version of this essay appeared as chapter 6 in Robin F. Bachin, *Building the South Side: Urban Space and Civic Culture in Chicago, 1890–1919.* © 2004 by The University of Chicago Press. All rights reserved. Used and adapted with permission from the University of Chicago Press.

1. Langston Hughes, *The Big Sea: An Autobiography* (New York: Alfred A. Knopf, 1945), 33.

2. *Chicago Defender*, June 18, 1910, April 9, 1910.

3. Donald Spivey, *Union and the Black Musician: The Narrative of William Everett Samuels and Chicago Local 208* (Boston: University Press of America, 1984), 38–39.

4. See Robin F. Bachin, *Building the South Side: Urban Space and Civic Culture in Chicago, 1890–1919* (Chicago: University of Chicago Press, 2004), for a broader examination of the relationship between race and the shifting definitions of public space.

5. For further discussion of the race riot, see Bachin, *Building the South Side*, 247–250, 290–295; Chicago Commission on Race Relations (hereafter cited as CCRR), *The Negro in Chicago* (Chicago: University of Chicago Press, 1922); Horace R. Cayton and St. Clair Drake, *Black Metropolis: A Study of Negro Life in a Northern City* (New York: Harcourt, Brace and Co., 1945), 65–73; James R. Grossman, *Land of Hope: Chicago, Black Southerners, and the Great Migration* (Chicago: University of Chicago Press, 1989), 178–180; Arnold R. Hirsch, *Making the Second Ghetto: Race and Housing in Chicago, 1940–1960* (Cambridge, UK: Cambridge University Press, 1983), 40–45, 68–69; Allan H. Spear, *Black Chicago: The*

Making of a Negro Ghetto (Chicago: University of Chicago Press, 1967); and William M. Tuttle Jr., *Race Riot: Chicago in the Red Summer of 1919* (New York: Atheneum, 1970).

6. Kevin J. Mumford, *Interzones: Black/White Sex Districts in Chicago and New York in the Early Twentieth Century* (New York: Columbia University Press, 1997), 27.

7. CCRR, *Negro in Chicago*, 79–80; Grossman, *Land of Hope*, 3–4; Spear, *Black Chicago*, 11–12; and Tuttle, *Race Riot*, 74–76.

8. Drake and Cayton, *Black Metropolis*, 1:178–211; Otis D. Duncan and Beverly Duncan, *The Negro Population of Chicago* (Chicago: University of Chicago Press, 1957), 89; Spear, *Black Chicago*, 20–21.

9. CCRR, *Negro in Chicago*, 117. See also Bachin, *Building the South Side*, 250–254, for additional discussion of restrictive covenants in Hyde Park and Kenwood.

10. CCRR, *Negro in Chicago*, 123.

11. Of the many discussions of the "Chicago School" of sociology, I found the most useful to be Robert C. Bannister, *Sociology and Scientism: The American Quest for Objectivity, 1880–1940* (Chapel Hill: University of North Carolina Press, 1987), 34–60; Martin Bulmer, *The Chicago School of Sociology* (Chicago: University of Chicago Press, 1984), 1–11, 34–36; and Dorothy Ross, *The Origins of American Social Science* (Cambridge, UK: Cambridge University Press, 1991), chapter 1.

12. For further discussion of definitions of "vice" and its relationship to an "informal" economy, see Cynthia Blair, "Vicious Commerce: African American Women's Sex Work and the Transformation of Urban Space in Chicago, 1850–1915," Ph.D. diss., Harvard University, 1999, 182–186; Timothy Gilfoyle, *City of Eros: New York City, Prostitution, and the Commercialization of Sex* (New York: W. W. Norton and Company, 1992); and Victoria W. Wolcott, *Remaking Respectability: African American Women in Interwar Detroit* (Chapel Hill: University of North Carolina Press, 2001), especially chapter 3.

13. William T. Stead, *If Christ Came to Chicago* (Chicago: Donnelley, 1894), 249–252.

14. Clifton R. Woolridge, *Hands Up! In the World of Crime* (Chicago: Police Publishing Company, 1901), 482–483.

15. Blair, "Vicious Commerce," 239–240. See also Herbert Asbury, *Gem of the Prairie: An Informal History of the Chicago Underworld* (DeKalb: Northern Illinois University Press, 1986), chapter 4; Mumford, *Interzones*, chapter 1; Walter C. Reckless, "The Natural History of Vice Areas in Chicago," Ph.D. diss., University of Chicago, 1925, 12.

16. Carter H. Harrison, *Stormy Years: The Autobiography of Carter H. Harrison, Five Times Mayor of Chicago* (New York: Bobbs-Merrill Company, 1935), 311.

17. *Chicago Record-Herald*, May 31, 1905. Historian Peter Baldwin argues that these efforts at segregating vice grew out of reformers' failures to completely eradicate it. Segregation, then, was a compromise between reformers and the political officials and owners of illicit businesses to address the problem of vice in the city. See Peter C. Baldwin, *Domesticating the Street: The Reform of Public Space in Hartford, 1850–1930* (Columbus: Ohio State University Press, 1999).

18. Chicago Vice Commission, *The Social Evil in Chicago* (Chicago: Vice Commission, 1913), 7–10.

19. For further discussion of the relationship among vice, interracial sex districts, and reform, see Blair, "Vicious Commerce," chapter 5; Mumford, *Interzones*, 18–35; and Gilfoyle, *City of Eros*, 209–215.

20. *Chicago Defender*, October 12, 1912.

21. Chicago League on Urban Conditions Among Negroes, "Suggestions for Block Visitors," Arthur Aldis Papers, Special Collections, University of Illinois at Chicago, Folder 6 [1917].

22. For further discussion of changing definitions of respectability, see Kevin K. Gaines, *Uplifting the Race: Black Leadership, Politics, and Culture in the Twentieth Century* (Chapel Hill: University of North Carolina Press, 1996); Stephanie Shaw, *What a Woman Ought to Be and to Do: Black Professional Women Workers During the Jim Crow Era* (Chicago: University of Chicago Press, 1996); and Wolcott, *Remaking Respectability*.

23. For further discussion of gender, race, and reform, see Evelyn Brooks Higginbotham, *Righteous Discontent: The Women's Movement in the Black Baptist Church, 1880–1920* (Cambridge, MA: Harvard University Press, 1993), 185–229; Anne Meis Knupfer, *Toward a Tenderer Humanity and a Nobler Womanhood: African-American Women's Clubs in Turn-of-the-Century Chicago* (New York: New York University Press, 1996); Elizabeth Lasch-Quinn, *Black Neighbors: Race and the Limits of the American Settlement House Movement, 1890–1945* (Chapel Hill: University of North Carolina Press, 1993); Shaw, *What a Woman Ought to Be*; Daphne Spain, *How Women Saved the City* (Minneapolis: University of Minnesota Press, 2001), 118–122; and Wolcott, *Remaking Respectability*, especially chapter 2.

24. *Broad Ax*, July 20, 1913. For further discussion of Ida B. Wells-Barnett, see Alfreda M. Duster, ed., *Crusade for Justice: The Autobiography of Ida B. Wells* (Chicago: University of Chicago Press, 1970); Linda O. McMurray, *To Keep the Waters Troubled: The Life of Ida B. Wells* (New York: Oxford University Press, 1998); and Patricia A. Schechter, *Ida B. Wells-Barnett and American Reform, 1880–1930* (Chapel Hill: University of North Carolina Press, 2001).

25. "Ida B. Wells—The Mother of Clubs," Ida B. Wells Papers, Box 10, folder 10, Special Collections, University of Chicago.

26. Schecter, *Ida B. Wells-Barnett*, 181.

27. *Chicago Defender*, February 28, 1920.

28. Victor F. Lawson to Ida B. Wells-Barnett, June 10, 1910, in Victor Lawson Papers, Newberry Library. See also Schechter, *Ida B. Wells-Barnett*, 189.

29. *Chicago Defender*, January 7, 1911, August 26, 1911, October 11, 1911.

30. Quoted in Grossman, *Land of Hope*, 142.

31. Christopher Robert Reed, *The Chicago NAACP and the Rise of Professional Black Leadership, 1910–1966* (Bloomington: Indiana University Press, 1997), 46. Newspapers like the *Chicago Defender* celebrated the success of both the Wabash YMCA and the Urban League and their roles in aiding new migrants both through securing housing and employment and in promoting uplift and respectability. Yet these two institutions also served to divert money away from the more neighborhood-based black civic institutions, like Wells-Barnett's Negro Fellowship League. See Schechter, *Ida B. Wells-Barnett*, 189–190.

32. *Chicago Defender*, August 17, 1918.

33. For a discussion of the efforts of the Detroit Urban League to provide wholesome recreation, see Wolcott, *Remaking Respectability*, 53–64.

34. *Chicago Defender*, May 21, 1910, July 2, 1910, August 5, 1911, September 23, 1911; Robert Peterson, *Only the Ball Was White: A History of Legendary Black Players and All-*

Black Professional Teams Before Black Men Played in the Major Leagues (New York: McGraw-Hill, 1984), 63–64; and Harold Seymour, *Baseball: The People's Game* (New York: Oxford University Press, 1990), 262. For further discussion of African Americans in baseball, see Phil Dixon with Patrick J. Hannigan, *The Negro Baseball Leagues, 1867–1955: A Photographic History* (Mattituck, NY: Amereon House, 1992); David Falkner, *Great Time Coming: The Life of Jackie Robinson from Baseball to Birmingham* (New York: Simon and Schuster, 1995); John B. Holway, *Blackball Stars: Negro League Pioneers* (Westport, CT: Meckler Books, 1988); Holway, *Black Diamonds: Life in the Negro Leagues from the Men Who Lived It* (Westport, CT: Meckler Books, 1989); Mark Ribowsky, *A Complete History of the Negro Leagues, 1884–1955* (Secaucus, NJ: Carol Publishers, 1995); Ribowsky, *The Power and the Darkness: The Life of Josh Gibson in the Shadows of the Game* (New York: Simon and Schuster, 1996); Sol White's *History of Colored Base Ball, with Other Documents of the Early Black Game, 1886–1936* (Lincoln: University of Nebraska Press, 1995); and Jules Tygiel, *Baseball's Great Experiment: Jackie Robinson and His Legacy* (New York: Oxford University Press, 1983).

35. *Chicago Defender*, June 18, 1910.

36. Leland Giants advertisement in the *Chicago Defender*, May 27, 1911.

37. Ad in *Chicago Defender*, April 23, 1910.

38. *Chicago Defender*, December 3, 1910.

39. *Chicago Defender*, July 13, 1912.

40. Randy Roberts, *Papa Jack: Jack Johnson and the Era of White Hopes* (New York: Free Press, 1983), 138. See also Blair, "Vicious Commerce," 359.

41. *Chicago Inter Ocean*, May 12, 1901.

42. Quoted in Travis, *Black Jazz*, 26.

43. For further discussion of policy in Chicago and its relationship to black business and politics, see Mark H. Haller, "Policy Gambling, Entertainment, and the Emergence of Black Politics: Chicago from 1900–1940," *Journal of Social History* 24, no. 4 (Summer 1991): 719–739. See also Cayton and Drake, *Black Metropolis*, 490–494.

44. *Broad Ax*, February 3, 1906, July 9, 1910. For further discussion of the origins of the Pekin, see William Howland Kenney, *Chicago Jazz: A Cultural History* (New York: Oxford University Press, 1993).

45. Duster, *Crusade for Justice*, 290.

46. The charity ball exposed some of the tensions within the black community over the role of commercial leisure spaces, especially cabarets, in the larger civic life of the South Side. Several black ministers protested the event, claiming that it was immoral to hold a charity event for a settlement organization in a space that promoted "low morals." For further discussion of this event, see Bachin, *Building the South Side,* 273–276.

47. Robert E. Weems, *Black Business in the Black Metropolis: The Chicago Metropolitan Assurance Company, 1925–1985* (Bloomington: Indiana University Press, 1996), 1–5. Robert A. Cole, who took over the funeral association, used his money to support the American Giants, keeping the team in black hands following the death of Rube Foster in 1930. Weems, *Black Business in the Black Metropolis*, 63.

48. *Chicago Daily News*, December 14, 1916. The other portion of Johnson's estate went to his sister Eudora, who married banker Jessie Binga.

49. Alberta Hunter, quoted in Nat Shapiro and Nat Hentoff, eds., *Hear Me Talkin' to Ya: The Story of Jazz as Told by the Men Who Made It* (New York: Dover, 1966), 88.

50. Frederic Ramsey Jr., "Going down State Street: Lincoln Gardens and Friar's Inn Set the Stage for Chicago Jazz," in *Jazzways*, ed. George S. Rosenthal and Frank Zachary (New York: Greenberg Publisher, 1947), 22–33.

51. Burton W. Peretti, *The Creation of Jazz: Music, Race, and Culture in Urban America* (Urbana: University of Illinois Press, 1994), 52. For a discussion of leisure sites in structuring black communal life, see Farah Jasmine Griffin, *"Who Set You Flowin'?": The African-American Migration Narrative* (New York: Oxford University Press, 1995). For further discussion of jazz clubs and their role in urban nightlife, see Lewis Erenberg, *Steppin' Out: New York Nightlife and the Transformation of American Culture, 1890–1930* (Chicago: University of Chicago Press, 1981), 129–130. There are two Web sites that are particularly useful for tracing the locations of dance halls and theaters in the Black Belt: the Chicago Jazz Archive site, which can be found through the University of Chicago's Web site at www.lib.uchicago.edu, and the Jazz Age Chicago Web site, created by Scott A. Newman, at www.suba.com/~scottn/explore/sites/ballroom.

52. *Chicago Defender*, January 23, 1915. See also Kenney, *Chicago Jazz*, 10.

53. Stanley Dance, *The World of Earl Hines* (New York: Scribner, 1977), 36.

54. Kenney, *Chicago Jazz*, 24.

55. Dance, *World of Earl Hines*, 36.

56. *Chicago Defender*, quoted in Rosenthal and Zachary, *Jazzways*, 27.

57. Alberta Hunter, quoted in Shapiro and Hentoff, *Hear Me Talkin' to Ya*, 87.

58. Earl Hines, quoted in Dance, *World of Earl Hines*, 36; Scoville Brown, quoted in Peretti, *The Creation of Jazz*, 138. In addition, Dan Jackson ran a policy wheel in a gambling house above the Dreamland Café. See Haller, "Policy Gambling," 725.

59. Alberta Hunter, quoted in Peretti, *The Creation of Jazz*, 68.

60. *Chicago Defender*, May 23, 1914.

61. "Chicago Jazz Spots, 1914–1928," in Paul Eduard Miller, Esquire *Magazine's 1946 Jazz Book* (New York: A. S. Barnes & Company, 1946). The map appears in a foldout in the back of the book.

62. For further discussion of white jazz, see Lewis A. Erenberg, *Swinging the Dream: Big Band Jazz and the Rebirth of American Culture* (Chicago: University of Chicago Press, 1998); Kenney, *Chicago Jazz*, chapters 3 and 4; and Peretti, *The Creation of Jazz*.

63. Bud Feeman, *You Don't Look Like a Musician!* (Detroit: Belamp, 1974), 7–8, quoted in Peretti, *The Creation of Jazz*, 88.

64. See Robin D.G. Kelley, " 'We Are Not What We Seem': The Politics and Pleasures of Community," in *Race Rebels: Culture, Politics, and the Black Working Class* (New York: Free Press, 1994), 35–53; and *Freedom Dreams: The Black Radical Imagination* (Boston: Beacon Press, 2002), 161–162, for further discussion of race, identity, and citizenship.

Michael Kahan

Rights of Passage

The Integration of Philadelphia's Streetcars and
Contested Definitions of Public Space, 1857–1867

Late one night during the Civil War, a certain Mrs. Derry was nursing wounded soldiers at a church in Philadelphia. On her way home at eleven o'clock, Derry, a light-skinned African American ("almost white," according to one observer), boarded a nearly deserted street railway car. This simple act was anything but routine in Philadelphia, where most streetcar lines refused to carry Black passengers.

After Derry had been seated for a few minutes, the conductor came and told her to leave, adding that "no damned niggers were allowed to ride on that line." Derry asked that he consider the hour and furthermore pointed out that there were only two or three other passengers in the car, and none had objected to her presence. When these arguments failed to persuade him, she "finally asserted her right to remain." As testimony in her lawsuit later revealed, "The conductor thereupon called in the aid of two friends standing upon a street corner, took off his coat, seized hold of her, struck, kicked and finally ejected her from the car with great violence, tearing her clothes and inflicting some personal injuries."[1]

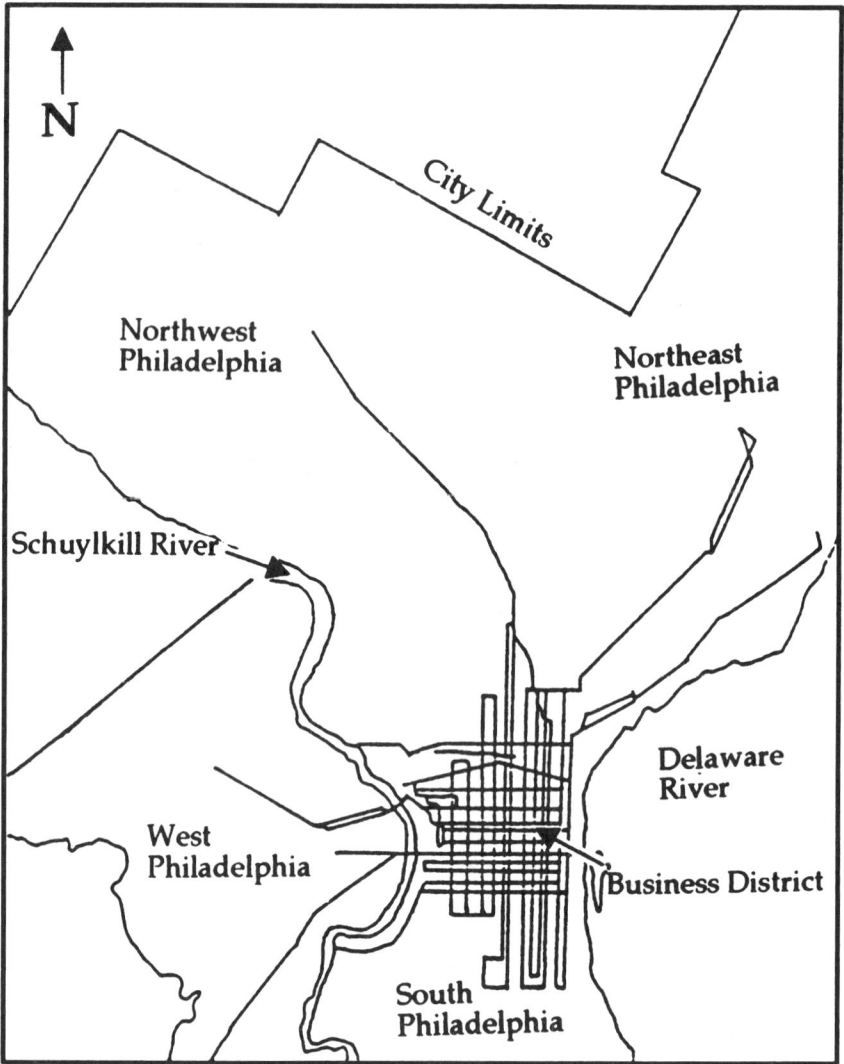

FIGURE 15.1.

Philadelphia street railway lines, 1860. (Adapted from
Roger Pierce Miller, "A Time-Geographic Assessment of
the Impact of Horsecar Transportation on Suburban Non-
Heads-of-Household in Philadelphia, 1850–1860," Ph.D.
diss., University of California, Berkeley, 1979, 269)

Although Derry won her lawsuit and $50 in damages, her case did not settle the hotly contested issue of whether African Americans had the right to ride in Philadelphia's streetcars. During and immediately after the Civil War, African Americans and their white allies used pamphlets, speeches, petitions, and lawsuits to make the case that streetcars should be open to all passengers, regardless of race. This essay interprets the struggle to integrate Philadelphia's streetcars as a contest over space by placing it in the context of a controversy that had occurred a few years earlier over whether the streetcar lines should be built at all. Both disputes raised questions that continue to echo today: Which spaces in the city were "public," and which were "private"? And what, precisely, did these designations signify?

Ironically, in the debate over racial exclusion from the cars, integrationists turned many of the streetcar companies' own arguments against them. Since the companies portrayed their franchises as public amenities, Black integrationists, together with some white Republicans, argued that African Americans could no more be excluded from the streetcars than from the public streets.

Ultimately, the battle to integrate Philadelphia's streetcars succeeded, with the passage of an 1867 law forbidding racial discrimination on all street railways in Pennsylvania. I suggest that this victory, although significant, was limited in several ways. First, many African Americans and others were still excluded from the streetcars by the price of the fare. Second, a standard of "respectability" that was enforced on the streetcars further limited access to the cars, especially by poor and working-class Philadelphians. Finally, the right to the streets was formulated as a right to transit, which opened the door to laws against non-transit-street uses such as begging, loitering, and making music. "Public" space remained contested terrain.

BLACK PHILADELPHIA IN THE CIVIL WAR ERA

Mrs. Derry was a member of the largest African American community in the North. In 1860, Philadelphia was the nation's second-largest city. However, its Black population of 22,185, or a bit less than 4 percent of the city's total population, was the largest, in both absolute and proportional terms, of any northern city. It was a city that one historian has described as a "contradiction" for African Americans. Economically, the city's employment structure severely limited opportunities for Black workers, resulting in a community marked by extreme poverty. Most Black Philadelphians worked as unskilled laborers or in some form of domestic or personal service to whites. At the same time, the city housed a small African American middle class, with some 15 percent of Black males listed as skilled workmen in 1860, and an even smaller but highly prominent professional and entrepreneurial elite.[2]

The economic situation of Philadelphia's African Americans had a strong effect on the community's spatial distribution. The largest concentration of African Americans was in the Fifth Ward, a neighborhood on the eastern edge of the downtown, convenient to waterfront opportunities for unskilled labor and to affluent residences where Blacks were employed in service positions. No ward, however, had a Black majority, and no ward was all white, suggesting the dispersion of much of the African American population throughout the city in housing in or near the homes of white employers.[3]

In spite of poverty and spatial dispersion, the Black community of Philadelphia was home to an array of vibrant community institutions, including churches, schools, mutual benefit societies, and an active antislavery movement.[4] Yet the "City of Brotherly Love" and the state of Pennsylvania were also known for virulent racism and severe limitations on the rights of African Americans. Black Philadelphians were barred from many theaters, restaurants, churches, schools, and other public or semi-public facilities.[5] The city saw outbreaks of anti-Black violence in 1834, 1838, 1842, and 1849. In 1838, the state legislature ratified a new constitution that repealed Black male suffrage, which had been permitted since 1790. In 1854 the state required separate schools for African American children in school districts with more than twenty Black pupils.[6]

In the racially charged years leading up to the Civil War, much of the discrimination and violence directed against Blacks centered on attempts to limit African American access to public spaces. Philadelphia bookseller John Campbell's racist tract *Negro-Mania*, published in 1851, asked rhetorically whether whites would "ever agree that blacks shall stand beside us on election day, upon the rostrum, in the ranks of the army, in our places of amusement, in places of public worship, ride in the same coaches, railway cars, or steamships."[7] It is significant that Campbell framed the question of equality in terms of spatial propinquity. His focus on spaces, particularly those of citizenship (such as the rostrum and the ranks of the army) and of public accommodation, reflects the strong connection between spatial access and racial equality in antebellum Philadelphia. It was in public spaces such as streets and squares that Philadelphians held civic celebrations and demonstrations, conducted much of their political discourse, and forged the city's identity. Access to such spaces was tantamount to membership in the public itself.[8]

During the Civil War, racial tensions over public space grew yet more pronounced. The Philadelphia-based *Christian Recorder*, the nation's only Black newspaper, noted in March 1863 that "in many places it is almost impossible for a respectable colored person to walk the streets without being assaulted."[9] In August, the mayor of Philadelphia, fearing an outbreak of racial violence in the wake of New York's draft riots of the previous month, refused to allow the Third U.S. Colored Regiment, based just outside Philadelphia at Camp William Penn, to parade in the city. In October, however, the Sixth Colored Regiment paraded in Philadelphia, scoring an important victory in the contest for access to the city's public spaces.[10]

PASSENGER RAILWAYS AND THE CREATION OF "PUBLIC" STREETS

By October 1863, Philadelphia African Americans could fight and die for the Union and could parade in dress uniform down the streets of the city, but they still could not ride the city's streetcars on equal terms with whites. To understand the controversy over streetcar integration, however, it is necessary to understand the debate that erupted around the grant of the original street railroad charters. In 1857, the Pennsylvania legislature considered chartering a corporation to operate a horse-powered street passenger railway in Philadelphia.[11] The idea raised a vocal protest among the city's residents. Two years later, after nearly twenty lines had been built (see Fig. 15.1), the mayor reflected that "perhaps no public improvement ever occasioned more contrariety of opinion than the occupation by the passenger railway system of the streets of this city."[12]

At the heart of the dispute was the question of who controlled the streets. As legal historian William Novak has argued, it was by no means self-evident in the nineteenth century that streets were "public" space. "The invention of public space was contested terrain," he writes. " 'Publicness' had to be constructed and defended in a political and social milieu fraught with conflict and tension."[13] In Philadelphia, the conflict over control of the streets involved three major actors: abutting property owners, the city, and the state. The struggle resulted in a victory for the state and the definitive creation of the streets as "public" space. Yet the state's triumph was also a victory for the street railways, private companies whose racial exclusivism illustrated the persistent limits of "publicness."

Debates over the street railways in Philadelphia illuminate the multiple and shifting meanings of the word "public." As both noun and adjective, the word was used with a variety of definitions by those on all sides. As a noun, the "public" was often said to mean "the people," "the whole people," or "the whole community." Yet even these seemingly straightforward definitions could raise more questions than they answered. Did the term refer to the people of the city or of the state? Did it truly encompass all the people or only a subset, such as those who voted, paid taxes, or owned property? Did it—indeed, could it—include women and people of color? As Katherine Masur has argued, African Americans in the era of the Civil War sought to widen the definition of the "public" served and protected by the government "to include all residents, not just the wealthy or the white."[14]

As an adjective, "public" could have broad and essentially positive connotations meaning "for all the people"; its opposite was "particular," which meant for the benefit of one or a few. But "public" could also have the narrower meaning of "government-related"; its opposite was "private," meaning simply "nongovernmental." Finally, it could have a negative connotation, particularly in the geography of gender: a "public woman" was sexually promiscuous. Many historians have identified the years around the Civil War as a crucial period of redefinition for the idea of the "public."[15] In the debate over Philadelphia's street railways, these shifting ideas helped structure the arguments of all parties; later, these ideas also shaped the debate over racial integration of the cars.

Property owners who objected to the street railways claimed that the streets were not "public" at all but were under the private control of the fronters, or owners of street-front property. Their claim rested largely on the fact that they often determined whether, when, and how improvements would be made to their street.[16] As in most American cities, fronters in Philadelphia paid for all new street pavements, curbstones, and sidewalks.[17] The system's emphasis on strong local control meant that abutting property owners felt entitled to a say in whether a passenger railway ran down the center of "their" street. Abutters on Chestnut and Walnut Streets saw no need to offer any specific reasons in one remonstrance against the railway; it was sufficient, they believed, to point out that the owners of the majority of "votable" footage and valuation opposed the railway.[18] Indeed, many fronters believed that the street was literally their property. Fronters on Third Street, for instance, filed suit in 1858 "based upon the assumption that constructing a railroad along Third Street would be taking their property for a public use."[19]

Yet fronters were not alone in their claim to control the streets. The city—or, more properly speaking, the municipal corporation—could tenably argue that it possessed the legitimate authority over the streets. After all, even if fronters decided when and how to pave the streets, they had to apply to the city councils for approval of their plans. The city's Highways Department, not the fronters, was in charge of paving intersections and crossings and of performing all repairs and repaving.

In fact, the city was bolstering its claim in the 1850s with a series of reforms that gave City Hall broader powers over the streets. The most important of these reforms was the consolidation of the City and County of Philadelphia in 1854, which gave the city greater control over an array of city services, including policing, paving, grading, cleaning, and lighting. In cities throughout America, the growth of these municipal services was linked with the creation of streets as "public" space.[20]

The increasing power of the city over the streets helped to erode the claims of the fronters; streets began to seem less like private property and more "public," in the sense of under government control. Yet the city, in its bid for control of the streets, was trumped by emerging legal doctrines regarding the power of the state over "its" cities. As legal historian Gerald Frug has explained, in the 1850s, cities throughout the United States began to lose local autonomy, particularly their ability to regulate businesses.[21] In Pennsylvania, the state legislature, heavily influenced by railroad investors, chartered twenty street railways for Philadelphia in the years 1858 and 1859. This liberality with charters angered the city councils, which would have preferred to control the population growth and property values that many expected to follow the railways. Yet in a critical 1858 case, a Philadelphia court ruled that the state legislature, not the city councils, spoke for "the people, the whole people" of the state and therefore retained the power "to direct how a highway shall be used by the public."[22] The court found the state's power over public highways "paramount" above that of the local authorities, and "supreme" to that of individual property owners. In other words, the court ruled that the streets were "public" in the senses both of belonging to the whole people of the state and of being under control of the state government.

In practice, the state's power over the streets had a clear result: the railways received their charters, over the objections of both fronters and the city councils. Streetcar lines sprang up rapidly, fueled by investors' eager speculation and aided by railway entrepreneurs' influence with (many said bribery of) state lawmakers. By 1876, Philadelphia had nineteen streetcar lines, with over 280 miles of track—more than New York City (which at that time covered only Manhattan) and Chicago combined.[23]

Less clear was what the railway charters meant for the status of the streets as public space. Railway proponents touted the charters as a great victory for the public. "As the street is the property of the whole community, and not of the few property owners fronting on it," wrote one street railway proponent, "it is not the community which must give way, but the privileged few whose property opens on the highway."[24] Opponents deplored the railways as private interests run amok: "Are the highways not 'public' highways?" asked one remonstrant rhetorically. "Can the authorities virtually compel the people to support a *particular line* of coaches?"[25]

Through this dispute, one can follow the shifting meanings of the term "public" in the mid-nineteenth century.[26] Railway companies used one definition to justify the building of the lines and another to justify exclusion of Black passengers. Integrationists insisted on a broad, democratic, and consistent definition of the whole community, and they sought to force the railways to adhere to the claim to serve "the public" in deed as well as word. Ultimately, the railways were compelled to integrate their cars. But this expansion of the boundaries of the public, although a victory for African Americans, was nonetheless limited and tenuous.

RACIAL INTEGRATION AND RIGHTS OF PASSAGE

From the beginning of Philadelphia's street railway system, the city's African Americans were excluded altogether from the cars on eleven of the city's nineteen lines. The other eight required African Americans to ride on the outside of the car with the driver. At least two companies tried running separate cars for African Americans, but these experiments apparently did not last long.[27] The policy of segregation became all the more intolerable to the city's Black population during the Civil War, when the poor treatment of colored troops preparing to fight for the Union and of Black women nursing the wounded came to symbolize the injustice of exclusion from streetcars.

Although African Americans were subject to a host of other injustices, streetcars were particularly visible, and therefore rankling, sites of "ritualized inequality."[28] Furthermore, streetcars were potent symbols of technological progress, urban growth, and individual freedom. Railroads and streetcars represented freedom of mobility, an especially significant right for African Americans in the mid-nineteenth century, both in slavery and in freedom. Furthermore, just as the railroad symbolized American expansion and the sense of a shared national destiny, so the streetcar represented the expansion of the city of Philadelphia and the 1854 consolidation of the city with its surrounding communities. Philadelphians' previous identification with a neighborhood or ward was expanding to become identification with the entire city. African American leaders understood that full citizenship in the city hinged on access to the transportation network that joined it together.[29]

In fighting the segregation of street railways, African Americans took arguments made earlier by the proponents of the street railways and turned these arguments against them. Just as the railways had argued in defense of their right to lay tracks in the streets, the anti-segregationists asserted that the streets were public space and therefore the property of the whole community, or, at the very least, all "citizens and taxpayers." William Still, a prominent African American community activist and businessman, voiced his contempt in particular for Quakers who were "so pre-eminently favorable to elevating the heathen in Africa, while forgetful of those in their very precincts—those who are taxed to support the very highways that they are rejected from."[30] Still implied that the economic power of African Americans as taxpayers entitled them to full membership in the public and unfettered access to public space. This property-based model of citizenship was exclusivist, but it articulated clearly the important connection between spatial access and municipal citizenship.

Benjamin Bacon, another Black activist, made a more radical argument in favor of streetcar integration: "Political equality everybody has the present or prospective right to demand—social equality nobody; for the barrier which separates the two is made up of private door-steps."[31] In other words, Bacon distinguished between access to private space and social equality on the one hand, which he viewed as privileges legitimately controlled by property owners, and access to public space and political equality on the other, which he viewed as universal rights. The streetcar, he asserted, was beyond the "private doorstep"; it lay in the public realm in which equal rights could be claimed by all.

The distinction between public and private, on which so much of the streetcar battle depended, inevitably raised issues of gender as well as race. In the mid-nineteenth century, American cities were undergoing a transformation in gender boundaries. As Mary Ryan and others have shown, from the 1840s onward, entrepreneurs and city leaders established new feminine spaces of commercial amusement, consumption, and recreation. These spaces, such as parks, department stores, and ice cream parlors, created new possibilities for women to venture out in public without losing their respectability. Yet the taint of the "public woman" remained a threat to any woman appearing in the street or other public space. Race intersected with gender in complex and contested ways. Many whites considered African Americans to be inherently morally dangerous, suspecting the men of sexual aggression and the women of loose morals.[32]

African Americans' claims to public space thus depended on reversing gender as well as racial stereotypes; white efforts to maintain segregation required upholding more traditional white ideas of both race and gender. Democratic mayoral candidate Daniel M. Fox thus boasted of his "manly" opposition to Negro equality, conflating white supremacy with masculinity.[33] (See Fig. 15.2.) Segregation of the cars, some whites suggested, was required to protect white women from the predations of Black men. Republican mayor Alexander Henry revealed the connection when he reportedly told a pro-integration committee that "I am not with you, gentlemen; I do not wish the ladies of my family to ride in the cars with colored people."[34] Benjamin Bacon confirmed in an anti-segregationist tract that the "fear of amalgamation" was a key motivation for excluding Blacks.[35]

Integrationists also sought to position themselves as protecting women from outrage by establishing that African American women were entitled to the protections and privileges accorded to white "ladies." At an anti-segregation meeting held in January 1865, those in attendance noted "with shame and sorrow" that "decent women of color have been forced to walk long distances . . . while visiting at our military hospitals, their relatives who have been wounded in the defence of the Country."[36] The case of Mrs. Derry, described at the outset of this

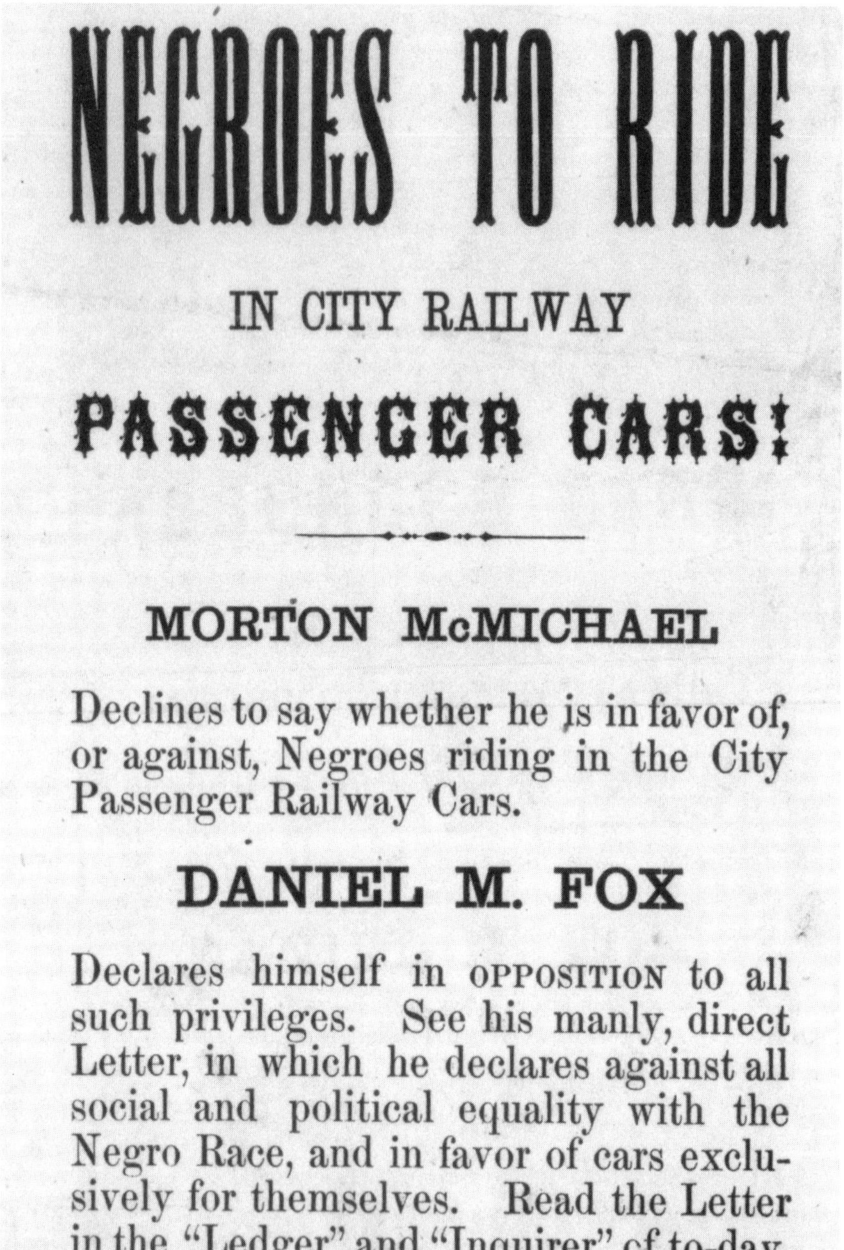

NEGROES TO RIDE

IN CITY RAILWAY

PASSENGER CARS!

MORTON McMICHAEL

Declines to say whether he is in favor of, or against, Negroes riding in the City Passenger Railway Cars.

DANIEL M. FOX

Declares himself in OPPOSITION to all such privileges. See his manly, direct Letter, in which he declares against all social and political equality with the Negro Race, and in favor of cars exclusively for themselves. Read the Letter in the "Ledger" and "Inquirer" of to-day.

FIGURE 15.2.
"Negroes to Ride in City Railway Passenger Cars!" Handbill apparently from Philadelphia mayoral campaign of 1865. (Courtesy of the Library Company of Philadelphia)

chapter, illuminated the links among gender, race, respectability, and the emerging role of the state in defining and regulating "public" space. In upholding the rights of this "respectable" African American woman, Judge Joseph Allison, a former Whig and American ("Know-Nothing") turned Republican, asserted that city railway companies, in their charters, were granted "the uses of the public highway of the city along and over which every person without distinction of age or sex, or nationality or color has a right to a free and unobstructed passage." "But," he continued,

> these grants by the Legislature were not intended to divert the highways of the city from the purpose for which they were established; . . . the object of the grant was in aid of this common right of passage upon and over the streets of the city; it was to render travel more easy and convenient to those to whom the right belonged, and this right is a common right; it belongs equally to the rich and to the poor, to the black man as much as to the white man.[37]

Allison here defined the right of passage in the street, and thus in the streetcars, as a "common right"—a phrase that occurs twice in this brief excerpt. In other words, he defined "public" highways as "common" in the broadest and most democratic sense of belonging to "every person."

The Republican *Evening Bulletin* endorsed the judge's reasoning.[38] Like Judge Allison, the newspaper explicitly connected the people's right to use the highways and the right of African Americans to ride the streetcars. "The public highways," the newspaper opined, "are not the exclusive property of persons of any particular shade of complexion." It went on to say that "the right of transit is not the exclusive privilege of any particular class, and the common carrier has no more right to refuse the privileges he pays for to the colored passenger, than he has a right to block his foot-passage through the common highway, or deprive him of the common blessings of light, air and water."[39] Again, the "public" highway was here a "common" highway, to be shared by the whole community.

The rhetoric recalled what the railways themselves had been saying a few years earlier. But now it was they, and not their opponents, being condemned as a privileged minority depriving the whole community of full use of the streets. The irony had little effect, however. Most of the railways did not admit Blacks on equal terms with whites until forced to do so in 1867. Philadelphia educator and activist Octavius V. Catto, together with other African Americans and white radical Republicans, pressed the Pennsylvania state legislature in 1866 to pass a statewide ban on streetcar segregation.[40] Facing the imminent passage of the Fourteenth Amendment, and with it the return of Black male suffrage for the first time since its elimination in the state constitution of 1838, Harrisburg banned discrimination by Pennsylvania street railways on March 22, 1867. According to B. P. Hunt, an activist who fought for integration, "exclusion from the cars continued in full force up to the last possible moment before the passage of the act" and "was even attempted after the act was signed. Cars were thrown off the track during the past winter because colored people were in them, sometimes in the presence of the police, and no effectual means were used to prevent it by [Republican] Mayor [Morton] McMichael."[41] Even if the streets were legally open to all, there was some distance to go before this ideal was achieved in fact.

CONCLUSION: A LIMITED VICTORY

For Philadelphia's African Americans, and for all who believed in public spaces accessible to the whole community, the 1867 law was a significant victory. However, this victory was limited in at least three important ways. First, unlike the streets, the cars were open only to those who could afford to pay the fare. As Theodore Hershberg and his fellow researchers have shown, paying streetcar fares, at least on a regular basis, was out of the question for most Philadelphians through at least 1880.[42] Thus, it was not entirely true that the right of passage on the streets belonged "equally to the rich and to the poor," as Judge Allison said in his charge to the jury.

In fact, even when poor and working-class Philadelphians found they could afford the price of a streetcar ticket, they encountered a second, more subtle, but no less real barrier: a standard of deportment and appearance known by the catchall term "respectability," which kept many off the cars or put them back on the outside platform. The street railways in their early years sought an elite ridership and took measures to ensure that their cars met strict standards of respectability. Many streetcar lines prohibited passengers to smoke or to board the cars while intoxicated.[43] Drivers were laid off for profanity or smoking.[44] Such efforts to attain respectability apparently succeeded; Sidney George Fisher, an upper-class Germantown resident, commented in 1859 that street railway cars "are now so comfortable that the most fastidious may endure them."[45] During the years of segregated streetcars, such fastidiousness, attributed to white women, was part of the rationale invoked for excluding Black riders. Benjamin Bacon mocked the attitudes of "the great, respectable, and intelligent portion" of Philadelphians who claimed that "they are not opposed, themselves, to riding with colored people—certainly not. The colored people may get into the cars if they can; they will not hinder it. But they do wish there were baths furnished at the public expense, for the use of these friends, in order that they might be made thereby less offensive to ladies." Black activists sought to turn this standard around, making it into a reason to include "respectable persons" of all colors, such as the 1865 lawsuit plaintiff Mrs. Derry, "a very respectable colored woman."[46]

After African Americans won the right to ride the streetcars, integrationists proudly pointed out that working-class Blacks had internalized the standard: "The conduct of our colored friends in the use of their newly acquired right has been all but faultless. . . . They resort to the cars sparingly, and, when not in clean clothes, voluntarily take their old places on the forward platform."[47] It is difficult to interpret such actions. Elsa Barkley Brown and Gregg D. Kimball remind us of the "fluidity of definitions of respectability," a value often attributed only to the middle class but rooted as well in working-class experience.[48] Indeed, African Americans have historically used claims to respectability to challenge negative stereotypes and thus subvert racial and gender hierarchies.[49] In this light, one might argue that Black passengers in dirty work clothes who decided to stand outside the car were not caving in to the expectations of white society; they were challenging those expectations, by showing, through their politeness, that they were not part of the "degraded class" of colored people.[50] In fact, they were overturning stereotypes by showing themselves superior to "the most offensive occupants of seats—the drunken, the profane, the tobacco-chewing, the unwashed, and the selfish" who were "of colors other than black or brown."[51] But the standard of "respectability" was a double-edged sword, which could exclude as well as include, demonize as well as elevate. Class divisions in Philadelphia, and especially within the Black community, could prevent working-class African Americans from enjoying the rights they had won.

In mid-nineteenth-century Philadelphia, access to "public" space and membership in "the public" were closely intertwined, and each underwent considerable redefinition in the crucible of war and reconstruction. The increasing "publicness" of the streets went hand in hand with a wider and more democratic public and thus with stronger rights for African Americans. But, in addition to class-based barriers, another trend threatened to undermine these expanding rights: the right to the streets, on which the integrationists' victory was premised, was already eroding. Judge Allison referred in his instructions to the "common right of passage upon and over the streets of the city"; the *Bulletin* similarly cited a "right of transit." Because the right to the street was only a right of passage or transit, however, it could be revoked from those who interfered with the efficiency of traffic circulation, such as corner loungers, street musicians, beggars, and street-corner orators. In the decades following the end of the Civil War, many such restrictions on the right to the streets were enacted in Pennsylvania and other northern states. As a final irony, although the right to use Philadelphia's streets for transit was established by the struggles of African Americans, many of the restrictions on other uses of the streets were inspired by the anti-vagrancy provisions of the South's Black Codes.[52] Thus, although

African Americans' victory in gaining equal access to the horsecars was a victory for the publicness of the streets, it was a narrow and vulnerable victory.

NOTES

1. *Derry v. Lowry*, Court of Common Pleas, Philadelphia County, May 1, 1865; bound as appendix with "In the Supreme Court, for the Eastern District of Pennsylvania, the *Philadelphia & Westchester Railroad Co. Plaintiffs in Error v. Mary E. Miles, Defendant in Error,* Brief of Argument for Defendant in Error" ([Philadelphia]: W. P. Kildare, 1865), 15. Also available at 6 Philadelphia Reports 30.

2. W.E.B. Du Bois referred to the period from 1850 to 1870 as the era of the "Guild of Caterers" in Philadelphia, an allusion to the Black entrepreneurs who amassed considerable fortunes in the catering business during this time. W.E.B. Du Bois, *The Philadelphia Negro: A Social Study*, with a new introduction by Elijah Anderson (Philadelphia: University of Pennsylvania Press, 1996 [1899]), 32. For population figures, see U.S. Census for 1860; J. Matthew Gallman, *Mastering Wartime: A Social History of Philadelphia During the Civil War* (New York: Cambridge University Press, 1990), 1; "contradiction" remark is in Philip Foner, "The Battle to End Discrimination Against Negroes on Philadelphia Streetcars: (Part I) Background and Beginning of the Battle," *Pennsylvania History* 40, no. 3 (July 1973): 261. See also Roger Lane, *Roots of Violence in Black Philadelphia, 1860–1900* (Cambridge, MA: Harvard University Press, 1986), 33–37; Theodore Hershberg, "Free Blacks in Antebellum Philadelphia: A Study of Ex-Slaves, Freeborn, and Socioeconomic Decline," in *Philadelphia: Work, Space, Family, and Group Experience in the Nineteenth Century*, ed. Theodore Hershberg (New York: Oxford University Press, 1981), 370–372.

3. *Population of the United States in 1860, Compiled from the Original Returns of the Eighth Census* (Washington, DC: Government Printing Office, 1864), 431–432; Lane, *Roots of Violence*, 20–21; see also Emma Jones Lapsansky, *Neighborhoods in Transition: William Penn's Dream and Urban Reality* (New York: Garland Publishing, 1994).

4. On community institutions, see Gary Nash, *Forging Freedom: The Formation of Philadelphia's Black Community, 1720–1840* (Cambridge, MA: Harvard University Press, 1988), especially chapter 6.

5. Lane, *Roots of Violence*, 17, 23–24; and Roger Lane, *William Dorsey's Philadelphia and Ours: On the Past and Future of the Black City in America* (New York: Oxford University Press, 1991), 170. On the notion of semi-public places (such as saloons and theaters), see Perry R. Duis, *The Saloon: Public Drinking in Chicago and Boston, 1880–1920* (Chicago: University of Illinois Press, 1983), 3.

6. Foner, "Battle to End Discrimination Against Negroes," 264.

7. John Campbell, *Negro-Mania: Being an Examination of the Falsely Assumed Equality of the Various Races of Man* (Philadelphia: Campbell and Powers, 1851), 545.

8. On the significance of public demonstrations in Philadelphia, see Susan G. Davis, *Parades and Power: Street Theatre in Nineteenth-Century Philadelphia* (Berkeley: University of California Press, 1988). On connections between public space and conceptions of "the public," see Laura K. Swartzbaugh, "Public/Private Geographies: Constructing Order in Chicago's Public Streets, 1893–1922," Ph.D. diss., University of Minnesota, 1997, especially chapter 4; and William R. Taylor, "The Evolution of Public Space in New York City,

the Commercial Showcase of America," in *Consuming Visions: Accumulation and Display of Goods in America, 1880–1920*, ed. Simon J. Bronner (New York: Norton, 1989), 287–309.

9. *Christian Recorder*, March 4, 1863, quoted in Gallman, *Mastering Wartime*, 184–185.

10. Gary Nash, *First City: Philadelphia and the Forging of Historical Memory* (Philadelphia: University of Pennsylvania Press, 2002), 230.

11. A note on terminology: "horsecar," "street passenger railway," "passenger railway," and simply "railway" are used interchangeably for horse-drawn streetcars running on rails for the purpose of intra-urban transit. A "railroad," in contrast, denotes a means of transport, usually powered by steam, for freight or inter-urban passengers.

12. Alexander Henry, *First Annual Message of Alexander Henry, with the Accompanying Documents* (Philadelphia: Crissy & Markley, Printers, 1859), 30.

13. William J. Novak, *The People's Welfare: Law and Regulation in Nineteenth-Century America* (Chapel Hill: University of North Carolina Press, 1996), 117.

14. Katherine Masur, "Reconstructing the Nation's Capital: The Politics of Race and Citizenship in the District of Columbia, 1862–1878," Ph.D. diss., University of Michigan, 2001, 160.

15. Philip J. Ethington, *The Public City: The Political Construction of Urban Life in San Francisco, 1850–1900* (New York: Cambridge University Press, 1994); Robin Einhorn, *Property Rules: Political Economy in Chicago, 1833–1872* (Chicago: University of Chicago Press, 1991); Novak, *People's Welfare*.

16. This provision was included in the Act of Consolidation as a gesture to the residents of the outlying districts who feared being taxed to pave the central city. On tensions between suburbs and center over paving, see Howard Gillette Jr., "The Emergence of the Modern Metropolis: Philadelphia in the Age of Its Consolidation," in *The Divided Metropolis: Social and Spatial Dimensions of Philadelphia, 1800–1975*, ed. William W. Cutler III and Howard Gillette Jr. (Westport, CT: Greenwood Press, 1980), 8; for the provision itself, see *A Further Supplement to an Act Entitled an Act to Incorporate the City of Philadelphia* . . . (Philadelphia: Crissy & Markley, Printers, 1861), 33, sec. 40.

17. On curbs and sidewalks in Philadelphia, see *Digest of the Acts of Assembly Relating to the City of Philadelphia* (Philadelphia: Crissy & Markley, Printers, 1860), 130–139. For other cities, see Robin Einhorn, *Property Rules*, 104–126; see also Clay McShane, *Down the Asphalt Path: The Automobile and the American City* (New York: Columbia University Press, 1994), especially chapter 4.

18. "Remonstrance of Property Owners on Chestnut and Walnut Streets, Against the Sanctioning by Councils of Any Act of the Legislature, to the Central Rail Road Company, Authorizing the Laying of Rails Through Said Streets" (Philadelphia: B. Franklin Jackson, Printer, 1858), 9–10.

19. *Faust et al. v. Passenger Railway Company*, 3 Phila. Reports, 169.

20. Novak, *People's Welfare*, 116.

21. Gerald Frug, "The City as a Legal Concept," *Harvard Law Review* 93, no. 6 (1980): 1108; see also Frug, *City Making: Building Communities Without Building Walls* (Princeton, NJ: Princeton University Press, 1999), chapter 2. For a detailed study of how this legal shift played out in one city, see Henrik Hartog, *Public Property and Private Power: The Corporation of the City of New York in American Law, 1730–1870* (Chapel Hill: University of

North Carolina Press, 1983). Howard Gillette has emphasized that Philadelphia municipal politics in the nineteenth century cannot be understood outside the context of state politics. Gillette, "Corrupt and Contented: Philadelphia's Political Machine, 1865–1887," Ph.D. diss., Yale University, 1970.

22. *Faust et al. v. Passenger Railway Company*, 166. In a separate case, the courts ruled that the same principle applied to the footway as well as the cartway: "A street railway company, in laying its tracks on a street, may take a portion of the footway at a point where it is necessary to make a curve. The footway of a public street is in no proper sense private property no more than is that portion of the street appropriated as a cartway." *Clark v. Second and Third Streets Passenger Railroad*, 3 Phila. 259 (1858), as quoted in Albert B. Weimer, *The Law of Railroads in Pennsylvania, Including the Law Relating to Street Railways*, vol. 2 (Philadelphia: T. & J. W. Johnson, 1893), 892.

23. Edmund Stirling, "Inside Transit Facts," *Philadelphia Public Ledger*, February 17, 1930, 3; and George E. Waring, *Report on the Social Statistics of Cities* (1880; reprint, New York: Arno Press, 1970).

24. Central Passenger Railway Company, "A Consideration of the Subject of the Central Passenger Railway, Being a Railway for Passengers Only, Proposed to Be Run from Second to Twenty-Third Street, via Walnut and Chestnut Streets, in the City of Philadelphia," 3rd ed. (Philadelphia: W. B. Zieber, 1858), inside back cover.

25. "Address and Remonstrance Adverse to Vacating the Licenses Granted to the Franklin Avenue Line of Omnibuses" (Philadelphia: Crissy & Markley, Printers, 1857), 2 (emphasis in original).

26. This was a time of significant flux in the legal meaning of "public"; for example, the distinction between public and private corporations, which had its roots in the late eighteenth century, became more salient in the 1850s, with significant consequences for the status of cities. See Frug, *City Making*, 39–45; and Morton J. Horwitz, *The Transformation of American Law, 1780–1860* (Cambridge, MA: Harvard University Press, 1977), 111–114.

27. The best secondary account of the desegregation of Philadelphia's streetcars is Philip S. Foner's two-part article, "The Battle to End Discrimination Against Negroes on Philadelphia Streetcars: (Part I) Background and Beginning of the Battle," *Pennsylvania History* 40 (July 1973): 261–292; and "(Part II) The Victory," *Pennsylvania History* 40 (October 1973): 355–379. The information in this paragraph is from 1:262, 268, and 286. For other accounts, see Frederic W. Speirs, *The Street Railway System of Philadelphia: Its History and Present Condition* (Baltimore: Johns Hopkins University Press, 1897), 23–27; Du Bois, *Philadelphia Negro*, 38; Stirling, "Inside Transit Facts," *Public Ledger*, February 15, 1930, 3; Lane, *Roots of Violence in Black Philadelphia*, 48–51.

28. Masur, "Reconstructing the Nation's Capital," 124.

29. John Hepp emphasizes the role that electric trolleys played in knitting together the spaces of the "bourgeois city" later in the nineteenth century. See Hepp, *The Middle-Class City: Transforming Space and Time in Philadelphia, 1876–1926* (Philadelphia: University of Pennsylvania Press, 2003), 25–48. On the importance of the freedom of mobility for African Americans, although with a focus on the South, see William Cohen, *At Freedom's Edge: Black Mobility and the Southern White Quest for Racial Control, 1861–1915* (Baton Rouge: Louisiana State University Press, 1991).

30. William Still, "A Brief Narrative of the Struggle for the Rights of the Colored People of Philadelphia in the City Railway Cars, and a Defence of William Still . . ." (1867; reprint, n.p., 1969), 3.

31. Benjamin Bacon, *Why Colored People Are Excluded from the Street Cars* (Philadelphia: Merrihew & Son, 1866), 24.

32. Mary Ryan, *Women in Public: Between Banners and Ballots, 1825–1880* (Baltimore: Johns Hopkins University Press, 1990), chapter 2. See also Masur, "Reconstructing the Nation's Capital," 111–123.

33. Morton McMichael and Daniel M. Fox, "Negroes to Ride in City Railway Passenger Cars!" Library Company of Philadelphia, 1865.

34. Bacon, *Why Colored People Are Excluded*, 3–4.

35. Ibid., 17, 24.

36. Colored People and Street-car Committee, "At a Meeting Held at Concert Hall," Library Company of Philadelphia, 1865, 1.

37. *Derry v. Lowry*, 16–17. On Allison, see Charles Morris, ed., *Makers of Philadelphia: An Historical Work* (Philadelphia: L. R. Hamersly, 1894), 75.

38. On the *Bulletin*, see J. Thomas Scharf and Thompson Westcott, *History of Philadelphia, 1609–1884* (Philadelphia: L. H. Everts, 1884), 3:2018.

39. Philadelphia *Evening Bulletin*, May 11, 1865; quoted in Foner, "Battle to End Discrimination," 2:360–361.

40. Harry C. Silcox, "Nineteenth-Century Philadelphia Black Militant: Octavius V. Catto (1839–1871)," *Pennsylvania History* 44 (January 1977): 65.

41. B. P. Hunt, "Report of the Committee Appointed for the Purpose of Securing to Colored People in Philadelphia the Right to the Use of the Street-Cars" (Philadelphia: Merrihew & Son, 1867), 5.

42. Theodore Hershberg et al., "The 'Journey-to-Work': An Empirical Investigation of Work, Residence and Transportation, Philadelphia, 1850 and 1880," in *Philadelphia*, ed. Hershberg, 143–147.

43. Alexander Easton, *A Practical Treatise on Street or Horse-Power Railways: Their Location, Construction, and Management* (Philadelphia: Crissy & Markley, Printers, 1859), 104.

44. Philadelphia City Passenger Railway Company, *Drivers Book*, 1883, in Railroad Papers, Dickinson College Archives, entries for J. Fleming, p. 69, and John Reed, p. 93.

45. Sidney George Fisher, *A Philadelphia Perspective: The Diary of Sidney George Fisher Covering the Years 1834–1871,* ed. Nicholas B. Wainwright (Philadelphia: Historical Society of Pennsylvania, 1967), 316, entry for February 1, 1859.

46. Foner, "The Battle to End Discrimination," 1:288–289; and *"Philadelphia & Westchester Railroad Co. Plaintiffs in Error v. Mary E. Miles, Defendant in Error,"* 15.

47. Hunt, "Report of the Committee," 6.

48. Elsa Barkley Brown and Gregg D. Kimball, "Mapping the Terrain of Black Richmond," *Journal of Urban History* 21, no. 3 (March 1995): 333–334.

49. Evelyn Brooks Higginbotham, *Righteous Discontent: The Women's Movement in the Black Baptist Church, 1880–1920* (Cambridge, MA: Harvard University Press, 1993), 188–195.

50. Still, "Brief Narrative," 4.

51. Hunt, "Report of the Committee," 6.

52. Amy Dru Stanley, "Beggars Can't Be Choosers: Compulsion and Contract in Postbellum America," *Journal of American History* 78 (March 1992): 1283–1293.

Michelle R. Scott

The "Sweetest Street in the World"

Recreational Life on Chattanooga's Ninth Street

Legendary 1920s blues singer Bessie Smith, "Empress of the Blues," is a prominent figure in American popular culture and African American history. The
depictions of Smith in a jeweled gown and feather headdress belting out the
blues are familiar images of the musical artist known for her renditions of "St.
Louis Blues" and "'Tain't Nobody's Bizness If I Do." Yet, Smith began her career
as an amateur performer on Ninth Street in Chattanooga, Tennessee, the city
of her birth. Ninth Street, or the "sweetest street in the world" to its African
American inhabitants, was the gateway to Chattanooga's entertainment and recreation scene. The restaurants, saloons, railway stations, and street corners of
Ninth Street were the physical spaces in which working-class African Americans
cemented their communal bonds and sought refuge from mainstream society.

On West Ninth the impoverished African American residents of Blue Goose
Hollow could cross paths with the elite white socialites of Cameron Hill as they
all traveled into the heart of the city. Some blocks farther down Ninth was the

FIGURE 16.1.
"The Sweetest Street," corner of Ninth and
Market Streets, Chattanooga, Tennessee.
(Courtesy of Library of Congress, Photos
and Prints Division, LCD4-19992)

commercial district, a place where "bankers and brokers, merchants and manufacturers, lawyers and doctors, and yes even politicians [could meet] on common
ground."[1] As one followed the bend in Ninth just past the Union Railroad station
and the elegant Read House hotel, East Ninth Street, the heart of downtown
black Chattanooga, came into sight. Although many of the commercial establishments of East Ninth generally catered to African American customers, a visitor could find Charles Zegelbaum's jewelry store, C. J. McFarland's shop, and
Shweidelson Brothers' ladies tailors in the same block as the offices of African
American lawyer J. W. White and the black hairdresser J. T. Higgins.[2] In the midst
of this medley of shops, professional offices, restaurants, and boardinghouses lay
the saloons and theaters that brought some of the most popular musical fare of
the period to the city. It was in the streets and sidewalks in front of these social
establishments that future entertainers, such as Bessie Smith, Lovie Austin, and
Roland Hayes, perfected their craft.

The adventures of Ninth Street called to Chattanooga residents as early as 1900. Interestingly, the twentieth-century status of East Ninth Street as a vibrant hub of black life can be traced to the early developmental years of the city. Prior to the Civil War, the area had been primarily waterlogged land that contained a pond local women used for washing clothes.[3] After the Civil War and the onset of emancipation, freedpersons settled in the area and eventually purchased small plots of this land, largely because of its undesirability to the general white population. As the black population grew in size, the East Ninth area became a hub for the newly built African American churches, businesses, and professional offices of the late 1890s.[4] By the onset of the twentieth century, the relatively self-sufficient community drew praise from the national African American press:

> It is simply amazing to note the progress of the people of Chattanooga, with their splendid business enterprises, standing as a monument to their thrift and energy. I was simply amazed when I was informed that a greater portion of them came from the lowest positions as menials on the farms and on the railroads, in the mines and in the foundries. . . . This much can be said of the business Negroes of Chattanooga, that they rank head and shoulder with those of any city of similar size in the country.[5]

It was the vast number of such institutions, including drugstores, physician's offices, restaurants, boarding homes, and churches, that led several residents to later refer to East Ninth as the "Big Nine." Indeed, Big Nine was a street that predated and, in many black Chattanoogans' eyes, rivaled Memphis's Beale Street.[6]

Just as Beale Street was home to the musical and recreational activities of Memphis blacks, so too was East Ninth Street a center of entertainment as well as commerce for African Americans in Chattanooga. The area's theaters, eating houses, and saloons hosted many of the nation's traveling revues as well as aspiring local entertainers. Remarkably, the early boom period of Ninth Street (approximately 1900–1917) coincided with a historical moment in which several African American musical genres were on the rise.[7] By the 1900s, locally rooted work songs and folk ballads collided with the golden age of black minstrelsy, ragtime, the dawn of black vaudeville theater, and a brass band movement to create an emerging blues music culture. It was during this period that Bessie Smith became aware of the secular musical life of the city.

AMATEUR MUSIC

Among the first elements of Chattanooga's musical culture one encountered were the sounds that emanated from the city's laborers—the community's work songs. As a child surrounded by washerwomen, including both her mother, Laura, and her sister, Viola, Bessie might have overheard the murmured tunes that many laundresses used to lessen the monotony of laundry work. Atlanta domestic Ella Mae Hendrix recalls that her mother would wash the family's laundry in the yard in front of their shotgun house while singing "I'm on the battlefield; I'm on the battlefield for my Lord."[8] Similarly, black entertainer Tom Fletcher recounted that his first musical encounters included hearing his mother intone spirituals like "Nobody Knows the Trouble I Seen" on wash day.[9] According to historian Lawrence Levine, African American work songs "were characteristically marked by a realistic depiction of the worker's situation."[10] Hence, Hendrix's mother's choice of singing "I'm on the battlefield" or Fletcher's mother's selection of "Nobody Knows" could represent how they and other laundresses felt about their work—that it was a "battle" to complete the burdensome task of washing and that "nobody" understood their plight of trying to support families on the incomes earned through arduous manual labor. Comparably, Bessie could have heard snippets of church hymns or even the wordless humming from her mother, sister, and other neighboring washerwomen. These melodies arguably offered some mental escape from the labor-intensive work at hand—a function of blues music. Although the "classic blues" format that Bessie and her counterparts later popularized in the early 1920s was just emerging as the twentieth century began, Bessie probably heard her first strains of the precursors to classic blues on the streets of her Blue Goose Hollow neighborhood in the form of washerwomen's work songs.[11]

Traveling through the Ninth Street area one would encounter other work songs and street cries from local laborers. One of the most noted figures in Chattanooga lore was the Rev. Addison Cole, known as Big Wheel. As both a pastor and general laborer he could be heard on West Ninth Street prior to 1910 in any parade, sounding the cry "Let Big Wheel roll on it," an adaptation of a work song he chanted while working at a wheelbarrow-manufacturing company.[12] Although his antics were remembered by local residents as quite eccentric, his familiar chant would draw people to him and perhaps they would remain to hear his street evangelizing. Other cries could be heard from street vendors or eating house (restaurant) operators like Rhoda Jennings, "Aunt Roddy," who called attention to her fish and chicken shack with her lively personality and songs.[13] Aunt Roddy's eating house stood on West Ninth between Poplar and Pine Streets and was frequented by both white and black customers.[14] Bessie would have encountered these and other songs that stemmed from the labors of working citizens, and these songs provided her with a foundation on which she could build her musical stylings.

Another type of music that Bessie was exposed to was the genre of popular tunes played at local rent parties, or "chittlin struts." Gwendolyn Smith Bailey,

Bessie's grandniece, maintained that rent parties, in which the resident of an apartment might charge ten cents for entry in exchange for an evening of music, dance, and food, was one of the most popular recreational outlets for the local lower-income black community, aside from theater shows and saloon entertainment.[15] Thomas Dorsey, a young pianist and composer who later met Bessie Smith and Ma Rainey on the black vaudeville circuit, recalled that a rent party was "a little get together, little functions, a few people give to sell their chitlins or sell their beans . . . you got all the food you could eat, all the liquor you could drink, and a good looking woman to fan you."[16]

PROFESSIONAL ENTERTAINMENT

Work songs of the street and popular party tunes attracted Bessie's attention, and she would additionally be mesmerized by the sights and sounds of the various minstrel shows, circuses, and vaudeville acts that traveled through the city on a regular basis. Traveling revues like the Thayer & Noyes Great U.S. Circus and mainstream minstrel shows like Bishop's Variety and Cumberland Minstrels had played in Chattanooga even prior to the end of the Civil War, and by the 1870s, colored minstrel acts like the Original Georgia Minstrels and Barlow, Wilson, Primrose and West's Minstrels played the City Auditorium in the downtown sector of the town.[17] By the 1890s, African American shows came to Chattanooga quite frequently, as evidenced by the 1893 theater season, which hosted over nine minstrel and variety shows in the midst of several dozen mainstream and classical performances.[18]

Chattanooga's geographic location and involvement in railway manufacture furthered the city's entertainment industry and aided the frequency in which troupes were able to visit the mid-sized southern city. With two railway stations, Union Station and Terminal Station, and as the terminus of ten railway lines, including the Nashville; Chattanooga & St. Louis; Chattanooga Southern; Alabama Great Southern; Tennessee Alabama & Georgia; Cincinnati New Orleans, & Texas; and Cincinnati Southern lines, Chattanooga was connected to most of the major cities in the nation.[19] Railway scheduling helped facilitate "layover" performances in which a musical troupe en route from a larger city like Atlanta, New Orleans, Memphis, or even New York might have just enough time to perform one show before moving on to a longer run in another city or state. Donald Clyde Runyan maintains that the city's New Opera Theater actually worked with rail lines in order to ensure that traveling acts could play the city "by occasionally timing trains to correspond within the hour of a performance."[20] Railroads further aided the city's entertainment in that porters could transmit knowledge of popular tunes from one city to another.[21] Hence, the latest sounds from Memphis's Beale Street, Atlanta's Decatur Street, or New

Orleans's Storyville district might be heard in a Ninth Street saloon if a porter brought the latest sheet music or personal knowledge of the new music with him from his city layovers.[22]

The traveling black revues were generally advertised in the *Chattanooga Daily Times*, in the African American newspaper *Blade,* and on billboards throughout downtown, particularly near the Union Station on Ninth Street. Often, traveling revues sent handbills ahead of their performance, alerting the city of their impending arrival. Show promoters wrote these handbills to raise the prospective audience's level of anticipation to the highest degree possible. For the 1901 season, George's and Hart's Minstrel Extravaganza distributed a brightly colored handbill that announced that the show was "En Route," was "Grand in Its Own Magnifigence [*sic*]," had a "Stupendous Aggregation of Colored Artists," and possessed the "Strongest Novelty Parade of the Season."[23] Handbills such as these were passed out to several dozen people and word of mouth further promoted news of the show throughout the rest of the city. By show day, eager crowds often flocked to the theaters to see if a show's grandiose claims of magnificence were indeed true.

Once off the train and in the city limits, African American shows performed in Chattanooga's segregated and exclusively African American theaters as well as in outlying parks. The segregated New Opera Theater (renamed the Lyric in the early 1900s) opened in October 1886 on Sixth and Market Streets and hosted dramatic, classical, and popular musical comedy groups.[24] For fifty cents, African Americans could enter the "colored balcony" and view the latest that the American stage had to offer.[25] As the 1900s progressed, African American theaters opened in the Ninth Street area, and by May 1910 the Ivy opened on 329 East Ninth Street and the Grand and Palace Theaters soon followed.[26] These black theaters primarily hosted African American variety acts and solo performers. Larger shows that did not fit in the city's theaters, like circuses and tent shows, often put up their mobile stages in the parks managed by the city.[27]

At fifty cents a ticket, or even less for outdoor performances, Bessie Smith had the opportunity to watch some of the most popular African American entertainers of the era. Primrose and West's Minstrels played Chattanooga theaters several times during the theater season and interestingly was one of the few troupes that featured a "gigantic organization of whites and blacks," who "overcrowded houses" every night of their run.[28] Additionally, the Al G. Fields Minstrels played the New Opera Theater frequently. Managed by Al "the Minstrel King" Fields, Fields Minstrels often opened Chattanooga's theater season.[29] Other nationally recognized African American minstrel and musical comedies that played to full Chattanooga audiences included Pat Chapelle's *A Rabbit's*

Foot and Sherman Dudley's *The Smart Set*, musical comedies that featured singers, dancers, and comedians.[30]

If the price of a theater ticket was unaffordable, a Chattanooga resident still could have witnessed the free, large pre-show parades that preceded a minstrel or variety show. A novelty parade roamed the city in hopes of increasing the audience for that night's engagement. The actors, singers, and band members advertised the show by marching up the most prominent street in the city, stopping at a central square, and playing medleys of classical and popular tunes from the show. They then paraded back to the theater, hopefully with hundreds of potential audience members in tow.[31] Trombone player Clyde Bernhardt described one of these pre-show parades with awe: "Colored people were all lined up along the curb . . . [S]uddenly, from around the corner marched these colored men. . . . The excitement was so great—the shining instruments, the music, real soldiers—I almost pulled my father's finger off asking fool questions."[32] The spectacle of the minstrel show parades was complemented by the elaborate holiday parades staged for the May Festival, the Fourth of July, and Labor Day, events that reinforced Ninth Street's role as the entertainment and social core of the black community.[33]

BESSIE SMITH ON HER STREET STAGE

The process of how black entertainers carved out performance space on Ninth Street can be more fully illuminated through an overview of Bessie Smith's adolescent performance history. With a variety of musical genres in her consciousness, a young Bessie decided to turn the streets that had been her playground into her "stage" and from the ages of ten to twelve began performing on the downtown avenues of Chattanooga.[34] In the aftermath of her parents' deaths, when Smith was only eight, Smith's eldest sister, Viola, had to take charge of her remaining Smith siblings. The Smith family lost their home from lack of income, boarded in the rooms of fellow community members, and Viola, a young woman in her twenties, became the head of the household.[35] To Bessie, entertaining appeared a far less strenuous way to bring some necessary supplemental income into the Smith home than helping Viola with laundry work.

As a young girl approaching adolescence, Bessie could not safely traverse Chattanooga's streets alone, and she did not take to performing solo; her eldest brother, Andrew, was at her side. Bessie and Andrew frequented downtown street corners in front of the shops, businesses, and eating houses that drew in the largest numbers of patrons. In 1902, there were nine saloons and eight eating houses between the 100 and 700 blocks of East Ninth Street alone.[36] Other key businesses like barbershops, tailors, grocery shops, and the City Auditorium, as well as private residences, were scattered among the saloons and eating shops of

Ninth Street—which ensured that sizable crowds would be present during the day.[37] Hence, Bessie and Andrew had several corners on which to perform their mobile show.

Bessie's "mobile show" typically consisted of Bessie dancing and singing popular tunes of the period as Andrew played guitar in the background. She placed some type of receptacle for money on the ground before her and took in whatever spare coins those who passed by threw her way. Yet street performing was not as simple as this basic description. Scholar Sally Harrison-Pepper contends that the success of a street performer is "partly measured by the ability to transform city 'space' into theater 'place,'" and that the "noise surrounding the performance space, the proximity of other performers, the social as well as the atmospheric climates are part of the street performer's daily, even minute to minute negotiations with a fluid and vital urban environment."[38] Thus, Bessie and Andrew had to make quick decisions about where to perform and about what type of material might draw in the most onlookers, while being mindful of other street performers around them. Businesses often relocated and others opened in their wake, which led Bessie and Andrew to move their act around accordingly.[39] Occasionally, when the Smiths preferred a more familiar and perhaps more receptive audience, Bessie and Andrew set up their traveling act in front of the White Elephant Saloon on the corner of Thirteenth and Elm, a few blocks from their Blue Goose Hollow neighborhood.[40] Fortunately, Bessie had an entertaining style that kept a crowd interested in whatever area of the city she performed. A friend of Andrew's, Will Johnson, recounted that Bessie often sang "Bill Bailey, Won't You Please Come Home," and although Johnson wasn't "impressed with her voice" in these early days, he did recall that "she sure knew how to shake money loose from a pocket."[41]

GENDERED SPACES ON NINTH STREET

Bessie Smith was not the only youth entertaining crowds on the city streets. Among her "competition" was famed classical tenor Roland Hayes. Prior to his formal training at Fisk University and in Boston, Hayes performed popular songs with his amateur Silver Toned Quartet on the "curbstones" and "railway stations" of Chattanooga.[42] Yet, although not an anomaly, a young girl making her livelihood by dancing and singing for spare change is still intriguing. If, as scholar Patricia Hill Collins argues, "male space included the streets, barbershops, and pool halls; female arenas consisted of households and churches," then where does Bessie, the Chattanooga street performer fit?[43] Furthermore, if "the streets of a city are the exhibition halls of its citizens, and walking through these public halls . . . the character and civilization of its people judged," as Chattanoogan Rev. Joseph E. Smith maintained, then how can a young woman negotiate the public sphere and still be "judged" to be respectable?[44] Fortunately for Bessie, the roles for women in public society had evolved as a result of the increase in industrialization and the subsequent surge in African American migration to the urban environment in the 1880s and 1890s. As previously discussed, the growth of manufacturing industries in the urban South had attracted thousands of African Americans eager to leave the poverty and racial violence of the rural South. Just as rapid migration changed the racial landscape of Chattanooga by raising the black population to over 40 percent of the city's total residents, so too did migration alter the gender landscape of the city. "Gender landscape" here refers not only to an increase in the proportion of African American women to black men in the city but also to a rise in women's status in the public environment as they entered retail and professional occupations.

The influx of migrants both necessitated that more service industries open to cater to the migrants and paved the way for women to be employed in several of these service occupations. Migrants who relocated to the city needed shelter, food, and other subsistence provisions, and the existing segregated housing and commercial establishments did not suffice as the black community reached over 13,000 persons by 1900 and nearly 18,000 by 1910.[45] Hence, many migrants who had arrived in the first surge in the 1880s created entrepreneurial opportunities for themselves by saving wages from manufacturing or domestic labor jobs and opening their own barbershops, dry goods stores, tailor shops, and other similar retail institutions.[46] African American women were a vital part of this growing population of small businesses operators. Although many female migrants transferred directly from sharecropping in rural areas to domestic service in the urban arena, just as the elder women in Bessie's family had, a select few accumulated a little capital from their domestic jobs and opened dressmaking shops, boarding homes, and eating establishments.

As the 1900s progressed, African American women in Chattanooga became increasingly visible as "petty entrepreneurs," the term historian Sarah Deutsch used in her discussion of women in Boston.[47] Many of these petty entrepreneurs based their businesses in the Ninth Street area to attract as many customers and patrons as possible. Women such as Celia Good, a former slave, opened a boardinghouse at 221 West Ninth Street and was said by the local community "to be as wealthy as any colored citizen in the city." Other women, such as Mrs. N. Morton and Rhoda Jennings, successfully operated grocery stores and eating houses on other blocks of the Ninth Street area.[48]

The overall increase in the black female presence on Ninth Street is evidenced in the compared demographics of Ninth Street in 1892, the year of Bessie's birth; 1902, the year Smith most likely considered entertaining in public; and 1908, one of the last years of Bessie's street performances. In 1892, five female heads of household resided on East Ninth, another four women operated eating houses, and an additional two ran dressmaking shops.[49] A decade later, a total of fifteen women headed households on East Ninth, yet only two operated eating houses.[50] By 1908, however, over thirty women headed households in the area, and five women operated eating houses, three managed boardinghouses, two ran dressmaking and pressing shops, and a final two ran a hairdressing shop and a grocery store.[51] Although these numbers in themselves are not overwhelmingly large (only 40 black women worked and resided on East Ninth out of a total of 155 black residences and shops in 1908), they attest to the reality that the Ninth Street area was not solely a male space. In whatever way possible, as owners, managers, and customers, African American women converged on Ninth Street and their presence made it more permissible for the young Bessie Smith to take her place on the street among them.

Another essential reason that Bessie was able to succeed in the predominantly male realm of public performing can be found in the gender shifts that occurred in the American entertainment industry near the close of the nineteenth century. Although African Americans ascended to the professional stage at the onset of emancipation, the roles for black women performers were severely restricted. The genres of sacred or classical music were deemed respectable for women's participation, but rarely were women in the mid-nineteenth century permitted to be in minstrel or variety shows.[52] Hence, classically trained African American women, such as Marie Selika Williams or Nellie Brown Mitchell, could reach prominence and be praised as "prima donnas" on the "high art" concert stage, but performance opportunities for black women elsewhere were not often available.[53] Prior to the late nineteenth century, working-class men took over even the audiences of musical theater, and many men feared that theater material would injure the delicate consciousness of women.[54] In Chattanooga, some shows were actually criticized for being "so tainted with an immoral, irreligious conception of wit . . . that the audience had felt its refinement insulted and its sensibilities shocked to a sense of disgust."[55]

The gender shift in entertainment occurred as women began to earn their own incomes and had the disposable income to spend on theater tickets, an occurrence that coincided with more women becoming petty entrepreneurs. Realizing the value of adding females to the audience, show producers actually changed the nature of the shows.[56] In 1900, African American shows like Mahara's Big Carnival Minstrels began to advertise themselves as acceptable for women and youth: "[S]trictly an entertainment for *ladies* and *children,* replete with choice music and melody, Strong singing features, magnificent choruses—not marred by loud mouthed comedians" [emphasis added].[57] Black women entered the audience en masse a few years after they joined the choruses and primary casts of major theater shows. In 1890, Sam Jack's "Creole Show" both bridged the gap between minstrelsy and black musical theater in its material and featured African American women in the chorus and in the typical lead minstrel role of the interlocutor.[58] By the turn of the twentieth century, theater troupes like Georgia-Up-Date Minstrels ran recruitment advertisements that read, "Wanted—colored performers, comedians, singers, dancers, musicians, *ladies* and gentlemen" [emphasis added].[59] Hence, as the shows of the twentieth century were no longer prohibited to women, Bessie was able to witness minstrel and variety performances on Ninth that might have influenced her own decision to become an entertainer.

RESISTANCE AND NINTH STREET'S SITES OF MELEE

Although the vibrant amateur and professional African American entertainment community opened its doors to include young black women in the 1900s, Bessie's choice of becoming a street performer and later a professional vocalist was not praised by all members of the Chattanooga African American community. Although Bessie and her entertaining counterparts often found receptive audiences among the crowds of West Thirteenth or Ninth Street, as evidenced by her continued performing efforts and modest profit, the recreational world patronized by lower-income African Americans—the storefront theater, rent party, tent show, and saloon—was not necessarily seen as respectable by elite society at large. As Bessie pursued dancing and singing on the street corners of East Ninth, she surely encountered many people, including many practicing Christians and culturally conservative African Americans, who did not reward her with spare change but looked upon her with dismay.

The popular musical landscape in which Bessie sang was criticized primarily because of where it was located and what institutions surrounded it. Crime was often rampant in the Ninth Street area. As late as the 1890s, the city maintained a reputation for being a "rough and ready place," where "saloons and all-night barrel houses" attracted visitors, African American and white alike.[60] Visitors could get off the train for a layover, be involved in a saloon brawl, and get back on the next train to escape repercussion. The eating houses, small theaters, and saloons that Bessie performed in front of were locations frequently plagued by arguments, drunkenness, and, at times, life-threatening violence. Saloons known by the names "Owl" and "Shamrock" repeatedly laced annual police reports as the central sites of "general melee" and locations of "extraordinary crime."[61] The variety or vaudeville theater also attracted a raucous crowd, and in some southern theaters, patrons were known to throw "sticks, bricks, spitballs, cigar butts, and peach pits" during a performance.[62] Prostitution houses lay near the outskirts of many recreational establishments on Ninth, particularly near Florence and Helen Streets, and were marked by "dark . . . stairways that led from the pavement to regions even darker . . . where human beings trafficked and traded with other human beings—sometimes colored and sometimes not."[63]

In spite of the often valid criticism the popular black recreational environment received from religious and uplift organizations, the storefront theaters, saloons, tent shows, and house parties—the same locations of "general melee"—served as a significant and distinct space for many poorer African Americans. In these spaces, impoverished African Americans could gather together outside of the gaze of oppressive white society and beyond the social confines of the "better class of negroes" to dance, listen to music, drink, and socialize.[64] Yet, these physical spaces on Ninth Street and the surrounding environments were also locations where lower-income African Americans carried out various acts of economic, political, and social resistance against racial oppression and the rise of Jim Crow segregation.

The recreational environment also brought in income for the Chattanooga community as a whole, much as it did in other cities with a sizable African American entertainment culture, such as Memphis, New Orleans, and Atlanta. The economic importance of the recreational environment was highlighted in an 1899 study on black businesses:

> The saloon, among these people, even more than among the Irish and other city groups, is a distinct social centre. In the country towns of the black belt, the field hands gather there to gossip, loaf, and joke. In the cities, a crowd of jolly fellows can be met there and in adjacent pool rooms. Consequently, the business has attracted Negroes with capital in spite of the fact that the Negro church distinctly frowns on the vocation, which means some social ostracism for the liquor dealer. Next to the saloons in importance come the traveling vaudeville shows. None of these are reported here, for having no permanent headquarters they are difficult to reach. . . . Most of them are compelled to have white managers in order to get entree into the theaters, but they are largely under Negro control and represent a considerable investment of Negro capital.[65]

Despite the opposition from the local churches, saloons, pool rooms, and small vaudeville theaters brought in revenue to black businesses in Chattanooga at a time when white-owned banks would not loan money to African American entrepreneurs.[66] John Lovell, the first African American saloon owner in Chattanooga, amassed $6,500 in property by the late nineteenth century, property purchased with the capital he earned in the leisure business.[67] With his earnings, Lovell supported other African American businesses in the city, in the process aiding in developing a self-sufficient black community, which was necessary with the advent of strict racial segregation. Lovell opened his saloon in the 1870s, and by

1902 there were ten African American–managed saloons in the city, including six in the Ninth Street area.[68]

The popular recreational environment surrounding the Big Nine also provided an arena for African Americans to plan small acts of political resistance against the rise of racial oppression in the city. Historian Robin D.G. Kelley maintains that black social spaces gave "African Americans a place to hide, a place to plan," and in select instances in southern cities, this is exactly what occurred.[69] Admittedly, African Americans did not plan grand acts of revolution against white supremacy in between dancing to blues songs and shooting pool. Nonetheless, social spaces allowed people to gather together and discuss the most pressing issues of the day in private. Blues composer W. C. Handy contended that on his travels as a minstrel troupe bandleader in Mississippi, he would also covertly sell copies of the *Chicago Defender*, *Indianapolis Freeman*, and *Voice of the Negro*, primary black periodicals of the era. Such information allowed African Americans to learn what their counterparts in other cities were doing and was a subtle form of resistance because black newspapers "were looked upon with strong disfavor by certain local powers" in Mississippi.[70] Yet, as an entertainer, Handy was never suspected of such a political act.

Similarly, as racial violence escalated to horrifying heights with the lynching of Chattanooga resident Ed Johnson, who was accused and convicted of raping a white woman in 1906, black saloons and eating houses became the locations where lower-income African Americans planned what should be done in response. Many of the black churches had become gathering places for some African Americans who, fearing for the overall safety of the black community, vowed to search out the "vicious and degraded negro" that Ed Johnson was purported to be.[71] Thus, when many of the African American factory laborers in the city went on strike on March 20, 1906 (the day after the lynching), to demonstrate their outrage at the murder, the strike was undoubtedly planned in the social spaces of the city, rather than at a church mass meeting.[72] So great was the fear that African Americans would retaliate with violence and that these violent plans would be crafted in black recreational spaces that the city's mayor "ordered all saloons frequented by black people to be closed" in the days following the lynching, but no restrictions were placed on similar white establishments.[73] Hence, even the Chattanooga community at large recognized the potential power black social spaces held in terms of political resistance.

One of the most significant functions of black social spaces was the opportunity they provided African Americans for spiritual renewal. At tent shows, saloon theaters, or house parties, blacks laughed, danced, sang, shed their communal worries, and bolstered themselves for the next workday. The ability of African Americans to have leisure time with each other is an example of covert resistance against a society that viewed black men and women primarily as laborers.[74] In many of the recreational environments along Ninth Street, African American patrons attempted to "transcend" the constant pain of poverty, racism, and oppression by dancing it away or, as author Albert Murray refers to it, "stomping on the blues."[75]

Laboring African Americans viewed Chattanooga's Ninth Street as a social center, a place to meet members of not only the local black community but surrounding black communities as well. Seamstress Tena Suggs recalled that she would leave her home on Lookout Mountain to attend vaudeville shows at the segregated Bijou Theater in downtown Chattanooga.[76] The city's saloons, theaters, and house parties drew in African Americans from Birmingham and Atlanta and afforded Chattanooga blacks the opportunity to congregate with other southern African Americans, and undoubtedly to form lasting bonds before the workweek forced them back to their jobs.[77] Ultimately, for many African Americans in Chattanooga, black social spaces were one of the few veiled environments in which they could be truly human, and this renewal of their humanity occurred on the Big Nine, the home of Bessie Smith's first performances and "the sweetest street in the world."[78]

NOTES

This chapter is an excerpt from the forthcoming manuscript titled *Blues Empress in Black Chattanooga* (Champaign: University of Illinois Press, 2008), which explores the early environment of legendary blues singer Bessie Smith and probes the differences between Smith's roles as the iconic "Empress of the Blues" and a southern working-class woman.

1. "Ninth Street in New Gown: Famous Thoroughfare Has Reformed," *Chattanooga Times*, September 2, 1917, 13.

2. *G. M. Connelley & Co.'s Alphabetical Directory of Chattanooga, Tennessee* (Chattanooga, TN: G. M. Connelley & Co., 1908), 903.

3. "History of the East Ninth Street Area," Chattanooga African American Museum Collection, n.d., 1.

4. By "the East Ninth Street area," I mean the central street itself, surrounding cross streets, and Gilmer Street (now East Eighth). See map insert in George C. Connor, *Historical Guide to Chattanooga and Lookout Mountain* (Chattanooga: T. H. Payne & Company, 1889).

5. R. J. Crawford, "Business Negroes of Chattanooga," *Voice of the Negro* 1, no. 11 (November 1904): 534, 537.

6. Interview with George A. Key by Chattanooga African American Museum Staff, August 1994; Interview with Ted Bryant by Paul Moss, June 9–10, 2000; Personal Interview with Leroy Henderson, November 11, 2000. Beale Street became the hub of black life in Memphis when prominent and wealthy black resident Robert Reed Church Sr. purchased land formerly ravaged by yellow fever and developed Church's Park, a black recreational center in 1899. After the 1910s, Beale Street became home to churches, shops, saloons,

and theaters patronized by African Americans. As a hub of black musical and recreational activity and the area where W. C. Handy resided when he first popularized written blues music, Beale Street became known to many as the street where "blues began" and a "Main Street of Negro America." See George Lee, *Beale Street: Where the Blues Began* (New York: Robert O. Ballou, 1934); and Margaret McKee and Fred Chisenhall, *Beale Street Black and Blue: Life and Music on Black America's Main Street* (Baton Rouge: Louisiana State University Press, 1981), 5–81.

7. "History of the East Ninth Street Area," 2; Travis Wolfe, "M. L. King Business Area Named to Historic Register," *Chattanooga Times*, April 24, 1984, B2.

8. Interview with Ella Mae Hendrix by Heather Biola in Heather Biola, "The Black Washerwoman in Southern Tradition," *Tennessee Folklore Society Bulletin* (March 1979): 25.

9. Tom Fletcher, *100 Years of the Negro in Show Business* (New York: Burge and Co., 1954), 214.

10. Lawrence W. Levine, *Black Culture and Black Consciousness: Afro-American Folk Thought from Slavery to Freedom* (New York: Oxford University Press, 1977), 214.

11. The classic blues format sung by Smith, Ma Rainey, Mamie Smith, Alberta Hunter, and other female vocalists had a twelve- or sixteen-bar format, had an AAB lyric structure, and was supported by a rhythm section of piano, drums, and brass instruments. By "bar," I refer to a measure or distinct unit of musical notes, and "AAB" refers to a lyric structure in which an opening line is sung twice followed by a response line: (A) I hate to see the evening sun go down / (A) I hate to see the evening sun go down / (B) It makes me think I'm on my last go around. See W. C. Handy, *St. Louis Blues* (Memphis, TN: Peace and Handy Publishing, 1914). For further information on the technical structure of the blues, see Eileen Southern, *The Music of Black Americans: A History,* 3rd ed. (New York: W. W. Norton & Company, 1997), 333–338.

12. "Looking Backward," *Chattanooga Daily Times*, July 1, 1952.

13. Ibid.; *G. M. Connelley & Co.'s Alphabetical Directory* (1908), 906.

14. "Looking Backward," July 1, 1952.

15. Interview with Gwendolyn Smith Bailey by James Hardy, October 16, 1986; Interview with Gwendolyn Smith Bailey by George Ricks and Suzanne Marcus, March 3, 1987.

16. Interview with Thomas Dorsey by Michael W. Harris, quoted in Harris, *The Rise of Gospel Blues: The Music of Thomas Andrew Dorsey in the Urban Church* (New York: Oxford University Press, 1992), 38–39.

17. Donald Clyde Runyan, "The Influence of Joseph O. Cadek and His Family on the Musical Life of Chattanooga, TN (1893–1973)," Ph.D. diss., Vanderbilt University, 1980, 140.

18. Ibid., 153–155; "Amusements," *Chattanooga Daily Times*, September–December 1893.

19. *Directory of Chattanooga and Its Suburbs, 1897* (Chattanooga: G. M. Connelly & Co., 1897), 20; Nashville, Chattanooga & St. Louis schedule, 1886, Railroad File, Warshaw Collection of Business Americana, Archives Center, National Museum of American History, Smithsonian Institution; "Railway Time Table," *Chattanooga Daily Times*, February 4, 1912.

20. Runyan, "Influence of Joseph O. Cadek," 19.

21. For further information on railroad porters and the transmission of culture, see David D. Perata, *Those Pullman Blues: An Oral History of the African American Railroad Attendant* (New York: Twayne Publishers, 1996).

22. Like Memphis's Beale Street, Decatur and Storyville were both centers of lower-income black entertainment in their respective cities. Decatur was home to popular black vaudeville theaters like the Eighty-One Theater and the Ninety-One Theater, whereas Storyville was a legendary red-light district in New Orleans in which several young jazz musicians got their start in the brothels and house parties of the area. See Harris, *Rise of Gospel Blues*, 30–31; James Lincoln Collier, *The Making of Jazz: A Comprehensive History* (New York: Delta Books, 1978), 64–65.

23. Handbill, George & Hart's Up to Date Georgia Minstrels Scrapbook, Archives Center, National Museum of American History, Smithsonian Institution.

24. James W. Livingood, *Hamilton County* (Memphis: Memphis State University Press, 1981), 316–317; John Wilson, *Chattanooga's Story* (Chattanooga, TN: Chattanooga Free Press, 1980), 315–317.

25. "New Opera House" advertisement, *Chattanooga Daily Times*, March 3, 1898.

26. Stage Section, *Indianapolis Freeman*, May 14, 1910; *Chattanooga Daily Times*, January 28, 1912; *Chattanooga Daily Times*, September 29, 1912.

27. Runyan, "Influence of Joseph O. Cadek," 28.

28. "Primrose and West Minstrels," *Chattanooga Daily Times*, January 8, 1898.

29. *Chattanooga Daily Times*, September 2, 1912; Runyan, "Influence of Joseph O. Cadek," 150–156; Charles C. Sweeley, *The Minstrel King March Two Step Sheet Music* (Williamsport, PA: Vandersloot Music Publishing, n.d.).

30. Theater Notices, *Indianapolis Freeman*, June 6, 1909; Theater Advertisements, *Chattanooga Daily Times*, February 18, 1912.

31. W. C. Handy, *Father of the Blues: An Autobiography* (New York: Macmillan, 1941), 34–36.

32. Clyde E.B. Bernhardt as told to Sheldon Harris, *I Remember: Eighty Years of Black Entertainment, Big Bands, and the Blues* (Philadelphia: University of Pennsylvania Press, 1986), 7–8.

33. *Chattanooga Daily Times*, January 16, 1898; "Chattanooga Items," *Indianapolis Freeman*, September 19, 1903; "May Festival," *Indianapolis Freeman*, May 5, 1900.

34. Smith's age at the time she began street performing, like her birth year, is an issue of debate. Newspaper articles on Smith reported that she was anywhere from seven to nine when she began her career, and Chris Albertson, Smith's most referenced biographer, contends that she became a street performer sometime after her mother's death "between the ages of eight and nine." See Mabel Chew, "Singer Began at Seven," *Baltimore Afro-American*, March 27, 1926; Allan McMillan, "New York Sees Bessie Smith; Wonders Where She's Been," *Chicago Defender*, March 28, 1936; Chris Albertson, *Bessie* (New Haven, CT: Yale University Press, 2003), 8. There is little evidence to suggest that Smith began performing before her mother's death, which was sometime in 1902, when Smith was ten years old. Bessie's interest in performing and her need to supplement the household income escalated when she watched her brother leave the household for the traveling stage in 1904, when Bessie was twelve years old. Smith most likely began her street performances during this time period.

35. *G. M. Connelley & Co.'s Alphabetical Directory of Chattanooga, Tennessee* (Chattanooga, TN: G. M. Connelly & Co., 1907), 590; *G. M. Connelley & Co.'s Alphabetical Directory of Chattanooga, Tennessee* (Chattanooga, TN: G. M. Connelly & Co., 1909), 623. The directories note Viola's and, later, sister Tennie's occupations as laundresses. Viola supported the household—which comprised herself and her younger siblings, Tennie, Lulu, Clarence, and Bessie—initially by working as a cook and later by following in her mother's path as a washerwoman. After Laura Smith's death in 1902 but before 1903, the Smiths no longer occupied the house on 100 Cross Street. Throughout Bessie's adolescence in Chattanooga, Viola moved from residence to residence, often boarding with others as opposed to renting or owning her own property; Tennie, Lulu, and Andrew also appear at several different addresses in the local city directories. Without the combined income of Laura Smith and her eldest children, it seems as if ownership of a family home proved quite difficult. Ultimately, by the age of ten, Bessie understood and had endured the instability that poverty can induce. See *G. M. Connelley & Co.'s Alphabetical Directory of Chattanooga, Tennessee* (Chattanooga, TN: G. M. Connelly & Co., 1908, 1909, 1910); Department of Commerce and Labor, Bureau of the Census, Thirteenth Census of the United States: 1910—Population Hamilton County, Chattanooga City, 1910, roll 1502, book 3, 164b; roll 1503, book 1, 67b.

36. *G. M. Connelley & Co.'s Alphabetical Directory, 1902*, 940–944.

37. Ibid., 940; *Plat Book of Chattanooga, TN* (Philadelphia: G. M. Hopkins Co., 1904), plates 2, 3, 4.

38. Sally Harrison-Pepper, *Drawing a Circle in the Square: Street Performing in New York's Washington Square Park* (Jackson: University of Mississippi Press, 1990), xv.

39. An example of how the commercial geography of a block changed is exemplified in the 600 block of East Ninth. In 1902, prominent on the 600 block was a black barbershop, an eating house, and ten African American residences, which were divided by a stockyard, a coal distributor, and white residences. By 1908, the same block comprised entirely African American residences and businesses, except for a white grocery store managed by W. M. Warren, the Lookout Transfer Company, and the G. R. Phillips Saloon. See *Directory of Chattanooga, Tennessee, 1902*, 940; *Directory of Chattanooga, Tennessee, 1908*, 904.

40. "Bessie Sang for Coins Along City's 'Big Nine,'" *Chattanooga Free Press*, April 10, 1994, A5.

41. Albertson, *Bessie*, 8.

42. MacKinley Helm, *Angel Mo' and Her Son, Roland Hayes* (Boston: Little, Brown and Company, 1942), 72, 97–99.

43. Patricia Hill Collins, *Black Feminist Thought: Knowledge, Consciousness, and the Politics of Empowerment* (New York: Routledge Press, 1990), 55.

44. Joseph E. Smith, "The Care of Neglected Children," in "Social and Physical Conditions of Negroes in Cities," May 25, 1897, in *Atlanta University Publications* no. 2 (New York: Arno Press and the New York Times, 1968), 41.

45. "Table II: Population by Race Per Cent Negro 1870–1946," in National Urban League, *A Study of the Economic and Cultural Activities of the Negro Population of Chattanooga, Tennessee*, 1947, National Urban League Papers, series 6, box 22, Manuscripts Division, Library of Congress.

46. See the biographical sketches in J. Bliss White, *Biography and Achievements of the Colored Citizens of Chattanooga* (Chattanooga, TN: J. Bliss Publishing, 1904), 23, 58.

47. Sarah Deutsch, *Women and the City: Gender, Space, and Power in Boston, 1870–1940* (New York: Oxford University Press, 2000), 115.

48. Crawford, "Business Negroes of Chattanooga," 536–537; White, *Biography and Achievements*, 58; "Looking Backward," July 1, 1952.

49. See *Directory of Chattanooga, Tennessee, 1892* (Chattanooga, TN: Connelly & Fais Publishers, 1892), 813–815.

50. *Directory of Chattanooga, Tennessee, 1902*, 940–944.

51. Ibid., 902–906.

52. Thomas Fletcher Marvin, "Children of Legba: African American Musicians of the Jazz Age in Literature and Popular Culture," Ph.D. diss., University of Massachusetts, 1993, 93–94.

53. Southern, *Music of Black Americans*, 244–248.

54. Richard Butsch, *The Making of American Audiences: From Stage to Television, 1750–1990* (Cambridge, UK: Cambridge University Press, 2000), 92.

55. "A Ringing Protest," *Chattanooga Daily Times*, January 28, 1898.

56. Butsch, *Making of American Audiences*, 112.

57. *Indianapolis Freeman*, January 13, 1900.

58. Marvin, "Children of Legba," 95; Henry T. Sampson, *Blacks in Blackface: A Source on Early Black Musical Shows* (Metuchen, NJ: Scarecrow Press, 1980), 6–7.

59. *Indianapolis Freeman*, February 10, 1900.

60. Centurion Committee, *Centurion: A History of the Chattanooga Police Department, 1852–1977* (Chattanooga, TN: Intercollegiate Press, 1976), 48.

61. Bureau of Police, *Seventh Annual Report of the City of Chattanooga, Tennessee* (Chattanooga, TN: Bureau of Police, 1899), 25.

62. Butsch, *Making of American Audiences*, 119.

63. Timothy Paul Ezzell, "Yankees in Dixie: The Story of Chattanooga, 1870–1898," Ph.D. diss., University of Tennessee, 1996, 56; "Ninth Street in New Gown," 13.

64. The phrase "better class of negroes" stems from an article concerning the Ed Johnson lynching of 1906 in which many African Americans affiliated with religious institutions condemned the supposed violent acts committed by Johnson. See "Better Class of Negroes Viciously Condemn Crime," *Chattanooga Daily Times*, January 26, 1906.

65. "The Negro in Business," May 30–31, 1899, in Atlanta University Press, *Atlanta University Publications*, Nos. 1, 2, 4, 8, 9, 11, 13, 14, 15, 16, 17, 18 (New York: Arno Press and the New York Times, 1968), 4:15.

66. Personal Interview with Vilma Fields, November 9, 2000; Interview with Theodore Bryant by Paul Moss, June 9–10, 2000.

67. Robert C. Kenzer, "Black Businessmen in Post Civil War Tennessee," *Journal of East Tennessee History* 66 (1994): 75.

68. *Directory of Chattanooga, Tennessee, 1902*, 940–944.

69. Robin Kelley, *Race Rebels: Culture, Politics, and the Black Working Class* (New York: Free Press, 1994), 51.

70. Handy, *Father of the Blues*, 79–80.

71. "Better Class of Negroes Viciously Condemn Crime," *Chattanooga Daily Times*, January 26, 1906.

72. Mark Curriden and Leroy Phillips Jr., *Contempt of Court: The Turn of the Century Lynching That Launched 100 Years of Federalism* (New York: Faber and Faber, 1999), 218.

73. Ibid., 220.

74. Ralph Ellison, "Richard Wright's Blues," in *Shadow and Act*, by Ralph Ellison (New York: Quality Paperback Book Club, 1994), 78.

75. For more on the function of dance and the blues environment, see Albert Murray, *Stomping the Blues* (New York: McGraw-Hill, 1976).

76. Interview with Tena Suggs by Chattanooga African American Museum Staff, August 1994.

77. Personal Interview with Vilma Fields, November 9, 2000; Personal Interview with James Bowles, November 9, 2000.

78. Interview with Theodore Bryant by Paul Moss, June 9–10, 2000.

PART VI

Churches and Sacred Spaces

Owen J. Dwyer

Putting the Movement in Its Place

The Politics of Public Spaces Dedicated to the Civil Rights Movement

Over the past twenty years, arguments over the meaning of the Civil Rights Movement have assumed a central place in debates over the role of race and racism in American society. For instance, both opponents and supporters of affirmative action draw on the movement's rhetoric of "equality" and "freedom" to support diametrically opposed positions, an irony that suggests the foundational status of the movement's legacy in contemporary racial politics.[1] In a move that both reflects and abets the growing rhetorical centrality of the movement, certain sites associated with its history are being commemorated with parks, monuments, and museums.[2] Conceived of as materialized discourses, public space is shaped by and in turn influences the society that produces it by conducting meaning through its representations of history and identity.[3] The narratives embedded at civil rights memorials are conditioned by the types of archival materials that survive, the intentions of their producers, and trends in contemporary historiography. In turn, through their symbolic power and the large number of visitors who travel to them, these landscapes play a role in reproducing society.[4]

Taken as a whole, these sites form the basis of an emerging landscape of civic spaces dedicated to the Civil Rights Movement. These sites play an important role in maintaining the movement's prominent place in the contemporary politics of memory. Their public situation and use of canonical media, in addition to the enormous outlays of financial and political capital such installations require, imbue them with an air of civic authority and permanence.[5] Relative to other representational media (e.g., television, music, films), these public spaces appear as lasting and official records of the past, above political bias and worthy of widespread admiration. Importantly, civil rights memorials are touted in tour books as prime destinations and annually visited by millions who regard their moral authority and historical accuracy as beyond reproach. Finally, these sites constitute a backdrop for everyday activity, accruing to these representations the naturalizing power of place.[6]

Beneath the appearance of historical consensus and stability, however, civil rights memorials, and by implication the meaning and significance of the events they represent, are the product of and conduit for ongoing political debate.[7] From their inception, these public spaces are designed and planned, with all of the narrative choices and biases this entails, by those who have the time, resources, and, commonly, a state mandate to define the past. Further, they are appropriated by groups across the political spectrum as sites for political rallies and protests. As major attractions in the growing heritage tourism industry, the history represented at these sites has been tailored to appeal to the broadest possible audience. Their reliance on state funding and corporate largess makes them further susceptible to influence. Far from neutral, consensual renderings of the "past," civil rights memorials are at once the product of and conveyance for contemporary politics associated with race, urban development, and collective memory.

This chapter examines the production of public spaces dedicated to the Civil Rights Movement in three southern cities—the King National Historic Site in Atlanta, the Birmingham Civil Rights District, and the National Civil Rights Museum in Memphis. In so doing, the relative location of these memorials is brought to the fore and examined in order to better understand the discursive framing that conditions what is remembered and forgotten at civil rights memorials. The development of these public spaces has an important relationship with their relative location. Rather than forming an inert backdrop for the public representation of history, the relative location of a memorial is an integral component of its meaning. In addition to employing the traditional materials and forms associated with the commemorative arts, these memorials draw meaning from their regional and local surroundings to communicate with their audiences.[8] Given the complex interplay of text and context that characterizes the relationship between a memorial and its environment, investigating the regional and urban situation—the relative location—of these civil rights memorials illustrates the claim that, although the events of the past have already happened, the political economy of memory that conditions their design and interpretation serves many, sometimes conflicting, interests in the present—a point that will be discussed further following a description of each site's development.[9]

THE SITE AND SITUATION OF CIVIL RIGHTS MEMORIALS

The production of a memorial landscape dedicated to the Civil Rights Movement is a watershed event in the commemoration of American history.[10] Prior to the late 1960s, when the first elements of the civil rights memorial landscape began to appear in the wake of Martin Luther King Jr.'s assassination, recognition of the contributions of African Americans to American history was relegated to the margins of public space or neglected entirely.[11] Unlike the majority of public representations of American history displayed, the civil rights memorial landscape presents an explicitly anti-racist rendering of the past. Whereas numerous studies of the cultural landscape have focused on its ideological role in masking power relations, civil rights memorials disclose the otherwise invisible presence of hegemonic conceptualizations of history and identity, in this case, those embedded in assumptions regarding the proper content of history.[12] In concert with broader trends in public history, these memorials embody the possibility of de-centering the legacy of American public history away from the hagiographic commemoration of elite individuals and their homes and toward the remembrance of more mundane, socially representative lives and landscapes. In essence, it is a movement against a version of history that underwrote white supremacy and toward one that celebrates its downfall.

Nevertheless, there are significant contradictions and exclusions in the memorial landscape's treatment of the civil rights era. Elements of the memorial landscape's representation of the movement reinscribe certain hegemonic norms characteristic of American public history.[13] For instance, the museums and monuments associated with the movement are major heritage attractions. Local and state governments as well as the tourism industry are responsible in part for their development and promotion. Their influence on memory's landscape requires careful consideration (Fig. 17.1). Additionally, at the country's largest civil rights memorials, there is a growing consensus as to what the movement stood for and who its protagonists were. This mainstream narrative is forcing women's, working-class, and local histories to the margins of the landscape in order to focus on charismatic leaders and dramatic events. Further, in

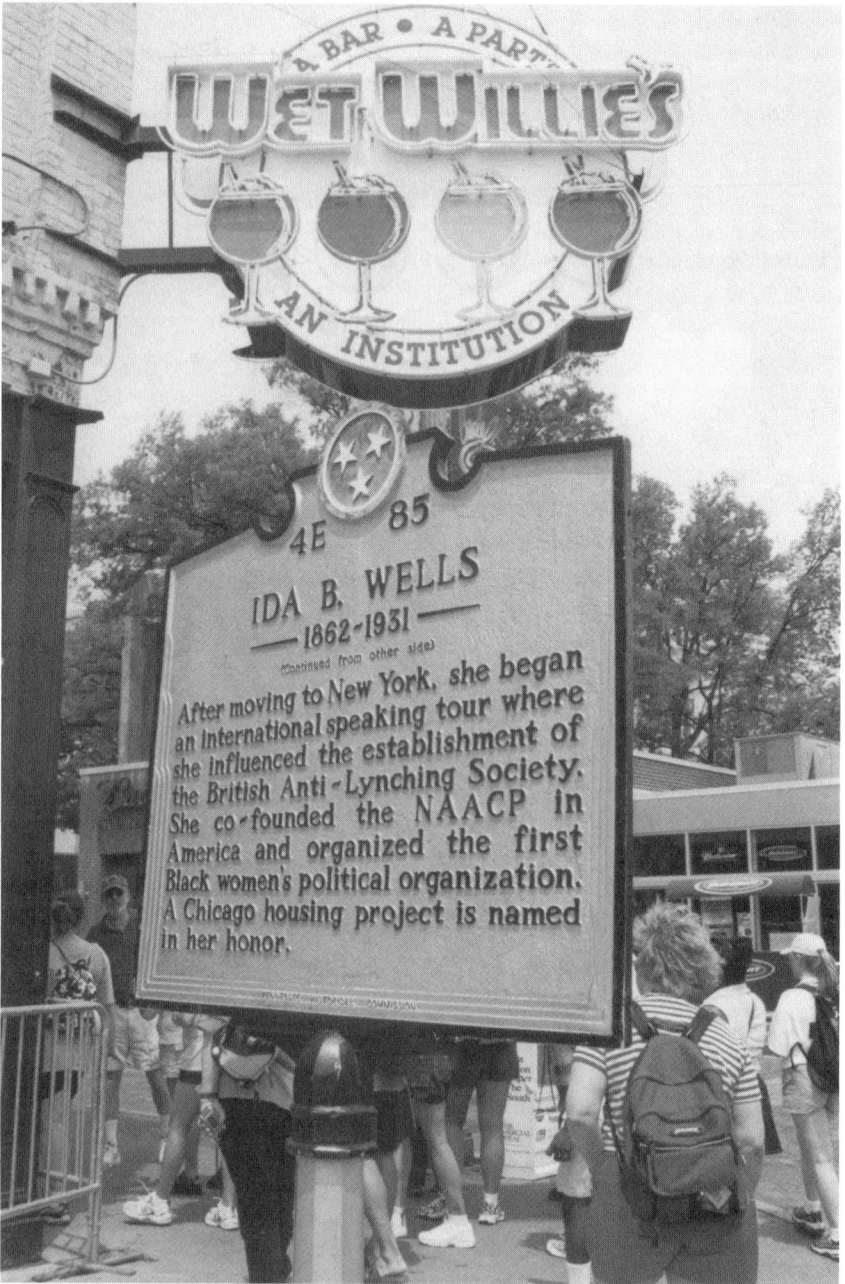

FIGURE 17.1.

This scene along Memphis's Beale Street illustrates the tension between commercialism and heritage tourism that characterizes many civil rights–related sites. (Photograph by author)

its treatment of racism, the landscape presents a simplified image that, although commendable for its unflinching portrayal of violence, nevertheless overlooks racism's more insidious elements. Thus, the civil rights memorial landscape is dominated by a politics of memory that elevates some individuals and ideas associated with the movement to the visual prominence formerly reserved for whites, while relegating others to the peculiarly racialized condition of formal invisibility and namelessness.[14] In effect, the canon of American public history has been desegregated but not overthrown.

The movement's memorial ambiguity, however, is not confined to its content alone. In all but a few cases, civil rights memorials are located amid the declining remains of segregation-era business districts and neighborhoods, characterized today by the scars of urban renewal campaigns, suburbanization, and structural inequality. Although the location of civil rights memorials in these places is historically consistent, the movement is not being commemorated at the traditional core of civic memorial space: city hall, the courthouse, or along Main Street. Importantly, this concern over the place of memory—why is civil rights history commemorated *here* and not *there*?—raises the issue of the social production of public space.

The most significant civil rights memorials, in terms of their size and audience, are located in Atlanta, Birmingham, and Memphis and are closely associated with the life and career of Martin Luther King Jr.[15] The following discussion describes the urban site and situation of these places. It draws on the idea that memory and place are always in a close, mutually constitutive relationship, one that is often at cross-purposes with the animating motivations of the parties responsible for producing civil rights memorials.[16]

ATLANTA

The location of the King National Historic Site in Atlanta is symbolic of the complexities that characterize public memory in the South. Several blocks to its east are the skyscrapers of Peachtree Street, the economic vitality of which made Atlanta the "city too busy to hate" during the 1960s.[17] A short distance to the west is the Carter Presidential Center, housing the Carter Center and the Jimmy Carter Library. The recently completed Freedom Parkway links the three sites, all of which are closely associated with the New South. At the same time, signs near the King National Historic Site and along the Freedom Parkway direct visitors to Stone Mountain State Park. It was from atop Stone Mountain that the Ku Klux Klan was reborn in 1915.[18] Into its granite face are carved the mounted figures of four Confederate generals. This poignant juxtaposition of iconic elements from the Old and New South underscores the site's position astride the fault lines of memory.

In more local terms, the King National Historic Site and its associated National Preservation District are located on Auburn Avenue, the onetime heart of the city's black community.[19] By the middle of the twentieth century, Auburn Avenue's concentration of segregated banks, insurance companies, professionals, and churches earned it the reputation as the "wealthiest Negro street in the world."[20] Shortly thereafter, the neighborhood began a slow decline. Many of its businesses and elite residents relocated to the neighborhoods associated with the historically black colleges and universities of Atlanta's West End. With the increasing mobility of the 1950s and 1960s came more opportunities to move from Auburn Avenue. Moreover, in the early 1960s, interstate construction bisected Auburn Avenue, effectively severing its remaining residential area from downtown businesses. By 1970, when King's tomb was moved from Southview Cemetery to grounds along the street near Ebenezer Baptist Church, where he had ministered alongside his father, the neighborhood showed the typical signs of social fragmentation and financial distress.

In contrast to the extensive interpretive presence currently provided by the Park Service, the site consisted of little more than small tours of King's birthplace and Ebenezer Baptist Church for nearly fifteen years after its establishment in 1980. Although willing to commission the site, Congress was unwilling to allocate funds to construct basic facilities, such as an exhibit hall, parking lot, and restrooms. Although the King National Historic Site attracted 350,000 visitors in 1984 and by 1991 was attracting two million annually, with a small interpretive presence and little to see or do, most visitors remained on-site for less than thirty minutes.[21] The large number of visitors overwhelmed the site's limited facilities and resulted in numerous inconveniences for neighborhood residents who were left to fend for themselves. Problems included the diesel fumes from idling tour buses, noise, and intense competition for parking.

Neglect of the site came to an end with Atlanta's successful bid in 1990 to host the 1996 Centennial Olympic Games.[22] National Park Service personnel deftly used the coming of the Olympics, and the international scrutiny that would accompany the event, to lobby for increased funding. Although the expected international visitors were generally unfamiliar with Atlanta, they were well acquainted with King's leadership, Nobel Peace Prize, and worldwide legacy. The mismatch between King's international stature and the ramshackle condition of the historic site threatened international embarrassment. Further, the paucity of the King site contrasted unfavorably with sites associated with the Confederacy and the Old South that dominated Atlanta's established memorial landscape at Stone Mountain and on the grounds of the state capitol. Additionally, given its proximity to the Olympic village and athletic venues, the site was expected to receive a large number of incidental visitors seeking public parking and restroom facilities—none of which existed on-site. These conditions provided potential fodder with which international news media could illustrate the neglect of African American history and continuing racism to a global audience.

In response to the impending crisis, Georgia's congressional delegation, the Atlanta Committee for the Olympic Games, and the National Park Service initiated intense lobbying efforts in search of funds to improve the site. At the heart of their plan, which totaled nearly $12 million, was the construction of a multimedia visitor center to be built on the site of the existing King Neighborhood Community Center.[23] The mayor's office and city council agreed to donate the community center and its parcel of land to the national historic site in return for the promise that a new community center would be built in the future with federal funds.[24] When this plan encountered opposition in Congress, the Georgia delegation confronted the House and Senate with budget figures demonstrating that even though King National Historic Site was one of the three most visited sites among the Park Service's urban parks, exceeded by only Independence Hall and the Statue of Liberty, it had received less than 20 percent of the funds spent developing comparable sites.[25] The stark contrast in funding, which implicitly leveled the charge of racist budgetary practices, persuaded Congress to apportion the necessary funds with the single caveat that no federal monies would be used to construct a replacement community center. Over a decade later the Park Service's promise to rebuild the community center has yet to be fulfilled and a site once dedicated to assisting the area's working-class African American residents now caters to middle-class tourists from home and abroad.[26]

A final hurdle to the completion of the proposed changes came in the form of direct opposition to the plan by the King family in 1994.[27] After initially supporting the plans for expanding the King National Historic Site, the family, led by Coretta Scott King, withdrew its support from the project when they learned that the visitor center would include an exhibit on King's life and career. In place of the National Park Service plan, the King family proposed building an interactive, edutainment center called "King Dream" and modeled after the Universal/MGM Studios venue in Orlando, Florida. The family urged that the proceeds from this venture be used to further King Center programs. The planned facility would depict the events from the Civil Rights Movement and its era via holographic and other multimedia exhibits and activity stations.[28]

In furtherance of its efforts, the King family barred the National Park Service from conducting tours of the King birth home, called for a halt in construction of the visitor center, and demanded that the Park Service abandon all of its activities and permanently leave the area. In response, the Park Service rescinded its $535,000 annual subsidy to the King Center. Members of the King family and

King Center staff argued that the Park Service was stealing the family's legacy and, further, as a federal agency, was not in a position to interpret "people's history."[29] Nonetheless, African American community leaders, local residents and business owners, city council representatives, the mayor, and state and federal representatives continued to back the Park Service's plan. Perhaps most critical in the eventual success of the Park Service plan was a series of editorials and opinion columns that appeared in newspapers and magazines across the country, lambasting the family as greedy. These were further bolstered by an *Atlanta Journal Constitution* investigation into King Center finances that revealed an institution beset by disorganization and improprieties.[30] In the face of such antagonism and lacking any outside source of funding for their proposed facility, the King family withdrew its protest of the visitor center. Since then, it has invited the Park Service to purchase the King Center property on Auburn Avenue and elsewhere.[31]

The new facilities and tours at the King National Historic Site opened several weeks prior to the beginning of the 1996 Olympic Games. Among the steps taken to introduce the improved site to an international audience, organizers placed prominent advertisements in the international terminal at Atlanta's Hartsfield Airport. Revealing the disjuncture between international and domestic memorial politics that allowed the site to languish originally, no similar advertisements were placed in the domestic terminal.[32]

BIRMINGHAM

In Alabama, the Birmingham Civil Rights District emerged from the efforts of a group of academic and legal professionals who aligned themselves with the city's first black mayor and, more broadly, the liberal coalition that dominated city politics beginning in the late 1970s. At the district's core are three sites closely linked by proximity, design, and the history of the 1963 campaign to desegregate the city: the Birmingham Civil Rights Institute, Kelly Ingram Park, and Sixteenth Street Baptist Church.

The original proposal for the Birmingham Civil Rights Institute was put forward in 1979 by the city's mayor, David Vann.[33] As a white liberal, Vann served as a mediator during the 1963 campaign and was party to the negotiations that followed the demonstrations. He was elected to city council in 1971 and to the mayor's office in 1975 by a coalition of black and white voters. During his first term, however, Vann's coalition fell apart in the wake of a police shooting of a young black woman and his subsequent refusal to suspend the offending officer.[34] Running behind in the polls with the next election approaching, Vann proposed a civil rights museum. In response, Birmingham's city council convened a committee to investigate the idea. Vann lost the election but the winner, Richard Arrington, the city's first black mayor, endorsed the idea of a museum.[35]

Despite a mayoral endorsement, the project suffered for lack of appropriations and stagnated in committee throughout Arrington's first term. This was due in part to opposition from some city council members to funding another museum.[36] Proponents of the museum argued that the city was best known for its civil rights history and that none of the city's existing museums reflected the African American heritage of Birmingham. Further opposition to the museum project stemmed from a general apprehension about examining the past. Running as an unspoken subtext throughout the on-again, off-again deliberations was the tacit wish of many in Birmingham to ignore the past for fear of attracting criticism or exacerbating existing racial tensions.[37] The mayor's executive secretary, Edward LaMonte, who was involved in the project over its thirteen-year history, remarked, "I've been surprised by the vehemence of some whites in saying 'Don't bring that up.'"[38] This feeling was pervasive enough that Arrington, who was elected by a narrow margin and felt his support among white voters to be tenuous, did not push for the museum with much determination.[39]

Arrington won reelection in 1983, as he would do five times over the course of two decades, and the museum project gathered momentum. Importantly, the project received the endorsement of the downtown business association, Operation New Birmingham. Created in the wake of the 1963 demonstrations, Operation New Birmingham brought together many of the city's most powerful corporate magnates, real estate agents, and attorneys for the specific purpose of addressing the city's poor public image and attracting commerce to the central business district. Although members of Operation New Birmingham recognized the district's potential for controversy given local opposition and institutional turf wars over limited funding for the arts, they backed the project's potential for improving the city's image and attracting visitors.[40] As was the case in Memphis, discussed below, the twin arguments of a need to rectify the city's image and the promise of tourist revenues helped secure several million dollars from corporate donors.[41]

In November 1985, the city allocated $500,000 for the purchase of a half-block parcel of land adjacent to Kelly Ingram Park and Sixteenth Street Baptist Church for the museum.[42] Early in the process, there had been some debate over the location of the museum. Some had lobbied for a parcel closer to the Fourth Avenue business district as a way of improving its sagging fortunes.[43] One white committee member suggested that few people would visit a museum located near Kelly Ingram Park due to that area's reputation as a dangerous part of town. He argued that the museum be placed at a site near the affluent, largely white suburb of Mountain Brook, along the city's border. He also suggested that the name of the museum drop any reference to civil rights and replace it with human rights.[44] Neither of these suggestions was adopted, and the eventual site chosen for the museum received the support of the city council and the museum board as well as the local editorial pages.[45] Pleased proponents described the area around the park and church as a "sacred space" in which the cause of freedom had been forwarded, likening its importance to that of Valley Forge in the country's democratic experience.[46]

Museum construction commenced in February 1991 but the project remained a controversial issue: the groundbreaking ceremony was protested by black activists who complained that working-class citizens had been left out of the planning of the museum. This prompted the city to hire two public relations firms to orchestrate the opening of the institute.[47] These consultants gauged public opinion, both locally and nationally. Locally, the fact that two bond issues were voted down by Birmingham's majority black electorate, combined with some critical editorial commentary, was cause for concern. Nationally, the city was viewed as a hotbed of racism, with its reaction to the planned museum interpreted as yet another indication of widespread bigotry. The firms decided to counter these opinions by focusing on the message that "Birmingham accepts its past, has begun the process of healing, celebrates its vital role in civil rights history, and continues to make progress toward improved race relations."[48] This idea was the central theme of a campaign that sought to position the institute as a tribute to the city's civil progress and as a boon for future development.

The Birmingham Civil Rights Institute opened in 1992.[49] The final cost of the project totaled $12 million, with the majority of funds coming from the city, a portion from Jefferson County, and a $4 million commitment from local corporations.[50] The result is a structure whose design elements echo those of the nearby Sixteenth Street Baptist Church and Kelly Ingram Park. Sitting on adjacent corners at the intersection of Sixteenth Street and Fourth Avenue, the three sites form a coherent whole. Originally, this area lay astride the boundary between white and black commercial districts. Today, in what has become a mostly black city surrounded by white suburbs, it sits at the intersection of the movement's success and failure.[51] The dilapidated condition of the area around the Civil Rights District contrasts sharply with the relative prosperity of the city's central business district and surrounding suburbs. As a result of the dismantling of legal segregation, the black businesses adjacent to the district lost their reason for existence as African American consumers, integrated with whites under the sign of the dollar, took their business elsewhere. Compounded with the difficulty of getting loans, neglect of property by absentee landlords, and suburbanization, the traditional black business district declined.[52]

That said, with the opening of the institute and the revival of the park and church, the largely African American Fountain Heights neighborhood has become the focal point of competing proposals to revitalize the area.[53] One proposal, backed by Operation New Birmingham and local real estate developers, calls for the removal of several rundown or abandoned residences to be replaced with upscale shops and townhouses along the lines of a new urban village.[54] The other proposal, put forward by a coalition of Fountain Heights residents, calls upon the city to fund new sidewalks, sewer repairs, streetlights, and a local police substation.[55] After several confrontational city council meetings and a protest march, the two sides reconciled over a proposed settlement.[56] Although the new upscale construction will occur, the city will ensure that the infrastructure upgrades are extended into the entire neighborhood and not just the part being gentrified.[57] For the time being, however, the Civil Rights District is likely to remain as it is—a landscape memorializing the very movement that inadvertently contributed to the negative consequences that now define the surrounding neighborhood.

MEMPHIS

In Memphis, the National Civil Rights Museum commemorates the site of King's assassination at the Lorraine Motel in 1968. At the time, the motel was owned by Walter and Loree Bailey. The couple purchased the motel in 1942 when it was one of the few available for African American travelers.[58] Immediately following the assassination, the Baileys, working in tandem with the Southern Christian Leadership Conference, memorialized the site with a plaque. Although thousands of tourists and pilgrims visited the site annually, subsequent efforts to create a more extensive memorial failed. The motel barely survived on a customer base undercut by integration and the declining fortunes of small, inner-city motels and faced the threat of foreclosure and possible demolition in 1982, when Bailey recruited a local radio station, WDIA, and a civil rights attorney, D'Army Bailey (no relation), to help him save the motel and transform it into a memorial befitting King's memory.[59] WDIA, the first radio station in the South to feature black disc jockeys, catered to the African American community in Memphis and had taken the lead in several high-profile fund-raising efforts.[60] Under D'Army Bailey's leadership, a nonprofit foundation was established for the purpose of purchasing the motel and creating a memorial to King. In addition to D'Army Bailey and WDIA's station manager, the foundation's board included the president of Memphis-based and black-owned Tri-State Bank, a local member of the state legislature, the president of Memphis's Lucky Heart Cosmetics, and the executive director of the American Federation of State, County, and Municipal Employees Union (AFSCME)—the union that emerged from the 1968 strike that King died supporting.

The foundation acquired the property at a foreclosure auction thanks to a last-minute loan from Tri-State Bank and outright donations from the union, the cosmetics company, and the holder of the building's mortgage. In early 1986, bills were introduced into the state legislature on behalf of the project, and after a bout of intense lobbying, a deal was struck among Tennessee, Memphis, Shelby County, and the Lorraine Foundation. The state agreed to pay half of the $9 million in capital costs, with the city and county accounting for the remainder. Funds for the creation of exhibits and operating costs were raised from local corporations, such as Federal Express and Browning Ferris Industries. The exhibit space portrays major events in the Civil Rights Movement and incorporates portions of the original motel, including the balcony on which King was shot and the room in which he stayed.[61] The museum also emphasizes international human rights by annually recognizing a leader in the field with its Freedom Award. Past winners include Yitzhak Rabin and Nelson Mandela. A new wing of the museum—funded entirely with private donations—incorporates the boardinghouse from which the assassin operated and presents information regarding various theories associated with King's murder.[62]

As with the Birmingham Civil Rights Institute, the National Civil Rights Museum attracted donations and praise from around the country while suffering the criticism of local opponents. Some argued that the site, a mark of civic shame, should be obliterated rather than transformed into a shrine/attraction.[63] Others, fearing a drain on the budgets of already existing cultural institutions in the city, argued that no public funds should be spent on the museum.[64] Finally, some charged that King's legacy would be more appropriately served by the creation of a job training center, homeless shelter, or school rather than a multi-million-dollar cultural complex (Fig. 17.2).[65]

The most outspoken proponent of this latter position is Jacqueline Smith, a poverty rights activist who protests the museum from a sidewalk encampment several feet from the entrance. A sign at her encampment succinctly expresses her sentiments:

> What Jacqueline Smith believes is that the Lorraine Motel should be put to better use such as housing, job training, free college, clinic, or other services for the poor. She also believes that the area surrounding the Lorraine should be rejuvenated and made decent and kept affordable and not gentrified with expensive condominiums that price the poor people out of their community.

Supporters of the museum counter these arguments by noting that preservation of the actual site of the assassination has provided an invaluable link to the past.[66] They argue further that in light of the thousands of visitors who annually made their way to the derelict site prior to its refitting, the absence of an appropriate memorial damaged the city's reputation.[67]

FIGURE 17.2.

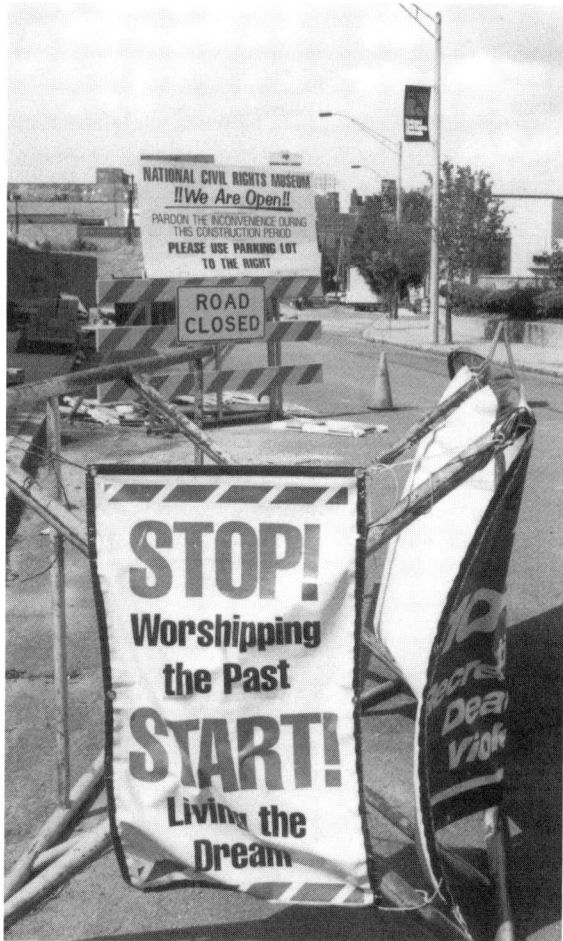

The juxtaposition of signs near the National Civil Rights Museum in Memphis poignantly calls attention to two different visions of how best to commemorate the Civil Rights Movement. *Foreground*, "Stop! Worshipping the past. Start! Living the Dream." *Background*, "National Civil Rights Museum !!We are open!!" (Photograph by author)

WHERE ARE THEY (NOT) LOCATED?

The history represented at civil rights memorials cannot be fully appreciated outside of the spatial context in which it is represented. Throughout the South, civil rights memorials tend to be located amid the declining remains of segregation-era black business districts and neighborhoods. These areas are characterized by the racialized aftershocks of suburbanization and so-called urban renewal programs: vacant lots and parking garages where there used to be neighborhoods and businesses, massive highway interchanges, low-end retail establishments and plummeting real estate values, warehouses and marginal industrial activity. The neighborhoods near most of the museums are predominantly African American, the conditions of which—dilapidated housing stock, high unemployment, poor transportation, declining schools, and violent drug trade—speak to the limitations of the very changes wrought by the events of the 1950s and 1960s and formally memorialized as the "Won Cause," a term coined by the historian Glenn T. Eskew to describe the triumphal telos of most civil rights memorials.[68] Although located in public space, civil rights memorials are not usually located in the traditional places of civic memory, calling attention to the racialized condition of public history on the urban landscape. In the three cities under study, the civil rights memorials and museums are in places that straddle the border between commemoration and condemnation insofar as they raise the question, Do these memorials celebrate these places or are they confined to them?

In the context of civil rights history, the location of these memorials is neither surprising nor inappropriate: these are sites at which history literally took place. Their location among black-owned businesses and churches affirms the central role played by these institutions in the movement. Mass meetings, the centerpiece of the movement's community building and instruction, were held in African American churches. Black-owned businesses were an important source of leadership and financial support. In contrast to African American teachers, for example, who were wholly dependent on white school boards and state legislatures for their existence and therefore at great risk of retaliation for participating in movement activities, businesses with a black clientele (e.g., beauty parlors) were somewhat insulated from the coordinated economic retaliation of the white citizens' council. Additionally, the representation of episodes from the civil rights era in these places complements their long history of anti-racism activism, practices that informed the movement and provided the context out of which it grew.

Thus, the location of civil rights memorials in historically black areas marks a point of convergence between practitioners of American public history—seeking to promote site-specific historical re-creations—and a storied history of resistance to and transgression of racist norms. Current trends in American public history emphasize site-based representations, as opposed to abstract sites of memory, in order to promote an authentic experience of the past.[69] These efforts to promote site-based public history intersect with the efforts of activists who seek to preserve places related to the movement in order to consolidate and extend the movement's achievements. Additionally, site-based public history and preservation offer a means of protecting against what activists interpret as efforts to dilute or co-opt the movement's legacy by commemorating it at sites removed from the actual events. Such was the case in Memphis, where memorial activists resisted the suggestion that the Lorraine Motel be torn down as a blemish on the city's reputation and King be remembered with a statue elsewhere in the city.[70] Although King's legacy is also commemorated downtown, activists considered it to be of the utmost importance to preserve the actual site of King's murder, in no small part because the visceral quality of place can be used to produce the sense of a tangible and immediate past. For those activists who want to simultaneously define the movement's legacy and organize a constituency around that legacy, the preservation of places associated with the movement is crucial.

As such, the location of memorial landscapes in historically black neighborhoods and business districts highlights the social-spatial context of memorial politics and its contemporary expressions. In a similar manner, their *non-location* relative to other memorial spaces in the city calls attention to the racialized geopolitics of public memory.[71] For instance, the movement is *not* being commemorated at the traditional core of civic memorial space in Atlanta, Birmingham, Memphis, and other cities across the South. Throughout the region, memorial spaces associated with city hall, the courthouse, and Main Street present an iconic legacy dominated by the city's preeminent white citizens, many of them dating from the antebellum or Civil War period. Historically, the outright absence or marginalized inclusion of African Americans at these sites inspired a memorial politics that sought to disclose the racial exclusivity of so-called civic memory. For instance, protests at the Lee monument in Richmond, Virginia, and at sites associated with Lincoln's memory called attention to the elision of black history from these places or its marginal inclusion in support of white achievements.[72]

The production of civil rights memorials outside of traditional memory space continues this politics of disclosing a history of elision and marginalization. The absence of civil rights memorials from the courthouse lawn and along Main Street subtly de-centers civic memory. In the process, this absence opens the racialized canon of public history to scrutiny and expands the traditional definition of civic space. Further, in light of the long-standing association between the state and traditional memorial space, commemorating the movement outside of these places offers a subtle rebuke to the antagonistic role played by the segregationist state during the movement. With all of the sites under study, the relocation of memory away from the main downtown park, surrounded by government buildings and dominated by war memorials, and toward the remnants of the black business district is part of a broader strategy for reconstituting a civic sphere via recognition of new civic memorial spaces.[73] In both Birmingham and Memphis, specific proposals for creating memorial landscapes and raising the funds to pay for them were couched in terms of coming to terms with the past in order to move beyond it.[74] Positioning these memorials on what were heretofore the edges of civic space commemorates the role played by the movement in which the putative center, compromised by segregationist doctrine and boss rule, was redeemed by forces operating from the margins of political power.

Nevertheless, the absence of civil rights history at city hall and along Main Street raises the concern that in addition to celebrating the movement's heritage sites, the memorials at issue may simultaneously be confined to them—*confined* in the sense that if organizers had so desired, could they have secured a site for these memorials outside of predominantly African American neighborhoods and placed them within the traditional core of civic memory? Research on the (re)naming of civic infrastructure, such as streets and schools, in honor of Martin Luther King Jr. suggests it is unlikely.[75] In the case of streets honoring King's legacy, proposals to rename major thoroughfares have faced insurmountable opposition, and minor streets or portions of large streets located in African American–dominated districts have been substituted. The most significant opposition to such plans has come from whites who claim that King is too narrowly "racial" to be commemorated in a public space meant to represent all citizens, the implication being that it would be racially partisan to commemorate him along Main Street and that his memory rightly belongs in the black part of town. Among its effects, the location of King Street—or other pieces of memorial architecture for that matter—in the black part of town perpetuates the white dominance of civic memorial space and further enunciates the social-spatial boundary between "white" and "not-white" places and identities. And although this place on the margins of civic space can be used as a site of leverage in order to substantiate calls for justice, it comes at the price of a location that can be ignored by elites and its radical meaning discursively contained as being "narrowly" racial.

CONCLUSION

The observation that in most cities King Street coincides with the bounds of the local African American community and only in rare instances continues into the central business district or the outlying suburbs is emblematic of the ambiguity that pervades the civil rights memorial landscape as a whole. The situation raises a hoary, perhaps intractable question, one that has been asked in the wake of all the country's social upheavals, including the Civil Rights Movement: After the revolution, to what extent has the country's collective sense of worth improved? Put in terms of civil rights commemoration, has our definition of a collective past been expanded to include, for instance, vernacular-built Baptist churches and now-derelict black business districts? Is this pervasive bounding of certain histories as "African American" a mark of pride, a sign that the canon of places considered to be properly historical is expanding away from the traditional white core? Or are we witnessing a subtle instance of racism in which civil rights history is put in its "place" by professional and public audiences that understand the 'hood and Main Street as racially polarized places, one suitable for "black" history and the other for "white"? Is it a sign that rather than integrate public memory at the courthouse, public square, and along Main Street, African American history has been, quite literally, ghettoized? Is it the case that the movement against segregation—widely, if erroneously, cheered as a success—has in turn found its memory segregated?

Ultimately, questions of this sort raise issues of intent and interpretation that cannot be answered in any satisfying way outside of the locally contingent circumstances that condition the production of these memorials. This ambiguous situation—involving as it does nebulous questions of motives as well as the problematic role of the state and private interests in their production—suggests the need to go beyond simply heralding the much-welcomed arrival of civil rights history on the memorial landscape and probe the condition of its production. In the case of the cities under study, diverse coalitions were responsible for making these memorials. The political-economic context of these public spaces offers points of both contrast and comparison. For instance, all three have struggled against opposition based on financial concerns, racial bias, and a reluctance to delve into what was perceived by some as an unpleasant story. Each coalition has overcome this opposition by developing broad support networks and constituencies. The constituent interests set aside their separate, sometimes conflicting desires (e.g., to improve a city's public image, advance an activist cause, or redeem the past from oblivion) and seized the common opportunity to shape the future by defining the past.

The production of these memorials is part of a larger movement in the public portrayal of American history from one that represented the past as white and elite to a more democratic vision of the past. That the Civil Rights Movement, an event so intimately associated with African Americans, has been able to claim public space suggests the extent of the movement's success; after all, it is the winners who write history. This success, however, does not remove these sites from the ongoing politics of representing and interpreting the movement. Taken as a whole, the public spaces associated with the Civil Rights Movement are sites at which the meaning of "civil rights," how they are achieved, their current status, and future promise, is currently undergoing active negotiation. In addition to challenging traditional conventions regarding whose history should be remembered as well as where and how that history should be commemorated, these memorials reinscribe certain hegemonic narratives.[76] For instance, as they write the past, the winners produce an unevenly developed memorial landscape, one that includes and excludes certain elements of the past. In contrast to most civil rights memorials, which represent the movement as a triumph, the decimated business districts that surround these sites offer a different vision of the changes wrought by the movement, namely, the social disintegration of black communities and the wholesale devaluing of the real estate on which they were built. Further, there are significant contradictions and exclusions in the memorial landscape's treatment of the civil rights era.[77] As a result, this landscape is characterized by deep ironies and cannot be considered static or finished.

Although commonly perceived as an objective recording of the past, inclusion and exclusion on the memorial landscape are closely associated with the political economy of commemoration. Examining the development and relative location of civil rights memorials pries open the conventional meanings embedded at these sites and acts as a reminder of the essentially unsettled condition of representations, of their constant vulnerability to multiple and sometimes contradictory interpretations. Location, understood in relation to multiple scales and referents, may confirm, erode, contradict, or render mute the intended meanings of the memorials' producers. Despite the best efforts of their producers, memorials cannot be insulated from the influence of relative location. The result is that the meanings of these memorials, and the political capital that can subsequently be derived from them, are produced intertextually via the interplay among authorial intentions, interpretive canons, and their social-spatial context. Rather than establishing the movement's public legacy once and for all, the creation of a memorial landscape ensures that debates over the movement's meaning will continue to play a role in contemporary politics of race, urban development, and memory.

NOTES

This chapter is a revised version of an article that originally appeared in *Urban Geography*, 23, no. 1 (2002): 31–56. I offer many thanks for the thoughtful comments and patient support of John Paul Jones III, Susan David Dwyer, Gerry Pratt, Dell Upton, Dana White, Bobby Wilson, the participants in Emory University's Center for the Study of Public Scholarship Spring 2000 seminar, and my colleagues from the University of British Columbia's Peter Wall Institute for Advanced Studies Junior Scholars Program. This research was supported by a Doctoral Dissertation Improvement grant, SBR-9811145, from the National Science Foundation and a Dissertation Research Grant from the Otis Paul Starkey Fund of the Association of American Geographers, as well as grants from the Office for Professional Development and the School of Liberal Arts at the Indianapolis campus of Indiana University.

1. Michael Omi and Howard Winant, *Racial Formation in the United States: From the 1960s to the 1990s* (New York: Routledge, 1994).

2. Derek H. Alderman, "Creating a New Geography of Memory in the South: (Re)Naming of Streets in Honor of Martin Luther King, Jr.," *Southeastern Geographer* 36, no. 1 (1996): 51–69; Derek H. Alderman, "A Street Fit for a King: Naming Places and Commemoration in the American South," *The Professional Geographer* 52, no. 4 (2000): 672–684; Robert. R. Weyeneth, "Historic Preservation and the Civil Rights Movement,"

CRM Bulletin 18, no. 4 (1995): 6–8; Jonathan Tilove, *Along Martin Luther King: Travels Along Black America's Main Street* (New York: Random House, 2003).

3. James S. Duncan, *The City as Text: The Politics of Landscape Interpretation in the Kandyan Kingdom* (Cambridge, UK: Cambridge University Press, 1990); Kenneth E. Foote, *Shadowed Ground: America's Landscapes of Violence and Tragedy* (Austin: University of Texas Press, 1997); Dolores Hayden, *The Power of Place: Urban Landscapes as Public History* (Boston: MIT Press, 1995); John Paul Jones III, "The Street Politics of Jackie Smith," in *The Blackwell Companion to the City*, ed. Gary Bridge and Sophie Watson (Oxford: Blackwell, 2000), 448–471; Scott A. Sandage, "A Marble House Divided: The Lincoln Memorial, the Civil Rights Movement, and the Politics of Memory, 1939–1963," *Journal of American History* 80 (1993): 135–167; Kirk Savage, "The Past in the Present," *Harvard Design Magazine* 9 (1999): 1–5; Richard H. Schein, "The Place of Landscape: A Conceptual Framework for Interpreting an American Scene," *Annals of the Association of American Geographers* 87, no. 4 (1997): 660–680.

4. Dolores Hayden, *The Power of Place: Urban Landscapes as Public History* (Boston: MIT Press, 1995); Jones, "Street Politics of Jackie Smith"; Savage, "Past in the Present."

5. Nuala C. Johnson, "Cast in Stone: Monuments, Geography, and Nationalism," *Environment and Planning D: Society and Space* 13 (1995): 51–65; David Lowenthal, "Past Time, Past Place: Landscape and Memory," *Geographical Review* 65, no. 1 (1975): 1–36; David Lowenthal, *The Heritage Crusade and the Spoils of History* (Cambridge: Cambridge University Press, 1998); James E. Young, *The Texture of Memory: Holocaust Memorials and Meaning* (New Haven, CT: Yale University Press, 1993).

6. James S. Duncan and Nancy Duncan, "(Re)Reading the Landscape," *Environment and Planning D: Society and Space* 6 (1988): 117–126; Schein, "The Place of Landscape."

7. Foote, *Shadowed Ground*; John R. Gillis, "Memory and Identity: The History of a Relationship," in *Commemorations: The Politics of National Identity*, ed. John R. Gillis (Princeton, NJ: Princeton University Press, 1994), 3–40.

8. Maoz Azaryahu, "McDonald's or Golani Junction? A Case of Contested Place in Israel," *The Professional Geographer* 51, no. 4 (1999): 481–492; Maurice Halbwachs, *The Collective Memory*, trans. F. J. Ditter and V. Y. Ditter (New York: Harper Colophon, 1980); Johnson, "Cast in Stone"; Claudia Koonz, "Between Memory and Oblivion: Concentration Camps in German Memory," in *Commemorations: The Politics of National Identity*, ed. John R. Gillis (Princeton, NJ: Princeton University Press, 1994), 258–280; Pierre Nora, "Between Memory and History: Les Lieux de Mémoire," *Representations* 26 (Spring 1989): 7–24.

9. Jonathan Boyarin, "Space, Time, and the Politics of Memory," in *Remapping Memory: The Politics of Timespace*, ed. Jonathan Boyarin (Minneapolis: University of Minnesota Press, 1994), 1–38; Reinhart Koselleck, *Futures Past: On the Semantics of Historical Time* (Cambridge, MA: Harvard University Press, 1985); David Lowenthal, *The Past Is a Foreign Country* (Cambridge, UK: Cambridge University Press, 1985).

10. Craig E. Barton, ed., *Sites of Memory: Perspectives on Architecture and Race* (New York: Princeton Architectural Press, 2001); Jonathan I. Leib, "Separate Times, Shared Spaces: Arthur Ashe, Monument Avenue, and the Politics of Richmond, Virginia's Symbolic Landscape," *Cultural Geographies* 9, no. 3 (2002); Fath Davis Ruffins, "Mythos, Memory, and History: African American Preservation Efforts, 1820–1990," in *Museums*

and Communities: The Politics of Public Culture, ed. Ivan Karp, Christine M. Kreamer, and Stephen D. Lavine (Washington, DC: Smithsonian Institution Press, 1992), 507–611; Kirk Savage, *Standing Soldiers, Kneeling Slaves: Race, War and Monument in 19th-Century America* (Princeton, NJ: Princeton University Press, 1997).

11. Donald W. Blight, " 'For Something Beyond the Battlefield': Frederick Douglass and the Struggle for the Memory of the Civil War," *Journal of American History* 75, no. 4 (1989): 1156–1178; John Bodnar, *Remaking America: Public Memory, Commemoration, and Patriotism in the Twentieth Century* (Princeton, NJ: Princeton University Press, 1992); David Burnham, *How the Other Half Lived: A People's Guide to American Historic Sites* (New York: Faber and Faber, 1995); Toni Morrison, *Playing in the Dark: Whiteness and the Literary Imagination* (Cambridge, MA: Harvard University Press, 1992); John P. Radford, "Identity and Tradition in the Post–Civil War South," *Journal of Historical Geography* 18 (1992): 91–103; Sandage, "A Marble House Divided"; Savage, *Standing Soldiers, Kneeling Slaves*.

12. Denis Cosgrove and Stephen Daniels, eds., *The Iconography of Landscape* (Cambridge, UK: University of Cambridge Press, 1988); Janice Monk, "Gender in the Landscape: Expressions of Power and Meaning," in *Inventing Places: Studies in Cultural Geography*, ed. Kay Anderson and Fay Gale (Melbourne: Longman Cheshire, 1992), 123–138; Tim Cresswell, *In Place / Out of Place: Geography, Ideology, and Transgression* (Minneapolis: University of Minnesota Press, 1996).

13. Owen J. Dwyer, "Interpreting the Civil Rights Movement: Place, Memory, and Conflict," *The Professional Geographer* 52, no. 4 (2000): 660–671.

14. Ibid.; Owen J. Dwyer and J. P. Jones III, "White Socio-Spatial Epistemology," *Social and Cultural Geography* 1, no. 2 (2001): 209–222.

15. Owen J. Dwyer, "Memorial Landscapes Dedicated to the Civil Rights Movement," Ph.D. diss., University of Kentucky, 2000.

16. Cresswell, *In Place / Out of Place*; Halbwachs, *The Collective Memory*; Yi-Fu Tuan, *Space and Place: The Perspective of Experience* (Minneapolis: University of Minnesota Press, 1977).

17. Alton Hornsby Jr., "A City That Was Too Busy to Hate," in *Southern Businessmen and Desegregation*, ed. E. Jacoway and D. R. Colburn (Baton Rouge: Louisiana State University Press, 1982), 120–136; Charles Rutheiser, *Imagineering Atlanta: The Politics of Place in the City of Dreams* (London: Verso, 1996).

18. James W. Loewen, *Lies Across America: What Our Historic Sites Get Wrong* (New York: New Press, 1999).

19. Robert W. Blythe, Maureen A. Carroll, and Steven H. Moffson, *Martin Luther King, Jr. National Historic Site Historic Resource Study* (Atlanta, GA: National Park Service, Southeast Regional Office, 1994); Lucy Lawliss, *Martin Luther King, Jr. National Historic Site Cultural Landscape Report: Birth-Home Block* (Atlanta, GA: National Park Service, Southeast Regional Office, 1995).

20. Rutheiser, *Imagineering Atlanta*.

21. National Park Service, *A Grand Endeavor for a Man with a Dream: The Story of the Martin Luther King, Jr., National Historic Site and Preservation District* (Washington, DC: Department of the Interior, 1997).

22. Ebba Hierta, "Overcoming the Odds," *National Parks* 70, nos. 7–8 (1996): 40–45;

National Park Service, *Grand Endeavor for a Man with a Dream*; Rutheiser, *Imagineering Atlanta*.

23. Hierta, "Overcoming the Odds"; Howard Pousner, "King Site Dream on Way to Reality," *Atlanta Journal and Constitution*, November 13, 1993.

24. Hierta, "Overcoming the Odds"; National Park Service, *Grand Endeavor for a Man with a Dream*; Ernie Suggs, "$1 Million Provided to Restore Church," *Atlanta Constitution*, January 18, 2000.

25. Hierta, "Overcoming the Odds."

26. Ibid.; National Park Service, *Grand Endeavor for a Man with a Dream*.

27. Howard Pousner, "King Family Plans Disney-Like Park," *Atlanta Journal and Constitution*, August 11, 1994.

28. National Park Service, *Grand Endeavor for a Man with a Dream*; Pousner, "King Family Plans Disney-Like Park"; Rutheiser, *Imagineering Atlanta*.

29. John Blake, "King Week '95: Q & A: Dexter King and Troy Lissimore: Main Figures in King Controversy Discuss Conflict over District's Future," *Atlanta Journal and Constitution*, January 15, 1995; Howard Pousner, "The King Site Fight," *Atlanta Journal and Constitution*, January 21, 1995; Rutheiser, *Imagineering Atlanta*.

30. Rutheiser, *Imagineering Atlanta*; Mark Sherman, "King Center Dips into Endowment," *Atlanta Journal and Constitution*, February 1, 1995; Mark Sherman and John Blake, "King Center's Finances: More Federal Funding May Be Difficult," *Atlanta Journal and Constitution*, February 1, 1995.

31. Interview by author, Frank Catroppa, June 9, 1999.

32. Interview by author, Robert R. Weyeneth, October 14, 1998.

33. Thomas H. Cox, "Interview with Odessa Woolfolk, President, Board of Directors, Birmingham Civil Rights Institute" (Birmingham, AL: Birmingham Civil Rights Institute, 1995); Glenn T. Eskew, "The Birmingham Civil Rights Institute and the New Ideology of Tolerance," in *The Civil Rights Movement in American History*, ed. R. C. Romano and Leigh Raiford (Athens: University of Georgia Press, 2006), 28–66; Jimmie Lewis Franklin, *Back to Birmingham: Richard Arrington, Jr. and His Times* (Tuscaloosa: University of Alabama Press, 1989).

34. Franklin, *Back to Birmingham*.

35. Sandy Coleman, "Birmingham's Civil Rights Institute Presents a Compelling History of the Movement," *Boston Globe*, February 26, 1995.

36. Terry Horne, "Rights Museum Remains a Dream," *Birmingham Post-Herald*, February 14, 1984.

37. William Booth, "Birmingham's Civil Rights Institute Is Tribute to a Not-So-Distant History," *Washington Post*, January 30, 1993.

38. Dave White, "Civil Rights Museum, Runway Beef-up Part of New City Thrust," *Birmingham News*, November 17, 1985.

39. Eskew, "The Birmingham Civil Rights Institute"; Horne, "Rights Museum Remains a Dream."

40. Cox, "Interview with Odessa Woolfolk"; Eskew, "Birmingham Civil Rights Institute."

41. Joe Nabbefeld, "Institute Should Have Strong Impact on City Economy," *Birmingham News*, November 15, 1992.

42. Dave White, "Council Votes to Buy Land for Rights Museum," *Birmingham News*, November 20, 1985.

43. Mitch Mendelson, "Black Business District Fights for New Life," *Birmingham Post-Herald*, January 28, 1981.

44. Horne, "Rights Museum Remains a Dream."

45. James R. McAdory, "Ideal Site for Museum," *Birmingham News*, November 23, 1985; White, "Civil Rights Museum"; White, "Council Votes to Buy Land."

46. Horne, "Rights Museum Remains a Dream."

47. PR News, "Case Study No. 2333: Intensive Media Campaign Fuels Support for Civil Rights Facility," *PR News*, January 25, 1993; Booth, "Birmingham's Civil Rights Institute Is Tribute"; Eskew, "Birmingham Civil Rights Institute"; Marcel Hopson, "The Grand Dedication and Opening Are Over; the Unfinished Agenda Must Now Include Roll Call of Unnamed 'Footsoldiers,'" *Birmingham World*, December 9, 1992; Nick Patterson, "Civil Rights Activists Want Stories Told," *Birmingham Post-Herald*, February 16, 1993.

48. PR News, "Case Study No. 2333."

49. Fredrick Kaimann, "A Dream Realized: Civil Rights Institute Opens," *The Birmingham News*, November 15, 1992.

50. Coleman, "Birmingham's Civil Rights Institute."

51. Bobby M. Wilson, *Race and Place in Birmingham: The Civil Rights and Neighborhood Movements* (New York: Rowman & Littlefield, 2000).

52. Mendelson, "Black Business District Fights for New Life"; Bobby M. Wilson, "Structural Imperatives Behind Racial Change in Birmingham, Alabama," *Antipode* 24 (1992): 171–202.

53. Interview by author, Bobby M. Wilson, June 22, 1999.

54. Anita Debro, "Residents Wary of Development," *Birmingham News*, January 12, 1999; Roy L. Williams, "Downtown Construction Revitalization Picks Up Zip," *Birmingham News*, January 11, 1998.

55. Anita Debro, "Fountain Heights Residents Still Oppose Downtown Revitalization Project," *Birmingham News*, January 24, 1999; Sherrel Wheeler Stewart, "Residents Protest Neighborhood Plan," *Birmingham News*, January 13, 1999.

56. Anita Debro, "Fountain Heights Demands Action," *Birmingham News*, February 24, 1999.

57. Ibid.

58. Alice Faye Duncan, *The National Civil Rights Museum Celebrates Everyday People* (Memphis, TN: Bridgewater Books, 1995).

59. Kenneth Roger Adderly, "Monument on the Mississippi: Background, Development, and the Rising Significance of the National Civil Rights Museum," Master's thesis, University of Memphis, 1997; D'Army Bailey, "Correspondence File: National Civil Rights Museum" (District Circuit Court, Chambers of Judge D'Army Bailey, Memphis, TN, 1998); D'Army Bailey, "D'Army Bailey Papers" (Mississippi Valley Room, McWherter Library, University of Memphis, 1998); Jerry Huston, "Site of Shame Now Glows as Beacon for Civil Rights," *The Commercial Appeal*, July 17, 1994; D. J. Miller and Associates, "Memphis Consortium Disparity Study" (Memphis, TN: Memphis Consortium, 1994); National Civil Rights Museum, "National Civil Rights Museum Archives," Memphis, TN, 1998; Wayne Risher, "Expert's Vision First Gave Form to Project in '86," *The Commercial*

Appeal, Spring 1991; Wayne Risher, "Museum Is Fruition of Dreams of Motel Owner, Many Others," *The Commercial Appeal*, Spring 1991; Mary B.W. Tabor, "King's Dream Lives Again at the Site of His Death," *New York Times*, July 1, 1991; William Thomas, "Building a Dream," *The Commercial Appeal*, September 28, 1991.

60. Tom Walter, "WDIA: 50 and Still Happenin'," *The Commercial Appeal*, October 22, 1998.

61. Bernard J. Armada, "Memorial Agon: An Interpretive Tour of the National Civil Rights Museum," *Southern Communication Journal* 63, no. 3 (1998); National Civil Rights Museum, "Review of Museum Exhibits" (Memphis: National Civil Rights Museum, 1991).

62. Deborah M. Clubb, "Museum Plan Will Tie Events Before, Since," *The Commercial Appeal*, April 4, 1998.

63. Adderly, "Monument on the Mississippi"; Foote, *Shadowed Ground*.

64. Adderly, "Monument on the Mississippi."

65. Armada, "Memorial Agon"; Jones, "Street Politics of Jackie Smith"; Eileen Loh-Harrist, "Vigil of a Lifetime: Jacqueline Smith's Views Are as Concrete as the Sidewalk Before the Civil Rights Museum," *The Memphis Flyer*, November 19–25, 1998.

66. "Editorial: Time to Come in, Jackie," *The Memphis Flyer*, November 19–25, 1998.

67. Huston, "Site of Shame Now Glows."

68. Joan T. Beifus, *At the River I Stand* (Memphis, TN: St. Luke's Press, 1990); Townsend Davis, *Weary Feet, Rested Souls: A Guided History of the Civil Rights Movement* (New York: W. W. Norton and Co., 1998); Tom Dent, *Southern Journey: A Return to the Civil Rights Movement* (New York: William Morrow and Company, 1997); Eskew, "Birmingham Civil Rights Institute."

69. Jennifer A. Amundson, "What's Behind the Wall: Why Progressive Public Memorials Are Designed for Private Commemoration," *Reflections: The Journal of the School of Architecture, University of Illinois, Urbana-Champaign* 10 (Spring 1992): 50–66; Dydia DeLyser, "Authenticity on the Ground: Engaging the Past in a California Ghost Town," *Annals of the Association of American Geographers* 89, no. 4 (1999): 602–632; Betsy Wade, "Preserving the Past in Places Where Work Goes On," *Pittsburgh Post-Gazette*, August 16, 1998.

70. Adderly, "Monument on the Mississippi"; Huston, "Site of Shame Now Glows."

71. Hayden, *The Power of Place*; Fath Davis Ruffins, "Culture Wars Won and Lost, Part 2: The National African-American Museum Project," *Radical History Review* 70 (1998): 78–101.

72. Blight, "'For Something Beyond the Battlefield'"; Eliot M. Rudwick and August Meier, "Black Man in the 'White City': Negroes and the Columbian Exposition of 1893," *Phylon* 26 (1965): 354–361; Ruffins, "Mythos, Memory, and History"; Sandage, "Marble House Divided"; Kirk Savage, "The Politics of Memory: Black Emancipation and the Civil War Monument," in *Commemorations: The Politics of National Identity*, ed. John R. Gillis (Princeton, NJ: Princeton University Press, 1994), 127–149; Jeffrey C. Stewart and Fath Davis Ruffins, "'A Faithful Witness': Afro-American Public History in Historical Perspective, 1828–1984," in *Presenting the Past: Essays on History and the Public*, ed. Susan Porter Benson, Steven Brier, and Roy Rosenweig (Philadelphia: Temple University Press, 1986), 307–338.

73. Richard Arrington, "Birmingham Now," *American Visions* 1, no. 1 (1986): 50–51.

74. Hierta, "Overcoming the Odds"; Huston, "Site of Shame Now Glows."

75. Alderman, "Creating a New Geography of Memory in the South"; Alderman, "Street Fit for a King."

76. Cresswell, *In Place / Out of Place*; Nuala C. Johnson, "Sculpting Heroic Histories: Celebrating the Centenary of the 1798 Rebellion in Ireland," *Transactions of the Institute of British Geographers*, New Series 19, no. 1 (1994): 78–93; Ruffins, "Mythos, Memory, and History."

77. Dwyer, "Interpreting the Civil Rights Movement."

Carroll Van West

Sacred Spaces of Faith, Community, and Resistance

Rural African American Churches in Jim Crow Tennessee

Upon freedom, African Americans of the 1860s quickly sought to create new physical spaces that belonged to them and reflected their values. Besides homes for their families, they rushed to create three institutions in particular: churches, cemeteries, and schools. African Americans typically clustered these institutions close together, with the church invariably as the focal point (indeed, it often doubled as the school building) surrounded by their homes and businesses. As freedpeople, they consciously redesigned the space of the antebellum South to carve out their own distinct community space within the larger built environment, and from these roots in the built environment they created stable neighborhoods and communities as well as safe havens from the very real threat of violence and retribution in the Jim Crow South.

During the Jim Crow era of segregation within the legal system, and within the land itself, these sacred places of faith and community became even more important. The churches, with their significant roles in religion, education, politics, music, and ethnic identity, served as the cultural heart of rural black communities. Their primacy in the community was further reflected in the placement of other key early institutions (cemeteries, schools, fraternal lodges, and African American commercial enterprises such as barbershops and funeral homes) on the church lot or on other immediately adjoining properties.[1]

Most writers who chronicled the South 100 years ago never noted these little worlds within the bigger world of the Jim Crow South—a blind spot that still remains for too many today. But as he taught school in rural DeKalb County, Tennessee, W.E.B. Du Bois noted and then wrote about the space created by African Americans within the larger village landscape of Alexandria, Tennessee. In the classic book *The Souls of Black Folk*, Du Bois described the African American side of Alexandria:

> Cuddled on the hill to the north was the village of colored folks, who lived in three- or four-room unpainted cottages, some neat and homelike, and some dirty. The dwellings were scattered rather aimlessly, but they centered about the twin temples of the hamlet, the Methodist, and the Hard-Shell Baptist churches. These, in turn, leaned gingerly on a sad-colored schoolhouse. Hither my little world wended its crooked way on Sunday to meet other worlds, and gossip, and wonder, and make the weekly sacrifice with frenzied priest at the altar of the "old-time religion." The soft melody and the mighty cadences of Negro song fluttered and thundered. I have called my tiny community a world, and so its isolation made it; and yet there was among us but a half-awakened common consciousness, sprung from common joy and grief, a burial, birth, or wedding; from a common hardship in poverty, poor land, and low wages; and above all, from the sight of the veil that hung between us and Opportunity.[2]

In describing the church at Alexandria, Du Bois observed, "[M]ost striking to me, as I approached the village and the little plain church perched aloft, was the air of intense excitement that possessed that mass of Black folk."[3] He eloquently described the church as a "central Club House" where secular and sacred groups met, where the community gathered for both joyous and somber events, where newcomers could discover the community, where those wanting work could find out about jobs, and where those in need could find assistance. The church embodied within its four walls a whole range of institutions that served these various functions for whites in the Jim Crow South.[4] As protective safe havens; as the grounds for adjacent cemeteries that documented the size, the diversity, and the growth of community; as complex institutions that provided social and cultural services when few, if any, public buildings were available; and as cultural memory palaces that nurtured pride, accomplishment, and promise for a better future, rural African American churches and their surrounding environs represent the most sacred, and oftentimes secular, spaces of African American institutional building in the Jim Crow South.[5]

The early churches of the 1860s were commonly first located where African Americans expected to have a degree of safety and freedom. Many stood on the outskirts of the large "contraband camps" created by the federal government to shelter and control the thousands of freedmen and freedwomen who rushed to federal encampments from 1862 to 1865. In Tennessee, the largest camps stood in Memphis, Nashville, and Chattanooga, where the federal army maintained large occupation forces. But federal officials also placed contraband camps in smaller towns, such as Grand Junction, Bolivar, Somerville, La Grange, Murfreesboro, Clarksville, Tullahoma, and Pulaski. In Murfreesboro, a large number of African Americans flocked to the camps of the Union army of Cumberland after the Battle of Stones River in late December 1862. They stayed after the battle and formed a community around the federal national cemetery. (The community was known as Cemetery.) Today, the Stones River United Methodist Church and Ebenezer Primitive Baptist Church mark the Cemetery community. They stand a few hundred yards west of the railroad and just north of the boundaries of Stones River National Battlefield. The creation of the national park in the 1920s displaced many African American residents but left the churches untouched.[6]

Freedmen and freedwomen created many churches within the protective view of occupation forces. At Jonesboro, the seat of pro-Union Washington County, residents established the early Jonesboro African Methodist Episcopal (AME) Zion Church directly parallel to the railroad tracks, where federal troops were stationed. At the small county seat of Dover, the location of the battle of Fort Donelson in February 1862, African Americans formed and located a Missionary Baptist church and a Methodist church on the outskirts of the town, immediately adjacent to some of the earthworks of the federally occupied fort. At Clarksville, where the federal army occupied and enlarged an earlier Confederate fort, a large black community called New Providence, with several extant churches, developed adjacent to the fort from 1862 to 1870, by which time most occupation forces had left the state.[7]

In other towns, freedpeople established early churches on a mere sliver of space in the local townscape. Sometimes their choice was due to the influence of a missionary group or a specific church. In other cases, whites donated or sold blacks poor land at a poor location—like at the local cemetery on the margins of town. On May 15, 1869, for instance, Alexandria town officials deeded a plot of three acres for a cemetery, church, and school to a group of African American trustees and the Methodist church. More likely, the town's transfer of this largely worthless property of limestone outcroppings and cedar breaks on top

FIGURE 18.1.
Pikeville AME Zion Church, Bledsoe County,
Tennessee, 1998. (Photograph by author)

of a prominent hill overlooking the village placed it in compliance with recently approved state laws commanding counties to create public schools for whites and blacks. (The local white Methodist church also initially sponsored the black Methodist congregation as a mission.) The school disappeared around 1930, when state money, African American donations, and the Julius Rosenwald Fund supported a new school on the opposite end of town. The church, later known as the Seay Chapel Methodist Church, remained active until the late 1990s. The large African American cemetery was only recently rediscovered under twenty years of neglect and overgrowth. The cemetery is not known to have ever had a proper name. It is known to this day as the "cemetery on the hill," according to an interview with resident Carrie Helen Smith, and was the only place that a black person could be buried in Alexandria from emancipation to the 1960s.[8]

Two of the earliest black church buildings in Tennessee—Pikeville AME Zion Church in Bledsoe County and St. Mark's Primitive Baptist Church in Spring Hill, Maury County, both circa 1870—also stand on the outskirts of white villages. Both were established after passage of the 1869 state law requiring funding for African American education, and both are plain, unpretentious buildings where function took precedence over form. Their lack of "architectural style" was one reason contemporary whites paid them little notice, and why much later historic preservationists and architectural history scholars failed to notice them in their surveys and studies.

The meaning of the descriptive category "vernacular architecture" has been a hotly debated topic for a generation, and most rural African American churches could be most conveniently classified as "vernacular." In applying that convenient term, however, it is most useful to follow an older definition of vernacular, one by American studies scholar John Kouwehoven. In his opinion, the words "resilient, adaptable, simple, and unceremonious" conveyed the attributes of vernacular design. The Tennessee survey identified some buildings with distinctive styles (typically either Gothic Revival or Classical Revival from 1880 to 1940 and then Colonial Revival after that), but most churches are largely one-story, unadorned gable-front buildings, with wings for classrooms and/or community rooms attached to the rear of the sanctuary. Their function and place—not style—within the larger space of African American institution building are what gave them distinction and primacy within the rural built environment. "The difference between style and form is the difference between a statement and a language," observes Stewart Brand. "An architectural statement is limited to a few stylistic words and depends on originality for its impact, whereas a vernacular form unleashes the power of a whole, tested grammar."[9] The churches, surrounding African American institutions, and the location of both within a larger white-dominated cultural landscape spoke a language of space, one that

FIGURE 18.2.
Republican Primitive Baptist Church,
Haywood County, Tennessee, 1998.
(Photograph by author)

conveyed faith, certainly, but also community, permanence, stability, and the feeling of a safe haven.

The form, function, and space in which the church is located are important indicators of the church's significance. In assessing the architectural significance of these buildings, the form and how it has changed over time within the context of Kouwenhoven's four terms of resiliency, adaptability, simplicity, and unceremoniousness may be usefully evaluated in tandem with the surrounding setting. An excellent example is the Beth Salem Presbyterian Church (circa 1920) in McMinn County. As a small frame building with a plain gable-front entrance, its unadorned yet dignified appearance certainly meets Kouwenhoven's tests of simple and unceremonious. That the building served on the same spot for two generations as a church and that it also doubled as the local school underscores its resiliency and adaptability, and its use today as a ceremonial setting for annual African American homecomings indicates both its resiliency and adaptability. Across the road is a small community cemetery; behind the church are wood boards on poles that serve as tables when community gatherings and homecomings take place. For those who once lived and toiled in this Appalachian county, Beth Salem is the place where dispersed people could weekly create community and nurture achievement, identity, and family. During the summer homecomings, Beth Salem is still that place, for families gather from many counties and many states to reconnect to this sacred space.[10]

When assessed within the social, cultural, and economic contexts in which they were created, church buildings can be recognized for what they are: purposeful, intentional attempts to create distinctive and meaningful places of worship within a social and built environment that, in most cases, was antagonistic to the notion that African Americans even deserved a spot in the landscape. The desire to practice their own faiths in the isolation left by the dominant culture gave African Americans an important degree of power and agency while these places also served as statements of resistance to the status afforded them. Often, in their very names, such as Fredonia or Promise Land, African Americans proclaimed their freedom and independence, and these political statements in the land, interestingly, remained outside of the vision of most whites as the legal and political system stripped away many rights of African American citizenship.

Their place and rights as citizens, however, became important messages consistently reinforced at rural African American churches during the workweek. If the Pikeville church or Beth Salem church looked like the unadorned one-room schools located across the countryside, there was a good reason: they were schools during the week, when they educated children, and then churches on the weekends, where lessons in citizenship were often extended to adults. The story of the Pikeville building is tied closely to this dual sacred and secular function. African American residents during the Reconstruction purchased a plot of land for a school but only paid about one-half of the purchase price. With the help of the Freedmen's Bureau, a school named Lincoln Academy was established, and church groups also used the building, with a AME Zion congregation, which called the building the Mount Zion AME Zion Church, being the primary user. In 1888, Alexander Browder and Elbert Henson raised the remainder of the purchase price and had the deed transferred to the Trustees of the AME Zion Church. But to settle a legal challenge the following year, the building continued as a school and union church, with all of the local African American congregations—including AME Zion, Missionary Baptist, Christian Disciples, and Cumberland Presbyterian—eligible to use the building. That arrangement remained in effect until 1925 when the new Rosenwald school—named Lincoln School after this building—opened on the opposite end of town.[11]

That churches served secular and sacred functions buttressed their symbolic role as distinct places of identity and culture for African Americans. In the Tennessee project, over fifty extant school buildings stood immediately on the church lot or were located next door because the church had either provided land or served as a major sponsor for the school's establishment. The schools' dates of construction range from the turn of the century to last-gasp attempts to maintain "separate but equal" facilities in the 1950s. For instance, in Rogersville a historic brick school building (circa 1920) that is associated with the Swift Memorial College lies between the Russell Chapel AME Zion Church and the Hassan Street Christian Church. Several schools are associated with the Rosenwald school building program of the late 1910s and 1920s. According to Mary S. Hoffschwelle (Chapter 11), church congregations played a key role in supporting and giving land for the Rosenwald schools. Rosenwald agent Robert E. Clay typically held his organizational meetings at a local church. Women church members, who supplied the labor and dedication for Sunday School programs, grasped similar leadership roles in the Rosenwald campaigns. They organized community suppers, entertainments, and fried fish and fried chicken feasts, usually at local churches. Denominational divisions between congregations sometimes led to local fights over the Rosenwald campaigns. Clay invariably returned to the communities and generally ordered the warring factions to stop and to work together, giving what he called a "frank" speech.[12]

Examples of the close relationship between churches and the Rosenwald program include Wingo, in Carroll County, where on the west side of the railroad tracks, at a local crossroads, is the Wingo Missionary Baptist Church (to the south) and immediately north is the Rosenwald school from 1920–1921. Immediately adjacent to the St. Paul Missionary Baptist Church, within a stone's throw from the Mississippi River in Tipton County, is a two-room early 1920s Rosenwald school, now used as a church-operated community center. Across from Goodes Temple AME Zion in Jefferson County, south of White Pine, is a circa 1919 two-room Rosenwald school. In Shelby County, where most Rosenwald schools were built in the state, the Oak Grove Missionary Baptist Church in Bartlett sponsored the school, and once the school closed, the church turned it into offices for community outreach programs. Other churches, such as Craigs Chapel AME Zion in Loudon County and Durham Chapel Baptist in Sumner County, also incorporated twentieth-century school buildings in their churches. Indeed, some congregations took over old schools, abandoned after consolidation or desegregation in the 1950s, and turned them into their churches. Toles Chapel Christian CME Church in Camden (Benton County), Union Hill Missionary Baptist in Elkton (Giles County), and Cumberland City Methodist Church (Stewart County) are good examples.

Historic cemeteries surrounded approximately one-fourth of the rural African American churches in Tennessee. The cemetery, according to folklorist John Michael Vlach, "has long had special significance. Beyond its association with the fear and awe of death, which all humans share, the graveyard was, in the past, one of the few places in America where overt black identity could be asserted and maintained."[13] Many have been in use since the 1860s and 1870s and most predate the actual church buildings, therefore representing the oldest institutions in their respective communities. What they lack in large, ornate headstones—the easiest way to distinguish a rural white cemetery from a rural black cemetery—they compensate for with clear African American patterns, from the older African tradition of burying a loved one with broken pottery and other items on the grave to a more modern treatment of low concrete vaults over the graves.

Fraternal lodges share land with, or lie adjacent to, church buildings at several sites across Tennessee. Three good examples are at St. Luke AME Church in South Fulton, Obion County, where the two-story concrete lodge of Jacksonville F&AM Lodge No. 50 is located next to the church; at Pleasant Grove Missionary Baptist Church in Grand Junction, Hardeman County, where the Frank Gibson Masonic Hall stands across the street from the church (and a 1950s school is nearby); and Third Avenue Baptist Church and Howard Chapel AME Church in Huntingdon, Carroll County, where the Golden Eagle Lodge No. 111 building stands on a lot behind the Baptist church and adjacent to the AME church. In the Jim Crow era, fraternal lodges transcended the function of group effort and race consciousness. According to Bobby Lovett, "blacks had no choice but to be racially conscious—a racist society and white-imposed Jim Crow rules dictated that for them." To Lovett, "lodges signaled the development of white and elite class structures in the post-Emancipation Negro communities, and often embodied the leadership" to build other civic and business institutions.[14] Historian Lester Lamon adds: "[I]n addition to creating occasions for socializing, the fraternal organizations usually provided small illness or death benefits, represented blacks in public celebrations such as Fourth of July parades, and served as important training grounds for black leaders."[15] Fraternal lodges also were major church builders in several areas of the state. Indeed, the United Sons and Daughters of Charity Lodge Hall in Bolivar (circa 1930) also served as a church building for congregations who lacked their own meeting place until the end of the twentieth century.

Typically, it took a generation to create this institutional network of churches, schools, cemeteries, lodges, and early businesses. The community stability provided by these institutions proved invaluable as rural African Americans withstood the onslaught of Jim Crow segregation from the late 1880s forward. This era was the nadir of race relations throughout the South. Violence and intimidation became increasingly common. From 1882 to 1932, a conservative figure counts at least 177 lynchings of African Americans in Tennessee; the last recorded lynching took place in 1940. As African American communities stabilized and the churches became resilient institutions, congregations built scores of new buildings that were larger and that often included additional space for community gatherings (rooms called fellowship centers or community halls). At the same time, segregation codes were being imposed across the state.

In the long Jim Crow era, churches were among the few public spaces where African Americans could and would gather for community-wide secular events. Unlike fraternal lodges, they were not gender-specific or limited to certain classes or trades. Schools were another option, but only for gatherings of an apolitical nature. Since public funding (albeit limited) was involved, schools were subject to political pressure from the white establishment. Churches were more independent, and as African American places of faith, they were more difficult for whites to influence, because they often did not even understand the meaning of the rituals and the music that made up the African American worship service.

Surrounded by lodges, schools, and cemeteries, rural churches nurtured African American identity and culture. The church and its grounds served as a public space where social and cultural rituals grounded in equality took place each Sunday. The churches, concludes historian William E. Montgomery, supported "people who struggled to maintain a positive self-concept against an onslaught of negative images and assertions emanating from the dominant white society."[16] Several of the larger churches met well into the evening, as historian Elisabeth D. Lasch-Quinn's description of alternative settlement school-like institutions suggests. And they often provided African American community services and worked toward social reform in the Jim Crow South. Rural African Americans, as Du Bois noted about Alexandria's community, created effective "little worlds" within the hostile dominant environment of that era.[17]

Alexandria was not the only such space within the state. In Sullivan County, freedpeople and veterans from the United States Colored Troops (USCT) established circa 1870 a freedmen's community soon known as Butterfly, the name given to a post office that existed there from 1883 to 1905. (In the twentieth century the community became known as Shinbone.) The community centered on a hill near Bays Mountain—where a concentration of Unionists lived in what was a mostly Confederate county. The centerpiece was the Pierce Chapel AME Church, a log building. Jerome Pierce, a mulatto who assisted Union forces (but did not formally join the USCT), began the church and is considered the community's founder. Surrounding the church was a large cemetery, and on the outskirts of the cemetery (which remains as the only rural African American cemetery in the county) were a handful of houses and a store that also served as the post office. The unadorned rectangular log building of Pierce Chapel was a place of worship on Sundays and Wednesday nights, but during the week, it was the local school from circa 1870 to the early 1920s, when the Douglass School was built in the nearby planned industrial town of Kingsport. As a result of the growth of Kingsport and the impact of the Great Depression of the 1930s, the rural African American community in the Bays Mountain area began to move away. Some went to Kingsport, where they lived in the New Deal's Riverview Homes public housing project. The new urban institution became the cultural heart of the local African American community and Pierce Chapel held only monthly meetings. Yet, the old church and cemetery remained a powerful metaphor of the community's beginnings. "On Memorial Day the families would gather at the cemetery with lunches to clean the graves of their loved ones with buttermilk and baking soda," recalled Anna Coley. The third Sunday in September was Homecoming Day, continued Coley, when "people came from all over the state for the services and to fellowship with their friends. They would put up tents and serve all kinds of foods. This all took place on the grounds of the church and cemetery."[18]

A similar pattern of growth in the early 1900s and relocation in the mid-century marks the history of Craigs Chapel AME Zion Church. Built in 1896 more than a mile south of the town of Greenback in Loudon County, the white frame, gable-front-entrance church stood on the margins of a larger, older white rural community. When built, with its steep gable-roof entrance standing tall, the church was a symbol of local African American achievement since emancipation. It remains today as a symbolic landmark of the African American community that existed in this portion of the Tennessee River valley before the 1950s. The church and its grounds soon became the center of a larger African American community. The congregation three years later—in 1899—built an adjacent school, and in 1903 the community formally established a cemetery between the school and the church. The three institutions maintained a close association with each other, sharing facilities for graduation services, community gatherings, school plays, fish fries, and cakewalks.

The Craigs Chapel AME Zion Church property is part of a larger historical landscape that has long held cultural significance for African Americans. An active area for Quaker abolitionism, with nearby settlements in Friendsville and Unitia, this area was the location for much antebellum antislavery activity. The family of William H. Griffitts, who lived only a couple of miles away, was active in the Quaker community and promoted social welfare, abolition, and education. The family is credited locally with attempts to assist fugitive slaves and other conscientious objectors. Local African Americans also associated their history with a nearby cave once linked to the Underground Railroad. The Craigs Chapel community considers the Underground Railroad tradition an integral piece of its history that adds to the symbolic importance they attach to the church and cemetery.[19]

The Craigs Chapel school served students from first through eighth grades. After eighth grade, African American students from Craigs Chapel attended the segregated black schools in neighboring counties. The original school building was physically connected to the church and was built after construction of WPA schools for both whites and blacks in Loudon County circa 1940. The building still serves as the church's fellowship hall.

To parishioner Grace Henry, Craigs Chapel meant so much because the school and church were completely organized, funded, and administered locally by the community. It was their place within a hostile outside world. Henry remembers her mother's employer offering to pay her poll tax on the condition that she would vote for a prescribed candidate. This kind of economic pressure made many rural blacks turn even more toward their church and school. Henry said that Loudon County African Americans did not want to "ruffle any feathers" by becoming civically involved in the white community because of the climate of intimidation that was present.[20]

Williamson Chapel Christian Methodist Episcopal (CME) Church at Needmore is hidden away at the corner where the counties of Davidson, Sumner, and Wilson meet in middle Tennessee. The community began circa 1850, when Dick Mastaman gave an acre of land to his slaves for the construction of a building that would be both a school and a Methodist church. Richard Williamson was the first teacher and pastor, and the building became known as Williamson Chapel Methodist Church in his honor. Williamson married a mulatto daughter of Dick Mastaman, named Cheney, at an unknown date; she gained freedom with the end of the Civil War. After 1865, several other freed families joined the community. In circa 1876, according to local tradition, the community name changed to Needmore, allegedly because an overabundance of young men "needed more" young women to take as brides. In 1876, the Williamson Chapel Methodist Church formally left the Methodist Episcopal Church, South, and joined the recently created Colored Methodist Episcopal (CME) Church. Richard and Cheney Williamson, also in 1876, transferred the one acre of church property to trustees Joe Johnson, Hiram Williamson (Richard's brother), Cal Gordon (the spouse of Lizzie Williamson, who was the daughter of Richard and Cheney), John Horton, and Jessie Parker.[21]

Near the end of the century, circa 1896, the congregation dismantled the original log church and replaced it with a new frame building, located "a few feet" from the original church site, according to a 1972 interview with Dillie Sellers-Davis. This original frame building remains intact today underneath the stone veneer added circa 1936. Its bell tower dates to circa 1930, and ringing the bell played an important communication role at Needmore. According to local historians,

> The bell was rung whenever the church doors were open for an occasion or event. If there was a death in the community the bell would be toned, no matter what time the death occurred. One of the older men in the community would go to the church to tone the bell, thereby informing the people in the community that a death had occurred. People would get up, find out who had died and go to the home of the deceased. No one knows why, but for some reason the toning of the bell was an act that was only performed by the older men who lived in the community.[22]

The church remained the local school until circa 1920 when community residents constructed a lodge hall, used by the Knights of Pythias and the Benevolent Society, next to the church. At that time, the school moved to the lodge hall. There was no public school building provided to the community until 1936, with the construction of the Needmore Elementary School across the road from the church.

The school's construction coincided with the appointment of John Henry Britton Sr. as the minister at Williamson Chapel. Britton was born in 1888 in the LaGuardo rural community of Wilson County; he grew up in the Andrews Tabernacle CME Church at LaGuardo. As a young man, he witnessed a white landowner humiliate his father, who was a sharecropper. From that point on, Britton was determined to better himself and gain an education, an income, and land to protect himself and his family as much as possible from the evils of the Jim Crow South. He also became a CME minister, pastoring first at Lane Tabernacle CME Church in East Nashville and then as presiding elder of the Clarksville District of the CME Church. His next major posting was also in Nashville, at St. Luke's CME Church. After a dispute with CME leadership, Britton lost his prestigious position and was sent instead to Needmore.

Britton accepted the 1936 appointment as a challenge and opportunity. He took steps to upgrade the appearance of the church building by hiring stonemasons Carmon Manning and Emmett Brown to add a stone veneer to the frame building, at a cost of $777.77. He then hired another mason, Pradie L. Tibbs, to design an arched stone entrance for the building.

Also in his first year at Williamson Chapel, Britton ended the decades-old practice of church elders leading the congregation in "the singing of line hymns. The church had no songbooks, so the singing was done from memory. The preacher would repeat the line hymn and the members would repeat after him in slow, mournful harmony. Or the songs would be joyous and hand clapping would be used as a means of staying in turn or keeping the rhythm."[23] Britton, who had once been a musician himself and who had enjoyed the large choirs at his Nashville churches, established a choir, a first for the church, and during the 1940s he hired Vinnie Mitchell as the church's first paid musician. Music became an important part of Williamson Chapel's religious traditions. Britton also organized traveling gospel groups; the two best known were the Greenlawn Four and the Wee Wee Jubilaires. Today, the inside of the church shows the typical bare interior with a plain pulpit; the loudspeaker and music system, at first glance, may seem out of place, but this equipment too is typical of many churches. (The pastor of Fredonia Baptist Church in Haywood County proudly told the author in 1998 that the sound system could be heard distinctly one-half mile away on Sunday mornings.)

In addition to his changes in the Sunday services at Williamson Chapel, Britton lobbied Wilson County education officials and wealthy white patrons for funds to construct a proper school. Needmore had not gained a new Rosenwald school during its large building program of 1917 to 1932. Britton was aghast at the poor facilities students faced at the lodge building, and he obtained funds from white public and private sources to build the Rosenwald-plan Needmore Elementary School. The school design reflected earlier Rosenwald plans in its unadorned architectural style, frame construction, banks of windows, and dual use as a school and community center. One of the more frequent public speakers was Wiley Bernard, the black extension agent. He and Britton joined forces to create the Needmore Civic Club, the precursor to the present Needmore Community Club. Another speaker was Datie Mai Drennon, who led the Needmore Home Demonstration Club.

Patricia Lockett and Mattie McHollin conclude that Britton was "mentor to the entire Needmore Community from 1936–1962." Community members assert that by turning his church into a self-contained small world for local residents, he "left a legacy of learning that continues even today with nurses, lawyers, engineers, preachers, historians, librarians, social workers and all manner of other professionals and tradesmen who were inspired and believed that they deserved all that the world had to offer."[24] Williamson Chapel CME Church, then, is both a monument to a free black community of the 1850s and a reflection of the impact of a reform-minded minister from the mid-twentieth century.

Woodlawn Baptist Church in Haywood County, a West Tennessee county with one of the state's highest percentages of African Americans, is a church with a similar grounding in both the days of slavery and the days when the shackles of Jim Crow were torn apart. Harden Smith, who secretly preached to other slaves before emancipation, established the church as the Woodlawn Missionary Baptist Church in 1865. Four years later, Issac Read sold to Dublin Shaw, William Evans, Isham Lankford, James Owens, Allen Peebles, Allfred Baucom, and Thomas Read, the trustees of the "Wood Lawn Colored Baptist Church," a 2.5-acre lot for the sole purpose of erecting a church, schoolhouse, and "burying ground." The construction of the initial brick church began in 1870, guided by former slave Will Wallace Brink, a master brick mason. In 1891, the church congregation had grown to such an extent that more land was required and an additional 2.5 acres were purchased from James D. and Lucy E. Read. This new addition later served as the location for the present church building.[25]

In the early twentieth century, Woodlawn's influence extended into the secular worlds of the blues and popular music. Artists associated with the church included blues artist Sleepy John Estes, the Bootsie Whitelow String Band, the Rev. Clay Evans, and Anna Mae Bullock (Tina Turner), whose family church was Woodlawn until her family joined the nearby Spring Hill Baptist Church, where Bullock could sing in the choir. The artistic roots of these individual artists, however, lay with two earlier Woodlawn Church bands, which performed from the late nineteenth century into the 1930s. The original Woodlawn band was composed of Prima Whitelow, Jim Green, George Peebles, Will Owens, Beab Daniels, and Lawrence Tyus. The second Woodlawn band, established in the 1920s, included Alan Tyus, Sewell Flagg Sr., Bootsie Whitelow, William E. Watkins, and Westley Watkins. The bands played blues, gospel, jazz, and black spirituals in churches and other venues. On June 18, 1950, the church hosted a Sunday program to honor the important gospel composer Lucy E. Campbell of Memphis.[26]

In 1927–1928, the congregation chose to build a new, larger brick church, with dual towers in Gothic Revival fashion, across from the cemetery. Harden Smith had retired in 1922; the decision to build a new church building at a new location was, in part, a deliberate act to symbolize that leadership of the congregation had passed into a new age. Woodlawn members, however, wanted to keep a close link to the past. L. V. Hill recalled, "[W]hen they started building the new church, I would leave school and come directly to the site and help my parents and the other people clean the bricks from the old church" so they could be reused in the new building. The Rev. A. L. McCargo was proud of how the members "formed a convoy of wagons and hauled the building materials from Brownsville."[27]

During the 1940s and 1950s, Woodlawn Baptist enhanced its reputation as a social, religious, political, and community center. During World War II, the church hosted meetings where members explained the course and developments of the war, as well as associated federal policies and programs, such as war bond drives. The American Red Cross held meetings at the church. During and after the war, the church also hosted local Home Demonstration Clubs and 4-H chapters as well as Community Club sessions where women members would be taught handicrafts, rug making, mattress making, and proper table manners and polite behavior. Woodlawn Baptist Church was one of the first places that held the early organizational meetings to raise money to build a black hospital, an initiative that grew into the Golden Circle Life Insurance Company, a large company that still operates today. There are few better Tennessee models of how a progressive African American church could be an alternative social reform institution, as Elisabeth Lasch-Quinn has pointed out, serving its community much like a settlement house in an urban area.[28]

Woodlawn's activism during the Civil Rights Movement also became an indelible part of the building itself and the church became a physical statement of African American resistance. The church was a place where residents could learn about meetings, events, and the latest news about the movement. In 1964, for instance, Mabel Beard Leigh, a granddaughter of Harden Smith, reported on recent developments. She observed: "Though the race question has important social implications, it is fundamentally a moral and spiritual issue. Only moral approaches provide a solution." At Woodlawn Baptist Church, meetings took place to teach residents how to register to vote; Elmer Beard of the church, the grandson of the founder, became the first African American voter in Nutbush since the late Victorian era.[29]

Symbolic of this activism and the renewed pride in race and achievement that occurred in African American communities throughout the civil rights era, the deacons at Woodlawn Baptist Church expanded and upgraded the facilities at the church. The congregation enjoyed increased economic opportunities due to the legal end of segregation, and it desired to make a statement with the building, similar to that of the congregation during the 1920s when it moved the building and built the present brick church. This new generation, which courageously led the congregation and the community into the Civil Rights Movement, also wanted their church building to be as progressive and comfortable as any other rural church in Haywood County. No longer did they need to downplay their wealth, their pride, or their heritage in order to avoid bringing too much attention to themselves. In 1966, the members added air-conditioning units, replaced the original windows from 1927–1928 with casement windows, and, most symbolically, added the Classical Revival–style portico. In the early twentieth-century South, the gleaming white columns of the Classical Revival style were closely associated with the imposition of Jim Crow segregation; in a phrase, white columns were equal to white supremacy.[30] African Americans at Woodlawn Baptist Church made their own cultural statement with the interior and exterior improvements at the church: they now had the power and freedom to have a church the equal of any rural white church. Travelers along Tennessee Highway 19 could see the gleaming white columns of the church; Woodlawn Baptist Church became an architectural landmark as well as an effective statement of cultural resistance in the landscape of West Tennessee. As the unpublished church history remarks, the congregation of Woodlawn Baptist Church in 130 years moved from a brush arbor to "a monumental historical edifice."[31]

Happy Hill Missionary Baptist Church—formally called First Baptist, Missionary Baptist, Lynnville—makes its own statement of African American sacred space not only through its twin towers but also through its location within the Giles County landscape. The county was notorious as the birthplace of the Ku Klux Klan, and black residents had ample reason to establish their own rural enclaves within the county. Built in 1901, Happy Hill Baptist sits in the middle of a small village of African American houses. Its hillside location overlooks Lynnville, and the half-mile distance between Happy Hill and the town physically reflects the chasm that developed between whites and blacks in the Jim Crow South. To reach this black neighborhood, one left the town entirely, crossed over a narrow bridge, and then followed a narrow lane for about one-half mile to the hill, where a dirt road took you to the church. From their hill, African Americans looked down on Lynnville, and the two tall white frame towers of the Happy Hill church faced the town, almost as if making the statement that the African Americans might be marginalized but they still had held true to their faith, pride, cultural identity, and achievement. The tower clearly marked the place as a safe haven and served as a sign for other African Americans who wished to find the church and the community and wanted to avoid the potentially hostile environment of Lynnville.

Within larger towns from 1900 to 1920, congregations with the funds and the ambition built their own urban landmarks in the form of large stylish brick churches. These buildings were testaments to their faith, marks of pride and achievement, and subtle statements of cultural resistance within the larger segregated landscape. The Mount Zion Missionary Baptist Church in Fayetteville was founded in 1873 by former slaves and their families, with Charles Taylor, Jack Williams, and James Rogers as trustees. Their lot was below the town square on an unimproved street named Mud Street. The church lot, however, served as the opening of the local black neighborhood. Adjacent was an African American barbershop; to one side was the local funeral home; and behind the church lot was the segregated school for African Americans. The original church building burned in the late 1890s (the exact date is not known), causing extensive damage. Five years later, under the leadership of the Rev. D. T. Carroway, efforts were made to raise funds not just from members but from the entire community. After finally negotiating a contract with a builder, Carroway issued an open letter to the public, requesting donations for rebuilding the church: "We are struggling to meet necesary [sic] payments," he wrote, "Being poor we . . . appeal to a generious [sic] public to help us. . . . The church must be built." The statement invited everyone to attend a daylong church dinner and prayer meeting and asked that they bring fifty cents or a dollar to contribute to the cause.[32]

In 1902, the congregation met its goal and the new church was completed. Its handsome appearance and stature sent a direct message from the African American community to the Fayetteville public. As pointed out by historian Teresa Douglass, "Gothic detailing and elements, popular architectural treatments often associated with Christianity in middle-class housing, signified that blacks were equally Christian as whites and perhaps served as a subtle lesson in morality." The church's massing and its brick and stone materials demonstrate the ideas of stability and permanence; whereas its tall bell tower was a landmark in the African American neighborhood, as well as housing the neighborhood's best communication device.[33]

Mount Zion Missionary Baptist Church continued its public role throughout the century, especially under the guidance of the Rev. Simmie Sanders, who was pastor from 1950 to 1980. Residents met at the church and organized the county's first NAACP chapter in 1964. The Rev. Sanders also supported the request of Fayetteville's Human Resource Agency, which provided aid and welfare, to operate from the church's basement from 1968 to 1982.

At another county seat, Covington, near the Mississippi River north of Memphis, Canaan Baptist Church, like Mount Zion Missionary Baptist Church, was an architectural landmark and the center of the downtown African American neighborhood. Located two blocks north of the courthouse square and flanked by a local funeral home on one side and a barbecue stand on the other, the church stands on the lot initially occupied by the white First Baptist Church of Covington. In 1885, white Baptists gave the lot and a frame church to the Canaan congregation. The transfer of land was part of a bigger shift in the growing town's built environment. Within ten years, Covington was rather clearly divided, with white denominations building churches south of the square and African Americans building their main churches—Missionary Baptist, AME, and CME—north of the square.[34]

In 1916 and 1917, Canaan's congregation, under the leadership of the Rev. W. J. Clark, made its own statement of resistance within the townscape by demolishing the old white church and replacing it with a grand brick building with a prominent bell tower. The new Gothic Revival–style church had pointed arched entries and windows and a castellated crest on the tower. It was the only African American building in the commercial district that had formal architectural styling—and it was also the largest black-owned building in the neighborhood.

The Rev. John Henry Seward, a dentist by professional training who served the congregation from 1931 to 1966, made the grand building a true community landmark. During his years, the congregation established several programs that enhanced its significant local role. The church was headquarters to the West Tennessee Leadership Training School, under the National Council of Churches in the United States of America, which promoted Christian education throughout Tipton County and inspired young people to pursue higher education or enter the ministry. The West Tennessee Association of Missionary Baptists held its quarterly board meetings at Canaan. Many secular groups, such as the Masonic Order, the Order of the Eastern Star, and the Legionnaires, held meetings at the church at various times. The Men's Club of the church sponsored the first African American Boy Scouts troop in Tipton County; whereas the Women's Club supported the first African American Girl Scouts troop. The Tennessee State Federation of Colored Women's Clubs started a chapter that met at Canaan and the Frazier High School in 1938. The club's purpose was to allow African American women to meet and promote citizenship in the community to advance the causes of African American women. In 1953, the state federation held its annual convention at Canaan.[35]

The county's NAACP chapter dates to the early 1950s and met at the church from about 1955 to 1975. Its second president was John "Mack" Edwards, a Canaan deacon, who later became a Tipton County constable and a city alderman. In 1963 and 1964, Edwards convinced Canaan to host mass civil rights meetings. By the late 1990s, Canaan had produced four of the first African American officials in Tipton County and Covington.[36]

In Fayetteville and Covington, the African American community commanded enough economic power—and whites exercised enough restraint—that a prominent, stylish church could stand as an institutional dividing line between the white and black sides of town. In more oppressive situations, however, the more stylish African American church stood away from the main road, almost hidden away in the black neighborhood. An excellent example is at Whiteville in Hardeman County, where the black neighborhood is on the town's northern outskirts. Two institutions on either side of the road—a local funeral home and the Lane Chapel CME Church—mark the neighborhood's boundary with the white world. Directly behind the church is the primary African American neighborhood of Whiteville, a residential area characterized by small homes, small lots, and narrow, poorly maintained streets. Lane Chapel CME thus serves as the public opening to the outside white world of an almost hidden African American world. Two blocks east of Lane Chapel CME is El Canaan Baptist Church, located on a small rise that is visible only within the African American neighborhood. Whereas Lane Chapel CME served as an African American public face to the outside white world, El Canaan Baptist was the center of the local African American public, cultural, and religious world. Built circa 1911, it is a large Gothic Revival–influenced brick building. Immediately north of the church is a deteriorating brick Rosenwald school, the Allen-White High School. It served as the county's only high school for African Americans—even attracting boarding students from neighboring counties and states—until 1959. Together the two churches define the public and private worlds of the local community.[37]

"As an institution managed and owned by black people," the African American church "by its very existence and democratic structure imparted racial pride and dignity, providing parishioners of all classes the opportunity to participate in its meetings and rituals and to exercise roles denied them in the larger society," observed Leon Litwack.[38] Today, the churches, especially when they are surrounded by other early institutions, like cemeteries, schools, and lodges, are powerful markers of the African American legacy and space in the southern landscape. Even when arsonists destroyed rural churches in Tennessee in 1995 and 1996, congregations immediately built new buildings on the ashes of the older buildings, keeping the link between past and present. In the rural South, the comments made by two Robertson County black writers in the Depression still ring true: "[T]he Negro church . . . is the most stabilized of our institutions, the Negro minister in the county is yet the recognized leader in his respective community, and . . . the majority of our people yet cling with faith to the church . . . we have God with us, we can hear the still, small voice whispering in the darkest hours of battle. 'I am with you always, even to the end of the world.'"[39] This faith and this optimism are what created these sacred—and secular—spaces over 100 years ago, and are what will sustain these spaces into the twenty-first century.

NOTES

1. Beginning in 1997, a group of historians, community activists, and historic preservationists at the Center for Historic Preservation at Middle Tennessee State University established the Tennessee Rural African American Church project, with the goal of identifying and documenting rural African American churches in all ninety-five counties. The project was created, with support of the Tennessee Historical Commission and Middle Tennessee State University, in reaction to a spate of rural church burnings in Tennessee the prior year. The project also was a reaction to the comments from some preservationists that perhaps nothing valuable historically or architecturally had been lost. On this point, see the excellent editorial, Nicholas Adams, "Churches on Fire," *Journal of the Society of Architectural Historians* 55 (September 1996): 236–237, 363. This systematic effort has, to date, surveyed over 400 properties and has begun the process of decoding the meaning of African American space within the larger built environment of the American South. First results of the survey and a National Register of Historic Places Multiple Property Submission for Rural African American Churches appear in Carroll Van West et al., *Powerful Artifacts: A Guide to Surveying and Documenting Rural African-American Churches* (Murfreesboro, TN: MTSU Center for Historic Preservation and National Trust for Historic Preservation, 2000). Also see Carroll Van West et al.,

"Rural African-American Churches in Tennessee, 1850–1970," National Register of Historic Places Multiple Property Submission Form, Tennessee Historical Commission, 1999. For scholarship on the significance of African American churches, see William E. Montgomery, *Under Their Own Vine and Fig Tree: The African-American Church in the South, 1865–1900* (Baton Rouge: Louisiana State University Press, 1993); Harry V. Richardson, *Dark Glory: A Picture of the Church Among Negroes in the Rural South* (New York: Friendship Press, 1947); C. Eric Lincoln and Lawrence H. Mamiya, *The Black Church in the African American Experience* (Durham, NC: Duke University Press, 1990); and Leon F. Litwack, *Trouble in Mind: Black Southerners in the Age of Jim Crow* (New York: Knopf, 1998), 379.

2. W.E.B. Du Bois, *The Souls of Black Folk* (New York: Penguin, 1995 [1903]), 102.

3. Ibid., 211

4. Ibid., 189, 213–214; W.E.B. Du Bois, "How I Taught School," *Fisk Herald* 4 (December 1886): 10.

5. The importance of the church in urban African American space has received more scholarly attention. See Armstead L. Robinson, "'Plans Dat Comed from God': Institution Building and the Emergence of Black Leadership in Reconstruction Memphis, 1865–1880," in *The Web of Southern Social Relations: Women, Family, & Education*, ed. John Wakelyn et al. (Athens: University of Georgia Press, 1985), 182–183; Carroll Van West and Jen Stoecker, "First Baptist, Lauderdale Church, Memphis, Tennessee," National Register of Historic Places Nomination Form, Tennessee Historical Commission, Nashville, 2001.

6. Bobby L. Lovett, "Contraband Camps," *Tennessee Encyclopedia of History and Culture*, ed. Carroll Van West and Connie L. Lester et al. (Nashville: Tennessee Historical Society, 1998), 203–204; Rutherford County Survey Files, Rural African-American Churches Collection, MTSU Center for Historic Preservation (hereafter cited as RAACC, CHP); Miranda Fraley, a historian at Stones River National Battlefield, has prepared an unpublished research report on the African American community at Cemetery, which is available in the research collections at the Stones River National Battlefield Visitor Center, Murfreesboro, Tennessee.

7. Susan Hawkins, "The African-American Experience at Forts Henry, Heiman, and Donelson, 1862–1867," *Tennessee Historical Quarterly* 61 (Winter 2002): 222–241.

8. DeKalb County Deed Book J, 1869, 517; Carrie Helen Smith Interview by Traci Nichols, June 1999, Alexandria Cemeteries Historic District, National Register Files, MTSU Center for Historic Preservation (hereafter cited as NR Files, CHP).

9. John A. Kouwenhoven, *The Beer Can by the Highway* (New York: Doubleday, 1961), 156; Stewart Brand, *How Buildings Learn* (New York: Penguin, 1994), 155.

10. Dorothy Hitchcock, a member of Beth Salem Presbyterian Church, to Carroll Van West, October 15, 1998, Beth Salem Presbyterian Church File, RAACC, CHP; David Hill, "Small Country Church Comes Alive for Homecoming," Athens *Daily Post-Athenian*, August 31, 1988; Carroll Van West, "Beth Salem Presbyterian Church," National Register of Historic Places Nomination Form, Tennessee Historical Commission, Nashville, 1999.

11. *Swafford, M. M., et al. v. Browder, Alexander, et al.*, July 3, 1889, Loose Papers, Bledsoe County Chancery Court, Pikeville; Mildred Bridgeman Interview by Carroll Van West at Pikeville Chapel AME Zion Church, June 1998; Mildred Bridgeman to Carroll

Van West, October 1998, in Pikeville Chapel AME Zion file, RAACC, CHP; Norma Brock Interview by Carroll Van West, at Pikeville Chapel AME Zion Church, June 1998, ibid.; Jan Galletta, "Images of Easter," Chattanooga *Free Press*, March 26, 1989; Paul D. Phillips, "Education of Blacks in Tennessee During Reconstruction, 1865–1870," *Tennessee Historical Quarterly* 46 (1987): 98–109; and "White Reaction to the Freedmen's Bureau in Tennessee," *Tennessee Historical Quarterly* 25 (1966): 50–62.

12. Mary S. Hoffschwelle, *Rebuilding the Rural Southern Community: Reformers, Schools, and Homes in Tennessee, 1900–1930* (Knoxville: University of Tennessee Press, 1998), 83–87.

13. John M. Vlach, *By the Work of Their Hands: Studies in Afro-American Folklife* (Ann Arbor: University of Michigan Press, 1988), 107.

14. Bobby L. Lovett, "Comments on Rural Church Nomination," October 1998, RAACC, CHP.

15. Lester C. Lamon, *Blacks in Tennessee, 1791–1790* (Knoxville: University of Tennessee Press, 1981), 45.

16. Montgomery, *Under Their Own Vine and Fig Tree*, 254–255.

17. Litwack, *Trouble in Mind*, 393; Kathy Bennett, "Lynching," *Tennessee Encyclopedia*, 560; Elisabeth D. Lasch-Quinn, *Black Neighbors: Race and the Limits of Reform in the American Settlement House Movement, 1890–1945* (Chapel Hill: University of North Carolina Press, 1993), 55–59, 149–150.

18. Anna R. Coley to Tennessee Historical Commission, August 17, 1998, Copy in Pierce Chapel AME Church Cemetery File, NR Files, CHP; Orvel Bond, Anna R. Coley, Theresa Dykes, Virginia Leiper, and Jack Pierce Interviews by Carroll Van West, October 21, 1999, at Pierce Chapel AME Church Cemetery, NR Files, CHP.

19. Jen Stoecker and Carroll Van West, "Craigs Chapel AME Zion Church and Cemetery," National Register of Historic Places Nomination Form, Tennessee Historical Commission, Nashville, 2000; Melanie Henry Interview by Jen Stoecker, February 28, 2000, at Craigs Chapel AME Zion Church, Craigs Chapel AME Zion Church File, NR Files, CHP; Carolyn Groves Interview by Jen Stoecker, April 18, 2000, by telephone, ibid.; Grace Henry Interview by Jen Stoecker, November 16, 2000, by telephone, ibid.

20. Grace Henry Interview.

21. Carroll Van West, "Williamson Chapel CME Church and Needmore School," National Register of Historic Places Nomination Form, Tennessee Historical Commission, Nashville, 2002; Patricia Ward Lockett and Mattie McHollin, *In Their Own Voices: An Account of the Presence of African Americans in Wilson County* (Lebanon, TN: Lebanon Democrat, 1999), 132–137; Woodrow Harris Interview by Carroll Van West, June 2000, Williamson Chapel CME Church, Williamson Chapel CME Church File, NR Files, CHP.

22. Lockett and McHollin, *In Their Own Voices*, 132.

23. Ibid., 135–136.

24. Ibid., 137.

25. Deed, Issac Read to Trustees of Church, filed January 1, 1870, Haywood County Deed Book 1, 636, Haywood County Courthouse, Brownsville; Deed, James D. and Lucy E. Read to Deacons, Woodlawn Baptist Church, March 2, 1891, Haywood County Deed Book 14, 363, Haywood County Courthouse, Brownsville.

26. Sharon Norris, "Nutbush: Of Cotton Fields, Butterflies, and Wild Onion Ridge" (Jackson, TN: unpublished manuscript, 1995), 86–87, 154–155, 167–168; *Haywood County Negro News*, June 11(?), 1950; on Campbell's importance, see Carroll Van West and Margaret D. Binnicker, eds., *A History of Tennessee Arts: Creating Traditions, Expanding Horizons* (Nashville: University of Tennessee Press, 2004), 409.

27. Norris, "Nutbush," 85–86.

28. Joint interview of Gladys E. Jones, Lollie Lee Mann, Sharon Norris, Earl Lee Reed, L. V. Hill, Sewell Flagg Jr., Opal Brack, and Sarah Doyle by Carroll Van West, October 20, 1995, Woodlawn Baptist Church, Woodlawn Baptist Church File, NR Files, CHP; *Haywood County Negro News*, April 14, July 5, 1950; Lasch-Quinn, *Black Neighbors*.

29. Norris, "Nutbush," 149; Joint Interview of Gladys E. Jones et. al.

30. Catherine Bishir, "Landmarks of Power: Building a Southern Past, 1885–1915," *Southern Cultures*, inaugural issue (1994): 27–28.

31. "Church History," unpublished document, Woodlawn Baptist Church, Haywood County, TN. A copy is in the author's possession; the author is unknown.

32. Rev. D. T. Carroway, "An Open Letter to the Public" (Fayetteville, TN), ca. 1900; Robert Eady Interview by Carroll Van West, June 1995, at Mt. Zion Missionary Baptist Church, Fayetteville, Mt. Zion M. B. Church File, NR Files, CHP; Robert Eady, "Mount Zion M. B. Church," *The Volunteer: Journal of the Lincoln County Historical Society* (Fall 1989): 14–18.

33. Teresa Douglass, "Mt. Zion Missionary Baptist Church, Fayetteville," National Register of Historic Places Nomination Form, Tennessee Historical Commission, Nashville, 1999.

34. Carroll Van West and Brad Wolf, "Canaan Baptist Church, Covington," National Register of Historic Places Nomination Form, Tennessee Historical Commission, Nashville, 1999.

35. Ibid.; John Mack Edwards Interview by Bradley Wolf at Canaan Baptist Church, October 16, 1995, Canaan Baptist Church File, NR Files, CHP; Mary Kent, "Canaan Baptist Church History," unpublished typescript, no date, copy at Canaan Baptist Church, Covington; Tennessee State Federation of Colored Women's Clubs, "Program of 1953 Convention," copy at Canaan Baptist Church, Covington.

36. Minnie Bommer and Tim Sloan, "NAACP at Canaan Baptist Church," unpublished typescript, 1997, Canaan Baptist Church File, NR Files, CHP; John Mack Edwards Interview.

37. Lane Chapel CME Church File and El Canaan Baptist Church File, RAACC, CHP; Neil R. McMillen, *Dark Journey: Black Mississippians in the Age of Jim Crow* (Urbana: University of Illinois Press, 1989), 12–14; Charles S. Aiken, *The Cotton Plantation South Since the Civil War* (Baltimore: Johns Hopkins University Press, 1998).

38. Litwack, *Trouble in Mind*, 391.

39. Jacob C. Morton and Virdner D. Moore Jr., comp., *Robertson County Negro Year Book* (Springfield, TN: privately published, 1938), 6.

Patrick Q. Mason

"In Our Image, After Our Likeness"

The Meaning of a Black Deity in the
African American Protest Tradition, 1880–1970

> And God said, Let us make man in our image, after our likeness. . . . So God
> created man in his own image, in the image of God created he him.
>
> GENESIS 1:26–27 (KJV)

In one of his numerous postmortem collaborations, popular hip-hop artist
Tupac Shakur—known more for his scrapes with the law and 1996 murder than
for his religiosity—includes a track titled "Black Jesuz." Along with fellow rap-
pers Outlawz, he calls on "Black Jesuz," who is "like a saint that we pray to in the
ghetto to get us through / Somebody that understands our pain . . . That understands where we coming from."[1] Tupac may or may not have known it, but his
appeal to a black Jesus came after more than a century of African American
churchmen and race leaders discussing that very topic.[2] Indeed, this example
illustrates a significant trend in twentieth-century American religious and cultural history, the debate over the nature of God and Jesus Christ and the attempt
by many in the African American community to depict the divine as black, both
in sympathies and in actual appearance.

Although paintings and murals of a black Christ, black Madonna, and black
saints date back to the early Christian era, such images had been generally

ignored or suppressed under white-dominated Euro-American Christianity. When African Americans were introduced to Christianity, usually in the shackles of slavery, they were presented with the religion of their masters, which included a blond-haired, blue-eyed Christ and an implicitly white God. Blacks adapted the Christian myths and doctrines they were taught, often syncretizing them with traditional African beliefs and rituals, to create their own distinctive brand of Christianity. This adoption and recapitulation of Christianity was an essential move in sustaining the psyche of African Americans, particularly through slavery. As Martha Blauvelt points out, in the antebellum period "religion provided blacks with a 'space' which made life more bearable."[3] The metaphysical space created by their own religious worldview also translated into the physical realm as blacks constructed religious spaces—such as the "hush arbors" of the plantation or the emerging institution of the independent black church—that helped them cope with the inequalities of American society. Nevertheless, for the most part they still worshipped the white God presented to them by white Christians.

Beginning in the late nineteenth century, however, certain black preachers and other community leaders renounced the images of a white Jesus that often adorned the walls of their churches. Both physically and spiritually they sought to reclaim their worship spaces for themselves and their race, replacing the whitened portraits of Jesus with artwork depicting a dark-skinned Christ and explicitly rejecting a white God in their sermons. Such a position was naturally controversial, especially in the face of the pronounced racism of the Jim Crow era, but believers in a black God and black Christ boldly resisted white ridicule and helped the doctrine eventually achieve widespread currency among the African American population. Collectively they made a bold assertion that they would no longer allow the cult of whiteness to invade their most private and sacred spaces, and that in their spiritual communion they would create a new theological space for a black God and thus uphold the dignity and even divinity of black people everywhere. Although many black theologians since the 1970s have incorporated the blackness of God and Jesus as a central theme in their writings, this essay does not assess their contributions. Rather, it traces how their predecessors in the struggle for African American liberation created the cultural, intellectual, and theological space in which the black theologians later formulated their arguments. These largely rhetorical and intellectual developments, which are the focus of this chapter, were essential steps in the development both of black churches as physical spaces where worship and protest blended seamlessly and of African American spirituality as a metaphysical space where a strong and positive sense of identity, self-esteem, and power could be maintained.

Numerous scholars have emphasized the importance of religion for African Americans as they protested and struggled against the institutions of American racism. Most accounts have employed, at least implicitly, a structural view of religion, focusing on the black church as a primary center of community pride and mobilization and giving less emphasis to the theological and ritual aspects of black religion.[4] In an important 1993 article, historian Robin Kelley admonished scholars to take more seriously actual religious belief and practice—what religious scholars call "lived religion"—and not merely structures. African Americans, he wrote, "understood and invoked" the spiritual and sacred as "weapons to protect themselves or to attack others." For black men and women, the spiritual world conferred "real power"—power that none of the various secular civil rights or labor organizations could boast. With the exception of Vincent Harding, Kelley regretted, no historian "since W.E.B. Du Bois has been bold enough to assert a connection between the spirit and spiritual world of African Americans and political struggle."[5] This is a step in that direction, seeking to understand how one particular religious doctrine and its implementation empowered the African American community both politically and spiritually.

Formulations of a racialized God were part of three separate but related attempts to claim "space," metaphysical and physical, for blacks in American society. First, the distinctive African American interpretation of Christianity that culminated in the rise of black theology in the late 1960s and 1970s was built on the cultural, intellectual, and theological space carved out by the proponents of and believers in a racialized God. Bold speeches by race leaders like Marcus Garvey and Malcolm X were bolstered by actions of "ordinary" people, such as one black woman who publicly refused to give money to preachers who worshipped a white Jesus, all of which anticipated the formal theology of scholars like James Cone. Second, the notion of a black deity helped in reclaiming their church walls and sanctuaries from the idolatry of whiteness. Although early spokesmen for a black God, such as Henry McNeal Turner, limited their struggle to the rhetorical claiming of theological space, later proponents of the idea actually created or reinvented their church congregations to focus on God's blackness, whether through the Garveyites' African Orthodox Church or through Albert Cleage's Shrine of the Black Madonna. Less obviously but perhaps even more significantly, belief in a black God reinforced the sanctity of the black body, a personal physical space that had been brutalized and desecrated by centuries of racist ideology and practice. Decades before the doll tests famously featured in *Brown v. Board of Education*, many African Americans began to recognize that they could hardly respect themselves if they despised the color of their own skin. In parallel fashion, they believed that they could never fully affirm their own dignity and equality while worshipping a God who looked more like and thus identified more fully with their oppressors than themselves.

Thus, in addition to the significant role of sustaining and nurturing their devotional life, the idea of a black deity was (and continues to be) important in the development of racial pride and solidarity among many blacks. African American efforts to racialize God were not merely abstract theological musings but instead represented an important form of protest against the idolatry of whiteness that extended into religious as well as political, economic, and social space. Discussions of God's color within the African American community were never limited to the shadowy realm of theory. Rather, denying God's whiteness and asserting his blackness played an important role in the movement to assert the dignity, and even divinity, of blackness by imbuing it with sacred character.[6]

Those who espoused the concept of a black God tended to come from the more radical segments of the African American population. Until the late 1960s, when black theology was by and large mainstreamed, the doctrine was espoused most fully by prophetic voices—including those of Father Divine, Alexander McGuire, and Albert Cleage—that remained somewhat on the fringes of the black community (as prophets usually do). Most mainline churches said little on the subject, either out of social conservatism or a built-in aversion to portraying visual images of the divine. That is not to say the idea was isolated or relatively unknown, as evidenced by the number of prominent race leaders who referred to a black God, including Henry McNeal Turner, Marcus Garvey, and Malcolm X, and the diverse range of groups who adopted the idea, such as Black Muslims, Christians of many affiliations, Harlem Renaissance literati, and various black nationalists. Each of these individuals and groups had their own notions about the most effective means of pursuing black liberation and equality, and so the methods and degree to which a racialized deity was employed changed significantly over time and varied according to circumstance. We should therefore not expect to find views of God's blackness to be monolithic or static.

In his article "The American Christ," historian Patrick Allitt provides an insightful survey of depictions of Jesus in popular literature during the past 150 years. He demonstrates that various authors have "invariably described a Jesus sympathetic to their own concerns"; thus, Jesus could be, besides son of God and savior of the world, a capitalist, urban reformer, socialist, executive, or feminist. Because the relatively ambiguous nature of the four Gospels makes it easy to manipulate the figure and character of Jesus to one's own liking, Allitt astutely observes that "most of these self-serving portraits of Jesus tell us more about the lives and times of their American authors than they do about Palestine two thousand years ago." The authors' motivations (whether conscious or not) are clear: "By identifying oneself with Jesus, one stands a good chance of seizing the American moral high ground."[7]

Allitt's thesis, originally applied to analyzing popular religious literature, takes on even greater proportions when framed in terms of the debate over the color of God. Instead of merely ensuring the "moral high ground," the question over whether God and Christ are white or black (or something else entirely) has very real implications for the emotional, spiritual, and psychological well-being of the African American community. Historian-theologian Kelly Brown Douglas has noted: "Identifying God and Christ as Black fosters Black people's self-esteem by allowing them to worship a God in their own image, and by signifying that Blackness is nothing to be detested. On the contrary it is a color and condition that even the divine takes on."[8] Thus, in addition to being central to the development of racial pride and self-esteem, the concept of a black deity has been an important aspect of sustaining and nurturing the personal devotional life of many African Americans in their search to know and understand God. An analysis of both of these aspects, placing them in their historical context, is essential in gaining a full understanding and appreciation of the long struggle of African Americans to identify the God they worship as one of their own.

The term "black theology" was not coined until the time of the Black Power movement of the late 1960s, but as a concept it is not unique to the last third of the twentieth century. Throughout the nineteenth century, black churchmen sought to understand the African American experience in terms of the race's relationship to God and his will. Prominent African American religious leaders such as Richard Allen, Prince Hall, Henry Highland Garnet, Alexander Crummell, and Edward W. Blyden all preached or wrote on the "Ethiopian prophecy" of Psalm 68:31: "Princes shall come out of Egypt; Ethiopia shall soon stretch out her hands unto God." While African Americans struggled to interpret two and a half centuries of bondage, many latched on to this prophecy as a sign of God's omnipresent care and the eventual triumph of African peoples. Many rationalized that their years in slavery were God's means of Christianizing the African race; rather than cursing God for their unparalleled burdens, most African Americans chose to adopt a longer view of providential purpose in their suffering.[9]

As African Americans redefined their own self-image in the post-Reconstruction United States, particularly in the South, they also made efforts to reshape the nature of their worship and the image of their God. By 1871, virtually all black Christians in the South had left the white churches and formed their own congregations and even denominations. Although whites often applied pressure for blacks to leave the churches, historian Katharine Dvorak demonstrates that in fact the primary drive behind the exodus was black initiative and their "own distinctive appropriation of Christianity."[10] The strongest voice to emerge from the black church in the face of the intensifying racial oppression of the 1880s and 1890s was African Methodist Episcopal (AME) bishop Henry McNeal Turner. An important leader within perhaps the most mainstream black Christian denomination at the time, Turner used his position and pulpit as a means of promoting economic, social, and political reform, placing him firmly in the tradition of other black ministers who used their influence in the community to push for black liberation and equality.[11]

Building on the black church's tradition of God's awareness of and sympathy for blacks' suffering, Turner was the first prominent African American leader to directly confront the issue of God's racial identity rather than simply reflecting on his divine commiseration with an oppressed people.[12] His theological rhetoric of racial uplift was centered on a rejection of perceiving the divine as exclusively white and the corollary that the demonic was necessarily black. Asserting that "[n]o race of people can rise and manufacture better conditions while they hate and ignore themselves," he believed that religious sensibilities were a key aspect of learning to "Respect Black."[13] In an 1884 article, Turner laid out his basic case: "In America black is supposed to symbolize the devil and white to represent God. But this is partially wrong, for the devil is white and never was black. . . . There are black worlds, and, I believe, millions of black angels in heaven. In fact, there are angels of all colors there."[14] Turner was confident that the religious beliefs of his people represented not just abstract theology but actually affected their political and institutional strength. In an 1890 open letter concerning African colonization, he berated those of his own race who continued to harbor sentiments of black inferiority, "who worship white gods, who would rather be a white dog on earth than a black cherub in heaven." Turner castigated those who he thought would not positively contribute to the progress of the race but would instead "be a curse to the [African] continent" because they "are fools enough to believe the devil is black, and therefore that all who are black are consanguinely related to him." These same people, he accused, "would rather go forty miles to hear a white ass bray than a hundred yards to hear a black seraph sing."[15]

The development of Turner's theology concerning the racial identity of God reached maturity in the mid- to late 1890s; it is not unreasonable to assume that his language became stronger in response to the dramatic increase in extremist racial violence in the South.[16] Turner's earlier rhetoric focused on general religious images of angels and devils and addressed God only in limited fashion, but his statements became increasingly pointed as the century came to a close. For a long time Turner hesitated to assign any specific color to God. As late as 1894, he wrote, "There is no such being as a white God; God is neither white nor black."[17] However, at an 1895 conference in Atlanta, a meeting that would prove key to the formation of the National Baptist Convention, he took the final leap and made his celebrated pronouncement that "God is a Negro."[18] Not surprisingly, the white press reacted with hostility, condemning both the statement and its author (who had been unpopular with local whites since the late 1860s due to his political activity on behalf of black civil rights). In a February 1898 editorial in the AME newspaper *The Voice of Missions*, Turner boldly responded to his critics. In his strongest statement on the subject, he proclaimed:

> We have as much right biblically and otherwise to believe that God is a Negro, as you buckra, or white, people have to believe that God is a fine looking, symmetrical and ornamented white man. . . . Every race of people since time began . . . have conveyed the idea that the God who made them and shaped their destinies was symbolized in themselves, and why should not the Negro believe that he resembles God as much so as other people? We do not believe that there is any hope for a race of people who do not believe that they look like God. . . . [W]e are no stickler as to God's color . . . but we certainly protest against God being a white man or against God being white *at all*. . . . The effect of such a sentiment is contemptuous and degrading.[19]

Turner was not arguing for an anthropomorphic God who was physically black or white; indeed, he fully subscribed to the traditional Christian tenet of God's spiritual immateriality. Primarily, he argued that God was colorless, and that Jesus—God's manifestation in the flesh—was certainly not white. (He refrained from commenting specifically on what color Jesus actually *was*, saying more comfortably what he *was not*.[20]) If races were staking claims on the divine, then African Americans had as much right to God as anyone else. Turner thus used theology in a plea for equality, asserting that God himself did not have color in the human sense, and if he did he was just as much black as he was white.

Turner's biographer, historian Stephen Angell, proposes that his "affirmation of a black God ought to be primarily understood as the strongest response he could fashion to the idolatry of whiteness that he saw all around him."[21] The bishop's intentions, in fact, were much broader. Rather than merely protesting against the dominant culture of whiteness, his rhetoric of a racialized deity was a conscious and proactive strategy to uplift the race through the creation of a more constructive, positive self-image. Nearly sixty years before similar arguments were made in *Brown v. Board*, Turner reflected on the psychological damage done to African Americans by their worship of whiteness: "Our Sabbath-school children, by the time they reach proper consciousness, are taught to sing to the laudation of white and to the contempt of black. Can any one with an ounce of common sense expect that these children, when they reach maturity, will ever have any respect for their black or colored faces, or the faces of their associates?"[22] For Turner, the issue was much larger than the debate over the hypothetical color of a spiritual (and thus inherently colorless) God. It was not a matter of esoteric theology but rather had profound implications for the emotional and psychological well-being of an entire race. Turner saw his discussions of God's color not as an end in and of themselves but rather as a means to the end of racial uplift by asserting the dignity of, and even sacralizing, blackness.

The absence of a single forceful leader in the African American religious community to carry on Turner's legacy after his death did not mean that the idea of a black God retreated into total obscurity. In fact, a number of emergent radicals and schismatics made Turner's rhetoric seem mild as they unequivocally asserted the blackness of Jesus, a subject Turner had hesitated to broach. For instance, the Church of the Living God maintained Jesus' color as a significant part of its theology. In addition to positively identifying Jesus as "a member of the black race," the church's catechism made the same claim for other biblical figures such as Moses' wife, David, Job, and Jeremiah.[23] The doctrine also found voice in non-Christian settings. Prophet F. S. Cherry, the leader of the Black Jews (Church of God), emphatically taught that Jesus was black. As a regular part of his services, he would shout, "Jesus Christ was a black man and I'm offering fifteen hundred dollars cash to anyone who can produce an authentic likeness of Jesus Christ and show I'm wrong!" Waving a picture of a white Jesus, he would exclaim: "Who the hell is this? Nobody knows! They say it's Jesus! That's a damned lie! Jesus was black!"[24] Not only was the doctrine of a black deity perpetuated after Turner's death, but it began to expand from a mainstream denomination (as represented by Turner's AME affiliation) into a wider segment of the population via the radical sects that gained some prominence in the early twentieth-century African American religious landscape.[25]

The next great expositor of God's blackness came not from America's shores but from those of its Caribbean neighbor, Jamaica. Influenced by the pan-Africanism of Alexander Crummell, Edward Blyden, and Henry McNeal Turner, and especially affected by Booker T. Washington's autobiography *Up from Slavery*, Marcus Garvey became convinced of the need to unite the black peoples of the world under a single political organization. A major part of Garvey's agenda was to carve out and reclaim space for African Americans. He sought to accomplish this economically through the Black Star Line and other business ventures; politically and socially through institution building, most notably through his Universal Negro Improvement Association (UNIA); and physically through repatriation to Africa. By 1919, Garvey claimed that membership in the UNIA exceeded two million, a number that had reportedly doubled by August 1920.[26] Although most scholars see the agenda of the UNIA and "Garveyism" as being chiefly concerned with political and economic goals, it is important not to overlook the strong religious aspects of both the organization and the ideology.[27] Central to Garvey's religious philosophy were his beliefs concerning the color of God, Christ, and the Virgin Mary. So along with his social, political, and economic goals, Garvey sought to reserve distinctive religious spaces for the blacks around the world, both in a theological sense and eventually in the very temporal sense of the creation of a new church whose God was as black as his worshippers.

In his speeches and writings concerning the color of the divine, Garvey used many arguments that paralleled those made a generation earlier by Turner. Remaining within the bounds of Christian orthodoxy, he carefully asserted that God was essentially colorless—definitely not white—and thus could justifiably be seen through the lens of any particular human experience, no matter the color.[28] He went further in countering the prevailing attitudes (among both whites and blacks) of the whiteness of the divine by pronouncing God's blackness as a rhetorical if not an actual fact.[29] Garvey's was an essentially pluralistic and multicultural God, one who could be seen through the "spectacles" of any race: "The white man knows there is no white God and the yellow man knows there is no yellow God, but in order to focus on their mental visions an image of God, they imagine him as looking like them. . . . Of course we all know that God is not physical, God is spiritual, we simply want to destroy that propaganda that God is a white man."[30]

Similarly, Garvey claimed Jesus as a necessarily universalistic figure. "Jesus Christ was not white, black or yellow," he insisted, but was instead "the embodiment of all humanity" because of the fact that "the line from which He came had connection with every race existing." Garvey's speculation about the universality of Jesus' heritage is significant, if genealogically problematic. In order for Christ to be a universal savior, Garvey theorized, he must have literally shared a racial identity with all those for whom he atoned. Thus, if claims were being made on the person of Jesus, blacks had just as much right to appropriate Christ's identity as any other racial or ethnic group: "If they reject God as a Spirit and Jesus Christ as the embodiment of all races," he proclaimed, "then the U.N.I.A. shall make God and Jesus Christ black."[31]

Garvey showed how an appeal to African Americans' devotional life could be a powerful avenue for fostering a sense of racial pride and unity in his listeners. Drawing on blacks' experience with whites in America, Garvey suggested that no white God would answer a black man's or woman's prayers. Indeed, a white God would be too tied up in "the affairs of these millions of white folks"[32]—an unattractive suggestion considering that the business of "white folks" in the early twentieth century too often meant segregation, disfranchisement, and lynching, in addition to less formal, everyday forms of racism.

In September 1921, the African Orthodox Church (AOC) was organized, with George Alexander McGuire, sometime–chaplain general of the UNIA, as bishop. Although the new church was not formally affiliated with the UNIA—a fact repeatedly emphasized by the latter—McGuire was inspired in large part by Garveyite ideology, and high-ranking UNIA officials were also prominent members of the church.[33] McGuire used the church as an institutional vehicle for both religious and racial indoctrination. His "Universal Negro Catechism" reinforced many of the principles taught by Garvey, specifically that God had no color but could be considered black "on the same basis as that taken by white people when they assume that God is of their color."[34] The catechism did not offer a historical explanation for God's color, instead presenting a rhetorical argument, one that was reactive to white perceptions rather than being an active assertion of distinctive doctrine. The primary purpose of the catechism was not to provide a precise theological statement on the color of God, however, but to instruct and to instill a sense of racial pride in the catechized. The racial self-esteem created through instruction in the catechism would naturally have had a religious foundation to it. Thus, McGuire (and, by extension, Garvey) recognized that an individual's perception of and relationship with the divine could have a strong influence on that same person's individual and racial self-esteem and place in the world.

Religion and racial politics came together in the convening of the Fourth International Convention of the Negro Peoples of the World, sponsored by the UNIA in August 1924. The announced program for the convention included numerous items of political, economic, social, and educational import, but Garvey emphasized that the most important points on the agenda were of a religious nature.[35] In addressing the delegates, he lamented the fact that most blacks still visualized God, Jesus, and Mary as white, whereas "hell and Satan and his imps" were imagined as being black, an individual and collective conviction that only resulted in "spiritual enslavement."[36] The convention sought to solidify, institutionalize, and diffuse the doctrine of an indisputably black Mary and Jesus (called the "Black Man of Sorrows") and of God as "a Creature of imaginary semblance of the black race, being of like image and likeness." McGuire instructed the delegates that "it was the height of stupidity and self-negation for negroes to worship a Caucasian deity." With dramatic flair, he cited the fallacy of allowing their children to be falsely indoctrinated by images of a white God and black devil and called for "the burning in a bonfire of all pictures of a white Jesus, a white God, a white Madonna, now in the homes of Negroes." In addition, portraits of a black Jesus and Madonna were to be commissioned and "immediately circulated among the Negro peoples of the world."[37] As the convention came to a close at month's end, McGuire triumphantly proclaimed, "No more white God, no more white Christ, no more white Madonna for me."[38]

Garvey's remarks throughout the convention were always framed in the larger perspective of race advancement and the creation of a space for distinctive black worship. "What can you expect to accomplish," he asked, "when your ideal is that of another race? If you make your God a white man, angels white, Christ white, it means you will go to hell as a race. . . . The hour has come for the Negro, like the Mongolian, like the Chinese and the Japanese and the Hindu to worship a God of their own."[39] Emphatically, he appealed to the convention delegates, as representatives of the entire race, to "let your God be as your image in as much as he made you in his own likeness." Putting a twist on the standard biblical creationist passage—"God said, Let us make man in our image, after our likeness" (Genesis 1:26)—Garvey declared that "we of the U.N.I.A. have elected to see God Almighty through our own creation."[40] The convention's preoccupation with the color of the divine, culminating in Garvey's call for a kind of reciprocal creation, was used as an effective tool in developing a greater sense of solidarity among the black peoples of the world. Garvey recognized that blacks' individual and collective devotional life was also an important aspect of their sense of racial pride, and he skillfully employed the discussion of the color of the divine to enhance both.

Popular responses to the adoption of a black God and Jesus were favorable among the UNIA's membership, according to indications in the *Negro World* and other accounts. Although the *Negro World*'s propagandist slant (as the official newspaper of the UNIA) must be taken into consideration, a number of letters to the editor and other articles indicate that the idea of a black deity was generally met with enthusiasm within the organization. A May 1924 letter to the editor firmly stated that blacks "must repudiate the white man's very conception of God." The writer refused to accept "a deity which condones segregation, lynching, social ostracism and other injustices done to Negroes" and declared that his entire race would "not accept a white tyrant or, equally repulsive, a supine being as our God."[41] Shortly after the August 1924 convention, another letter thanked UNIA leaders for their religious platform, suggesting a sense of intellectual and spiritual enlightenment and even liberation: "We have heard so much in the past of a white God, white angels, and the great white throne that we had almost lost our identity by thinking white, seeing white and depreciating everything black. But, thank God, many of us have caught the spirit of this movement. We are now thinking of the black angels, the great black throne and the Deity having the semblance of the black race."[42] In a particularly poignant example of popular reaction to the "new" doctrine, George Alexander McGuire told of an elderly black woman who approached a preacher during his sermon on the black Christ. She offered the preacher five dollars, exclaimed that "[n]o white man would ever die on the cross for me," and returned to her seat as a "tumult of applause" drowned out the preacher's voice.[43]

Garvey did not stand alone in his comments on the color of the divine in his era, although the UNIA probably reached more people than any of the other

African Americans who had similar reflections. The idea of God's blackness was also taken up by the other major cultural movement to capture the imagination of New York's African American community in the 1920s. Various Harlem Renaissance authors and artists employed images of a black God and Jesus in their work, sometimes prominently so. For instance, Countee Cullen's epic poem "The Black Christ" attempted to make an existential connection between Christ's crucifixion and the suffering of blacks in America, specifically through the story of a black man's struggle of faith as he witnesses the lynching of his brother.[44] Another Cullen poem, "Heritage," expressed a heartfelt longing, "Wishing He I served were black."[45] John Henrik Clarke, in his powerful short story "The Boy Who Painted Christ Black," tells of a black school principal who steps forward to defend his prized student's painting of a black Christ to his unappreciative white supervisor and in turn loses his job.[46]

The two authors who grappled with the meaning of the color of the divine more than any others were Langston Hughes and W.E.B. Du Bois. Hughes's most controversial offering in this vein was his poem "Christ in Alabama," which boldly depicted Jesus as a "nigger" and a "bastard" and used metaphor to closely identify Jesus with blacks as fellow sufferers at the hands of their oppressors.[47] But his most poignant explorations of the subject came in short stories, when he considered the psychological effects of African Americans associating whiteness with everything heavenly. One of his recurring characters, Simple, observes:

> I never did see a Sunday School card with no dark angels with white wings on it. . . . Every time I went to Sunday School when I was a little boy, they come handing me a card with white angels and a white Moses and white Adams and white Eves on it. I thought everybody in heaven was white. And we was always singing, "You shall be whiter than snow." I used to wonder about that—because I would not know my own mother if I went to heaven and she come running to meet me *white.*[48]

In another story, Simple, still ruminating on his Sunday School experience, remembers that the Jesus he was introduced to there "was the color of the white folks that black folks worked for in our town."[49]

Du Bois, whose eminent career began long before any of the other participants in the Harlem Renaissance, noted that slavery constituted a kind of spiritual and social death among Africans and later African Americans: "Nothing was left; nothing was sacred. . . . Nothing—nothing that black folk did or said or thought or sang was sacred."[50] Du Bois spent most of his life trying to recover the dignity, even sacredness, of blackness. As early as 1899, he wrote a poem that paralleled what Turner was doing at the same time, turning color conceptions on their head: "I am carving God in night, I am painting hell in white."[51] Du Bois continued the same project in *Darkwater*, a collection of stories and poems published at the dawn of the Harlem Renaissance in 1920. In "Jesus Christ in Texas," he portrays Jesus as a mulatto in Waco, Texas, who, after being accepted by local blacks and rejected by whites (including a minister, who muses: "[S]omehow I thought I knew that man. I am sure I knew him once"), is eventually hung on a burning cross. Du Bois even more directly confronts God's color in "A Litany at Atlanta," when he prays, "Surely Thou, too, art not white, O Lord, a pale, bloodless, heartless thing!"[52]

In his collection of Du Bois's writings on religion, historian Phil Zuckerman argues that "Du Bois understood how powerful a symbol Jesus Christ was to suffering black Americans; they could relate their agony to his and in such relation feel a sense of worth, comfort, and even godliness."[53] Because of the nature of their writings, it is difficult to tell whether Du Bois and the other Harlem Renaissance writers personally saw God's blackness as mere symbol or as something more literal. Regardless, historian Sterling Stuckey's insight about Du Bois applies equally to all of them: "Du Bois transforms blackness into a desirable characteristic, inverts the qualities usually associated with whiteness, suggesting the blackness of God and the whiteness of hell. . . . He was attempting to strengthen the Afro-American's acceptance of being black, of being Negro."[54] It is significant that Du Bois, Hughes, Cullen, and other black literati of the early twentieth century used images of a black God and Jesus in their struggle for "civil rights by copyright."[55] By the 1930s, the notion of a black deity not only had permeated African American religious communities and popular Black Nationalist organizations but had also achieved currency among African American moderates and intellectuals, who likewise used the doctrine as a means of enhancing racial pride and dignity.

The period in between the world wars was an era of soul-searching and uncertainty for all of America. In this period, African Americans struggled to find a collective voice and to identify effective strategies to secure greater rights for themselves and their children. Their struggles were marked by great divergence of thought as they searched for acceptable and effectual avenues leading toward full equality in American society. A multitude of possible race leaders (both people and organizations) emerged and vied for ascendancy, including the NAACP, Urban League, Marcus Garvey, Harlem Renaissance elites, and A. Philip Randolph.

Another alternative voice, one that took a firm hold of the idea of a black deity and then significantly added to its development, came from the religious arena—not from within the Christian tradition but from Islam, which experienced a kind of rebirth among African Americans in the early twentieth century, especially in urban settings. The largest and most prominent of these Islamic— or "pseudo-Islamic," in the words of one scholar[56]—organizations was the

Nation of Islam, which emerged in Detroit in the midst of the Great Depression. The Nation of Islam began under the direction of W. D. Fard (later known as Fard Muhammad), who initially presented himself as an intermediary between humans and God but eventually came out to declare that he was in fact Allah.[57] It was under the leadership of Fard's handpicked successor, Elijah Muhammad (formerly Poole), and his chief disciple, Malcolm X, that the Nation of Islam gained widespread public attention and attracted tens of thousands of members and even more sympathizers, especially in the 1950s and 1960s.[58] This organization was attractive to inner-city blacks for a number of reasons, including their efforts to rebuild and revitalize African American urban neighborhoods, but at the heart of all their institutional work and reclamation projects (both of individuals and physical space) was their message. The fundamental tenets of the Nation of Islam were simple enough: that Allah, as manifested in Fard Muhammad, was a black man (curiously, Fard is described as "a short, fair-skinned man with dark, straight hair . . . difficult to distinguish from a white man"); that "the Messenger of Allah," Elijah Muhammad, was a black man (although at least two of Elijah's great-grandfathers were white);[59] and that, collectively, whites were a race of devils who were "directly *responsible* for not only the *presence* of this black man in America, but also for the *condition* in which we find this black man here."[60]

De facto spokesman for the Nation of Islam Malcolm X's public rhetoric was primarily oriented toward African Americans' woeful political, social, and economic circumstances. As one of his biographers insists, however, Malcolm's life and rhetoric cannot be seen only as political in nature but must also be considered for their genuine religious qualities—"he was a man who was as concerned with redemption as with revolution."[61] The repudiation of a white God and white Jesus, along with a call to repentance to those blacks who had been "brainwashed" into believing in and worshipping such false gods, was a frequently recurring theme in Malcolm X's speeches. In a typical sermon, Malcolm would try to convince his listeners that "the white man has brainwashed us black people to fasten our gaze upon a blond-haired, blue-eyed Jesus! We're worshiping a Jesus that doesn't even *look* like us! . . . The blond-haired, blue-eyed white man has taught you and me to worship a *white* Jesus, and to shout and sing and pray to this God that's *his* God, the white man's God."[62] Malcolm often pointed out the inconsistencies of black people worshipping a white deity. He equated being "down on our knees looking up and praying to a picture of a white, blond and blue-eyed Jesus" with "worshiping the white man," an act that ranked among the most vile of all sins in his estimation.[63]

Malcolm was convinced of the psychological and spiritual damage done by believing in and worshipping a deity that took on the form of one's enemy and oppressor. He diagnosed some of the symptoms of such "wrongheadedness," asserting that believing in a white God would naturally lead African Americans to associate white with good and black with evil, on a subconscious basis at the very least. Rather than taking pride in one's own blackness, then, one would despise one's self and one's kind, glorifying white and valuing a lighter complexion as more beautiful, more natural, more divine.[64] The purpose of Malcolm's preaching was clear: to urge African Americans to admire, respect, and love themselves, a major part of which involved worshipping a God that looked like them and not like the race that had oppressed them for some three and a half centuries in America.

When Malcolm X was assassinated in February 1965, the Civil Rights Movement had been in full swing for over a decade, and thanks in part to Malcolm's leadership, many blacks were becoming increasingly radical, forming the core of the nascent Black Power movement. There were a number of radical black leaders who were well prepared to step into the void left by Malcolm's death, although none could duplicate the natural gifts that Malcolm (by then known as El-Hajj Malik El-Shabazz) had so well exhibited and magnified. Those leaders who did vie for ascendancy among black radicals glorified the memory of Malcolm, often trying to appropriate his message and even suggesting that had he still been alive, he would be in their camp. Among the most prominent of these emergent voices was that of the Rev. Albert B. Cleage Jr.

Originally a United Church of Christ pastor, Cleage transformed his Detroit congregation into the Shrine of the Black Madonna and became nationally prominent with the publication of his book *The Black Messiah* in 1968.[65] In *The Black Messiah*, Cleage asserted that Jesus "was the non-white leader of a non-white people struggling for national liberation against the rule of a white nation."[66] Like that of Turner, Garvey, and Malcolm before him, Cleage's alternative theology was not an end in itself but rather a component part of his black nationalism, a means toward achieving the greater goal of racial enlightenment and advancement.[67] Cleage called the notion of a white Christ "the crowning demonstration of [Americans'] white supremacist conviction that all things good and valuable must be white." This "lie" had resulted in blacks' "spiritual bondage to the white man" and a feeling that they did not have a "right to first-class citizenship in Christ's kingdom here on earth."[68]

For Cleage, it was essential that African Americans not only reject the white Christ but also embrace his true black identity. After all, he noted, "You can't build dignity in black people if they go down on their knees every day, worshipping a white Jesus and a white God."[69] He pointed out that at least some degree of respect for one's own blackness had to precede the notion of assigning that same color to deity: "Our rediscovery of the Black Messiah is part of our rediscovery of ourselves. We could not worship a Black Jesus until we had thrown off the shackles of self-hate."[70] In many ways, his entire program was succinctly stated in a prayer he offered to God at the conclusion of one of his sermons, "Help us come forward and say: 'I am not ashamed to worship a black Jesus.'"[71]

Cleage's argument for Christ's identity as the Black Messiah was grounded in history, or at least his own unique interpretation of the historical record. Looking to the Old Testament and employing a fairly loose geographical definition of Africa, he concluded: "The Nation Israel was not at any time a white nation. Where could they have picked up any white blood, wandering around Africa?" The Jews at the time of Jesus were thus a black people, and the color of Jesus was a matter of simple genetics: "Jesus was born to Mary, a Jew of the tribe of Judah, a non-white people; black people in the same sense that the Arabs were black people, in the same sense that the Egyptians were black people. Jesus was a Black Messiah born to a black woman."[72]

Cleage took his conclusions about the color of Jesus and applied them to deduce the color of God. "Jesus was the Son of God," he affirmed. "Do you dare face the implication of this? . . . Then don't tell me God doesn't have any color. There had to be a seed there."[73] In addition, he asserted: "If God created man in his own image, then God must be some combination of this black, red, yellow and white. In no other way could God have created man in his image."[74] Whereas Turner and Garvey had "only asserted the black man's right to view God through his own spectacles and to depict him accordingly," Cleage insisted on a more radically literal interpretation of God's identification with the various races.[75] It was not just that the different races had a right to see God through their own experience but that God literally comprised a combination of the races. This interpretation served two related purposes: it definitely identified God with the nonwhite peoples of the world, and it disproved any exclusive claims made by whites as to the color of the divine.

By the late 1960s, as Mark Chapman has noted, African Americans faced a "basic theological dilemma" as to "whether Christianity [was] a source of black liberation or oppression." With increasing intensity, many African Americans, such as Stokely Carmichael, were questioning whether Christianity was really capable of effectively addressing the race problem in the United States.[76] Part of Cleage's importance, then, is that he countered Elijah Muhammad's claim that Christianity was a white man's religion with a white man's God, inherently bankrupt and serviceable only in the propagation of white supremacy. Cleage's platform, that "Christianity is essentially and historically a black man's religion,"[77] appealed to the "many Blacks, young and old, [who] would not follow Malcolm into the Nation of Islam, but believed he spoke the truth about Christianity being a religion for White people."[78] In his actions as well as his words, Cleage showed radical and even militant blacks that Christianity still formed a viable framework in which the African American protest could be staged.[79]

In contrast to the Nation of Islam, Cleage and other radical churchmen like him did not reject Christianity as propaganda of, by, and for the white man. Instead, they redefined Christ and Christianity in new terms, simultaneously rejecting white images of Jesus and further nurturing the seeds of the black Jesus ideal that had been planted in American soil three-quarters of a century earlier by Henry McNeal Turner. Indeed, Cleage went beyond asserting the historical and theological reality of the Black Messiah and made it a matter of action. Theologically and spatially, Cleage converted his local pastorate in Detroit from the Central United Church of Christ to the Shrine of the Black Madonna. The most visible step in this transformation was the commission of a chancel mural of the Black Madonna, nine feet wide by eighteen feet high, which replaced stained glass depicting the Pilgrims' landing at Plymouth Rock.[80] Just as medieval Christian architects designed churches to instruct the faithful with tangible symbols of God's redemption, Cleage worked to make theology a physical reality by altering the space in which his congregation worshipped. The renovation of both physical and metaphysical space helped lay the groundwork for the emergence of black theology, which began as a loose group of radical clergy but in the 1970s became widely accepted by mainline black churches.[81] Decades of social conservatism followed by the Civil Rights Movement thus helped black Christianity in America find a new identity in its historical balancing act as a site of both spiritual refuge and sociopolitical protest.

For over a century, leaders in the African American protest tradition have repudiated white images of deity and endorsed black images of God, Jesus, and other religious figures. Typical of the black radical tradition in which it found its greatest voice, the discussion of the color of the divine provides a strong example of race trumping all other considerations in American culture, in this case denominational and even interfaith differences. The arguments for a black deity became increasingly radical as they evolved over time, moving from a relatively tame and reactive denunciation of the whiteness of God to more proactive statements describing his rhetorical, existential blackness and finally to a potentially disruptive and subversive assertion of his literal blackness. Thus, as African Americans struggled to assert a more positive image of themselves, they correspondingly changed the image of their God. A new space for asserting the divine dignity of blackness was thus constructed.

Promoting the idea of a black God and black Jesus not only worked to improve race pride on both a group and an individual basis but also fulfilled a related but separate role in enhancing the devotional life of African Americans by providing them with a deity that looked like them and whom they could thus identify with on a more personal and intimate basis. On an even deeper level, though, the idea of a black God undermined the privileges of whiteness that lay at the core of American racism. The logic created by centuries of reasoning connecting religion and racism was turned on its head when Henry McNeal Turner boldly stated that "God is a Negro," even if at the time the statement was not meant in a literal sense. In the end, those who preached the doctrine of a black deity not only sought to affirm the social and cultural implications of humankind being created in God's image and likeness but also asserted the right of African Americans, like all other peoples, to create their God in their own image and likeness.

NOTES

This essay is a revised version of a paper presented at the Second Annual Graduate Student Conference in African-American History at the University of Memphis, October 20–21, 2000. The author thanks Howard McOmber, Brian Cannon, the Colloquium on Religion and History at the University of Notre Dame, George Marsden, Richard Pierce, and Angel David Nieves for their helpful insights and suggestions. Since I originally wrote this essay, two fine books chronicling the various depictions of Jesus in American history have appeared. Both books treat African American images of Jesus, but they approach the topic from the perspective of religious history rather than African American history or the carving out of a distinctive religious "space." See Stephen Prothero, *American Jesus: How the Son of God Became a National Icon* (New York: Farrar, Straus and Giroux, 2003), especially chapter 6, "Black Moses"; and Richard Wightman Fox, *Jesus in America: Personal Savior, Cultural Hero, National Obsession* (San Francisco: HarperSanFrancisco, 2004).

1. 2Pac + Outlawz, "Black Jesuz," *Still I Rise*, Amaru / Death Row / Interscope, 1999.

2. The use of the gender-specific word "churchmen" here is intentional. Although I fully recognize that women have always been at the forefront of African American spiritual and church life, this essay relies almost exclusively on men's voices, especially in the primary sources. Although such leading women as Maria Stewart, Jarena Lee, Sojourner Truth, Nannie Helen Burroughs, and Anna Julia Cooper all had a faith-based approach to their various forms of sociopolitical struggle and thus contributed to the beginnings of black feminist theology, the particular topic of this essay—the color of the divine and its meaning to the black community—was rarely addressed in black women's writings until after 1970, when this chapter stops. So although this essay admittedly has a heavy male bias, I contend that the voices here are still generally representative of the African American community (or at least a particular leader's constituents) as a whole. In addition, all of my references to God are masculine, reflecting the unanimous belief among the subjects in this study. For an excellent treatment of the feminist theology developing among black Baptist women in the late nineteenth century, see Evelyn Brooks Higginbotham, *Righteous Discontent: The Women's Movement in the Black Baptist Church, 1880–1920* (Cambridge, MA: Harvard University Press, 1993), 120–149.

3. Martha Tomhave Blauvelt, "Slaves and Gentlemen: Religion in the Antebellum South," *Reviews in American History* 7 (September 1979): 351. In this essay I employ a simi-

lar definition and usage of religious "space," which can be either theological or physical (or both), and which aided African Americans both in coping with racial injustice and in combating it.

4. A few examples of the structural approach to the black church's role as a vital center of the African American community include Aldon Morris, *The Origins of the Civil Rights Movement: Black Communities Organizing for Change* (New York: Free Press, 1984); Gary B. Nash, *Forging Freedom: The Formation of Philadelphia's Black Community, 1720–1840* (Cambridge, MA: Harvard University Press, 1988); Higginbotham, *Righteous Discontent*; William E. Montgomery, *Under Their Own Vine and Fig Tree: The African-American Church in the South, 1865–1900* (Baton Rouge: Louisiana State University Press, 1993); James Oliver Horton and Lois E. Horton, *In Hope of Liberty: Culture, Community, and Protest Among Northern Free Blacks, 1700–1860* (New York: Oxford University Press, 1997); Janet Duitsman Cornelius, *Slave Missions and the Black Church in the Antebellum South* (Columbia: University of South Carolina Press, 1999).

5. Robin D.G. Kelley, "'We Are Not What We Seem': Rethinking Black Working-Class Opposition in the Jim Crow South," *Journal of American History* 80 (June 1993): 88. See also Vincent Harding, *There Is a River: The Black Struggle for Freedom in America* (New York: Harcourt Brace Jovanovich, 1981).

6. Mark L. Chapman makes a similar point in writing about the black theologians of the late 1960s and 1970s: "[They] did not emphasize blackness simply because they thought it would be an interesting theological concept to discuss and write books about; rather, they believed the celebration of blackness was an essential part of black liberation." Chapman, *Christianity on Trial: African-American Religious Thought Before and After Black Power* (Maryknoll, NY: Orbis Books, 1996), 117.

7. Patrick Allitt, "The American Christ," *American Heritage* (November 1988): 128. See also Prothero, *American Jesus*; and Fox, *Jesus in America*.

8. Kelly Brown Douglas, *The Black Christ* (Maryknoll, NY: Orbis Books, 1994), 30–31. Similarly, Gayraud Wilmore links ideas about a black God and Jesus to twentieth-century sociopolitical and religious radicalism in the African American community: "[T]he willingness to speculate about the 'color' of God and the meaning of a black Christ [was among the] developments and tendencies [that] gave inspiration and ideological substance to the evolution of black consciousness and nationalism, a heightening sense of racial identity and messianism wherever blacks writhed under the heel of white oppression." Wilmore, *Black Religion and Black Radicalism: An Interpretation of the Religious History of African Americans*, 3rd ed., rev. and enl. (Maryknoll, NY: Orbis Books, 1998), 161.

9. See Wilmore, *Black Religion*, 145–149. See also Wilson Jeremiah Moses, ed., *Classical Black Nationalism: From the American Revolution to Marcus Garvey* (New York: New York University Press, 1996). W.E.B. Du Bois commented on how the freedmen perceived God's hand in their suffering: "But to most of the four million black folk emancipated by civil war, God was real. They knew Him. They had met Him personally in many a wild orgy of religious frenzy, or in the black stillness of the night. His plan for them was clear; they were to suffer and be degraded, and then afterwards by Divine edict, raised to manhood and power." W. E. Burghardt Du Bois, *Black Reconstruction: An Essay Toward a History of the Part Which Black Folk Played in the Attempt to Reconstruct Democracy in America, 1860–1880* (New York: Harcourt, Brace & Co., 1935), 124.

10. Katharine L. Dvorak, *An African-American Exodus: The Segregation of the Southern Churches* (Brooklyn, NY: Carlson Publishing, 1991), 2.

11. For background biographical information on Turner, see Stephen Ward Angell, *Bishop Henry McNeal Turner and African-American Religion in the South* (Knoxville: University of Tennessee Press, 1992); Henry J. Young, *Major Black Religious Leaders: 1755–1940* (Nashville: Abingdon, 1977), 140–142; and Edward L. Wheeler, *Uplifting the Race: The Black Minister in the South, 1865–1902* (Lanham, MD: University Press of America, 1986), 61–65.

12. Although Turner is credited with being the church leader who brought the notion of a black God to prominence, he was not the first to suggest the idea. For instance, the Rev. Samuel Cox's preaching that Christ was a "colored man" contributed to the 1834 anti-abolition riots in New York City. See David Grimsted, *American Mobbing, 1828–1861: Toward Civil War* (New York: Oxford University Press, 1998), 36.

13. "The Democratic Victory," *AME Church Review* 1, no. 3 (January 1885): 248, reprinted in Edwin S. Redkey, ed., *Respect Black: The Writings and Speeches of Henry McNeal Turner* (New York: Arno Press, 1971), 72. In the late nineteenth century, a number of African American leaders, men and women, began to emphasize the importance of "respectability" in the search for racial equality. This quest for respectability often took on a spatial dimension, with the establishment of black schools, businesses, fraternal organizations, and cooperatives, in addition to churches. See Kevin Gaines, *Uplifting the Race: Black Leadership, Politics, and Culture in the Twentieth Century* (Chapel Hill: University of North Carolina Press, 1996).

14. *Baltimore American*, May 12, 1884, reprinted in Redkey, *Respect Black*, 73.

15. "Open Letter to Blanche K. Bruce," *Washington Post*, March 17, 1890, reprinted in Redkey, *Respect Black*, 76–77.

16. By W. Fitzhugh Brundage's count, there were 50 lynchings of blacks in Turner's native Georgia in the 1880s, 105 in the 1890s, and 98 in the opening decade of the new century. See Brundage, *Lynching in the New South: Georgia and Virginia, 1880–1930* (Urbana: University of Illinois Press, 1993), 270–276.

17. Turner, introduction to *The Black Side*, by E. R. Carter (Atlanta: n.p., 1894), viii, quoted in Angell, *Bishop Henry McNeal Turner*, 261.

18. *Voice of Missions*, November 1895, quoted in Angell, *Bishop Henry McNeal Turner*, 261.

19. "God Is a Negro," *The Voice of Missions*, February 1898, reprinted in Redkey, *Respect Black*, 176–177 (emphasis in original).

20. See also *The Voice of Missions*, March 1896.

21. Angell, *Bishop Henry McNeal Turner*, 261.

22. Turner, "The American Negro and His Fatherland," in *Africa and the American Negro*, ed. John W.E. Bowen (Atlanta: Gammon Theological Seminary, 1896), 195–198, reprinted in Redkey, *Respect Black*, 169–170, and Moses, *Classical Black Nationalism*, 225.

23. In Wilmore, *Black Religion*, 182–183. The catechism's biblical references are, respectively, Matthew 1, Numbers 12:1, Psalms 119:83, Job 30:30, and Jeremiah 8:21.

24. Quoted in Wilmore, *Black Religion*, 186.

25. Other sectarian movements that are often thought of in this context include those led by Father Divine and Daddy Grace. They are not included here because not

only did they downplay race as a meaningful category but they were more intent on deifying themselves than creating a purposeful program for the advancement of African Americans as a race per se. See Wilson Jeremiah Moses, *Black Messiahs and Uncle Toms: Social and Literary Manipulations of a Religious Myth* (University Park: Pennsylvania State University Press, 1982), 11–12. Jill Watts further argues that Father Divine's theology was ultimately of little use in the black struggle for equality. He denied the very reality of race, arguing it was a damaging artificial construct of the mind (he refused to let his followers refer to themselves in racial terms) and maintained that social, economic, and political problems were simply products of negative thinking. See Jill Watts, *God, Harlem U.S.A.: The Father Divine Story* (Berkeley: University of California Press, 1992).

26. See Young, *Major Black Religious Leaders*, 152–155. Garvey was not, of course, the first person who believed that social and religious institution building would be a key element in uplift; indeed, he drew on a long history that stretched back to the "hush arbors" of slavery and continued through Reconstruction and the Jim Crow era. For a good local study of how African Americans built a variety of institutions to serve their own social, cultural, religious, and political needs, see Armstead L. Robinson, "Plans Dat Comed from God: Institution Building and the Emergence of Black Leadership in Reconstruction Memphis, 1865–1880," in *Toward a New South? Studies in Post–Civil War Southern Communities*, ed. Orville Vernon Burton and Robert C. McMath Jr. (Westport, CT: Greenwood Press, 1982), 71–102.

27. A good treatment of the religious aspects of Garvey's movement is Randall K. Burkett, *Garveyism as a Religious Movement: The Institutionalization of a Black Civil Religion* (Metuchen, NJ: Scarecrow Press, 1978). He addresses Garvey's theology of God and Christ on pages 46–55.

28. Garvey speech, August 2, 1921, in *Negro World*, August 13, 1921, quoted in Robert A. Hill, ed., *The Marcus Garvey and United Negro Improvement Association Papers*, 4 vols. (Berkeley: University of California Press, 1983–1985), 3:603 (hereafter cited as Garvey papers).

29. For instance, see Garvey speech, February 4, 1921, in *Negro World*, February 26, 1921, quoted in Garvey papers, 3:161–162; *Gleaner*, March 26, 1921, quoted in Garvey papers, 3:283.

30. Garvey speech, August 2, 1921, in *Negro World*, August 13, 1921, quoted in Garvey papers, 3:603; Garvey speech, June 1922, quoted in Garvey papers, 4:656–657.

31. *Gleaner*, March 26, 1921, quoted in Garvey papers, 3:283.

32. Garvey speech, June 1922, quoted in Garvey papers, 4:656–657.

33. For an overview of the complicated relationship between Garvey and McGuire (and the UNIA and AOC), see Burkett, *Garveyism as Religious Movement*, 88–99. He asserts that Garvey did not particularly desire to have his own church but rather envisioned "one great Christian confraternity without regard to any particular denomination" (97). One of Burkett's contributions is showing how the UNIA largely succeeded in its ecumenical ambitions, attracting leading churchmen from a wide variety of churches, both mainstream and sectarian (see chapters 4–5).

34. Quoted in Garvey papers, 3:302–303. The entire catechism is on pages 302–319.

35. *Negro World*, June 7, 1924, front page.

36. Report of the proceedings of the Fourth International Convention of Negroes of the World, Tuesday evening, August 5, 1924, in *Negro World*, August 16, 1924, 3.

37. "Negroes Acclaim a Black Christ," *New York Times*, August 6, 1924, 7; *Negro World*, August 9, 1924, 2, 7, 9; *Negro World*, August 16, 1924, 3.

38. "Religious Ceremony at Liberty Hall That Corrects Mistakes of Centuries and Braces the Negro," *Negro World*, September 6, 1924, 5.

39. *Negro World*, August 9, 1924, 7.

40. "Religious Ceremony at Liberty Hall . . . ," *Negro World*, September 6, 1924, 5.

41. Martin DeVere Stuart, letter to the editor, *Negro World*, May 24, 1924, 12.

42. William F. Clarke, letter to the editor, *Negro World*, September 13, 1924, 16.

43. "Negroes Acclaim a Black Christ," *New York Times*, August 6, 1924, 7.

44. Countee Cullen, "The Black Christ" (January 31, 1929), in *The Black Christ & Other Poems* (New York: Harper & Brothers, 1929), 69–110; and *On These I Stand: An Anthology of the Best Poems of Countee Cullen* (New York: Harper & Row, 1947), 104–137.

45. Countee Cullen, "Heritage," in *On These I Stand*, 27.

46. John Henrik Clarke, "The Boy Who Painted Christ Black" (1940), reprinted in Clarke, ed., *American Negro Short Stories* (New York: Hill & Wang, 1966), 108–114.

47. Langston Hughes, "Christ in Alabama," in *The Panther and the Lash: Poems of Our Times* (New York: Alfred A. Knopf, 1967/1987), 37. Hughes explained that "Christ in Alabama" was "an ironic poem inspired by the thought of how Christ, with no human father, would be accepted were He born in the South of a Negro mother." When Hughes visited the University of North Carolina shortly after publishing the poem, one local politician said that he should be run out of town before he had a chance to speak: "'It's bad enough to call Christ a bastard,' he cried, 'but to call Him a nigger—that's too much!'" In Hughes, *I Wonder as I Wander: An Autobiographical Journey* (1956; reprint, New York: Octagon Books, 1974), 46. (Page citations according to reprint editions.)

48. Hughes, "Whiter Than Snow," in *Simple Takes a Wife* (1953), reprinted in *The Return of Simple*, ed. Akiba Sullivan Harper (New York: Hill & Wang, 1994), 154. In another story, Simple wondered if he would recognize "all my relatives setting up in heaven washed whiter than snow." "God's Other Side," in *Simple's Uncle Sam* (1965), reprinted in *The Return of Simple*, ed. Harper, 193 (emphasis in original).

49. Hughes, "Empty Houses," in *Simple's Uncle Sam*, reprinted in *The Return of Simple*, ed. Harper, 190.

50. Du Bois, *Black Reconstruction*, 39, 125.

51. Du Bois, "The Song of the Smoke," originally in *Horizon* (1899), reprinted in Sterling Stuckey, *Slave Culture: Nationalist Theory and the Foundations of Black America* (New York: Oxford University Press, 1987), 276.

52. Du Bois, *Darkwater: Voices from Within the Veil* (New York: AMS Press, 1969 [1920]), quotes from 128 and 27, respectively; also see "The Prayers of God" in the same volume.

53. Phil Zuckerman, ed., *Du Bois on Religion* (Walnut Creek, CA: AltaMira Press, 2000), 10.

54. Stuckey, *Slave Culture*, 276.

55. See David Levering Lewis, *When Harlem Was in Vogue*, with new preface (New York: Penguin Books, 1997 [1981]).

56. Louis A. DeCaro Jr., *Malcolm and the Cross: The Nation of Islam, Malcolm X, and Christianity* (New York: New York University Press, 1998), 3–4.

57. See Claude Andrew Clegg III, *An Original Man: The Life and Times of Elijah Muhammad* (New York: St. Martin's Press, 1997), chapter 2.

58. For various estimates on membership in the Nation of Islam, see Clegg, *Original Man*, 114–115. For Malcolm X's account of his conversion to the Nation of Islam, see Malcolm X and Alex Haley, *The Autobiography of Malcolm X* (New York: Grove Press, 1965), chapter 10.

59. Clegg, *Original Man*, 21, vii. As one might expect, Malcolm had an answer for those who scoffed at the Nation of Islam's ideas about Allah being a black man: "When we tell you that Allah is a supreme black man, you laugh, because you can't conceive of God as black. But when the white preacher tells you that Jesus had blue eyes and stayed in the ground for three days and got up and went to heaven, you believe it. Now, which is more ridiculous?" Quoted by C. Eric Lincoln in Peter Goldman, *The Life and Death of Malcolm X*, 2nd ed. (Urbana: University of Illinois Press, 1979), 91.

60. Malcolm X and Haley, *Autobiography*, 269 (emphasis in original).

61. Louis A. DeCaro Jr., *On the Side of My People: A Religious Life of Malcolm X* (New York: New York University Press, 1996), 2.

62. Malcolm X and Haley, *Autobiography*, 222 (emphasis in original).

63. "God's Angry Men," *Los Angeles Dispatch*, March 27, 1958, quoted in James H. Cone, *Martin & Malcolm & America: A Dream or a Nightmare* (Maryknoll, NY: Orbis Books, 1991), 173. Also see *Playboy* interview with Malcolm X by Alex Haley (May 1963), reprinted in G. Barry Golson, ed., *The Playboy Interview* (New York: Playboy Press, 1981), 50.

64. "This religion taught the 'Negro' that black was a curse. It taught him to hate everything black, including himself. It taught him that everything white was good, to be admired, respected, and loved. It brainwashed this 'Negro' to think he was superior if his complexion showed more of the white pollution of the slavemaster" (Malcolm X and Haley, *Autobiography*, 164). See also "Twenty million Black people in a political, economic, and mental prison," January 23, 1963, reprinted in Bruce Perry, ed., *Malcolm X: The Last Speeches* (New York: Pathfinder, 1989), 31.

65. Albert B. Cleage Jr., *The Black Messiah* (New York: Sheed and Ward, 1968; reprint, Trenton, NJ: Africa World Press, 1989), page citations according to the reprint edition. A collection of sermons rather than a single monograph, *The Black Messiah* was extremely controversial in both the black and white religious communities. Even ten to fifteen years after its publication, scholars were still issuing their critiques of the book, its theology, and its author. Wilson Moses called it "a transparent attempt to appeal to emotional black militants by distorting the essential message of the Gospels" (Moses, *Black Messiahs*, 222). James Cone said the book was "seriously limited by its rhetorical and sermonic style, the historical and theological problems associated with his use of the terms 'Black Nation' and 'Black Messiah,' and the absence of an ecumenical vision in his theological perspective" (in Gayraud S. Wilmore and James H. Cone, eds., *Black Theology: A Documentary History, 1966–1979* [Maryknoll, NY: Orbis Books, 1979], 611). Finally, Gayraud Wilmore, the most complimentary of the three but still reserved in his praise, commended Cleage for his consistency and then observed that "Cleage may have gone too far, but no one has made a greater contribution to the decolonization of the minds of Black Christians, and no institution has sought more seriously to demonstrate the implications of Black

Theology for local congregations than his Shrine of the Black Madonna" (in Wilmore and Cone, *Black Theology*, 251–252).

66. Cleage, *Black Messiah*, 3. Recurring criticisms of Black Nationalist ideology (of which Cleage is but one voice in a long history) were that it did not have a consistent geographic dimension and that it neglected diversity within the black community. See Moses, *Classical Black Nationalism*, 5.

67. Cleage readily acknowledged the influence of Malcolm X and Marcus Garvey in the formation of his own theology. Regarding Malcolm, he said: "I cannot resist the temptation to compare Brother Malcolm to Jesus. . . . We believe that the things which Brother Malcolm taught, Jesus taught two thousand years ago" (Cleage, *Black Messiah*, 186). He praised Garvey as "the only black leader in this country to meet this problem [of the color of Jesus] head-on" (198). He regretted the fact that "[f]orty years ago black Americans apparently were not ready for Garvey's religious ideas" (8). On issues of race uplift and Black Nationalism, see Angel David Nieves, " 'We Are Too Busy Making History . . . to Write History': African American Women, Constructions of Nation, and the Built Environment in the New South, 1892–1968," Chapter 12, in this volume.

68. Cleage, *Black Messiah*, 3.

69. Ibid., 98–99.

70. Ibid., 7.

71. Ibid., 114.

72. Ibid., 39–40, 42. The life of Jesus as found in the Gospels of Matthew, Mark, and Luke (Cleage rejected John as spurious) was portrayed in this same color framework. According to Cleage, Jesus' teachings were primarily concerned with "telling black people how to fight white people" (156): He was "a powerful black man" not "the weak little mamby-pamby white Jesus" (86); He drove the "Uncle Tom" moneychangers out of the temple for "exploiting their own people with the connivance and support of the white Gentile oppressors" (45); and eventually He was sold out by his own people and crucified by white Romans for being a "dangerous revolutionary" trying to liberate the oppressed black nation Israel (67).

73. Ibid., 86. According to Cleage's logic, since sons look like their fathers, if Jesus was the son of God and He was black (an indisputable fact for Cleage), then according to simple genetics God had to be black as well. One of Cleage's most intriguing arguments in justifying his conclusions about the blackness of God turned the American legal definition of blackness on its head: "In America, one drop of black makes you black. So by American law, God is black, and by any practical interpretation, why would God have made seven-eighths of the world non-white and yet he himself be white? That is not reasonable. If God were white, he'd have made everybody white. And if he decided to send his son to earth, he would have sent a white son down to some nice white people. He certainly would not have sent him down to a black people like Israel" (43).

74. Ibid., 42.

75. Moses, *Black Messiah*, 223. Reinforcing his thesis of the literal blackness of Jesus, Cleage said in an interview, "When I say that Jesus was black, that Jesus was the black Messiah, I'm not saying, 'Wouldn't it be nice if Jesus was black?' or 'Let's pretend that Jesus was black' or 'It's necessary psychologically for us to believe that Jesus was black.'

I'm saying that Jesus *WAS* black. There never was a white Jesus." In Alex Poinsett, "The Quest for a Black Christ," *Ebony* 24 (March 1969): 174 (emphasis in original).

76. Chapman, *Christianity on Trial*, 1–5, quote from p. 3. Also see "An Epistle to Stokely," in Cleage, *Black Messiah*, 35–47. James Baldwin's writings also reflect this anger toward historic (European) Christianity. In *The Fire Next Time* (1963), he wrote: "If the concept of God has any validity or any use, it can only be to make us larger, freer, and more loving. If God cannot do this, then it is time we got rid of Him" (reprinted in Baldwin, *Collected Essays* [New York: Library of America, 1998], 314). Even more poignantly, in his 1964 play *Blues for Mister Charlie*, one character rails against "this damn almighty God who don't care what happens to nobody, unless, of course, they're white. . . . It's that damn white God that's been lynching us and burning us and castrating us and raping our women and robbing us of everything that makes a man a man for all these hundreds of years. Now, why we sitting around here, in *His* house? If I could get my hands on Him, I'd pull Him out of heaven and drag Him through this town at the end of a rope" (Baldwin, *Blues for Mister Charlie* [New York: Dial Press, 1964], 4).

77. Cleage, *Black Messiah*, 39.

78. Wilmore and Cone, *Black Theology*, 69.

79. See Chapman, *Christianity on Trial*, 98–99.

80. "Black Madonna," *Liberator* 7 (May 1967): 14. At about the same time Cleage established his Shrine of the Black Madonna, another Detroit congregation, St. Cecelia's Roman Catholic Church, "unveiled a striking dome of a thick-lipped, kinky-haired *Black Christ*, surrounded by a veritable United Nations of angels of different races and ethnicities. In 1969, St. Cecelia's *Black Christ* appeared on the cover of *Ebony* magazine" (Prothero, *American Jesus*, 200). The *Ebony* cover was on the March 1969 issue, accompanied by Alex Poinsett's article "The Quest for a Black Christ," cited above.

81. This mainstreaming of the Black Theology movement, as developed by the National Conference of Black Churchmen and articulated by a new class of African American scholars and theologians such as James H. Cone and J. Deotis Roberts, eventually became intolerable to radicals such as Cleage, who denounced the movement as "Black schoolmen's theology . . . written for white acceptance." Wilmore and Cone, *Black Theology*, 6, 67.

Andrea E. Frohne

Reclaiming Space

The African Burial Ground in New York City

The African Burial Ground located in Lower Manhattan was used by Africans and people of African descent from approximately 1700 until 1790. Containing perhaps the remains of between 10,000 and 20,000 persons, the African Burial Ground covered five to six acres. A small portion of it was unearthed in 1991 when General Services Administration (GSA) began and completed construction of a thirty-four-story federal office building at 290 Broadway. The area lies in Lower Manhattan's Civic Center, surrounded by City Hall, Federal Plaza, and the Supreme Court. Because the land occupies prime real estate, it was initially treated as such rather than as a sacred, historical burial site. Throughout the 1990s and into the twenty-first century, African Americans and other concerned citizens in New York City fought GSA for respectful treatment of the space to such an extent that the burial ground became a contested terrain at both the local and national levels.[1]

How has the African Burial Ground been reclaimed, first in the eighteenth and then in the twentieth and twenty-first centuries? The first section of this essay explores the engagement of the burial ground by early Africans and its mapping by colonial Europeans. The second section moves to the twentieth century to consider an attempted denial of space until present-day African Americans and their allies fought governmental politics surrounding the site. As well as political victories, the essay explores how space has been reclaimed through remembering and reinventing spirituality at the burial ground.

In this discussion, space is understood as ever mutable and unfixed.[2] The notion of space as used here recognizes the indeterminacy of the burial ground because of its immaterial, spiritual component and because to this day, the exact physical boundaries of the five- to six-acre area remain unknown. This is a space that is still being defined through the process of reclamation where memories continue to be formulated. Furthermore, space is not static, but it is "constructed and produced and is a social experience."[3] Since the realm of the spatial is inevitably politicized, explorations of the spiritual space at the African Burial Ground both in the eighteenth and twentieth centuries involve politics of power, race, identity, memory, and dispossession. In considering these various aspects of reclamation and dispossession of space, I introduce the term "spirituality of space." First, the African Burial Ground is contextualized through a lens of spirituality because as a cemetery, the space is naturally sacred. Second, the term enables an African-based understanding of spirituality at the site. The African Burial Ground has been surrounded by an African discourse from the culturally diverse, early Africans who held nightlong funerals in which they remembered and reinvented traditions that honored the departed—from the libations and offerings left for ancestors during vigils and ceremonies by African Americans today to commissioned artworks that reference the African spirit world at 290 Broadway.

The expression "spirituality of space" can be understood as a personal or collective interaction, recognition, or reference to a spiritual entity in a space. The word "spiritual" impresses that a space may be imbued with spirits, and it emphasizes interaction between the spirit world and the physical. Rather than let the notion of spirituality stand alone, it is conjoined with space to ground the metaphysical in the physical. Therefore, I consider tensions involved with reclamation of the burial ground in terms of its physical as well as metaphysical space.

THE COLONIAL SPACE

Africans were introduced to the island of Manhattan in 1626 by the Dutch West India Company. The company's objective was to supply slaves to perform the backbreaking labor necessary to build the infrastructure of the New Amsterdam colony while European settlers pursued the lucrative fur and beaver trade. As the population grew, a cemetery reserved for Africans and people of African descent came into use during the late seventeenth or early eighteenth century.[4] It was Trinity Church that perhaps instigated use of the African Burial Ground, although it may have been in use prior to the church's October 1697 proclamation. The Trinity Church minutes of October 25, 1697, state:

> Ordered, that after the expiration of four weeks from the date here of no Negroes be buried within the bounds and limits of the church yard of Trinity Church, that is to say, in the rear of the present burying place and that no person or Negro whatsoever, so presume after the term above limited to break up any ground for the burying of his Negro, as they will answer it at their peril, and that this order be forthwith publish'd.[5]

It is unknown whether the Africans claimed their own space for the burial ground or if it was assigned to them. Although racism and the institution of slavery played a role in forcing the issue, I argue that early Africans claimed their own space for burying the dead, honoring the ancestors, and remembering cultural funerary traditions. Nineteenth-century city clerk and New York City historian David Valentine documented one of the few descriptions of the site:

> Beyond the commons [now City Hall] lay what in the earliest settlement of the town had been appropriated as a burial place for the Negroes, slaves and free. It was a desolate, unappropriated spot, descending with a gentle declivity towards a ravine which led to the Kalchhook Pond. . . . Many of them were native Africans, imported hither in slave ships, and retaining their native superstitions and burial customs, among which was that of burying by night, with various mummeries and outcries. . . . The lands were unappropriated, and though within convenient distance from the city, the locality was unattractive and desolate, so that by permission the slave population were allowed to inter their dead there.[6]

Valentine used the word "appropriate," which means either to take for one's own or to set aside for a specific use or person. Did the government appropriate the land for the Africans? Or did early Africans appropriate it for themselves? In his last sentence, Valentine noted that enslaved people used the land "by permission." This crucial sentence suggests that Africans themselves chose the land and requested permission from the city government to use it. Also, Valentine stressed that Europeans held no interest in the swampy, undesirable land that lacked real estate value, and he noted twice that this land north of the city limits was initially "unappropriated," or vacant.

There are a plethora of reasons why the early Africans would have selected this area for a communal cemetery. The African burying place was located on the outskirts of the city several blocks north of Wall Street and what is now City Hall Park in Lower Manhattan. A number of Africans lived in this area surrounding the cemetery, as they had been granted farms in the seventeenth century. For instance, in 1644 the Dutch West India Company granted half freedoms to the first eleven males who had been brought to New Amsterdam in 1626 when they, along with their wives, petitioned for freedom from enslavement. Each petitioner was granted freedom and a deed for between one and twenty acres of land. However, the following provisions were also made initially: any living or yet-to-be-born children of freed slaves were still slaves to the company, and 22½ bushels of maize, wheat, peas, beans, and one hog had to be paid each year to the Dutch West India Company.[7] Although it was unusual for former slaves to become landholders during slavery in general, the company, as well as private enslavers, benefited, as they did not have to house or care for the nonproductive elderly former slaves. Moreover, the land grants were so far out of town that they served as a protective buffer against attacks from Native Americans provoked by the Dutch. The African-owned lots were sold off to the encroaching white population, the last African-owned lot sold by a Peter Santomee in 1716.[8] This part of the island had traditionally been African-identified space—a home, as such—and thus may have been considered appropriate ground for African burials.

With the cemetery at the edge of town and actually in a ravine, it was also beyond the surveillance of Europeans. Here, mourners could likely hold funeral ceremonies as they wished, remembering past traditions and creating new ones. In this space of spirituality, burials became a time for meeting, mourning, and remembering. Dislocated Africans and people of African descent recalled and reinvented the sacred practices that they remembered, that were passed down to them by family members, or that they learned from others. Valentine corroborates this by his description of the people. Additionally, David Humphreys wrote in 1730: "They were buried by those of their own country or complexion in the common field, without any Christian office, perhaps some ridiculous heathen rites were performed at the grave by some of their own people."[9] The sounds, songs, and words were foreign to Europeans because the practices were carried over from Africa, and their scorn reflects their racism and ignorance of indigenous traditions. However, Humphreys and Valentine, perhaps inadvertently, contributed to a collective memory of the African Burial Ground by remembering night funerals held in native African languages. Eventually, restrictions were placed on funerals by British-enacted laws in 1722. One law ordered that funerals for African and Native American slaves dying "on the South side of the fresh water [the exact location of the burial ground] be buried by daylight at or before sunset."[10] A later law stipulated that only twelve Africans attend a funeral. Out of fear of rebellion, whites attempted to restrict group gatherings that were out of town, during the night, and therefore beyond their surveillance. These laws, however, are evidence of memories of funerary practices because all-night funerals with large gatherings of people must indeed have occurred at the burial ground if laws were enacted to attempt to quell them. Documents of punishment recount resistance to the laws. There were Africans and people of African descent who did not follow curfew, gathered in groups, participated in "unlawful" entertainment, stole, or committed arson out of retaliation.[11]

Finally, Africans may have selected this space for a communal cemetery because of its proximity to water. As illustrated in the Maerschalk Plan of 1755, it is clearly evident that the burial ground lay adjacent to a major body of spring-fed water called Collect Pond or Fresh Water Pond. This location southwest of the body of water may have been of spiritual benefit from an African perspective. In African (such as Kongo and Igbo, for example) and diasporic cultures, water can connote the passage to, or realm of, the dead. Water has been associated with the space one travels to the next world, the realm of water spirits, or the land of the dead.

Francis Maerschalk was a surveyor and cartographer for the city of New York who mapped the "Negroes Burying Ground" in his 1755 plan of New York (a second version was published in 1763). His plan was one of the very few colonial-era documents to acknowledge the existence of the cemetery. For urban New World cartography of this era, it was common practice to map religious places of worship (e.g., the 1763 plan lists Trinity Church, Old Dutch Church, French Church, New Dutch Church, Presbyterian Meeting, Quaker Meeting, Baptist Meeting, Lutheran Church, Jews Synagogue, and Moravian Meeting). Perhaps Maerschalk recognized the cemetery as a sacred site connected to religious expression and therefore included it in his representation of New York City.

In addition to the above account of the physical location of the burial ground, burial excavations attest to the metaphysical nature of the space and illustrate that it was shaped by African tradition. Europeans, Native Americans in North America and the Caribbean, Afro-Caribbeans, and the African descendant community in New York also contributed to the funerary traditions of the African Burial Ground. Allowing for such variation, it is difficult to assume that any one aspect of the New York burial ground specifically derives from one African culture. Even in Africa, one particular culture never exists in isolation; there are always interactions, intermarriages, interlocutors, trade, and travel occurring between communities, countries, and continents. Nonetheless, those at the burial ground hailed directly from Africa or were of African heritage. In fact, the African Burial Ground in New York is the largest and earliest known cemetery of African descendants in North America.[12]

An examination of the slave trade helps to determine African cultures that were most likely represented in New York. When New Amsterdam was under Dutch control (1626–1664), the majority of Africans were brought from Angola, the Kongo area, Guinea, Calabar in Nigeria, the Gold Coast, and Curaçao.[13] The Dutch colony of New Amsterdam was renamed New York City under the British (1664–1776), who transported Africans primarily from Madagascar, Jamaica, Barbados, and Antigua. The points of origin from Africa to the Caribbean included Calabar, Guinea, Angola, the Kongo area, and the Gold Coast. From 1644 to 1659, approximately 1,840 Africans were brought over.[14] Between 1700 and 1774, at least 6,800 enslaved were brought to New York.[15] The slave population reached 3,137 by 1771 and comprised 14.3 percent of New York residents. In 1790, slaves were owned by about 40 percent of the white households around New York City, with blacks comprising nearly one-quarter of the urban population.[16] This proved to be the highest number of enslaved blacks outside of South Carolina during the eighteenth century.[17] Enslaved people in New York City did not work on plantations, as was typical of southern labor. Research reveals that they helped to build the physical colonial infrastructure, laboring to such an extent that some were literally worked to death.[18] In fact, at least five women had fractures at the base of their head. In addition, between 45 and 50 percent of the excavated burials were of children under the age of twelve.[19]

A brief description of excavated burials profoundly illustrates that the site was indeed a space of spirituality for the eighteenth-century population in which African funerary traditions were remembered and reinvented. These explicit associations between early blacks in America and Africa reveal the emergence of an African American population and the continuation of an African cultural and philosophical identity in colonial New York City. It was with these forced cultural concurrences that Africans developed an African diasporic society through negotiation, cooperation, and reinvention of cultural, artistic, and religious traditions. The 419 burials that were excavated in the early 1990s date from roughly between 1720 and 1760.[20] The majority of interred bodies faced east, were wrapped in white shrouds and pinned with copper pins, and were placed in wooden coffins without any names. Some were buried with copper coins placed over the eyes or hands, and shells were included in other coffins. Also recovered were coral, quartz crystal, glass, buttons, pipes, pearlware ceramics, beads, sleeve links, and a silver earbob. Several people who were born in Africa had teeth filed in various African ethnic styles. One older woman around fifty-two years of age with filed teeth bears the burial number 340. She wore a belt of a few cowrie shells and 111 beads, mainly blue and gold, around her waist and possibly more beads around her wrist. Waist beads were and still are today worn by women in many parts of Africa, and anthropologist Cheryl LaRoche believes that "the burial ground waistbeads represent a cultural continuum" from Africa.[21] This older woman, who held the status of an elder, warranted a funerary tribute from Africa that would have been particularly prized in the New York community.

Another burial, numbered 434, contained at least one bead that was manufactured in West Africa. Anthropologist Christopher DeCorse determined that this type of glass bead hailed from southern Ghana, where they are still made to this day.[22] Such a bead has also been found in Barbados at Jerome Handler's excavation of the Newton plantation cemetery, a site roughly contemporaneous with the African Burial Ground.[23]

Burial 101 possesses traits that link him to his African homeland and African spirituality but also tell a story about his life in New York City as an enslaved person because his vertebrae were fractured from the middle down to the bottom, probably as a result of lifting.[24] Details confirm that burial 101 was born in Africa. He had a tropical skin disease that he must have contracted there.[25] Also, burial 101 had filed teeth, a practice performed in Africa that was discontinued in New York. This arthritic elder over sixty years of age was honored with a *sankofa*, or Akan ideographic symbol from Ghana, tacked into the lid of the coffin. The *sankofa* denotes a specific proverb that translates into "it is not a taboo to go back and retrieve if you forget," or look to the past to inform the future.[26] In Ghana, a *sankofa* is stamped onto an *adinkra*, or funerary cloth. This cloth bears a conglomerate of black stamps that represent a variety of proverbs relating to wisdom, state power, and history. Because the adinkra is worn to honor the ancestors, there is an underlying notion that the living gain wisdom and knowledge from the deceased. The garb offers a visual expression of death as a transition in the fluid cycle of life. Interestingly, the *sankofa* from the African Burial Ground has been adopted as the motto for the project. It graces newsletters from the Office of Public Education and Interpretation (OPEI) for the burial ground and is found on many handouts and announcements. In reclaiming the site, people working on the project today have also reclaimed aspects of African spirituality.

The African Burial Ground has also been remembered in a select number of colonial maps. Whereas the Maerschalk Plan may have appreciated the site's religious significance, a map by David Grim marked a space of violence instead. Cartography operates as a means for creating a representation of space that recalls, redefines, or deletes a space from existence. Therefore, production of knowledge and politics of power are significant considerations for interpreting representation of space. David Grim offered a specific example through his map from 1813 of New York City that depicts the years 1742 through 1744. He elected to remember the burial ground area not as a cemetery but as a place of execution. The map legend reads "(#55) Plot Negro's burnt here" and "(#56) Plot Negro Gibbeted." "Plot Negro" refers to the 1741 conspiracy in which fear of a slave rebellion created mass hysteria resulting in executions of the accused. As relayed by sixteen-year-old indentured servant Mary Burton, the supposed conspiracy of blacks and poor whites who had planned to burn the city cost many in the African community their lives.[27] The hanging and burning at the stake took place in the City Commons (now City Hall Park) near the African Burial Ground, where the dead were likely buried. Grim marked the site of the burial ground as a place of "conspiracy" with written text, adding small images of a gibbet and people in flames next to Collect Pond. In the Grim map of 1813, images of control and oppression are mapped in relation to the African presence in New York, as opposed to his mapping the sacred space where the executed were buried. In his preciseness, the Remmey and Crolius Pottery firm (#44) is documented. This pottery business occupied a portion of the burial ground and shards of its pottery were disposed of in the cemetery.

At the close of the eighteenth century, the burial ground was physically eradicated from existence as Manhattan expanded northward. As streets were laid and buildings constructed, a sacred space was obliterated from sight and, over the course of 200 years, erased from memory. In both 1785 and 1795, sections of the burial ground were surveyed and separated into lots for residential and commercial development. The land had become de facto property of the Common Land of the City of New York, whereupon the city then designated land for a new African burial ground on Chrystie Street in 1795.[28]

Around 1794, Chambers Street was laid, which was named after John Chambers, a lawyer, corporation counsel, alderman, and Supreme Court judge from 1727 to 1765. The burial ground was also covered or bordered by Duane and Reade Streets. James Duane was an attorney and U.S. District Court judge who served as the first mayor of New York after the British left in 1783. Joseph Reade was a member of the governor's council and/or a warden of Trinity Church.[29] Thus, in the area's transformation from a sacred space to the epicenter of a white city government, the City of New York inscribed its top legendary officials onto the space.[30] The area now carefully and purposefully memorialized upper-class white men rather than those who had buried their dead there for a century before. By the end of the twentieth century, the forgotten cemetery was still situated beneath the heart of New York's governmental district, surrounded by buildings including Federal Plaza, the Supreme Court, City Hall, Tweed Courthouse, U.S. Courthouse, U.S. Appeals Court, and U.S. District Court.

The now polluted, stagnant Collect Pond was filled in by 1811, and by the 1820s, the hilly land had been graded and leveled.[31] To this end, archaeological excavations of the burial ground revealed that between sixteen and twenty-five feet of fill had been added above the graves, ultimately protecting them. Thus, several basements of buildings erected later penetrated only the fill and did not necessarily disturb the burials.[32]

It is interesting to compare the eradication of space at the African Burial Ground with the preservation of space at a contemporaneous cemetery belonging to Trinity Church.[33] A ten-minute walk south of the burial ground will lead you to the graves of Trinity Church, which have remained undisturbed for 300 years. The still-legible gravestones bear witness to people's lives, dates of birth and death, and names. Why is it that Trinity's graves remain intact for people to honor and visit, whereas the African graves were forgotten and then exhumed to make way for an office building? Politics of power and racism are entwined in these two spaces of spirituality. Trinity Church was purposefully built at the head of Wall Street to dominate the financial center, and it remains in a position of power and economic wealth to this day. Meanwhile, structures were built over the exploited and enslaved people of the African Burial Ground. Ironically, Trinity Church became an important rallying point during a pivotal 1992 New York town meeting when prominent politicians and concerned citizens discussed the plight of the burial ground. Through ambitious struggle and resistance, inequity and amnesia were coming undone.

THE CONTEMPORARY SPACE

The burial ground remains a dynamic site caught between performances of spirituality and politics of power as its erasure was attempted in the twentieth century. Today, the area between Duane and Reade Streets just off Broadway reveals the remains of once-oppressed and marginalized peoples buried in the heart of contemporary New York City. The disputed terrain of the burial ground reflects battles over capitalism, racism, marginalized identity, and spirituality. A detailed recounting of these issues epitomizes the African American struggle to reclaim the sacred space at 290 Broadway as the African Burial Ground. As in the eighteenth century, the modern reclamation involves a space of spirituality comprising an African-based discourse.

The story begins when GSA purchased two plots of land from New York City for $104 million for the purpose of constructing a federal office building at 290 Broadway as well as a federal courthouse at Foley Square in 1990. Although the necessary salvage archaeology was performed by a firm named Historic Conservation and Interpretation (HCI) and the location of the burial ground was generally determined through historical maps and documents, purchase and construction commenced without alternative strategies if burials were indeed unearthed, as GSA presumed the burial site had already been destroyed by urban development.

Before GSA commenced construction of the $276 million, thirty-four-story office building, they again hired HCI to physically probe for the possibility of undisturbed burials. Intact burials were in fact located during summer 1991. Ultimately, 419 burials were excavated. Not only was construction concurrent with excavation, but GSA's inexperienced archaeological teams worked hastily to excavate several hundred skeletons and artifacts before office building construction was to begin. Major recovery errors included the destruction of several burials due to a digging accident and damage to about twenty burials when concrete was poured on them. The large volume of bones and artifacts stored at Lehman College in the Bronx were wrapped in newspaper and placed in cardboard boxes, so that mold formed until the city's Metropolitan Forensic Anthropology Team (MFAT), hired by GSA, could clean and study the remains. Representatives of the African American community asked to review the process. "We kept asking them [MFAT], 'Can we go up there?' And that involved more waiting, more delays. . . . It wasn't that we were against Lehman, we just wanted to see how our ancestors were being stored," explained community activist Miriam Francis.[34] Public dissatisfaction escalated to outrage as European Americans again controlled the fate of African and African American ancestors. Along with others, Francis challenged Euro-American control: "If it was an African find, we wanted to make sure that it was interpreted from an African point of view."[35]

The public protested vehemently against disrespectful treatment and against GSA's reluctance to recognize or commemorate the sacred site that it had disturbed. Concerned citizen Onaje Muid explained at a public forum in April 1999: "I am appalled that the federal government built on land that is the ancestral burial land of my people. Those Africans were captive in this country and never had a voice. You must talk about the pain, the degradation. They gave their lives in the most desperate way so that I can be here today."[36] Journalist and OPEI employee Emilyn Brown understood that everything the interred "had lived for and possibly died for was being minimized for the sake of a building."[37] Activist Donna Cole, an employee of OPEI, lamented: "So what if you paid X amount of dollars for it? Once you discovered it was a burial ground, you basically should have left it alone."[38] An interviewer for the broadcast of *Like It Is* questioned in 1992, "[I]s it right to put a building on a gravesite?" In the program, Noel Pointer, a well-known jazz musician and burial ground activist, explained that GSA initially professed they had neither the authority nor the funding to put a national cemetery in a federal building, that is, no on-site reburial and minimal memorialization. Pointer commented that this was "absolutely ridiculous . . . because in fact they're putting a federal building in a cemetery."[39] The space of the African Burial Ground proved to be a contested terrain as conflict erupted over the development of prime real estate versus proper treatment of a sacred, historically valuable site. Although plans for the building could not be withdrawn, questions remained over how the site would be remembered and honored.

Initially, GSA regional administrator Bill Diamond expressed willingness to contribute $250,000 to an interpretive display within the office building, an appropriate plaque on the exterior of the building, and reinterment of the remains in a public park (fifty yards away and outside federal lands) for memo-rialization of the African Burial Ground.[40] There was much contention over on-site reinterment, a quintessential goal for African Americans fighting for sacred treatment of the land. In fact, a petition circulated in 1992 contained 100,000 signatures arguing for reburial on the site.[41] Activist Herman Howard com-mented, "Someone's going to tell you that the remains of your ancestors are not more important than getting up this office building?"[42] Diamond acknowledged the differences between the community and GSA but requested that the public acquiesce: "I'm hoping that the community will buy into the American system of settling differences peaceably."[43] In other words, GSA intended for the plot of land at 290 Broadway to exist as a federal office space. However, those who endeavored to reclaim the space fought for transformation so that 290 Broadway could be recognized as an African cemetery of historical and spiritual import. The demand for memorialization and reburial on that space forced the issue.

The office building was in fact constructed above the African Burial Ground and opened at the end of 1994. Activists' hard work eventually caught the atten-tion of politicians at the local, state, and national levels, including Mayor David Dinkins, Senator David Paterson, Congressperson Charlie Rangel, City Council member Kathryn Freed, and Manhattan Borough president Ruth Messinger. It was Illinois representative Gus Savage who held a hearing in July 1992, threat-ening to suspend future funding for GSA projects. His hearing resulted in the successful achievement of community activists' demands, including African American scientific control of the remains, a plan for scientific research, reburial of the bones and artifacts on the site, significant memorialization of the cem-etery, and abandonment of a proposed pavilion, adjoining the office tower, where a majority of burials were located. Excavation was halted on July 19, 1992. HCI was replaced by the respected firm John Milner Associates, and Dr. Michael Blakey, based at Howard University in Washington, DC, was hired to research skeletal remains. Additionally, after considerable community pressure and President George H.W. Bush's eventual forced intervention, $3 million was appropriated for memorialization. The money has been used to commission art-ists for artworks inside the lobby of the office building, an Interpretive Center that will open in the lobby, and an exterior memorial that will be located behind the office building.

COMMEMORATING THE SPACE

The politics and controversies surrounding the African Burial Ground in the twentieth and twenty-first centuries challenged citizens to consider the signifi-cance of a spiritual space. People questioned whether the land was still sacred if it bore a multimillion-dollar high-rise. Was this a secular office building or sacred space? Was a plot of land interred with once-forgotten, unmarked bodies still a cemetery? How could the burial ground be reclaimed and represented, and how could its historical erasure be transformed to contemporary prominence?

In wrestling with these questions, people organized creative means for memorializing the African Burial Ground. The following multifarious examples of memorialization that I offer exemplify the significance of recognizing, remembering, and reclaiming the burial ground. The memorials themselves, both inside and outside of the office building, are defined through African conceptions of the ancestral realm. Before summarizing the altars and offerings constructed on the space at the African Burial Ground, I offer a specific African metaphysical example of how and why the spirit world is honored since this discourse pervades the burial ground. A number of cultural groups and cosmological systems within Africa could be posited as examples. Here, I select the Akan for a variety of reasons, although this is not meant to serve as the only possible example. Akan is the linguistic name for a group of people who live in central and southern Ghana and parts of Côte d'Ivoire. Akan people and their descendants have been dispersed throughout the African diaspora because of the slave trade. They were brought to New York in the colonial era, as is evident from the presence of the *sankofa* on the coffin lid. More recently, people from Ghana and Côte d'Ivoire have emigrated to New York City during the last century, with continuations of traditions such as holding a swearing-in ceremony for the new Asantehene (ruler) and Queen Mother in Manhattan, as was done in 2003.

A summary of Akan metaphysics in Ghana offers a specific notion of African spirituality.[44] These specifics also outline general characteristics of African spirituality, such as the recognition of and interaction with the ancestral world, as seen at the African Burial Ground. The Akan recognize a supreme being named Nyame, who created the sky, earth, spirits, and order instantaneously and is the creator of everyone and everything, seen and unseen. Attesting to Nyame, omnipresent and all-pervasive, a proverb states, "If you want to tell God anything[,] tell the wind."[45] Like Nyame, wind is intangible, but its effects are visible all around you.[46] Akan people use this analogy for other spirit entities as well. They are ever conscious of the spirit world, recognizing that spirits, the physical world, nature, and society are dynamically related, whether visible or not.[47]

The essence of Nyame is generally present among humans through the *abosom*, or deities.[48] The *abosom* were created by Nyame and also have their own identities, as is evident in their shrines and varying modes of human veneration. Other spirits are recognized as dwelling in rivers or trees. If a spirit dwells in a particular river, it is paid the necessary respect. Stones and living trees and plants are not considered inanimate, but their existence is defined either through the state of being or having *sunsum*. *Sunsum* is the spirit or essential defining component that pervades both living and inanimate objects and derives from Nyame.[49]

Ancestors are a crucial component to Akan metaphysics.[50] Among the Akan, ancestors are honored locally in household shrines. They are quite "person-like," living close to the realm of humans and continuing to be members of the family left behind.[51] Ancestors protect, watch over, and advise the living and can be especially called upon by trained priests to effect a change or settle a dispute in a client's life. In return, the living offer libations and invite them to participate in family or community affairs.[52] Ancestors can reincarnate if they wish, usually electing to return to their families, although they are not bound to do so.[53] Thus, for Akan people, the spirit world is not a realm outside or beyond human experience.[54] They do not recognize any bridge or distance between two worlds, but the two are part of a continuous reality.[55]

Although not necessarily specifically Akan, there has been a similar regard for the ancestral world in New York City. Acts of building altars and leaving offerings at the African Burial Ground have contributed to the space of spirituality associated with the site. For instance, at the excavation site of the office building, an altar was erected against a wall away from pedestrians. The shrine consisted of two bottles of Florida water, a sweet potato, plums, a calabash, sunglasses, and a cup of coffee.[56] Another altar at the excavation site held red and white carnations and a light orange rose in a glass vase along with pears, pinecones, apples, bananas, and a glass container of water. There was also a large clay vessel. Alagba Egunfemi Adegbalola, a priest in Oyatunji (an African village in South Carolina), attended to another shrine. He poured a libation onto a mound with cowrie shells outlining eyes, nose, and mouth. The priest then smoked a cigar and added that to the shrine. Typically, the cowrie-shell face represents Esu, the trickster Yoruba deity who mediates the crossroads between the living and dead, with tobacco being one of Esu's favorite offerings. The shrine also held a container of water, carnations, and green plants. At the altar, Chief Adegbalola declared: "All around the world, you do not violate the cemetery. It is our last place to rest."[57]

Community members strove to assert the spiritual significance of the cemetery and its ancestors throughout their struggle against GSA. An altar was set up at Lehman College, where the excavated remains were first stored. People visited the remains to pay their respect or perform ceremonies. Also, MFAT opened a repository where visitors left offerings of drawings, shells, mementos, candles, and dried flowers.[58] An African American activist explained at a conference that it was during this time that she *learned* African religious practices and had not known them before her involvement in the African Burial Ground project.[59] The process of spiritualizing the African Burial Ground space has led to

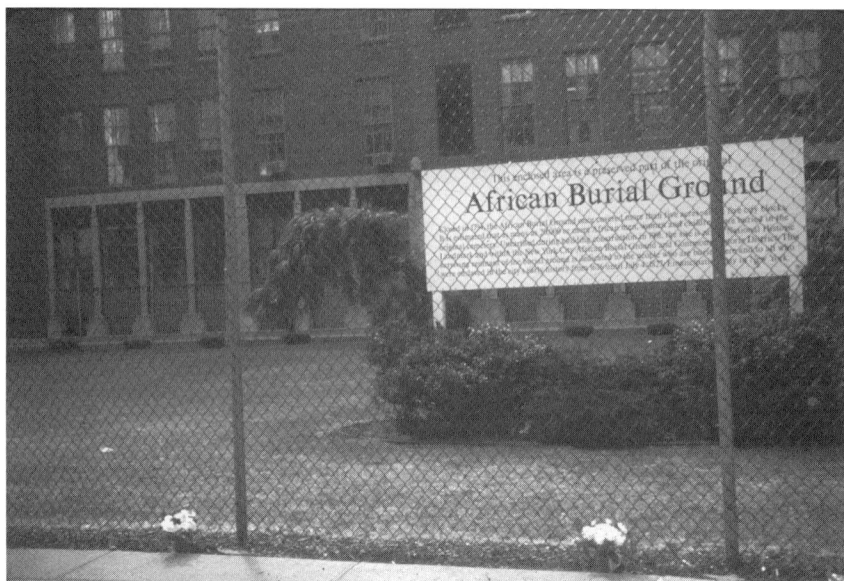

FIGURE 20.1.
Two vases of white flowers left in water to honor the
ancestors, February 2000. (Photograph by author)

teaching traditions, sharing knowledge, and exchanging cultural and spiritual information.

As well as building altars, visitors create personal ways for reclaiming the space as sacred. A grassy, fenced plot of land is located directly behind the office building at 290 Broadway. A metal chain-link fence prohibits public access to this area, which contains the reburied remains as well as approximately 200 unexcavated burials. The area will eventually bear an exterior memorial, although GSA is several years behind schedule in constructing it. On several occasions, I have passed the space to discover informal personal offerings that, by honoring the dead, also demarcate the area. On February 23, 2000, two glass jars of water were filled with white peonies and placed on the far side of the sidewalk right up against the chain-link fence behind the office building (Fig. 20.1). The visitor intended for the flowers in full bloom to remain there for more than a day since they had water to sustain them. This aesthetically beautiful offering was left to activate a sacred space spiritually—a cemetery that naturally warranted flowers for remembering the ancestors. Another time that I passed by the site in June 1999, an orange had been left alongside the fence. In May 2000, there were three apples, one yellow between two red ones. Fruit is a typical offering placed on altars or left for spirits among the Yoruba of Nigeria, as well as for Africans in the diaspora who practice Santería, Candomblé, and Orisha worship, among others. In fact, schoolchildren who visited the site in June 1999 were taught by their teacher to honor their ancestors by depositing fruit outside the fence. By the next day, the offering was cleared away. In fact, all of the objects described above were gone by the next day because objects seemingly discarded on the ground countered Western aesthetics of a pristine lawn.

One person was successful in leaving an offering for longer than a day. Two slim, handmade brown pouches covered with white squares of fabric connected by a leather string were tied into the fence behind the office building. One end faced outward to Elk Street, and one end was tied to face inward to the cemetery. The small, barely noticeable pouches remained threaded through the fence for many months during spring 2000. These pouches are similar to gris-gris used in West Africa. People, or spiritual specialists visited by a client, insert requests or messages from the Koran into a leather pouch to petition for something such as protection. The gris-gris offer protection when worn on the body or tied onto a mode of transportation, for example.

Such practices of honoring the dead are certainly not limited to the African world. The honoring of the departed at the burial ground can be contrasted with that at other spaces that are defined by national recognition and commemoration. For instance, the Vietnam Veterans Memorial and the initial memorialization of the World Trade Center are accepted sites of national and personal mourning. These two examples are offered not to compare actual events but to illustrate the fundamental, if not universal, human aspiration to honor the dead. These are natural expressions for humans and it therefore follows that there is a desire to create and engage spaces that honor the dead. In memorializing the loss of life, people leave offerings such as flowers, candles, and written messages to the dead. Why is this practice accepted for some spaces and not others?

Visitors from all around the world travel to the Vietnam Veterans Memorial in Washington, DC, to remember the dead, at any hour night or day. Many of them communicate with the deceased through messages and gifts left at the wall. Articles are cleared away twice a day and placed in a storage space after they are tagged and catalogued. However, this was not always the case. The Park Service that maintains the memorial initially gathered up the objects—such as letters, toys, badges, medals, liquor, tobacco, marijuana, personal memorabilia, photographs, and Easter baskets—and classified them as "lost and found."[60] This practice illustrates the authorities' inability to recognize the memorial as a space for remembering and communicating with the dead. But by the sheer magnitude of the number of objects left as offerings, they were forced to reconsider classifying these objects as "lost." Now, visitors simultaneously "leave a piece of memory" and articulate a part of history.[61]

The World Trade Center disaster invoked a natural and national (as well as international) desire to leave offerings to the victims. Candles, messages, flowers, flags, and photographs appeared all over New York City in public spaces where thousands pass. Objects continued to be added to the Times Square subway station and Union Square weeks after the disaster occurred. Even when a metal fence surrounding Ground Zero became the focal space to visit, visitors continued to bring memorabilia, leave flowers as offerings, and write messages to the dead on the fence. But although aesthetics of "order" were overturned during this intense period of personal and public mourning, they have since been restored by and large. By July 2006, official signage attached to the fence now reads: "Please understand all articles left behind must be removed" and "Please do not write anywhere on the viewing fence." Again, I scrutinized the space for evidence of offerings and have photographed small ribbons, carnations, gum wrappers, small messages, and a pair of Christian icons threaded through the fence.

The Vietnam Veterans Memorial and the post-9/11 World Trade Center site illustrate the need to create and engage spaces to honor the dead. At 290 Broadway, and now at Ground Zero, spiritual engagement and reclamation of the space have been suppressed and offerings continue to be discouraged and discarded. Yet it is these offerings that help to mark the space as sacred.

A milestone for the African Burial Ground project occurred in October 2003, when all of the excavated bones and funerary objects were reburied at 290 Broadway behind the office building. The remains traveled along the East Coast, from Howard University in Washington, DC, where Michael Blakey and his team had completed researching the bones, to New York City, with several stops in cities along the way. The entire event encouraged public and personal expressions of spirituality. The Manhattan event began at South Street Seaport. Thousands of schoolchildren, drummers, and citizens followed horse-drawn carriages with coffins up Broadway to the final resting place (Fig. 20.2). An all-night vigil brought out performers, dancers, poets, and singers. One woman fell into possession, a diviner from Côte d'Ivoire performed a divination, and many brought gifts of fruit, flowers, water, coins, and written messages to place among the coffins. In this case, the public was informed that all offerings would be buried with the coffins and therefore were expected and accepted for the weekend. A final formal tribute in Foley Square included presentations by the Harlem Boys Choir, Maya Angelou, Amadou Diallo's mother, and others.

The 2003 reburial marked a major reclamation of space and public performance of spirituality both for the people who once toiled in New York and were buried in the African Burial Ground and for African Americans who fought so hard to protect and memorialize those who had come before them. As Katharine

FIGURE 20.2.
Drummers preparing for the reburial
of all excavated remains, October
2003. (Photograph by author)

Hodgkin and Susannah Radstone write, "If what is disputed is the course of events—what really happened—new answers, particularly by groups whose knowledge has previously been discounted, may challenge dominant or privileged narratives."[62] Hegemonic narratives have certainly been challenged by previously discounted voices to such an extent that there have been numerous acts of reclamation at the African Burial Ground. African American intervention and resistance against GSA's politics began reclamation from a secular office-building site back to a sanctified space such as had been claimed by early Africans and their descendants. Despite attempts to deny the existence or memory of the space in both the eighteenth century and contemporary society, the African Burial Ground has successfully been constituted as an African-based space of spirituality. Hodgkin and Radstone continue, "Contests over the meaning of the past are also contests over the meaning of the present and over ways of taking the past forward."[63] The cemetery continues to be reclaimed politically and spiritually despite politics of power, dispossession, and race that circumscribe the space. Like the *sankofa*, it is in that reclamation that new knowledge is learned and remembered in order to share with future generations.

NOTES

1. In writing this chapter, I do not mean to suggest that the burial ground is only for African Americans or was reclaimed only by African Americans. The majority of the leaders and people involved, however, were and still are African American.

2. Don Mitchell, *Cultural Geography: A Critical Introduction* (Oxford: Blackwell Publishers, 2000), 214.

3. Phil Hubbard et al., *Thinking Geographically: Space, Theory, and Contemporary Human Geography* (London: Continuum, 2002), 14.

4. The earliest written document recognizing the existence of the burial ground is by a British chaplain. Anglican missionary John Sharpe had noted in 1712: "They are buried in the Common by those of their country and complexion without the office, on the contrary, the Heathenism rites are performed at the grave by their countrymen." John Sharpe, "Proposals for Erecting a School, Library and Chapel at New York," 1712–1713, *New-York Historical Society Collections* 13 (1880): 355.

5. *Trinity Church Minutes*, October 25, 1697.

6. David T. Valentine, "History of Broadway," *Manual of the Common Council of New York* (New York: D. T. Valentine, 1865), 567.

7. Morton Wagman, "Corporate Slavery in New Netherland," *Journal of Negro History* 65, no. 1 (1980): 39; Graham Russell Hodges, *Root and Branch: African Americans in New York and East Jersey, 1613–1863* (Chapel Hill: University of North Carolina Press, 1999), 34–36.

8. Peter R. Christoph, "The Freedmen of New Amsterdam," *Journal of the Afro-American Historical & Genealogical Society* (n.d.): 150.

9. David Humphreys, *An Historical Account of the Incorporated Society for the Propagation of the Gospel in Foreign Parts to Instruct Negroes* (1730; reprint, New York: Arno Press, 1969), 93–95.

10. City of New York, *Minutes of the Common Council of the City of New York, 1675–1776*, vol. 3 (New York: Dodd, Mead, and Co., 1905). Also cited in Edwin G. Burrows and Mike Wallace, *Gotham: A History of New York City to 1898* (New York: Oxford University Press, 2000), 129.

11. Thomas Joseph Davis, "Slavery in Colonial New York City," Ph.D. diss., Columbia University, 1974, 134.

12. Few African cemeteries are known to exist in the Americas. The only other excavated eighteenth-century urban cemetery for enslaved people is St. Peter's Cemetery in New Orleans, where twenty-nine people were exhumed. Quite a few nineteenth-century urban African cemeteries, usually related to churches, are known. Not many have been explored, although the First African Baptist Church cemetery in Philadelphia has been excavated. The site dated from the 1820s to 1840s, with over 140 burials (U.S. Department of the Interior, National Park Service, *African Burial Ground National Historic Landmark Registration Form*, Prepared by the New York City Landmarks Preservation Commission [Jean Howson and Gale Harris] [New York, November 9, 1992], 21–22). A small number

of burials have been excavated from rural sites (usually associated with plantations), save for the Newton Plantation in Barbados. It dates from the seventeenth to nineteenth centuries and had at least 101 people in it. For information about existing African American cemeteries across the country, see Roberta Hughes Wright and Wilbur B. Hughes III et al., *Lay Down Body: Loving History in African American Cemeteries* (Detroit: Visible Ink Press, 1996).

13. African places of origin are evident by the names given to the first eleven males stolen off a Portuguese ship and brought to New Amsterdam in 1626: Simon **Congo**, Peter **Santomee** (probably the phonetic spelling of São Tomé), Gratia **D'Angola**, and Paulo **Angola**. For further information on the slave trade to New Amsterdam / New York, see Joyce D. Goodfriend, "Burghers and Blacks: The Evolution of a Slave Society at New Amsterdam," *New York History* (April 1978): 125–144; Willie F. Page, *The Dutch Triangle: The Netherlands and the Atlantic Slave Trade, 1621–1664* (New York: Garland, 1997); James G. Lydon, "New York and the Slave Trade, 1700–1774," *William and Mary Quarterly* 35, no. 2 (April 1978): 375–394; and Leslie M. Harris, *In the Shadow of Slavery: African Americans in New York City, 1626–1863* (Chicago: University of Chicago Press, 2003).

14. Page, *Dutch Triangle*, 199; and Sherrill D. Wilson, *New York City's African Slaveowners* (New York: Garland, 1994), 22.

15. Vivienne L. Kruger, "Born to Run: The Slave Family in Early New York, 1626–1827," Ph.D. diss., Columbia University, 1985, 79.

16. William D. Piersen, *From Africa to America: African American History from the Colonial Era to the Early Republic, 1526–1790* (New York: Twayne Publishers, 1996), 63.

17. Ibid.

18. Mark Mack, Edna Medford, M. C. Hill, Jean Howson, Lisa King, Warren Perry, and Leslie Rankin-Hill, "Toiling Through Our Troubles: Exploitation and Resistance of African New Yorkers in the Eighteenth Century" (paper presented at the Fourteenth Congress of Anthropological and Ethnological Sciences, Williamsburg, Virginia, July 28, 1998), 6.

19. Michael Blakey, presenter at the "African Burial Ground Project OPEI 8th Annual Open House," New York City, May 20, 2000.

20. The New York African Burial Ground Final Reports were published following the writing of this essay and so their content is not reflected here. They are available online in their entirety at http://www.africanburialground.com/ABG_FinalReports. htm. Each of the 419 burials is numbered in the order it was excavated and is referred to by its number.

21. Cheryl J. LaRoche, "Beads from the African Burial Ground, New York City: A Preliminary Assessment," *Beads: Journal of the Society of Bead Researchers* 6 (1994): 8.

22. Michael Blakey, presenter at the "African Burial Ground Project OPEI 8th Annual Open House," New York City, May 20, 2000.

23. For more information, see Jerome S. Handler, "An African-Type Healer/Diviner and His Grave Goods: A Burial from a Plantation Slave Cemetery in Barbados, West Indies," *International Journal of Historical Archaeology* 1, no. 2 (1997): 91–130.

24. Michael Blakey, presenter at the "African Burial Ground 7th Annual Open House," New York City, May 22, 1999.

25. Ibid.

26. Edna Medford, Edna Greene, Warren Perry, Selwyn Carrington, Linda Heywood, Fatimah Jackson, S.O.Y. Keita, Richard Kittles, and John Thornton, "The Transatlantic Slave Trade to New York City: Sources and Routing of Captives" (paper presented at the Fourteenth Congress of Anthropological and Ethnological Sciences, Williamsburg, Virginia, July 28, 1998), n.p.

27. Although actual conspiracies may have existed, there is no question that Burton embellished and fabricated her story under pressure. At one point, just under half of the males over sixteen were in jail. All in all, 160 blacks and 21 whites were arrested, 4 whites and 17 blacks were hanged, and 13 blacks were burned at the stake. Another 72 were ostracized from the city and sent to the West Indies and Madeira. After the executions, Burton began recounting names of prominent New York citizens in connection to the conspiracy. This prompted the court to close the case quickly so that the public would not question the veracity of the proceedings, whereupon she was exiled from the community. For further details concerning the 1741 conspiracy, or the Great Negro Plot, see Herbert Aptheker, *American Negro Slave Revolts* (New York: International Publishers, 1967); Mike Fearnow, "Theatre for an Angry God: Public Burnings and Hangings in Colonial New York, 1741," *The Drama Review* (Summer 1996): 15–36; Daniel Horsmanden, *The New-York Conspiracy, or, A History of the Negro Plot with the Journal of the Proceedings Against the Conspirators at New-York in the Years 1741–2* (New York: Southwick & Pelsue, 1810); and Jill Lepore, *New York Burning: Liberty, Slavery, and Conspiracy in an Eighteenth-Century Manhattan* (New York: Alfred A. Knopf, 2005).

28. Interestingly, it was an accepted practice to incorporate cemeteries into urban expansion. In some instances, bodies were moved and in others they were built over. *Memorialization of the African Burial Ground: Recommendations to the Administrator, General Services Administration, and the United States Congress*, prepared by Peggy King Jorde, Weil, Gotshal & Manges, Counsel, and the Federal Steering Committee (August 6, 1993), 27. For instance, the dead had been removed from the French Episcopal Church on Pine Street and the Presbyterian burial ground on Nassau Street. For the Lutheran burying ground at the corner of Broadway and Rector Street, the "bones in open box carts [were carted off] promiscuously, and fragments of bones and coffins were dumped into the North River" in 1805–1806 for the construction of Grace Church. Similarly, bones and rubbish of the Quaker burial ground were carried away in carts, and the Jewish burying ground on Oliver Street was also dug up. Cited in *Memorialization of the African Burial Ground*, 27n100. Finally, the Old Dutch cemetery on lower Broadway had been sold off as lots for development as early as 1677.

29. Henry Moscow, *The Street Book: An Encyclopedia of Manhattan's Street Names and Their Origins* (New York: Fordham University Press, 1978), 37.

30. This transformation was gradual. By 1802, the newly divided block of residences was rented by people of African descent and whites. The block could be described as ranging from a "solidly respectable Broadway façade to the city's industrial core." Marjorie Ingle, Jean Howsen, and Edward S. Rutsch, S.O.P.A. of Historic Conservation and Interpretation, Inc., *A Stage IA Cultural Resource Survey of the Proposed Foley Square Project in the Borough of Manhattan, New York, NY*, for Edwards & Kelcey Engineers, Inc. (September 1989, revised May 1990), 90.

31. For details, see *Reconstruction of Foley Square: Historical and Archaeological Resources Report,* prepared for the City of New York Parks and Recreation by Joan H. Geismar (December 1993), 8–9.

32. U.S. Department of the Interior, National Park Service, African Burial Ground National Historic Landmark Registration Form, prepared by the New York City Landmarks Preservation Commission, Jean Howson and Gale Hanis (New York, November 9, 1992), 4.

33. Another prominent cemetery still in existence is the First Cemetery of the Spanish and Portuguese Synagogue, which is the oldest intact burial ground in New York, dating from 1656. It is probably significant that since both Spanish and Portuguese Jews and British Anglicans procured wealth through the slave trade, their graves are among those still preserved.

34. Spencer Harrington, "Bones and Bureaucrats: New York's Great Cemetery Imbroglio," *Archaeology* (March–April 1993): 35.

35. Ibid., 34.

36. Debbie Officer, "Uproar and Protest at African Burial Ground Meeting," *Amsterdam News,* April 21, 1999.

37. Susan C. Pearce, "Africans on This Soil: The Counter-Amnesia of the New York African Burial Ground," Ph.D. diss., New School for Social Research, 1996, 122–123.

38. Ibid., 122.

39. Gil Noble, Sherrill Wilson, Noel Pointer, and David Paterson, "Negro Burial Ground," *Like It Is,* TV show on WABC TV, August 2, 1992.

40. *The African Burial Ground: An American Discovery,* pts. 1–4, dir. and prod. David Kutz, assoc. prod. and writer Christopher Moore, 2 hrs., U.S. General Services Administration, 1994, videocassette.

41. Pearce, "Africans on This Soil," 76.

42. Ibid.

43. Ibid.

44. Information is based on research I performed in Ghana in 1995 and written scholarship.

45. Kwabena Amponsah, *Topics on West African Traditional Religion* (Accra, Ghana: Adwinsa Publications, 1977), 26, quoted in J. O. Kayode, *Understanding African Traditional Religion* (Ile Ife, Nigeria: University of Ife Press, 1984), 27.

46. Kwame Gyekye, *An Essay on African Philosophical Thought* (Cambridge, UK: University of Cambridge Press, 1987), 70.

47. Kofi Asare Opoku, "The World View of the Akan," *Tarikh* 7, no. 2 (1982): 62.

48. J. G. Platvoet, *Comparing Religions: A Limitative Approach, An Analysis of Akan, Para-Creole, and IFO-Sananda Rites and Prayers* (The Hague: Mouton Publishers, 1982), 41.

49. Helaine K. Minkus, "The Concept of Spirit in Akwapim Akan Philosophy," *Africa* 50, no. 2 (1980): 182.

50. Gyekye, *Essay on African Philosophical Thought,* 86.

51. Kwasi Wiredu, *Cultural Universals and Particulars: An African Perspective* (Bloomington: Indiana University Press, 1996), 47.

52. Opoku, "World View of the Akan," 65.

53. Anthony Ephirim-Donkor, *African Spirituality: On Becoming Ancestors* (Trenton, NJ: Africa World Press, 1997), 38. For a clear, detailed explanation of the ancestors and how the living relate to them, see A. K. Quarcoo, "Akan Visual Art and the Cult of the Ancestors," *Research Review* 9, no. 3 (1973): 48–82.

54. Wiredu, *Cultural Universals and Particulars*, 50, 52.

55. W. Emmanuel Abraham, "A Paradigm of African Society," in *Readings in African Philosophy: An Akan Collection*, ed. Safro Kwame, 39–65 (Lanham, MD: University Press of America, 1995), 49.

56. Sharon Fitzgerald, "Sacred Ground," *Essence* 24, no. 5 (September 1993), http://referenc.lib.binghamton.edu:2076...Fmt=3&Sid=4&Idx=43&Deli=1&RQT=309&Dtp=1 (accessed October 13, 2000).

57. Kutz, *African Burial Ground*.

58. Tureka Turk, "Dispute Stops Progress on African Burial Study," *Michigan Citizen*, May 22, 1993, 3; *Ethnic Watch*, CD-ROM, Softline Information, 1995.

59. The conference was titled "Uncovering Connections: Cultural Endurance Between Africa, the Americas, and the Caribbean," Medgar Evers College, New York City, March 2003.

60. Marita Sturken, "The Wall, the Screen and the Image: The Vietnam Veterans Memorial," in *The Visual Culture Reader*, ed. Nicholas Mirzoeff (London: Routledge, 1998), 173.

61. *Offerings at the Wall: Artifacts from the Vietnam Veterans Memorial Collection* (Atlanta: Turner Publishing, 1995), n.p.

62. Katharine Hodgkin and Susannah Radstone, eds., *Contested Pasts: The Politics of Memory* (New York: Routledge, 2003), 1.

63. Ibid.

Leslie M. Alexander is Associate Professor of History at the Ohio State University. She received her B.A. with honors from Stanford University, her M.A. from Cornell University, and her Ph.D. from Cornell University. Most recently, she published her first monograph, titled *African or American? Black Identity and Political Activism in New York City, 1784–1861* (University of Illinois Press, 2007). A recipient of several prestigious fellowships, including the Ford Foundation Postdoctoral Fellowship and the Ford Foundation Dissertation Fellowship, Alexander has presented her research at the annual meetings of the Association for the Study of African American Life and History, the Association for the Study of the Worldwide African Diaspora, the American Historical Association, the Organization of American Historians, the African Heritage Studies Association, and the Caribbean Studies Association. In 1999, she was elected to the executive board of the African Heritage Studies Association. Her next research project, titled " 'To Leave the House of Bondage': African American Internationalism in the Nineteenth Century," is an exploration of early African American foreign policy, which seeks to investigate how African Americans in the antebellum and early postbellum eras viewed political issues throughout the African diaspora, particularly antislavery struggles and resistance movements in Haiti, Cuba, and Brazil.

Robin F. Bachin is the Charlton W. Tebeau Associate Professor of History and Director of the American Studies Program at the University of Miami. She received her B.A. from Brandeis University and her M.A. and Ph.D. degrees from the University of Michigan. Her areas of research and teaching include American urban, environmental, immigration, sport, and cultural history. Her first book, *Building the South Side: Urban Space and Civic Culture in Chicago, 1890–1919*, was published by the University of Chicago Press in 2004 and won the Award for Outstanding Contribution to Illinois History and Heritage. Her current book project, "Home Away from Home: The Transformation of Seaside Recreation on the East Coast, 1865–2000," focuses on the rapid commercialization of seaside resorts in the late nineteenth and twentieth centuries.

Stefan Bradley is Assistant Professor in the Department of Historical Studies at Southern Illinois University–Edwardsville. He graduated with a B.A. in history from Gonzaga University in 1996, an M.A. in twentieth-century U.S. history with an emphasis on the black experience from Washington State University in 1998, and a Ph.D. in twentieth-century U.S. history with an emphasis on the black experience from the University of Missouri–Columbia in 2003. His research interests include black student activism at Ivy League universities. He teaches courses titled Black Student Power and Race and Athletics. Bradley currently resides in Alton, Illinois.

Ann Denkler is Assistant Professor of History and Director of the Public History Program at Shenandoah University.

Michael Dennis is Associate Professor of History at Acadia University in Nova Scotia.

Owen J. Dwyer is Associate Professor of Geography at Indiana University's Indianapolis campus, where he teaches about cities, cartography, and cultural landscapes. Before arriving in Indianapolis, he was a postdoctoral fellow at Emory University and the University of British Columbia. In the course of his research on the politics of public space and commemoration, he has conducted dozens of interviews, solicited hundreds of surveys from visitors, and spent many hours observing civil rights memorials in Atlanta, Birmingham, Memphis, Montgomery, and Selma. His dissertation fieldwork was supported by the Rockefeller Foundation as well as a grant from the National Science Foundation, the results of which were selected by Columbia University's Graduate School of Architecture, Planning, and Preservation for inclusion in its biannual Temple Hoyne Buell Colloquium on American Architecture. Since then, he has published a number of research articles and book chapters and has consulted with civil rights museums about visitor demographics and evaluations.

Andrea E. Frohne teaches African Art History in the School of Interdisciplinary Arts and in Art History at Ohio University. She has held visiting positions at Cornell University, Pennsylvania State University, and Dickinson College. Her manuscript being prepared for publication is titled "Space, Spirituality, and Memory: The African Burial Ground in New York City."

Scott Hancock is currently Associate Professor in the History Department and the Africana Studies Program at Gettysburg College. His research has explored how from the seventeenth century up to the eve of the Civil War, African Americans in the North used the law in a variety of ways. He is particularly interested in how this interaction with the law, from small disputes in lower courts to using constitutional law and legal ideologies, affected the formation of black identity over the course of 200 years.

Mary S. Hoffschwelle is Associate Professor of History at Middle Tennessee State University. She is author of *The Rosenwald Schools of the American South* (University Press of Florida, 2006) and *Preserving Rosenwald Schools* (National Trust for Historic Preservation, 2003). Her research on Rosenwald schools began with her doctoral dissertation at Vanderbilt University, which was published as *Rebuilding the Rural Southern Community: Reformers, Schools, and Homes in Tennessee, 1900–1930* (University of Tennessee Press, 1998).

Michael Kahan is Associate Director of the Urban Studies Program at Stanford University. Prior to joining Stanford, he worked as a lecturer at the University of Pennsylvania and taught courses in nineteenth- and twentieth-century urban and social history. He completed his doctoral work in history at the University of Pennsylvania, where his research focused on street life in Philadelphia from the 1850s through the 1920s.

Kevin M. Kruse is Associate Professor of History at Princeton University. He is the author of *White Flight: Atlanta and the Making of Modern Conservatism*

(Princeton University Press, 2005) and co-editor, with Thomas J. Sugrue, of *The New Suburban History* (University of Chicago Press, 2006). Kruse has written several articles and chapters on issues such as civil rights and the courts, the connections between the desegregation of urban spaces and the politics of suburban conservatism, and the ideology and strategy of segregationist resistance. He is currently working on a book that locates the origins of the modern Religious Right in postwar America.

Patrick Q. Mason is Coordinator of the Program on Religion, Conflict, and Peacebuilding at the Joan B. Kroc Institute for International Peace Studies at the University of Notre Dame. He earned his Ph.D. in U.S. history from Notre Dame in 2005. His dissertation focused on violence against religious outsiders in the American South from 1865 to 1910.

Megan Kate Nelson is Assistant Professor of History, specializing in nineteenth-century American cultural history at California State University, Fullerton. She received her B.A. in history and literature magna cum laude from Harvard University and her Ph.D. in American studies from the University of Iowa. The University of Georgia Press published her book *Trembling Earth: A Cultural History of the Okefenokee Swamp* in April 2005. She teaches undergraduate and graduate classes in Nineteenth-Century America, the American Civil War, Environmental History, the U.S. South, and Cultural History.

Angel David Nieves is currently Assistant Professor in the School of Architecture, Planning, and Preservation at the University of Maryland, College Park. In fall 2006, he began his new role as Director of Graduate Research and Training at the Consortium on Race, Gender, and Ethnicity (CRGE) and as a Resident Fellow at the Maryland Institute for Technology in the Humanities (MITH). He is an affiliate faculty member in the Departments of American Studies, Women's Studies, African American Studies, and Anthropology. He is also an affiliate member of the Center for Heritage Resource Studies and the Program in LGBT Studies. He completed his doctoral work in architectural history and Africana studies at Cornell University in 2001. He was Assistant Professor of Black Studies, Women's Studies, and Geography in the Department of Ethnic Studies at the University of Colorado at Boulder from 2001 to 2003. His book manuscript "'We Gave Our Hearts and Lives to It': Black Women, Industrial Schools, and Nation-Building in the New South," is currently being revised for publication by Duke University Press. His scholarly work and activism critically engage with issues of heritage preservation, gender, and nationalism at the intersections of race and the built environment in the Global South.

Carla L. Peterson is Professor in the Department of English at the University of Maryland and affiliate faculty of the Women's Studies and American Studies Departments as well as the Afro-American Studies Program. She is the author of *"Doers of the Word": African-American Women Speakers and Writers in the North (1830–1880)* (New York: Oxford University Press, 1995). Peterson has also published numerous essays on nineteenth-century African American literature and literary history. Her current project, "Family History in Public Places," is a social and cultural history of African American life in nineteenth-century New York City as seen through the lens of family history.

Mark Santow is Assistant Professor of American History and a fellow at the Center for Policy Analysis at the University of Massachusetts, Dartmouth, specializing in twentieth-century American urban history, politics, and social policy. He has taught at the University of Pennsylvania, Fordham University, and Gonzaga University and has published numerous essays on segregation, urban policy, and the "war on poverty." His book *Saul Alinsky and the Dilemmas of Race in the Post-War City* will be published by the University of Chicago Press in 2008.

Michelle R. Scott is Assistant Professor in History and Women's Studies at the University of Maryland, Baltimore County. Her book *Blues Empress in Black Chattanooga: Bessie Smith and the Emerging Urban South* is forthcoming from the University of Illinois Press, and she has contributed to the Martin Luther King Jr. Papers Project volumes and the recently published *The Columbia Guide to African American History Since 1939*. She has been awarded a Mellon-Mays / Social Science Research Council Grant, a Ford Foundation Predoctoral Grant, a Smithsonian Institution Research Grant, and a Woodrow Wilson–Andrew W. Mellon Career Enhancement Postdoctoral Fellowship.

Carroll Van West is a Professor of History and the Director of the Center for Historic Preservation at Middle Tennessee State University. He serves as the Senior Editor of the *Tennessee Historical Quarterly* and the *Tennessee Encyclopedia of History and Culture*, an online reference published by the University of Tennessee Press. He also directs the Tennessee Civil War National Heritage Area, which is a partnership unit of the National Park Service.

Derrick E. White is currently Assistant Professor in the Department of History at Florida Atlantic University. He received his Ph.D. from the Ohio State University in 2004. His research examines the history of ideas, primarily during the Civil Rights Movement and Black Power era. He was the 2003–2004 recipient of the University of California–Santa Barbara Department of Black Studies Dissertation

Fellowship. He currently has a manuscript on the Institute of the Black World, a black think tank in Atlanta, under review by the University of Georgia Press.

Andrew Wiese teaches at San Diego State University, where he specializes in American urban history. His interests include the history of suburbanization, housing, and landscape and the role of space in the production of race and class. He is the author of *Places of Their Own: African American Suburbanization in the 20th Century* (University of Chicago Press, 2004), which won the award for Best Book in North American Urban History from the Urban History Association and the John G. Cawelti Prize for Best Book in American Culture Studies from the American Culture Association. He is also the co-editor, with Becky Nicolaides, of *The Suburb Reader* (Routledge, 2006), a volume on the history of American suburbia. Wiese has served on the board of directors of the Urban History Association and the Society for American City and Regional Planning History.

Barlow, Wilson, Primrose and West's Minstrels, 397

Barnett, Ferdinand, 357

Barney, James, 29

Barzun, Jacques, 330

Baseball, 359, 360, 361

Baucom, Allfred, 452

Beacon Hill, 144

Beadle, Lottie Q., 287

Beale Street (Memphis), 406–7(n6), 418(fig.)

Beard, Elmer, 454

Beck, Shepherd, 237, 239

Beekman, James, 7, 36–37, 45(n43)

Benevolent Society, 451

Bennett, Lerone, 181(n18); "The Challenge of Blackness," 173; Gary Convention, 178

Bernard, Wiley, 452

Bernhardt, Clyde, 399

Berry family, 29

Bethel AME Church, 358

Beth Salem Presbyterian Church, 443–45

Big Grand Theater, 368

Big Sea, The (Hughes), 351

Binford, George, 115, 122

Binga, Jessie, 364, 365, 373(n48)

Birmingham, civil rights memorials, 16, 422–25, 429

Birmingham Civil Rights District, 416, 422–25

Birmingham Civil Rights Institute, 422–24

Bishop, Edward, 149

Bishop's Variety show, 397

Black Belt (Chicago), 14, 351, 354; identity, 369–70; recreation in, 358, 361–68; services in, 368–69; social geography of, 352–53; vice in, 356–57

"Black Christ, The" (Cullen), 474

Black Consciousness Movement, 177, 178

Black Freedom Struggle, 9, 172, 175, 341

"Black Holiday Inn," 10

Black Jews (Church of God), 470

Black Madonna, 479

Black Messiah, 477–79

Black Messiah, The (Cleage), 477, 485–86(n65)

Black Musicians' Union 208, 352

Black Muslims, 466. See also Nation of Islam

Blackness, 5, 184(n54); and IBW goals, 173–74

Black Power, 169–71, 178, 183(n52), 331–32, 477; and Columbia University, 337, 339

Black Power: The Politics of Liberation (Ture and Hamilton), 170, 171

Black Studies programs, 172, 173, 177, 178, 179, 181(n18), 182(n22)

Black University project, 169, 171–72

Blackwood family, 263–64

Blaine, Mrs. Emmons, 359

Blakeley, Ulysses, 77, 78

Blakey, Michael, 499

Bledsoe County (TN), 441, 443

Blockbusting, in Atlanta, 199–21

Blue Goose Hollow, 393, 396

Blyden, Edward W., 467

B'nai B'rith chapter, 203

Bolivar (TN), 441, 447

Bombings, in Chicago, 354

Booth, William H., 340

Borders, William Holmes, 215, 220(n35)

Boston, 156; court system in, 138–46, 148–55, 157, 158–60, 162(n10), 164(nn23, 30), 165(n38); justice-of-the-peace in, 147–48; public conduct issues, 137–38

Boston Police Court, 142, 146, 148, 151–52, 153, 158, 162(n10); reporting on, 155, 159–60

Bowers, John, 137

"Boy Who Painted Christ Black, The" (Clarke), 474

Brazier, Arthur, 77, 88, 90; Black Self-Determination, 83

Breckinridge, Sophonisba, 359

Brevard Rosenwald School, 292

Brickell, John, 253–54

Brink, Will Wallace, 453

Britton, John Henry, Sr., 451–52

Brooks, Deton, 86

Brooks, Margarette, voter mobilization, 118–19

Brothels: in Chicago, 355–56; mob raids on, 143, 144

Brow, Florence, 226

Brow, Grover, 226

Browder, Alexander, 445

Brown, Caleb Gregory, 123

Brown, Emilyn, 498

Brown, Elsa Barkley, "Mapping the Terrain of Black Richmond," 4–5

Brown, John, 195

Brown, John (slave), 260, 268–69(n23)

Brown, H. Rap, 339, 341–42

Chicago League on Urban Conditions Among Negroes, 357

Chicago's Great Question, 72, 95(n1)

Chicago Vice Commission, 356

Cholera, 61

Christianity, racialization of, 17, 56, 57, 463–75, 477–80, 485–86(n65)

Christian Methodist Episcopal (CME) Church, 287, 288

"Christ in Alabama" (Hughes), 474, 484(n47)

Churches, 240, 439; black, 467–68; and cemeteries, 446–47; in Chicago, 78, 91; community organizing, 77–78; in Jim Crow South, 439–41; New York City, 24–25, 28–29, 54; as public spaces, 313, 448; rural, 16–17; and schools, 445–46; Tennessee, 441–45, 449–53

Citizens Housing and Planning Council of New York, 333

Citizens Trust Company, 211

City College of New York, 105

City parks, New York, 34–35, 327

City planning, New York City, 328–29

City Planning Commission (CPC), 80

City Planning Department (Chicago), 80

Civic education program, 112, 119, 132–33(n46); in Virginia, 115–16, 120, 121, 122–25

Civic life, 15; commercial leisure and, 363–65

Civil rights, 50, 124, 125, 130(n24), 170, 309, 456, 475; activism, 111, 126–27; education in, 104–5

Civil Rights Movement, 2, 9, 16, 74, 127, 178, 184(n63), 331; in Chicago, 83, 84; Martin Luther King Center, 172, 176; memorials, 415–30; public space, 431–32; rural churches and, 17, 454

Civil War, 375; conscription during, 50–51; Fernando Wood during, 38–39; Philadelphia, 377–79, 382, 383

Claflin University, 315

Clark, W. J., 456

Clarke, John Henrik, "The Boy Who Painted Christ Black," 474

Clay, Robert E., 446

Cleage, Albert, Jr., 465, 466, 478–79, 486–87(nn66, 67, 72, 73, 75); The Black Messiah, 477, 485–86(n65)

Cleveland, 223–24, 227–28, 239, 240

CME. See Christian Methodist Episcopal Church

Coalition for the Future of Manhattanville, 344

Codozoe, Art, 366

Cole, Addison (Big Wheel), 396

Cole, Donna, 498

Coley, Anna, 449

Collect Pond, 493, 496

College of Pharmacy of the City of New York, 49, 63, 64, 66

Colonies: Georgia, 252–53, 254–55; New Amsterdam, 490–93; New York, 494–95

Colonial Williamsburg, mock slave auction, 10

Colonization movement, 7, 74; in New York City, 32, 36–37

Colonization Society, 37

Colored American, The (newspaper), 54

Colored Orphan Asylum, 49, 55, 56

Colored School No. 3, 30, 43(n21)

Columbia-Community Athletic Program, 334, 335

Columbia University: and Black community, 13–14, 105, 329, 330, 340, 344–45; and Harlem, 333–34, 337–38; land acquisition and use, 325–27, 333–36, 338–39; as landlord, 332–33; Morningside Heights, 328, 341; protests at, 341–44

Comedies, 398–99

Commemorations, 311; African Burial Ground, 499–500; Civil Rights Movement, 415–27

Communities, 75, 310; in New York City, 6–8, 13–14, 31, 60–61, 333–34, 344–45; black suburbs and, 223–24; Chagrin Falls Park, 233–34; freedmen, 448–51; role of schools in, 280–81; self-determination and, 6–7; utopian, 317–18; Woodlawn development as, 77–78

Community Action Agencies (CAAs), 86–87

Community Action Program (CAP), 82, 86, 90, 94

Community Board #9 (CB9), 344

Community Housing Corporation (Atlanta), 203–4

Community Planning Council (Atlanta), 203

Community School Plans (Rosenwald program), 278, 283–84, 291, 292, 293

Commuters, working-class, 230–31

Concerned Citizens for Equality (CCE), 188, 191–92

Pinkster festival, 143
Pittsburgh, 235
Place, race and, 73–74. *See also* Space
"Plans Dat Comed from God" (Robinson), 4
Plantations. *See* Rice plantations
Pleasant Grove Missionary Baptist Church, 447
Plunkett, Moss, 112, 120
Political activism/engagement, 5, 8–9, 405; education and, 104–5; in Revolutionary America, 143–44; in Seneca Village, 33–34; in Virginia, 106, 109–24
Politics, 27, 50, 103, 178, 419; Chicago, 90, 91, 92; marginalization in, 143–45; and religion, 465, 472–73; women's participation in, 232–33
Poll tax, in Virginia, 109, 123, 124
Pompeii Club, 365
Pooler, Nelly, 265
Pool halls, in Chicago, 368
Popular Front ethic, 111
Pounds, Annie, 237
Pounds, Mattie, 237
Poverty, 82, 184(n63), 241, 378; Chicago's programs on, 86–87, 89, 90; War on, 85–86
"Poverty, Power and Race in Chicago" (TWO), 87
Power relationships, 90, 331–32; strategic, 52–53
Prejudice, against blacks, 50
Price, Robert, 330
Primrose and West's Minstrels, 398
Princeton University, 168
Principals, school: civic education, 112, 114, 115–16, 121; voter registration, 116–17
Prizefighting, 361
Prisoners, 175
Progressive era, school construction, 278–79
Progressive Party, 123
Propaganda campaign, for Central Park, 39–40, 46(n55)
Property, 7; private vs. public, 380–81; use of suburban, 235–36
Property ownership, 142; Chagrin Falls Park, 234–35; in New York City, 24–26, 36, 37, 62; Philadelphia street railways, 380–81; suburban, 235–36; and voting rights, 27, 33–34
Property rights, 5, 10–11
Prosperity (SC), 290
Prosperity school, 289

Prostitution, 154; in Chattanooga, 403–4; in Chicago, 355–56, 362, 366
Protests, Columbia University, 341–44
Public conduct: court system, 155–56; legal system and, 137–38, 145, 147
Public domain, 336
Public performance: antebellum blacks, 155–57; court system as, 158–59
Public-private partnerships, TWO, 92–93
Public School Society, 49
Public space(s), 14, 15, 141, 309, 321(n27), 336, 390(nn22, 26); in Atlanta, 419–22; campus quadrangles, 315–16; Civil Rights Movement memorials, 415–17, 419–32; controlling, 309–10; courts as, 154–55, 157–59; in Jim Crow South, 448–49; performance in, 155–56; in Philadelphia, 377, 378–79, 379–83, 385–86, 387–88; women in, 232–33
Pullman Company, George, 358

Quadrangle, as public space, 155–56
Quakers, 449
Quincy, Josiah, 144, 158

Rabbit's Foot, A (Chapelle), 398–99
Race, 3, 4, 8, 72, 106, 145, 150, 227, 360, 369; caste system, 5–6; consciousness, 30–32; ecological theories of, 252, 253–54; and religion, 472–73; suburban life, 239–40; and urban space, 74–75, 160–61
Racial geography: of Chicago, 92, 93–94; urban renewal, 76–77
Racism, 3, 4, 175, 205, 378, 414, 485(n64); Central Park development, 36–37, 39–40; Columbia University expansion, 326, 340; in New York City, 7–8, 34–39, 45(n51), 57; suburban development and, 229–30; urban renewal, 76–77
Radical activism, 9, 174–75, 477
Railways/railroads, in Chattanooga, 397–98. *See also* Street railways
Randolph, A. Phillip, 110, 475
Randolph, T. A., 117
Rangel, Charlie, 499
Ranson, Reverdy, 358
Ray, Charles, 33
Read, Isaac, 452
Read, James D., 453
Read, Lucy E., 453

St. Michael's Protestant Episcopal Church, 29

St. Paul Missionary Baptist Church, 446

St. Philip's Episcopal Church, 25, 48, 49, 54, 55, 67; draft riots and, 59–60, 63; High Church ideals in, 58–59; role of, 56–57; sacred space, 57–58

Saint Shuttle, 362

St. Simons Island plantation, 251, 257

Salary equalization cases, 119–20, 132(n42), 134(n58)

Saloons, in Chattanooga, 404–5

Sampson, 259–60, 270(n37)

Samuels, William Everett, 352

Sanctuary, Florida as, 262–63

Sanders, Simmie, 456

Sanitation, in New York City, 61

Santomee, Peter, 492

SAS. *See* Students' Afro-American Society

Savage, Gus, 499

Savannah, 253, 265, 271(n45); fugitives around, 259, 264

Savannah Light Infantry, 259

Scholars, 167, 168

Schools, 84, 104, 126, 130(n25), 132–33(n46), 184(n63), 229, 297(n26), 302(n69), 306, 308, 310, 315, 439, 444; in Atlanta, 206, 213; community role of, 280–81; funding for, 286–88; in New York City, 49–50; Rosenwald, 12–13, 275–76, 277–80, 281–84, 285–86, 288–90, 298–99(n34), 300–301(nn47, 50), 302(nn64, 66), 303(n72), 443, 458; Seneca Village, 28, 42(n2), 43(n21); Tennessee, 445–46, 449, 450, 451, 452; Virginia, 114–15; white control of, 280–81

School settlements, 317

Schorling, John, 360

Schwarzhaupt Foundation, Emil, 79

Scott, Clyde, 122

Scott, William A., Jr., Mozley Place home, 206–8

SDS. *See* Students for a Democratic Society

Seagrove, James, 264, 265

Seaman's General Outfitting Store, 60

Seaman's Homes for Colored Sailors, 48, 49, 54, 60

Seay, C. W., 119

Second Great Migration, 76

Segregation, 4, 8, 17, 94, 121, 127, 130(n25), 131(n28), 241, 299(n41), 306, 309, 398; in Atlanta, 10–11, 206–7, 210–13, 214–16, 217(n2), 420; in Chicago, 14, 76, 78, 84, 90–91, 94, 353–54; perpetuation of, 91–93; racial, 8, 10, 90–91; school, 126, 213, 229; in Philadelphia, 375, 377, 382–83; in Tennessee, 447–48

Self-determination, 1, 72, 104, 314; community and, 6–7; segregation and, 8, 126; TWO, 74–75, 81–82, 84, 85, 87–88

Self-help, 291, 307, 316, 357; Rosenwald school program and, 286–88

Sellers-Davis, Dillie, 450

Seminoles, 259, 270(n35), 271(n45)

Senate Buffet and Lakeside Club, 365

Seneca Village, 6–7, 26, 42(n2), 43(n10), 48–49; anti-abolition riots and, 32–33, 57; and Central Park, 23, 24, 34–36, 39–40, 46(n55); churches, 28–29; education, 29–30; inhabitants of, 27–28; land condemnations, 40–41, 46(n60); political activism, 33–34; racial consciousness in, 30–32

Settlement houses, 355

Seward, John Henry, 456–57

Seymour, Horatio, 50

Shakur, Tupac, 463

Shaw, Dublin, 452

Shelby County (TN), 446

Shell, Chester, 288, 289

Shenandoah Valley, 190

Shiloh AME Church, 289

Shiloh School, 289

Shinbone (TN), 448–49

Shrine of the Black Madonna, 465, 477, 479

Shrines, at African Burial Grounds, 501–3

Silvan, Charles, 27

Sims, Janie, 116, 117

Sims, John, 311

Single-room occupancy (SRO) buildings, 329–30, 332–33

Sixteenth Street Baptist Church (Birmingham), 422, 423, 424

Sixth Colored Regiment, 379

Slave auction blocks, 197(n4); in Luray, 187–88, 189–91; as memorials, 10, 193–94; symbolism of, 195–96

Slavery, 5, 10, 37, 49, 190, 464; freedom from, 260–61; reminders of, 30–31; rice plantations, 251, 252, 254–55; spirituality and, 474–75

War of Jenkin's Ear, 260

War on Poverty, 85–86, 90

Washington, Booker T., 12, 74, 285, 286, 314, 318; school building program, 275–77, 281, 282, 284, 289, 295(n4); *Up From Slavery,* 315

Washington, Booker T., Jr., 280

Washington County (TN), 441

Watkins, Westley, 453

Watkins, William E., 453

Watson, James L., 334

WDIA, 425

"'We Are Not What We Seem,'" (Kelley), 4

Web sites, Rosenwald schools, 293–94

Webster, George, 27

Wedgeworth (AL), 286

Weevis, William, 159

Wee Wee Jubilaires, 452

Welfare Council of Metropolitan Chicago, 76

Welfare: housing issues, 240–41; segregation in, 91–92

Wells-Barnett, Ida B., 167, 357, 358, 364; commemoration of, 418(fig.)

West, Cornel, 168

West End, housing in, 202

West Harlem Environmental Action, 345

West Tennessee Leadership Training School, 457

West Virginia, 317

White, Mr., 158, 159

White, Philip Augustus, 48, 49, 52, 53, 56, 58, 67; community affairs, 60, 61–62, 63–66

White City, 308

White Elephant Saloon (Chattanooga), 400

White flight, 72, 74; from Atlanta, 210–11; from Chicago, 76, 78; from Woodlawn, 75–76

Whitehead, John, 24

Whitelow, Prima, 453

Whitelow String Band, Bootsie, 453

Whiteness, 73–74

Whites, 7, 13, 318, 352, 353, 369; in Atlanta, 202, 204, 205, 206–9, 210–12, 213–14; at Columbia University, 341–42; as patrons, 54–55; St. Philip's Episcopal Church and, 56–57

White supremacy, 104, 131(n28)

Whiteville (TN), 457–58

Whitson, J. H. "Lovie Joe," 366

Whittaker, J. P., 203

Wilberforce (Ohio), 317

Wilkes, W. R., 203

Williams, Andrew, 7, 24, 26, 27, 40

Williams, Bert, 364

Williams, Eugene, 14, 352

Williams, Jack, 455

Williams, Marie Selika, 402

Williamson, Cheney, 450

Williamson, Hiram, 450

Williamson, Richard, 450

Williamson Chapel Christian Methodist Episcopal (CME) Church, 450–52

Wilson (Ark.), 286

Wilson, Cicero, 326

Wilson, J. R., 210

Wilson, Sarah, 28, 29

Wingo (TN), 446

Wingo Missionary Baptist Church, 446

Witten, Prince, 263

Witten family, 263

Wolfe Realty, J. L., 210

Woman's Era, 307

Women, 154, 247(n28), 316, 383; as entertainers, 400–406; and legal system, 143, 144, 145, 149; public roles, 232–33, 312–13; race, 307, 311–13, 318; reformers, 13, 358; suburban, 231–32; as theater-goers, 402–3; voter registration, 116–17, 133(n51)

Wood, Fernando, 7, 50; Alinsky's program for, 78–79; racism of, 34, 36, 37–39, 45(n51)

Woodlawn, 72, 92, 351; black migration into, 75–76; citizen-based urban planning for, 81–82; community organizing in, 77–78; integration project in, 78–80; relocation housing, 82–83. *See also* Temporary Woodlawn Organization

Woodlawn Baptist Church, 452–55

Woodlawn Plan, 80

Woodson, Carter G., 107, 109; *The Mis-Education of the Negro,* 171

Woolley, Celia Parker, 359

Woolridge, Clifton, 355

Work, suburban patterns of, 230–32, 239, 247(n28)

Working class, 5, 51, 214; in Chagrin Falls Park, 227–31, 245(n14); commuters, 230–31; property ownership, 234–35; suburbs, 11, 224–26, 230–32, 240, 241

Works Progress Administration, 291